Growth and Development
of Children

GROWTH AND DEVELOPMENT OF CHILDREN

George H. Lowrey, M.D.
Professor of Pediatrics, School of Medicine,
University of California, Davis

SEVENTH EDITION

YEAR BOOK MEDICAL PUBLISHERS, INC.
CHICAGO · LONDON

Library of Congress Catalog Card Number: 77-83308
International Standard Book Number: 0-8151-5644-8

To my wife
PATRICIA
and
To my children
PATRICIA GAIL, THOMAS and GEOFFREY

Preface

The study of normal and abnormal growth and development of children has become an increasingly important part of the practice and teaching of pediatrics and of research in all fields related to child health. All of the dynamic anatomic, physiologic and psychologic changes taking place from conception, or before, to maturity must be considered in an attempt to understand the growing individual. Improvements in the prevention and treatment of infectious diseases and the simplification of infant feeding, have permitted greater concentration upon the many aspects of growth and development. During the past two or three decades there has been a greatly increasing amount of literature published upon every aspect of the subject. This is in marked contrast to any similar period in the first half of this century. As with previous editions, the author's purpose has been to attempt to collect and summarize that widely scattered material and present it in an easily available form. Personal experience has had some influence on the choice of material as well as its presentation.

In the selection of references considerable effort has been made to choose review articles or texts. Some older references have been retained either because they are classics in their field or because more recent publications on the same subject fail to present anything really new and are less well written. In many chapters, half or more of the references are new or different from the previous edition. It was impossible to prevent lengthening the list for most chapters and to increase the text material. An earnest attempt has been made to keep the book a convenient size despite many additions.

The changes from previous editions are too numerous to list in detail. They are the result of recent developments and research, critical reviews by journals as well as individuals and the desire to make the book more thorough in coverage. The accomplishment, if it can be so called, has been very time consuming, including a first time sabbatical leave. But, the author is more than compensated by the opportunity to make an uninterrupted review of the field and to learn a great deal by virtue of expanding several topics or preparing material for some subjects not covered before. Hopefully the result is a more complete and current presentation of growth and development.

New or greatly expanded material includes placental development, amniotic fluid, causes of congenital anomalies, updated material on physical measurements, the low birth weight infant, cognitive development, maternal-child relationship, additional items for evaluating behavior, the adolescent (physical and psychologic), development of immunity, endocrinology of growth, nutritional influences on growth and development and facial growth.

Unfortunately, Dr. Hilda Knobloch, who has made substantial contributions to Chapter 6 in the past, was unable to comply with my request for a revision this time. Her material on measuring behavior in the 6th edition has been used as the nucleus for the discussion of that topic in the present edition. I would like to again acknowledge my gratitude for her help and trust that my modifications have not distorted her message.

Dr. Ralph Gibson, Assistant Dean and Professor of Psychology, University of Michigan Medical School, revised and added to his section in Chapter 6 on Evaluation of Intelligence Testing. As in previous editions, it is a pleasure to express my appreciation for his most valuable contribution.

The Year Book Medical Publishers were again most cooperative and helpful in the preparation of this edition. Their encouragement has always been a welcome stimulus. Last, but far from least, I would like to express my gratitude to Mrs. Jean M. Ostlind for her fine secretarial work. In addition, she made many valuable suggestions to improve clarity or correct errors. The author, however, assumes full responsibility for those errors that remain and hopes they will be brought to his attention for future correction.

GEORGE H. LOWREY, M.D.
El Macero, California

Table of Contents

1 / History and Introduction

Historical Background

THE EARLIEST RECORDS concerning the science of child health were primarily concerned with the preservation of life and therefore describe in some detail the proper methods of infant rearing and the diseases common to that age. Until fairly recent times the study of growth and development would have been considered a luxury, in view of the more pressing problems of decreasing the infant and child mortality rates. In the works of Greek, Roman and Arab physicians there was considerable discussion of education, which included sports and preparation for military service. Nutrition received much attention, but little of this literature could be considered as based upon any kind of sound observation, such as the effect upon weight or height. Superstition and religious dogma played a major part in the rules laid down for bringing up the child. Often the old texts would give an account of the preparation for birth, the care of the newly born baby, nursing, and the introduction of other foods, and then deal with the diseases of infants. It was a situation in which the only measurement of good health was survival.

Although records were incomplete, it is estimated that only one of every two children born in America 200 years ago would live to reach the age of 21 years. Infectious diseases were the major reason for this mortality, of which diarrhea and enteritis were the leading causes.[30] As recently as 1910, 30% of all infant deaths were caused by diarrhea and enteritis. Most mothers breast-fed their infants but this was often supplemented with milk or water from contaminated sources. Wet-nursing was not uncommon since women did not hesitate to suckle each other's children. The superstition that the milk might be responsible for passing on the characteristics of the woman supplying it was so strong that it imposed considerable limitations to a practice that might have saved more lives. The time of weaning was one of worry since many ills had their onset then.[31]

Substitutes for breast milk included the milk from cows, goats or asses, and occasionally other animals. These animals often were easier to obtain and cheaper than human wet nurses. One of the first texts on child care, published in this country in 1825, called attention to the value of various

1

animal milks in infant feeding.[32] Some authorities in America and Europe considered the use of a specific animal's milk, added to the diet, as having remedial qualities. Well into the present century, a major portion of time in pediatric training was devoted to the preparation of infant formulas.

Reduced infant morbidity and mortality from contaminated formulas was the result of a number of important developments beginning at the end of the 19th century. The recognition of bacterial origins of disease resulted in improved public health measures including milk and water inspection. The advent of nearly universal pasteurization, and shortly after, the availability of refrigeration further improved the situation for the infant and child.

The first publication about the anatomic differences of the child and the adult, with some references to developmental anatomy, was by Gabrielo de Zerbis in 1502.[1] The total number of publications on growth and physical development between 1500 and 1700, collected by Scammon[1] after an exhaustive search, was 41. Still, some knowledge of the normal and abnormal is very apparent from the art of this period. Several of the paintings of Diego Velázquez (1599–1660) are beautiful examples of children in good health as well as of several types of dwarfism, including achondroplasia. *The Anatomy Lesson of Doctor Frederick Ruysch* by Jan van Neck, painted in 1683, depicts the famous physician dissecting a newborn baby with the cord and placenta attached. In one corner of this masterpiece is the articulated skeleton of an infant. Ruysch is best remembered for his studies of the anatomy of the vascular system, including the association of the fetal and maternal vessels in the placenta.

In 1651 William Harvey, better known for his work on the circulation, published his *Exercitationes de Generatione Animalium,* which, although not entirely accurate, helped to dispel the concept that the human embryo was completely preformed from the time of conception and helped to launch embryology as a science. François Mauriceau[2] was the first to give accurate descriptions and illustrations of the proportions of the fetus and newborn. His book, which included some information concerning the physical measurements of infants, was printed in 1694. Although Mauriceau was the greatest French obstetrician of his time, his observations were not free from error. The average weight of the newborn was given as between 14 and 15 lb (based on our present standards). This error was perpetuated in many translations and was not properly challenged until the German J. C. Roederer read a paper in 1753 before the Royal Society of Göttingen. This work may be considered the first to record normal birth weight and length accurately.[2]

Albrecht von Haller (1708–77), the great Swiss physiologist, had published a similarly correct indication of birth weight a year prior to Roederer, but his observation was an isolated one and his method of arriving at the figure was not given. In England Joseph Clarke had the distinction of being the first to report correct figures for weight at birth and also normal head circumferences at this age. His paper was presented at a scientific meeting in 1786 and was based, for the first time, on what we would consider to be adequate data.[3]

The oldest, and still one of the best, longitudinal studies of the growth of a child was that by Count Philibert Gueneau de Montbeillard, which was completed in 1777 but was published by his friend, Buffon, in 1837. This was a curve of the body length of his son from birth to 18 years, recorded every six months. This study is often quoted as a classic accomplishment, and justifiably so.[4] Buffon was the first to postulate the seasonal changes in growth, based on the figures that were then available to him. He also reported on the smallest adult dwarf so far recorded, a man 36 years of age who was only 16 in. (39 cm) tall.

John Hunter (1728–93) was a very colorful figure in the history of English medicine, and his fame is based upon his discoveries relative to surgical procedures and investigations of infections. However, his interests were broad and included records of measurements of the human body. His museum in London contained a number of skeletons of dwarfs and giants. The most renowned was that of the Irish giant O'Brien. The story of Hunter's acquisition of the body against O'Brien's last wishes and carefully laid plans makes fascinating, though macabre, reading. An apt pupil of Hunter was Samuel von Soemmerring (1775–1830), from Poland. He first described in detail the condition of achondroplasia with measurements and drawings, which were published in an atlas of congenital anomalies in 1791.

Certainly we owe the credit for the first complete study of the physical growth of children to the Belgian astronomer and statistician Lambert Adolphe Jacques Quetelet (1796–1874). He was director of the Royal Observatory in Brussels for many years and contributed a large number of articles on many scientific subjects during his life. Possibly because of his failure to find satisfactory material on growth in his search of the literature up to that time, he carried out extensive studies of heights and weights of male and female subjects of all ages. These findings were published in 1835.[6] His figures of body dimensions have been used for comparative purposes in growth studies until recent times. The term *anthropometry* was also originated by Quetelet.

To Guillot (1852) goes the distinction of being the first to advocate the use of periodic weighing of infants and children as a means of evaluating their general health.[2] Furthermore, he emphasized the value of this method in estimating the adequacy of the breast-milk feeding.

A very complete statistical study of the growth of children from the Boston, Massachusetts area was made by H. P. Bowditch[7] in 1875. Bowditch was the grandson of Nathaniel who was a famous mathematician and navigator. His graduation from Harvard Medical School in 1868 was delayed for four years because of his participation in the Civil War as a member of the Massachusetts Cavalry. After a brief period of study in Europe, he returned to Harvard to become a member of the faculty and established the first physiology laboratory for students in the United States. Later, as dean of the school, he became an influential leader in medical education. Bowditch's observations on growth were made on several thousand individuals classified according to age. In a number of subsequent publications, he presented numerous tables and analyses pertaining to height and weight, nationality, economic backgrounds and the patterns followed by each sex. We can be thankful that a man of his caliber carried out these studies, because he set a sterling example for those who followed him in similar endeavors. His published material served as the usual guide for comparison in most of the standard pediatric texts until well into the 20th century.

William Camerer,[25] in Germany, collected important data relating to various aspects of metabolism and energy requirements for growth from birth to adult size. These studies were published over a period from 1880 to 1896. Camerer's material included physical measurements for infants and children younger than those included by Bowditch. Together, the work of these two constituted the standards used for measuring physical growth for nearly half a century.

In 1921 and 1922, respectively, R. M. Woodbury and B. T. Baldwin[8] published new charts depicting the growth of children in the United States from birth through adolescence. The former's material consisted of a widespread population of children under six, while the latter's consisted of the entire age range, but of a more homogeneous socioeconomic group. A large number of growth charts have been published in this country and abroad in the past 50 years. A few of these are described in some detail in Chapter 4.

The great increase in interest in physical growth and development that was taking place at this period was evident from the appearance between 1900 and 1925 of nearly 3,000 published titles on the subject.[1] Krogman[9] collected over 2,000 references published between 1914 and 1940. The bulk of work following World War I began to shift from Europe to the United States and has continued so until very recent times. Part of this undoubtedly was a result of the aftermath of the war, but much of it resulted from the change in the character of the approach to children's health and the rapid growth of American medicine. More and more emphasis was being placed on a sound knowledge of the subject in the fields of pediatrics, preventive medicine and education. The very essence of preventive medicine in children has as its goal normal growth and development.

Purely anatomic studies of the infant and child began in the fourteenth and fifteenth centuries. Modern anatomy in this field was largely confined to the

European literature, mainly German, until after World War I. Among such works may be mentioned Henke's *Anatomie des Kindesalters* (1873), Ribemont's *Recherches sur l'anatomie topographique du fétus* (1878), Symington's *The Topographic Anatomy of the Child* (1887) and Stratz's *Der Körper des Kindes* (1904). Scammon's summary of anatomy in Abt's *Pediatrics* is a rich and valuable compilation printed in 1923.

A number of research centers for the study of growth and development were established as early as the 1920s, including the Iowa Child Welfare Research Station, the Brush Foundation at Western Reserve University, the Yale Clinic of Child Development, the Child Health Division of the Harvard School of Public Health, the Child Research Council of the University of Colorado and the Fels Research Institute for the Study of Human Development, Antioch College. One of the important reasons for the creation of such centers was the longitudinal study of the child. Although cross-sectional studies have value, more detailed knowledge can be obtained by following individual children throughout part or all of their growing period. In 1923 the National Research Council sponsored a Committee on Child Development to foster and coordinate the rapidly growing research in this field. The White House Conference of 1930, and the resulting publications, may still be considered one of the finest sources for material on growth and development of children.[13] Although all of the pediatric journals carry articles on the subject, special publications now came into existence. *Growth: A Journal for Studies of Development and Increase* appeared in 1937, and *Child Development* a few years prior to that.

In 1895 the discovery of x-rays and their properties by Roentgen offered a means of studying the growth of the bony structure of the body in the living. Since then great advance has been made in standardization of techniques of roentgenology and in the appraisal of bone growth. Preston Hickey of Detroit in 1904 reported on his studies of the skeletal maturation of the fetus, infant, child and adolescent. Pryor (1905)[10] and Thomas Rotch (1907)[5] were the first to show the usefulness of this method in estimating maturation by the examination of the number of bones and their size and shape in the hand. Rotch, who was the first professor of pediatrics at Harvard University, also made other researches on the "physiologic" age of children. Although T. Wingate Todd published his well-known *Atlas of Skeletal Maturation* in 1937 as a result of his studies carried on at the Brush Foundation, similar but less complete outlines were available previously, based on the work of Baldwin and his co-workers (1928), P. C. Hodges (1933) and C. D. Flory (1936). It is interesting to note that at the same time Pryor and Rotch were discussing physiologic age in terms of skeletal development, an educator, C. W. Crampton,[11] was discussing the same subject in terms of body development, especially the appearance of secondary sexual characteristics. The latter author is credited with being the initiator of the term *physiologic age* (1908).

The first paper to describe the roentgenologic appearance of the fetus was printed the year following the discovery of the x-ray and was written by E. P. Davis of New York. Escherich of Graz, Austria, presented the initial lengthy report on x-ray examination in infants and young children and discussed its potentials as a diagnostic tool (1898).[12] Reyher's monograph of 1908 was the first review of the literature in German, and Rotch's *The Roentgen Rays in Pediatrics* appeared two years later in the United States. Subsequently a number of fine texts have been published, of which Caffey's *Pediatric X-Ray Diagnosis* is outstanding (first edition, 1945).[12]

The concept of types of structure of the body and their possible relationship to specific growth patterns, personality and predisposition to disease is an ancient one. Hippocrates[33] described the tall thin type as *habitus phthisicus* with an increased incidence of tuberculosis; the short obese person was designated *habitus apoplecticus* with susceptibility to vascular accidents. Shakespeare alludes to the personality of different types in *Julius Caesar:*

> Let me have men about me that are fat
> Sleek-headed men, and such as sleep o'nights.
> Yond Cassius has a lean and hungry look;
> He thinks too much: such men are dangerous.

Leo Rostan of France in 1828[14] proposed that people be classified in terms of body build under one of four categories: *digestif* (short and obese), *musculaire* (solid and muscular), *respiratoire* (combination of *musculaire* and *cerebral*) and *cerebral* (tall and thin). Nearly one hundred years later, Ernst Kretschmer,[15] in Germany, described three body types and related them to personality traits and mental diseases. The round-faced, well-nourished person was called *pyknic* and characterized as an extrovert. Manic-depressive psychosis was more commonly found in this group according to Kretschmer. *Asthenic* was the term applied to the tall and thin person who was introverted and the type in which the schizoid person was identified. Between these two in temperament and physique was the *athletic* type. Although little credence is given today to the association of somatotype with specific personalities or diseases, its rough clinical evaluation may have some value in predicting growth patterns.

A few comments may be given to the history of growth studies of special age groups. Although a number of treatises had been written on fetal growth prior to Von Baer's important work of 1829 describing the germ layers and their formation in the embryo, these earlier works broke no new ground not explored by Mauriceau in the late 17th century. It was not until after the formulation of the cell theory by Schleiden and Schwann (1839) that the significance of Von Baer's work was appreciated. A classic summary of anatomy of human embryos (*Anatomie menschlicher Embryonen*) was brought out by His of Germany in 1880. After the turn of the century Dafner of Germany and Mall in the United States supplied us with accurate figures on the age, growth and external form of the human embryo.[26] From here to the premature infant would seem but a short step. However, growth and development of these "problem children" resisted concentrated attention until late in the 19th century, when Camerer brought attention to them in his studies, already mentioned. Ylppö[17] of Finland published in 1919 the first comprehensive report of the physical growth of the premature infant through childhood with many tables of measurements. Hess[18] of Chicago wrote about his experiences with a group of premature babies followed for several years; this was in 1934. Although recent work has thrown some doubt upon certain conclusions of these men, their studies are of more than historic interest.

Charles-Michel Billard, who died at the age of 32, published in Paris in 1828 the first monograph on the newborn infant, which began with a careful consideration of the expected height and weight and color of skin, attitudes and pulse rate. This text, *Traité des maladies des enfants nouveau-nés et à la mamelle*, long remained the standard and was translated into several languages. Another milestone in pediatric literature was August von Reuss's *Krankheiten des Neugebornen*, printed in Vienna in 1914. Like Billard's book, it was primarily concerned with disease but outlined normal growth, development and the meager knowledge then available of physiology of the neonatal period. Unique in this field was the first edition of Clement A. Smith's *The Physiology of the Newborn Infant*, which immediately became a classic upon publication in 1945.

Separation of the period of adolescence from other growth periods is of relatively recent origin. Vierordt (1818–84) of Tübingen, one of the most important contributors in the early studies of growth, divided periods of development according to age and other aspects of maturation and, along with Bowditch, recognized the adolescent spurt and also the fact that girls enter this period sooner than boys.[19] The two volumes on adolescence by Stanley Hall,[22] published in 1904, were especially complete for their time. In 1919 the Scandinavian Schiötz wrote one of the first detailed analyses of physical growth during pubescence.[8] In the United States Shuttleworth and Stuart, and in Great Britain Tanner,[16] have made particularly large contributions on the subject of the adolescent.

Physiologic and biochemical differences among infants, children and adults were relatively recent subjects of interest. It should be recalled that physiology passed beyond metaphysics and speculation as recently as the first half of the 19th century. This change was due mainly to the efforts of the Frenchmen François Magendie (1783–1855) and Claude Bernard (1813–78). Both insisted upon proof of facts by the experimental technique. Special study of the body functions of the pediatric age group became well established in Germany in the last half of the 19th century. At first this was primarily concentrated upon nutrition and related aspects of physiology. In 1878 Friedrich Ahlfeld emphasized the relationship of an infant's weight to adequate nutrition. At the same time, Joseph Forster studied the respiratory gases in the newborn and showed that they produced more carbon dioxide per unit of weight than the adult. Shortly after this, Camerer introduced the scientific investigation of infantile metabolism with special reference to energy requirements. Max Rubner and Otto Heubner in 1898 published *Die natürliche Ernährung eines Saüglings*, which is often considered the starting point of all modern work on infant metabolism. Rubner also was among the first to relate rate of energy metabolism to surface area. Heubner later became the director of the Pediatric Clinic in Berlin and was given the first full professorship in Germany in 1894. Adalbert Czerny of Prague made many contributions in regard to infant feeding and was among those first interested in the products of intermediate metabolism. He also anticipated the modern behaviorists in his teachings on child rearing. In 1913 he assumed the chair of pediatrics in Berlin, following Heubner. In his time Czerny was undoubtedly the European leader in pediatrics, and his influence was felt throughout the world.[20]

In the United States John Murlin, Fritz Talbot and Francis Benedict made particularly significant contributions to the understanding of energy metabolism in the early years of the present century. It is beyond the scope of this review to mention all of the important work in this and related biochemical fields, and new developments of today are changing previously held concepts at a rapid rate. It would be an unpardonable omission, however, not to acknowledge the work in chemistry of John Howland (1873–1926) of Johns Hopkins University and William McKim Marriott (1885–1936) of Washington University in St. Louis. These two men were directly responsible for emphasizing the importance of laboratory methods in studying clinical problems, a concept that is largely taken for granted now.

The behavior and psychologic development of the child was first approached on an educational basis. The general attitude until quite recent times was that children were inferior objects and did not warrant any special study. Education was important only because it aided the child in assuming the tasks of the adult and becoming a dependable parent. Johann Amos Comenius (1592–1670), a Moravian bishop, published several works on education and first emphasized the individuality of children and that education should be directed according to ability rather than to a desire to mold into a socially acceptable pattern. The philosophical implications of Jean Jacques Rousseau (1712–78) have carried considerable weight upon ideas of children's behavior and methods of teaching. He extolled natural methods as opposed to the disciplinary ones practiced in teaching at that time. "Nature never deceives us; it is always we who deceive ourselves." He wrote that the child has ways of observing, thinking and feeling that are peculiar to him or her. In Germany Friedrich Froebel (1782–1852), the father of the kindergarten, preached much the same concept in his attempt to reform contemporary education, basing his ideas upon careful observations of children in the school and the home.

Child rearing in America from colonial times to the beginning of the present century was often influenced by superstition and religious dogma.[31, 34] Relatively minor mishaps or events occurring during pregnancy were blamed for hemangiomas or congenital malformations in the infant. The exact (astrological) time of birth could account for future personality traits, mental or physical illness. To many parents, the infant was born in sin and was in urgent need of being saved from Hell. Many children were, some few still are, raised in the strict observance of religious taboos and received severe punishment for often trivial misbehaviors. Play of any kind on the Sabbath was forbidden. The content of children's books was more often moralizing in character than educational or for pleasure. Educators and education for children were given very low priorities except among the wealthy who could afford to hire tutors or send their offspring to private schools. Until the early 1920s school health programs were virtually nonexistent.

In the latter part of the 18th century, interest in studying the child turned from a purely educational approach to biographic methods. Johann Heinrich Pestalozzi (1746–1827), from Switzerland, was noted for his ideas concerning education and greatly influenced Froebel. In addition, he wrote the first well-documented developmental biography of a child, his own son, which may be considered the initial scientific record of this kind. In 1787 the German physician Tiedemann published similar but more complete observations on the development of his children. However, his work was long neglected and required republishing more than a hundred years later to attract attention. In 1877 Charles Darwin wrote his delightful and instructive *A Biographical Sketch of an Infant*. Wilhelm Preyer's *Die Seele des Kindes* first appeared in 1882 and reached eight editions.

The limitations of the biographic approach to the study of behavior were recognized and have been largely replaced by longitudinal and experimental methods. Reflex behavior, or the response to specific stimuli, was the subject of a monograph by Adolf Kussmaul in 1859. Kussmaul, who became professor of medicine at four German medical schools, made numerous im-

portant contributions including the first use of thoracentesis and esophago-
scopy and wrote the description of the respiratory pattern seen in diabetic
acidosis which bears his name. In 1918, Ernst Moro, a German pediatrician,
noted the reflex now known by his eponym. The sensorimotor responses in
infants were described by the Shermans[21] in 1925. A very productive period
of study of infant and child behavior occurred in the 1930s and 1940s resulting in publications by Nancy Bayley, Arnold Gesell, M. B. McGraw, and M.
M. Shirley. Each of these Americans, working independently, was largely
responsible for cataloging the expected norms of behavior at various stages of
development that are now in common use.

Jean Lamarck (1744–1829), the famous French naturalist, attributed the
maturation of behavior to the inheritance of acquired traits. Although subsequent studies threw considerable doubt upon the validity of these concepts, it was not until the late 1800s and early 1900s that new theories
concerning child behavior were formulated. Sigmund Freud (1856–1939)
reported his controversial ideas about infantile sexuality and its influence
upon behavior in 1908. Even though modified or entirely unaccepted by
some psychologists and psychiatrists, these theories have had great influence
in stimulating thought and methods of investigation. Not so startling were
the concepts of the school of "behaviorism" led by John Watson. He introduced many new experimental technics. In 1914 he began publishing a
series of works on child behavior that largely denied the existence of instinct
and consciousness and therefore were antagonistic to Freud. Among other
contributions to a discussion of personality development was the monograph
by Stanley Hall on the psychology of adolescence (1904).[22] This was a truly
monumental work, and it maintains a place of eminence in the field. Although this was not the first material to call attention to the relationships of
physical to mental development, it had the greatest influence on those interested in the study of the growth of the whole child. Hall was largely
responsible for the formation of the National Association for the Study of
Children, the first child study society in America (1893). The first international Child Study Congress was held in Berlin in 1906.

Until the early part of the 20th century the measurement of mental growth
occupied almost no place in the scientific literature. To the American James
Cattell must go much of the honor for the concept of mental testing, which
he outlined in 1890.[24] Binet and Simon, in Paris, were carrying out similar
experiments about the same time, and in 1908 they published what must be
considered the first adequate test scale. Goddard, in this country, was an
important figure in making these experiments available and promoting their
use. Lewis M. Terman was instrumental in introducing mental tests into the
schools and in developing further refinements of the methods (1916–37).
The "developmental" tests of Gesell are now well known and nearly univer-

sal in their use. Several test methods are now available for specific age groups and are also used to aid in attempting more definitive diagnostic criteria.

As a final note in this review, attention should be called to an international foundation for the study of the growth and development of children, the Centre International de l'Enfance, which was opened in Paris in 1953. The center has sponsored studies in a number of countries, holds regular meetings to promote knowledge, understanding and cooperation and has released a number of important publications.

Some Principles of Growth and Development

The terms *growth* and *development* are often used interchangeably, and it is certainly true that each depends on the other for fruition. In the normal child each parallels the other, and any separation would be an artificial one. For convenience, however, we may distinguish between them. We restrict, when possible, the term *growth* to mean an increase in physical size of the whole or any of its parts. Growth, therefore, may be measured in terms of inches or centimeters and pounds or kilograms. It can be measured also in terms of metabolic balance, i.e., retention of calcium and nitrogen by the body. *Development* is used to indicate an increase in skill and complexity of function. The individual develops neuromuscular control, he develops dexterity and he develops character. Maturation and differentiation are frequently used as synonyms for development. Used in this sense, it is evident that development is related to growth but is not the same.

Comparative aspects of growth and development are of special interest. Some of the lower forms of life, particularly certain species of insects, emerge from the egg in a fully mature state, capable of carrying on all of the activities of the adult, including reproduction. Even among some higher forms a considerable degree of maturity is rapidly attained. The newly born guinea pig can shift for himself three days after birth. Man is set apart from other animals by the protracted period of infancy and childhood. Nearly one third of man's life span is spent in preparation for living the latter two thirds. It is as though nature, cognizant of man's unique cerebral attributes, provides a long training period. He is essentially a learning animal, and biologically speaking he develops so slowly that his mental processes are enabled to use and absorb the cumulative experiences of all who have gone before him. In some animals, the potential for growth never ceases. In the cold-blooded or poikilothermic species, growth slows with age but is never-ending during life. In the rat the epiphyses never close, which makes this animal unique and, incidentally, somewhat of a problem for the interpretation of growth studies. Only the primates appear to have the second period of accelerated growth that we associate with early adolescence in man. Other animals follow a relatively smooth decelerating curve with advancing age until adulthood.

The basic process of protein synthesis is shared by every living thing on earth. All cells have ribosomes, consisting of two dissociable bits of ribonucleoprotein which form the workshop of protein manufacture. All cells have *transfer* RNA and *messenger* RNA (see Chapter 2), and their function in transmitting the genetic code is a universal one. In fact, experiments have been carried out in which transfer RNA from bacteria were used with messenger RNA from reticulocytes of a rabbit to make hemoglobin.[29]

At fertilization two very important events occur. The egg is provided with a paternal genome and metabolic processes are initiated which are required for renewed cell division and cell differentiation. Until the multicelled blastocyst becomes implanted in the uterine wall, cell division is accomplished with little or no protein synthesis and each new cell is smaller than its parent cell. This is the only time in human development when cell division is not preceded by growth in size and protein synthesis. Differentiation must depend upon changes in the protein content of developing cell populations. An important aspect of messenger RNA is that it is unstable, with a relatively short half-life. Thus a continuing supply of it is necessary to maintain protein synthesis. This permits alterations in the programs for ribosomes to produce a variety of proteins according to cellular need or function. It also permits changes in the rate of production of a specific protein, since rate depends upon the concentration of messenger RNA. In differentiation an important aspect of the development of specialized cells is the production of proteins that permit realization of their unique role. For example, stem cells which are precursors of those blood cells that will become erythrocytes during maturation convert to cells in which most of the messenger RNA codes for hemoglobin. The number of identifiably different proteins increases rapidly with the length of gestation in the early embryonic period.

It has been demonstrated that the production rate, and therefore quantity, of ribosome RNA varies with the course of development regardless of chronologic age. Embryonic cells disturbed from forming the gastrulation stage will not synthesize ribosome RNA at the same rate as chronologically equal cells that have been permitted to reach gastrulation.[29]

Chemical controls of growth mechanisms also play an important role early in development. Once an enzyme molecule has been formed by the ribosome, its metabolic activity will modify the substrate. This in turn will increase or decrease the activity of the indicated enzyme, as well as possibly modify other enzymes. There is some evidence that induction or activation of an enzyme is dependent upon a critical concentration of a specific substrate. In this way the checks and balances of growth become established.

Little is known about how growth and physiologic activity are mediated in various tissues. Muscle, bone, nerve and skin are types of tissue that may be stimulated by local influences, or inhibited by them. In the case of muscle, stimuli could result from nerve impulses. Blood pressure changes in the heart and larger vessels and stress upon bones might represent important influences upon growth. Physical features such as temperature, total mass and surface area may affect the ultimate rate or direction of growth.

Immediately following fertilization, all cells of the organism divide at an equal rate. Differential and nonrandom proliferation very quickly replace the former pattern. Renewing cell populations consist of stem cells that divide to yield new stem cells and also differentiating cells. In turn, some of these cells eventually become senile cells that have lost the ability to divide and are removed from the population. It is likely that much of the growth control is exerted by *chalones*. These substances, which inhibit cell proliferation, have been reportedly isolated from a number of tissues. The implication is that cells of a specific organ would multiply indefinitely unless prevented by the chalone. It is postulated that this substance is produced by many, perhaps all, cells but it remains inactive as long as it is within the cell. In the course of growth, as the number of cells increases, the amount of chalone released from dying cells also increases. Once in the circulation in sufficient quantity, it inhibits further increase in cell population by influencing receptors on the cell surface. These polypeptides are stated to be organ-specific.[35]

An example of a highly specific growth-promoting factor is found in erythropoietin (ESF). This substance is produced by the kidney, and stimulates both the production of erythrocytes and their release from the marrow to the circulation. The stimulus for release of this protein hormone is renal hypoxia, either by reduced blood flow or decreased oxygen saturation of the blood. Erythropoietin is present in the circulation from the time of late fetal development.

Among other interesting theories proposed to explain growth regulation are those based upon functional demand and total body mass, each with their specific feedback mechanisms.[35] (See also Chapter 9.)

The inherent urge to grow and develop is very strong in children. It can be blighted by many factors, e.g., malnutrition, acute and chronic infections, endocrine disturbances, congenital malformations and genetic defects. Prenatal influences determine to no small extent the size, viability and general health of the newborn infant. Whether or not complete recovery and normal development will occur following an insult depends upon several factors. The nature, severity and duration of the incident are of obvious importance. In most animals the timing is important; the earlier the insult, the more likely it is to cause permanent harm. The term *criticial period* is often used to describe the time of greatest sensitivity of an organ or system to a specific action. Absence of fetal testicular hormone at the critical period of differentiation and development of the wolffian duct system will result in its degeneration and permit predominance of the müllerian ducts. This situation can be accomplished by castration in animals. A delay of a few days in the operative procedure will not interfere with full male ductal system development. Artificially supplying the hormone after the critical period is passed will not cause a reversal of the degenerative process.

If an insult occurs at a less crucial time and it does not persist, recovery is possible. Temporary deprivation of adequate nutrition in an older child may markedly retard growth in height and weight. When normal food intake is resumed, there usually follows a period of rapid recovery until former levels of height and weight are attained. The accelerated growth period is referred to as *catch-up growth* and is a common phenomenon experienced by most children following major illnesses.

In subsequent pages an attempt is made to emphasize the individuality of growth and development. No single schedule can be anticipated for any one child. When this is properly understood and given due consideration, many errors can be avoided in evaluating a child. For instance, we would not expect comparable accretions of height and weight for two children, one of whom was born of Japanese parentage and the other of English parentage, even though both were reared in a similar environment. Likewise, we cannot establish a common calendar for the events of maturation that characterize adolescent development. First, there is a difference between the sexes; second, in the same sex there can be considerable variation within normal limits; finally, various organ systems and functions within the individual reach maturity at different times. This concept of individuality has gained great impetus resulting in the use of graphs and charts on which each child establishes his or her own pattern of development. However, the concept of the usual range or distribution of physical, mental or physiologic attributes is important and it is desirable to compare each measurement of the child under observation with this distribution rather than with any single norm. Obtaining and interpreting such measurements improve clinical judgment and may bring to one's attention characteristics which might otherwise be overlooked. The first indication of disease may be failure to gain or actual loss of weight or failure to increase in stature. Some phases of development do not lend themselves to easy or simple methods of measurement, for example, personality and emotional behavior. This does not decrease their importance in considering the child as a whole individual. In some fields of behavior we do have fairly well-defined or expected patterns of behavior and, as with physical or biochemical measurements, these are useful as guiding principles, especially in the counseling of parents.

Every child has the privilege and the right to develop to the limits of his capacity. It is the great responsibility of physicians, parents, educators and public health and social service workers to see that the child is given the best opportunity to carry this privilege and this right through to completion. It is hoped that the information presented in the following pages may serve as a guide to the accomplishment of these ideals. It is only through the continued study of children that optimal levels may eventually be defined and attained.

Although there is great variation, it may be helpful for purposes of discussion to divide the periods of growth. Several different lists have been given by various writers; the following grouping seems satisfactory. Such a division of periods will also acquaint the reader with the terms used hereafter.

Growth Period	Approximate Age
Prenatal	From 0 to 280 days
Ovum	From 0 to 14 days
Embryo	From 14 days to 9 weeks
Fetus	From 9 weeks to birth
Premature infant	From 27 to 37 weeks
Birth	Average 280 days
Neonate	First 4 weeks after birth
Infancy	First year
Early childhood (preschool)	From 1 to 6 years
Later childhood (prepubertal)	From 6 to 10 years
Adolescence	Girls, 8 or 10 to 18 years Boys, 10 or 12 to 20 years
Puberty (av.)	Girls, 13 years Boys, 15 years

Each of the periods has one or more characteristics relative to growth and development that set it apart from the others, aside from the chronologic differences. There is no sharp line dividing the periods; they blend imperceptibly from one into another. Prenatal and postnatal growth are one continuous process, but the incident of birth and the beginning of extrauterine existence is an important dividing point. The period of the ovum is characterized by increase in complexity and cell multiplication with little increase in total size. For a part of this time the new organism is self-sufficient, living on its own food stored in the yolk sac. The embryo is parasitic and derives its nutrition from the maternal organism, as does the fetus. It is during the embryonic period that rapid differentiation takes place and all of the organ systems are established. During fetal life there is further development, and early functional activities are apparent. Most pronounced is the rapid increase in body mass.

At birth the parasitic existence is terminated, and as a result there are the initiation of respiration; changes in the circulatory system largely related to the onset of pulmonary function; dependence on an external source of nutrition and upon the digestive system for assimilation of the offered food; dependence upon the organism's own resources to maintain proper body heat; and finally, the excretion of unwanted metabolic substances. It is during this time that the greatest risk to life is experienced, and this fact has stimulated an intense amount of research. Infant mortality rate is regarded as a sensitive index of a country's or community's concern with its health. It is also this period and that of early infancy that many investigators consider to be the most critical relative to the lasting effects of serious injury or disease. Rapid growth and continued maturation proceed during infancy, especially by increase in the functions of the nervous system. It is important to note that very little cell division occurs in the human brain after five months of age and further growth results from increase in cell size. Another interesting fact is the noisiness of the human infant as compared to infants of nearly all other species. At no other time is the velocity of growth so great. Throughout both early and late childhood growth is relatively slow but steady. Only the lymphoid tissue continues to accelerate. There is increasing coordination of functions with the development of skills and intellectual processes. Emotional development is undergoing constant fluctuations and perhaps represents the least stable factor in the entire period.

The period of adolescence has had many definitions. By general use, however, the term is associated with accelerated growth in height and weight, appearance of sexual characteristics and the decelerating growth curve which follows and is terminated in the union of the epiphyses. The ability to reproduce is the culmination of sexual development. More briefly, but less exactly stated, adolescence represents the period of "growing up" or the change from child to adult. There are no sharp lines of demarcation at the start or end of this time interval, and for each subject the chronologic ages may vary. Puberty refers to the time of appearance of dark, pigmented pubic hair in both sexes and includes the age of menarche in girls. Ovulation and the ability to reproduce follow some time after the first menstrual period in most girls. On the average puberty is assumed to take place about two years later in boys than in girls. The "adolescent spurt" of growth is steroid-(sex-hormone) mediated and is more pronounced in boys, who also grow for a longer total period than girls.

Boys have a larger muscle and skeletal mass at all ages and a larger energy requirement for both maintenance and growth. These sex differences are increased during adolescence. Girls constantly have a more advanced skeletal maturity (bone age) and are ahead of boys in most psychomotor skills in the earlier years. Contrary to the usually accepted ideas of growth, increase in stature may continue through age 25. The median age for American children at which statural growth ceases is 21.2 years for boys and 17.3 years for girls.[36] Increase in muscle mass usually continues into the 20s and increase in skeletal mass into the 30s in both sexes.

Each growth period produces some behavioral characteristics; however, these are not necessarily the same for each child. Along with increasing motor skills and gain in self-confidence, the 3-year-old becomes more sociable and is able to share and take turns. Physical size and function have important influences on status with peers and on the individual's approach to people and situations. For the adolescent there is the combination of "threat" of separation and the "joy" of independence from parents. Facing the world as an individual rather than as a member of the family is a step usually accomplished comfortably by virtue of adequate preparation. Sexual development, with its implications of assuming the responsibilities of partner and parent, normally produces some anxieties that in turn have been and will be influenced by society and the world as it is.

REFERENCES

1. Scammon, R. E.: The literature on the growth and physical development of the fetus, infant, and child: A quantitative summary, Anat. Rec. 35:241, 1927.
2. Cone, T. E.: The history of weighing the newborn infant, Pediatrics 28:490, 1961.
3. Clarke, J.: Observations on some causes of the excess of mortality of males above that of females, Trans. R. Soc. (London) 76:358, 1786.
4. Scammon, R. E.: The first seriation study of human growth, Am. J. Phys. Anthropol. 10:329, 1927.
5. Garrison, F. H.: History of Pediatrics, in Abt, I. A. (ed.): *Pediatrics*, Vol. I, (Philadelphia: W. B. Saunders Company, 1923), Chapter 1.
6. Quetelet, L. A. J.: *Sur l'homme et le développement de ses facultés, un essai de physique sociale* (2d ed.; Brussels, 1869).
7. Bowditch, H. P.: *Eighth Annual Report, State Board of Health, Mass.* (1875).
8. Baldwin, B. T.: *The Physical Growth of Children from Birth to Maturity* (Iowa City: State University of Iowa Press, 1922).
9. Krogman, W. M.: *Bibliography of Human Morphology, 1914–1939* (Chicago: University of Chicago Press, 1941).
10. Pryor, J. W.: Development of the bones of the hand as shown by the x-ray method, Bull. State Coll. Kentucky, 1905.
11. Crampton, C. W.: Physiological age, a fundamental principle, Am. Phys. Educ. Rev. vol. 13, nos. 3–6, 1908.
12. Caffey, J.: *Pediatric X-Ray Diagnosis* (6th ed.; Chicago: Year Book Medical Publishers, Inc., 1972).
13. *White House Conference on Child Health and Protection*, Sect. I: Part I, Growth and Development; Part II, Anatomy and Physiology (New York: Century, 1933).
14. Rostan, L.: *Cours élémentaire d'hygiène* (Paris, 1828).
15. Kretschmer, E.: *Körperbau und Charakter* (Berlin: A. Springer, 1921).
16. Tanner, J. M.: *Growth at Adolescence* (Springfield, Ill.: Charles C Thomas, Publisher, 1955).

17. Ylppö, A.: Das Wachstum der Frühgeborenen von der Geburt bis zum Schulalter, Z. Kinderheilkd. 24:111, 1919.
18. Hess, J. H., Mohr, G. J., and Bartelme, P. F.: *The Physical and Mental Growth of Prematurely Born Children* (Chicago: University of Chicago Press, 1934).
19. Vierordt, K.: Physiologie des Kindesalters und Wachstum, in Gerhard, C. (ed.): *Handbuch der Kinderkrankheit* (Tübingen, 1877).
20. Veeder, B. S. (ed.): *Pediatric Profiles* (St. Louis: C. V. Mosby Co., 1957).
21. Sherman, M., and Sherman, I. C.: Sensori-motor responses in infants, J. Comp. Psychol. 5:53, 1925.
22. Hall, G. S.: *Adolescence: Its Psychology and Its Relations to Physiology, Anthropology, Sociology, Sex, Crime, Religion and Education* (New York: Appleton-Century-Crofts, Inc. 1904).
23. Hoefnagel, D., and Lüders, D.: Ernst Moro (1874–1951), Pediatrics 29:643, 1962.
24. Cattell, J. McK.: Mental tests and measurements, Mind 15:373, 1890.
25. Camerer, W.: Bermerkungen über Wachstum, Z. Biol. 36:24, 1880.
26. Mall, F.P.: On measuring human embryos, Anat. Rec. 1:129, 1907.
27. Caffey, J.: The first sixty years of pediatric roentgenology in the United States—1896 to 1956, Am. J. Roentgenol. 76:437, 1956.
28. Smith, R. M.: Fifty years of medical progress: Medicine as a science: Pediatrics, N. Engl. J. Med. 244:176, 1951.
29. Malt, R. A. (ed.): *Macromolecular Synthesis and Growth* (Boston: Little, Brown & Company, 1967.)
30. *Child Health in America* (Washington, D.C.: U.S. Dept. of Health, Education and Welfare, Public Health Service, 1976.)
31. Radbill, S. K.: Colonial pediatrics, J. Pediatr. 89:3, 1976.
32. Radbill, S. K.: The Role of Animals in Infant Feeding, in Hand, W. D. (ed.): *American Folk Medicine* (Berkeley: University of California Press, 1976), p. 21.
33. Hippocrates: *The Genuine Works of Hippocrates*, trans. by F. Adams (New York: William Wood, 1886).
34. Black, H.: Childhood in the early colonial period, Pediatrics 54:71, 1974.
35. Goss, R. E. (ed), *Regulation of Organ and Tissue Growth*, (New York: Academic Press, 1972).
36. Roche, A. F., and Davila, G. H.: Late adolescent growth in stature, Pediatrics 50:874, 1972.

2 / Heredity and Environmental Factors

Heredity

THE MATERIALS with which embryonic life is begun consist of the cytoplasm and the nucleus of the fertilized egg, received from the two parents. The nucleus contains the genes, which differ much in each individual, and these differences affect all of the characteristics of the organism. The manifestations of the results of differences among the genes are known as *heredity*. Obviously one cannot hope to cover this broad field in a few paragraphs, and the purpose of this discussion is to point out the more important known factors and to attempt to evaluate them in relation to growth and development.

One of the fundamental properties of life is the ability to reproduce. Reproduction is always of the organism's own kind, so there is a very close resemblance between parent and progeny. This is also true of individual cells in the replacement of loss due to ordinary "wear and tear." Rarely, as in some nervous tissues, with complete maturity reproductive abilities may be lost. There is, therefore, continuity of the total organism as well as its separate parts. The material in cells responsible for the continuity is deoxyribonucleic acid (DNA), which makes up the chromosomes and the genes.

The molecular model of DNA consists of two helical chains of alternate sugar (deoxyribose) and phosphate. These chains are linked, similarly to rungs in a ladder, by pairs of nitrogen bases which are bonded to the sugar molecules. The nitrogen bases have been identified as purines, adenine and guanine, and pyrimidines, cytosine and thymine. The pairs of bases are joined by hydrogen bonds (Fig 2–1). The DNA molecules are extremely large, with a molecular weight probably in the millions.

The pairing of the bases is always the same, adenine with thymine and cytosine with guanine. Consequently, if the order in one helix is known, the order in its matched pair can easily be deduced. This sequence is the basis of the *genetic code.* At the time of the reduction division (*meiosis*) of the sperm

Fig 2–1.—A schematic diagram of the double helix of deoxyribonucleic acid (DNA). The outside chains consist of alternating sugar *(S)* and phosphate *(P)* molecules. On the inside of the cylinder are the bases *(B)*, of which thymine and adenine are examples. The *double bars* indicate hydrogen bonds between the bases.

and egg, the DNA splits into single chains. These single chains then attract from the environment the appropriate bases to build two copies which are spatially the exact duplicates of the original double helix. Fertilization of the germ cell is at least one of the stimuli for the initiation of this replication.

The chemical identity of human genes has not been ascertained, but probably they consist of several nucleotides (a base plus a sugar and phosphate molecule). There are potentially thousands of genes to each DNA molecule, and the total number of genes in man has been estimated to be not less than 100,000.[6, 21]

All of life's functions are dependent upon protein synthesis. Proteins are composed of several or many units of polypeptides. The polypeptides are made up of amino acids linked in chains. There are 20 amino acids, but since 1 polypeptide may contain more than 200 amino acids in a number of different sequences, the possible variations for protein structure are nearly unlimited. The structure and function of a protein depend upon the amino acid sequence.

The arrangement of the bases in the chain of the ribose phosphate of the

DNA acts as a template for protein synthesis and the order of the amino acid sequence. The genetic information is carried from the gene, found in the nucleus, to the cytoplasm by a specific type of ribonucleic acid called *messenger* RNA. This is a much smaller chain than DNA, very labile and with a half-life measured in minutes or hours. The messenger RNA is synthesized by the DNA strand with a complementary pairing of the bases, except that uracil replaces thyamine. The messenger RNA passes from the nucleus to the cytoplasm in which are located the ribosomes, which appear to be the main site of synthesis of the final protein. From the cytoplasm are drawn the amino acids used as building materials. It is believed that the free amino acids are attached to, and some orderly arrangement is made by, another ribonucleic acid referred to as *transfer* RNA. These are very short chains. In order, then, the DNA makes messenger RNA, which gives the code to transfer RNA, which conveys the selected amino acids to the ribosomes where they "line up" according to the template and linkage occurs. Still another ribonucleic acid, *ribosome* RNA, is responsible for the product produced.

We can now go one step further in our understanding of the action of the genes. All biologic reactions are catalyzed by enzymes. An enzyme is a protein which may be specific to one reaction and one substrate or may catalyze a group reaction, such as the oxidation of all aldehydes by aldehyde oxidase. Each enzyme has a specific structure and, as noted, a specific function. All biochemical processes are resolvable into a series of individual reactions, each dependent on the preceding reaction. Each reaction is, in turn, under the influence of a different enzyme. Since the enzyme is an individual protein, it will be modified in its structure by the genes. Finally, it seems well established that a change (mutation) of a single gene results only in an alteration in the ability of a cell to carry out a single chemical reaction. This postulate of one gene for one enzyme appears to be valid under all circumstances so far tested.[35]

An example is the difference between normal hemoglobin and the abnormal hemoglobin of sickle cell disease in man. The sequence of amino acids in the abnormal hemoglobin varies from that in normal hemoglobin only in the substitution of a single valine for a glutamic acid in each half molecule. This apparently slight change produces a difference in certain properties, including solubility, leading to morbid consequences in the individual who is homozygous for the abnormal hemoglobin.

The nuclear substance of the zygote and of all the somatic cells derived therefrom contains 46 chromosomes. The germ cells (spermatocyte and ovum) contain half as much chromatin material, due to the reduction division, or meiosis. The union of the two gametes (germ cells) re-establishes in the fertilized cell the number of chromosomes characteristic of the somatic cells of the species. Of the 46 chromosomes, 23 are of paternal origin and the other half are of maternal origin. Each series of chromosomes contains a complete assortment of genes and therefore a complete set of developmental potentialities. The paternal and maternal chromosomes can be grouped into 22 homologous pairs containing 22 sets of genes. These chromosomes are termed *autosomes*. In addition, there are two *sex chromosomes*, homologous in the female (XX) and nonhomologous in the male (XY). Every hereditary trait is under the influence of a pair of genes, but other influences, possibly including other gene pairs, may modify their action. In general, the two members of a pair have a similar principal function. However, they may or may not differ in their qualitative or quantitative potentialities. An individual who carries a pair of genes which tend to produce very similar or identical results is said to be *homozygous* with regard to genes and the trait. On the other hand, if the members of the pair tend to produce different results, the individual is *heterozygous*. If one of the genes has a more potent influence than the other, it is said to be *dominant,* and the relatively weaker gene is called *recessive*. A recessive gene can express its characteristic fully only when paired with a similar gene or in a homozygous person.

To express the difference in appearance as determined by genes, the term *phenotype* is used. This indicates the morphologic or perhaps physiologic characteristic of an individual. *Genotype,* on the other hand, expresses the genetic make-up of the individual, or the combination of genes present. When the pair of genes influences a certain physiologic or anatomic characteristic in different ways, i.e., tallness or shortness, they are referred to as *alleles*. These genes are believed to occupy the same relative positions in the paired chromosomes.

The formation of germ cells is preceded by a so-called reduction division in which the members of each chromosome pair separate and pass into two different mature germ cells. Each germ cell in man, therefore, contains 23 chromosomes. There are free intermingling and segregation of what were originally maternal and paternal chromosomes, and the variant germ cells may contain all possible combinations in accord with the laws of chance. With man's 46 chromosomes it has been estimated that some 17,000,000 different combinations are possible at the time of the reduction division.[1]

When one gene has a greater capability in producing its own effect than another, the former is dominant over the latter. In different pairs of alleles there will be found a wide spectrum of such dominance relationships. A completely dominant gene, by definition, will achieve the type effect regardless of the nature of its allele. An incompletely dominant gene acts in the direction of the type effect, but requires support from its allele in order to produce the full type. These are sometimes referred to as genes of *intermediate dominance*. A person who has a strongly dominant abnormal trait is usually heterozygous. The abnormal person has one dominant, abnormal gene (A) and one recessive, normal gene (n) for the trait under discussion. The individual shows the pathologic trait because the normal gene is suppressed. Such an individual has the genotype (An). If this individual has children by a person without the abnormal trait, the following offspring result:

Parents	(An)		×	(nn)	
Germ cells	A	n		n	n
Offspring	(An)	(An)		(nn)	(nn)

One half of the offspring will be heterozygous and show the abnormal trait. The other half will be homozygous and normal.

There are some situations in which heterozygous individuals show the phenotype of both, and true dominance is not apparently manifested by either gene. The person with blood type AB is such an example. There are also genes that appear to have an intermediate dominance in their effect. The sickle cell hemoglobinopathies serve as a good example. The substitution of a single valine molecule for glutamic acid has already been noted as the cause for change in properties of the abnormal hemoglobin. The basic defect arises from a mutation in an autosomal gene. The heterozygous occurrence of the sickle gene is associated with a clinically benign course, even though 30–45% of the red cell hemoglobin is of the sickle type. Such a person is said to have "sickle cell trait." The homozygous individual with 100% abnormal hemoglobin suffers from a severe, chronic hemolytic anemia and has "sickle cell disease."

It may be of value to outline some characteristics of conditions inherited in a dominant manner. The dominant pathologic traits and diseases outnumber those due to recessive genes, and in contrast to these they have a tendency to a later age of onset and are less severe. They would naturally appear in more than one generation, but unless one parent has the disease they are seldom found in a sibship, only one of the brothers and sisters usually having the condition. There is likely to be considerable variety among the affected members of a family with regard to degree or severity.[19] Marfan's syndrome and osteogenesis imperfecta are typical examples of dominant genes in heterozygotes.

A heterozygous individual with an abnormal recessive gene may appear normal owing to dominance of the normal gene. However, if that person has offspring by another heterozygous individual, one fourth of the progeny will display the abnormality and three fourths will carry the abnormal genotype.

Assuming N to be the normal dominant and p the abnormal recessive gene, the pattern of heredity will be:

Parents	(Np)		×	(Np)	
Germ cells	N	p		N	p
Offspring	(NN)	(Np)		(Np)	(pp)

Only the genotype (pp) will show the abnormality. It is much more likely for such a pairing of abnormal recessive genes to take place in consanguineous marriages than in normal marriages.

When a person who is homozygous for a pathologic trait marries a person with normal phenotype but heterozygous genotype for the same trait, one half of the children will be abnormal, and the other half will appear normal but will be carriers of the recessive pathologic trait. Such an example follows:

Parents	(Np)		×	(pp)	
Germ cells	N	p		p	p
Offspring	(Np)	(Np)		(pp)	(pp)

Superficially such a family (two generations only) may appear to represent a pattern of a dominant pathologic trait such as the first diagram showed. Only a careful and complete study of more than two generations will reveal the true state of affairs.

If a homozygous normal (NN) marries a homozygous individual with abnormal recessive genotype (pp), all the offspring will appear normal but will carry the abnormal trait.

Most of the so-called inborn errors of metabolism are due to recessive genes. In contrast to the characteristics of the dominant traits, these diseases are more severe and usually have an early age of onset, and the distribution within a family is such that several siblings are often affected. The victims of such diseases are often sterile or less fertile than the normal population. Phenylketonuria is such a condition. The child has a block in the synthesis of tyrosine from phenylalanine owing to the loss of activity of the enzyme system involved. There is an accumulation of phenylalanine and other precursors, apparently resulting in neurologic damage and some loss in pigment formation. If untreated, these children early in life manifest mental retardation and light hair and pale blue eyes. It is interesting to note that some heterozygotes, although showing no evidence of disease, when given a large intake of phenylalanine cannot convert it as completely or as rapidly to tyrosine as a normal individual. Here again we are probably dealing with a gene that is not completely recessive, just as some dominant genes are not completely dominant.

The mode of inheritance may be a guide in the analysis of the basic defect in genetic disorders. A gene-determined enzyme deficiency is likely to be reflected in the phenotype only when homozygogenicity exists. When the mutation concerns a nonenzyme protein, e.g., a structural protein like collagen, that change in the protein will very probably alter physical properties to such an extent as to produce a typical phenotype even though only half the protein is of the mutant type. This implies, as suggested above, that all inborn errors of metabolism will be recessive and most purely anatomical errors will be dominant. There are some exceptions for the anatomical errors, but none for the biochemical or metabolic.[6]

Hereditary factors may depend on their expression upon a number of variables in addition to a gene. Diabetes mellitus is a good example of this. It is certainly a familial-oriented disease, yet the time of clinical onset, even in identical twins, will vary considerably. The environment, in the form of infection, nutrition or emotional stress may individually, or in combination, play a role in the final results of heredity.

Still another phenomenon is the quality of *pleiotropy*, that condition wherein a single gene has a number of different effects on different organ systems. Marfan's syndrome, previously mentioned, is such an example. Here a single mutant gene causes alterations in several organ systems. The tubular bones are elongated, the musculature is hypotonic, the subcutaneous fat is decreased, the lens of the eye is dislocated, retinal detachment is often found, and malformations of the aorta and aortic valves are frequently present.

It was previously mentioned that only 22 pairs of the human chromosomes are homologous. The remaining pair are the sex chromosomes. In the male these are unequal in size; the larger is designated X and the smaller Y. In the female they are equal, and both are termed X chromosomes. In reduction division in the male, one germ cell receives the X chromosome and one the Y chromosome. Fertilization may result in combination of X and Y and the production of a male, or the combination may be (XX), resulting in a female. Since the genes of the X chromosome in the male are not matched by an equal number of homologous genes in the smaller Y chromosomes, the genes in the former are in a unique position to exert influence on the developing organism. Thus, recessive traits in the X chromosome of the male are not dominated by a corresponding gene in the Y chromosome. In the female such a recessive gene is usually overbalanced by its partner in the second X chromosome. Certain hereditary traits may therefore appear only in the male. Hemophilia and color blindness are well known examples of this pattern of sex-linked inheritance.

Mutation is defined as a permanent transmissible change in the character of an offspring from either of its parents. Little is known of the cause and nature of mutation in man. Radiation* has long been known as an effective agent in lower forms of life and has been postulated as an important cause in man.[20] A purely theoretical figure has been arrived at of 3×10^{-5} as the average mutation rate per locus (position of a single gene) per generation in man. It should be emphasized that although many diseases and malformations are caused by mutant genes, they also are the material on which heritable variation is made and permit evolution and species formation.

By special techniques the number and morphology of each of the 46 chromosomes can be ascertained in cells from many kinds of tissue. The term *karyotype* designates this mapping of the chromosomes. Deviations from the normal number, or the addition or subtraction of a portion of a chromosome, have been associated with clinical syndromes. In 1959 it was first reported that an individual with mongolism (Down's syndrome) had an extra autosomal chromosome, or a total of 47. Subsequently this was identified as trisomy 21 (the presence of three number 21 chromosomes). This is the most common autosomal abnormality in humans, with a frequency of 1 in 668 live births. Other examples of chromosomal polymorphism have been described, and in nearly every instance, this has resulted in gross abnormality. Retardation of both physical growth and mental development is quite characteristic, and all three germinal layers are usually involved. The severity of the involvement usually helps to distinguish these abnormalities from gene mutations.[15, 49, 50]

The sex chromosomes may similarly be involved in abnormalities.[51] Indications of such abnormalities were first appreciated from a study of cells in subjects with intersex problems. A deeply staining intranuclear body resting against the wall of the nucleus was seen in a large percentage of the cells from tissue of a normal female, whereas this structure was very rarely observed in male cells.[38] This heavily staining material has been designated *sex-chromatin body*. When this is absent, the individual has been termed *chromatin-negative*—a characteristic of the normal male's cells. It should be emphasized that this term is to be preferred to *sex-negative* or *male-*

---

*The possible method by which mutations are caused by radiation has been reported by Puck.[36] Radiation or ionizing rays disturb the structure of the atom by knocking out an electron and leaving the atom unbalanced in its electrical charges, with one less negative than positive charge; i.e., it is ionized. The atom with the lost electron responds by shifting electrons to fill all but the outermost shell of electrons. This produces the most stable energy state within the atom, but to maintain balance, the outer shell of electrons must be filled. This eventually leads to union with another atom and a sharing of electrons. Radiation thus changes the binding capacity of atoms and therefore their molecular structure. When this occurs in the gene, the change is transferred to the next generation of cells, provided the mutation is not lethal. The amount of radiation necessary to produce such a change in human cells may be quite small, and embryonic tissue is more susceptible than mature tissue to this change.[46]

somatotype when referring to the chromatin body. The presence of two X chromosomes is necessary for the formation of chromatin-positive cells. The incidence of chromatin-positive cells from the buccal mucosa, the most frequently used source for these studies, may be significantly lower for the first three or four days of life in normal female infants. The reason for such a peculiarity is not known, but it indicates caution in the interpretation of such cells obtained before 5 days of age.

Klinefelter's syndrome is displayed by chromatin-positive phenotypic males. The external genitalia appear to be those of a normal male, but during adolescence gynecomastia appears and female distribution of pubic hair occurs. These individuals are sterile due to aspermatogenesis secondary to atrophic and sclerotic changes in the small testes. The urine contains an increased amount of gonadotropins (follicle-stimulating hormone, or FSH). Studies have revealed that 47 chromosomes are present, with the extra one being a sex chromosome (XXY).

Turner's syndrome is characterized by moderate dwarfism, lack of sexual development at the expected time of puberty, and often other abnormalities such as congenital webbing of the neck, cubitus valgus, and mental retardation. The appearance of the external genitalia is female. These individuals have chromatin-negative cells and a karyotype with 45 chromosomes, the single sex chromosome being X (usually designated XO). The ovaries are rudimentary and do not contain normal follicular structures. (See also Chapter 13.)

As another example of syndromes displayed by persons with abnormal karyotypes, we can mention the clinical picture of combined Klinefelter's syndrome and mongolism. As could be predicted, these persons have an extra autosome, and the sex formula is XXY, with a total of 48 chromosomes present.

Most geneticists explain the variations in chromosome number as being a result of a mechanism known as *nondisjunction*. In preparation for division of the cell, duplicate chromosomes align on the equatorial plate. Then they separate, and members of each pair go to opposite poles. If nondisjunction occurs, both chromosomes of the pair go to the same pole, resulting in an extra chromosome in one of the daughter cells and a deficiency in the other daughter cell. If this unequal division takes place during the formation of gametes, either in mitosis of ancestral cells or during meiosis, the abnormality is passed on to the next generation.

In some patients with chromosomal abnormalities, the abnormality will be demonstrable in only one type of cell. Cultures of white blood cells might demonstrate an abnormal number, while cultures from skin or mucosa would be normal in the same individual. Such a phenomenon is known as *mosaicism*. Most often, all cells are similar in their chromosome content.

The following outline may be helpful in describing some of the presently known chromosomal abnormalities and examples of the associated syndromes[13, 54]:

A. Aneuploidy—abnormality of number of chromosomes
   1. Monosomes—absence of one of a pair of chromosomes (Turner's syndrome)
   2. Trisomy—triplicate chromosomes (mongolism, Klinefelter's syndrome)
   3. Polyploidy—more than one added chromosome (few live-born with autosomal excess, some live with excess sex chromosomes as in XXXY Klinefelter's syndrome)
B. Structural—abnormal morphology
   1. Deletions—absence of part of chromosome (cri-du-chat syndrome and others)
   2. Translocation—portion of one chromosome attached to another (mongolism)
   3. Inversion—following two breaks, a new alignment of the three segments (various anomalies)
   4. Isochromosomes—horizontal instead of vertical division with fusion of the two long and the two short arms (mostly sex chromosomes and intersex anomalies)

It should be pointed out that, of the many congenital malformations studied, few have been associated with an abnormality of a chromosome.[16, 49] It is estimated that between 15 and 25% of all conceptions end in spontaneous abortion.[5] One quarter of these aborted fetuses have chromosomal abnormalities. The earlier in pregnancy the abortion occurs, the more likely the association with an abnormality of the chromosomes. Gross congenital malformations have been reported in from 16 to more than 30% of abortuses and stillborn infants. Of viable newborn infants, approximately 5% will have structural malformations, but less than 1% will have chromosomal errors. Stating these facts in a different way may help to clear some of the confusion. About 7.5% of all human conceptions have chromosomal anomalies. About 10% of these will be normal by all present standards, 80% end in abortions and another 10% survive for some period of time.[4, 5, 40, 53]

Another approach to this problem as well as an aid to understanding the nomenclature is the following[42]:

BIRTH DEFECT CATEGORY	INCIDENCE IN LIVEBORN
Structural malformations	1 per 20
Mental retardation	1 per 30
Genetic disorders	1 per 100

Chromosomal errors	1 per 200
Congenital deafness	1 per 1,000
Congenital blindness	1 per 7,000

The fact that slightly different figures are given by different authors probably reflects the particular population studied. In the above list, a child with more than one defect would be listed in each category.

Among the structural malformations, the etiology is unknown in 70%, genetic transmission is responsible for 20%, chromosomal abnormalities account for 5%, environmental factors (infection, radiation, drugs and chemicals) complete the list for the remaining 5%. Of the children with major structural malformations, nearly half are also mentally retarded.

Although we have used as examples mainly pathologic traits, the same rules hold for variations of normal traits. Through the processes of blending and the additive effects of genes, each individual has a great tendency to follow a predestined pattern of growth and development which is very similar for all children. Although considerable variation does occur, the more or less common design which is inherited by the vast majority of persons is extremely important to realize. In studying the abnormal subject, one is apt to forget the equally fascinating normal subject. The inheritance of the urge to grow normally and the overall similarity of development among children have received little attention from a hereditary standpoint. The problem is indeed complex, but the implications are great.

The physical resemblance of family members is too well known to merit extended comment. There exists a fairly high correlation with regard to stature and weight of siblings, and there is evidence that rates of growth are more alike among siblings than among nonrelated individuals. In certain families accelerated growth and early maturation are the rule, while in others growth is slow and maturation is delayed. For stature, sitting height, head length and breadth, the correlation between monozygotic twins is higher than between fraternal twins and between siblings. These dimensions tend to hold true even when the twins are reared apart. Such a relation does not hold for weight.[11, 42]

The search for size factors in mammals has shown that various genes are pleiotropic in their effects, affecting size as well as some other characteristic. There are some types of dwarfism and giantism in which inheritance is perfectly marked and definite.[4] (These are described in some detail in Chapter 13.) Most important for the physician to remember is that some children are small because of their genetic constitutions and not because they have endocrine or nutritional disturbances, and that other children may be of above average size or development because of heredity. In some cases only a careful study of the child and family will reveal that heredity can offer the only explanation for seeming abnormalities.

From studies of sex chromosome abnormalities, it appears that the Y chromosome confers extra stature. Children and adults with Turner's syndrome are abnormally short. The XYY male is often in excess of 6 ft tall, and the addition of further Y chromosomes has further similar influence. Along with the height increase, there is often an associated aggressive personality with antisocial behavior.[11]

Bakwin[24] made some interesting observations on the growth of African pygmies. He noted that there was a lack of adolescent growth spurt in this race and that growth in height lagged behind that of American children at every level but was more exaggerated from the sixth year on than before this time. The author made similar observations of the Negrito race in the Philippines. The average adult height was 55 in. for the male. Figures for average birth weight were not available but were considerably below those for the Filipino population or the white races. The children had a fairly normal weight and height gain for the first year, although less than American children, and then a rather pronounced slowing down. No adolescent spurt was present, although secondary sex characteristics appeared at an average of 11 to 13 years with menarche at 14 years in the small group available for study. Genetic factors appear to be responsible for lack of response of an end organ to normal growth hormone levels in the circulation (see Chapter 13).

Since different populations, even within a single geographic or national area, are subject to much variability in their environment, it is difficult to determine the degree of the effect of the genotype upon growth. American white and black children ultimately reach the same height and weight as adults. Their rates of growth and body proportions will differ slightly. The Japanese child will never have the relatively long legs of the white child, let alone the even longer legs of the native African. Thus, we must conclude that there are indeed subtle but definite racial differences in the pattern of growth.[10]

The role of genetics in the development of mental characteristics is still a hotly debated subject. There can be little doubt that heredity plays an important part, but the organism is also strongly influenced by environment. The tremendous effect of malnutrition and associated disadvantaged socioeconomic factors on both intellectual and physical development have been, and will be, referred to many times. In a study of American children with superior intelligence, a favorable parental social and educational background was the single best correlate.[72] As indicated with earlier studies of gifted children, both physical and mental growth were above average at all ages.[73] Personality characteristics, such as timidity or aggressiveness, are probably more strongly influenced by environment than by heredity. Delinquent behavior, mental retardation and tall stature in phenotypic males with XYY genotypes are rare but well-recognized entities.[43]

Prenatal Environment

It has been estimated that in the normal prenatal period 44 successive cell divisions take place and that an equivalent of only 4 additional divisions is necessary to change the newborn to adult size. The velocity of cell multiplication is particularly rapid in the first eight weeks, during which time the zygote is converted into the fetus, an organism possessing all of the essential features of an adult human being. Although the genes may be said to contain the plan of the future organism, this plan can be variously modified by environment. Differentiation, for instance, does not depend on genes alone. The type of cell developing in a certain part is determined by the close interaction of the nuclear material (containing the genes) with the internal (nucleus plus cytoplasm) and the external environments. Development consists of countless physicochemical processes. Whether the genes act as enzymes or catalysts, their normal mode of behavior depends on the presence of a normal cytoplasm and a normal external environment. So integrally related are inherent and environmental influences that it is impossible, except under controlled experimental conditions, to differentiate their respective contributions to the development of an organism.

Anomalies of the environment or of the genes may lead to faulty development or to malformations. Certain genetic as well as environmental changes may, therefore, result in a very similar congenital defect. It should be emphasized that it is not a simple matter to classify a given congenital anomaly as "hereditary" or "nonhereditary." Between conception and birth the growing organism may be injured by many external factors. If injury occurs during the embryonic period, the result is arrest of development and often irreparable malformation. During the fetal period (ninth week to birth) injuries result in changes more closely resembling those of postnatal damage, such as mutilations and scars. Apparently the various organs are more sensitive to noxious agents at the time of rapid differentiation or maturation which occur during the embryonic period than they are later. The following prenatal environment factors include most of those either established or suspected of having important influences during pregnancy: (1) nutritional, (2) mechanical, (3) chemical, (4) endocrine, (5) actinic, (6) infection, (7) immune reactions and (8) anoxia.

Although there is no direct proof that vitamins influence human prenatal development, there are at least bits of experimental evidence that strongly suggest such a relationship. Warkany[16] has been able to produce congenital anomalies in animals by feeding the pregnant mothers diets severely deficient in certain vitamins. The types of malformation could be predicted by the omission of a specific vitamin. Other food elements have also been implicated by this investigator. In Chapter 3 we shall see that there is strong evidence that poor diet during pregnancy may result in a high incidence of stillbirths and neonatal deaths. That they are all due to anomalies of the fetus has not been conclusively shown, but the importance of proper maternal diet to normal intrauterine growth and development is established. Finally, it is known that when malnutrition becomes sufficiently severe, conception is prevented altogether. In this regard one might quote Warkany, who said: "The most serious congenital malformation is never to be conceived at all."

In the discussion of the low birth weight infant (Chapter 5) it will be pointed out that small infants are born to small mothers who come from lower socioeconomic groups. It may well be that the mother's growth during childhood might have a very great influence on her offspring, regardless of the social stratum she occupies at the time of her pregnancy.

Mechanical factors, particularly abnormalities of fetal position and oligohydramnios, have been blamed for such congenital malformations as clubfoot, congenital bowing of the legs and micrognathia.[3] Such fetal anomalies are of relatively minor character or severity, probably because they have their pathogenesis late in intrauterine life. Faulty implantation of the ovum, which might be considered a mechanical factor, may interrupt the nutrition of the embryo, with resulting disturbance of development. Occasionally in twins placental development of positioning on the uterine wall will result in a much richer supply of essential nutrients to one of the twins at the expense of the other. This may result in twins of great dissimilarity in size. As with the very small premature infant, or in the syndrome termed "intrauterine dwarfism," these infants may remain relatively small all of their lives and, in addition, may suffer some degree of mental retardation.[58]

At the time the first edition of this book was published in 1951, there was little solid evidence that chemical agents might act as teratogenic factors in man, although this was a well-established fact in experimental animals. Now a long list of chemical agents has been shown to cause some degree of intrauterine abnormality, from severe malformation to mild growth retardation.[16, 66, 67] In some instances, the exposure in utero may become manifested years later, as in the occurrence of adenocarcinoma of the vagina in young women exposed to stilbestrol administered to their mothers during the pregnancy. The most notorious of these agents is thalidomide, which may cause a number of severe defects in the fetus if taken early in pregnancy. Among the malformations reported are phocomelia, heart defects, and anomalies of the brain and special sensory organs. Harelip, cleft palate, hydrocephalus and cranial dysostosis have followed the use of a number of cancer chemotherapeutic drugs, such as aminopterin and the nitrogen mustards.[39] Tetracycline causes less severe changes including mildly retarded skeletal growth and staining of primary teeth with varying degrees of poor enamel formation. Many other drugs and chemicals could be added. The factors involved in the manner and degree of response include dosage, the developmental stage of the embryo or fetus and the duration of exposure to the potential teratogen.[52]

Exposure of the fetus to the commonly used narcotics, e.g., heroin and morphine, are often associated with intrauterine growth retardation, prematurity and postdelivery withdrawal symptoms in the infant. Congenital anomalies do not appear to be increased in frequency. A very interesting observation is the fact that mothers who had used heroin only prior to pregnancy also had babies of low birth weight. Infants born to mothers on methadone maintenance during pregnancy also were of lower than average weight, but were significantly less severely affected than infants whose mothers abused heroin.[69] The effects of maternal use of lysergic acid diethylamide (LSD) is not clear, since claims have been made and denied that it causes congenital deformities.[70]

Low birth weight, subsequent slow physical growth and developmental delay have been described as a fairly frequent consequence of severe alcoholism during pregnancy. Common additional features of this syndrome include microcephaly, small palpebral fissures and maxillary hypoplasia.[62]

Excessive smoking by the mother during pregnancy is associated with a reduced birth weight. This has been ascribed to the vasoconstriction caused by nicotine and the resulting relative placental insufficiency. No malformations have been attributed to the use of tobacco.

Pregnancies maintained at high altitudes are known to lead to newborn infants of a lower mean size than the average population.

In many instances where a specific environmental influence has been cited as giving rise to a cause-and-effect phenomenon, it is often difficult, if not impossible, to eliminate important socioeconomic factors with their additional influence upon the fetus. To illustrate the complexity of the problem with a single example: a pregnant narcotic addict is often the recipient of poor prenatal care, is subject to many infections and suffers from malnutrition.

Although endocrine factors may harmfully affect the fetus, few well-substantiated reports of such cases can be found in the literature. Endemic cretinism is more probably the result of an iodine deficiency in the maternal diet than the result of endocrine influence. Mothers suffering from hypothyroidism and Addison's disease have borne apparently normal children when under proper therapy. The adrenogenital syndrome is caused by excessive androgenic hormone production from the adrenal cortex. In the female the effect of this hormone leads to anomalies of the external genitalia with hypertrophy of the clitoris and often the formation of a common urogenital tract into which both the vagina and urethra open. The term "pseudohermaphrodite" has been used for this condition but should more properly be applied to a purely anatomic variant unassociated with the adrenogenital syndrome. Virilizing tumors of the adrenals or ovary and administration of androgenic hormones as well as the synthetic progestins have resulted in masculinizing the genitalia of female infants.

The newborn infants of diabetic or prediabetic mothers frequently display macrosomia, cardiomegaly, adrenal hyperplasia and extramedullary erythropoiesis with erythroblastosis. There may also be hyperplasia of the islets of Langerhans and resultant hypoglycemia. The infants often have respiratory difficulty and progress poorly during the neonatal period. Some of these conditions cannot be explained on the basis of hypoglycemia alone. They may be the result of abnormal endocrine influences on the fetus, nutritional disturbances on the basis of carbohydrate metabolism or genetic factors not yet clearly understood, or may be the result of two or more of these factors in combination. The incidence of congenital malformations in children of diabetic mothers is about 10 times greater than the average.[8, 16]

The average age of mothers at the birth of infants with mongolism (Down's syndrome) and some other congenital anomalies is significantly higher than that of mothers at the birth of normal children. The finding of an extra autosome (trisomy) in the chromosome pattern of the infant with mongolism has been previously noted. In the karyotypes of adults' blood there is an increasing frequency of abnormalities with age, most often aneuploid cells involving the sex chromosome. These changes are very prominent by the fifth and sixth decades. These findings parallel the occurrence of mongolism in an unselected population where the incidence is about 1 in 700 in women in the twenties but rises to 1 in 70 in the early forties.[4]

Older paternal age is a major factor relative to the frequency of fresh gene mutation in man. As with mongolism related to female aging, there is a tenfold increase in the occurrence of achondroplasia, hemophilia A, Crouzon's syndrome and some other anomalies in families as the father passes from the third to the sixth decade.[68]

Injudicious use of radium or roentgen ray therapy during pregnancy has resulted in malformation of the fetus. Microcephaly, spina bifida, mental retardation and deformities of the extremities have been described in such instances.[16]

A tragic lesson concerning the effects of atomic radiation on the fetus was learned at Hiroshima, Japan.[18] If exposure to the atomic blast took place within the first 20 weeks of gestation and the mother was within 1,200 meters of the hypocenter, the chances of delivering a normal baby were indeed small. Seven of 11 mothers so exposed delivered children with diagnoses of microcephaly and mental retardation. Other anomalies in other fetuses less severely exposed because of greater distance from the hypocenter included congenital dislocation of the hip, congenital malformations of the eyes, congenital heart disease and mongolism. Children who were exposed in utero and who did not show immediate evidence of anomalies at birth have often shown subsequent slower physical growth than controls, as indicated by a low value for height, weight and head circumference.[57] A study of children exposed to heavy fallout on the Marshall Islands revealed that nine years later growth was retarded, as well as skeletal maturation, if they had been under age 5 years at the time of exposure.[56] It is of considerable interest, and also curious to note, that in both of these observations boys were more affected than girls.

Although the fetus is susceptible to a number of virus infections, relatively few of the hundreds to which humans are constantly exposed are transmitted to the fetus. Bacterial infections rarely, if ever, cross the placental barrier, though they may infect the uterine contents as an ascending process through the lower reproductive tract. Viral agents which have been associated with abortion, stillbirth, intrauterine infection or congenital malformation are given in the following list with their most frequent effect.[14, 17, 64, 65]

VIRAL AGENT	DISEASE
Influenza	Abortion
Mumps	Abortion
Rubeola	Abortion
Vaccinia	Abortion
	Congenital vaccinia
Varicella-zoster	
Poliovirus	
ECHO	Congenital infections
Coxsackie	
Equine encephalitis	
Cytomegalovirus	Congenital infection
	Microcephaly
	Deafness
	Mental retardation
Rubella	Abortion
	Congenital infection
	Congenital malformations of heart, eyes, ears, brain

There is some question of the association of the herpes and Coxsackie viruses with true congenital anomalies. Only those infections during the first trimester are apt to cause morphologic abnormalities, but later periods of infection may result in low birth weight and delayed physical and mental development.

Toxoplasmosis, as a prenatal infection during the first months of pregnancy, may cause the classical triad of chorioretinitis, cerebral calcification, and hydrocephaly. It has been estimated that approximately 2% of severe mental retardation in the United States is the result of congenital toxoplasmosis. Congenital syphilis, which had nearly disappeared following World War II, has recently increased in incidence along with other venereal diseases. The spirochete is transmitted by hematogenous spread across the placenta. If promptly recognized and adequately treated, no sequelae result.

The ability of the fetus to respond to these infections with the production of specific immunoglobulins, such as IgM and others, is of utmost importance diagnostically, and will be given further consideration in Chapter 7.

The conditions of erythroblastosis and kernicterus due to red blood cell incompatibility between fetus and mother are so well known that they need be discussed but briefly. In barest outline, the fetus inherits a blood type (Rh, A, B, AB, etc.) which differs from the mother's type. If cells from the fetus enter the mother's bloodstream, or if she has been previously sensitized by transfusion, antibodies to the fetal red cells are produced, which then cross the placental barrier and cause hemolysis. Hyperbilirubinemia and some anemia as well as other pathologic changes result. If these changes are of sufficient degree, especially the hyperbilirubinemia, permanent damage may result, with the brain being especially susceptible (kernicterus).

Regional and seasonal variations in the occurrence of some congenital anomalies have been reported, as well as a suggested increase in their incidence in the lower socioeconomic classes. It must be admitted that no single major cause of developmental defects has been found.

Parity, or order of birth of the child, may affect size at time of delivery as well as some aspects of intellectual functioning later in life. The average birth weight increases with increasing order, i.e., the birth weight and linear dimensions of the firstborn are less than those of subsequent infants. The weight of infants of parity order 5 averages about 100 gm more than that of infants of parity 2–4.

A study of the relation of birth order and family size to intellectual competence was made of the total population of 19-year-old men of the Netherlands.[63] For both mean family size and birth order, there was a consistent gradient in the level of performance: as the test scores became poorer, mean family size and birth order became progressively larger. These results were obtained in all of three social groups into which the subjects were divided.

The effects of racial differences upon birth weight are often difficult to assess because of additional factors that may be involved. These include nutritional habits of the mothers, adequacy of perinatal care and geographic differences. The frequency of low birth weight (less than 2,500 gm) in various areas of the world is briefly discussed in Chapter 5. Within the boundaries of the United States, the incidence of low birth weight babies is approximately twice as great in blacks as in whites. Among primiparous mothers, the mean birth weight is roughly 250 gm greater for white compared to black infants. A gestational period that averages 8 days less in the black mother is an important contributing factor to this difference.[75]

The relationship between size at birth and size at a later age, including the adult, has received considerable attention. Illingworth,[41] in a study of English children, found a fairly high correlation between birth height and weight and height and weight at subsequent ages through the 14th year. The children with the smallest birth weight tended to remain the smallest, and this was especially true in early childhood. Many investigators have found that the smallest of the low birth weight infants (whether premature or not) remain small throughout all of their childhood. Falkner concluded that the size of the newborn and infant, excluding low birth weight infants, is not strongly related to size in the future. However, after any prenatal influences have largely been eliminated, there is a good correlation between height at age 2 or 3 years and adult height.[44] Such factors as socioeconomic environment or frequency and severity of illness have seldom been studied for their possible effects upon final size. In one study[45] of low birth weight infants, it was found that the mothers were significantly shorter than the control group of mothers who delivered babies of normal size. It was also found that the low weight infant is more frequently born into a low socioeconomic group, further jeopardizing his chances of optimal growth and development. In summary, birth length relates predominantly to maternal height, and by 2 years of age and thereafter, the length or height correlates best to the mean parental height.[71]

In Chapter 3, on fetal growth and development, other important points not discussed here receive consideration. We have attempted to show in the foregoing paragraphs that nothing is produced by the genes without intra- and intercellular factors playing an important role. Anyone desiring to understand completely the growth and development of children must be aware of this interesting field in which new observations are constantly modifying old concepts and perhaps pointing to new potentialities in the realm of practical therapeutics.

Postnatal Environment

Environment after birth may be varied in so many ways that well-controlled studies are exceedingly difficult to make. Most of our knowledge is based on very gross differences that are easily apparent. Children vary in their potentialities for modification. These remain used or unused to the extent that the environment offers opportunity for their realization. As mentioned in Chapter 1, the human organism has a long period of immaturity which gives time for the development of many qualities, good and bad, necessary or detrimental to survival.

Children are not all alike, and consequently we cannot expect exactly similar responses to similar changes in environment either in single individuals or in groups of individuals. Further, we know that the continuity of growth implies a resistance to displacement (both mental and physical) and a tendency to restoration of the normal pattern of development for a given child. An excellent example of this is shown by the premature infant. Early in life its measurements of physical growth are below those of the term infant, but in a relatively short time there is little difference between them, and thereafter the growth of one parallels that of the other for all practical purposes. Differences in nutrition or environment may either speed up or slow down the period before equality is reached, but the tendency to convergence toward average trends will always hold.

Some of the more clearly understood environmental factors are discussed here; others are considered in the chapters that follow.

Geographic variations appear to be of little importance within the boundaries of the United States. Mills[9] has stated that children living in tropical regions show retarded growth and inferior adult size. However, since such children frequently suffer from poor diets and other poor socioeconomic factors, one can doubt that climate alone is responsible for the differences noted. Mills also found that full sexual maturity is reached later in the tropical and frigid zones than in the temperate zones. We feel that this statement needs further clarification. Among Filipino girls born and raised in tropical conditions and receiving good nutrition and medical care the average age of menarche was just over 13 years, which compares very favorably with average American girls. The observations of Ellis[26] and Tanner[27] support the fact that climate has little effect on adolescent development.

There is considerable evidence to show that the growth rates of weight and height are influenced by the seasons of the year and that these differences are particularly striking in older children. Growth rates in weight are at a minimum in the spring and early summer and are maximal during late summer and autumn. Conversely, growth in height is greatest in the spring in this country.[74]

Measurements of infants born in a poor socioeconomic group are in general inferior to similar measurements of infants born in a high socioeconomic group. In many countries throughout Europe and in this country it has been shown that the stature of adult laborers is inferior to that of students, who presumably represent a more prosperous group. The rate of growth of children both of whose parents were unemployed was found to be inferior to that of children with one employed parent. Thus socioeconomic factors are of great importance in determining the physical status of children.[7, 10] In the 1940s the growth and development of American-born Japanese children in California were compared with those of children of the same sex and age in Japan. There was a striking superiority in regard to weight, height, and skeletal age for the California-born children. Inferior diet and other unfavorable environmental conditions found in Japan at that time undoubtedly were responsible.[47] A contemporary study indicates no differences between American-born and Japanese-born Japanese children.[10]

There is also an increasing accumulation of evidence that mental development is related to socioeconomic factors. The concept that some children are functioning at substandard levels because of faulty nutrition and other adverse environmental conditions is relatively new. Whether actual intelligence is influenced or whether it is the ability to use the inherited potentialities that is affected remains to be proved. Another point to be considered is the possibility that genetic potentialities are such that the child born in the lowest socioeconomic group has less chance to raise himself above this level than the child born in a better environment. The important point introduced by several studies is that children's behavior should be interpreted with a knowledge of the interrelation of growth and organic development. As we will repeat again and again, significant advances in the study of child development can be made only with a careful correlation of all of the apparently isolated facts.

Over the past century or more, there has been a general trend toward increases in height and weight with each succeeding generation in the more developed nations.[27, 28, 30] This trend has been noted within the first few months of life and persists throughout the entire growing period. For example, selecting boys aged 14 with similar ethnic backgrounds and living in the United States, in 1877 the average height was 145 cm and weight 39 kg; by 1920 they were 155 cm and 45 kg and in 1970 they were 163 cm and 51 kg respectively. The average height and weight of the United States Army recruit was 4 cm and 4.5 kg greater in World War II than in World War I.

The acceleration of growth is also shown in the trend of age of menarche. Tanner[27] gathered statistics from several northern European countries and found a marked similarity in all. In the period from 1850 to 1950 there was an average decrease in the age of the first menses from over 17 to 13.5 years, or a reduction of nearly one-half year for each decade. In the United States one study showed menarche took place at about 14.5 years in 1900 but in the same area now occurs at an average of 13 years.[29] There is also evidence that the adolescent spurt of growth occurs sooner and final stature is attained at an earlier age than in previous generations.[27] Just as menarche occurs at an earlier age, so menopause occurs at a later one. Compared to a century ago, the delay is between 4 and 5 years in areas where statistics are available.[59, 60]

These changes in growth have been noted over a period of at least 100 years. The beginning may be marked by the emergence from the lowest levels of the Industrial Revolution. For the countries that are more fortunate in terms of good health care, there is some evidence that the trend is slowing and perhaps near-optimal levels have been reached. There appears to be little difference in the average figures for height in children in the United States today as compared to a generation ago.

In both man and lower animals the capacity for growth is very great. If the rate of growth in a child is retarded temporarily, as by illness from infection, starvation or hypothyroidism, and this is corrected, an accelerated rate of growth then takes place. This rate may exceed normal for height and skeletal maturation by three- or fourfold. Once the child's normal levels have been attained, the velocity decreases to that which had been present before the illness.[55] If interference with statural growth takes place over a long period of time, this is usually accompanied by a similar delay in bone maturation, resulting in an actual lengthening of the growing period. If a child is held at a constant weight by underfeeding, he will again gain weight if no further decrease in his food intake occurs. Such studies portray the tremendous impetus to grow and develop despite adverse environmental conditions. They re-emphasize the resistance to displacement from an average trend.[12]

Exercise may also be an important factor in the complete picture of development and growth. Growth processes are inseparable from dynamic processes, and physiologic activity of protoplasm favors its further development. The disuse atrophy and weakness of an immobilized limb are examples of this important principle. The development of "skills" through practice might serve as still another illustration.

Practical Applications

It is no longer believed that the child has inherited certain traits as finished products. What the child does inherit is a large assortment of genes which determine his make-up. Each of the many genes influences some particular part of the developing embryo and child. From the time of conception until death each phase of development is influenced by the interplay of the inherited genes and the many environmental factors whose roles begin at fertilization. Growth, both mental and physical, is constantly creating its own new conditions as it proceeds. In appraising development we must consider all factors: family tree, cultural milieu, siblings, sickness, nutrition, sunshine, education and all other possible influences.

Since a new combination of genes is formed with every child, there may be great diversity among siblings or between parents and the child. However, in general it may be stated that the child will show genetic characteristics similar to those of his relatives if he comes from a distinctly superior or inferior family. But there is no such thing as certainty in predicting the characteristics of children from knowledge of the family, with the possible exceptions of some of the congenital anomalies previously mentioned in which the mode of inheritance is known.[6]

If a child is born with a deficient genetic constitution, a change in environment will not go far toward improving him. On the other hand, individuals with superior gene combinations are precisely those who may take advantage of the opportunities which environment presents to them. Still other individuals seem to have inherited strong tendencies in particular directions. Here environment may have a good effect by assisting in the further development of the beneficial tendencies and/or repressing undesirable ones.

With increasing knowledge and improvements in technics more and more congenital anomalies are subject to remedy or improvement. However, therapeutic measures and environmental correction cannot cure defectiveness of genes. Nature's frequent remedy for this situation is to "neutralize" the defective genes by pairing them with normal genes from the other parent. The fact remains, however, that they are carried to future generations. The only method of preventing this is to prevent propagation by the individuals who carry the defect. It can be seen that the problem becomes extremely complex when the physician is confronted with a request for advice regarding adoption or advisability of parenthood. The interested reader should consult the references at the end of this chapter for further discussion of these very real problems.

Man may be considered the most successful product of biologic evolution so far. From his obscure beginning as a rare animal in an isolated area, most probably Africa, he multiplied to become one of the most numerous of mammals. Although numbers may not be an unaltered blessing, they are an important measure of biologic success. In man alone, adaptation can occur through alteration of culture as well as by natural selection. Technology not only has improved environment (e.g., heat and clothing) but has permitted persistence and increase of abnormal genes (e.g., diabetes mellitus), neither of which was in the realm of any creature before man. Regulation of population size cannot be postponed much longer, and the genetic problem will have to be met. As Dr. Dobzhansky[48] has written, "The question how many people and what kind of people will be solved together, if they are solved at all."

SUMMARY OF THE FACTORS WHICH INFLUENCE GROWTH

Genetics

This may influence the response of end organs to all sorts of stimuli, e.g., hormones, nutrients and external environment. In addition it may influence growth profoundly through congenital malformations of the end organ, as in achondroplasia.

Nutrition

This may include quantitative and qualitative amounts of the building materials, i.e., protein, carbohydrate, fats, minerals and vitamins. Nutrition may also be influenced by diseases of the gastrointestinal tract, e.g., diarrhea and celiac disease. Finally, local or general nutritional failure may result from circulatory changes such as congenital heart disease.

Internal milieu

Optimal growth presupposes normal function of all organs and normal metabolism. Severe liver or kidney insufficiencies are examples of conditions that preclude normal growth due to impairment of tissue metabolism of all parts of the body.

Hormones

Secretions of the endocrine glands act as catalysts to the normal growth potentials of the body. Some are growth-promoting, as the pituitary growth-stimulating hormone and androgens. Others cause maturation—thyroid hormone, androgens and estrogens. Some may be antagonistic to growth but useful in other ways when in proper balance—the adrenal glucocorticoids, for example.

Environment

Severe disease may influence ultimate growth. There are definite seasonal variations in increments of weight and height. Emotional disturbances may affect growth, e.g., anorexia. Socioeconomic aspects may be important in relation to nutrition, clothing, disease, etc. Such factors as fetal position, faulty implantation of the ovum, rubella during pregnancy, etc., are among the earliest adverse environmental influences on the growing organism.

REFERENCES

1. Stern, C.: *Principles of Human Genetics* (2d ed.; San Francisco: W. H. Freeman & Company, 1960).
2. Polani, P. E.: The incidence of chromosomal malformations, Proc. R. Soc. Med. 63:14, 1970.
3. Chapple, C. C., and Davidson, D. T.: A study of the relationship between fetal position and certain congenital deformities, J. Pediatr. 18:483, 1941.

4. Court Brown, W. M.: *Human Population Cytogenetics* (Amsterdam: North Holland Publishing Company, 1967).
5. Reid, D. E.; Ryan, K. L.; and Benirschke, K.: *Principles and Management of Human Reproduction* (Philadelphia: W. B. Saunders Company, 1972).
6. Erbe, R. W.: Current concepts in genetics, principles of medical genetics, N. Engl. J. Med. 294:381, 1976.
7. Meredith, H. V.: Stature and weight of children of United States, with reference to influence of racial, regional, socioeconomic and secular factors, Am. J. Dis. Child. 62:909, 1941.
8. Gellis, S. S., and Hsia, D. Y.: The infant of the diabetic mother, A. M. A. Am. J. Dis. Child. 97:1, 1959.
9. Mills, C. A.: Climatic Factors in Health and Disease, in Glasser, O. (ed.): *Medical Physics*, Vol. I (Chicago: Year Book Publishers, Inc., 1944), p. 232.
10. Eveleth, P., and Tanner, J. M.: *Worldwide Variations in Human Growth* (London: Cambridge University Press, 1976).
11. Gall, J. C.: Genetic factors in physical growth and development, Mich. Med. 67:1209, 1968.
12. Robbins, W. J., Brody, S., Hogan, A. G., Jackson, C. M., and Greene, C. W.: *Growth* (New Haven, Conn.: Yale University Press, 1928).
13. Summitt, R. L.: Abnormalities of the autosomes and their resultant syndromes, Pediatr. Ann. 2:40, 1973.
14. Swan, C., Tostevin, A. L., Mayo, H., and Black, G. B.: Further observations on congenital defects following infectious diseases during pregnancy with special reference to rubella, Med. J. Aust. 1:409, 1944.
15. Fishbein, M. (ed.): *Second International Conference on Congenital Malformations: Papers and Discussions Presented* (New York: International Medical Congress, Ltd., 1964).
16. Warkany, J.: *Congenital Malformations* (Chicago: Year Book Medical Publishers, Inc., 1971).
17. Siegel, M., and Fuerst, H. T.: Low birth weight and maternal virus diseases, J.A.M.A. 197:88, 1966.
18. Plummer, G.: Anomalies occurring in children exposed in utero to the atomic bomb in Hiroshima, Pediatrics 10:687, 1952.
19. Ford, C. E., and Hamerston, J. L.: The chromosomes of man, Nature 178:1020, 1956.
20. Levine, H.: *Clinical Cytogenetics* (Boston: Little, Brown and Co., 1971).
21. McKusick, V.: *Mendelian Inheritance in Man* (Baltimore: The Johns Hopkins Press, 1971).
22. Neel, J. V., and Schull, W. J.: *Human Heredity* (Chicago: University of Chicago Press, 1954).
23. Reed, S. C.: *Counseling in Medical Genetics* (2d ed.; Philadelphia: W. B. Saunders Company, 1965).
24. Bakwin, H.: Child care in Uganda and the Belgian Congo, J. Pediatr. 45:430, 1954.
25. Browne, D.: Congenital deformities of mechanical origin, Arch. Dis. Child. 30:37, 1955.
26. Ellis, R. W. B.: Age of puberty in the tropics, Br. Med. J. 1:85, 1950.
27. Tanner, J. M.: *Growth at Adolescence* (2d ed.; Springfield, Ill.: Charles C Thomas, Publisher, 1962).
28. Meredith, H. V.: Measurements of Oregon school boys, Hum. Biol. 23:24, 1950.

29. *Age at Menarche: United States,* (Washington, D.C.: U.S. Dept. of Health, Education and Welfare, Public Health Service, 1973).
30. Meyers, E. S. A.: Height-weight survey of New South Wales school children, Med. J. Aust. 1:435, 1956.
31. McKusick, V. A.: Approaches and methods in human genetics, Am. J. Obstet. Gynecol. 90:1014, 1964.
32. Hewitt, D., and Stewart, A.: A study of the influence of social and genetic factors on birthweight, Hum. Biol. 24:309, 1952.
33. Warkany, J. (ed.): Congenital malformations (a series of papers by various authors on various aspects), Pediatrics 19:719, 1957.
34. Stern, C.: *Principles of Human Genetics* (2d ed.; San Francisco: W. H. Freeman & Company, 1960).
35. Jukes, T. H.: The genetic code, Am. Sci. 53:477, 1965.
36. Puck, T. T.: Radiation and the human cell, Sci. Am. 202:142, 1960.
37. Norris, A. S.: Prenatal factors in intellectual and emotional development, J.A.M.A. 172:413, 1960.
38. Barr, M. L.: Sex chromatin and phenotype in man, Science 130:679, 1959.
39. Warkany, J., Beandry, P. H., and Hornstein, S.: Attempted abortion with aminopterin (4-aminopteroylglutamic acid): Malformations of the child, A.M.A. J. Dis. Child. 97:274, 1959.
40. Carr, D. H.: Genetic basis of abortion, Ann. Rev. Genet. 6:65, 1971.
41. Illingworth, R. S.: Birth weight and subsequent weight, Br. Med. J. 1:96, 1950.
42. Flynt, J. W.: Extent of the birth defects problem, Pediatr. Ann. 2:10, 1973.
43. Hook, E. B.: Behavioral implications of the human XYY genotype, Science 179:139, 1973.
44. Falkner, F.: Some physical measurements in the first three years of life, Arch. Dis. Child. 33:1, 1958.
45. Drillien, C. M.: A longitudinal study of the growth and development of prematurely and maturely born children, Arch. Dis. Child. 33:423, 1958.
46. Ruch, R.: X-irradiation effects on the human fetus, J. Pediatr. 52:531, 1958.
47. Greulich, W. W.: Growth of children of the same race under different environmental conditions, Science 127:515, 1958.
48. Dobzhansky, T.: Man and natural selection, Am. Sci. 49:285, 1961.
49. Smith, D.: *Recognizable Patterns of Human Malformation* (2d ed.; Philadelphia: W. B. Saunders Co., 1976).
50. Holmes, L. B.: Inborn errors of morphogenesis, a review of localized hereditary malformations, N. Engl. J. Med. 291:763, 1974.
51. Gerald, P. S.: Current concepts in genetics, sex chromosome disorders, N. Engl. J. Med. 294:706, 1976.
52. Sutherland, J. M., and Light, I. J.: The effect of drugs upon the developing fetus, Pediatr. Clin. North Am. 12:781, 1965.
53. Bauld, R., Sutherland, G. R., and Bain, A. D.: Chromosome studies in investigation of stillbirths and neonatal deaths, Arch. Dis Child. 49:782, 1974.
54. Summitt, R. L.: Chromosome nomenclature, J. Pediatr. 76:314, 1970.
55. Prader, A., Tanner, J. M., and von Harnack, G. A.: Catch-up growth following illness or starvation, Pediatrics 62:646, 1963.
56. Sutow, W. W., Conrad, R. A., and Griffith, K. M.: Growth status of children exposed to fallout radiation on Marshall Islands, Pediatrics 36:721, 1965.
57. Burrow, G. N., Hamilton, H. B., and Hrubec, Z.: Study of adolescents exposed in utero to the atomic bomb, Nagasaki, Japan, J.A.M.A. 192:357, 1965.

58. Babson, S. G., Kangas, J., Young, N., and Bramhall, J. L.: Growth and development of twins of dissimilar size at birth. Pediatrics 33:327, 1964.
59. Bakwin, H.: The secular change in growth and development, Acta Paediatr. Scand. 53:79, 1964.
60. Frommer, D. J.: The changing age of the menopause, Br. Med. J. 2:349, 1964.
61. Day, R. L.: Factors influencing offspring, Am. J. Dis. Child. 113:179, 1967.
62. Tenbrinck, M. S., and Buchin, S. Y.: Fetal alcohol syndrome, J.A.M.A. 232:1144, 1975.
63. Belmont, L., and Marolla, F. A.: Birth order, family size and intelligence, Science 182:1096, 1973.
64. Overall, J.C., and Glasgow, L. A.: Virus infections of the fetus and newborn infant, J. Pediatr. 77:315, 1970.
65. Hanshaw, J. B., Scheiner, A. P., Moxley, A. W., Gaev, L., Abel, W., and Scheiner, B.: School failure and deafness after silent congenital cytomegalovirus infection, N. Engl. J. Med. 295:468, 1976.
66. Wilson, J. G.: Present status of drugs as teratogens in man, Teratology 7:3, 1973.
67. Herbst, A. L., Poskanser, D. C., Robby, S. J., Friedlander, L., and Scully, R. E.: Prenatal exposure to stilbestrol, N. Engl. J. Med. 222:334, 1975.
68. Jones, K. L., Smith, D. W., Harvey, M. A. S., Hall, B. D., and Quan, L.: Older paternal age and fresh gene mutation: Data on additional disorders, J. Pediatr. 86:84, 1975.
69. Kandall, S. R., Albin, S., Lowinson, J., Berle, B., Eidelman, A. I., and Gartner, L. M.: Differential effects of maternal heroin and methadone use on birthweight, Pediatr. 58:681, 1976.
70. Evans, H. E., and Glass, L.: Perinatal Medicine (Hagerstown, Md.: Harper & Row Publishers, Inc., 1976).
71. Smith, D. W., Truog, W., Rogers, J. E., Greitzer, L. J., Skinner, A. L., McCann, J. L., and Harvey, M. A. S.: Shifting linear growth during infancy: Illustration of genetic factors in growth from fetal life through infancy, J. Pediatr. 89:225, 1976.
72. Fisch, R. O., Bilek, M. K., Harrobin, J. M., and Chang, P.: Children with superior intelligence at 7 years of age, Am. J. Dis. Child. 130:481, 1976.
73. Terman, L. M., and Oden, M. H.: The Gifted Child Grows Up (Stanford, Calif.: Stanford University Press, 1947).
74. Marshall, W. A.: The relationship of variations in children's growth rates to seasonal climate variations, Ann. Hum. Biol. 2:243, 1975.
75. Niswander, K. R., and Gordon, M.: The Collaborative Perinatal Study of the National Institute of Neurological Disease and Stroke: The Women and Their Pregnancies (Washington, D.C.: U.S. Dept. of Health, Education and Welfare, 1972).

3 / The Placenta and Fetal Development

The Placenta

THE PLACENTA is an organ of exceptional accomplishments. It can perform some of the functions of the liver, intestinal mucosa, lung, kidney, and several endocrine glands. In addition it has some characteristics which are unique. Because of its profound influence on the earliest stages of growth and development with respect to nutrition, excretion, hormonal relationships, and immunity, the placenta merits some discussion before proceeding to the subject of the fetus.[22, 25]

The fetal portion of the placenta develops from a combination of the two primary fetal membranes, the allantois and the serosa. These fuse to form the chorion, which in turn fuses with the lining of the uterus. The serosa is made up of an outer cell layer termed the trophoblast and can be recognized at a very early stage as cells extending outward from the earliest cell mass. Shortly thereafter a second layer of mesodermal cells reinforces the trophoblast, and the two layers form the trophoderm. Almost as soon as the hindgut of the embryo is formed, a diverticulum, the allantois, arises. The human allantois exhibits only a rudimentary lumen confined to the belly stalk region, but its mesoderm, or supporting tissues and blood vessels, grows out beyond the lumen and spreads over the inner surface of the trophoderm. The fusion of the allantois and serosa brings to the latter a highly vascular layer which is connected to the vascular supply of the embryo. Later this connection is maintained through the umbilical arteries and vein. Once the embryo is implanted, there follow rapid changes in both chorion and endometrium. As early as the second week after implantation, villi have formed from the trophoderm. The villi are fingerlike projections with a vascular core. Through continuous branching and invasion of the endometrium by the villi, growth and complexity of the placenta increase. Erosion of maternal vessels produces small pools of blood which form the intravillous spaces. It is estimated that at term the fetal surface of the placenta is approximately 10 sq m, with only a very thin tissue layer separating fetal and maternal circula-

47

tion. The trophoblast undergoes considerable modification and toward term largely disappears, and only the syncytium remains of the chorion.

Certain aspects of the structure of the placenta are not yet defined. Furthermore, as the placenta ages, its structure changes. These details are beyond the scope of this book. One important factor, however, should be brought out. The structure of the human placenta is sufficiently unique that experiments carried out with other species must be applied or interpreted with great caution in terms of the human organism.

The placenta functions as the main organ of homeostasis for the fetus. It serves as the organ of respiratory exchange. In some aspects it is an immunologic barrier between mother and fetus, yet there is evidence that some fetal portions of the placenta may enter the maternal circulation during normal pregnancy and, possibly by this method, establish tolerance to the fetus. It is an alimentary organ supplying proteins, lipids, carbohydrates, minerals and water required for growth and development. As an excretory organ it functions as a kidney for the fetus. As an endocrine gland it synthesizes gonadotropins, progesterone, estrogens, and other steroids whose actions are still not certain. With increasing age several of these functions undergo distinct changes which are not necessarily related to changes in vascularity or permeability of the membranes.

Simple diffusion from maternal to fetal circulation is exemplified by oxygen, carbon dioxide, water and urea. Increased permeability during most or all of pregnancy is true for most minerals except iron, zinc and iodides. An active gradient from fetus to mother is present for bilirubin, adrenal steroids and thyroxin. Active transport exists for amino acids, glucose, fatty acids, water-soluble vitamins, iron and certain of the antibodies.

In discussing the placental role in the nutrition of the fetus, Dancis[21] concluded that the transfer rate of sodium across the placenta progressively increases during the course of gestation, paralleled by increased vascularization of the fetal membranes. Terminally the transfer rate decreases. With regard to both water and sodium, considerably more is transferred than is retained by the growing fetus. Phosphorus, iron and iodine are relatively more concentrated on the fetal side, indicating an active transfer of these substances. With regard to iron, it was found that in infection of the mother iron transport is decreased, but with hemorrhage it is increased. Like the liver, the placenta contains ferritin, the chief storage form of iron, which is a protein complex. The blood concentration of calcium is higher in the fetus than in the maternal organism, but the filtrable, or ionizable, calcium is equal, indicating the possibility of a greater binding capacity of fetal blood for this element.

The water-soluble vitamins are found in higher concentrations in fetal than in maternal blood, whereas the reverse is true of the fat-soluble vitamins.

Glucose is the principal source of energy for the fetus. Throughout pregnancy the fetal blood level of glucose is lower than in the mother (Table 3–1). This is not a result of fetal consumption alone, but because the placenta maintains a gradient in that direction. Placental content of glycogen stores increases during the early stages of pregnancy and then rapidly falls. It has been postulated that this source of carbohydrate, although small in comparison to the total quantity required, is made available to the fetus during its period of rapid growth. The net transfer is in the direction of the fetus, and near term the placenta must transfer more than 20 mg of glucose per minute. The placenta is stereospecific and otherwise selective in its transport mechanism. For instance, D-xylose passes much more rapidly than L-xylose, and glucose more rapidly than fructose.[3, 21, 28]

Very early in gestation there is a dependence on maternal sources for lipids. The placenta can metabolize and transport fatty acids. However, the fatty acid concentration in fetal blood is much lower than in the mother and fluctuations in maternal fatty acid content are not reflected in the blood of the fetus. Triglycerides do not cross the placenta. The fat content of fetal tissues increases nearly 300-fold from the second to the ninth month of pregnancy, by far the greatest increase occurring during the final trimester. The lipid concentration and the fatty acid composition do not vary significantly throughout that period.[40, 48] Lipid synthesis by the fetus, primarily from glucose, is well established early in gestation and the rate of production parallels the rate of growth of the fetal organs.

Amino acids easily and quickly pass from the mother to the fetus, and their concentration is usually higher on the fetal side. They can readily be incorporated into protein. The placenta transfers intact proteins in a highly selective manner. The only source of gamma globulin until well after birth is the maternal organism. At birth the fetal and maternal levels are equal. Small but significant amounts of albumin cross the placenta from the mother, even though the fetus is very capable of manufacturing his own. There is some

TABLE 3–1.—RELATIVE CONCENTRATIONS OF
SOME SUBSTANCES IN MATERNAL AND CORD
BLOOD INDICATING CERTAIN ASPECTS OF
PLACENTAL AND FETAL FUNCTIONS

HIGHER IN FETUS	EQUAL	LOWER IN FETUS
Phosphorus	Urea	Total lipids
Calcium	Uric acid	Cholesterol
Potassium	Creatine	Glucose
Lactic acid	Magnesium	Albumin
Amino acids	Chloride	
Water soluble vitamins	Sodium	
	Gamma globulin	

evidence that the placenta can synthesize proteins, but the value of this to the fetus remains obscure. (See also discussion on development of immunity, Chapter 7.)

Proof of the existence of any mechanism other than simple diffusion for the exchange of oxygen and carbon dioxide has not been established. All indications are that the fetus exists in utero under conditions that are hypoxemic by postpartum standards. Oxygen saturation near term is considerably below that found shortly after birth, but provided there is a large enough systemic blood flow to fetal tissues and the oxygen-carrying capacity of the blood is great enough, this saturation of the fetal blood is clearly sufficient to supply tissue needs with some margin of safety. Maternal arterial blood at term has a PO_2 of 95 mm Hg while umbilical venous blood has a PO_2 of 28 mm Hg. Two factors contribute to the adequacy of fetal tissue oxygenation. The oxyhemoglobin dissociation curve for fetal blood is shifted to the left in comparison to adult blood. Thus, oxygen saturation of fetal hemoglobin can be accomplished at a much lower PO_2 level. The actual hemoglobin concentration is considerably higher in the fetus than in the adult, a hematocrit of 53 at term for the fetus compared to an average of 44 for an adult female. In addition, the metabolic rate of the fetus is relatively low since there is no thermal loss and little physical activity.

The placenta has a high rate of metabolism, being comparable to active adult organs such as the liver and the kidney. It can carry on a wide spectrum of anabolic and catabolic reactions, including a glycolytic cycle, the Krebs tricarboxylic acid cycle and the synthesis of fatty acids and proteins from small precursors. Approximately 60 enzymes have been identified in the placenta.[38] Active transport involves enzymatic action against a gradient. In the case of large molecules, e.g., gamma globulins, pinocytosis is the mechanism of transfer.

The placenta is a major endocrine organ that is known to produce at least three protein hormones de novo, analogues of pituitary hormones and, from chemical precursors of fetal and maternal origin, the steroids progesterone and estrogens.[25, 27, 60] Human chorionic gonadotropin (HCG) is produced in very large quantities in early gestation, and then drops off to maintain a slightly fluctuating, but still much higher than normal maternal serum level, for the remainder of gestation. HCG closely resembles luteinizing hormone (LH) produced by the pituitary. Although its physiologic functions are not completely understood, especially in view of the early very high levels, HCG appears to maintain the action of the corpus luteum during the transition from the menstrual cycle to pregnancy. It has also been noted that HCG may play a role in blocking maternal immunological responses directed against the fetus, thus preventing a reaction similar to graft rejection.

A second protein hormone produced by the placenta has both growth hormone and prolactinlike activities. Originally referred to as the placental lactogenic hormone, it is now identified as the human chorionic somatomammotropin (HCS). Maternal serum levels of HCS rise at a steady rate throughout gestation, fairly accurately paralleling placental weight. It does not cross the placenta. It is postulated that it functions in the maternal organism to maintain positive nitrogen balance, mobilize fat stores and raise serum glucose levels. All of these results are analogous to those of pituitary growth hormone actions (see Chapter 9). The end result is to supply the fetus with adequate quantities of glucose and amino acids at minimal expense to the mother. This hormone plays an additional role, with several other hormones, in preparing the breasts for lactation.

The third protein hormone closely resembles pituitary thyrotropin (TSH), and our knowledge of its function is still too meager to warrant further comment.

Of the estrogens synthesized by the placenta, one of great importance is estriol. Despite considerable ignorance of its physiologic role, maternal urine or serum levels of estriol are a valuable index of the status of the fetus. An essential precursor for the production of this steroidal hormone comes from the fetal adrenal gland. In normal pregnancy, during the final trimester, there is a slow but steady increase in its production. In anencephaly, associated with lack of development of a functional adrenal cortex, levels remain low. In threatened abortions with a poor prognosis for fetal survival, the levels are below normal, but if survival occurs and pregnancy proceeds, the levels will be normal and a steady increase will ensue.[25, 39] The amount of urine estriol excretion appears to correlate accurately with fetal weight.

Progesterone, another steroid hormone produced by the placenta, is important in maintaining the endometrium for the continuation of gestation. Maternal cholesterol is the basic building block for the synthesis. There is a steady rise in the maternal serum and urine as pregnancy progresses. It has been postulated that progesterone, crossing to the fetus, serves as the precursor for the male fetus to manufacture testosterone, and therefore plays an important role in sexual differentiation and development.

The relationship of changes of structure and function in the placenta to the growth and development of the fetus, infant or child is difficult to define in many circumstances. The study of the placental changes in morphology throughout pregnancy and the establishment of adequate normal standards are of recent origin. Most of the studies so far published describe rather gross changes in the placenta associated with fetal abnormality. As our ability to measure more subtle changes improves, the list of insults to the fetus resulting from placental insufficiency will undoubtedly expand.

Using weight versus time as the criterion, the placenta grows most rapidly during the first trimester of pregnancy, and then the rate drops off rather quickly. In contrast, the fetus grows slowly initially and then rapidly in the final trimester. The fetus and placenta are equal in weight at $3^{1}/_{2}$ months, but at term the placenta is about 12–15% of the infant's weight. Although there is a direct relationship between placental and fetal size, there is a surprising frequency of exceptions to the rule.

Low birth weight, when associated with low socioeconomic status and maternal malnutrition, does appear to correlate with a low functional placental mass. Morphologically, this is accompanied by a diminution in the vascular area available for exchange. By necessity, human studies of placental size and presumed function have been limited in number, and control groups used for comparison have often been poorly selected. If indeed there is such an entity as placental insufficiency, then questions must be asked as to the etiology. Is the major cause maternal malnutrition, a genetic or chromosomal abnormality in the fetus, chronic illness in the mother, the long-term effect of many generations of deprivation including small size of the mother, or an actual anatomic and physiologic defect in the placenta?[24, 33, 34, 36]

Recent studies have established that placentas from infants with "intrauterine growth failure" have fewer cells when compared to controls. These findings were true whether the cause of the infant's smallness was malnutrition, intrauterine infection or a chromosomal disorder. In many of the organs of these infants there was a significant reduction in cell numbers. Data from laboratory animals have shown similar results and also indicate that even with optimum conditions following birth there remains a deficit in cell number. These findings suggest that early programming of ultimate cell numbers of various organs, including the brain, takes place in utero and may be unchangeable despite subsequent events.[42, 43]

A pregnancy that extends beyond the calculated date of confinement (290 days) has been the subject of controversy for a long time. The questions asked refer to the existence of such a clinical entity as postmaturity (placental dysfunction) and whether a fetus can be adversely affected by such circumstances.[3] The newborn infant said to result from such a pregnancy lacks the usual amount of subcutaneous fat and vernix caseosa and has meconium-stained skin. He appears thin and undernourished with wrinkled skin having a parchmentlike quality. No definite placental abnormalities are identifiable in the majority of cases.[24] Morbidity and mortality are higher than normal with autopsy of stillbirths revealing findings consistent with asphyxia. Hypoglycemia is a particularly common risk in these infants, very possibly as a result of decreased glycogen and fat storage.[32, 33] There is also increasing evidence that a considerable number of these infants may have neurologic abnormalities later in life.

In mothers who develop hypertension and toxemia of pregnancy, placental size is reduced and the vascularity of the villi is curtailed.[33] Similar changes with thrombotic lesions have been described in pregnancy associated with the diabetic who has developed degenerative vascular complications.[31] Abnormalities in the fetuses of such pregnancies are frequent. Nodularity of the placental surface and oligohydramnios in the condition termed *amnion nodosum* are frequently seen with renal agenesis or polycystic kidney in the fetus.[35] The small size of both placenta and newborn has been repeatedly noted when a chromosomal abnormality existed.

The occurrence of a single umbilical artery is about 1% in all pregnancies. The incidence is slightly higher in whites than in blacks and is more frequent in low birth weight infants. Although originally thought to be more common in twin pregnancies, this now seems doubtful. Statistics vary in different studies, but from 30 to 40% will be associated with recognizable congenital anomalies, of which a quarter will die in early infancy.[29, 59] The organ systems most frequently involved are the cardiovascular and the genitourinary. It is interesting, and fortunate, to note that follow-ups of surviving children indicate they have essentially normal growth and development, even though they will have a higher incidence of some malformations than the general population.[58, 59]

Vascular anastomoses in monochorionic twin pregnancies may lead to plethora in one twin and anemia in the other. The donor twin is always considerably smaller and may remain so for many years.[35]

Amniotic Fluid

The growing fetus is surrounded by amniotic fluid which aids in maintaining a steady body temperature, protects from physical injury and serves as a media for fluid exchange. In early pregnancy the amniotic fluid contains little protein and is probably a dialysate of maternal serum. Later the fluid becomes hypotonic as it becomes diluted with fetal urine. Maximum volume of approximately 1,400 ml is reached at the seventh month and then decreases to about 800 ml in uncomplicated term pregnancies. The turnover rate of amniotic fluid is around 600 ml per hour, at least 75% of this exchange being through the fetus and placenta by swallowing and excreting a urine that is essentially a glomerular filtrate. These facts explain the frequent complication of polyhydramnios with congenital obstructive lesions of the gut. In contrast, oligohydramnios is seen with renal aplasia or urethral obstruction. Average values for some components of the fluid near term are: protein; 100–500 mg/100 ml; nonprotein nitrogen, 25 mg/100 ml; uric acid, 4.5 mg/100 ml and glucose, 20–60 mg/100 ml.[3]

Examination of the amniotic fluid by abdominal amniocentesis has been established to be of value in the diagnosis and/or prognosis of the fetal condition. More than 30 different inborn errors of metabolism are potentially identifiable by specific enzyme measurement of cultured desquamated skin fibroblasts. Over half of these have now been reported in the literature as confirming antenatal diagnoses. Examples of some of the most frequently encountered are: Tay-Sachs disease, Gaucher's disease, Krabbe's disease, Fabry's disease, glycogen storage disease, galactosemia and Hurler's disease. By determination of the presence of abnormal amounts of specific metabolic products in amniotic fluid, other diagnoses can be made. A fetus with the adrenogenital syndrome (adrenal hyperplasia) will excrete high levels of 17-ketosteroids, and their precursors, which are readily measurable. Changes in the optical density of the fluid are associated with anencephaly and erythroblastosis. Antenatal diagnosis of heritable disorders has become an integral part of human genetics.[14, 19, 20]

Throughout pregnancy, as increasing amounts of fetal urine are excreted, the creatinine concentration rises in the amniotic fluid. A level above 2 mg/100 ml is taken as an indication of at least 36 weeks of gestation. As the fetus and the lungs mature, surfactant phospholipids are found in increasing amounts in tracheal fluid. Since there is continuity between the fetal lung and amniotic fluid, concentration of the phospholipids in that fluid can be used as a measure of the degree of maturation. Determinations are usually made of the lecithin/sphingomyelin ratio since the change in that ratio is an accurate reflection of physiologic maturity. Ratios of less than 1 persist until about 30 weeks of gestation. In normal pregnancy, the ratio rises to 2 by 35 weeks. The method has been of great value in predicting the probability of the occurrence of the respiratory distress syndrome (see Chapter 5). The ideal ratio sought in elective deliveries would be a value of 2 or greater.[17]

Not related to amniocentesis, but equally important, are some other biochemical determinations. One is the finding of abnormally elevated maternal serum levels of alpha-fetoprotein when the fetus is anencephalic or has spina bifida.[37] The use of urine estriol levels has been mentioned as another tool in antenatal evaluation of the progress of pregnancy. Such methods alert the physician to prepare for abortion or exceptional therapeutic measures.

Fetal Monitoring

In recent years a number of new techniques have been developed, in addition to amniocentesis, as aids in antenatal diagnosis or as determinants of the course of fetal growth and development. A relatively safe and noninvasive method is the use of ultrasound (sonography) based upon the principles of pulse-echo and the Doppler phenomenon. Using the latter, one can monitor the fetal heart rate which is a sensitive indicator of fetal viability and stress. The pulse-echo permits evaluation of fetal position and size, and cardiovascular and other organ system sizes and functioning. It has also been found very useful in determining placental position before attempting amniocentesis. Direct fetal heart rate monitoring, through application of electrode to the scalp after rupture of the membranes, has proved to be a valuable means of determining such conditions as cord compression, uteroplacental insufficiency and simple head compression with uterine contractions. Standards of changes of heart rate and time intervals have been established in relation to each uterine contraction.[12] Usual methods of radiology as well as fetography (injection of radiopaque material in amniotic fluid) have also been used.[3] These have the added risk of radiation exposure.

Fetal Growth

That growth and development do not begin at the time of birth is quite obvious, but for the pediatrician birth marks the onset of growth and development from a clinical standpoint. To provide a clear understanding of these phenomena after birth, the changes that occur before birth and continue to take place in the postnatal period are reviewed here.

Life as a new individual commences at the moment of fertilization. Growth becomes an inherent force in that individual and continues, in stature at least, until the average postnatal age of about 20 years unless disease, accident, or death interferes. During this time there are also marked changes in differentiation or maturation of specific organs as well as in the body as a whole.

Figure 3–1 shows the curves for length, surface area and weight for a normally developing fetus. The steepness of the curves is better appreciated when it is realized that growth is plotted by monthly increments, rather than by yearly increments as is commonly done for the postnatal period. During the second month the embryo tends to grow about 1 mm a day in "sitting height" and thereafter averages 1.5 mm per day.[9] In comparison, a 10-year-old child who had continued to grow at the rate of 1.5 mm a day would be 20 ft tall.

The increase in weight is even more surprising. From birth to maturity the weight is increased 20-fold. From the time of fertilization to birth the increase in weight is approximately 6 billion times.

The rate of growth of total body mass constantly increases during intrauterine life, and for several years after birth the curve of growth shows a steady decline. Maximal linear growth during gestation occurs in the sixth and seventh months and decelerates during the last two months of the fetal period.[10]

Figure 3–2 shows the relative proportions of different parts of the body during fetal and postnatal life and portrays the changes taking place with growth better than any written discussion. It is not until the third month that

Age lunar mo.	Length (L.) Cm.	Surface Area (S) Sq. cm.	Weight (W.) Grams
Ovum	$\frac{1}{93}$	$\frac{1}{38,000}$	$\frac{1}{1,700,000}$
2	2.6	--	--
3	9.0	42.	19.
4	16.7	171.	100.
5	24.3	402.	312.
6	31.1	706.	667.
7	37.1	1055.	1151.
8	42.4	1430.	1754.
9	47.0	1809.	2396.
10	51.0	2178.	3087.

$$L. = 107.3 \epsilon^{-\frac{208.2}{T(days)}}$$

$$S. = 0.2808 L.^{2.278}$$

$$W. = 0.26 L.^{3.108} + 4.6$$

Fig 3–1.—Curves of prenatal growth: length (crown-heel), surface area of the body and weight from time of conception to birth. (From Patten[9]; after Edith Boyd.)

the fetus definitely resembles a human being. The head is disproportionately large, and the umbilical herniation is reduced due to the return of the intestine into the abdominal cavity. The nails are forming, and sex can be determined. At 5 months hair is present on the head and body, and shortly thereafter eyebrows and eyelashes form. At 7 months the fetus looks like a dried-up old man with red and wrinkled skin. The eyelids are no longer fused. By the eighth lunar month subcutaneous fat begins to accumulate, and the nails are completely formed. The major changes from this time until birth are due to progressive accumulation of fat, and the downy hair coat is shed.[1, 9, 10]

In the following chapters will be found brief references to fetal organ development, and they will not be reported here. By the end of the second fetal month definition of the permanent organs is so far advanced that the

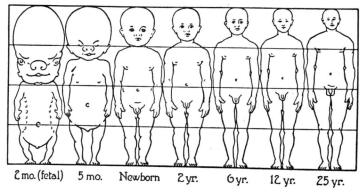

2 mo. (fetal)   5 mo.   Newborn   2 yr.   6 yr.   12 yr.   25 yr.

Fig 3–2.—Stages of growth—relative proportions of head, trunk and extremities for different ages. (From Robbins, W. J., et al.: *Growth* [New Haven, Conn.: Yale University Press, 1928].)

subsequent growth of the fetus is devoted to the development of parts already formed. In general, the growth of organs during prenatal life follows an accelerating smooth curve which is in marked contrast to the divergent growth curves following birth (see Fig 7–7).

Some aspects of human fetal development are outlined in the following tabulation. The figures in parentheses refer to fetal age in months of gestation.[1, 9]

Integument	Three-layered epidermis (3)
	Body hair begins (4)
	Skin glands form, sweat and sebaceous (4)
Mouth	Lip fusion complete (2)
	Palate fused completely (3)
	Enamel and dentin depositing (5)
	Primordia of permanent teeth (6–8)
Gastrointestinal	Bile secreted (3)
	Rectum patent (3)
	Pancreatic islands appear (3)
	Fixation of duodenum and colon (4)
Respiratory	Definitive shape of lungs (3)
	Accessory nasal sinuses developing (4)
	Elastic fibers appear in lung (4)
Urogenital	Kidney able to secrete (2½)
	Vagina regains lumen (5)
	Testes descend into scrotum (7–9)

Vascular	Definitive shape of heart ($1^{1}/_2$)
	Heart becomes four-chambered ($3^{1}/_2$)
	Blood formation in marrow begins (3)
	Spleen acquires typical structure (7)
Nervous	Commissures of brain complete (5)
	Myelinization of cord begins (5)
	Typical layers of cortex (6)
Special senses	Nasal septum complete (3)
	Retinal layers complete, light-perceptive (7)
	Vascular tunic of lens pronounced (7)
	Eyelids open (7–8)

Fetal Behavior

Behavior depends to a great extent on morphology and structure, and one cannot discuss behavior without also discussing developmental anatomy. There are regulating growth mechanisms which govern the order in which successive patterns of behavior emerge. Most fundamental are the structures of the muscle and nerve cells and the manner in which these structures come into functional relationship.

Fetus at 8 Weeks

The major components of both trunk and limb musculature are evident in the embryo at the end of the second fetal month.[6] The nerves as yet have no anatomic or physiologic connections with either smooth or striated muscle. During this time the embryo has floated quiescently in the amniotic fluid. However, movement has already taken place in this new individual. Since 4 weeks of age the heart has been beating at a fairly regular rate.[16] Skeletal muscle may have developed an intrinsic tonus by this time also. The available evidence indicates that the fetus becomes capable of responding to tactile stimulation at $8^{1}/_2$ weeks. The trunk flexes and the head extends. Anatomically, by this time, there are found all of the necessary components of the reflex arc.[6]

Fetus at 12–14 Weeks

With increasing age and maturation of the neuromuscular system the movements spread caudally and become more pronounced in the lower trunk. Then discrete reflexes appear, accompanying spread of the skin areas sensitive to stimulation. By 14 weeks the human fetus has largely ceased to exhibit the earlier, more generalized responses and activity becomes less stereotyped.[6]

Windle[16a] has stated that behavior, in general, goes through five stages: (1) myogenic responses: (2) neuromotor responses; (3) reflex responses; (4) integration of simple reflexes; (5) integration and control from higher centers. From this it can be seen that behavior follows closely the differentiation of structures in the fetal nervous system. Evidence concerning the functions of the central nervous system during prenatal life indicates that behavior, until about the beginning of the sixth month, is largely controlled by spinal mechanisms.[8] At a slightly later period there are indications that the medulla and lower brain centers participate in the control of specific reflex activities. (It is possible that a strong stimulus may affect the medulla before this, however, as indicated by the respirationlike movements which may occur at 20 weeks). There is no evidence that the cerebral cortex exerts any specific influence on behavior until some time after birth.[8]

By the end of the first trimester the fetus makes brief jerky movements without artificial stimulation. By the twentieth week the sucking reflex is present and the first patterns of respiratory movements manifest themselves.[5, 16]

Fetus at 28 Weeks (Viable)

The fetal age of 28 weeks approximately demarcates the zone between viability and nonviability. The following outlines of behavior are based on the observations of Gesell[5] in premature infants from fetal ages of 28 to 40 weeks. He states that this behavior probably varies only slightly from that which would take place in utero. To support this contention he was able to demonstrate: (1) that all infants of the same fetal age follow a very similar pattern of behavior, (2) that, in general, the week-old neonate exhibits a behavior picture remarkably like that of the mature "fetal-infants," and (3) from previous studies, that in older premature infants the fundamental rates and patterns of development are little disturbed by displacements of birth.

Fetus at 28–32 Weeks

Movements meager, fleeting, poorly sustained
Lack of muscular tone
Mild avoidance responses to bright light and sound
In prone position turns head to side
Palmar stimulation elicits barely perceptible grasp
Breathing shallow and irregular
Sucking and swallowing present but lack endurance
No definite waking and sleeping pattern
Cry may be absent or very weak
Inconstant tonic neck reflex

Fetus at 32–36 Weeks

Movements sustained and positive
Muscle tone fair under stimulation
Moro reflex present
Strong but inadequate response to light and sound
In prone position turns head, elevates rump
Definite periods of being awake
Palmar stimulation causes good grasp
Good hunger cry
Fairly well established tonic neck reflex

Fetus at 36–40 Weeks

Movements active and sustained
Muscle tone good
Brief erratic following of objects with eyes
Moro reflex strong
In prone position attempts to lift head
Active resistance to head rotation
Definite periods of alertness
Cries well when hungry and disturbed
Appears pleased when caressed
Hands held as fists much of time, good grasp
Tonic neck reflex more pronounced to one side (usually right) than to the
    other
Good, strong sucking reflex

Each infant in Gesell's series showed individuality as well as a general
sameness of overall behavior pattern. It can be seen that the development of
fetal behavior lays a necessary foundation for the later development of postnatal behavior, the latter not merely being imposed on the former but arising
from it by a process of maturation of existing activities.

Metabolism of the Fetus

In utero the fetal temperature is about 0.5 C above the maternal temperature. Environmental temperature for the fetus is unfluctuating, and ambient
temperature control puts little metabolic demand upon the organism. Little
physical activity, depressed muscle tone and insulation against heat loss all
contribute to a relatively low metabolic rate. During normal gestation the
oxygen consumption of the fetus, based upon weight, remains relatively
constant and at a level of approximately one third that of the newborn. A

large proportion of the caloric intake of the fetus is used to satisfy growth requirements, about 50% of the total in contrast to 15 to 20% in a 10-year-old child.[16, 22]

Newborn babies with fetal growth retardation, regardless of cause, have relatively low rates of oxygen consumption for gestational age, but high rates for body weight. It has been suggested that this reflects recovery from fetal malnutrition and rapid increase in tissue (cell) growth.[61]

Nutrition of the Fetus

The normal physiologic processes of the body are considerably altered during pregnancy, and additional demands are imposed upon the maternal organism during this period. It is well established that the state of maternal nutrition influences the nutrition and subsequent growth and development of the child.[2, 3, 41] If the need arises, the fetus is to a certain extent provided for at the expense of the mother. Growth of the placenta is closely tied into that of the fetus and shares a similar preferential position. When the maternal intake of iron, calcium or phosphorus, as examples, is inadequate, the fetus draws on her stores to supply its own requirements. Iron-deficiency anemia is, therefore, rare in the early stages of infancy. A severe reduction in protein intake, as in starvation, will lead to a lower-than-average weight, length and head circumference in the newborn.[2, 51, 52] When starvation is sufficiently severe, sterility of the potential mother may result, but abortion and malformation do not appear to increase. Infants born to mothers on good diets during the pregnancy usually are superior in general health and vigor during early infancy, in comparison to those infants of mothers on poor diets. Although stillbirths, prematurity, congenital anomalies and early neonatal death have been blamed upon maternal malnutrition, the evidence supporting such claims is very poor. It is difficult, if not impossible, to separate the effects of poor nutrition from those of other factors associated with a low socioeconomic status. Inadequate medical attention could constitute a very major role and would include prevention and treatment of infection, among other things.

Although many reports indicate the harmful results of a poor or marginal maternal diet on fetal growth and development, the differences between such infants and those exposed to an adequate diet are often minimal. The striking results that can be produced in the experimental animal are almost never seen in man. Total, or nearly total, withholding of essential nutrients is seldom obtained in pregnant women. In the human, fetal growth is very slow. In the mouse, by comparison, the weight of a litter is 30% of the mother's weight and is reached in 3 weeks. In man, the weight of the newborn is 5% of the mother's, and this is reached in 40 weeks. The rate of metabolic changes in one as compared to the other is obviously great. The relatively gradual development may serve to protect the human fetus and limit the deleterious effects of a poor diet. In fact, most studies indicate, the major effect of maternal malnutrition occurs during the rapid growth period of the final trimester, long after the critical period of organogenesis.[50, 52] Toward the end of gestation, the fetus lays down 500 mg of nitrogen, 300 mg of calcium and about 200 mg of phosphorus each day. It has been estimated that the fetus requires 5% of the total calcium in the plasma of the mother every hour during the last 3 months. The whole body of the fetus has about 9 gm of carbohydrate at 33 weeks of gestation and 34 gm at term.

The critical issues relate to the long-term effect of maternal undernutrition. There is general agreement that small physical size of the newborn is a result. Some continued relatively slow growth and delayed maturation may occur, but normal, or near normal, adult size can be expected unless there is continued poor food intake.[44-49] Subsequent development of the central nervous system and intellectual performance is a subject upon which there is some disagreement. Unfortunately, the elimination of continued exposure of the infant and young child to a poor socioeconomic climate is not always possible in evaluation studies. The selection of properly matching control subjects for comparison is not an easily accomplished task. The conditions under which such studies must be carried out is far from ideal in most instances. Therefore, we must state opinions with reservations. The effects suffered by a fetus from a single maternal episode of undernutrition, as in the Netherlands in 1944–45, may not be properly equated with multiple generations of malnutrition as experienced in some of the developing countries. In the former, i.e., a single episode of maternal undernutrition, the fetus would appear to suffer only temporary slowing of physical development.[54, 56, 57] In the situation where multiple factors may be involved, and where poor nutrition is essentially chronic, the results of maternal malnutrition may be an important factor contributing to premature delivery, small size at birth, slowed physical development, compromised intellectual development and possibly decreased immunologic protection.[44-49, 53]

In the newborn infant small for the time of gestation, the possible role of the placenta is still somewhat of a riddle. We are often at a loss as to the etiology, although we use such terms as "placental dysfunction" and "placental dysmaturity." The reason the small and apparently poorly functioning placenta became that way is far from clear. One can ask whether the placenta is small because of the small fetus and reduced requirements, or whether the fetus is small because the placenta is inadequate.[24]

Teenage pregnancies often occur among those of a low-income group who often neglect their own health. This combination of low socioeconomic status and biologic immaturity is often associated with a low birth weight and increased perinatal morbidity.

The size of the newborn infant, to a large extent, determines its functional maturity and ability to survive. Even a small reduction of the time spent in utero will make a considerable difference at birth because of the rapid gains made just before term. Babies small at birth often remain small as children and as adults.

The effect of specific vitamin deficiencies is not so well known. There have been isolated reports of infants born with beriberi,[15] rickets[3] and scurvy.[7] As mentioned previously, Warkany produced congenital malformations of the eyes and other tissues in animals by depriving the mother of vitamin A. He has also shown a relationship between riboflavin deficiency in the rat and certain congenital skeletal defects.

It may be concluded that the pregnant woman requires more calories, minerals, vitamins and protein than the nonpregnant woman to insure proper or optimal growth of the fetus.

At the 15th week the placenta and fetus are equal in weight and contain similar amounts of glycogen, fat, phosphorus and potassium. As the end of gestation is approached, the fetus weighs 6–7 times as much as the placenta, and the concentrations of glycogen, fat, calcium, and phosphorus in the fetus exceed those of the placenta. The concentrations of sodium and potassium remain the same. Table 3–2 indicates the changes occurring in fetal growth relative to concentrations of some substances.[18]

The human fetus begins to lay down fat at a weight of 800–1,000 gm or around the sixth lunar month of pregnancy. At a weight of 3,000 gm the body contains an equal amount of fat and protein, but from this point on the fat exceeds the protein.[18] Fat deposition, especially in the subcutaneous tissues, as an insulating material to conserve body heat is very important. The fat of the fetus and newborn differs from that found later in life in having a higher melting point, greater saturation and a higher content of palmitic but less stearic and oleic acids. By midfetal life deposits of brown fat are evident, and these increase quantitatively until birth. Brown fat is an important ther-

TABLE 3–2.—CONCENTRATION OF
SUBSTANCES IN THE FETUS DURING LATE
PREGNANCY AND IN THE NEWBORN

SUBSTANCE	FETUS 1,500 GM	FETUS 2,500 GM	TERM INFANT 3,500 GM
Protein	11.6	12.4	12.0
Fat	3.5	7.6	16.2
Water	82.5	77.3	68.8
Sodium	0.23	0.21	0.19
Calcium	0.68	0.76	0.81
Iron	7.10	7.40	7.52

Values are expressed as gm per 100 gm body wt. except for iron, which is mg.

mogenic source in response to cold and thus differs considerably in its function, in contrast to the more metabolically stable white fat. (See also Chapter 10.)

Internal Environment

As growth progresses, the relative content of the total body water decreases. The 6-week-old fetus contains about 97% water, the newborn about
72% and the adult about 60%. With the loss of water there results a proportionate loss of sodium and chloride (Fig 3–3). The reduction of fluid content of the body is due almost entirely to a reduction of extracellular fluids.
Since the concentration of sodium and chloride in the extracellular fluid is
the same for the fetus, the newborn infant, and the adult, the total body
content of these minerals changes with growth in order to maintain this
even concentration. The percentage of total body content of chloride is:
fetus, 0.27; newborn, 0.25; adult, 0.21.[11]

With the increase in tissue mass that occurs with growth there is an
increase in the total amount of intracellular fluid. To maintain ionic and
osmotic equilibrium, the increase in potassium content of the body parallels

Fig 3–3.—Total mineral content of the body at different periods of development; trace elements are not represented. The apparent excess of positive ions is compensated for by organic acids and protein. (From Shohl.[11])

TABLE 3–3.—CHANGES IN DISTRIBUTION OF WATER AND POSITIVE IONS THROUGHOUT LIFE

| | TOTAL BODY WATER | | TOTAL BODY FLUID | |
	Na^+, mEq/kg	K^+, mEq/kg	EXTRA-CELLULAR, %	INTRA-CELLULAR, %
Fetus	125	52	71	29
Newborn	97	63	63	37
Adult	67	95	42	58
Adult (corrected for intracellular sodium)			30	70

the increase in intracellular fluid. Table 3–3 shows these changes. The sodium and potassium ion concentrations are given for the whole body. The percentages of extracellular and intracellular water are computed on the basis that the sodium is entirely extracellular and the potassium intracellular.[11] The sum of the two cations in the total body fluids equals approximately 162 mEq/kg of water throughout life. These figures show that as growth continues and the number of cells increases, an ever-increasing amount of water becomes intracellular.[20]

Practical Applications

Recently the role of the placenta in embryonal and fetal growth and development has received considerable interest. It is recognized that this organ of chemical exchange between mother and fetus displays a remarkable degree of selectivity that bears little resemblance to a passive semipermeable membrane. During its brief existence it acts as an important depot for glycogen and synthesizes hormones that are important in maintaining the pregnancy and may have other important metabolic functions relative to fetal development. As a means of gaseous exchange it compares favorably with the lung. Careful study of structure and physiology of this long-neglected organ, upon which fetal survival is absolutely dependent, has led and will continue to lead to an improved understanding and prognosis for intrauterine life.

Growth and development have progressed to a considerable degree before birth. All the organ systems are well established by the second fetal month, and at no time after birth is growth as rapid as during the prenatal period. Through an understanding of fundamental embryology a better concept of congenital anomalies is obtained, as well as an appreciation of future trends in growth and development. We have seen that most of the vital reflexes are well established and prepared for the initial shock of extrauterine existence. Behavior depends on functional and morphologic development and is influenced by regulating growth mechanisms which determine the pattern of behavior both pre- and postnatally. Behavior may well be a better criterion of the degree of maturity than physical measurements during the neonatal period.

The availability of techniques to make antenatal diagnosis of congenital malformations and heritable metabolic diseases may alert the physician to prepare for a therapeutic abortion or for special and energetic methods of treatment. The counseling of families in such situations involves the complex interplay of ethics, genetics and knowledge of the extent of medical abilities to influence end results in the infant, child and adult.

The importance of maternal nutrition during pregnancy has been stressed because there is little doubt that this factor influences the development of the fetus and the well-being of the organism for some time after birth. A better knowledge of the physicochemical changes that take place just before and after birth will aid us in further reducing neonatal mortality.

REFERENCES

1. Moore, K. L.: *The Developing Human, Clinically Oriented Embryology* (Philadelphia: W. B. Saunders Company, 1973).
2. Burke, B. S., Harding, V. V., and Stuart, H. C.: Nutrition studies during pregnancy: IV. Relation of protein content of mother's diet to birth length, birth weight and condition of infant at birth, J. Pediatr. 23:506, 1943.
3. Reid, D. E., Ryan, K. J., and Benirschke, K.: *Principles and Management of Human Reproduction* (Philadelphia: W. B. Saunders Company, 1972).
4. Warshaw, J. B.: Factors Affecting Fetal Growth, in Gluck, L. (ed.): *Modern Perinatal Medicine* (Chicago: Year Book Medical Publishers, Inc., 1974).
5. Gesell, A.: *The Embryology of Behavior* (New York: Harper & Brothers, 1945).
6. Hooker, D.: Reflex Activities in Human Fetus, in Barker, R. G., et al. (eds.): *Child Behavior and Development* (New York: McGraw-Hill Book Company, Inc., 1943), p. 17.
7. Jackson, D., and Park, E. A.: Congenital scurvy: Case report, J. Pediatr. 7:741, 1935.
8. Munn, N. L.: *Psychological Development* (Boston: Houghton Mifflin Company, 1938).
9. Patten, B. M.: *Human Embryology* (3d. ed. New York: McGraw-Hill Book Company, Inc., 1968).
10. Scammon, R. E., and Calkins, L. A.: *The Development and Growth of the External Dimensions of the Human Body in the Fetal Period* (Minneapolis: University of Minnesota Press, 1929).
11. Shohl, A. T.: *Mineral Metabolism,* Am. Chem. Soc. Monogr. Ser. (New York: Reinhold Publishing Corporation, 1939).
12. Evans, H. E., and Glass, L.: *Perinatal Medicine* (Hagerstown, Md.: Harper and Row Publishers, Inc., 1976).
13. Smith, C. A.: Effects of maternal undernutrition upon the newborn infant in Holland (1944–1945), J. Pediatr. 30:229, 1947.
14. Gardner, D. M.: Antenatal diagnosis of genetic defects, J. Reprod. Med. 10:261, 1973.
15. Van Gelder, D. W., and Darby, F. V.: Congenital and infantile beriberi, J. Pediatr. 25:226, 1944.

16. Dawes, G. S.: *Foetal and Neonatal Physiology* (Chicago: Year Book Medical Publishers, Inc., 1968).

16a. Windle, W. F.: *Physiology of the Fetus* (Philadelphia: W. B. Saunders Company, 1940).

17. Gluck, L., and Kulovich, M. V.: The Evaluation of Functional Maturity in the Human Fetus, in Gluck, L. (ed.): *Modern Perinatal Medicine* (Chicago: Year Book Medical Publishers, Inc., 1974).

18. Wharton, B. A.: Child Health and Nutrition, in Apley, J. (ed.): *Modern Trends in Pediatrics* (London: Butterworths, 1970).

19. Emery, A. E. H.: *Antenatal Diagnosis of Genetic Disease* (Edinburgh: Churchill Livingston, 1973).

20. Thompson, J. N.: Antenatal detection of heritable disorders in man, Pediatr. Ann. 2:83, 1973.

21. Dancis, J.: Placental Function and Fetal Nutrition, in Villee, C. A. (ed.): *The Placenta and Fetal Membranes* (Baltimore: Williams & Wilkins Company, 1960), Chapter 6.

22. Villee, C. A.: *The Placenta and Fetal Membranes* (Baltimore: Williams & Wilkins Company, 1960), pp. 131–244.

23. Clifford, S. H.: Postmaturity, in Levine, S. Z. (ed.): *Advances in Pediatrics*, Vol. IX (Chicago: Year Book Medical Publishers, Inc., 1957), Chapter 1.

24. Gruenwald, P.: Placental insufficiency—a questionable concept, Arch. Dis. Child. 49:915, 1974.

25. Jaffe, R. B.: Endocrine interactions and the placenta, Hosp. Pract. 12:71, 1971.

26. Hendricks, C. H.: Discussion, in *Physiology of Prematurity, Transactions of the Fifth Conference* (New York: Josiah Macy, Jr., Foundation, 1961), p. 217.

27. Goebelsmann, V., Freeman, R. K., Mestman, J. H., Nakamura, R. M., and Woodling, B. A.: Estriol in pregnancy, Am. J. Obstet. Gynecol. 115:795, 1972.

28. Dancis, J.: The role of the placenta in fetal survival, Pediatr. Clin. North Am. 12:477, 1965.

29. Bourne, G. L., and Benirschke, K.: Absent umbilical artery: Review of 113 cases, Arch. Dis. Child. 35:534, 1960.

30. Gruenwald, P., and Minh, H. N.: Evaluation of body and organ weights in perinatal pathology, Am. J. Obstet. Gynecol. 82:312, 1961.

31. Driscoll, S. G.: Pathology and the developing fetus, Pediatr. Clin. North Am. 12:493, 1965.

32. Wigglesworth, J. S.: Fœtal growth retardation, Br. Med. Bull. 22:13, 1966.

33. Aherne, W., and Dunnill, M. S.: Morphometry of the human placenta, Br. Med. Bull. 22:5, 1966.

34. Behrman, R. E.: Placental function and malnutrition, Am. J. Dis. Child. 129:425, 1975.

35. Wilson, M. G.: Placental abnormalities and fetal disease, Am. J. Dis. Child. 108:154, 1964.

36. Laga, E. M., Driscoll, S. G., and Munro, H. N.: Comparison of placentas from two socioeconomic groups, Pediatrics 50:24 and 33, 1972.

37. Wald, N. J., Brock, D. J. H., and Bonner, J.: Prenatal diagnosis of spina bifida and anencephaly by maternal serum-alpha-fetoprotein measurement, Lancet 1:765, 1974.

38. Barnes, A. C.: *Intrauterine Development* (Philadelphia: Lea & Febiger, 1968).

39. Green, O. C.: Steroid metabolism in the fetus and the newborn infant, Pediatr. Clin. North Am. 12:615, 1965.

40. Robertson, A. F., and Sprecher, H.: A review of human placental lipid metabolism and transport, Acta Paediatr. Scand. (suppl.) 183:3, 1968.

41. Singer, J. E., Westphal, M., and Niswander, K.: Relationship of weight gain during pregnancy to birth weight and infant growth and development in the first year of life: Report from collaborative study of cerebral palsy, Obstet. Gynecol. 31:417, 1968.

42. Naeye, R. L.: Prenatal organ and cellular growth with various chromosomal disorders, Biol. Neonate 11:248, 1967.

43. Winick, M., and Rosso, P.: The effects of severe early malnutrition on cellular growth of human brain, Pediatr. Res. 3:181, 1969.

44. Lechtig, A., Delgado, H., Lasky, R., Yarbrough, C., Klein, R. E., Habitch, J., and Behar, M.: Maternal nutrition and fetal growth in developing countries, Am. J. Dis. Child. 129:553, 1975.

45. Sinclair, J. C., and Saigal, S.: Nutritional influences in industrial societies, Am. J. Dis. Child. 129:549, 1975.

46. Rush, D.: Maternal nutrition during pregnancy in industrial societies, Am. J. Dis. Child. 129:430, 1975.

47. Naeye, R. L., Diener, M. M., Harcke, H. T., and Blanc, W. A.: Relation of poverty and race to birth weight and organ and cell structure in the newborn, Pediatr. Res. 5:17, 1971.

48. Roux, J. F., Takeda, Y., and Grigorian, A.: Lipid concentration and composition in human fetal tissue during development, Pediatrics 48:540, 1971.

49. Simpson, J. W., Lawless, R. W., and Mitchell, A. C.: Responsibility of the obstetrician to the fetus. II. Influence of prepregnancy weight and pregnancy weight gain on birthweight, Obstet. Gynecol. 45:481, 1975.

50. Naeye, R. L., Blanc, W., and Paul, C.: Effects of maternal nutrition on the human fetus, Pediatrics 52:494, 1973.

51. Stein, H.: Maternal protein depletion and small-for-gestational-age babies, Arch. Dis. Child. 50:146, 1975.

52. Stein, Z., and Susser, M.: The Dutch famine, 1944–45, and the reproductive process. Effects on six indices at birth, Pediatr. Res. 9:70 and 76, 1975.

53. Birch, H. G.: Functional effects of fetal malnutrition, Hosp. Pract. 3:134, 1971.

54. Stein, Z., Susser, M., Saenger, G., and Marolla, F.: Nutrition and mental performance, Science 178:708, 1972.

55. Chase, H. P., Welch, N. N., Dabiere, C. S., Vasan, N. S., and Butterfield, L. J.: Alterations in human brain biochemistry following intrauterine growth retardation, Pediatrics 50:403, 1972.

56. Babson, G. S., and Henderson, N. B.: Fetal undergrowth: Relation of head growth to later intellectual performance, Pediatrics 53:890, 1974.

57. Fujikura, T., and Froehlich, L. A.: Mental and motor development in monozygotic co-twins with dissimilar birth weights, Pediatrics 53:884, 1974.

58. Froehlich, L. A., and Fujikura, T.: Follow-up of infants with single umbilical artery, Pediatrics 52:6, 1973.

59. Bryan, E.M., and Kohler, H. G.: The missing umbilical artery II. Paediatric follow-up, Arch. Dis. Child. 50:714, 1975.

60. Friesen, H. G.: Placental Protein Hormones and Tissue Receptors for Hormones, in Gluck, L. (ed.): *Modern Perinatal Medicine* (Chicago: Year Book Medical Publishers, Inc., 1974).

61. Sinclair, J. C.: *Energy Metabolism and Fetal Development* (New York: McGraw-Hill Book Company, Inc., 1970).

4 / Normal Physical Measurements

THE RELATIONSHIP of the rate of growth and adequacy of body development to physical fitness is generally recognized. By comparison of the physical measurements of a given child over a period of time with those of other healthy children it is possible to determine, within limitations, whether he is doing as well as should be expected. The purpose of this discussion is to present normal body measurements and charts illustrating their use in the evaluation of progress of normal growth. It should be kept in mind that such measurements are made to reinforce and improve clinical judgment and not to displace it. The methods or technics used in obtaining measurements of physical growth must be followed closely to ensure adequate comparison with the standards established. When a child is being evaluated in the usual clinic setting, by far the most common reason for an unexpected deviation in weight, height, head circumference, etc. is due to an error in obtaining the measurement. Several excellent monographs on methodology are available.[15, 16, 20, 43]

In the recent literature on measurements of children it has become common practice to use one of two different standards as a means of assigning a given individual some point of reference relative to the group of his age. One method uses a mean value and one or more standard deviations. Such a system of presenting figures gives a good indication of just where a given child is in relation to the so-called normal group. One standard deviation includes 66.6% of the total number, two standard deviations include 95% and three include 99.7%. Many of the tables presented here are given in this form. The other method of presenting such data is in percentiles. The number of the percentile indicates the position which a measurement would hold in a typical series of 100 (100%). Thus the 10th percentile gives the value for the 10th child of a group of 100. Nine children will be smaller in the measurement under consideration, and 90 will be larger. At the 50th percentile an equal number of children will be smaller or larger than the measurement. Tables 4–4 and 4–5 (pp. 84–85), for height and weight, were constructed according to this method. Both the percentile and the standard deviation method are of value in estimating where a given child stands relative to a large group of the same age and sex. In some of the material presented in this chapter neither method has been used because the group studied was too small to give reliable trends or it was believed that these technics would add little of value to simple averages from a purely practical standpoint.

It is difficult to select truly representative figures of measurements in children. Many of the tables commonly used as acceptable standards are out of date so far as today's children in this country are concerned. Some figures are of doubtful value because of the selection of subjects used for the study, e.g., children from a special socioeconomic group or from a limited geographic area. Furthermore, there are few studies pertaining to racial groups or to one race in different environments. The use of standards such as those outlined in the foregoing paragraph does not rule out the objection that such tables are usually compiled from a more or less heterogeneous population in which many of the individuals are below optimal development. The tables used here are from relatively recent sources and represent measurements of children reared under relatively satisfactory conditions. Within the boundaries of the United States they can probably be considered adequate for clinical purposes.

Differences between populations in the size and shape of adults depends upon the variations in their gene pools and the influence of their environments. Differences in size and shape of children have a similar basis, plus the added effect arising from variations in the rate of maturation. Two populations may reach nearly identical adult size, but the children of one may be larger because they have a more rapid growth, enter puberty earlier and stop growing earlier. Such differences are present, to a mild degree, in the black and white populations in the United States. Physical measurements and assessments of development of all countries and of ethnic groups within a country are highly desirable. The accumulation of this kind of material in a convenient form is just beginning to be realized.[24, 25] Tanner[54] has emphasized the need of such studies and has also pointed out some of the difficulties in the interpretation of results. The response of the individual and of the population have separate counterparts in the study of growth. An example is the superiority in height and weight of Japanese children born and raised in California as compared to those born and raised in Japan a generation ago. Differences in tempos and patterns of development would become better known and, hopefully, their significance would be understood. Another example to illustrate the point relates to the time of onset of menarche among different racial groups. Among European girls, menarche occurs just after the peak of the adolescent growth spurt, while in Nigerians it appears near the end of growth in height. Still another observation indicates that throughout childhood Chinese girls (Hong Kong) have skeletal maturation behind that of American girls until the age of 12 years when the Chinese forge ahead. This results in earlier completion of growth and a mean adult height that is shorter.[37, 38]

The recently completed studies of American youth have revealed some most interesting data as well as making available, for the first time, adequate figures for the black population.[3, 5, 7, 26] There was a marked diminution and near cessation of the trend to constantly increasing size of successive generations of American children. In this population, the so-called secular trend has come to an end. Only a small portion of children at the lower ends of the height and weight charts moved up the scale in the past couple of decades. When socioeconomic standards are analyzed and applied to this data, Hamill et al.[3] make the following comment, "When the stragglers will finally achieve their genetic potential to full stature can probably be better predicted by economic and social factors than by biologic ones."

Individual Growth Patterns

When the growth and development status or level of a given child is being appraised, the physician must keep in mind that this child, like all others, has his own growth pattern. His growth will resemble that of other children, but his timetable is strictly his own. For this reason mean or average values for height and weight should not be considered more than points of reference. When sequential measurements can be made, the percentile method of recording height and weight is much more useful than tables stating means and standard deviations. It is more important to know that a child is consistently maintaining a given relationship (in height and weight) to other children of his sex and age than it is to know that he is tall or short. The progress of growth (height and weight) is predictable for a given child once his approximate percentile position or channel is established.

General Body Configuration

Alteration of body configuration results from selective regional rate of growth at different stages during the developmental period. In infancy the head grows at a relatively rapid rate, so that during the first year the head circumference is greater than that of the chest. Thereafter the chest circumference becomes increasingly larger in proportion, since growth of the head after the first year is slow. Some exceptions to this rule may normally exist, and for this reason absolute measurements of the head have greater value than do proportions. The extremities are shorter than the trunk at birth but grow more rapidly later. During adolescence the major gain in height is due to growth of the lower segment of the body; however, growth of the legs slows and ceases somewhat sooner than that of the trunk.[22] The ratio of the distance from crown to symphysis to that from symphysis to sole of the foot relates the trunk-extremity proportion. This proportion decreases from approximately 1.7 at birth to near unity at 10 years and is thereafter maintained. The changing ratios in trunk and extremity length are also reflected in the measurements of span compared to height. In boys the span exceeds standing height after the 10th birthday and in girls after the 14th birthday.

During most of childhood growth appears to be primarily linear. In the adolescent, growth assumes more of a process of "filling out." Linear growth does not cease entirely until maturity is reached, at about age 17 in girls and 21 in boys. However, after a rather short period of rapid linear growth at puberty, linear increase diminishes quite abruptly and tapers off to an insignificant amount by about age 16 in girls and 18 in boys. For purposes of predicting eventual height in the early-maturing girl, it can be stated that growth in height is seldom more than 3 in. after menarche. (See also discussion and Fig 9–4, p. 324). During adolescence girls show an increase in breadth relative to height from about age 11, whereas boys maintain a relatively constant ratio.[22] These changes are easily demonstrated by use of the width-length index, obtained by dividing the pelvic bicristal diameter (pelvic breadth or intercristal width) by the standing height (Table 4–1). (It has also been stated that this index is one of the most reliable measures for estimating body build or physique.[9]) On the other hand, shoulder breadth is found to expand more rapidly in boys than in girls. These and other differences in rates of growth account for the differences in average size, physique and contour between the sexes in adult life.

Longitudinal studies have demonstrated that children pass through the phase of accelerated growth associated with adolescence at widely different

TABLE 4–1.—WIDTH-LENGTH INDEX
FOR BOYS AND GIRLS AT DIFFERENT
AGES*

AGE	BOYS	GIRLS
Under 1 yr	0.173	0.175
1 yr	.168	.172
3 yr	.166	.168
5 yr	.161	.161
7 yr	.159	.159
9 yr	.157	.159
11 yr	.157	.161
13 yr	.156	.163
15 yr	0.155	0.164

*From Lucas and Pryor.[9] The figures express the mean for normal subjects.

chronologic ages, but that they follow the same pattern or sequence for any particular measurement. In general, the sooner the phase is entered, the sooner growth (in height and weight) is completed. Children who enter the period early are apt to be slightly shorter as adults than are those who enter the period later. The stimulus to advanced or retarded growth is a general one and affects all dimensions.

The apparent smooth and gradual adolescent growth curves seen on most charts can be very deceiving. Each percentile line represents an average for a large number of children who may have entered the growth spurt at many different ages covering at least a 6-year span of time. Plotting this phenomena for a single individual may indicate a much more abrupt change, which appears to be more rapid and of shorter duration than a cross-sectional representation.

Some of the many different measurements suggested for proper evaluation of growth in children have considerable importance to the research worker. A volume which purports to be brief and practical is of necessity selective, and the measurements included in this chapter are believed to represent the most significant ones because experience has shown them to be most reliable. They are based on easily accessible bony landmarks and therefore are least subject to errors of interpretation or to variation of muscle tonus. In addition to linear or weight measurements alone, various authors have used indexes in an attempt to demonstrate body proportions better. Two examples have been given: the trunk-extremity proportion and the width-length index. Both may be useful in determining certain factors in the maturation of children. As a single example, it is known that the trunk-extremity index remains high in untreated children with hypothyroidism; i.e., infantile proportions are maintained. Other useful indexes are referred to at various points in the discussion which follows.

Constitutional (Somatic) Types

Since ancient times, attempts have been made to associate distinctive body types with personality traits or with predilection to specific diseases. At times these efforts have been pushed to extremes. However, some of these correlations have stood up better than others. In the study of the epidemiology of obesity, it appears that one has a good chance of predicting the obese adult from the body habitus of the infant and child (see Chapter 13).

In this country, Sheldon[36] has suggested the classification of endomorphy, mesomorphy and ectomorphy. In the first of these, the person is stocky with abundant subcutaneous fat. Sheldon felt such individuals had a predominance of structures derived from the endodermal embryonic layer. Mesomorphy shows a predominance of muscle, bone and connective tissue.

Fig 4-1.—Somatotyping. In a general way the photographs above illustrate the different body builds which have been described as somatotypes. All are 16-year-old girls. **Left,** this girl conforms roughly to the endomorphic type and may be designated 7 1 1. **Center,** this girl is a mesomorphic or athletic type and can be designated 1 7 1. **Right,** this girl is a linear type, though she should be taller to be the typical 1 1 7 type of Sheldon.

"Athletic" is a word commonly applied to this habitus. Ectomorphy, corresponding to the habitus phthisicus of Hippocrates, is characterized as thin, linear and poorly muscled.

Sheldon has popularized the use of several techniques for somatotyping; principal among these is the use of photography of the nude subject standing before a calibrated grid. Certain technical details are necessary to avoid errors of parallax. In addition careful anthropometric observations are made, including widths of the head (bitemporal), of the shoulders (biacromial), of the hips (bi-iliac and bitrochanteric). With these are included circumference measurements of neck, biceps, midthigh, calf, ankle and estimation of thickness of the fat layer made with special tension calipers. Complete somatotyping according to the 20-odd measurements made by Sheldon is quite an undertaking and probably should be reserved for the serious student of anthropology.

Sheldon devised a numerical scale by means of which measurements could be made to yield a somatotype for any given individual. The somatotype is usually expressed by a series of three numerals, each of which expresses the relative strength or preponderance of one of the primary components— endomorphy, mesomorphy or ectomorphy. The numerals are either 1, 4 or 7, and are always written one after another from left to right, the first numeral indicating the degree of endomorphy present, the second, mesomorphy and the third, ectomorphy. Number 1 indicates less preponderance, number 4, medium and number 7, maximum preponderance. It can thus be seen that the endomorphic type would be expressed by the numeral 7 followed by the numerals 1 or 4, depending upon the examiner's estimate of those structures derived from the mesodermal layer, and that this numeral would, in turn, be followed by a 1 or 4, depending upon the degree of development of structure derived from ectoderm. Thus the extreme endomorph is 7 1 1. The extreme athletic type is 1 7 1, and the extreme ectomorph is 1 1 7 (Fig 4–1). The pediatrician and general practitioner are more likely to depend on such simple measurements or estimations as height, weight, head and chest circumferences and a rough estimate of the thickness of the subcutaneous fat layer.

Photography

Good photographs may be of considerable aid as an accessory in growth studies. The graphic record of change afforded by photographs of a subject often portrays points difficult to show by figures, description or curves. Such photographs should be made with the subject nude, in anterior and lateral views, with a measured grid as a background that will show up well in the print (Fig 4–1). The child should stand as close as possible to the grid to avoid large errors from parallax. If the camera is high, near the eye level of the subject, the error due to parallax is minimized for those attempting to read actual height directly from the background grid.

Head Measurements

One of the most important measurements in the evaluation of children is the circumference of the head, because this is related to intracranial volume and permits an estimation of the rate of brain growth. It is a measurement having a relatively narrow range for any age group, with a standard deviation that remains small and nearly constant for the entire growing period. There is almost no variation based on racial, national or geographic factors.[47] Although there is a slight difference between the sexes, the circumference of males being greater, the difference does not exceed 1 cm for the mean at any age. Table 4–2 is constructed using a mean of both sexes and is adequate for any clinical appraisal. Sequential measurements of the head circumference plotted on a graph may reveal significant abnormal trends not apparent in an isolated value. A rapid increase, although remaining within the limits of two standard deviations, may be the first indication of hydrocephalus. This is

TABLE 4–2.—AVERAGE HEAD
CIRCUMFERENCE OF AMERICAN
CHILDREN

	MEAN		STANDARD DEVIATION	
AGE	IN.	CM	IN.	CM
Birth	13.8	35	0.5	1.2
1 mo	14.9	37.6	0.5	1.2
2 mo	15.5	39.7	0.5	1.2
3 mo	15.9	40.4	0.5	1.2
6 mo	17.0	43.4	0.4	1.1
9 mo	17.8	45.0	0.5	1.2
12 mo	18.3	46.5	0.5	1.2
18 mo	19.0	48.4	0.5	1.2
2 yr	19.2	49.0	0.5	1.2
3 yr	19.6	50.0	0.5	1.2
4 yr	19.8	50.5	0.5	1.2
5 yr	20.0	50.8	0.6	1.4
6 yr	20.2	51.2	0.6	1.4
7 yr	20.5	51.6	0.6	1.4
8 yr	20.6	52.0	0.8	1.8
10 yr	20.9	53.0	0.6	1.4
12 yr	21.0	53.2	0.8	1.8
14 yr	21.5	54.0	0.8	1.8
16 yr	21.9	55.0	0.8	1.8
18 yr	22.1	55.4	0.8	1.8
20 yr	22.2	55.6	0.8	1.8

especially true during infancy, when normal growth is relatively fast (Fig 4–2,A and B).

Any disturbance in the growth of the brain or injury to it may result in such varied conditions as microcephaly and hydrocephaly. During the early months of life, when maturation and growth of the brain proceed at a rapid rate, it may be easier to detect such anomalies or abnormalities from excessive variations in head circumference than from other means of evaluation, including a neurologic examination or observation of performance level. It should be pointed out, however, that visual inspection alone may be misleading, and it is not uncommon to suspect hydrocephalus in the low birth weight infant when accurate measurements will dissipate such errors. It is in such subjects that the proportions of head to chest or trunk may cause ungrounded fears. (See also Chapter 5.)

Head circumference is measured by passing a tape measure over the most prominent part of the occiput and just above the supraorbital ridges. This is not necessarily the "maximum head circumference" which has been incor-

Fig 4–2, A.—Head circumference for boys from birth to 18 years. (From Nellhaus.[47])

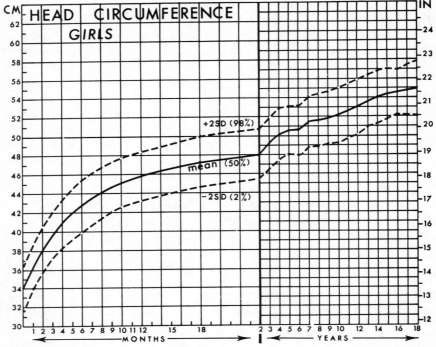

Fig 4–2, B.—Head circumference for girls from birth to 18 years. (From Nellhaus.[47])

rectly used by some for evaluation. Growth is very rapid during the early months of life, and then there is deceleration. There is a 5-cm increase in the first four months, or about ½ in. a month. A second increase of 5 cm is not completed until the end of the first year. From then until age 18 there is only another 10-cm increase. The slight but definite increase that occurs during adolescence and early adult life reflects a greater thickness of cranium and cutaneous tissues rather than any change in brain size.

A number of studies have been published indicating that a large percentage, as high as 80%, of children whose head circumferences fall below the 2 percentile measurement will have mental retardation.[2, 29, 39, 51] Studies by the author indicate that there are some interesting and important exceptions. A relatively large number of children with severe congenital heart disease, and resultant retarded growth, maintained head circumferences well below that expected for their chronologic ages, but only rarely did they manifest any neurologic deficit. A small number of children with moderate to severe degrees of malabsorption syndrome, stunted growth and head circumferences below 2 standard deviations, had normal psychometric testing. Similar findings have been reported by others.[28] It may be that prenatal interference, e.g., maternal malnutrition or intrauterine infections, associated with microcephaly, offers a greater threat to the central nervous system than postnatal interference. Nevertheless, it must be recognized that a small head circumference, regardless of cause, is often associated with other evidence of neurologic impairment.[42]

By contrast, children with superior intelligence have head circumferences that are usually well above the mean, but within the normal 2 standard deviations. These studies indicate that a larger head size from one year of age is an early finding associated with superior intelligence.[39, 57]

The shape of the adult head differs conspicuously from that of the infant, the cranium being much more prominent in the latter (Fig 4–3). Separation of the cranial bones during the neonatal period is not uncommon, nor is a slight degree of overlapping (see also Chapter 12). If these changes are marked or if some other abnormality of the shape of the skull exists, e.g., oxycephaly, scaphocephaly, or brachycephaly, then measurements will not indicate the true volume of the cranial vault. During the first week after birth, there may actually be a very slight decrease in head circumference possibly related to fluid loss or redistribution.[8]

A measurement commonly used for obstetrical purposes and to estimate the degree of maturity at birth is the occipitofrontal diameter. The range for full-term infants is 10.5–13 cm (4–5 in.). Owing to molding during labor, much variation can result that tends to invalidate the use of this method in

Fig 4–3.—The skull of a newborn infant **(left)** and an adult **(right)** drawn to the same scale. The changes due to the differences in growth are apparent in the relatively large cranial vault of the infant and the greater increase in size of the facial bones in the adult. The *horizontal lines* cross the same bony landmarks in each illustration.

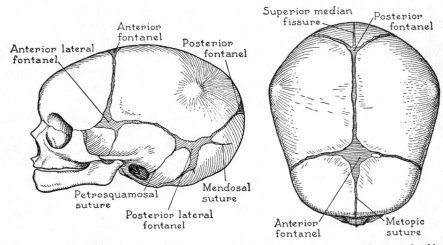

Fig 4–4.—The cranium at birth, showing major sutures and fontanels. No attempt is made to show molding or overlapping of bones, which sometimes occurs at birth. (From Caffey.[58])

the early neonatal period. At age 1 year the mean diameter is 16 cm (6½ in.), at age 2, 17 cm (7 in.) and at age 18, approximately 19 cm (8 in.).

Attempts have been made to establish some reliable measurement standards for size of the fontanels, especially the anterior one. For a number of reasons this has not been found practical. Definitive points to use for the measurements have not been uniformly agreed upon. There is great variation in the size and shape of the fontanels within the limits of normal. Other methods are available and more reliable than estimating the significance and/or cause for a large or small fontanel. Since the fontanel is covered by a soft and pliable tissue, it can be used as a kind of manometer to judge intracranial pressure. If there is abnormally increasing pressure the fontanel becomes tense, palpable arterial pulse is obliterated, and, finally, bulging occurs. Normally the anterior fontanel is closed to palpation by 12–18 months, though a slight depression may still be evident. Sutures cannot be felt after the first few months, but they are not anatomically obliterated until 12–15 years (Figs 4–3 and 4–4).

Chest Measurements

Measurements of the chest should be taken with the subject recumbent at the level of the nipples midway between inspiration and expiration. Mean values are given in Table 4–3. At birth the transverse and anteroposterior

TABLE 4–3.—AVERAGE CHEST CIRCUMFERENCE AND
INTERCRISTAL WIDTH OF AMERICAN CHILDREN

AGE	CHEST CIRCUMFERENCE		PELVIC BICRISTAL DIAMETER	
	IN.	CM	IN.	CM
Birth	13.7	35	3.2	8
3 mo	16.2	40	4.3	11
6 mo	17.3	44	4.8	12
1 yr	18.3	47	5.1	13
18 mo	18.9	48	5.5	14
2 yr	19.5	50	6.0	15
3 yr	20.4	52	6.2	16
4 yr	21.1	53		
5 yr	22.0	55	7.2	18
6 yr	22.5	56		
7 yr	23.0	57	8.2	20
8 yr	24.0	59		
9 yr	24.5	60	8.5	21
10 yr	25.1	61		
12 yr	27.0	66	9.0	22
14 yr	29.0	72	11.0	28
16 yr*	31.0	77		
18 yr*	33.0	82	12.2	31
20 yr*	34.5	86	12.6	32

*Males only.

diameters are nearly equal. The thoracic index, which is the ratio of the former to the latter, at this time is 1.0. The transverse diameter increases more rapidly than the anteroposterior, so that at age 1 year the index is 1.25 and at 6 years, 1.35. The ratio changes little thereafter.

Abdominal and Pelvic Measurements

During infancy and early childhood the abdomen is more prominent than at subsequent ages. The circumferences of the abdomen and thorax are about equal until age 2 years; after this time the abdominal circumference is considerably less than the thoracic. Because the abdominal circumference is influenced by the phase of respiration, the degree of voluntary and involuntary muscle tone and possible gaseous distention, it is a variable and relatively unreliable measurement.

A measurement less subject to variations in posture or tone of the musculature is the pelvic bicristal diameter. This represents the maximal distance between the external margins of the iliac crests, measured by calipers with the child in a recumbent position. Older children may be measured in erect position. The breadth of the pelvis usually reflects quite well the general stockiness of the child. Average values for different ages are recorded in Table 4–3.

Weight and Height

In any group of measurements that of the body weight, because it sums up all the increments in size, is probably the best index of nutrition and growth. This is particularly true in infancy. In any period of life there are wide variations within normal limits. Careful clinical evaluation of the subject is necessary to avoid errors. The obese infant, although he weighs more than a healthy one wisely fed, is certainly not in a better state of nutrition. Infants in whom edema is developing will show a gain which is quite misleading in the absence of frank edema. Such factors, and more could be listed, must be recognized in order to evaluate properly the meaning of an individual's weight.

During the first few days of the neonatal period some loss of weight is normal, usually less than 10% of birth weight. This is accounted for by the initial loss of meconium and urine and by the inadequacy of the milk supply from the breast at this time. In some infants, particularly prematures, some of this loss may be due to disappearance of a "physiologic" edema during the first week. Birth weight is generally regained by the 10th day. Thereafter, in healthy infants, a steady gain ensues. The mean birth weight is usually given as 7–7^1/$_2$ lb (3.4 kg). During the first three months, the average baby gains close to 1 kg (2.2 lb) a month, or nearly 30 gm (1 oz) a day. More than half of healthy infants will have doubled their birth weight within 3 to 4 months. Generally, weight gain is slightly greater in the formula-fed as compared to the breast-fed baby. By 6 months the average gain per month is down to 0.5 kg (1 lb). Birth weight is usually tripled by the end of the first year and quadrupled by the end of the second year. During the second year, the average monthly increment is about 0.25 kg, the rate of gain steadily decreasing. The older the child, the less regular is the increase in weight, and it may remain stationary for weeks at a time in perfectly healthy subjects. After age 2, the approximate annual increment in weight will be 2.3 kg (5 lb) until the individual begins his adolescent growth spurt.

The time of onset of rapid gain in weight during adolescence corresponds closely in both sexes with the gain in height. The duration of the gain in weight, however, covers a longer span.[22] The adolescent acceleration occurs earlier in girls than in boys, the most rapid spurt beginning in girls at 10–12 years and in boys two years later. This rapid growth is greatest the year before menarche.

All weight measurements should be obtained with the subject undressed and upon scales that are checked for accuracy periodically. Although these statements seem axiomatic, it must be emphasized that failure to observe both constitutes a common source of error.

Unlike those in weight, the annual increments in height continually diminish from birth to maturity, except for a short period referred to as the adolescent spurt of growth. The average birth length is about 50 cm (20 in.). By the end of the first year the infant has increased his birth length by about 50%. He has doubled it by age 4 years. During the early school years the curve of height increments is nearly flat, and the average annual gain is 5 cm (2 in.) or a little better. By the 13th year the birth length has trebled.

In girls the adolescent acceleration of growth in length occurs from approximately age 10 to 12 years, whereas for boys the acceleration is usually from age 12 to 14. From age 13 years in girls and 15 years in boys the rate of growth in stature rapidly decelerates. Growth ceases in girls at age 17–19 years but may continue in boys at a very slow rate beyond the 20th birthday.[10] In each individual child the rapid spurt of growth is most pronounced during the earliest period of the acceleration. It is only when a cross-section of many children is considered that the curve is broadened.[22] Thus the individual grows at a much more rapid rate and for a relatively shorter time than a composite curve would indicate. The menarchial relationships to the time of attainment of terminal height are the same as those described for weight. Of course, there is variation in the annual increments of stature among children of the same age. For any given year a child's gain in height may be very small and still be normal for him, even though others of his age are becoming taller. Apparent growth retardation is most significant at the stages when growth should be accelerated. For instance, during infancy failure to grow in stature should be regarded with suspicion even in the absence of obvious disease.

The United States Public Health Service recently reported a survey of height and weight and other measurements of children in the United States.[3-5, 26] This consisted of examinations of over 7,000 children in the age range 6–18. The project covered the entire geographic area of the United States and, for statistical purposes, divided the groups into white and black. Though other races were included, their numbers were too small to be significant. This material was supplemented by other studies of equally recent origin to adequately cover the entire age span of childhood. All measurements were done between 1962 and 1974. In comparison of mean height and weight, or 50th percentiles, it is surprising how similar the USPHS figures are to the material from Simmons's study published in 1944[16] or the Stuart and Meredith statistics published in 1946.[30] In height there is virtaully no difference at any age for boys in the three studies. For girls, the differences are never greater than 2.5 cm. There is considerably greater variability in weight, but even here the differences probably have little or no clinical significance in their use as a means for comparison in the evaluation of a single child. The most recent study does indicate some increase in stature in the lower percentiles. Essentially no differences are present be-

GROWTH AND DEVELOPMENT

TABLE 4–4.—WEIGHT AND HEIGHT PERCENTILE TABLE:
BOYS (BIRTH TO AGE 18)

WEIGHT IN LB			WEIGHT IN KG			AGE	HEIGHT IN IN.			HEIGHT IN CM		
10%	50%	90%	10%	50%	90%		10%	50%	90%	10%	50%	90%
6.3	7.5	9.1	2.86	3.4	4.13	Birth	18.9	19.9	21.0	48.1	50.6	53.3
8.5	10.0	11.5	3.8	4.6	5.2	1 mo	20.2	21.2	22.2	50.4	53.0	55.5
10.0	11.5	13.2	4.6	5.2	6.0	2 mo	21.5	22.5	23.5	53.7	56.0	60.0
11.1	12.6	14.5	5.03	5.72	6.58	3 mo	22.8	23.8	24.7	57.8	60.4	62.8
12.5	14.0	16.2	5.6	6.3	7.3	4 mo	23.7	24.7	25.7	60.5	62.0	65.2
13.7	15.0	17.7	6.2	7.0	8.0	5 mo	24.5	25.5	26.5	61.8	65.0	67.3
14.8	16.7	19.2	6.71	7.58	8.71	6 mo	25.2	26.1	27.3	63.9	66.4	69.3
17.8	20.0	22.9	8.07	9.07	10.39	9 mo	27.0	28.0	29.2	68.6	71.2	74.2
19.6	22.2	25.4	8.89	10.7	11.52	12 mo	28.5	29.6	30.7	72.4	75.2	78.1
22.3	25.2	29.0	10.12	11.43	13.15	18 mo	31.0	32.2	33.5	78.8	81.8	85.0
24.7	27.7	31.9	11.2	12.56	14.47	2 yr	33.1	34.4	35.9	84.2	87.5	91.1
26.6	30.0	34.5	12.07	13.61	15.65	2½ yr	34.8	36.3	37.9	88.5	92.1	96.2
28.7	32.2	36.8	13.02	14.61	16.69	3 yr	36.3	37.9	39.6	92.3	96.2	100.5
30.4	34.3	39.1	13.79	15.56	17.74	3½ yr	37.8	39.3	41.1	96.0	99.8	104.5
32.1	36.4	41.4	14.56	16.51	18.78	4 yr	39.1	40.7	42.7	99.3	103.4	108.5
33.8	38.4	43.9	15.33	17.42	19.91	4½ yr	40.3	42.0	44.2	102.4	106.7	112.3
35.5	40.5	46.7	16.1	18.37	21.18	5 yr	40.8	42.8	45.2	103.7	108.7	114.7
38.8	45.6	53.1	17.6	20.68	24.09	5½ yr	42.6	45.0	47.3	108.3	114.4	120.1
40.9	48.3	56.4	18.55	21.91	25.58	6 yr	43.8	46.3	48.6	111.2	117.5	123.5
43.4	51.2	60.4	19.69	23.22	27.4	6½ yr	44.9	47.6	50.0	114.1	120.8	127.0
45.8	54.1	64.4	20.77	24.54	29.21	7 yr	46.0	48.9	51.4	116.9	124.1	130.5
48.5	57.1	68.7	22.0	25.9	31.16	7½ yr	47.2	50.0	52.7	120.0	127.1	133.9
51.2	60.1	73.0	23.22	27.26	33.11	8 yr	48.5	51.2	54.0	123.1	130.0	137.3
53.8	63.1	77.0	24.4	28.62	34.93	8½ yr	49.5	52.3	55.1	125.7	132.8	140.0
56.3	66.0	81.0	25.54	29.94	36.74	9 yr	50.5	53.3	56.1	128.3	135.5	142.6
58.7	69.0	85.5	26.63	31.3	38.78	9½ yr	51.4	54.3	57.1	130.6	137.9	145.1
61.1	71.9	89.9	27.71	32.61	40.78	10 yr	52.3	55.2	58.1	132.8	140.3	147.5
63.7	74.8	94.6	28.89	33.93	42.91	10½ yr	53.2	56.0	58.9	135.1	142.3	149.7
66.3	77.6	99.3	30.07	35.2	45.04	11 yr	54.0	56.8	59.8	137.3	144.2	151.8
69.2	81.0	104.5	31.39	36.74	47.4	11½ yr	55.0	57.8	60.9	139.8	146.9	154.8
72.0	84.4	109.6	32.66	38.28	49.71	12 yr	56.1	58.9	62.2	142.4	149.6	157.9
74.6	88.7	116.4	33.84	40.23	52.8	12½ yr	56.9	60.0	63.6	144.5	152.3	161.6
77.1	93.0	123.2	34.97	42.18	55.88	13 yr	57.7	61.0	65.1	146.6	155.0	165.3
82.2	100.3	130.1	37.29	45.5	59.01	13½ yr	58.8	62.6	66.5	149.4	158.9	168.9
87.2	107.6	136.9	39.55	48.81	62.1	14 yr	59.9	64.0	67.9	152.1	162.7	172.4
93.3	113.9	142.4	42.32	51.66	64.59	14½ yr	61.0	65.1	68.7	155.0	165.3	174.6
99.4	120.1	147.8	45.09	54.48	67.04	15 yr	62.1	66.1	69.6	157.8	167.8	176.7
105.2	124.9	152.6	47.72	56.65	69.22	15½ yr	63.1	66.8	70.2	160.3	169.7	178.2
111.0	129.7	157.3	50.35	58.83	71.35	16 yr	64.1	67.8	70.7	162.8	171.6	179.7
114.3	133.0	161.0	51.85	60.33	73.03	16½ yr	64.6	68.0	71.1	164.2	172.7	180.7
117.5	136.2	164.6	53.3	61.78	74.66	17 yr	65.2	68.4	71.5	165.5	173.7	181.6
118.8	137.6	166.8	53.89	62.41	75.66	17½ yr	65.3	68.5	71.6	165.9	174.1	182.0
120.0	139.0	169.0	54.43	63.05	76.66	18 yr	65.5	68.7	71.8	166.3	174.5	182.4

TABLE 4–5.—WEIGHT AND HEIGHT PERCENTILE TABLE:
GIRLS (BIRTH TO AGE 18)

WEIGHT IN LB			WEIGHT IN KG			AGE	HEIGHT IN IN.			HEIGHT IN CM		
10%	50%	90%	10%	50%	90%		10%	50%	90%	10%	50%	90%
6.2	7.4	8.6	2.81	3.36	3.9	Birth	18.8	19.8	20.4	47.8	50.2	51.0
8.0	9.7	11.0	3.3	4.2	5.0	1 mo	20.2	21.0	22.0	50.4	52.8	55.0
9.5	11.0	12.5	4.1	5.0	5.8	2 mo	21.5	22.2	23.2	53.7	55.5	59.6
10.7	12.4	14.0	4.85	5.62	6.35	3 mo	22.4	23.4	24.3	56.9	59.5	61.7
12.0	13.7	15.5	5.3	6.2	7.2	4 mo	23.2	24.2	25.2	59.6	61.0	64.8
13.0	14.7	17.0	5.9	6.8	7.7	5 mo	24.0	25.0	26.0	60.7	64.2	67.0
14.1	16.0	18.6	6.4	7.26	8.44	6 mo	24.6	25.7	26.7	62.5	65.2	67.8
16.6	19.2	22.4	7.53	8.71	10.16	9 mo	26.4	27.6	28.7	67.0	70.1	72.9
18.4	21.5	24.8	8.35	9.75	11.25	12 mo	27.8	29.2	30.3	70.6	74.2	77.1
21.2	24.5	28.3	9.62	11.11	12.84	18 mo	30.2	31.8	33.3	76.8	80.9	84.5
23.5	27.1	31.7	10.66	12.29	14.38	2 yr	32.3	34.1	35.8	82.0	86.6	91.0
25.5	29.6	34.6	11.57	13.43	15.69	2½ yr	34.0	36.0	37.9	86.3	91.4	96.4
27.6	31.8	37.4	12.52	14.42	16.96	3 yr	35.6	37.7	39.8	90.5	95.7	101.1
29.5	33.9	40.4	13.38	15.38	18.33	3½ yr	37.1	39.2	41.5	94.2	99.5	105.4
31.2	36.2	43.5	14.15	16.42	19.73	4 yr	38.4	40.6	43.1	97.6	103.2	109.6
32.9	38.5	46.7	14.92	17.46	21.18	4½ yr	39.7	42.0	44.7	100.9	106.8	113.5
34.8	40.5	49.2	15.79	18.37	22.32	5 yr	40.5	42.9	45.4	103.0	109.1	115.4
38.0	44.0	51.2	17.24	19.96	23.22	5½ yr	42.4	44.4	46.8	107.8	112.8	118.9
39.6	46.5	54.2	17.96	21.09	24.58	6 yr	43.5	45.6	48.1	110.6	115.9	122.3
42.2	49.4	57.7	19.14	22.41	26.17	6½ yr	44.8	46.9	49.4	113.7	119.1	125.6
44.5	52.2	61.2	20.19	23.68	27.76	7 yr	46.0	48.1	50.7	116.8	122.3	128.9
46.6	55.2	65.6	21.14	25.04	29.76	7½ yr	47.0	49.3	51.9	119.5	125.2	131.8
48.6	58.1	69.9	22.04	26.35	31.71	8 yr	48.1	50.4	53.0	122.1	128.0	134.6
50.6	61.0	74.5	22.95	27.67	33.79	8½ yr	49.0	51.4	54.1	124.6	130.5	137.5
52.6	63.8	79.1	23.86	28.94	35.88	9 yr	50.0	52.3	55.3	127.0	132.9	140.4
54.9	67.1	84.4	24.9	30.44	38.28	9½ yr	50.9	53.5	56.4	129.4	135.8	143.2
57.1	70.3	89.7	25.9	31.89	40.69	10 yr	51.8	54.6	57.5	131.7	138.6	146.0
59.9	74.6	95.1	27.17	33.79	43.14	10½ yr	52.9	55.8	58.9	134.4	141.7	149.7
62.6	78.8	100.4	28.4	35.74	45.54	11 yr	53.9	57.0	60.4	137.0	144.7	153.4
66.1	83.2	106.0	29.98	37.74	48.08	11½ yr	55.0	58.3	61.8	139.8	148.1	157.0
69.5	87.6	111.5	31.52	39.74	50.58	12 yr	56.1	59.8	63.2	142.6	151.9	160.6
74.7	93.4	118.0	33.88	42.37	53.52	12½ yr	57.4	60.7	64.0	145.9	154.3	162.7
79.9	99.1	124.5	36.24	44.95	56.47	13 yr	58.7	61.8	64.9	149.1	157.1	164.8
85.5	103.7	128.9	38.78	47.04	58.47	13½ yr	59.5	62.4	65.3	151.1	158.4	165.9
91.0	108.4	133.3	41.28	49.17	60.46	14 yr	60.2	62.8	65.7	153.0	159.6	167.0
94.2	111.0	135.7	42.73	50.35	61.55	14½ yr	60.7	63.1	66.0	154.1	160.4	167.6
97.4	113.5	138.1	44.18	51.48	62.64	15 yr	61.1	63.4	66.2	155.2	161.1	168.1
99.2	115.3	139.6	45.0	52.3	63.32	15½ yr	61.3	63.7	66.4	155.7	161.7	168.6
100.9	117.0	141.1	45.77	53.07	64.0	16 yr	61.5	63.9	66.5	156.1	162.2	169.0
101.9	118.1	142.2	46.22	53.57	64.5	16½ yr	61.5	63.9	66.6	156.2	162.4	169.2
102.8	119.1	143.3	46.63	54.02	65.0	17 yr	61.5	64.0	66.7	156.3	162.5	169.4
103.2	119.5	143.9	46.81	54.2	65.27	17½ yr	61.5	64.0	66.7	156.3	162.5	169.4
103.5	119.9	144.5	46.95	54.39	65.54	18 yr	61.5	64.0	66.7	156.3	162.5	169.4

tween the white and black races relative to height. Black girls do begin the pubertal acceleration of growth at a slightly earlier age than white girls, and for a brief period are slightly taller. Both black boys and girls weigh slightly less than their white peers between the ages of 6 and 12. It does not appear necessary to publish separate standards for black and white children based upon the differences cited.[27, 35, 53, 56]

The changes in body proportions that follow the growth in height are important. At birth the sitting height represents 70% of the total length, but decreases to only 57% by age three, and roughly 50% by adulthood. Black children have slightly shorter sitting height but have longer lower extremities than white children at all ages.[5, 34]

Some boys and girls may be taller and heavier than the average from early childhood for genetic reasons. They also will mature more rapidly and complete their linear growth sooner. Conversely, genetically slow children will follow another pattern of growth at a lower level on the growth chart. The fact that other members of the family have experienced similar patterns of growth is helpful in arriving at the correct diagnosis in such situations. The child born small for gestational age is prone to grow more slowly than his peers and even remain small as an adult.[32, 45]

Common sources of error or confusion in comparing measurements obtained at different times result from poor technique. It is highly desirable to use reclining length for the first three years and thereafter standing height. The table or stand must be solid and firm, and the equipment used must not contribute to the problem, as is true of most measuring devices attached to weight scales found in many physicians' offices.

By the correlation of the height-age and weight-age data, a number of tables have been constructed which present mean weight for sex-age-height groups. Given the age, sex and height of a child, the expected weight may be ascertained. This expected weight is the average for a large group of children. Several objections have been raised to the use of such tables in the appraisal of physical status: (1) There is a difference of opinion concerning the amount a given child may deviate from the mean figures before he should be considered abnormally over- or underweight for his age, sex, etc. (2) Unless deviations from the usual physique are excessive, they are apt to be overlooked. (3) Furthermore, such tables fail to present a graphic picture of the mean against which the individual's progress may be compared. The mean itself may be criticized as an undesirable standard because it is based on a child population that includes different levels, many of which are not optimal. Such tables do provide, nevertheless, a convenient standard and are frequently used.

Tables 4–4 and 4–5 give data for weight and height in percentiles, based on anthropometric charts, against which a child's development may be observed. Weight measurements for a child usually fall in the same percentile group at succeeding ages or change only gradually from period to period. Height and weight often differ in their actual percentile positions, but tend to maintain the same general relationships from period to period. Eighty percent of the weight measurements of children at a given age would be expected to fall between the 10th and 90th percentiles. Allowance must, of course, be made for the adolescent spurt in girls between ages 10 and 14 and in boys between 11 and 16. Children with weight and height measurements

Fig 4–5.—A, percentile curves for measurements of girls from birth to 3 years. Length was obtained in a recumbent position during the first 3 years, thereafter as standing height. Where the length and height measurements overlap, the results have been modified to result in a smooth uninterrupted curve. (The growth charts, Figs 4–5 and 4–6, are reproduced by permission of the National Center for Health Statistics.[3]) *(Continued.)*

which (1) fall in different percentile groups, (2) shift percentile groups or (3) fall near to or outside the 10th and 90th percentile should be reviewed for growth abnormalities.

Height-Weight Curves

The presentation of norms in terms of curves has a decided advantage, providing a running account of the individual's measurements plotted against the pattern of growth of a large group of his own age. A child growing normally tends to maintain his relative position (percentile level) with respect to his age group. His growth trend as compared with the growth trend

Fig 4–5 (cont.).— B, percentile curves for measurements of girls from 2 to 18 years.

of other children is represented in such a way that deviations from the norm may become apparent earlier than otherwise.

Once the measurements are plotted, one looks at a picture of growth with the intermediate numerical steps dispensed with once and for all. Patterns of growth of the individual are compared with curves of the chart: levels of growth attained by the individual are examined in relation to the levels of the different percentiles of the chart. The weight-age curve is compared with the height-age curve to determine the subject's build and nutritional status. Any marked deviation from the curves of the chart must be interpreted in the light of the medical and social history of the child and the results of physical examination (Figs 4–5 and 4–6).

Fig 4–6.—A, percentile curves for measurements of boys from birth to 3 years. See legend for Figure 4–5, A. *(Continued.)*

Fig 4–6 (cont.).—B, percentile curves for measurements of boys from 2 to 18 years.

Velocity of Growth

The rate or velocity of growth is an extremely important aspect of the evaluation of any child. This is especially so if information on the longitudinal growth is meager or absent for a particular subject. Growth is not constant and is characterized by periods of acceleration occurring at different times but in similar sequences for healthy children. The velocity of growth is most rapid immediately after birth and then falls off rapidly (Table 4–6). From age 2 until about 11 in girls and 13 in boys the rate or velocity continues slowly decelerating, and then the adolescent increase begins. For girls this peaks at approximately age 12 and for boys at 14. Except for infancy, the usual time interval used in measuring either height or weight velocity is one year. It should be pointed out that the adolescent peak for weight in girls follows

TABLE 4–6.—EXPECTED INCREMENTS IN
WEIGHT AND HEIGHT*

AGE		WEIGHT, KG		HEIGHT, CM	
0–1	mo	0.64		3.8	
1–3	mo	1.54		6.1	
3–6	mo	1.77		6.4	
6–9	mo	1.36		4.6	
9–12	mo	1.00		4.1	
12–18	mo	1.40		6.6	
18–24	mo	1.22		5.6	
24–30	mo	1.04		4.8	
30–36	mo	0.95		4.3	
36–42	mo	1.04		3.8	
42–48	mo	0.95		3.6	
48–54	mo	1.09		3.6	
54–60	mo	1.00		3.3	
60–66	mo	1.14		3.6	
66–72	mo	1.18		3.3	
		BOYS	GIRLS	BOYS	GIRLS
6–7	yr	2.2	2.1	6.1	5.8
7–8	yr	2.4	2.4	5.6	5.6
8–9	yr	2.5	2.5	5.6	5.6
9–10	yr	2.7	2.8	5.1	5.3
10–11	yr	2.5	3.5	5.1	5.8
11–12	yr	3.0	4.5	5.1	6.4
12–13	yr	4.1	5.1	5.6	6.6
13–14	yr	5.5	4.3	7.2	5.1
14–15	yr	5.1	2.3	5.8	2.5
15–16	yr	4.5	1.8	5.1	2.0
16–17	yr	3.2	1.2	3.8	0.8

*Data represent averages from several sources.

height by about one year, or at age 13, while the peaks occur nearly simultaneously in boys.

In velocity standards a child does not have the same tendency to stay in the same percentile position from one age to another as in the usual height or weight versus age graphs. He may occupy a relatively high or low position at one stage of his development, but if he enjoys good health, he will tend to move toward a more central or average rate of increment in the following stage.

When considering height velocity, two important facts must be remembered as they apply to the individual child. The adolescent peak (time of most rapid increase in height growth) will occur at different ages for each subject, depending upon his rate of sexual maturation. The relative velocity for boys is greater than for girls; an increase of 7.3 cm as compared to 6.5 cm in the maximal year are mean figures, based on Tanner's work[55] (Fig 4–7).

Fig 4-7.—Velocity curves for length and height for boys and girls based upon intervals of one year. They indicate the rapid deceleration following birth and the relatively short duration of the adolescent acceleration. Each curve represents the mean of the sex and the mean for age and height increase. Normal variations from these are to be expected, but the relative shape of the curve will be followed by each child. The shape of the curve for the adolescent growth "spurt" for an individual child will usually be narrower (less time) and higher (more accumulated height) than the mean illustrated.

Comparisons of percentile positions held by measurements at repeated periodic examinations indicate adherence to or possibly significant deviation from previous percentile positions. In normal circumstances one expects a child to maintain a similar position from age to age, i.e., on or near one percentile line or between the same two lines. Occasional sharp deviations or gradual but continuing shifts from one percentile position to another call for further investigation as to their causes.

Mnemonics

Anyone who has occasion to appraise the growth and development of children realizes the need for some system of remembering approximate

TABLE 4–7.—WEIGHT PREDICTION FROM AGE
(3–12 MONTHS)

AGE, MO	WEIGHT, LB MITCHELL-NELSON		HOLT-McINTOSH		GRAND AV., LB	PREDICTED BY FORMULA, LB
	BOYS	GIRLS	BOYS	GIRLS		
3	12.6	12.4	14.3	13.0	13.1	14
6	16.7	16.0	18.7	17.0	17.1	17
9	20.0	19.2	21.7	19.7	20.2	20
12	22.2	21.5	23.8	21.9	22.4	23

Formula: weight = age + 11

heights and weights of various ages. One such aid in general use has been the statement that at age 2 years the child is probably one-half as tall as he will be at maturity. Others are that at age 3 years the child is 3 ft tall, or at 4 years is 40 in. tall; or at age 3½ years the average child weighs 35 lb and at 7 years weighs seven times his birth weight.

Weech[40] has added several mnemonics to those already in use and tested them against tables of height and weight in the Holt and McIntosh (12th edition) and Mitchell-Nelson (7th edition) textbooks. Tables 4–7 to 4–11 contain Weech's mnemonic formulas and illustrate how values obtained by these formulas compare with those in the aforementioned texts.

There is need for a formula for predicting the size and shape of the adult-to-be from measurements made in infancy or childhood. It is general knowledge that height and body build (somatotype) are strongly influenced by heredity. As Weech has pointed out, the heights of the parents should be

TABLE 4–8.—WEIGHT AS FUNCTION OF AGE

AGE, YR	AVERAGE (OR MEDIAN) VALUES, LB MITCHELL-NELSON		HOLT-McINTOSH		GRAND AV., LB	PREDICTED BY FORMULA, LB* (6 × AGE) + 12	(7 × AGE) + 5
	BOYS	GIRLS	BOYS	GIRLS			
4	36.4	36.2	38.1	37.2	37.0	36	
5	40.5	40.5					
5	42.8	41.4	42.8	42.3	41.9	42	
6	48.3	46.5	48.2	48.3	47.8	48	
7	54.1	52.2	54.2	54.5	53.8	54	
8	60.1	58.1	61.0	61.9	60.3	60	61
9	66.0	63.8	68.4	69.6	67.0		68
10	71.9	70.3	76.8	78.1	74.3		75
11	77.6	78.8	85.6	88.4	82.6		82
12	84.4	87.6	95.2	100.4	91.9		89
13	93.0	99.1	105.7	110.5	102.1		96
14	107.6	108.4	119.1	120.1	113.8		103

*Weight from age 4 to 8 years is approximately 6 times the age plus 12. From 8 to 12 years the formula would be 7 times age plus 5. Here both formulas apply to age 8 years, yielding substantially the same figure.

TABLE 4–9.—MNEMONIC FORMULAS FOR PREDICTING WEIGHT

AGE	WEIGHT, LB
Birth	7.35
3–12 mo	Age (mo) + 11
30 mo	30
3.5 yr	35
4–8 yr	(6 × age) + 12
8–12 yr	(7 × age) + 5

Average growth in weight—girls and boys (Mitchell-Nelson; Holt-McIntosh).

considered in any formula for calculating eventual height of a growing child. Bayer and Bayley[43] have made the stage of osseous development an important determinant in estimating height at maturity from early measurements (Figs 4–8 and 4–9). The commonly accepted statement that the child at age 2 is one-half his final height holds up well enough for boys but gives a value from which 10–12 cm should be subtracted for girls. An approximation of final height can be had when the length at 3 years is known by multiplying by 1.87 for boys and 1.73 for girls. However, it is easier to remember 2 times length at 2 years (2 × 2). Tanner et al.[41] found in the Aberdeen growth study that height at age 3 years showed better correlation with height at maturity than at any other age. The correlations of childhood measurements with

TABLE 4–10.—HEIGHT AS FUNCTION OF AGE

AGE, YR	AV. (OR MEDIAN) VALUES, IN.				GRAND AV., IN.	PREDICTED BY FORMULA, IN.
	MITCHELL-NELSON		HOLT-McINTOSH			
	BOYS	GIRLS	BOYS	GIRLS		
2	34.4	34.1	34.4	33.9	34.2	35.0
3	37.9	37.7	38.0	37.6	37.8	37.5
4	39.7	40.6	40.9	40.7	40.5	40.0
5	42.8	42.9				
5	43.8	43.2	43.6	43.5	43.4	42.5
6	46.3	45.6	46.3	46.3	46.1	45.0
7	48.9	48.1	48.7	48.7	48.6	47.5
8	51.2	50.4	51.1	51.1	51.0	50.0
9	53.3	52.3	53.3	53.3	53.1	52.5
10	55.2	54.6	55.2	55.5	55.1	55.0
11	56.8	57.0	57.4	58.1	57.3	57.5
12	58.9	59.8	59.6	60.7	59.8	60.0
13	61.0	61.8	62.0	62.8	61.9	62.5
14	64.0	62.8	64.9	64.1	64.0	65.0

Formula: height = $(2^{1}/_{2} \times \text{age}) + 30$

TABLE 4–11.—WEIGHT AS FUNCTION OF HEIGHT
(2–12 YEARS)

AGE, YR	GRAND AV. FOR BOYS AND GIRLS (MITCHELL-NELSON; HOLT-MCINTOSH)		PREDICTED BY FORMULA, LB
	HEIGHT, IN.	WEIGHT, LB	
2	34.2	27.9	27.8
3	37.8	32.5	32.5
4	40.5	37.0	36.9
5	43.5	41.9	42.6
6	46.1	47.8	48.2
7	48.6	53.8	54.3
8	51.0	60.3	60.8
9	53.1	67.0	66.9
10	55.1	74.3	73.1
11	57.3	82.6	80.4
12	59.8	91.9	89.3
13	61.9	102.1	97.2
14	64.0	113.8	105.6

Formula: $\text{weight} = 48 + \left(\dfrac{\text{height}}{2} - 23\right) \cdot \left(\dfrac{\text{height}}{10}\right)$

adult height were: birth, 0.27; 1 year, 0.67; 2 years, 0.75, and 3 years, 0.79. There was no increased correlation between height at 4 years and final height, and the correlation using length at 5 years was slightly less.

Tanner's[41] formulas:

Adult height (cm) = 1.27 × H_3 + 54.9 cm (males)
Adult height (cm) = 1.29 × H_3 + 42.3 cm (females)

Tanner's formulas fail at the extremes of length, and it is when these extremes are feared that parents ask, "How tall will she be?" This question is frequently asked by anxious mothers of early-maturing girls because the 10- or 11-year-old girl, already much larger and heavier than her peers, seems likely to grow a lot larger before reaching final height. Excessive height is a most unwelcome attribute in young women. A less well-known aphorism of growth is one which says that after menarche a girl is not likely to grow more than 3 more in. in height. Usually this will be found to be true, but like all rules it has exceptions.

There is obviously a correlation between height of parents and height of their children. Weech offers formulas using the average height of the parents as one of the variables entering into calculation of final height. He found that using the averages of the parents' heights correlated better than use of the height of either parent.

GROWTH AND DEVELOPMENT

Ht. (inches)	Skeletal Age 6-0	6-3	6-6	6-9	7-0	7-3	7-6	7-9	8-0	8-3	8-6	8-9	9-0	9-3	9-6	9-9	10-0	10-3	10-6	10-9	11-0	11-3	11-6	11-9	12-0	12-3	12-6	12-9	13-0
% of Mature Height	68.0	69.0	70.0	70.9	71.8	72.8	73.8	74.7	75.6	76.5	77.3	77.9	78.6	79.4	80.0	80.7	81.2	81.6	81.9	82.1	82.3	82.7	83.2	83.9	84.5	85.2	86.0	86.9	88.0
41	60.3																												
42	61.8	60.9	60.0																										
43	63.2	62.3	61.4	60.6																									
44	64.7	63.8	62.9	62.1	61.3	60.4																							
45	66.2	65.2	64.3	63.5	62.7	61.8	61.0	60.2																					
46	67.6	66.7	65.7	64.9	64.1	63.2	62.3	61.6	60.8	60.1																			
47	69.1	68.1	67.1	66.3	65.5	64.6	63.7	62.9	62.2	61.4	60.8	60.3																	
48	70.6	69.6	68.6	67.7	66.9	65.9	65.0	64.3	63.5	62.7	62.1	61.6	61.1	60.5	60.0														
49	72.1	71.0	70.0	69.1	68.2	67.3	66.4	65.6	64.8	64.1	63.4	62.9	62.3	61.7	61.3	60.7	60.3	60.0											
50	73.5	72.5	71.4	70.5	69.6	68.7	67.8	66.9	66.1	65.4	64.7	64.2	63.6	63.0	62.5	62.0	61.6	61.3	61.1	60.9	60.8	60.5							
51	75.0	73.9	72.9	71.9	71.0	70.1	69.1	68.3	67.5	66.7	66.0	65.5	64.9	64.2	63.8	63.2	62.8	62.5	62.3	62.1	62.0	61.7	61.3	60.8					
52	76.5	75.4	74.3	73.3	72.4	71.4	70.5	69.6	68.8	68.0	67.3	66.8	66.2	65.5	65.0	64.4	64.0	63.7	63.5	63.3	63.2	62.9	62.5	62.0	61.5	61.0	60.5		
53	77.9	76.8	75.7	74.8	73.8	72.8	71.8	71.0	70.1	69.3	68.6	68.0	67.4	66.8	66.3	65.7	65.3	65.0	64.7	64.6	64.4	64.1	63.7	63.2	62.7	62.2	61.6	61.0	60.2
54	79.4	78.3	77.1	76.2	75.2	74.2	73.2	72.3	71.4	70.6	69.9	69.3	68.7	68.0	67.5	66.9	66.5	66.2	65.9	65.8	65.6	65.3	64.9	64.4	63.9	63.4	62.8	62.1	61.4
55	80.9	79.7	78.6	77.6	76.6	75.5	74.5	73.6	72.8	71.9	71.2	70.6	70.0	69.3	68.8	68.2	67.7	67.4	67.2	67.0	66.8	66.5	66.1	65.6	65.1	64.6	64.0	63.3	62.5
56			80.0	79.0	78.0	76.9	75.9	75.0	74.1	73.2	72.4	71.9	71.3	70.5	70.0	69.4	69.0	68.6	68.4	68.2	68.0	67.7	67.3	66.7	66.3	65.7	65.1	64.4	63.6
57				80.4	79.4	78.3	77.2	76.3	75.4	74.5	73.7	73.2	72.5	71.8	71.3	70.6	70.2	69.9	69.6	69.4	69.3	68.9	68.5	67.9	67.5	66.9	66.3	65.6	64.8
58					80.8	79.7	78.6	77.6	76.7	75.8	75.0	74.5	73.8	73.1	72.5	71.9	71.4	71.1	70.8	70.6	70.5	70.1	69.7	69.1	68.6	68.1	67.4	66.7	65.9
59							79.9	79.0	78.0	77.1	76.3	75.7	75.1	74.3	73.8	73.1	72.7	72.3	72.0	71.9	71.7	71.3	70.9	70.3	69.8	69.3	68.6	67.9	67.0
60								80.3	79.4	78.4	77.6	77.0	76.3	75.6	75.0	74.4	73.9	73.5	73.3	73.1	72.9	72.6	72.1	71.5	71.0	70.4	69.8	69.0	68.2
61									80.7	79.7	78.9	78.3	77.6	76.8	76.3	75.6	75.1	74.8	74.5	74.3	74.1	73.8	73.3	72.7	72.2	71.6	70.9	70.2	69.3
62											80.2	79.6	78.9	78.1	77.5	76.8	76.4	76.0	75.7	75.5	75.3	75.0	74.5	73.9	73.4	72.8	72.1	71.3	70.5
63												80.9	80.2	79.3	78.8	78.1	77.6	77.2	76.9	76.7	76.6	76.2	75.7	75.1	74.6	73.9	73.3	72.5	71.6
64														80.6	80.0	79.3	78.8	78.4	78.1	78.0	77.8	77.4	76.9	76.3	75.7	75.1	74.4	73.6	72.7
65																80.5	80.0	79.7	79.4	79.2	79.0	78.6	78.1	77.5	76.9	76.3	75.6	74.8	73.9
66																		80.9	80.6	80.4	80.2	79.8	79.3	78.7	78.1	77.5	76.7	75.9	75.0
67																						81.0	80.5	79.9	79.3	78.6	77.9	77.1	76.1

Fig 4-8.—Percentages and estimated mature heights for boys with skeletal ages one year or more retarded for their chronologic ages. This is one of several tables published by Bayley and Pinneau, by means of which an estimate of the height at maturity is made from present height and skeletal age. Skeletal age is determined from an x-ray wrist plate (Fig 4–9) and use of the Greulich-Pyle Atlas. Using this table, we see that the patient shown in Figure 4–9, who is now 58 in. tall and who has a skeletal age of 12 years, 3 months, has achieved only 85.2% of his expected growth and should eventually be approximately 68.1 in. tall. Bayley and Pinneau found an error of less than 1 in. in prediction of final height in boys 14½ years of age. (From Bayer and Bayley.[43])

Fig 4–9.—Boy, age 14$^1/_2$. Complaint: smallest boy in his class. Height: 58 in.; weight: 91 lb. Bone age: 12 years, 3 months by Greulich-Pyle Atlas.[42] Height at 2 years: 34$^1/_4$ in.; at 3 years: 37$^1/_4$ in. Height of father: 6 ft. Height of mother: 5 ft 3$^1/_2$ in. The problem is one of predicting final height. It is obvious that reassurance can be given the patient and his family if it appears that final height will be satisfactory and that the present shortness is one of delayed velocity rather than dwarfism. The following calculations illustrate several different methods of estimating this boy's final height from measurements taken early in life. In the formulas below, H_m equals height at maturity, H_2 equals height at 2 years of age and H_3 equals height at 3 years of age. As can be seen, all the methods indicate a satisfactory height for this boy eventually.

Tanner: H_m (cm) = 1.27 × H_3 + 54.9 cm (males)
$\qquad$ H_m = 175 cm or 69.8 in.
Weech: H_m = 0.545 H_2 + 0.544 A + 14.84 in.
$\qquad$ H_m = 70.3 in.
Bayley: (See Fig 4–8) = 68.1 in.
Traditional concept: 2 × H_2 = H_m
$\qquad$ 2 × 34$^1/_4$ = 68$^1/_2$ in.

Weech's formulas*:

$$H_m = 0.545H_2 + 0.544A + 14.84 \text{ in. (boys)}$$
$$H_m = 0.545H_2 + 0.544A + 10.09 \text{ in. (girls)}$$

---

*H_m = height at maturity $\qquad$ H_2 = height at 2 years $\qquad$ A = average of parents' height

Using Weech's formula against data collected at the University of Michigan Elementary School, we were able to validate the formula satisfactorily, finding that the standard deviation of the differences of actual over predicted heights in 62 boys and girls was approximately 1 in. This was true for both sexes.

Garn and Rohmann[49] have emphasized the interaction of nutrition and genetics as determinants of growth and as factors influencing the timing of growth. They use midparent stature (the average of father's and mother's statures in the fourth decade) in preparing parent-related age-size standards for children. They used the Fels Longitudinal Studies data to compile tables which should be more helpful in predicting probable age-height and final height values for individual children. Figure 4–10 clearly shows the effect of parental size on the stature of children. Tables 4–12, A and 4–12, B provide a more precise reference than do conventional age-size standards long in general use. For example, the 10-year-old boy of parents whose average (midparent) stature is 163 cm would be expected to be near 132.5 cm tall, whereas a boy of the same age whose parents averaged 178 cm would be expected to be more than 10 cm taller. Within the first few years of life the children

Fig 4–10.—Effect of parental size on the statural growth of children. Child no. *356,* whose midparental (average of both) stature was 180 cm, was considerably taller than subject no. *127,* whose midparental stature was 156 cm (From Garn and Rohmann.[49])

who were offspring of tall parents were taller than those of shorter parents. With increasing age these differences become more apparent.

It seems fair to say that the final word on formulas to predict final height from early measurements has not yet been spoken. Certainly three variables appear to be important enough to include in such calculations. These are the height of the parents, the bone age of the child at varying ages and the age of the mother at menarche (especially related to time of onset of maturational changes in boys).

Individual differences in growth become accentuated with the onset of adolescence. The variations of heights and weights and degree of maturation seen in schoolchildren, sixth through tenth grade, are enormous. The girl who matures early is much larger than average at age 11 but will usually be shorter than the average at maturity, whereas the girl who matures later will, in most physical measurements, be smaller than average until age 14 or 15 years but will continue to grow for a longer time and is likely to be taller than average when growth is completed. This tendency for early maturation to bring about early curtailment of growth is much more marked in girls than in boys. It is generally accepted that female sex hormones (estrogens) will cause epiphysial closure and cessation of statural growth once they reach the levels seen with onset of menses. The presence or absence of secondary sexual characteristics, such as pubic and axillary hair, size of the male genitalia and degree of breast development, are valuable adjuncts in the clinical estimation of future growth potentials. Using a grading system based upon the stages of development, some authorities contend that quite accurate predictions can be made.[52]

Growth as a Whole

Olson and Hughes,[12, 13] of the University of Michigan Laboratory School, have devised a table to show the longitudinal development of the child as a whole. On one table are plotted measurements of various mental and physical attributes. These workers feel that by using such a method they have the "life history of any given child over a significant age span" and also a table which takes into consideration the interrelationship of many factors of development. The unit of description is age, and each measure is converted into an age value. Using this principle, one can plot height, weight, number of erupted teeth, strength of grip, carpal age, mental age (Kuhlmann-Binet), educational age (Stanford), social age (Doll) and many others against a common scale. A manual has been compiled to assist in the translation of the various measurements into age units (reprinted from Olson and Hughes[13]).

Data so far acquired by the use of this table have shown a remarkable

TABLE 4–12, A.—FELS PARENT-SPECIFIC STANDARDS FOR HEIGHT: GIRLS' STATURE BY AGE AND MIDPARENT STATES*

AGE	\multicolumn{10}{c}{PARENTAL MIDPOINT, CM}									
	161	163	165	167	169	171	173	175	177	178
Birth . .	47.3	48.9	49.0	49.2	49.2	48.8	49.7	49.1	49.0	47.5
0–1 . . .	53.0	53.4	54.2	52.0	53.3	53.1	53.5	53.2	55.8	52.8
0–3 . . .	57.4	58.4	59.6	57.4	59.4	59.6	59.4	58.0	61.5	57.6
0–6 . . .	64.4	64.7	65.6	65.7	64.6	66.5	66.6	67.4	67.3	65.8
0–9 . . .	68.2	69.0	70.2	70.1	69.8	71.5	71.5	71.0	72.2	69.8
1–0 . . .	72.3	73.0	73.8	74.0	74.0	75.2	75.5	74.6	77.3	73.2
1–6 . . .	78.8	79.5	80.6	81.4	80.2	81.7	82.6	81.6	84.0	81.0
2–0 . . .	84.6	84.0	86.5	87.4	85.5	88.8	88.7	88.2	89.5	87.6
2–6 . . .	89.1	87.2	91.0	91.6	89.9	93.2	92.9	92.6	93.9	92.0
3–0 . . .	93.2	90.4	94.5	95.8	93.8	97.1	96.5	96.5	98.5	96.2
3–6 . . .	96.7	93.5	98.3	99.6	97.8	101.4	100.3	102.0	102.4	103.0
4–0 . . .	100.1	96.8	102.4	103.5	103.9	104.9	104.0	103.8	105.8	104.3
4–6 . . .	103.5	100.2	106.0	106.7	105.8	108.6	107.5	107.4	109.4	108.0
5–0 . . .	106.8	103.5	108.9	109.9	109.1	111.6	110.9	111.0	112.6	111.7
5–6 . . .	110.0	107.0	112.2	113.2	112.0	114.8	114.4	114.2	115.8	115.4
6–0 . . .	113.2	110.2	115.0	116.2	115.0	118.2	117.8	117.3	119.1	118.8
6–6 . . .	116.1	113.4	117.8	119.4	117.6	121.6	121.2	120.8	122.6	122.3
7–0 . . .	118.8	116.5	120.6	122.4	120.2	124.4	124.4	124.0	125.0	125.5
7–6 . . .	121.7	119.4	123.5	125.7	122.9	127.6	127.6	127.3	127.8	128.7
8–0 . . .	124.6	122.4	126.3	128.8	125.8	130.7	130.8	130.2	130.8	132.0
8–6 . . .	127.3	125.5	129.4	131.8	128.5	133.8	133.8	133.4	133.9	135.0
9–0 . . .	130.1	128.6	132.2	134.7	131.4	137.1	136.7	136.6	137.0	138.2
9–6 . . .	132.7	131.6	135.6	137.5	134.2	140.2	139.8	139.8	139.9	140.9
10–0 . . .	136.0	135.1	139.0	140.3	136.9	143.8	142.9	143.1	143.8	143.6
10–6 . . .	139.1	138.5	142.3	143.2	140.0	147.4	146.0	146.6	147.4	146.4
11–0 . . .	141.9	141.6	145.9	146.0	143.4	150.3	149.0	149.6	151.3	149.4
11–6 . . .	145.0	144.8	149.4	148.9	146.6	153.2	152.1	152.8	155.3	152.2
12–0 . . .	148.0	147.8	152.8	151.8	150.3	156.4	155.2	155.8	159.0	154.9
12–6 . . .	150.8	151.1	155.8	154.4	154.0	159.0	158.2	158.8	161.1	158.0
13–0 . . .	152.9	154.2	158.8	157.0	157.0	161.0	161.1	161.7	162.3	160.5
13–6 . . .	154.5	157.2	161.0	159.1	159.0	163.0	163.3	164.0	163.0	162.5
14–0 . . .	155.4	158.8	161.7	160.9	160.4	163.7	165.0	165.9	163.9	164.1
14–6 . . .	155.7	159.4	162.2	162.5	161.5	164.0	166.2	167.4	164.5	165.5
15–0 . . .	155.9	159.8	162.6	163.7	162.2	164.0	167.1	168.4	165.0	166.5
15–6 . . .	156.1	160.1	162.7	164.7	162.9	164.0	167.5	169.2	165.3	167.8
16–0 . . .	156.0	160.5	162.8	165.5	163.4	164.1	167.8	169.7	165.5	168.7
16–6 . . .	156.1	160.7	162.9	166.1	163.8	164.2	167.8	170.3	165.6	169.4
17–0 . . .	156.2	160.8	163.0	166.5	164.0	164.3	167.9	170.9	165.7	170.0
17–6 . . .	156.2	160.9	163.0	166.9	164.2	164.4	167.9	171.4	165.7	170.4
18–0 . . .	156.2	161.0	165.0	167.2	164.3	164.4	167.9	171.8	165.7	170.8

Note: no attempt to eliminate sampling fluctuations.
*From Garn and Rohmann.[49]

TABLE 4–12, B.—FELS PARENT-SPECIFIC STANDARDS FOR HEIGHT:
BOY'S STATURE BY AGE AND MIDPARENT STATES*

AGE	PARENTAL MIDPOINT, CM									
	161	163	165	167	169	171	173	175	177	178
Birth	47.1	49.7	50.3	50.0	48.3	50.7	50.0	51.5	51.4	
0–1	52.7	54.6	54.7	57.6	53.2	53.6	52.2	55.6	55.9	
0–3	58.9	60.8	60.0	62.2	57.4	60.8	61.2	61.4	62.6	
0–6	65.1	66.2	66.8	67.4	65.8	70.2	69.0	70.2	70.3	
0–9	70.7	72.9	73.8	73.2	71.0	74.8	75.2	77.1	75.7	
1–0	73.1	75.6	75.7	75.1	73.4	76.6	77.1	79.6	77.8	
1–6	79.9	82.4	81.7	82.0	81.2	82.6	83.4	86.8	85.2	
2–0	85.4	87.2	87.0	87.4	87.8	88.0	88.9	92.0	91.3	
2–6	88.8	91.3	92.0	92.1	93.2	93.5	94.0	96.7	96.0	
3–0	93.2	94.9	96.1	96.0	97.2	98.1	98.3	100.7	99.9	
3–6	96.3	98.4	100.0	99.5	101.0	102.3	102.6	104.5	103.5	
4–0	99.5	102.2	103.5	103.1	104.6	106.0	106.3	108.0	107.0	
4–6	102.7	105.4	107.1	106.6	108.0	109.6	109.6	111.4	110.4	
5–0	105.6	108.5	110.6	110.0	111.5	113.2	112.7	114.6	113.8	
5–6	108.3	111.3	113.4	112.7	114.5	116.3	115.8	117.4	116.8	
6–0	110.9	114.1	116.4	115.4	117.4	119.4	118.7	120.4	119.8	
6–6	113.6	116.9	119.3	118.4	120.3	122.4	121.7	123.4	122.8	
7–0	116.2	119.7	122.3	121.3	123.2	125.6	124.6	126.4	125.6	
7–6	118.9	122.5	125.1	124.3	126.1	128.8	127.6	129.5	128.4	
8–0	121.6	125.0	127.8	126.8	128.8	131.6	130.4	132.8	131.6	
8–6	124.2	127.6	130.7	129.3	131.5	134.9	133.2	135.9	134.6	
9–0	126.9	130.4	133.3	131.9	134.1	138.0	136.0	138.8	137.5	
9–6	129.9	132.9	136.1	134.6	136.9	141.0	138.8	142.0	140.5	
10–0	132.5	135.8	138.8	137.4	139.8	143.8	141.5	145.3	143.2	
10–6	135.6	138.8	141.5	140.3	142.6	146.8	144.3	148.6	146.0	
11–0	138.5	141.8	144.1	143.0	145.4	149.9	146.8	151.9	148.9	
11–6	141.6	144.9	146.9	145.6	148.3	152.8	149.6	155.4	151.6	
12–0	144.7	148.0	149.7	148.4	151.4	155.7	152.4	158.8	154.5	
12–6	147.7	151.1	152.6	151.6	154.6	158.3	155.8	162.6	157.5	
13–0	151.0	154.2	155.7	154.9	158.0	161.7	159.6	166.3	160.5	
13–6	154.5	157.7	158.9	158.1	161.6	164.6	163.6	170.1	163.8	
14–0	158.8	161.7	162.3	161.6	165.7	167.6	167.8	173.4	166.9	
14–6	162.6	164.9	165.9	164.8	169.6	170.3	172.0	175.2	171.3	
15–0	165.8	168.1	169.1	167.9	172.9	173.0	174.7	176.4	175.2	
15–6	168.0	171.3	172.0	170.6	174.5	175.6	175.8	177.0	178.6	
16–0	169.4	173.3	174.3	172.8	177.3	177.5	176.6	177.4	181.2	
16–6	170.3	174.2	175.8	174.4	178.4	178.7	177.3	177.4	182.8	
17–0	170.9	174.7	176.8	175.4	179.2	179.4	177.8	177.5	184.3	
17–6	171.2	174.9	174.4	176.0	180.0	179.9	178.2	177.6	185.4	
18–0	171.5	175.0	177.9	176.2	180.5	180.2	178.6	177.6	186.3	

*From Garn and Rohmann.[49]

Fig 4-11.—Curves showing similarity of growth patterns of brothers born 33 months apart. Course of growth is shown for mental age, *MA*, reading age, *RA*, carpal ossification, *CaA*, height, *HA*, weight, *WA*, and dental development, *DA*. (Fom Olson and Hughes.[13])

correlation of all of the measures used; i.e., in most instances there is a marked homogeneity of all measures of physical and mental growth.* Studies of siblings have shown a high degree of similarity in the pattern of growth (Fig 4-11). Finally, the diverse data for each subject are averaged from all of the age levels, and this is plotted against chronologic age. This average for the individual has been termed the "organismic age" by Olson and Hughes. They state that the liberty taken in averaging these diverse data is based on the hypothesis that all data are samples of structures and functions of the organism and that individuals having different patterns may be "organismically" equal. "Organismic age" divided by chronologic age equals the "organismic quotient" which can be used to determine, in general, the status of any child. Figure 4-12 shows the data and the table of one subject

---

*In a study of gifted children (those with an IQ of 140 and over) Terman and Oden[23] found that both physical and mental development were above the average and that this superiority continued into adult life. They believe that favorable environment alone cannot explain these observations.

studied who exhibited an accelerated total growth and of another subject with slow growth.

In general, when a wide scattering of the several elements which are measured is maintained throughout several successively plotted points, it can be postulated that the inherited characteristics have been variable. For

Fig 4–12.—The Olson-Hughes growth chart. Various physical and mental measurements plotted, **A,** for a girl above average, and **B** *(page 104),* for a boy slightly below average. On the abscissa *A, B* and *C* represent advancing degrees of breast development; pubic hair development is indicated as *I* present, *II* pigmented, and *III* pigmented and curly; *M* indicates menarche. The straight, unbroken diagonal line represents average course for all measurements. For both children the homogeneity of all the factors measured is clearly apparent. The table on page 104, for chart **A,** shows the functions measured at the chronologic age of 108 months. The figures in the right-hand column are obtained from a manual (see text) giving age equivalents, and these are plotted on the ordinate opposite the chronologic age on the abscissa. (From Olson and Hughes.[13]) *(Continued.)*

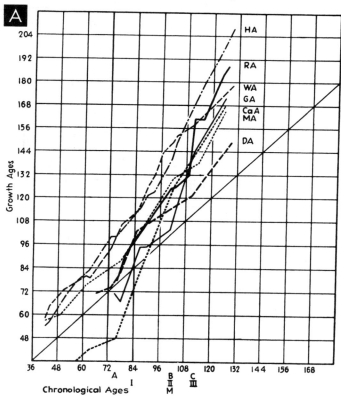

FUNCTION MEASURED	RAW SCORE	ABBREVIATION	AGE EQUIVALENT
Height	60.4 in.	HA	160
Reading	28 items correct	RA	130
Weight	96 lb	WA	156
Strength of grip	19.7 kg	GA	130
Ossification of hand and wrist	X-ray	CaA	135
Mental capacity	Tests passed	MA	134
Dental eruption	16 permanent teeth	DA	119
Organismic age		OA	138
Variability		AD	11.7
Chronological age		CA	108

Fig 4–12 (cont.).— B. (From Olson and Hughes.[13])

example, when the parents of a child are of widely different physical builds, there may be a wide range in the different physical measurements of the child. The lines of height, weight and carpal age may fall far apart on the table. Disease and emotional stress are quickly reflected by a lowering of all or some of the elements measured. The authors cite one example in which death of the mother resulted in a drop in weight and "reading age" over a period of six months until a suitable adjustment was accomplished.

Olson and Hughes have applied statistical tests to many similar systems of curves for individual children and have concluded that in all growth there is an underlying unity. They also believe that achievement in school is a function of the total growth of the child, and they doubt that school achievement is primarily a matter of curriculum and method, provided environment is suitable. When the "organismic age" for a child is calculated for successive life ages and the points are plotted and connected, much stability and predictability of trend are revealed. As a matter of fact, each child tends to grow in a more steady and orderly manner when the average values for "organismic age" are used than when a single attribute is plotted. This type of evidence suggests some "central maturational tempo or release of energy at a steady rate, with a tendency toward a balancing of the various aspects of the whole."[12]

The Fels Composite Sheet

The Fels method makes use of variability units to describe growth in many factors relative to time.[19] The mean and standard deviations of each measure (height, weight, ossification, dietary adequacy, biochemical values, performance tests, etc.) are first calculated by age and sex. Thereafter any measurement obtained can be described or plotted in terms of variability rather than in terms of the absolute value of the units used in originally collecting the data. With this method the average is always arbitrarily placed at 50 and the scale is then laid out in terms of variability units. One standard deviation above the average or mean is always 60; two standard deviations above are 70, etc. A single standard deviation below would then be 40. The score for any measure is called the T-score, average T-score being 50. In the plotting of this material, the abscissa represents age in years (or months) and the ordinates are in units of T-score and sigma (units of standard deviation). The advantage of the standard deviation method is that many measures which do not show an age trend but which do reveal individual differences can be plotted to show relative status in the group. By plotting a series of determinations, profiles at various ages on a vertical axis will be obtained (Fig 4–13).

Examples of many other tables and curves could be presented, many of

Fig 4–13.—The Fels composite sheet, showing growth of a girl from birth to age 10. The abscissa is in units of chronologic age. The left ordinate is expressed in units of 1 or more standard deviations *(sigma)* of expected values for a specific age on the abscissa; the right ordinate, in units of the T-score in which 50 represents the expected mean. At birth the child was 2 sigmas below the mean for height and weight, but by 4 years was above the mean in weight and near the mean in height. From this record one can conclude that at birth she was small but well proportioned and at 4 was of stocky body build. Various other factors are indicated according to the key below the chart. (Form Sontag and Reynolds.[19])

which have considerable merit. However, those described seem to represent fairly the basic principles that have been used in an effort to answer that most important question, "Is this child growing normally?" Again it should be emphasized that an adequate clinical history is vital for an understanding and proper interpretation of somatic and mental growth. Deviations from the expected average are without meaning unless such factors as illness, emotional trauma, nutrition and genetics are all properly evaluated.

Practical Applications

Measurements of physical growth may give a very general indication of a subject's health when other more detailed methods are not available, as in schools where the medical personnel is limited. This monitoring function of periodic measuring as a screening process is common, but its yield in identifying previously unidentified abnormality is not readily available. It must be admitted that growth deviations from normal often accompany or follow, rather than herald, diseases. The development of the methods and the accumulation of data have added immeasurably to our understanding of the growth and development of children. Though given tables or graphs do not indicate or define the optimum, they have revealed such interesting trends as the so-called secular changes during the past decades.

Cross-sectional tables and curves are inferior to longitudinal studies of the individual child. The former do not indicate the variability of rates of maturation, which may be earlier or later than the average, nor do they portray the individual variations in rate of growth. They may even give a false sense of security when a single measurement of a child falls within the "normal" range.

Considerable value may be realized from their use as a graphic means of presentation to parents. Showing a mother that her child is following or deviating from the expected curve is often more convincing than a purely verbal explanation. Also, in evaluating the effect of treatment on growth, the availability of standard curves is most helpful.

Posture

In the past 20 years our ideas concerning correct posture have changed greatly. The physical educators and hygienists were once dogmatic about it, and rigid standards were established. We have since become aware that no one posture can be termed the "correct" one. We now recognize that it is a functional attribute and that posture depends on the age, the occupation, the physique and the health of the individual. Furthermore, the general consensus seems to be that so-called "poor" posture is seldom detrimental unless, of course, it is the result of some pathologic condition. Good posture, as opposed to that which is both functionally and esthetically bad, is certainly desirable. It looks well and therefore promotes self-respect. It may also aid in physical efficiency and general well-being. To define "good posture" is probably an impossibility in view of our present knowledge; at least, no one definition can be said to hold for all individuals.

Posture changes with age.[1, 12] There are many factors involved, but at least two important ones are the variations in the curves of the vertebral column and the shifting center of gravity. At birth the entire presacral vertebral column is extremely flexible, and no particular curve may be described as truly characteristic since the curve depends entirely on the position of the infant. At age 3 or 4 months, when the infant begins to hold up his head, an anterior convexity of the cervical portion appears. Nevertheless, the cervical vertebrae remain freely movable and at no time become fixed in any one position. By the time an upright posture is assumed the forward lumbar convexity develops, but it is not far advanced for several years. An important contribution to this curve is the fact that the anterior portion of the last three lumbar vertebrae become increasingly thicker than the posterior portions. Even the intervertebral disks in this region develop similar inequalities. The tilting of the pelvis and the pull of the psoas muscles in an erect position tend to maintain the lumbar curvature. In the thoracic region growth of the vertebral bodies is the reverse of that of the lumbar area; i.e., the posterior portions of the bodies are thicker than the anterior portions, resulting in a forward concavity. The sacral curve is present from birth but contributes little to posture except in maintaining the position and relationship of the pelvis. The only two relatively fixed curves of the vertebral column involved in the posture of the child are the lumbar and the thoracic, and even these can be said to show great flexibility throughout the entire growing period.

Since the proportions of head, trunk and extremities vary so greatly with growth, it is natural that the center of gravity of the body changes with age.* The location of this point is relative not only to posture but to all functions in which balance is involved. In the newborn in an erect position the center is near the level of the xiphoid, and throughout early childhood it remains above the umbilicus. At 5–6 years it is just below the umbilicus and is below the crest of the ilium by 13 years. With increasing age there is also an increasing ability to maintain balance because of muscle coordination and strength. Although posture may be said to have some basis in nutrition and exercise, it is strongly influenced by the unfolding design of growth of skeletal, muscular and neuromuscular mechanisms.

During the first 2–3 years after an erect posture is assumed, the feet are relatively flat; there is a tendency to inward bowing of the legs from knee to ankle; some lordosis is apparent, which varies a great deal from child to child, and the abdomen is prominent. In the early school period the shoulders are "rounded," and this is little influenced by exercise. A "military" posture of head high, shoulders back and chest equal with the plane of the abdomen comes with adolescence. In general, a satisfactory posture may be said to exist at this time if a straight line passes from in front of the ear through the shoulder and the greater trochanter to the anterior part of the longitudinal arch of the foot. Such a posture distributes the weight equally to the balls of the feet and permits an erect yet comfortable standing position.

---

*Center of gravity may be determined by the formula $y = 0.557 \cdot X + 1.4$ cm, where y equals distance of the center above the soles and X equals height in centimeters.[14]

Fig 4–14 (above).—A, normal feet and legs of 13-month-old child just beginning to walk, the stance giving the appearance of genu valgum and some pronation. Observation of the child in action indicated good sturdy legs and feet. **B,** simple flatfoot with resulting genu valgum. Whole foot rotates outward, the longitudinal arch disappears, heads of the astragali thrust medially and the heel is everted.

Fig 4–15 (left).—Pigeon-toed foot. Ankle and knee of a boy of 13 months are in normal relationship, but forefoot deviated medially and is rotated. This foot seems far worse than it really is, and the boy could walk with support.

Forcing such an attitude on a child, however, is hardly to be advised. Posture, to a degree, reflects strength and health, and these factors are the more basic conditions which should receive our consideration.

To the clinician a peculiarity of posture may be viewed as a sign of simple fatigue or of some more definite organic or mental disturbance. It must be emphasized that both the general and the detailed forms of the body are highly variable. We cannot assume that there is a single correct posture any more than we can assume that there is a single correct height or weight. The old idea of admonishing school children to "stand straight" or "sit straight" in the interest of better posture often confuses cause and effect. A child typically adopts that posture which keeps the parts of his body in proper balance. Frequent action and change of activity in school are excellent preventives of faulty posture.

Growth and Development of Legs and Feet

The legs and feet grow more rapidly than the trunk during childhood. Both legs and feet respond to some degree to external factors which may be operative before or after birth. Bowed tibiae have been attributed to abnormal and restricted positioning in utero. Many varieties of clubfoot are seen at birth, some of which seem rather clearly to be due to abnormal positioning

Fig 4–16.—Physiologic bowing of the legs. **A,** film of legs of healthy 18-month-old boy. By inspection the legs appeared to be bowed. X-rays show thickening of medial tibial cortex, flaring and exaggerated recurving of medial lips of femoral and tibial metaphyses at the knees. The distal femoral epiphyses are wedged. **B,** the same child 3 years later. Clinical and roentgenologic appearance is entirely normal; recovery was spontaneous. (From Holt and Watson.[48])

Fig 4–17.—Brother of boy whose x-rays appear in Figure 4–16. **A,** legs at 10 months and **B,** at 3 years. This change was spontaneous and accompanied by x-ray findings like those shown in Figure 4–16.

or pressures in utero. Imbalance of muscle groups and muscle pull will produce grotesque anomalies of foot or leg, as in arthrogryposis.

The normal foot of the newborn infant is proportionately fatter and wider than that of the adult. Fat pads obliterate the longitudinal arch, giving the appearance of "flatfoot," and this is accentuated by normally pliant muscles. Fetal positioning, dorsiflexion of the foot on the tibia, stretches the Achilles tendon thus making it impossible to elicit that tendon reflex for several months. As the infant learns to walk, the apparent pronation is further exaggerated by abduction of the foot and eversion of the heel (Fig 4–14). A well-formed arch is not visually obvious until most children are 3–4 years of age.[31]

Toeing in or "pigeon-toe" is not uncommon in the early stages of walking, and is seldom a serious problem (Fig 4–15). It is often associated with tibial torsion, itself a benign condition that corrects with normal growth. True adduction of the forefoot, metatarsus adductus, is due to a boney deformity and requires specific treatment of plaster casting.[33]

Physiologic bowing of the legs is a normal variant and is self-correcting (Figs 4–16 and 4–17). It is present at birth but may become evident only as the infant stands and begins to walk. Radiologic examination indicates thickening of the medial tibial cortex as well as the bowing (see Fig 4–16, A). None of the typical findings of rickets are present, the abnormal condition with which it is most often confused.[48]

REFERENCES

1. Appleton, A. B.: Posture, Practitioner 156:48, 1946.
2. Winick, M., and Rosso, P.: Head circumference and cellular growth of the brain in normal and marasmic children, J. Pediatr. 74:774, 1969.
3. Hamill, P. V. V., Drizd, T. A., Johnson, C. L., Reed, R. A., and Roche, A. F.: *NCHS Growth Charts, 1976,* Monthly Vital Statistics Report (Washington, D.C.: U.S. Dept. of Health, Education and Welfare, 1976).
4. *Height and Weight of Children: Socioeconomic Status, United States* (Washington, D.C.: U.S. Dept. of Health, Education and Welfare, Public Health Service, 1972).
5. *Body Weight, Stature, and Sitting Height: White and Negro Youths 12–17 Years, United States* (Washington, D.C.: U.S. Dept. of Health, Education and Welfare, Public Health Service, 1973).
6. Harris, J. A., Jackson, C. M., Paterson, D. G., and Scammon, R. E.: *The Measurement of Man* (Minneapolis: University of Minnesota Press, 1930).
7. *Body Dimensions and Proportions, White and Negro Children 6–11 Years, United States* (Washington, D.C.: U.S. Dept. of Health, Education and Welfare, Public Health Service, 1974).
8. De Souza, S. W., Ross, J., and Milner, R. D. G.: Alterations in head shape of newborn infants after caesarean section or vaginal delivery, Arch. Dis. Child. 51:624, 1975.
9. Lucas, W. P., and Pryor, H. B.: Range and standard deviations of certain physical measurements in healthy children, J. Pediatr. 6:533, 1935.
10. Meredith, H. V.: *The Rhythm of Physical Growth,* State Univ. of Iowa Stud. Child Welfare, Vol. 11, no. 3, 1935; Boynton, B.: State Univ. of Iowa Stud. Child Welfare, Vol. 12, no. 4.
11. Meredith, H. V.: A "physical growth record" for use in elementary and high schools, Am. J. Public Health 39:878, 1949.
12. Olson, W. C.: *Child Development* (Boston: D. C. Heath & Company, 1949).
13. Olson, W. C., and Hughes, B. O.: Growth of the Child as a Whole, in Barker, R. G., et al. (ed.): *Child Behavior and Development* (New York: McGraw-Hill Book Company, Inc., 1943), Chapter 3.
14. Palmer, C. E.: Study of the center of gravity in the human body, Child Dev. 15:99, 1944.
15. Shuttleworth, F. K.: *The Adolescent Period: A Graphic and Pictorial Atlas,* Monogr., Soc. Res. Child Dev., Vol. III, no. 3 (Washington, D.C.: National Research Council, 1938).
16. Simmons, K.: *Growth and Development,* Monogr., Soc. Res. Child Dev., Vol. IX, no. 1 (Washington, D.C.: National Research Council, 1944).
17. Simmons, K., and Greulich, W. W.: Menarcheal age and height, weight and skeletal age of girls age 7 to 17 years, J. Pediatr. 22:518, 1943.
18. Simmons, K., and Todd, T. W.: Growth of well children: Analysis of stature and weight, 3 months to 13 years; growth, J. Pediatr. 2:93, 1938.
19. Sontag, L. W., and Reynolds, E. L.: The Fels composite sheet: I. A practical method for analyzing growth progress; II. Variations in growth patterns in health and disease, J. Pediatr. 26:317, 1945.
20. Owen, G. M.: The assessment and recording of measurements of growth of children: Report of a small conference, Pediatrics 51:461, 1973.
21. Stuart, H. C.: Observation of growth of children in pediatric practice, Am. J. Dis. Child. 57:1417, 1939.

22. Stuart, H. C.: Normal growth and development during adolescence, N. Engl. J. Med. 234:666 and 732, 1946.
23. Terman, L. M., Oden, M. H., et al.: *The Gifted Child Grows Up* (Stanford, Calif.: Stanford University Press, 1947).
24. Eveleth, P., and Tanner, J. M.: *Worldwide Variations in Human Growth* (London: Cambridge University Press, 1976).
25. Snyder, R. G., Spencer, M., Owings, C., and Van Eck, P.: *Source Data of Infant and Child Measurements* (Bethesda, Md.: Children's Hazard Division, Food and Drug Administration, 1973).
26. *Height and Weight of Children, United States* (Washington, D.C.: U.S. Dept. of Health, Education and Welfare, Public Health Service, 1970).
27. Wingerd, J., Schoen, E. J., and Solomon, I. L.: Growth standards in the first two years of life based on measurements of white and black children in a prepaid health care program, Pediatrics 47:818, 1971.
28. Martin, H. P.: Microcephaly and mental retardation, Am. J. Dis. Child. 119:128, 1970.
29. Pryor, H. B., and Thelander, H.: Abnormally small head size and intellect in children, J. Pediatr. 73:593, 1968.
30. Stuart, H. C., and Meredith, H. V.: Use of body measurements in the school health program, Am. J. Public Health 36:1365, 1946.
31. Miller, W. R.: Observations on the examination of children's feet, J. Pediatr. 51:527, 1957.
32. Lacey, K. A., and Parkin, J. M.: The normal short child; community study of children in Newcastle upon Tyne, Arch. Dis. Child. 49:417, 1974.
33. Compere, E. I.: Foot problems in the young child, Rocky Mt. Med. J. 47:747–751, October, 1950.
34. *Selected Body Measurements of Children 6–11 Years, United States* (Washington, D.C.: U.S. Dept. of Health, Education and Welfare, Public Health Service, 1973).
35. Garn, S. M., and Owen, G. M.: Growth standards for American Negro (black) boys and girls, J. Pediatr. 84:160, 1974.
36. Sheldon, W. H.: *The Varieties of Human Physique* (New York: Harper & Brothers, 1940).
37. Meredith, H. V.: Findings from Asia, Australia, Europe and North America on secular change in mean height of children, youths and young adults, Am. J. Phys. Anthropol. 44:315, 1976.
38. Meredith, H. V.: Body size of contemporary groups of eight-year-old children studied in different parts of the world, Monogr. Soc. Res. Child Dev. 1:34, 1969.
39. Nelson, K. B., and Deutschberger, J.: Head size at one year as predictor of 4-year I.Q., Dev. Med. Child Neurol. 12:487, 1970.
40. Weech, A. A.: Signposts on highway of growth, A.M.A. Am. J. Dis. Child. 88:452, 1954.
41. Tanner, J. M., Healy, M. J. R., Lockhart, R. D., MacKenzie, J. D., and Whitehouse, R. H.: Aberdeen growth study I, Arch. Dis. Child. 31:372, 1956.
42. Babson, S. G., and Henderson, N. B.: Fetal undergrowth: Relation of head growth to later intellectual performance, Pediatrics 53:890, 1974.
43. Bayer, L. M., and Bayley, N.: *Growth Diagnosis* (Chicago: University of Chicago Press, 1959).
44. Garn, S. M.: Physical growth and development, Am. J. Phys. Anthropol., N.S. 10:1969, 1952.

45. Falkner, F.: Velocity growth, Pediatrics 51:746, 1973.
46. Tuddenham, R. D., and Snyder, M. M.: *Physical Growth of California Boys and Girls from Birth to Eighteen Years* (Berkeley: University of California Press, 1954).
47. Nellhaus, G.: Head circumference from birth to eighteen years, Pediatrics 41:106, 1968.
48. Holt, J. F., and Watson, E. H.: Physiologic bowing of the legs in young children, J.A.M.A. 154:390, 1954.
49. Garn, S. M., and Rohmann, C. G.: Interaction of nutrition and genetics in timing of growth, Pediatr. Clin. North Am. 13:353, 1966.
50. Heimer, C. B., and Freedman, A. M.: The physical development of prematurely born Negro infants, Am. J. Dis. Child. 109:500, 1965.
51. O'Connell, E. J., Feldt, R. H., and Stickler, G. B.: Head circumference, mental retardation and growth failure, Pediatrics 36:62, 1965.
52. Gallagher, J. R., and Seltzer, C. C.: Maturity ratings and the prediction of height of short 14-year-old boys, Pediatrics 27:984, 1961.
53. Scott, R. B., Hiatt, H. H., Clark, B. G., Kessler, A. D., and Ferguson, A. D.: Growth and development of Negro infants, Pediatrics 29:65, 1962.
54. Tanner, J. M.: Growth and Physique in Different Populations of Mankind, in Baker, P. T., and Weiner, J. S. (ed.): *The Biology of Human Adaptability* (Oxford: Clarendon Press, 1966).
55. Tanner, J. M.: Standards from birth to maturity for height, weight, height velocity, and weight velocity: British children 1965, Arch. Dis. Child. 41:613, 1966.
56. Malina, R. M.: Growth and physical performance of American Negro and white children, Clin. Pediatr. 8:476, 1969.
57. Fisch, R. O., Bilek, M. K., Horrobin, J. M., and Chang, P.: Children with superior intelligence at 7 years of age, Am. J. Dis. Child. 130:481, 1976.
58. Caffey, J.: *Pediatric X-Ray Diagnosis* (6th ed.; Chicago: Year Book Medical Publishers, Inc., 1972).

5 / Low Birth Weight and Premature Infants

FROM THE STANDPOINT of morbidity and mortality, low birth weight represents the most important problem of the neonatal period. A birth weight of less than 2,500 gm is a direct cause, or is associated with other conditions as a cause, of approximately 80–90% of infant deaths in the United States. It is estimated that as many as one third of the survivors have significant mental or motor handicaps.[1, 6] Although many different factors are involved, it is recognized that the smaller the infant, the less are his chances for survival. The problems of low birth weight must be approached from two aspects: prevention, and extension of our knowledge of these infants so improvement in care will be possible. An obvious part of this necessary knowledge pertains to growth and development. In the following paragraphs the physical growth and development of low birth weight infants are summarized, and some of the more important physiologic differences between them and the normal term infants are outlined.

DEFINITION.—As a term of general use *low birth weight infant* has replaced the term *premature infant,* since the former includes all infants with a birth weight of less than 2,500 gm regardless of the duration of gestation. *Premature* should be used to indicate a period of gestation of 37 weeks or less. (The weeks of gestation are counted from the first day of the last menstrual period.)

Because estimations of the duration of pregnancy, based upon history, are often inexact, more objective measures of prematurity are commonly sought. In Chapter 2 some discussion was given to the use of amniocentesis, sonography and amounts of estriol excreted during pregnancy as means of estimating fetal age. The ratio of lecithin to sphingomyelin in amniotic fluid was pointed out to be a particularly valuable guide to fetal lung maturity. A gradually increasing number of lipid-containing cells and an increase in the creatinine content in amniotic fluid correlate well with gestational age. Exposure of the fetus to radiation, as well as the great variability in interpretation, has discouraged roentgen examination of the fetus for size or bone

TABLE 5–1.—REPRESENTATIVE PHYSICAL SIGNS AT DIFFERENT GESTATIONAL TIMES

	28 WEEKS	32 WEEKS	36 WEEKS	40 WEEKS
Skin	Transparent, veins numerous, dark red, edema of hands and feet, no subcutaneous fat	Transparent, veins numerous, pink, no edema, no subcutaneous fat, lanugo abundant	Few vessels seen, pale pink, lanugo thinning, some subcutaneous fat	Few vessels indistinct, pale, pink palms, soles, lips and ears, lanugo patchy, abundant subcutaneous fat
Plantar creases	None	Single anterior crease	1/2–2/3 of anterior covered with creases	All of sole covered with creases
Eyes	Lids just separating, pupillary membrane complete	Lids open, central clearing of pupillary membrane	Pupillary membrane absent	
Ears	Pinna, soft, flat, no recoil to folding	Soft, easily folded, slow recoil	Cartilage to edge but soft, moderate recoil	Pinna firm, outer edge folded along upper portion, prompt recoil to folding
Breasts	Nipple present, no areola, no nodule	Areola smooth and flat, breast nodule < 0.5 cm diameter	Areola stippled, < 0.75 cm diameter, breast nodule 0.5–1.0 cm diameter	Areola raised, > 0.75 cm diameter, breast nodule > 1.0 cm diameter
Genitalia Female (hips abducted)	Labia majora separate, labia minora exposed		Labia majora cover labia minora	
Male	Testes undescended	Testes may descend, scrotum smooth	At least one testis in scrotum	Scrotum wrinkled, testes descended

TABLE 5–2. — REPRESENTATIVE NEUROLOGIC SIGNS OR REFLEXES AT DIFFERENT GESTATIONAL TIMES

	28 WEEKS	32 WEEKS	36 WEEKS	40 WEEKS
Posture and tone	Hypotonic	Thighs begin flexion	Flexion of 4 limbs, tone moderate	Flexion of 4 limbs, tone strong
Moro reflex	Weak or absent	Present, may not repeat promptly	Present and repeat elicited easily	Present and repeat elicited easily
Popliteal angle*	Reaches 150 degrees	Reaches 110 degrees	Reaches 100 degrees	Less than 100 degrees
Scarf sign†	Lack of tone permits full scarf position	Tone limits arm extension	Extension limited so elbow just past midline	Elbow just short of midline
Neck position on lifting from supine	No tone, head drops	Neck muscles contract but head drops	Head lags, comes forward abruptly	Head may follow trunk and briefly holds position
Rooting reflex	Response slow and incomplete	Response prompt	Response prompt and sustained	Response prompt and sustained
Glabella tap reflex (blinks)	Absent	Inconstant	Present	Present
Palmar grasp reflex	Rarely present	Present but weak	Present	Present
Stepping movements	Absent	Inconstant	Usually present	Present
Head rising prone	Absent	Absent	Weak or absent	Present

*Position assumed while in supine position and with maximum flexion of the hips.
†Scarf sign is elicited by throwing arm across chest with full extension and elbow below the chin, similar to the position of a scarf.

maturation. Once delivered, the criteria given in Table 5–1 and Table 5–2 have proved to be of considerable aid in estimating gestational age.[2, 5, 8]

Neurologic development and the changes in the electroencephalogram are among the most reliable indicators of maturational age. This assumes, of course, that no major anomalies or diseases are present. Before 28 weeks of gestation the EEG is polymorphic with long silent periods. The waves that appear are slow and diffuse. After 28 weeks the pattern becomes simpler and the voltage of activity bursts are lower than before. They are regular rhythmic theta waves lasting 1 or 2 seconds.[38] Between 30 and 34 weeks there emerges a new pattern of slow activity superimposed on rapid rhythms, and the bursts last 3–10 seconds. The right and left electrodes for the first time are isopotential. After 32 weeks the pattern becomes more continuous with delta waves added, and the occipital area no longer predominates. Between 37 and 40 weeks of conceptional age the most dramatic change is the appearance of a difference between the waking and sleeping tracings. The response of the EEG to an auditory stimulus also changes with maturation and may prove of value in judging gestational age.[3, 39]

Another method of value in assessing the degree of maturity is the measurement of motor nerve conduction velocity.[41, 42] The conduction velocity of nerve depends on the thickness of the myelin sheath. The degree of myelination of peripheral nerve increases with age, but the changes are most pronounced during the end of gestation and throughout the early years of life. The slower conduction time seen in the less mature newborn will persist for as long as a year and affords an objective measurement of maturity of the infant and his nervous system.

Although charts showing intrauterine growth in length, weight and head circumference for each geographic area and socioeconomic class of population would be highly desirable in the proper evaluation of the low birth weight infant, the records prepared by Lubchenco et al. seem adequate for almost all clinical situations (Fig 5–1).[9, 10, 21, 22]

The neurologic examination may be of little value during the first few hours after birth for determining gestational age, due to the "shock of birth." Since the very small infant may subsequently suffer problems that influence neurologic responses, the interpretation may be difficult. Nevertheless, the evaluation of muscular tone and reflexes may be helpful in arriving at an estimate of the duration of pregnancy. At 28 weeks the angle measured at the popliteal fossa with the leg extended and the pelvis fixed in supine position is 180 degrees, but by 37 weeks this narrows to about 100 degrees. By 34 weeks the heel-to-ear maneuver, which previously was easily accomplished, becomes increasingly difficult. General muscular tone and recoil to extremity extension increases with gestational age and are minimal at 24–26 weeks but pronounced by 37–38 weeks. The Moro reflex is first elicited at 28–29

Fig 5–1.—Curves of intrauterine growth in length, weight and head circumference. The subjects were all live-born, white and mainly from middle-class society in the United States. The estimated week of gestation was obtained by careful history. The weight-length ratio is indicative of adequacy of intrauterine nutrition when high and of insufficiency when of a low value. (Modified from Lubchenco et al.[21])

weeks. The walking reflex is not present before 34 weeks but is usually well established by 37–38 weeks. The grasp reflex is feeble before 28 weeks, present and strong by 34 weeks and sufficiently powerful by 37 weeks to lift the infant partially or totally from the bed surface.[3, 37]

The total incidence of prematurity is extremely difficult to determine. Estimates in the United States are usually about 75% of all low birth weight infants.[4, 5] On the basis of weight alone the incidence of hospital births below 2,500 gm in the United States is approximately 7.6%, in Great Britain 6.5%, in Sweden 5.5%, in France 7%, in Japan 10% and in a geographic area of India over 35%. The problem of evaluating such figures becomes apparent when it is realized that the average birth weight cited in that area of India was 6 lb (2.7 kg).[7] The incidence of premature births versus low birth weight caused by fetal malnutrition in the underdeveloped countries is virtually impossible to assess, but in areas of India, Africa and Latin America, where some analyses have been attempted, it would appear that chronic malnutrition of mothers may be a highly significant cause of decreased fetal size. Socioeconomic and racial factors undoubtedly play a role.

Synonyms which have been used to designate the condition of the low birth weight infant include the following: small-for-date, intrauterine growth retardation, fetal malnutrition, dysmaturity and pseudomaturity.

The causes of low birth weight have been discussed by numerous investigators from many countries.[5, 7, 11-15] The incidence is higher in countries with low socioeconomic levels. Although fetal undernutrition in man could result from conditions which affect maternal nutrition or general health, the human fetus seems to be largely protected from any deleterious effects of maternal malnutrition.[16] The frequency of associated malformations in small neonates also suggests that either genetic or early embryonic influences are more important as a factor in intrauterine growth retardation than deficient nutrition. There is a definite correlation with an increasing frequency of congenital anomalies as the weight for gestational age decreases. There is also a higher incidence of mental and neurologic impairment in association with these anomalies.

Drillien's survey[16, 17] indicated that the height of the mother was highly correlated with the social class of her own childhood and that this correlation carried over to the size of her newborn. Infants whose birth weight for gestational age was below the 10th percentile were predominantly from short mothers (155 cm [61 in.] or less). There is a tendency for recurrence of small newborn infants in some women. Twins and other multiple births are almost always small for their gestational age; frequently one infant is considerably smaller than the other or others. Extremes of age in the mother, under 16 and over 40 years, are a definite contributing factor. Toxemia is a frequently associated condition and in the past was considered the single most important cause.[8] Maternal infection, maternal-fetal blood incompatibility, genetic abnormalities (especially in chromosome structure or numbers) and cigarette smoking have all been substantiated as causes. Metabolic diseases in the mother, e.g., diabetes mellitus, renal failure and possibly others, have been associated with smallness in babies.

The incidence of placental lesions with small infant size is relatively high, as much as 50% in some studies.[12, 14] The most commonly associated abnormalities were anomalous insertion of the umbilical cord, abruptio, infarction and circumvallate placenta with a weight more than two standard deviations below normal for the period of gestation.

The interrelationship of these various factors is difficult to evaluate. The so-called critical period for the fetus (see Chapter 1) has never been clearly established, and many safeguards are provided. Placental lesions, maternal undernutrition and vascular incompetence may all theoretically interfere with fetal nutrition and growth. There are abundant animal studies supporting this concept. However, experience in human models does not always lend strong support to undernutrition as the main etiology. It is also important to recognize that the length of insult, as well as the time of its occurrence, will influence the final outcome. In the United States, based on the clinical evaluation of the newborn infant, the evidence indicates that between 25 and 35% of low birth weight babies are small for gestational age. The incidence must be considerably higher in the areas of the world where adequate nutrition and prenatal care are minimal. Where therapeutic abortion is permitted and widely practiced, the incidence of both prematurity and small-for-gestational-age infants appears to be declining.[5, 18-20]

Physiologic Handicaps

Immaturity renders the premature infant's physiologic functions less well equipped to cope with external hazards encountered at birth, with the result that capacity for adaptation is low. The small but gestationally older infant appears to have fewer handicaps, and his initial survival and development are less precarious.[43]

The following outline is far from complete but hopefully will serve the purpose of identifying the more important problems facing the clinician.

RESPIRATION. — The respiratory pattern of the premature infant is irregular, rapid, often shallow with periods of apnea. The shorter the gestational period, the more irregular is the pattern. Cyanosis is common and easily precipitated by slight changes in environment. Among the recognizable causes of respiratory difficulty are: (1) high threshold of the respiratory center in the brain, requiring stronger afferent stimuli for response; (2) reduced number of capillaries in the lung, impeding gas exchange and possibly other chemical factors responsible for activating enzymes; (3) sparsity of pulmonary elastic tissue and decreased "surfactant," leading to slower and often incomplete expansion of the lungs; (4) feeble muscle strength and tone of thoracic cage and diaphragm, together with (5) a soft cartilaginous cage, resulting in reduced intrathoracic pressure changes with respiratory efforts; (6) the fact that fetal hemoglobin releases oxygen less readily; (7) deficiency of some enzymes, such as carbonic anhydrase, was once considered to interfere with gaseous exchange, but there is almost total lack of evidence to support this.[45, 46]

The respiratory distress syndrome (hyaline membrane disease) is certainly one of the most common causes of death in prematurely born infants. The incidence varies, but in the smaller subjects may exceed 50%. The basic defect is inadequate pulmonary exchange of oxygen and carbon dioxide. Metabolic acidosis eventually develops. During fetal life blood bypasses the lungs. With the first breath the pulmonary circulation increases and vascular resistance decreases normally. In the respiratory distress syndrome pulmonary vascular resistance is higher than normal, probably secondary to arteriolar constriction. Consequently, blood shunts from the pulmonary circulation and the foramen ovale remains fully functional. Hypoxia, cyanosis and respiratory distress follow. Since hypoxia causes an increased secretion of epinephrine and norepinephrine and these agents further constrict the pulmonary arterioles, a vicious cycle results. Atelectasis and alveolar coating with transudate increases the difficulty of gas exchange between the blood and alveoli. Fibrin and other protein products from the transudate are responsible for the formation of the hyaline membrane, which does not form unless the infant lives for at least a few hours.

The lungs have a developmental sequence during the fetal period. If this is shortened or interrupted, the immaturity may be life-threatening to extrauterine existence. On expiration, after the first breath, the lungs retain considerable air in the normal-term infant. This lessens the required effort to fill the lungs with any subsequent breathing. Present in the airway, and especially in the alveoli, is pulmonary surfactant, which, by virtue of its effect on surface tension, stabilizes these fine air spaces and prevents their collapse. As pointed out in Chapter 3, pulmonary surfactant appears late in fetal life and usually does not attain adequate functional levels until about the 34th or 35th week of gestation. Without it, the alveoli tend to collapse following each inspiration. The hyaline membrane is of secondary importance though it may add further impediment to respiratory efforts. It is interesting to note that fetal surfactant maturation can be accelerated by stress, such as premature rupture of the membranes, or administering large doses of glucocorticoids to the mother or fetus.[45, 47, 56] The condition of respiratory distress syndrome is more common in male than in female neonates.[57]

TEMPERATURE CONTROL. — Reasons for faulty control of body temperature of the premature infant are discussed in some detail in Chapter 10. It appears from most recent work that failure to maintain an ideal body temperature in these babies leads to a number of metabolic disturbances that may play a prominent role in morbidity and mortality. Among the changes are a slower rate of recovery from asphyxia, rapid exhaustion of lipid and glycogen stores and an increased risk of hypoglycemia.

IMMUNITY. — Both the premature and small-for-date baby have decreased resistance to infection when compared to the normal newborn.[26, 50] There does not appear to be a greater liability dependent upon longer or shorter gestation. This observation does not correlate well with the concentrations of gamma G and gamma M immunoglobulins. The initial levels of G do correlate with the gestational age; the longer the time, the higher the concentration. Infants of very short gestational age have a relatively poor capacity to synthesize gamma M.[48] Phagocytosis has also been demonstrated to be reduced in the circulating cells of premature infants.[49] Thin and fragile skin increases the liability of the short-gestation baby to superficial infections.

NUTRITIONAL METABOLISM. — Of the main foodstuffs, the premature infant seems to be intolerant only of large amounts of fat, which is adequately split but is largely excreted in that form in the stool.

Hypoglycemia is a common finding in small-for-date infants.[51] At least two factors are important: rapid exhaustion of hepatic and muscle stores of glycogen and glucose, and rapid utilization by the relatively large brain, which is almost totally dependent upon glucose. Inadequate exogenous sources can be partially corrected by early feeding or parenteral glucose administration.[52] Observations by a number of investigators have indicated that early feeding of carbohydrate may not only enhance glucose homeostasis but benefit acidosis and hyperbilirubinemia.[53, 54] Hypoglycemia, as does asphyxia, appears to add an important additional threat to the prognosis of the low birth weight baby. Central nervous system damage is found more often in subsequent years in these children than those who escaped the low blood sugar.[5, 58]

BLOOD-VASCULAR SYSTEM. — Owing to the reduced antenatal storage of iron, anemia is common in nearly all prematures at some time during the early months of life. Marrow studies of normal compared to low birth weight infants reveal no essential differences. The life-span of the red cell which contains fetal (F) hemoglobin is much shorter than the one containing adult (A) hemoglobin. The shorter the period of gestation, the greater the amount of F hemoglobin, which may exceed 90% at birth. This rapid turnover of red cells does not appear to be a factor in the anemia.

Hemorrhagic manifestations may be slightly more frequent in the premature infant as compared to the small-for-date infant due to increased capillary fragility. A rare form of true hemorrhagic disease that occurs exclusively in prematures is characterized by prolonged bleeding time and diminished factor V. It is not prevented by use of vitamin K.

The normal hypercoagulable state found in the neonate is exaggerated in the preterm infant. Babies who die within the first few weeks of birth have a high incidence of hemorrhagic lesions, such as intraventricular bleeding associated with subependymal infarction. Renal thrombosis and thrombotic complications of indwelling venous or arterial catheters are not uncommon. A low level of the naturally occurring anticoagulant, antithrombin III, is closely related to gestational age, and may contribute to these complications.

RENAL FUNCTION.—The kidneys in the premature are less efficient excretory organs than in the mature newborn or small-for-date baby. Available evidence suggests this deficiency is due to a decreased glomerular filtration rate. Under stress this may lead to water and electrolyte imbalances and edema or dehydration.

Even though the majority of premature infants are unable to concentrate the urine beyond 700 mOsm/kg this limit is seldom reached, let alone exceeded. Since half of the renal solute load resulting from breast or cow's milk is usually diverted into forming new tissue, as long as growth occurs there is little danger of surpassing renal ability.[59]

Prognosis: Physical and Neurologic

The prognosis for the smallest of the surviving low-birth-weight infants relative to physical and mental development is less favorable than for those of normal weight. There may be a birth weight below which normal development is not possible. In a number of animal species perinatal undernutrition will retard growth in both cell numbers and cell size.[20] If the insult is either prenatal or postnatal, the reduction is nearly the same, but if both periods are combined, the resulting retardation is more severe than the sum of the two independently. Some organs are more vulnerable than others. Thymus, spleen and liver are most influenced, while the heart and brain are less so. Decrease in placental size in these animals is clearly evident. Experimental vascular deficiency to the pregnant uterus results in similar findings, except that the brain is completely spared. Though exact comparisons to the human fetus and neonate cannot be drawn, there is evidence that the differences may not be great. Study of human placentas has revealed similar diminution in size (cell number and cell size) with severe malnutrition. Infants who have died as a result of undernourishment during the first year have a decrease of 15–20% in total brain cell number, as well as a reduction in body size. In prematurely born infants (by weight), who then suffered malnutrition and death, the reduction in brain cell number was 60%. As in the experimental animal, doubling the insult may more than double the effect.

It is difficult to select truly representative statistics for survival of low birth weight infants. All such figures indicate that the percentage of deaths is inversely proportional to the weight at birth. In the United States there has been a steady upward trend of survival over the past 20 years. As shown in

TABLE 5-3.—SURVIVAL OF LOW
BIRTH WEIGHT INFANTS

| BIRTH WEIGHT GROUP, GM | SURVIVAL, % | |
	1945	1975
2,001–2,500	94	99
1,501–2,000	84	94
1,000–1,500	53	82
Under 1,000	10	45

Table 5–3, the improvement has been most pronounced among the smaller infants. With the increase in number of intensive care units for newborn infants and the improvement in available therapeutic procedures, there are indications that the number of handicapped children associated with low birth weight is decreasing.[26]

Early in this century, Ylppö[24] compared his data from observations of "premature" babies with the available data on intrauterine growth and concluded that the premature infant tends to follow the laws of growth corresponding to conceptional age. More recent studies have indicated that there are two fairly distinct patterns of growth found in the low birth weight infant. If the baby is premature, but appropriate weight for gestational age, after a period of adjustment following birth, he or she will exhibit some "catch up" or accelerated growth followed by a rate that parallels that of full-term infants. The lower the birth weight and the shorter the gestational age, the lower the percentile curve followed in subsequent growth. The infants who are small for gestational age do not have the potential for "catch up" growth exhibited by the prematurely born of normal weight for duration of gestation. In height, weight and head circumference, the measurements of children who were born small for gestational age remain further behind those who were born prematurely or who were within the normal range at birth.[5, 16, 17, 61]

Infants born with a weight of less than 1,500 gm, or a gestational age estimated to be under 32 weeks, have not only a greater liability for survival but also a greater liability to attain a normal physical growth pattern. Recent improvements in care of such infants would appear to be offering considerable improvement in the outcome of these infants. Figures concerning such children born 20 years ago would place mean height and head circumference for the group at age 17 years at about the 10th percentile of the normal distribution curve.[5]

Evidence continues to accumulate that two factors are of utmost importance in improving both the physical as well as the neurologic prognosis in these infants. One is to promptly supply adequate caloric intake and car-

bohydrates to minimize the readjustments required in extrauterine existence and hypoglycemia. To these nutritional needs must be added a favorable environment in the home. A good socioeconomic level in the family,
both before and after birth, greatly enhances the outcome.[13, 62, 63] With satisfactory early care and a favorable environment, excluding associated pathology, both the premature and small-for-date infant are usually well established in their growth patterns by 18–24 months of age (Fig 5–2).

As will be discussed later when intellectual development is considered,
the eventual outcome cannot be divorced from etiologic factors. If fetal
undernutrition was severe during pregnancy, the prognosis for normal
growth and development must remain guarded.[18]

Central nervous system damage in the perinatal period is of primary importance in causing neonatal mortality, mental retardation, cerebral palsy
and epilepsy. The incidence of each of these is greater in low birth weight
babies as compared to the general population. In autopsy material, approximately 75% of low birth weight infants will have evidence of central nervous
system lesions. In order of frequency, the most common are: subdural
hemorrhage, spinal cord and brain stem damage and deep cerebral and
cortical infarctions.[44] The long duration of many of these lesions would indicate they existed prior to birth. Intrauterine hypoxia and "placental insufficiency" have been described as causing such lesions, as well as severe
hypoglycemia following delivery.

A number of studies have indicated that a low birth weight is a liability to
intellectual development, the smaller the weight and briefer the gestation
the greater the chance of handicap. Knobloch et al.[34] found that only half of
the infants who weighed less than 1,500 gm, could be considered normal at
one year. A quarter of the infants had demonstrable moderate-to-severe
neurologic abnormality. This was in contrast to the finding of only 7% of
similar abnormalities in infants with birth weights between 1,500 and 2,500
gm. Children weighing more than 2,500 gm at birth had an incidence of less
than 2% of abnormalities. Another study,[36] carried out at about the same
time in the 1950s, found that at age 4 years the average IQ of 116 selected
children whose birth weight was less than 1,000 gm was 94, compared to
normal siblings used as controls, who had an average IQ of 107. Of an
additional 43 low birth weight children who might have been included,
none were available for testing, but it was known that 19 of these were severely retarded. Lubchenco[5] and others[31] indicate that a gestational age of
under 28 weeks and birth weight less than 1,200 gm each carry a greater than
70% risk of moderate-to-severe handicap. A gestational age between 28 and
31 weeks or a birth weight between 1,200 and 1,500 gm has a risk of about
50%. If there is an associated perinatal history of asphyxia, hypoglycemia or

Fig 5-2.— Growth curves for premature infants divided in four groups depending on birth weight. It will be noted that as the end of the first year of life is reached there is a definite tendency for convergence of all the groups in body length, **A**, and head circumference, **B**. (Modified by smoothing the curves from Woolley and Valdecanas.[28])

any physical anomaly present, the risk increases by a very considerable extent.[58, 60]

There does not appear to be a clear-cut difference in the prognosis of mental performance of the premature, as compared to the small-for-date infant of the same birth weight.[44, 55] Both types of infants appear to experience an increased incidence of learning and reading difficulties in the usual school situation.[31] Anticipation of such difficulties can often help to avoid associated emotional problems.

An important question relates to the time (age) at which a reliable prediction can be made of future development based upon available information. Prenatal history, duration of gestation, birth weight and presence or absence of any congenital anomalies are important pieces of information usually helpful to the clinician. Unfortunately, the neurologic examination during the initial neonatal period is often equivocal. Suggestive signs at one or three months often disappear at 12 months. Approximately 20% of low birth weight children may appear to have normal development until they reach 4–6 years of age, at which time mild indications of diplegia or ataxia, with or without hypotonia, become evident. The neurologic evaluation of the newborn is often helpful in the evaluation of gestational age but is extremely equivocal in predicting future mental development.[3, 27, 40, 49]

A number of investigators have reported an increased incidence of behavior disorders in children of low birth weight.[7, 16, 32, 64] The possibility that such traits may be related to the mother's long separation from the infant and the apprehensive state that birth engendered in the parents cannot be ruled out. Drillien[16] found that when children reached school age, behavior problems increased at a much higher rate in low birth weight children, especially in males. Her comments about the differences in teachers' attitudes toward the sexes is most interesting, and is an indication of the care one must exercise in drawing conclusions based upon random samples. It has already been pointed out that a favorable socioeconomic environment is a great benefit to the low birth weight child in terms of his or her future.[60] There can perhaps be no more poignant reminder of this than to point out that the incidence of the "battered child syndrome" is considerably greater among low birth weight children than is found in the general population.[64]

Practical Applications

We now appreciate that many infants may represent a deviation of intrauterine growth. They appear to fall into three major categories in the low birth weight group. Infants born to mothers with toxemia, renal disease, advanced hypertension, severe diabetes mellitus and "insufficient placentas," constitute one category with a generally favorable outcome, though physically on the small side of the scale, if of very low birth weight. The second category is the premature, an infant of appropriate size for gestational age who is born too soon. Such an infant suffers some of the disadvantages of experiencing an extrauterine environment before being physiologically ready for it. Although there are distinct differences in their future growth and development, they do not follow greatly dissimilar patterns. Each is subject to very specific risks depending upon their degree of physiologic maturity, nutritional competence, and absence of other complications.

A third category, fortunately rare, includes infants born with one of a variety of chromosomal abnormalities, the association of severe but non-fatal teratogens administered to or used by the mother, and intrauterine infections, most notably rubella. Their prognosis depends upon etiology, but is often poor.

Of very great concern is the relatively high incidence of permanent neurologic complications in those who survive. A question that is difficult to face is whether the improved methods of care to reduce mortality are worth the price to increase the number of children who may be incompetent in our social milieu. This question particularly pertains to the very low birth weight and/or very premature infant. Both cell size and number may be so compromised in these individuals that future growth and development cannot rectify the consequences nor permit recovery to a normal status.

REFERENCES

1. Quilligan, E. J., Paul, R. H., and Sacks, D. A.: Results of Fetal and Neonatal Intensive Care, in Gluck, L. (ed.): *Modern Perinatal Medicine* (Chicago: Year Book Medical Publishers, Inc., 1974).
2. Usher, R., McLean, F., and Scott, K. E.: Judgment of fetal age. II. Clinical significance of gestational age and an objective method for its assessment, Pediatr. Clin. North Am. 13:835, 1966.
3. Koenigsberger, M. R.: Judgment of fetal age. I. Neurologic evaluation, Pediatr. Clin. North Am. 13:823, 1966.
4. Silverman, W. A., and Sinclair, J. C.: Infants of low birth weight, N. Engl. J. Med. 274:448, 1966.
5. Lubchenco, L. O.: *The High Risk Infant* (Philadelphia: W. B. Saunders Company, 1976).
6. *Vital Statistics Report: Summary Report, 1971* (Washington, D.C.: U.S. Dept. of Health, Education and Welfare, Public Health Service, 1974).
7. Corner, B.: *Prematurity, The Diagnosis, Care and Disorders of the Premature Infant* (Springfield, Ill.: Charles C Thomas, Publisher, 1960).
8. Evans, H. E., and Glass, L.: *Perinatal Medicine* (Hagerstown, Md.: Harper & Row Publishers, Inc., 1976).
9. Tanner, J. M.: Standards for birth weight or intrauterine growth, Pediatrics 46:1, 1970.
10. Freeman, M. G., Graves, W. L., and Thompson, R. L.: Indigent Negro and Caucasian birth weight—gestational age tables, Pediatrics 46:9, 1970.

11. Fischer-Rasmussen, W.: Causes of low birth weight in infants, Dan. Med. Bull. 13:1, 1966.
12. Naeye, R. L.: Malnutrition, probable cause of fetal growth retardation, Arch. Pathol. Lab. Med. 79:284, 1965.
13. Drillien, C. M.: The small-for-date infant: Etiology and prognosis, Pediatr. Clin. North Am. 17:9, 1970.
14. Shanklin, D. R.: The influence of placental lesions on the newborn infant, Pediatr. Clin. North Am. 17:25, 1970.
15. Battoglia, F. C., Frazier, T. M., and Hellegers, A. E.: Birth weight, gestational age, and pregnancy outcome, with special reference to high birth weight–low gestational age infant, Pediatrics 37:417, 1966.
16. Drillien, C. M.: *The Growth and Development of the Prematurely Born Infant* (Edinburgh: E. & S. Livingstone, Ltd., 1964).
17. Drillien, C. M.: Later development and follow-up of low birth weight babies, Pediatr. Ann. 1:44, 1972.
18. Scott, K. E., and Usher, R.: Fetal malnutrition: Its incidence, causes and effects, Am. Obstet. Gynecol. 94:951, 1966.
19. Cassady, G.: Bromide space studies in infants of low birth weight, Pediatr. Res. 4:14, 1970.
20. Winick, M.: Cellular growth in intrauterine malnutrition, Pediatr. Clin. North Am. 17:69, 1970.
21. Lubchenco, L. O., Hansman, C., Dressler, M., and Boyd, E.: Intrauterine growth as estimated from liveborn birth weight data at 24 to 42 weeks' gestation, Pediatrics 32:793, 1963.
22. Lubchenco, L. O., Hansman, C., and Boyd, E.: Intrauterine growth in length and head circumference as estimated from live births at gestational ages from 26 to 42 weeks, Pediatrics 37:403, 1966.
23. Lubchenco, L. O.: Assessment of gestational age and development at birth, Pediatr. Clin. North Am. 17:125, 1970.
24. Ylppö, A.: Das Wachstum der Frühgeborenen von der Geburt bis zum Schulalter, Ztschr. Kinderh. 24:111, 1919. (Much of this material will also be found in the English translations by Peterman et al. of Pfaundler and Schlossmann: *Diseases of Children*, Vol. 1 [Philadelphia: J. B. Lippincott Company, 1935], pp. 473–504.)
25. Gordon, H. H., Levine, S. Z., and McNamara, H.: Feeding of premature infants: A comparison of human and cow's milk, Am. J. Dis. Child. 73:442, 1947.
26. Yerushalmy, J.: The classification of newborn infants by birth weight and gestational age, Pediatrics 71:164, 1967.
27. Speirs, A. L.: An anthropometric study of prematurely born children at the age of 5 years, Arch. Dis. Child. 31:395, 1956.
28. Woolley, P. V., and Valdecanas, L. Q.: Growth of premature infants, Am. J. Dis. Child. 99:642, 1960.
29. Harper, P. A.: Discussion, in *Physiology of Prematurity, Transactions of the Fifth Conference* (New York: Josiah Macy, Jr., Foundation, 1961), pp. 218–221.
30. Dunham, E. C.: *Premature Infants, A Manual for Physicians*, Children's Bureau Pub., no. 325 (Washington, D.C.: U.S. Government Printing Office, 1948).
31. Rubin, R. A., Rosenblatt, C., and Below, B.: Psychological and educational sequelae of prematurity, Pediatrics 52:352, 1973.
32. Benton, A. L.: Mental development of prematurely born children: A critical review of the literature, Am. J. Orthopsychiatry 10:719, 1940.

33. Hess, J. H., Mohr, G. J., and Bartelme, P. F.: *The Physical and Mental Growth of Prematurely Born Children* (Chicago: University of Chicago Press, 1934).
34. Knobloch, H., Rider, R., Harper, P., and Pasamanick, B.: Neuropsychiatric sequelae of prematurity, J.A.M.A. 161:581, 1956.
35. Knobloch, H., and Pasamanick, B.: Environmental factors affecting human development, before and after birth, Pediatrics 26:210–218, 1960.
36. Dann, M., Levine, S. Z., and New, E. V.: The development of prematurely born children with birth weights or minimal postnatal weights 1,000 grams or less, Pediatrics 22:1037, 1958.
37. Amiel-Tison, C.: Neurologic problems in perinatology, Clin. Perinatol. 1:33, 1974.
38. Dreyfus-Brisac, C.: The Bioelectric Development of the Central Nervous System during Early Life, in Falkner, F. (ed.): *Human Development* (Philadelphia: W. B. Saunders Company, 1966), p. 286.
39. Graziani, L. J., Weitzman, E. D., and Velasco, M. S. A.: Neurologic maturation and auditory evoked responses in low birth weight infants, Pediatrics 41:483, 1968.
40. Thomas, A., Chesni, Y., and St. Anne Dargassies, A.: *Examen neurologique du nourrison* (Paris: La Vie Médicale, 1955).
41. Ruppert, E. S., and Johnson, E. W.: Motor nerve conduction velocities in low-birth-weight infants, Pediatrics 42:255, 1968.
42. Blom, S., and Finnstrom, O.: Motor conduction velocities in newborn infants of various gestational ages, Acta Paediatr. Scand. 57:377, 1968.
43. Van den Berg, B. J., and Yerushalmy, J.: The relationship of the rate of intrauterine growth of infants of low birth weight to mortality, morbidity and congenital anomalies, J. Pediatr. 69:531, 1966.
44. Towbin, A.: Central nervous system damage in the human fetus and newborn infant, Am. J. Dis. Child. 119:529, 1970.
45. Avery, M. E.: *The Lung and Its Disorders in the Newborn Infant* (3d ed.; Philadelphia: W. B. Saunders Company, 1974).
46. Dawes, G. S.: *Foetal and Neonatal Physiology* (Chicago: Year Book Medical Publishers, Inc., 1968).
47. Gluck, L.: The Evaluation of Functional Maturity in the Human Fetus, in Gluck, L. (ed.): *Modern Perinatal Medicine* (Chicago: Year Book Medical Publishers, Inc., 1974).
48. Berg, T.: Immunoglobulin levels in infants with low birth weights, Acta Paediatr. Scand. 57:369, 1968.
49. Brazelton, T. B.: *Neonatal Behavior Assessment Scale* (Philadelphia: J. B. Lippincott Company, 1973).
50. Overall, J. C.: Neonatal bacterial meningitis, Pediatrics 76:499, 1970.
51. Shelley, H., and Neligan, G. A.: Neonatal hypoglycemia, Br. Med. Bull. 22:34, 1966.
52. Avery, M. E., and Hodson, W. A.: The first drink reconsidered, J. Pediatr. 68:1008, 1966.
53. Beard, A. G., Panos, T. C., Marasigan, B. V., Kennedy, H. F., and Lamb, J.: Perinatal stress and the premature neonate, J. Pediatr. 68:329, 1966.
54. Rabor, I. F., Oh, W., Wu, P. Y., Metcoff, J., Vaughn, M. A., and Gabler, M.: The effects of early and late feeding of intra-uterine fetally malnourished infants, Pediatrics 42:261, 1968.
55. Wiener, G.: The relationship of birth weight and length of gestation to intellec-

tual development at ages 8 to 10 years, J. Pediatr. 76:694, 1970.

56. Fencl, M. de M., and Tulchinsky, D.: Total cortisol in amniotic fluid and fetal lung maturation, N. Engl. J. Med. 292:133, 1975.

57. Lee, K., Eidelman, A. I., Tseng, P., Kandall, S. R., and Gartner, L. M.: Respiratory distress syndrome of the newborn and complications of pregnancy, Pediatrics 58:675, 1976.

58. Pildes, R. S., Cornblath, M., Warren, I., Page-El, E., Meuza, S., Merritt, D. M., and Peeva, A.: A prospective controlled study of neonatal hypoglycemia, Pediatrics 54:5, 1974.

59. Ziegler, E. E., and Ryer, J. E.: Renal solute load and diet in growing premature infants, J. Pediatr. 89:609, 1976.

60. Francis-Williams, J., and Davies, P. A.: Later intelligence in low-birth-weight infants, Dev. Med. Child. Neurol. 16:709, 1974.

61. Cruise, M. O.: A longitudinal study of the growth of low-birth-weight infants: I. Velocity and distance growth, birth to 3 years, Pediatrics 51:620, 1973.

62. Miller, H. C., Hassanein, K., Chin, T. O. Y., and Hensleigh, P.: Socioeconomic factors in relation to fetal growth in white infants, J. Pediatr. 89:638, 1976.

63. Schaffer, A. J., and Avery, M. E.: *Diseases of the Newborn* (Philadelphia: W. B. Saunders Company, 1971).

64. Klein, M., and Stern, L.: Low birth weight and the battered child syndrome, Am. J. Dis. Child. 122:15, 1971.

6 / Behavior and Personality

No FIELD RELATED to growth and development of children is in a greater state of flux than that of behavior, including personality and intelligence. There are several reasons for this. In contrast to the physical aspects of child development, our methods of measurement are inexact, controversial and greatly influenced by personal prejudices. There are nearly as many theories on cognitive development as there are authors who choose to write about it. The same may be said about the subject of personality. For most of the present century arguments have been very heated as to whether genetic or environmental influences, nature versus nurture, are most important in shaping the minds of our children.

Behavioral development obviously is dependent upon the growth and functional maturation of the central nervous system. In the evaluation of the infant or child there is considerable overlapping of the neurologic with the behavioral aspects. The behavioral or developmental assessment is used to measure a person's achievements or accomplishments in functional areas. This involves a steady, largely predictable, increase of abilities with increasing age as a result of interaction between the nervous system and environmental experiences. The neurologic assessment measures the integrity of neural mechanisms appropriate to the age of the subject. Although these two different assessments will usually parallel or complement each other, exceptions can exist. A child with cerebral palsy might have some neurologic abnormalities but the developmental evaluation could be entirely normal.

Some aspects of the development of the central nervous system and of the special senses are discussed in Chapter 7.

Neonatal Development

The use of representative reflexes and neurologic signs in determining gestational age is outlined in Chapter 5. It is important to reiterate that in the evaluation of the neonate it is assumed that the infant has not suffered unusual trauma from the delivery nor experienced the effects of drugs that could influence his responses to stimuli. The environment for any testing situation, infant or child, must be such as not to distract nor interfere with accurate observation. The infant should be awake. Reflex response is greatly modified by the state of sleep or wakefulness of the baby and failure to recognize this has resulted in inconsistent and unpredictable behavior standards.

The fetus exhibits reflex movement of a very crude order as early as 8 or 9 weeks. These consist of flexion of the trunk, retraction of the head, and retraction or backward movement of the arms. By 14–16 weeks the fetus is quite active, showing elementary movements of short excursion involving extremities, trunk, and neck. The motor and most of the reflex behavior in late fetal life is mainly under control of the medulla and spinal cord. Many of the so-called primitive reflexes, especially those involving the extremities, depend upon the tonic and myotactic reflex, i.e., recoil from stretch. These appear by or after 32 gestational weeks. (See Chapter 5, Table 5–2.)

At birth tonicity and activity are equal bilaterally, and the resting position assumed is one in which there is a tendency for all extremities to be flexed in an attitude of the fetal position. Most of the time the hands are tightly fisted. Spontaneous rotation of the head in supine and prone positions occurs and assures the ability of the newborn infant to free his nose of obstruction and maintain his airway. There is usually good tone throughout the body, and this is partly exemplified by the resistance to extension of all the extremities. The presence or lack of this tone is a useful method in evaluating gestational age. An object placed in the hand of the mature newborn infant stimulates a strong grasp, sometimes of such magnitude that the baby can be lifted free of the surface of the table.[2, 23] This grasp reflex is present by 32 weeks of gestation, but is less sustained and weaker then.

The tonic neck reflex of Magnus and de Kleijn is inconstant in the newborn but assumes a predictable reaction in the normal month-old infant. When the head is turned forcibly to one side while the infant is in the supine position, the arm, and less consistently the leg, of the side to which the head is turned will extend, and the opposite arm and leg will be flexed. This is often described as the "fencing position" and will persist until 4–6 months.[7]

Both premature and term infants respond to a sudden change in position, jarring or a loud noise by a startle response consisting of increased muscle tone and some extension of the extremities. Of much greater significance is the Moro reflex, which is elicited by abrupt removal of support of the infant's head when held in a supine position. Infants of less than 35 weeks of gestation extend and abduct the upper extremities only. After 35 weeks the extension is followed in one continuous movement by adduction and flexion. This has been described as an embracing action. Normal infants lose this reflex by 5 months.[24]

When the newborn is supported vertically and the plantar surfaces of the feet are placed on a flat surface, the legs become extended and partially support the infant. If the infant is then lightly propelled, he makes walking movements with good coordination and relatively steady positioning of the feet in a "stepping movement." This reaction persists for about 6 weeks.

One of the earliest reflex patterns to crystallize is that of sucking. By 14–16 weeks the fetus will protrude his lips in unmistakable preparation for sucking. Tongue and pharynx can adequately adapt to swallowing by this time. The full-term newborn and all but the smallest premature infant suck vigorously upon a fingertip introduced into the mouth. When the cheek is lightly touched, the infant turns his head toward the stimulus and purses his lips. This reaction has been termed the rooting reflex.

Shortly before term reflex blinking to strong light is present, and a similar response is elicited by a loud noise. Light reflex action of the pupil is present as early as 32 weeks of gestation. Sneezing in response to nasal irritation as well as bright light is found in the newborn. Both coughing and the gag reflex are elicited by appropriate stimuli by 32 weeks of gestational age.

Repeated pricking of the skin between the costal margin and the iliac crest causes a concave curving in of the trunk on the stimulated side. This persists from birth through the second month and then reappears much later.[2]

The Babinski reflex is variable, and the response is subject to different interpretations. If plantar flexion of the great toe in response to a stroking of the lateral plantar surface from heel to toe is termed "positive," then more than 90% of infants in the late fetal and newborn period have a positive Babinski. Wakefulness, supine position and neutral attitude of the extremities are important prerequisites in evaluating the response. Fanning of the toes is not often present. This type of response often lasts throughout the first year.[10]

The deep tendon reflexes are usually easily elicited at birth. These may be more brisk than in the adult throughout early childhood. If the baby is born with a positional marked dorsiflexion of the feet, the resulting stretching of the Achilles tendon may obviate the ankle jerk. Some ankle clonus, less than 10 contractions, may be found in normal infants for a year or more. Sustained clonus is abnormal.

Rhythmic or clonic movements, elicited by stimuli or spontaneous, occur in many infants. They are often associated with crying and are stronger and more sustained in term than in preterm infants. The parts involved include all of the extremities and the chin. Though the reaction is usually symmetrical, not all parts are always participating. With increasing age there is decreasing frequency and disappearance by 6–7 months.

Most of the superficial, cutaneous reflexes are present at birth or before. These include the abdominal, sphincter, cremasteric, as well as the rooting and sucking responses already described.

In the behavioral examination, the baby's state of consciousness and reaction to specific stimuli are evaluated. In the Brazelton[13] examination there are graded series of procedures, e.g., sounds, pulling to sitting position, restraint, etc., and the response is recorded on a point system. The reaction to a small bell ring may be used as an example of the scoring system.

1. No reaction
2. Either respiratory change or blink
3. Quieting plus item 2
4. Stills, brightens
5. Shifts eyes, turns toward sound plus item 4
6. Alert, eyes and head turn
7. Alert, head turns, eyes search
8. Prolongation of item 7
9. Turning and alerting on both sides with every presentation of stimulus

It is sometimes difficult to break down the response to such a fine distinction as 9 points in some of the suggested procedures. Brazelton points out that repeated tests over several days on a baby enhance the value of the examination and that results are reproducible among trained examiners.[13]

Typical procedures in the assessment scale include the following: response to bright light, response to pin prick, response to inanimate visual object, response to human voice, pull-to-sit position and covering face with cloth.

In addition to the specified items listed in the assessment scale, the examiner notes other aspects of behavior and records these in a similar manner. Among these are: consolability, irritability (to aversive stimuli), tremulousness, amount of startle response and hand-to-mouth facility.

In all, there are a total of 27 major items to be scored. The author claims no attempt was made to create a summary score that would indicate optimal development. An average score would be 5 for each item.

The ultimate value of the Brazelton scale or other methods in predicting the future intellectual competence of neonates or older infants has yet to be determined. Some discussion of this point will be considered later in this chapter. There does seem to be general agreement that reflex behavior, sensorimotor development in early life, the changing patterns of sleep (to be discussed) and the EEG (electroencephalogram) are strongly dependent upon gestational age.

Behavior and Environment

The human organism is remarkably plastic in its adaptability and is extremely dependent on social interaction for its specifically human qualities. From birth onward it needs a close interrelationship with protective and responsive adults in order to gain the type of maturity of personality for which we all strive. All personality is both genetically and environmentally influenced. The former influence is responsible for the limitations of the central nervous system typical of the individual, even though these restrictions are quite broad and allow great latitude in the response to environment.

In a sense environment begins before birth. The feelings and attitudes of the pregnant woman toward her unborn child are of utmost importance. Such factors as desire for pregnancy, the economic status of the home and attitudes toward birth, such as fear or misunderstanding of the birth process, will influence her acceptance or rejection of her condition. Physical and psychologic factors, such as severe nausea or discomfort and the reaction of her husband to her condition, play important roles and in large or small part carry over into the period after parturition. A strong desire for an infant of a particular sex is still another example of the psychologic influences beginning before the infant enters the world.

Often a mother's acceptance of her child will not come immediately. Doubts and actual fear of her ability to assume the new role may present themselves to the mother after delivery. There is strong evidence that early and repeated physical contact with her baby is an important element in allaying such fears and doubts.[16] How closely the infant matches or differs from her fantasy of him or her becomes a factor in how the mother handles and stimulates the infant. Many of her original attitudes will change, but the original feelings will continue to influence her throughout her entire association. The very fact that the child changes through growth and development causes a constant reevaluation among all members of the family.

Affectional ties can be disturbed, perhaps permanently, by illness in the newborn. Even minor problems, such as feeding difficulties, may cause residual anxieties that will influence her attitudes for years unless a satisfactory resolution is achieved before baby and mother leave the hospital. Obviously a major illness, e.g., marked prematurity or severe congenital anomalies, present a far greater problem often resulting in prolonged separation and worry. The high percentage of unfavorable behavior outcomes in high-risk infants often cannot be completely explained by the physical injury, brain damage, sensory loss, etc., that may be present. Often, as in prematurity, there is no physical evidence of abnormality. There is growing belief that the interruption of or impairment of the reciprocal interactions that establish and refine the infant's communication with his mother early in life are at fault.[16, 19]

The development of attachment between infant and mother has been described in four phases.[9] During the first 2–3 months the infant has the range of sensorimotor mechanisms to orient himself to his social environment but is essentially *undiscriminating* in social responsiveness. Any person that will satisfy hunger, comfort and furnish tactual-kinesthetic stimulation will do. The second phase is *discriminating* as the baby begins to differentiate his mother from others and manifests this by rather specific types of smiling, vocalization and crying in response to her presence or voice or lack of it. The third phase begins after 6 months with more explicit proximity-seeking and contact-maintaining behavior. All of the earlier attachment activities are still present but added to them is ambulation which facilitates proximity and contact. The infant's signals, vocal as well as body movements, are more effective and often used to evoke a response from the mother or other caretaker. Ainsworth calls this the phase of *active initiative in seeking proximity and contact.* As the child grows older and his thinking encompasses more complex ideas he becomes able to anticipate his mother's goals and actions. This may well correlate with Piaget's developmental stage when internalization of thought becomes apparent at around 2–3 years of age.[52] Now the child begins to attempt to alter the mother's goals and he plans to improve his own position in regard to contact, proximity and interaction. This phase has been described as that of *goal-corrected partnership.* It has been postulated that there may be a critical period for the interaction between baby and mother to form attachment, and that if it does not occur by 18–24 months it will never occur.[9] Very important for this development is the sensitivity and responsiveness by the mother to the infant's signals and communication. Routine care is not sufficient though it is important as a means to provide for the interaction.

Two important points need to be made at this time. It is not necessary or even optimal for mother and child to form an exclusive partnership. A spreading of secondary attachments over other figures is probably healthy and beneficial for complete development. Brief separations from the mother are eventually well tolerated if the maternal bond is a secure one. Where the relationship is tentative, separation becomes very stressful to the child. The second point is that fostering maternal-infant attachment does not "spoil" the child. A sure way to cause overdependent reactions and increase the amount of crying is to ignore the crying and/or react in a perfunctory manner.

One result of secure bonding is the earlier and more aggressive exploratory behavior of the infant and young child. In an older individual we would probably refer to this as self-confidence. It is certainly suggestive, though perhaps more difficult to prove, that a good mother-child attachment is a necessary preliminary to a satisfactory adjustment to society. Nonacceptance by the parent, especially the mother, during the first 2–3 years is said to be associated with increased frequency of both withdrawn-neurotic behavior and antisocial aggressiveness later in life.[19]

Studies comparing two groups of primiparous women revealed that those experiencing close and extended physical contact with their newborn infants had a far superior record of absence of child abuse and neglect than those mothers experiencing a more traditional and limited exposure. These observations were continued for at least 2 years following birth. The assignment of the mothers to each group was purely random and their educational and socioeconomic backgrounds were similar.[91] An increased degree of intimacy with the mother at this time may also result in improved competence in communications by the child later in life.[86]

Kagen,[28] on the other hand, has seriously questioned the permanence of any ill effect of maternal deprivation or lack of early stimulation. He cites a number of studies that indicate neither intellect nor behavior are impaired if remedial efforts are made to correct past deficits. Furthermore, these efforts can accomplish excellent results even if delayed for some time after infancy or early childhood. Kagan does point out that the deprived subjects may lag behind their peers for a considerable period before catching up. It should be pointed out that even though there was considerable recovery, Kagan's deprived subjects never attained the average level in IQ testing as did the controls. Both the tests for measurement of IQ as well as the selection of controls may have prejudiced the results in favor of the control subjects. Perhaps the most important information that can be derived from such observations is that a child has great resilience and that he can benefit from programs designed for cognitive stimulation.

Many investigators have emphasized the beneficial results of good child rearing in the first few years of life relative to intellectual attainment and social adjustments.[27, 44, 64] A satisfactory parental environment has the potential to minimize the effects of prematurity, low birth weight and other perinatal complications and to maximize the reservoir of intellectual abilities.

If there is no other depriving condition, Rabin[61] found that mother sharing in the kibbutz resulted in no marked differences of personality or intelligence as compared to a conventionally raised control group of children. Similar findings have been emphasized for adopted children.[28] Provided there is sufficient contact (no author has offered to define "adequate" or "optimal" in this relationship) between parent and child, the effects of maternal employment,[65] communal child rearing[66] or day care[67] have not been demonstrated to endanger the well-being of the child. Lacking in most of these studies are long-term follow-ups, adequate evaluations of critical ages of the children, parental attitudes and the influence of the socioeconomic status of the families.

It has been pointed out that the low language skills of the underprivileged are not due to a quantitative lack of exposure, but rather to the chaotic and undisciplined nature of the stimuli.[60] If Piaget and other investigators are correct in the emphasis they put upon the role played by language in cognitive development, then indeed these children are at a great disadvantage. By the age of three years the specific information and ideas furnished and fostered by the parents or caretakers become increasingly important to mental growth. The more extensive the education (not necessarily formal), the richer the reservoir of ideas and information that can come from the parents. There is a large and still growing literature supporting the concept that family social differences and language have enormous influence upon intellectual performance of the child.[28, 68-71] Whether the measurement of social class is by occupation, income or educational background, the higher the rating of the parents the stronger will be the child's school performance, the higher will be his IQ scores, the greater his language skills. Regardless of birth history or early (first 2 years) developmental history, the intelligence of the teenager is more clearly related to his social class than to any other factor.[28, 70] For the mother, the incidence of poor prenatal care, undetected infections and poor nutrition during childhood, as well as during pregnancy, is greater in the economically disadvantaged. For the child, these factors contribute to a lowered potential even before the exposure to an impoverished environment. Such conditions seriously impair the opportunity for the quantity and quality of stimulus needed for normal development. Delay or poor timing of the stimulus may be partly correctable.[28]

Size of family is also related to intellectual ability. A recent study indicates that the larger the family and the higher the birth order the lower will be the score on standardized intelligence testing. The authors of the study postulate, but do not conclude, that dilution of parental attention or economic factors may play a part.[72]

Cross-cultural study is interesting as a means of comparing some aspects of environmental influence upon behavior.[70, 73] Traditionally reared rural infants accomplished motor milestones of development more rapidly than "westernized" urban infants in Africa. This persisted throughout the first year. ("Traditional" refers to a relaxed and leisurely attitude by parents with few expectations. Breast feeding on demand, nearly constant body contact with an adult caretaker, no toilet training, lack of clothing and membership in a large stable family are typical features.) On the average, all native African children achieved motor milestones at an earlier age than Caucasian children. During the second year progress in language and adaptive behavior (Gesell and Bayley items) were slower in the African children as compared to the Caucasian. Since weaning usually takes place for the black infants at about 12–18 months, Werner[73] attributes some of the relative decline to the onset of poor nutrition and infections, especially parasitic. In those cultures characterized by isolation of infants and absence of any type of stimulation, motor and language development was considerably delayed. In the Kauai study[70] a 10-year follow-up of several ethnic groups was possible.

The incidence of serious school problems was quite high, but 90% of school failures were unrelated to any deleterious perinatal condition. Children with poorly educated parents and unstable homes, at age 10 had lower IQ scores, had a high percentage of disturbed social and emotional development, and lacked communication skills. These findings were more common in children from Filipino, Hawaiian and Portuguese descent than those from an Anglo-Saxon or Japanese family. An analysis of early family environment showed that parental language styles, attitude about achievement and concern for the young child have a very significant impact upon its future. The pattern of development during the first two years seems interrelated to ethnicity, caretaker attitudes, nutritional status and socioeconomic position. The Kauai study further supports the concept that to be productive enrichment programs must begin early.

The sexual role assimilated by the child appears to become deeply imbedded by the third or fourth year. Recent studies now give great force to the idea that sexual orientation almost exclusively is determined by the mode of rearing. The child assumes the assigned sex and all of its psychologic attitudes regardless of the hormonal, genital or gonadal sex. These findings were made possible by the study of children of varying ages in which true or gonadal and chromosomal sex was opposite to that assigned them because of congenital anomalies of the external genitalia or hormonal aberrations, as in the adrenogenital syndrome in girls. Their parents had regarded them as normal boys or girls and treated them accordingly. The children responded by establishing a pattern of psychosexual behavior conforming to the demands of their culture. When attempts were made to change their gender after the third year, in almost every case there was great psychologic difficulty. This gender orientation is certainly a strong example of the fact that psychic influences are durable and extremely potent.[74]

Fetal hormonal sex exercises some influence on sexual pathways in the hypothalamus and related limbic structures of the brain (see Chapter 9). Girls who become virilized in utero as a result of exposure to androgens (iatrogenic or the adrenogenital syndrome) will definitely show a tendency in their behavior to "tomboyism." In view of their medical history, parents often become disturbed. With adequate counseling, child and parents can make satisfactory adjustments. Such girls can adequately assume the female role in lovemaking and marriage, though they may persist in preferring competitive sports and choosing less feminine dress, hobbies, etc. Money[74] points out that there is no corresponding term for "tomboy" to apply to boys who may be artistic and sensitive and dislike athletic pursuits. In our present society it is more difficult for the unmasculine man to gain acceptance than it is for the unfeminine woman.

The sex roles of parents and other members of society are important in conditioning the child in his or her own sex role. Children demonstrate in their play and conversation at an early age recognition that the male is expected to be physically stronger, more aggressive and more punitive while the female is more dependent and passive. This image is still dominant today, though perhaps the degree of contrast in America is less than it was a decade or two ago. Parents set the pattern throughout childhood by assigned dress, toys and duties, and physical differences are recognized by children as early as three years. Sex role behavior is largely determined throughout early childhood by parent models. The effect of a fatherless family upon boys is variable and seems to reflect the results of loneliness, anxiety and social adjustment in the mother as well as the absence of a father figure. If the fatherless child is sufficiently exposed to other males, of all ages, his sex identity is usually undisturbed.[75]

Cognitive Development

Cognition is the means by which an individual accumulates organized knowledge of the world and the use of that knowledge to solve problems and modify behavior. There are numerous theories about how a child thinks and about his cognitive development. The author will attempt to make an outline of ideas common to most of these theories and discuss two of them in some detail.

In the neonate there is little evidence from behavior of anything that could be termed cognitive, yet there is evidence that some perceptual (visual) choices are made when confronted with different patterns. Later in infancy selective attention is given to familiar objects and anticipatory behavior is apparent as demonstrated by quieting upon the approach of the mother. Another early indication of cognitive development is curiosity and exploration of surroundings and perceived objects. By the second to third year the intellectual progress is dominated by language. This is communicative in reporting with some accuracy internal requirements such as hunger and the need to eliminate. The language is also referential as the names for objects and activities begin to be cataloged. Not until after five is language used as a conceptual tool for reasoning and thinking and problem-solving. Standards for behavior are established in the preschool years. The child begins to understand the viewpoint of others and to take his or her turn. Discrimination of some abstract ideas now appears, e.g., fair-unfair, near-far, fast-slow and masculine-feminine. Language gains are in grammar, vocabulary and pronunciation.

A very significant change occurs in the increased capacity for thought and reasoning between the ages of 6 and 11. Learning becomes systematic and selective and is applied with increasing ease to a variety of contexts. Thought becomes more inductive and insightful with increasing abilities to deal with abstractions. Increasingly refined use of language is an important element of these developments leading to improved verbal reasoning and the use of symbolic and graphic representations. There is an understanding of the relevance of new information and improved discrimination of levels of abstraction and generalities.

Most investigators agree upon the units involved and the basic process of cognition although there may be some disagreement in the use of terms. The units or media are usually designated: *images, symbols* (which includes language) and *concepts*. Images are mental representations of objects and happenings. The use of symbols or language in thinking is a way of managing the vast amount of coded information that has accumulated in the mind. Concepts are the characterizations of an action or a thing. A concept stands for a set of common attributes. Justice may be conceptualized as the defeat of evil and the victory of good.

Cognitive processes begin with the *perception*, or comprehension, of a question or problem. The next step involves *memory*—whether the problem resembles a past experience. The third process is the *generation of ideas* to bring about a possible solution. In order to produce good ideas the child must have accurate perception and possess the right set of images, symbols and concepts. The child wishes to resolve uncertainties and to understand. In order to find an answer he reaches into his store of knowledge for information that will aid him in explaining a new event. Finally there is *evaluation* as the child measures the accuracy of his conclusions. The application of the two processes, generation of ideas and their evaluation, toward the solution of a given problem is the very essence of thinking.[28, 76]

Piaget,[52, 53, 78] a physiologist, has theorized that cognitive development occurs in three stages throughout infancy and childhood. In each stage there is a period of genesis resulting in specific attainments. The order of the stages is constant, since the development of a new attainment depends upon the completion of past ones. The reader may also wish to follow the same stages as related to Piaget's ideas about personality development outlined later in this chapter.

Stage one occupies approximately the first 2 years and is called *sensorimotor*. During this time the child explores his surroundings. Early reflex activity gives way to purposeful movement and repetition of activities. Relations are established between objects and persons and the child's own body. The last development in this stage is the initiation of manipulating the environment and imitating other people.

Stage two is the period of *concrete operations*, which ends with the attainment of true reversibility of mental operations. Early in this period the child's activity consists primarily of symbolic play by imitating and representing what others do. Language development is considerable, but remains egocentric until near the end of this period when it gradually evolves into social speech. Until about 7 years, thought remains largely oriented around immediate experiences and does not follow logical paths of reasoning. From 7 to 11 years the child begins to perform logical operations which can be described as a system for logical notation. Genuine objectivity becomes apparent in respect to objects, space, time, causality, etc. It is a time of refinement of concepts and their use in thinking. By reversibility, a factor used in describing this stage, Piaget means the ability to make mental transformation of concrete material into its inverse state, e.g., for any operation there may exist another operation that cancels it.

Stage three begins at about 11 years and is designated as the period of *formal thinking operations*. The stage ends at around 15 years with an attained equilibrium that will last indefinitely. It should be emphasized that the three stages are cumulative and none displaces the attainments of its predecessor. This last period is characterized by the use of hypothetical reasoning and methods. Due consideration is now given to the possible and what might be. Thinking also becomes propositional and the child uses methods of extrapolation to reach conclusions. A third property of formal operations is that they are reflective. The adolescent can not only apply a set of solutions to a specific problem but can consider the effects of all possible variables. Reflective thinking makes possible a great gain in efficiency by permitting the elimination of inconsequential variables and concentrating on those that matter.

Two major criticisms of Piaget's theories have been expressed. One is that he ignores the cumulative effect of experience in cognitive development with excessive emphasis upon maturation as outlined in his stages. The second points out the lack of experimental evidence and too great a reliance upon speculation. It should be mentioned that none of the experimental data so far available have disproven any of the proposed concepts.

Bruner,[76, 77] an educator, differs from Piaget in his ideas of the growth of cognitive thought in his greater emphasis upon the part played by the environment and experience. He was influenced by his background in teaching and his observations of perceptual suppression or discrimination as a possible tool in education.

Both in animals and in man there may occur a centrally mediated suppression of peripheral sensory activity. This suggests the possibility of cortical control over the selection of cues. Both spatial proximity of stimulus as well as time proximity can be shown to reinforce learning efficiency by increasing attention and reducing distraction.

Selective memory phenomena may have a similar role in cognitive development. There are two kinds of memory, long and short. Short memory lasts only a few seconds. The inability to recall the color of an automobile just passed or a once-used phone number are typical examples. Obviously methods can be used to reinforce memory and make it more lasting.

Bruner contends that cognitive development from infancy to the mature level is shaped by "technological" advances in the use of the mind, and depends upon a mastery of techniques which are transmitted by the culture in which the person lives. With advancing age language plays a larger and larger role as an implement of knowing. By translating experiences into words (or other symbols) the child achieves remote references, transformations and combinations. Intellectual activity is accomplished primarily through the medium of language. This facilitates the development of propositional and reflective thought in a manner very similar to Piaget's stage three. Bruner, however, suggests that in making use of past experience it must be organized, condensed and cataloged. Selectivity is already present at the time of the perception of a given experience. The child learns to manipulate his store of information in line with his existing cognitive structure to cope with problems met.

From an educational point of view, Bruner's theories indicate that a child's cognitive abilities can be improved by greater attention to learning experiences. There is some experimental support of this.

Early Social Behavior

Social behavior has been discussed in several sections of this chapter as related to parents, sex, personality, adolescence and other age groups. A few important points not covered elsewhere will be considered here.

Voice and physical contact can elicit responses in the neonate including visual, auditory and consoling or quieting activity. Between 2 and 3 months parents are recognized by sight and voice with appropriate reactions such as smiling, cessation of crying or reaching. Social laughing is present by this time also. By 7 or 8 months fear of strangers is manifested by visual avoidance, frowning, crying, reducing physical activity and clinging to a parent. This apparent fear seems to reach a peak between 9 and 12 months and usually subsides by 18–24 months. Some children will find separation from a parent or parents, e.g., baby-sitter or day-care center, a very distressing experience until after three years.

At one year simple tricks or games such as peek-a-boo are enjoyed. The 18-month infant is fairly self-contained and, if the caretaker is in close proximity, can spend long periods alone with toys. By two years there is usually considerable emotional equilibrium and decreasing number of tantrums which reached a peak at 18 months. The two-year-old uses tone and loudness of voice symbolically. He likes to show off and he can be coy.

At three years cooperative and group play are possible. The child is ritualistic in many activities which include dress, arranging toys and the pattern of going to bed. There is increasing evidence of the desire to please parents and one manifestation of egocentricity is jealousy of siblings. To an increasing extent, a child's conception of himself is related to his skills. He has an opportunity to test his skills against those of his peers and he adds to the conception of himself as his peers react to his skills. It is through continuing ego development that socialization becomes a prominent part of the child's life. Recognition of self as a complete entity permits this phase of development.

The psychoanalyst emphasizes that the ritualistic and repetitive play that is so characteristic of the 3- and 4-year-old are simply methods of gaining confidence and self-assurance. The strongest fears at this time are those of separation from parents and self-injury. These fears are usually satisfactorily resolved by the well-adjusted 6- to 7-year-old. It seems reasonable to delay elective hospitalization and surgery until such resolution takes place.

Although the 4-year-old may appear argumentative, this ploy is often used in a desire to experience new actions and new words and as a test of parental reaction. Boasting, exhibitionism, exaggeration of humor, physical aggressiveness, verbal profanity and excessive pride in accomplishments are some of the difficulties parents must expect at this age. There is a strong feeling of "me," "mine" and "I" but a continuing recognition of other people as social entities. There is even the first glimmer of self-criticism.

Play and Discipline

Until fairly recent times no serious thought was given to the significance of play in the child's development. In fact, it was often looked upon as a pleasant but unnecessary or superfluous part of early life and was to be discouraged so that the more serious role of learning and work could be attended to. It is now recognized that play is an extremely important activity beginning in infancy and progressing through a series of overlapping stages which can be readily documented and which appear to be essential for normal developmental maturation.[19, 30, 53]

Many of the important contacts between the child and the environment take place through the medium of play. The pleasure this activity provides, in the presence or absence of adults and peers, serves to discharge tension and permits him or her to exercise imagination. Social play, sometimes with imaginary people, is essential for the development of the personality by modifying egocentric concepts with exposure to the feelings and behavior of others. The child assumes many different roles in his play, which is an important preparation for entering adult life. Early in life play is a useful means of decreasing dependence upon parents and serves as a way for the catharsis of strong emotional reactions.

The earliest manifestations of play can be observed between 3 to 4 months when the infant first laughs aloud. Some authors consider the earlier appearance of the smile as a social reaction to be differentiated from the kind of response resulting in the laugh. Next he discovers and manipulates his hands and fingers and then his feet. By 7 months he vocalizes to his toys which includes squealing, laughing and imitative sounds. By 9 months his repertory includes the nursery games of pat-a-cake and waving bye-bye, and he can accomplish a broad spectrum of facial expressions both as a means of stimulus as well as a response to stimuli. At 14–15 months play includes activity with a favorite doll or stuffed toy with much conversation and the beginning of role-taking. This is further elaborated by the child's assuming the role of the parent at around 2 years of age. The previous undirected play of the baby merges into practice play with evident objectives. He repeats because he enjoys the pleasantly familiar and because he is becoming goal-oriented. The child watches, listens and imitates. Repetition and imitation constitute important aspects of play throughout life.

Learning what he must do and how he must act to obtain a pleasant sensation is also the beginning of discipline. The child's relation to parents involves his need for acceptance by them. He wants to learn how to control his actions so that life is happy. As he becomes ambulatory he also becomes exploratory, inspecting his environment with all of his senses. This inevitably leads to some conflicts with parents and siblings and the increasing application of discipline.

By 2 years the child plays for relatively long periods independently of mother. The sensory pleasures of play and consistent discipline condition the child to an appreciation of the joys of learning. But he now experiences some anxieties in the conflicts between his sensory pleasures and that discipline. In a normal setting the child can cope with these disturbing emotions and they do not destroy his desire to continue to explore the world. One method for coping with moderate degrees of anxiety is through symbolic play. He will relieve his frustrations and anger by acting out or dramatizing his feelings. He may spank his "mother" doll or scold another one for behaving badly. In the fantasy of play he does many of the things he does not dare to do in real life. In much of this type of symbolic play the child is not always aware of what or why he is acting out. This is in contrast to the imaginative play where he pretends to be an airplane but knows that he is not.

Not until 3 years of age is the average child sufficiently mature to enter into cooperative play which involves sharing and taking turns. From this age on few normal children will actively avoid social contact with their peers, though there are wide ranges of how aggressively he or she will pursue such contacts.

The type of play entered into by the early school years is characterized by the need for conformity and tends to follow a ritualistic pattern. This is especially true of games which have fixed and unvarying rules. Play by this time, and for the remainder of childhood, often leads to the acquiring of many skills. This leads to self-confidence as he gains stature with his peers. Not all play is directed toward games. As children grow older they become interested in many other pursuits which may include music, art, sewing, cooking, etc. This is also the time of collecting. At first the collections may be an odd assortment of objects and are not well organized, but later in the school years more meaningful objects are accumulated and often carefully cataloged, such as stamps, books or records.

Parents' understanding, usually an intuitive one, of the importance of play is essential for a satisfactory child-parent relationship. The child learns by experimenting and from that gains competence. He constructs new abilities from past experiences and enjoys each new achievement. Parents should be supportive without fostering excessive dependence or inhibiting the development of skills. Completing a task for a child without allowing adequate experimentation or time to find his own solution, if done repeatedly, could lead to lack of development of autonomous abilities. At the other extreme are parents who constantly set difficult goals for their children and then deride them for their failures. Both types of parents are found fairly often among the children with learning difficulties in school.

No grand plan for child rearing exists. Parents who are aware of the developmental continuum experienced by all children are better able to cope with behavior problems as they arise. Mothers and fathers should be encouraged to manage their children in terms of their present capabilities, their cultural heritage and anticipation of developing requirements. The ultimate aim is to achieve security and independence that is commensurate with the child's level of development.

The child, to become an accepted member of the community, must acquire a set of socially desirable traits. Such traits can usually be obtained by systematic reward without resorting to punishment. Reward in this connotation means the showing of approval and affection. Firm, but reasonable, expectations of behavior are effective means of guiding children. Without guidelines, without limits established by parents and consistently followed, the infant and child feels helpless and unloved. When discipline must be enforced, the child must understand the reason for it. Its administration should not be unduly delayed beyond the time of the event which necessitated it. Discipline which is consistent, firm, friendly and which does not ask the impossible is seldom unsuccessful. Discipline which is administered in an unpredictable (at least to the child) fit of anger and threatens the withdrawal of parental love is poorly accepted and creates unnecessary fear and anxiety. An explanation to the child that one can understand his feeling of anger or frustration but that his behavior was unacceptable is an important measure to assure him of continued affection by the parent.

Measuring Behavior

Intelligence (associative memory) of a high order and quality characterizes man. Growth of this attribute in the child is eagerly anticipated by the parents and looked for by the physician. Considerable variation in intelligence is noted, but the limits of normal are generally accepted. Understandably, intelligence above the normal range is welcomed, while a failure of growth of intelligence to keep pace with chronologic age causes alarm. Sooner or later the child with subnormal intelligence will be recognized as being retarded, the time of recognition depending on the degree of retardation and on the ability of parents or physician to recognize abnormal behavior.

When slowness of neuropsychologic development is suspected, the physician is usually consulted, and he sets about making a diagnosis much as he does when looking for diseases in other organ systems. A careful history with emphasis on pregnancy, delivery, neonatal period, and course of development is obtained. The status of hearing, sight, and motor control must be established, as serious impairment in any may distort the manifestation of normal developmental potential. A check for evidence of metabolic diseases known to be associated with slowed mental development should be routine. Hypothyroidism, phenylketonuria, and galactosemia are examples of conditions that should be diagnosed at the earliest possible moment, since treatment is available which may prevent or minimize their deleterious effects on mental development. Hurler's syndrome (gargoylism) and Down's syndrome (mongolism) are representative of conditions associated with mental deficiency, and although corrective measures are not available, it is important to the family that these conditions be recognized early enough to permit suitable counseling and advice.

Because of the rapidity of development and the wealth of complex integrations about which data are available, infancy is the period in which deviations from normal are most easily detected. This is particularly true of those relatively minor deviations for which compensations occur but which may have lasting effects on the later organization of learning and behavior.

The developmental examination and/or screening inventory is a standardized clinical procedure which can be adapted to the needs of the child. The examination situations and test objects are so designed that characteristic responses are expected at each developmental stage (Gesell) or the expected percentile at a given chronologic age range (Thorpe and Frankenberg). Systematic observations of large numbers of normal and abnormal infants have demonstrated that development proceeds in an orderly and predictable fashion. Although there are some differences in the age norms given by different authors, the spread is seldom very large.[7] Explanations for the differences may be due to variations in methods of standardization, recording, and in the definition of test items or techniques. In some items, but not all, cultural differences have substantial influence. Especially in motor development and language, acceleration may result from environmental stimulation.

Neurologic and developmental assessment are inseparably related and should be evaluated together. Some of the screening examinations combine the two, e.g., reflexes plus functional items, but there may be a dilution of each as a result. The material which is included in this text is a combination of a number of tests which the author has found of greatest value in his own practice. The largest percentage of items come from Gesell[6] but also include some from Thorpe,[79] Frankenburg,[80] Bayley[81] and Illingworth.[82] Since growth is a complex process and behavior an expression of complex interactions, diagnosis depends upon the total picture presented. A complete knowledge of normal growth and development is the basis for the detection of abnormality. The discussion that follows is restricted to a consideration of a small number of selected behavior patterns which can be used as reference points in *screening* children. This is not intended to represent a diagnostic examination but a method to alert the examiner to the need for further evaluation.

Epidemiologic investigations indicate the narrow range of variability in behavior in infancy.[38] During the first year the effects of racial and socioeconomic factors are minimal. Only 1.8% of the usual infant population has a developmental quotient (see below) under 85, compared to 14% in a group of white children of school age. In the small percentage with below-average intellectual functioning there was a high incidence of organic disease including low birth weight, bleeding, and toxemia during pregnancy, and both physical and neurologic abnormality in early infancy. In later childhood, by age 3, a sharp division along socioeconomic lines is present. The changes predominate in the fields of adaptive behavior and language.[40] Except for a relatively small number of hereditary diseases giving rise to mental deficiency, the genetic factors which are present cannot be considered as primarily responsible for significant differences in behavioral functioning, according to Knobloch and Pasamanick.[6, 40] Man's structure and basic functions are genetically determined; it is his sociocultural milieu which modifies his behavior and makes one individual significantly different from another.

Most investigators feel that the predictive value of early developmental screening, or even more thorough examination, is not very high. Not only are tests carried out during the first 2 years unreliable in predicting scores at school age, but individual infants may have high scores in one category at one time and low results in the same category 6, 12 or 18 months later.[68, 83, 84] It should be emphasized that infant tests are most useful in identifying defective development resulting from organic pathology. The child's development after the first 2 years is determined largely by his environment and no test can be expected to predict that variable.

Behavior, for testing purposes, is usually divided into four major categories: motor, adaptive, personal-social and language. Gesell divides motor into fine and gross, while Frankenburg combines fine motor and adaptive. Thorpe enlarges the language category to include all communication skills. Bayley uses two separate scales, one motor, one mental development. All authors emphasize the importance of observing such factors as emotional stability, span of attention and the nature of the attentional pattern, muscle tone and control, perceptual abilities (these include vision and hearing), fatigue and general appraisal of health status.

Gross motor behavior includes the control of the head, trunk, and extremities, and fine motor behavior pertains to the achievement of the control of fine movements of the fingers. Although it is true that there is no evidence that any thinking has taken place unless there is some observable motor reaction, it is important to avoid the mistake of using acquisition of motor control as the criterion of intellectual ability. Motor behavior is most important in the evaluation of neurologic integrity and may sometimes be so disordered that the evaluation of intellectual potential is extremely difficult. Acceleration in motor development does not contribute to intellectual abilities, nor does motor defect necessarily mean that there is a concomitant defect in intelligence.

Language behavior includes the production of sounds, single words and combinations of words, facial and gestural expressions and understanding of the communications of others. Just as motor behavior in infancy is incorrectly used as an important criterion of intelligence, language behavior is somewhat similarly misused later in the preschool period as a sole index. A child who can neither talk nor understand the language he hears is not necessarily mentally defective. There is considerable variation in the time of the appearance of the "talking" aspects of language, and they may be delayed in otherwise entirely normal children with good developmental potential. Normal speech production will occur if a child hears, understands the language of others (is not aphasic) and has no intellectual or neurologic defect.

Personal-social behavior has the widest variation of all of the fields and depends to a larger extent on culture and environment, but its expression is also a function of neuromotor maturity. It includes such things as feeding and sleep habits, bladder and bowel function, identification of objects and persons and the ability to work and play with others and to adapt to the regulations imposed by society.

Adaptive behavior includes manipulation and exploitation of objects, the use of motor capacities in the execution of practical situations, as well as the utilization of past experience in the solution of new problems.

Adaptive behavior is the most important field; judgment of intellectual potential is based largely on the adaptive maturational status. However, intellectual potential takes into account not only the developmental level but also the quality of behavior. The concept of intellectual potential is concerned with prognosis and implies that if nothing happens to damage the infant organically, socially or psychologically, his future development will be at an essentially constant rate in terms of an overall level of adaptive functioning. This level is related to, but not equated with, school age or adult tests of intelligence. Intelligence tests as now constituted tend to measure limited functions; and the downward trend in test results between infancy and childhood that occurs largely in the lower socioeconomic groups would indicate that these children have less exposure to the kinds of experience that later tests are designed to evaluate. The upward spreading in the curve can be explained adequately only on the basis of learning; but even learned behavior, though it is greatly modified by environmental factors, must be dependent on the basic integrity of the central nervous system.

The developmental quotient is a clinical estimate of maturity based on the overall picture and is a guide to the rate of developmental progress, which can be different for each of the fields of behavior.

$$DQ = \frac{\text{maturity age}}{\text{chronologic age}} \times 100$$

A diagnosis does not result from a DQ score. An adequate history and physical examination are necessary as well as evaluation of emotional aspects of development for a final diagnosis.

Development progresses in a cephalocaudal and proximodistal direction. Control of the eyes and the head is achieved in the first quarter of the first year, that of the upper trunk and arms in the second quarter, that of the lower trunk and the use of the fingers for fine prehension in the third quarter, and integration of the legs in the erect posture begins in the last quarter of the first year of life. Figure 6–1 illustrates the general trend and the major achievements, primarily in motor behavior, at the various age levels. The differences which can be found in the literature on the age of attaining various developmental milestones can usually be explained by differences in defining the behavior that is meant. Sitting may be accomplished with support by leaning forward on the hands for brief periods, which occurs at 28 weeks, or indefinitely and steadily without the use of hands for support,

STANDS
12 ALONE

WALKS WITH
11 SUPPORT

10 CRUISES

9 PULLS UP

8 CREEPS

SITS
7 BRIEFLY

TRANSFERS
6 OBJECTS

ROLLS
5 OVER

HOLDS
4 HEAD

TURNS
3 HEAD

2 SMILES

1 REGARDS

BIRTH 1 2 3 4 5 6 7 8 9 10 11 12 13 14
AGE IN MONTHS

Fig 6–1.—Developmental diagram for the first year of life. The infant's figure represents a diagonal line on which is plotted the progress of behavior (right of the diagram) against chronologic age. The cephalocaudal pattern of behavior is diagrammatically illustrated by position of the figure. (After Aldrich.[3])

which occurs at 40 weeks. Thus definition of terms is essential.

In the first year of life development is estimated in terms of weeks rather than months because it progresses so rapidly that the use of monthly intervals may be misleading. "Four months" may mean just over 17 weeks or almost 22 weeks of age, and the developmental change in this period of time is tremendous. Further, the chronologic age must be corrected for the amount of prematurity, since development must really be measured from the time of conception and premature birth does not confer any advantage to the maturing nervous system. The "key ages," which are at 12-week intervals in the first year, represent turning points and major integrative periods in the developmental paths and correspond roughly to the quarters of the year mentioned above.

It should be understood that the behavior patterns given below represent the average performances for a large group of healthy subjects. An individual pattern might deviate 20–25% from these standards and still be within normal limits. Nevertheless, it is important to emphasize that norms for neuropsychologic behavior are as essential as are norms for any of the other aspects of development discussed in this book.

It is important to understand just what it is an infant evaluation predicts. It is not meant to assign a precise quotient, a number that will not change with time. What happens to the infant and the influences to which he is exposed before he reaches school age will affect his ability to perform on an intelligence test at that time. Unless qualitative changes in the central nervous system are caused by noxious agents or gross changes in milieu alter major variables of function, his Stanford-Binet IQ will be above 85, provided it can be stated in infancy that he has no neuromotor impairment and has an intellectual potential within the normal range. In actuality the predictions are much more precise than this clinically acceptable statement, and the Gesell developmental examination performs as reasonably in predicting in infancy as other examinations do at later ages. Its usefulness goes beyond what one expects of a clinical neurologic method: namely, identification of the abnormal infant with a below-average potential, usually on an organic basis, and definition of the nature of his abnormality.[50]

The screening should be done in a quiet, comfortable and isolated environment. If the mother is present she should be told not to correct answers or persuade the child in any manner. The infant or child should be awake and not fatigued, nor should the examination displace nap time. The examiner should permit the child a brief examination of the room, but items used in the tests should be introduced only as needed, and then removed before progressing to the next part. Verbal or other instructions should be given slowly, deliberately and in terms the child is sure to understand. In presenting tasks in any category, the initial level should be one easily accomplished to prevent discouragement or boredom. The examiner should be completely familiar with the method of presenting the test items. Some may be introduced first with an opportunity for spontaneous response, failing which, verbal instructions or demonstration may be used. Both by facial expression as well as tone of voice, the examiner should acknowledge the response as being acceptable, whether or not it is correct. An achievement observed should carry greater significance than one obtained by history from a parent or caretaker.

Developmental Screening Inventory*

4 Weeks

Motor: Gross   1. Asymmetrical tonic neck reflex positions predominate
                2. Head sags forward in sitting

---

*Much more detailed inventories are available and should be consulted by anyone who plans to participate in screening technics. A number of teaching films have also been prepared.[13, 51, 79, 81] The age placement of an item is that at which roughly 50% of infants and children achieve success.

Fine	1. Hands fisted
	2. Hands clench on contact
Adaptive	1. Regards object in line of vision only
	2. Follows to midline
	3. Drops toy immediately
Language	1. Vague indirect regard
	2. Small throaty noises
Personal-social	1. Stares indefinitely at surroundings
	2. Regards observer's face and diminishes activity

16 Weeks

Motor: Gross	1. Symmetrical postures predominate
	2. Head steady in sitting
	3. Head lifted 90 degrees when prone; on forearms
Fine	1. Hands engage
	2. Reaches, grasps objects, brings to mouth
Adaptive	1. Eyes follow slowly moving object well
	2. Arms activate on sight of dangling toy
	3. Regards toy in hand and takes to mouth
	4. Regard goes from hand to object when sitting
Language	1. Laughs aloud
	2. Excites and breathes heavily
Personal-social	1. Spontaneous social smile
	2. Hand play with mutual fingering
	3. Pulls dress over face
	4. Anticipates food on sight

28 Weeks

Motor: Gross	1. Sits briefly leaning forward on hands
	2. Supports large fraction of weight in standing
	3. Bounces actively in supported standing
	4. Rolls over
Fine	1. Has radial palmar grasp of toy
	2. Rakes at small pellet with whole hand
Adaptive	1. One-hand approach and grasp of toy
	2. Bangs and shakes rattle
	3. Transfers toy from one hand to the other
Language	1. Vocalizes "m-m-m" when crying
	2. Talks to toys

Personal-social	1. Takes feet to mouth
	2. Reaches for and pats mirror image

40 WEEKS

Motor: Gross	1. Sits indefinitely steady
	2. Creeps and pulls self to feet at rail
Fine	1. Crude release of toy
	2. Plucks pellet easily with thumb and index finger
	3. Exploring poke with forefinger
Adaptive	1. Matches 2 objects in hands
	2. Index finger approach
	3. Spontaneously rings bell
Language	1. Says "mama" and "dada" with meaning
	2. One other "word"
Personal-social	1. Waves "bye-bye" and pat-a-cakes (or other nursery trick)
	2. Feeds self cracker and holds own bottle

52 WEEKS

Motor: Gross	1. Walks with 1 hand held
	2. Stands momentarily alone
	3. Cruises
Fine	1. Neat pincer grasp of pellet
Adaptive	1. Tries to build tower of 2 cubes
	2. Releases cube in cup (after demonstration)
	3. Serial play with objects
Language	1. Two words besides "mama" and "dada"
	2. Gives toy on request or gesture
Personal-social	1. Offers toy to image in mirror
	2. Cooperates in dressing

15 MONTHS

Motor: Gross	1. Toddles independently
	2. Creeps upstairs
Fine	1. Puts pellet into bottle
Adaptive	1. Builds tower of 2 cubes
	2. Puts 6 cubes in and out of cup
	3. Incipient imitation of stroke

Language	1. Jargons
	2. Four to 6 words, including names
	3. Follows simple commands
Personal-social	1. Says "thank you" or equivalent
	2. Points or vocalizes wants
	3. Indicates wet pants
	4. Casts objects in play or refusal

18 Months

Motor: Gross	1. Walks, seldom falling
	2. Seats self in small chair and climbs into adult chair
	3. Hurls ball in standing position
Fine	1. Turns pages of book 2–3 at once
Adaptive	1. Builds tower of 3–4 cubes
	2. Imitates stroke with a crayon and scribbles spontaneously
	3. Dumps pellet from bottle
Language	1. Has 10 words
	2. Looks selectively at pictures and identifies 1
	3. Names ball and carries out 2 directions ("on the table," "to mother")
Personal-social	1. Pulls toy on string
	2. Carries and hugs doll
	3. Feeds self in part with spilling

24 Months

Motor: Gross	1. Runs well, no falling
	2. Walks up and down stairs alone
	3. Kicks large ball on request
Fine	1. Turns pages of book singly
Adaptive	1. Builds tower of 6–7 cubes
	2. Aligns cubes for train
	3. Imitates vertical and circular strokes
Language	1. Uses pronouns
	2. Three-word sentences; jargon discarded
	3. Carries out 4 directions with ball ("on the table," "on the chair," "to mother," "to me")
Personal-social	1. Verbalizes toilet needs consistently
	2. Pulls on simple garment

3. Inhibits turning of spoon in feeding
4. Plays with domestic mimicry

30 MONTHS

Motor: Gross	1. Jumps up and down
	2. Walks backward
Fine	1. Holds crayon in fist
Adaptive	1. Copies crude circle, closed figure
	2. Names some drawings: house, shoe, ball, dog
Language	1. Refers to self as "I"
	2. Knows full name
Personal-social	1. Helps put things away
	2. Unbuttons large buttons

3 YEARS

Motor: Gross	1. Alternates feet going upstairs
	2. Jumps from bottom step
	3. Rides tricycle, using pedals
Fine	1. Holds crayon with fingers
Adaptive	1. Builds tower of 9–10 cubes
	2. Imitates 3-cube bridge
	3. Names own drawing
	4. Copies circle and imitates cross
Language	1. Uses plurals
	2. Gives action in picture book
	3. Gives sex and full name
	4. Obeys 2 prepositional commands ("on," "under")
Personal-social	1. Feeds self well
	2. Puts on shoes

4 YEARS

Motor	1. Walks downstairs alternating feet
	2. Does broad jump
	3. Throws ball overhand
	4. Hops on one foot
Adaptive	1. Draws man with 2 parts
	2. Copies cross

3. Counts 3 objects with correct pointing
4. Imitates 5-cube gate
5. Picks longer of two lines

Language
1. Names 1 or more colors correctly
2. Obeys 5 prepositional commands ("on," "under," "in back," "in front," "beside")

Personal-social
1. Washes and dries face and hands; brushes teeth
2. Distinguishes front from back of clothes
3. Laces shoes
4. Goes on errands outside of home

5 YEARS

Motor
1. Skips, alternating feet
2. Stands on 1 foot more than 8 seconds
3. Catches bounced ball

Adaptive
1. Builds 2 steps with cubes
2. Draws unmistakable man with body, head, etc.
3. Copies triangle
4. Counts 10 objects correctly

Language
1. Knows 4 colors
2. Names penny, nickel, dime
3. Descriptive comment on pictures
4. Carries out 3 commissions

Personal-social
1. Dresses and undresses without assistance
2. Asks meaning of words
3. Prints few letters

6 YEARS

Motor
1. Advanced throwing
2. Stands on each foot alternately, eyes closed
3. Walks line backward, heel-toe

Adaptive
1. Builds 3 steps with blocks
2. Draws man with neck, hands, and clothes
3. Adds and subtracts within 5
4. Copies diamond

Language
1. Uses Stanford-Binet items (vocabulary)
2. Defines words by function or composition, e.g., "house is to live in"

Personal-
social

1. Ties shoelaces
2. Differentiates A.M. and P.M.
3. Knows right from left
4. Counts to 30

The Structure of Behavior

The development of cube behavior is presented here in some detail to illustrate how behavior grows, the complex neuromotor mechanisms involved, the interrelationships between patterns and the importance of accessory supporting behavior in the emergence of specific patterns during the course of the developmental process. It shows also how many details of development are known; such a fine dissection has been done not only in the field of cube behavior but in many of the other aspects of growth as well.[6]

Not until age 12 weeks does the infant sit supported with his head bobbingly erect and fix his eyes more than momentarily on so small an object as a 1-in. cube; this involves both control of the eye muscles and some control of the neck muscles. At 16 weeks, in the supine position, he is able to rotate his head freely a full 180 degrees, but without this accessory support in the sitting position, he holds his head steady only so long as it is set forward, and he does not turn it to one side. Macular vision has developed, and he regards the cube promptly and for prolonged periods. The eyes still have the lead, but the beginnings of eye-hand coordination are seen as he looks from hand to cube and back again. When he is supine and able to move his arms more freely because his head is supported by the crib platform, he activates his arms at the sight of a dangling object; but he is unable to do this in a sitting position until age 20 weeks. By then his head is held in the axis of his body, and he can turn it to the side without losing control of it. Consequently, he has more freedom of movement of his arms, and there is even the very beginning of finger movements in conjunction with the gross movements of the arms. He scratches at the tabletop as he regards the cube, and as he moves his arms under the influence of the symmetrotonic reflex, they come together toward the midline and approach the cube. But only if his hand comes in contact with the cube does he close on it and grasp it. When it is placed in his hand, he holds it precariously with an ulnar-palmar grasp. Simultaneously with the achievement of control of the arms, grasp is moving across the palm toward the eventual specialization of the radial digits. At 24 weeks approach and grasp occur as one movement—on sight of the cube the arms go out and pick it up. It is still a crude bilateral corralling motion, although the grasp itself is now palmar. With the emergence of vertical movements in addition to the symmetrical in-and-out activity in a horizontal plane characteristic of the earlier ages, he takes the cube to his mouth and retrieves it if he drops it.

At 28 weeks the symmetrotonic reflex has disappeared, and the asymmetry necessary for more complex movements is present. Eye-hand coordination is very well developed, and the infant makes an immediate one-hand approach and grasp on sight of the cube, with further specialization, since grasp, although still palmar, is now at the radial side of the palm. The beginning of handedness now appears, but in a very rudimentary stage, and the 28-week-old infant shows his bilaterality in his transfer of the cube from one hand to the other. Just prior to this stage one hand pulls an object out of the other in a very crude transfer. But at 28 weeks simultaneous grasp and release are still reflex, as shown by transfer and the dropping of a cube held in one hand as the other hand goes out to pick up a second cube being presented. The combination of perception and manipulation is very active, and the infant regards the cube intently as he takes the cube from mouth to tabletop with each hand alternately.

At 32 weeks there is the first inhibition of the simultaneous grasp and release reflex as the infant picks up and holds the first and then the second cube presented. But the inhibitory aspects are so strong that he is unable to drop one of these cubes to pick up a third. Not until 36 weeks is there the first voluntary release as the infant drops one of the cubes he is holding to pick up the third cube. This release is extremely crude, for it is indeed only an opening of the hand and dropping the cube from it.

Concomitantly there is differentiation in the stimulus value of objects, particularly in relation to size, and in the ability to encompass more than one object at a time. At the earliest age (12 weeks), the infant can contact only the large cup, then the massed cubes (20 weeks), and finally (24 weeks) a single cube. The larger objects have the greater stimulus value, and not until 32 weeks does the infant retain a cube when the cup is presented. At 28 weeks only if the massed cubes are presented does he grasp and hold a cube with each hand more than momentarily. As already indicated, not until 36 weeks is there enough inhibition of reflex activity so that the infant can exploit more than two objects in succession. At 36 weeks, also, his horizon is widening, and he combines an object in his hand with another on the tabletop, hitting cube against cube or cube against cup. Until greater control is achieved, the concept of "more than one" is restricted to one object only in his hands, so long as very active manipulation such as banging is prominent.

There are two other diverse threads to be picked up which are also being incorporated into the behavior picture simultaneously. So far as cube behavior is concerned, radial specialization has been achieved, and the radial digits, not the palm, are used in manipulation. Further specialization of the radial digits is concerned with precise manipulation of small objects, which lags behind the facile use of the fingers for larger objects. The other thread concerns the relation of the arms to trunk control. The arms are free for such complex manipulations only if the trunk is supported, either by fastening the child into a specially constructed infant Morris chair or by holding him on someone's lap. Otherwise, both hands at first, and then one hand, must be used to support the body in the sitting position.

At 40 weeks he has new achievements, but they are limited by new restrictions. He now combines two objects more definitely, holding a cube in each hand and matching both together. Crude release, independent of grasp, is present; he no longer merely opens his hand to let the cube drop, but puts it down on the tabletop and removes his hand from it. A dim awareness of dimension is developing—he first notices the cube which the examiner has dropped into the cup, and he reaches in and fingers it. It is less mature to grasp than to release, as development up to now has indicated, and at 44 weeks he removes the cube from the cup; but within its confines he is unable to release, and he merely thrusts hand and cube together into the cup. By 52 weeks release has developed to the point where he puts a cube into the cup after demonstration; but fine motor control is still too imprecise to enable him to release one cube on top of another, and his attempts to build a tower fail. At 56 weeks he has coordinated his understanding and his ability to release well enough so that he puts one cube into the cup on request.

By 15 months release has come sufficiently under voluntary control to allow him to build a tower of two cubes. He exhibits his new-found power by casting cubes to the floor and putting five or six cubes into the cup. Here again the integration of more than one simultaneously developing pattern appears. At the earlier age of 48 weeks he also begins to encompass a series of objects; his horizons are widening. Rudiments of sequential behavior appear as he takes the cubes in succession from the table to the crib platform. Further elaboration of the sequential cube behavior results from an increasing attention span and greater fine motor skill in release. At 15 months his attention is easily distracted by new stimuli, and his drive is not sustained, so that he begins to take the cubes out of the cup again after the fifth or sixth one. Not until 18 months does he have the prolonged attention for and sense of completing a task so that he fills the cup with the cubes. He now builds a tower of three or four cubes before it falls; but this fine motor control grows slowly, and it takes him another six months to add three more cubes to his tower, making a tower of six or seven cubes at 24 months. Not until 36 months is he precise enough to add the final three cubes for a tower of nine or ten.

Human Figure Drawings

Young children use drawings to express their ideas. In addition, there is a progressive improvement with age in both detail and complexity. Using the human figure as the subject, Goodenough and Harris[41] developed a point system for scoring in which a single point is awarded for each of a series of body parts or features. A total score is achieved by summing the individual

TABLE 6–1.—SCORING ITEMS FOR FIGURE DRAWING

1. Head present (outline and some features)
2. Arms present
3. Legs present
4. Trunk present
5. Trunk length greater than width
6. Shoulders indicated
7. Attachment of arms and legs to trunk
8. Feet present
9. Neck present
10. Eyes present
11. Nose present
12. Mouth present
13. Nostrils indicated
14. Hair present
15. Hair more than on crown
16. Nose two-dimensional
17. Mouth two-dimensional
18. Clothing indicated (buttons, belt, tie, etc.)
19. At least 2 articles of clothing (hat, dress, coat)
20. Costume complete (at least 4 articles)
21. Fingers present (add point for correct number)
22. Hand distinct from arm and fingers
23. Limb joints indicated (point for upper, point for lower)
24. Proper proportion of head to body
25. Proper proportions of all parts of body
26. Hip indicated
27. Heel indicated
28. Ears present
29. Eye details (one point each: pupils, lashes, brows)
30. Points added for increased detail and avoiding irregularities such as transparencies or overlaps

Point score	= Mental age in years
2	3
6	4
10	5
14	6
18	7
22	8
26	9
30	10

Fig 6–2 (left).—Drawing by girl aged 4 years 9 months. Point score of 12 for the items credited as numbered in Table 6–1. Credit for 1, 2, 3, 4, 5, 8, 10, 11, 12, 14, 21 and 28. This would indicate a mental age of 5 years and 6 months.

Fig 6–3 (right).—Drawing by boy aged 7 years. Point score of 21 for the items credited as numbered in Table 6–1. Credit for 1, 2, 3, 4, 5, 7, 8, 10, 11, 12, 14, 16, 17, 18, 21 (2 points), 22, 24, 25, 28 and 29. This would indicate a mental age of 7 years 9 months.

parts and this total score, can then be translated into mental age. This is based upon the accumulated experience of the authors and comparing results with other intelligence tests. This method of testing has several advantages. Instructions are simple, brief and readily understood. The child usually enjoys drawing and does not feel the stress usually associated with an examination. It is a performance test which enhances its value for the subject with hearing or speech difficulties. Between the ages of 5 and 11 years there is good correlation with other measures of intellectual development.[85] As described here, the test should be considered only as screening procedure in a manner similar to the developmental inventory.

Instructions given to the child should be straightforward and simple, e.g., "On this paper I want you to draw a picture of a person. Make the very best picture you can and take your time." When the picture is completed the child is asked to tell the examiner about the drawing.

The 30 items listed in Table 6–1 are not all-inclusive but should give some indication as a guide to scoring. Each item in the list is worth a single point. See Figures 6–2 and 6–3 for examples of scoring.

Evaluation of Intelligence Testing*

The intelligence test has two functions: diagnosis and prediction. Prediction requires knowledge of what a particular test score means. For example, if a test has proved reliable in predicting school performance and a child obtains a low score, we need know nothing about the reason for the low score to predict low school performance. However, if diagnosis is the goal of testing, it is important to know what characteristics of the child caused the low score. The intelligence test is a procedure for comparing the behavior of two or more persons and for standardizing clinical observation of behavior. It can be evaluated quantitatively and qualitatively.

The quantitative evaluation subserves the function of prediction. Once the score, or IQ, is obtained, it is necessary to relate it to the norm group. It is assumed that in a random population the distribution of scores can be plotted on a normal curve, as are measurements of biologic characteristics such as height and weight. Following this basic assumption it becomes imperative that certain facts about the particular test be known: the variability of IQ scores around the mean, the reliability of the scores, and the validity of the scores.

When the standard deviation is known, a particular IQ score can be assessed in comparison to the norm group. Thus, on the 1960 revision of the Stanford-Binet Intelligence Scale the standard deviation is 16 IQ points. On the Wechsler Intelligence Scale for Children-Revised[43] the standard deviation is 15 IQ points. Therefore, an IQ score of 90 obtained on either test would fall within one standard deviation below the mean of an IQ of 100.

When, in addition to the standard deviation, the reliability coefficient or the accuracy of the measure is known, the error of the IQ score can be determined. The score on the test is determined principally by the ability or knowledge of the child who takes it, but the score is also affected by the inaccuracy of the test itself. The reliability coefficient shows the extent to which errors of measurement influence scores on the test. The complexity of factors which may influence scores on a test is indicated in the following list prepared by R. L. Thorndike.[42]

---

*Pages 165 through 172 were prepared by Ralph Gibson, Ph.D.

Possible Sources of Differences in Performance on a Test

 I. Lasting and general characteristics of the individual
  A. General skills and techniques of taking tests
  B. General ability to comprehend instructions
  C. Level of ability on one or more general traits which operate in a number of tests

 II. Lasting but specific characteristics of the individual
  A. Specific to the test as a whole (and to parallel forms of it)
   1. Individual level of ability on traits required in this test but not in others
   2. Knowledge and skills specific to particular form of test items
  B. Specific to particular test items
   1. The "chance" element determining whether the individual does or does not know a particular fact

III. Temporary but general characteristics of the individual (factors affecting performance on many or all tests at a particular time)
  A. Health
  B. Fatigue
  C. Motivation
  D. Emotional strain
  E. General test-wiseness (partly lasting)
  F. External conditions of heat, light, ventilation, etc.

IV. Temporary and specific characteristics of the individual
  A. Specific to the test as a whole
   1. Comprehension of the specific test task (insofar as this is distinct from I-B)
   2. Specific tricks or techniques of dealing with the particular test materials (insofar as distinct from II-A-2)
   3. Level of practice on the specific skills involved, especially in psychomotor tests
   4. Momentary "set" for a particular test
  B. Specific to particular test items
   1. Fluctuation and idiosyncrasies of human memory
   2. Unpredictable fluctuations in attention or accuracy

 V. Variance not otherwise accounted for (chance)
  A. Luck in the selection of answers by "guessing"

Another very important source of differences in performance resides in the relationship between the child and the examiner. The test is basically a standardized interview in which the psychologist serves in the role of a participant observer. This implies that he is not only observing the child's behavior, including the test responses, but is also contributing something of a negative or positive value to the child's willingness to exhibit a representative sample of his behavior. In order to obtain a valid test, the psychologist must endeavor in various ways to meet the child's immediate emotional needs. The psychologist can begin with a nonverbal test for a child who is anxious about talking to a stranger, can begin with easier items with a child who is greatly concerned about failure and needs to experience immediate success, or can begin by responding to and possibly interpreting feelings expressed by the child's behavior or conversation. It is apparent that in order to obtain a valid result, the psychologist must be well grounded, not only in testing procedures but in the psychodynamic aspects of the emotional development of children.

Reliability coefficients estimate the extent to which some or all of the factors cause random changes in the score. The reliability coefficient, however, has two drawbacks: (1) its numerical value depends, to a large extent, on the spread of the scores, and (2) it does not help directly in evaluating the obtained score. Unfortunately, there is no practical method to determine the precise amount of error in an individual case. Statistical methods have been developed, however, for estimating the margin of error that should be allowed in test scores. One of the most useful of these is the standard error of measurement. If we know the exact obtained score and the standard error of measurement of the particular test, we can define the limits around the obtained score within which we would be reasonably sure to find the true score. For two thirds of all children tested the observed score will lie within one standard error of measurement of the true score, and for 19 out of 20 children the observed score will not be more than two standard errors away from the true score.

When the precision of the Binet IQ is determined by comparing Form L and Form M IQs obtained a few days apart, a correlation of about .91 is obtained. Thus the Stanford-Binet test is established as one of the most reliable intelligence tests. However, the average shift of IQs from form to form is substantial: 5.9 for IQ 130, 5.1 for IQ 100 and 2.5 for IQs below 70. Thus the test is more precise for low IQs. However, for a child with an IQ of 130 on Form L, the quotient on Form M a few days later may range from 124 to 136 if we accept one standard error as a reasonable limit.

On the Wechsler Intelligence Scale for Children-Revised, the average reliability coefficients and standard error of measurements for the verbal

IQs, performance IQs and full scale IQs are reported by Wechsler[43] as follows:

	VERBAL IQ	PERFORMANCE IQ	FULL SCALE IQ
Reliability coefficient	0.94	0.90	0.96
Standard error of measurement	3.60	4.60	3.19

Thus, if we were to accept one standard error as a reasonable limit, we could state if a child obtains a verbal IQ of 89, the true score lies between 85 and 93, a performance IQ of 89, the true score lies between 84 and 94, and a full scale IQ of 89, the true score lies between 86 and 92.

From our discussion it should be clear that the smaller the standard error of measurement, the more confident one can be that the obtained score approximates the true score and that a prediction based on the obtained score is warranted.

Knowledge of the validity of the intelligence test is the final and pivotal information necessary in order to carry out the predictive function. A test is valid to the degree that we know what it measures or predicts. A vast body of literature clearly shows that mental ability is significantly related to school performance, vocational success, etc. Thus both the Stanford-Binet test and the Wechsler Intelligence Scale for Children-Revised are positively related to school achievement. However, intelligence is only one facet of individuality to be considered in a practical decision about a child.

A special problem of prediction is encountered in the assessment of the intelligence of infants. There has been no clear evidence in the literature that test results in infancy correlate significantly with intelligence test scores in later childhood, adolescence and adulthood. However, infant intelligence scales are widely used in clinical situations to assess the current developmental status of babies. In the author's experience, these scales can provide pertinent information regarding deviations in development that necessitate further medical evaluation, educative counseling of parents and frequent medical evaluation of the infant's development. However, one must be constantly aware of the caveat suggested by Lewis and McGurk,[84] who state, "This use of infant intelligence scales is justified only if, in interpreting the result scores, the scores are regarded solely as measures of present performance and not as indices of future potential." The author is in complete accord with the view enounced by Schwartz and Elonen[90] based on their longitudinal study of adopted and nonadopted children. At the time of each psychological examination, records were made of such pertinent facts concerning the child's life and family as accidents, deaths, moves, adoption, birth or adoption of a sibling and the child's reactions to these events. The reports were obtained in interviews with family members as well as with the child. The children were evaluated first when they were under twelve months of age and the final evaluation done when they were over sixteen years of age. The IQ test scores varied over time and in some instances quite dramatically. However, the investigators were able to associate the variance with developmental transitions in cognitive, emotional and social function and with unevenness in cognitive development and significant life events and experiences. Thus, the assessment of the child did not stress IQ scores per se but rather fitted intelligence into the process of adaptation, and the issue of the predictive validity of infant intelligence tests was not the primary concern.

The classification of intelligence by IQ score is very misleading and tends to give a picture of rigidity of score and ability. However, since the classification is so widely used in the reporting of intelligence testing, it is given with the hope that its operational limitations will be kept in mind.

The clinical usefulness of the intelligence test is particularly outstanding when its second function, diagnosis, is explored. It is at the level of diagnosis that the need for remedial measures can be seen. It is the qualitative evaluation of the test performance that is particularly helpful in total clinical evaluation of behavior. The emphasis in the diagnostic function is to describe how the child arrived at the obtained IQ score. Consideration is given not only to the various aspects of the test performance but also to the behavior exhibited by the child during the course of the examination.

IQ	CLASSIFICATION
120 and above	Superior
110–119	Upper average or bright normal
90–109	Average
80–89	Dull average or dull normal
70–79	Borderline
69 and below	Mental defective or retarded

The need for complete evaluation of all clinical and laboratory data in addition to the intelligence test score is highlighted by taking as illustrations 8 children aged 7 years who obtain an IQ of 92 on a given test of intelligence. They are functioning toward the lower end of the average range of intelligence. Their true scores fall somewhat below or above the obtained scores, depending on the standard error of measurement of the test used. One can predict a lowered degree of school achievement on the basis of the known relationship between obtained scores on the test and school achievement.

When we analyze the test performance of child A, it is immediately apparent that he was unable to demonstrate any abilities or pass any items commensurate with his age level. He shows relative lag in all abilities underlying the test items. His range of successes, whether in terms of age levels on the Stanford-Binet or in terms of scaled scores on the Wechsler Intelligence Scale for Children, is relatively narrow. This qualitative analysis suggests that the reason that child A is having school difficulty is basically because his ability level is low average and he might well be competing with children who are better than average. By noting his reactions to failure during the course of the examination, one might ascertain whether or not any reported distractibility or inattention is secondary to his lowered ability to compete with good average children.

In the case of child B an analysis of the test performance might reveal consistent difficulty on all the test items related to perceptual abilities. On the other hand, items related to other abilities might be passed at or above the level of expectancy for the child. In addition, the child may manifest considerable distractibility and/or hyperactivity during the testing session. The behavior may appear on close observation to be unrelated to interpersonal problems. In fact, the parents often report that the behavior has been characteristic of the child since birth. In general, this is the type of child identified as the "brain-injured child." It should be quickly pointed out that in many cases the medical history and neurologic examination will be entirely negative for organic brain pathology. However, operationally the child does have a rather specific deficit in intellectual functioning, which can be further demonstrated by specific tests designed to measure perceptual abilities.

In the case of child C an analysis of the test performance might reveal consistent difficulty in abstract reasoning ability, i.e., the ability to generalize and to conceptualize relationships. On the other hand, items related to language skills, general comprehension, memory, and perceptual abilities may be near or beyond the expectancy level of the child. The deficit can be further demonstrated by specific tests designed to measure abstract reasoning ability. This child may exhibit distractibility, hyperactivity and negativism, which should be evaluated in terms of their relationship to his deficit and the parental reactions and attitudes toward the child.

In the case of child D the analysis of his test performance might indicate significant difficulty on items related to memory, in contrast to average or above-average performance on items related to other abilities. This, then, is another type of deficit pattern. At the present time it is not possible in the case of children to turn to a specific test of memory to confirm the impression gained from the intelligence test.

Another type of deficit pattern might be exhibited by child E. The analysis of the test performance might indicate significant difficulty on all items involving language. The problem could range from that of having difficulty in naming pictures to being unable to communicate information and comprehension verbally in a meaningful way. In such a case it would be necessary to administer a nonverbal test of intelligence in order to obtain a valid picture of the child's intellectual abilities.

In the case of child F a basic reading deficit might be revealed and reading retardation would be suspected. Three major diagnostic groups of children exhibiting reading retardation have been identified. One group consists of those children in whom the capacity to read is impaired by frank brain dysfunctioning manifested by clear-cut neurologic deficits. The second group consists of those children in whom the capacity to read is impaired with no definite brain dysfunctioning being suggested either in the medical history or on the neurologic examination. The defect lies in the inability to deal with letters and words as symbols, with decreased ability to integrate the meaningfulness of written material. The reading problem appears to reflect a basic disturbed pattern of neurologic organization. Because the cause is endogenous, these children are diagnosed as exhibiting *primary reading retardation*. These children also exhibit language and conceptual difficulties and in this sense are like child C and child E. The third group consists of children whose capacity to learn to read is intact but is utilized insufficiently for the child to achieve a reading level appropriate to his basic intellectual ability. The causative factor is exogenous, as represented by interpersonal difficulties like those of child G or limited opportunities for schooling. The children who exhibit the deficit patterns described are often diagnosed as exhibiting minimal brain dysfunction or learning disability. However, these diagnostic terms are used interchangeably to describe a child who is not grossly impaired but does exhibit cognitive and behavioral deviations. While an underlying central nervous system dysfunction is implied, in most cases it cannot be proven. Unfortunately, it is the author's opinion that these diagnoses are made too often without a careful evaluation of the child's total home and school adjustment.

In the case of child G an analysis of the test performance might reveal no single area of consistent difficulty but marked inconsistency. This would be the situation in which relatively easy items are failed and relatively difficult items are passed. Attention difficulties might be characteristic of the child's behavior. The intrusion of personalized material might characterize the test responses. This pattern we characterize by the term "variability." In general, it is observed in children with various degrees of interpersonal difficulties and resultant emotional disturbance.

Finally, in the case of child H an analysis of the test performance might suggest a pattern of emerging abilities. On all intelligence tests the child is required to pass a specified number of subparts of an item in order to get credit for it, to perform the item correctly within a specific time limit or to respond in such a way that the answer is similar to the ones given by the standardization population. However, sometimes a child passes fewer of the subparts on items than expected, gives the correct answers beyond the time limit or answers so that the response is not quite comparable to the expected one. In each instance it is apparent that the child exhibits some basic comprehension of the items, and it might be expected that the qualitative understanding would approach the qualitative criteria in the course of subsequent development. This is the typical pattern exhibited by the average normal child.

While tests[45, 46] have been devised to measure a specific deficit in perceptual motor integration, no adequate measure of abstracting ability in children has been forthcoming. However, the author would propose the Leiter International Performance Scale as such a test. In studies of children with hydrocephalus with and without meningocele,[47] postencephalitis syndrome, posttraumatic head injuries and poorly controlled convulsive disorders,[48] the Leiter score has been found to be consistently significantly below the score on the Stanford-Binet[49] and the Weschler Intelligence Scale for Children. However, a deficit in abstract reasoning is suggested by both of the last-mentioned tests. In contrast, children diagnosed as hebephrenic, prepsychotic or neurotic tend to do significantly better on the Leiter test. At least part of the difference seems to be due to the fact that the Leiter test involves no verbal directions by the examiner and no verbal responses by the child. Furthermore, the items minimize interpersonal material. Thus, the child whose disturbance is based upon interpersonal experiences is better able to demonstrate his ability on this test, which places a minimum emphasis on the interpersonal factor.

The foregoing qualitative analysis of the test performances of eight children with an IQ of 92 points up the "kind" of intelligence the children possess. An understanding of the qualitative differences between children with the same score is a prerequisite for counseling parents and helping educators to provide the best possible educational setting for the child.

Psychoanalytic Theories of Personality Development

There are a number of reasons for considering the theories of personality development as advanced by psychoanalysts. Although they have not been universally accepted, these concepts have become very useful tools in terms of reference and in approach to therapy. Criticisms of the theories have emphasized that they are narrowly bound from a cultural standpoint and that they are based on suppositions that cannot be proved. A further weakness is that the theories are direct statements about, or personifications of, attributes of personality rather than an explanation of *raison d'être*. However, nowhere else in the psychologic literature does there appear a complete set of hypotheses on how personality is formed.

One of the basic principles of living organisms is the constant adjustment to environmental changes, with achievement of a satisfactory state of existence. As a result of these adjustments, conflicts may develop between the outside forces and inner forces, or instincts. Instincts are somatically based urges arising in the body and seeking gratification. (The term *instinct* as used by Freud[34] refers to such things as hunger and erotic urges and does not, as often in biology, indicate a stereotyped behavior.) Much of personality development arises through such conflicts and the resolution of them.

The structure of personality consists of three parts. At the time of birth personality is made up primarily of the *id*. The id is the reservoir of the instincts, or their mental representative. The newborn infant has only the barest nucleus of an *ego*.[31] From this nucleus the ego grows and expands and gains ever greater mastery over the id. The ego is the seat of consciousness and serves as the mediator between the inner instinctual desires and the outer world. It is that part of the personality we refer to as "I" or "me." Furthermore, it is the receiving center for the five special senses. It controls voluntary movements and is concerned with memory and judgment. One of the major functions of the ego is the formation of the mechanisms of defense.[30, 31] These mechanisms are the means by which the ego wards off unconscious and unwelcome instinctual impulses. As the development of the personality is described, we will note these mechanisms of defense in relation to the stage of development at which they appear and their changes with age.

According to Freud, a large area of mental functioning always remains beneath conscious awareness. Between the ego and the id are formed the boundaries of the conscious and unconscious. The division between these two in the infant is very indistinct, but as growth progresses and the ego grows, the division becomes ever more clear. The outer world has little influence on the unconscious, and time and logic do not affect it. These are important aspects, as they account for the apparent emergence of long-repressed and illogical memories in their original strength.

The third division of the personality is the *superego*, which acts as a censor concerning the acceptability of thoughts, feelings and behavior. This portion of the personality develops last, with the child's parents serving as an external superego in the early years. The permanent structure of the superego does not begin to form until after age 3 or 4 years and then becomes increasingly important as the judge over actions, thoughts and feelings. Clear separation of ego and superego is not always possible. However, only a portion of the latter is conscious. The superego is built up of all types of experiences and exposures—teaching, reading, etc.—and is responsible for that very uncomfortable feeling of guilt.

One common misunderstanding should be avoided before progressing further. The term *sexual* indicates anything pleasurable and includes "love" in a limitless sense or any positive creative force. The infant who enjoys sucking his thumb is experiencing sexual pleasure in the psychoanalytic sense.

Children are said to pass through five stages of psychosexual development, but it is emphasized that each phase blends into the next without clear separation.[31] Also, children vary in regard to the relative prominence of each stage and in the way a particular one is manifested. The *oral phase* covers the first year of life and is so termed because the mouth is the primary erotic (pleasure) zone. The infant associates the pleasure of hunger satisfaction with oral stimulation, and he soon learns to stimulate his mouth for pleasure even though no nutrition is accomplished, as in thumbsucking. Less often in the oral phase physical stimulation of other anatomic parts, e.g., ear or nose, may replace or accompany oral stimulation. During the first six months the infant is relatively parasitic in his adjustments and emotionally is very dependent. In the second half of the first year, especially with the eruption of teeth and increasing muscular control, there begins a more aggressive approach to his environment. To some extent adults perpetuate this oral phase, the best example being smoking. The psychoanalysts refer to this as "oral dependency."

Previously we stated that the establishment of defense mechanisms of different kinds is characteristic of the maturation of the personality. *Projection* is one of the earliest and most primitive of defense mechanisms. The infant's immature ego conceives of everything pleasurable belonging to him and that which is unpleasant being outside of him. In the older child this same mechanism is often seen but is more clearly understood because it is given verbal reference. As an example, the boy working with a piece of wood has such difficulty that he makes an error and calls the wood "stupid" or "no good." He is projecting his feeling of inadequacy in order to feel more comfortable.

The *anal phase* follows the oral phase and remains through the next two to three years. The child now becomes ambulatory. His interests widen, his pleasures are not so closely associated with oral stimulation and the primary erotic zone changes to the anal region. The functions of elimination take on new importance. Pleasure is found not only in defecation but in the retention of feces, and this leads to some of the difficulties experienced in toilet training.

There is a diminishing dependency on parents, and obstinacy becomes quite apparent. The 2-year-old is extremely selfish. He manifests a certain amount of sadism, which arises from two sources.[34] The first is the feeling of mastery or superiority engendered by cruelty to dolls, animals or even playmates. Freud feels that this is justly suspected of emanating from the erogenous zones and must be considered as a kind of sexual activity. (Once again it should be pointed out that Freud's use of the term "sexual" is related to any feeling of pleasure or satisfaction.) Secondly, the sadism arises from curiosity and the resultant investigative activity which becomes so evident at this time.

Identification is one of the mechanisms of defense which assumes prominence at this phase of personality development. It refers to the assumption of the qualities of someone else. The toddler, for example, recognizing the power of the adult, attaches himself to the adult, but in such a way that the latter is the all-powerful person and the child is only a dependent. A child may also act out an unpleasant experience in reverse, using a doll, sibling or smaller playmate as the focus of his aggression. An example would be the girl who assumes the role of the mother who recently punished her and in turn punishes her doll. This is an attempt to relieve the emotion of the original traumatic situation. In later childhood the boy or girl identifies with the parent of the same sex and attempts to copy him or her.

A common occurrence during the anal phase is a relapse in behavior to a more infantile manner. Confronted by a new baby in the home and the threat this makes to his security, the child reverts to enuresis, encopresis, demands for bottle feeding and "baby talk." Such a defense mechanism is termed *regression* and can occur when any anxiety-producing situation arises, such as moving to a new neighborhood, starting school or the birth of a sibling.

In the third phase the primary erotic zone shifts to the genital area, and it will remain there. This period, covering from approximately 3 or 4 to 6 years of age, is termed the *phallic*, or *genital, phase*. The child begins to attribute greater importance to the anatomic difference between the sexes. The beginning inquisitiveness, described in the preceding anal phase, continues, and especially turns to the genitalia. This may be combined with some exhibitionism, as though the child hopes that this will lead to a sharing of exposure and therefore of knowledge. During this time the Oedipus complex develops, and genital masturbation increases over that previously apparent.

The *Oedipus complex* is the feeling in the child of possessiveness toward the parent of the opposite sex and rivalry toward the parent of the same sex. The boy observes that his father has many privileges with his mother from which he is excluded. He is envious of his father, not only because of these liberties but because the father has a larger penis. The boy develops some anxiety about his own genitalia in this relationship. He fears any paternal retaliation may involve this most prized anatomic part. This anxiety has apparent foundation, by his own reasoning, in the fact that some people do not have such parts, namely girls. This fear is termed the *castration complex* and, according to the psychoanalytic school, is manifested not only in relation to the genitalia but also in the child's preoccupation with any bodily injury that is so evident during these years. The boy finally resolves the Oedipus dilemma by renouncing his erotic feelings toward his mother and identifying himself with his father. He will be like his father and marry someone like his mother.

The young girl at this time feels that she has been cheated and is inferior to boys because she has no penis. The girl assumes castration has taken place and holds her mother responsible. This resentment causes her to turn favorably toward her father, first in the hope that he will give her a penis and later that he will give her a baby. The girl's Oedipus complex does not come to such a sharp end point as the boy's, for the resolution of the penis envy is more difficult than the resolution of the castration complex. The normal girl goes through a considerable period of being a "tomboy" and is said to completely accept her femininity only when her first child is born.[31, 34]

In addition to the defense mechanisms previously described, *reaction formation* is especially characteristic of this age. This is the development of behavior which is the opposite of that dictated by the unconscious impulses. The perfectionistic child is often used as an example. His unconscious anality includes impulses toward messiness, sadism and selfishness, but on the surface his character appears to be the opposite, and he is overly clean and thoughtful.

Repression is another mechanism of defense first apparent at this age, but it is common to all phases that follow. Repression is purposeful, unconscious forgetting. It involves the consigning of ideas and emotions to the unconscious and, according to Freud, the use of energy to keep this material out of consciousness. The relatively complete inability to recall memories from early childhood, especially the Oedipus years and before, is due to repression. This concept forms a major part of the whole psychoanalytic movement.

The next phase is called *latency* because the previous libidinal and aggressive drives become latent. Anna Freud[33] describes this period as one of a truce in the battle between the id and the ego; and puberty sees the end of that truce once again. At the beginning of the latency phase the superego becomes more firmly internalized. Children's intellectual thinking at this time is apt to be concrete, useful, earthbound and rather closely associated with the everyday events of their lives. Normally, social adjustment is more homosexual than heterosexual. Increasing accumulation of knowledge increases the child's independence from his parents and broadens his outlook.

He can compete and lose more gracefully than before. In general, he accepts his parents and their authority with little question.

By the time of the latency phase the mechanisms of defense used by each individual are well developed and characteristic. Some of these, for any one individual, may have been used but later discarded as inadequate. Two mechanisms that have not been previously considered require our attention. *Rationalization* is the mechanism closest to the conscious level and is used by everyone to some degree. This is the endeavor to provide an acceptable reason for doing something that is motivated by an unacceptable reason. Fear of failure, for example, in carrying out some project will make a child refuse to do it, but he cannot admit this as the reason for his refusal. Instead, he excuses himself on the basis of having to do something else more urgent or important. The avoidance of many uncomfortable situations is rationalized, but if carried to an extreme degree, rationalization can have a very stultifying effect.

Probably the most satisfactory mechanism of defense is *sublimation*, because it allows the discharge of instinctual impulses in an acceptable form. Sublimation primarily involves those drives observed prior to the genital phase: childish curiosity, sadism, exhibitionism, destructive curiosity, etc. The exhibitionist becomes an actor and the sadist a butcher. The adolescent sublimates his sexual drives in athletic pursuits. All other mechanisms of defense either distort reality or are considered to be energy-wasting.

Adolescence is the last phase in personality development to be discussed. It has been described as the time when infantile sexual drives assume their final shape. The subordination of other erotogenic zones to the genital area, the establishment of new sexual aims differing in boys and girls and the finding of new love objects outside the home have been considered the main events of this period. Temporarily the ego is inadequate to meet the demands of defense in the reopening of its battle with the id. The physiologic changes occurring at this time and all of the associated social and psychologic consequences are the causes of this reawakening of the struggle. The inadequacy of the ego reveals itself in many ways, but perhaps Anna Freud[33] has stated it as well as any when she points out that the atmosphere in which the adolescent lives is characterized by ". . . anxieties, the height of elation or depth of despair, quickly rising enthusiasm, the utter hopelessness, the burning—or at other times sterile—intellectual and philosophical preoccupations, the yearning for freedom, the sense of loneliness, the feeling of oppression by the parents, the impotent rages or active hates directed against the adult world, the erotic crushes, and the suicidal fantasies." The hectic intellectual activity is closely related to the defense mechanism of intellectualization (similar to rationalization), which is an attempt to master the danger of instinctual drives by means of thought. These thoughts may be abstract, useless and at variance with actual behavior, in great contrast to the concreteness of the latency phase. The adolescent may cover up and minimize his anxieties in the sexual sphere by concentrating on problems that are often beyond him in the area of social issues. This is the time of utopias and remaking the world.

Devaluation of parents accompanies the detachment from them. Friendships, often homosexual in the early part of this phase but becoming more heterosexual later, are a striking phenomenon of adolescence and an aspect of the struggle to attain a firm sense of self. The ideals of the leader of the group are accepted wholeheartedly and without criticism. All of these characteristics often lead to conflicts with parents or other adults, adding further to the child's anxieties.

Even the best-informed girl will experience menstruation to some degree as trauma to her body. Some feelings formerly attached to the shame and disgust of elimination may reappear at menarche. Disappointment occurs also when she realizes that she is not going to be accepted as an adult equal despite the onset of this long anticipated physiologic change. Hypochondriacal tendencies are not unusual and are more common in girls than boys.

Masturbation is practiced by most adolescents, but to a greater degree by boys, as a release of sexual tensions. The boy, being more aggressive, may be able to sublimate these tensions in sports or social activities. The dominance of passivity in the feminine personality favors the development and utilization of fantasy in the release of sexual tensions. The earliest love objects of the girl seem by necessity to be unattainable, e.g., a movie star, and are frequently changed, which in itself is a disturbing thing and plagues her with feelings of self-doubt and guilt.

Occasionally the sexual drives are strongly repressed with asceticism. Such boys or girls renounce all interest in sex and often in social intercourse as well. In the extreme they become cold and analytical and develop a contemptuous attitude toward their peers and most adults. Only in a pathologic condition does this persist into adult life.

Although the turmoil of adolescence is inevitable, according to the psychoanalytic theory, resolution of the conflicts takes place with continuing maturity. The censorship of the superego becomes one that is acceptable to the individual and to the society in which he lives. The feud between id and ego never ends but becomes less tumultuous through the use of defense mechanisms, most of which can be guided into useful channels.

Piaget's Theories of Personality Development

Piaget[52, 53] has introduced some concepts of personality development that differ in many points from those of Freud. The self and personality have different stages or levels of development. In infancy and early childhood the individual is entirely egocentric and self-centered, but this changes with age so that he can share another's point of view. The true or final personality is not formed until his thoughts are integrated and his feelings about himself take into account his total life perspective, including all of his environment. Only a brief survey of some of the more important ideas offered by Piaget will be presented. Along with his concepts of cognitive development, outlined above, these theories are considered by many to be the most significant since those of Freud.

In essence, the mental development of the child passes through four stages. No external or internal act is executed except as a reaction to motive or a need (an elementary need, an interest, a question, etc.). Human action consists of a continuous readjustment or equilibration. The infant is entirely egocentric. All of his sensorimotor activity is self-related, and there is no conceptualization that is beyond self. Dissociation of the external environment from self is not present. As he begins to grasp and manipulate and develop language, his potentiality for entering the next stage begins.

With the appearance of language the possibility of socialization enters the behavior pattern. More importantly, the development of internalization of words or thought begins. Piaget emphasizes that thought and language are different in their origins, but if symbolism is included as a kind of language, it is this development which marks the next stage and profoundly modifies behavior effectively and intellectually. This stage lasts from approximately ages 2 to 7 years. Egocentricity prevails. When speaking, the conversation is rudimentary and is almost as though the child were speaking to himself. The child still cannot project himself into the thoughts of another. His environment, the world, was made for him, and things are often conceived of as living and having intent.

The first moral precept of the child is obedience. Parents are loved and considered always correct. In play with others the "rules" are inviolate, though they may be poorly understood. "Truth" is a "must," but if lies must be told, the child will accept punishment. All of his moral values are those of adults, especially his parents.

The next stage, from 7 to 12, sees the child capable of cooperation because he distinguishes his own point of view from that of another. True discussion is now possible. He searches for logical explanations and justifications, and the animism of early childhood disappears. He can now completely dissociate himself from another person, and his language reflects this. "The child of seven or eight thinks before acting and thus begins to conquer the difficult process of reflection."[52]

These changes lead to important moral concepts that characterize this period. As a function of cooperation among children the feeling of mutual respect arises. Honesty and obeying the "rules" is now based on agreement and esteem among peers. The relationship with parents also changes as the child differentiates between submission and justice.

The adolescent stage is characterized in Piaget's conceptions by still further maturation of thought processes that are only modified to a degree by the physiologic changes of this period, including sexual changes. In this Piaget differs considerably from Freud. What is particularly striking is the development of the elaboration of abstract theories. This is a continuation of the relatively concrete thinking of middle childhood, which now progresses to reflection no longer attached to external reality. Thinking becomes both hypothetic and deductive. Perception of problems involving spatial relationships, size and quantitation is possible on a level not previously attainable.

Personality achieves its final form in adolescence. It begins, according to Piaget, in late childhood with the autonomous organization of rules and values. Personality is said to exist as soon as a "life plan," which is both a source of discipline for the will and an instrument of cooperation, is formed. This presupposes the intervention of thought and reflection and therefore is not possible before the stage of adolescence. The adolescent sees himself as equal to his elders but different. He desires to correct society's errors and is filled with generous and altruistic projects. His megalomania leads to visions of great accomplishments on his part. The adolescent therefore contacts adult society by means of ideas of social reform, theoretical systems and "life plans." Social interaction of younger children occurs largely through the team game, while for the adolescent it is more often through discussion. True adaptation to society results when the adolescent reformer attempts to put his ideas to practical use.

The conception that abstract operational thought of older children and adults has its beginnings in the earliest sensorimotor reactions of the infant has led some psychologists to use Piaget's observations to support their view that there are *critical* or *sensitive* periods in human cognitive development. Mental development is construed as the creation of an ever-growing and necessarily more complex copy of the external world through the addition of more and more information. In this view, each of the stages of development must be attained (learned?) at a critical period or time. If this opportunity is missed, the child may fail to realize his full intellectual potential. Further support was implied from the "imprinting" phenomenon observed in some lower animals in which a single opportunity must be experienced during a narrow time span. If this does not happen, the "learning" (imprinting) either never occurs or is poorly established. The importance of these concepts as related to child development is especially pertinent in considering the neglected or underprivileged. Are learning disabilities and intellectual retardation due to missed learning opportunities?

Piaget never stated that there were "critical periods," though he implied the sequence of developmental stages was important. Available evidence does not support the view that there are such critical periods during which children must be exposed to a given learning procedure or forever after suffer some intellectual deficit.[60]

Language Development

Speech is a function that is unique to man and sets him apart from the lower animal forms. The attainment of speech is one of the most important achievements of childhood. The coming of language occurs at approximately the same age in every healthy child throughout the world, strongly supporting the concept that genetically determined processes of maturation rather than environmental factors are the foundation for speech and verbal comprehension.[21] Early aspects of language development are now considered as a biologic phenomenon similar to the development of walking and other predominantly innate varieties of neuromotor coordination. There are morphologic studies to support this concept. The phenomenon of cerebral dominance occurs in no mammal other than man. The dominance of the left side of the brain for speech (Broca's area) is a most striking example. There is a definite anatomic asymmetry between the temporal speech region on the left and the corresponding region of the right hemisphere.[62]

In the newborn infant evoked auditory responses, as measured by the EEG, are most marked to frequencies found in the human voice. The voice thus qualifies as a potent stimulus with resulting favorable influence in the formation of human bonds of affection.[23] Speech and behavior between mother and child, as long as 2 years later, are modified by the degree of intimacy permitted in the immediate postnatal period.[20] An analysis of mother-infant communication patterns at 12 weeks indicated they were predictive of later language competence.[86]

It is important to consider the functions of speech and its relationship to the total development of the child.[25, 54] The functions can be divided into two categories, which are interrelated and not mutually exclusive: personal and social. The personal functions of speech include emotional expression, self-communication (note Piaget's reference to this earlier in the chapter), dramatic expression and vocal play. Primitive forms of speech are evident in the early vocalizations of infants. They coo and gurgle by the sixth week. Syllablelike babbling begins to replace cooing by the fifth to sixth month. These sounds are apparently made for sheer enjoyment and have little communicative value. The cries of displeasure or pain are obvious, as are the sounds of pleasure and contentment. With increasing age the verbalization of emotion serves to neutralize some of the intense feelings and permits symbolization so that social living becomes possible. In the absence of language man would command a very meager catalog (recall and classification) of experiences for subsequent reference and comparison. Children learn language in the first 2 years for coding what they know of the world of objects, events and relations. They apparently know a great deal more than they are able to talk about.[5]

The social functions of speech are more evident, but not necessarily more important, than the personal ones. These include communication with others on a purely social level, the exchange of ideas or information and the modifying influences of language on behavior and attitudes of others. It is impossible to think of any culture or civilization without language.

Verbal communication requires the coordination of neuromotor and neurosensory systems with higher centers involving perceptual and conceptual abilities as well as appropriate social and emotional responses. Within 2–3 years a high degree of specificity has been attained which is largely automatic. By the time the average child has completed his 5th year, the basic elements of verbal behavior have become established.[21, 63] Syntax, semantics and phonology are important parts of language that are continuing to improve throughout the school years. During this time the child increases his ability to use the linguistic code, both to speak and understand messages, independently of the states or conditions or circumstances in which speech occurs.[5]

An interesting observation related to these facts is the learning of a foreign language. At age 3 or 4 practically every child entering a foreign community learns to speak the new language rapidly and without accent. This facility declines slowly with age until the early teens when nearly every child loses the ability to speak a new language without an accent and does not learn as rapidly as when younger.[21] Aphasia due to damage to Broca's area in a child can usually be reversed without residual evidence of speech problems. Such a lesion occurring after puberty results in incomplete recovery.

Early levels of development are fairly easily differentiated. Localization of sound stimuli is present in the first few weeks of life, and differentiation of sounds is demonstrated by the second or third month. Vocalization of pleasure-related sounds is apparent by the second or third month in association with vegetative activities. At this level there is a response to appropriate stimuli which is almost at a reflex level.

The ability to integrate sensory stimuli into patterns occurs by age 4 or 5 months. This is manifested by increases in variety and quality of emitted sounds, including babbling and echolalia. Some rudimentary imitation of sounds occurs from the third to tenth month. The development of memory for auditory stimuli is demonstrated by the child's imitation of bisyllabic and trisyllabic sounds near the end of the first year. Between 12 and 18 months the child responds to auditory stimuli as symbols, and he learns to make sound patterns as symbols. He comprehends and creates language. At first the symbolization is attached to easily identifiable objects or actions, while less concrete objects and activities (articles, prepositions, etc.) are learned by repeated exposures and associations. Among the highly complex mechanics of speech is the automatic control of respiration necessary to accomplish it. While talking one inhales slightly faster but exhales much more slowly, resulting in a greatly reduced respiratory rate. The appropriate positioning of lips, tongue, and teeth is further evidence of the intricate neuromuscular coordination necessary for normal language behavior.

Nearly all observers agree that comprehension of spoken language precedes its use by a considerable span of time. There is probably comprehension of gestures and actions before that of language. Nevertheless, there is certainly definite response to the human voice by the second or third month. Truly differential response to different words is present in the normal 9- and 10-month infant. At this time also one notes imitation of syllables and words. Adequate response to simple commands may appear at this time. McCarthy[22] states that symbolic gesture is used long before language proper, but that these overt movements may be accompanied by vocalizations. In the usual process of maturation the child's use of gesture gradually recedes, and its place is taken by real language. Language retardation in some cases is quite correctly attributed to the fact that the child may develop an elaborate system of gesture language (sometimes associated with a "sound language all his own") which is so well understood by parents and siblings that his wants are well satisfied. This tends to occur a little more frequently in families with several children. As a matter of fact, studies indicate that only children are often considerably more advanced in their language development than are children with siblings at home.

The first words are usually made up of monosyllables or reduplicated monosyllables such as *dada, mama* and *bye-bye*. They often are strongly affective, expressing wishes, needs and feelings. There are marked individual variations in the sizes of vocabularies at any age. Very cautiously we offer a vocabulary development table (Table 6–2), recognizing the limitations and vagaries in its interpretation, but still feeling that it has usefulness in evaluating this phase of development.

Articulation of speech develops slowly at first. So-called baby talk is used by most children during the early years. At 2 years of age about one third of the number of sounds are given correctly, at 4 years, about 75% and by 6 years, 89%. The observation of the length (number of words) of sentences has some value as a measure of speech maturation. In general a child of 18 months is at the one-word sentence stage. By 2^1/$_2$ years an average sentence contains three words, and in another year four words. By 6^1/$_2$ years the mean

TABLE 6–2.—VOCABULARY
DEVELOPMENT OF CHILDREN
TO AGE 6

AGE		NUMBER OF WORDS
YR	MO	
1	0	3
1	3	19
1	6	22
2	0	272
2	6	446
3	0	896
3	6	1222
4	0	1540
5	0	2072
6	0	2562

length of sentences becomes five words and at 9½ years has increased to six or seven words. Grammatically complete sentences are usual by 4 or 5 years, but seldom before this age.[17] (Table 6–3).

By 2 years all vowel sounds are used and many of the consonants including *b, p, k, g, w, m, h, n, t* and *d.* The final consonant in a word is often omitted. By 4 years the consonant sounds *b, t, d, k* and *g* are mastered but combinations such as *tr, pr, bl* and *gr* are apt to be faulty. Between 5 and 6 years the former combinations are pronounced well but some trouble with blending *thr, shr, sk, sh, ch, s* and *z* may persist until 7 to 8 years.

By the age of 4 recognition of plurals, sex differences and pronouns is comprehended. A year later the child uses plurals and pronouns in his everyday speech as well as many adjectives and some adverbs, conjunctions and prepositions. He correctly uses "I" instead of "me" or his name, i.e., "I want a cookie" instead of "me want a cookie."

Stuttering, a repetition of syllables and words, is normal in young children. The commonest form is that in which the whole word is involved, e.g., "Mother-mother may I go out-out." Ordinarily this occurs late in the second or early in the third year and may last from a few weeks to a year or two. Bloomer[25] points out that stuttering normally is seen when the child first puts words together in phrases or simple sentences and that this characteristic of speech has a tendency to disappear and reappear until the fifth year. Persistence into the sixth year can usually be considered outside the realm of normal. At first the child seldom is concerned with his stuttering, and at this early age it simply represents a lack of maturation of speech centers. Often it may indicate that thought processes are ahead of the child's vocabulary or ability to express himself clearly.

TABLE 6-3.—PATTERN OF NORMAL LANGUAGE DEVELOPMENT

AGE	VOCALIZATION AND SPEECH	RESPONSE AND COMPREHENSION
1 mo	Much crying and whimpering; produces some vowel and few consonant sounds.	Smiles; decreases activity; startles at loud sounds.
3 mo	Different cries for pain, hunger, and discomfort; decreased crying time; some repetitive sounds ("ga, ga, ga"); coos and sighs.	Vocal gurgle in response to soothing voice; some imitative response to speech.
5 mo	Babbles; vocal play; many repetitive sounds; all vowels, m, k, g, b and p; laughs out loud.	Imitative response to speech decreased; turns and looks to sound; recognizes familiar voice; vocalizes displeasure.
7 mo	Considerable variety in babbling, loudness and rhythm of all vocalizations; adds d, t, n and w to repertory of sounds; talks to toys.	Gestures increase as part of vocal responses to stimuli; response to sound is increasingly influenced by visual factors.
9 mo	Cries to get attention; increasing variations in pitch; "mama," "dada" and "baba" part of vocal play but not associated with a person or object.	Retreats from strangers, often accompanied by crying; may imitate hand clapping.
11 mo	May use one word correctly; imitates sounds and correct number of syllables; little crying.	Comprehends "no no"; responds to "bye-bye" or "patty-cake" with appropriate gestures.
1–2 yr	Much unintelligible jargon; all vowels present; improves articulation so that 25% of words intelligible; names many objects by 24 mo; much echolalia.	Recognizes 150–300 words by 24 mo; responds correctly to several commands, e.g., "sit down," "give me that," "stand up," "come here," etc.
2–3 yr	Tries new sounds but articulation lags behind vocabulary; 50–75% of words intelligible; often omits final consonants; jargon nearly absent.	Comprehends 800–1,000 words by 3 yr; responds to many commands using "on," "under," "up," etc.
3–4 yr	Speech nears 100% intelligiblity; faulty articulations of l and r frequent; uses 3–4 words in sentences; uses a few plurals by 4 yr.	Recognizes plurals, sex differences, adjectives and adverbs; comprehends complex sentences.
4–6 yr	Syntax correct by 6 yr; forms 5- or 6-word sentences that are compound or complex (with some dependent clauses); fluent; articulation good except for sh, z, ch and j; can express temporal relations; voice well modulated in conversation.	Understands 2,500–3,000 words; carries out commands involving 3–4 actions; comprehends "if," "because" and "why."

Some other characteristics of speech at different ages have been recorded by Metraux.[26] At 24 months speech is repetitive and is almost compulsive in quality. Screaming and squealing are common as a method of expression. At 3 years the inflection of the voice is unstable and poorly controlled, and gross motor movement often accompanies speech in situations where there is strong emotional feeling. The pronoun "I" is very prominent. By $3^{1}/_{2}$ years a high, full-volumed yell is often assumed as the normal speaking voice. Stuttering is common and probably reflects the general increase in rate or speed of talking in contrast to earlier months. By $4^{1}/_{2}$ years the voice is quite well modulated. Often a sentence is preceded with the sound "m" much as the adult uses "ah" when hesitating or searching for words. At this age the child also shows a real interest in words, repeating new ones and asking that they be repeated so he gets them right.

From the time the child enters school his reading skill will be the predominant factor determining his success or failure.[17] Unfortunately our knowledge concerning the development of reading skills is very meager. It is closely related to the development of speech and depends upon the maturation of perceptual and cognitive abilities. Many educators use the term "reading readiness" to indicate the stage or age level when reading skills begin to form. The chronologic age will vary significantly, but for most starts between 5 and 6 years and reaches considerable proficiency by age 8. Some very normal children can read by 4 years while a few do not develop the skill until 10 or 11. The reason for the wide variation is unknown. There is some relationship with intelligence. Seldom does a child with an IQ of 70 or below become an adequate reader. It is rare to find reading disabilities in children with superior intelligence.

The basic skill in reading is the transformation of visual symbols into auditory symbols, even though the process of speech is not involved. In the act of reading one thinks with words which have been learned through auditory channels. Many children with reading difficulties have had or do have some deviations from normal speech development. Severe articulatory problems are often associated with reading difficulties. Still, there are children whose oral language has developed in a normal pattern and who are unable to read at a satisfactory level.

The Child during the Early School Years

In the period from age 6 to about 11 years the child learns about the outside world and becomes increasingly independent of his parents. He develops a conscience or a sense of responsibility about matters that to him seem important. These are the years when closely knit groups are formed, such as clubs and gangs. During this period the child is introduced to the culture of his society through the public or private school. These are important years for learning how to get along with other people and to abide by the rules of society.

The child's independence of his parents is manifested by his gaining a feeling of individuality and by his desire to be treated as a person rather than as a possession. He is apt to show some impatience toward his parents, who keep telling him the right things to do. Although he loves them as much as ever, he dislikes emotional display about himself. Joining a club is simply another means of showing his ability to accomplish things independently of adults.

His sense of responsibility is manifested in competitive types of games or ones that require some skill. He becomes a small businessman by setting up a lemonade stand or by starting a garden. He may not carry many of these enterprises through to completion, but the urge to do them is present.

Toward the end of this period he thinks in terms of cause and effect and acquires an insight into the actions of machines and some of the fundamentals of human relationships. The desire to accomplish great things occupies his mind when he is not doing school- or homework. He dreams of bold adventures, and one of his favorite heroes may well be a character in a comic strip or story where right always wins. Besides the comics, books, radio, television and motion pictures furnish him with his ideals.

Because of his desire for independence he may be irritating to his parents and present a problem in discipline. The adult must try to overlook some of his less serious bad habits and, when giving orders, try to be matter-of-fact and friendly. Most obnoxious to the child is "bossiness" or a nagging voice, which one should strive to avoid. School problems are best taken up with the teacher or school authorities. Poor work in school may be due to many causes such as physical defects, poor eyesight or hearing and poor attention. The highly intelligent child may be bored with his schoolwork, while the child with a low intelligence cannot comprehend his studies. Finally, the school system may be at fault. One should carefully examine and eliminate any or all possible causes instead of punishing the child.

In the following paragraphs are given guides to expected behavior in children to each of the ages listed. It must be stressed that each child has an individual pattern of growth which is unique to him or her. The traits listed, therefore, are not to be taken too rigidly or as absolute models that all children will follow. They illustrate the behavior trends for each age. Such an outline may aid a physician or other interested person in judging very roughly the maturity level of a particular child. Under each age heading are two brief paragraphs. The first describes various factors of behavior such as play, eating, habits and relations to society. The second lists a few of the more readily tested accomplishments that can be used to appraise normality of development.

Five Years Old

Appetite is usually good, except perhaps for breakfast. The child is slow but persistent in eating and many other activities. He has considerable motor ability and skill. He is poised and controlled. He loves his home and persons and objects associated with it. The stage of the 4-year-old runaway is passed. The outstanding fear of the 5-year-old is loss of his mother. Fears of ghosts or bogeymen and unreal objects have greatly diminished in the past year. The child is serious about himself and concerned with his own ability. He wants to assume responsibilities. He usually gets along with adults very well, although shy at the initial meeting. His memory for past events is surprisingly accurate. Play is apt to follow domestic patterns in both sexes. Both like to "play house," and dolls are favorite objects. The child makes a good adjustment to school and enjoys the routine of planned programs.

He can name four or more colors, repeat a sentence of 10 or more syllables, tell which is the heavier of two weights or objects, reconstruct a rectangular card which has been cut diagonally into two pieces, draw a recognizable picture of a man with a body, head, etc., and can identify penny, nickel and dime.

Six Years Old

This is a period of physical and psychologic change. It is apt to be a difficult period for the parent who does not understand this transition. The child is restless and has difficulty in making decisions. Activity is almost constant. Appetite continues to be good. A characteristic in eating and nearly all other activity is that he is good at starting things but poor at finishing them. Accidents—spilling of milk, stuffing the mouth too full of food, etc.—are common at the table. Enuresis is rare now. The growing vocabulary includes slang and swearing. "Emotional storms" such as temper tantrums reach a peak at this age and may be difficult to control. Rudeness is another common and difficult problem. Behavior patterns are often explosive and seemingly unpredictable. Jealousy toward siblings is the rule, and sibling play should be supervised. All play is more vigorous than in the 5-year-old, and imagination is a big factor. Several favorite radio or TV programs are followed religiously by many children. The majority like school and want to "learn." Parental love and praise are extremely important throughout this difficult period of growing up.

A vocabulary of about 2,500 words has been acquired. The child can define simple objects in terms of what they are used for, can count correctly to 20 or 30, knows right and left parts of body, knows number combinations making up to 10, draws a man with hitherto unadded features, e.g., neck, clothing, and hands, and differentiates A.M. and P.M.

Seven Years Old

Play is approached more cautiously than when the child was 6. In all respects he is less of a "problem child" than one year before. Although he has definite likes and dislikes, he is less vehement in expressing them: this is true of food, clothing, friends, play, and the like. The child needs only slight help in dressing and undressing and preparing for bed. Bowel and bladder training are complete, and little conversation is directed toward these functions. He or she is aware of and sensitive about sex and in front of the opposite sex avoids self-exposure. Seven becomes a cooperative member of the family group. Neatness and alacrity in dressing or carrying out parental commands are frequently wanting. He is not entirely self-contained, but he is very introspective and desires the approbation of his group and of his parents. One might call the seventh year a pensive one.

He can count by 2s and 5s and grasps the basic idea of addition and subtraction, can tell time, often knows what month it is, can copy a diamond accurately, repeats five numbers in series, e.g., 4, 7, 9, 3, 2, and repeats three of them backward.

Eight Years Old

The 8-year-old's movements increase in "smoothness" and "poise." These words in a large measure describe this age. Yet unsupervised play of a large group may become extremely rowdy, with reversion to "animal spirits." He dislikes being alone and wants his companions to take an interest in his activities, either actively or as interested observers. Segregation of the sexes for the first time becomes important in the choice of playmates and groups. He is becoming more resentful of parental authority. His best behavior is often away from home or when strangers are in the home. Television may occupy much of the child's spare time, but reading interests are expanding and are often related to special interests or hobbies. Eight enjoys school and dislikes staying at home. Individual differences are great, but in general this is an age of broadening experiences and exploration intellectually.

The 8-year-old knows the days of the week; he can count backward from 20 to 1; he can make correct change for small amounts of money; comprehension of time and place has begun; he appreciates the difference between a real or historic character versus a fictitious one in cinema and television; he can describe differences and similarities between two things from memory, e.g., bird and butterfly, dog and cat or wood and stone.

Nine Years Old

This is an intermediate age—between childhood and the beginnings of adolescence. The child has better control of himself, is seeking and acquiring new forms of independence. He has a growing capacity to complete tasks that he sets for himself or that are expected from him. Even short interruptions will not interfere, for he will return to his work or play. He looks to the future and plans ahead for work and play. He is mature enough to accept blame, and alibiing of the infantile type is less indulged in than formerly. He is essentially truthful and honest. Eating is much neater than formerly, and manners are usually well observed. Dressing is completed without aid. He obeys well and can assume many responsibilities. He will show disgust at both siblings and parents if they do not act as he feels they should. Hero-worship has become prominent. The 9-year-old is self-sufficient, self-critical, but not severely so, and he is anxious to please. The sexes remain well separated at parties and other social gatherings. It is usually not difficult to discipline him. His reading material is more realistic than before, although he may still enjoy comic books. His literary interests reflect his general character, a fluctuation between childhood and youth in his thoughts and actions.

He describes objects in detail and does not just tell what they are used for; he knows the day of the month and year, tells time well, arranges weights in the order of heaviness and can do simple multiplication and division.

Ten Years Old

A very fundamental change that occurs at this age is the beginning of differences in attitudes toward sexuality. The girl is usually more mature socially and more poised than the boy. Sexual maturation has often started in girls, seldom in boys. Both are beginning to think about social problems and are eager to discuss them. There is a strong tendency to categorize civic and school leaders as well as events as either "good" or "bad," though they are apt to select other words. The concept of individuality and singularity of self and of others is becoming well developed. Teamwork and willing submission to fixed rules in play is now possible. Formation of lasting friendships is evident and moving to a new and distant home is often quite traumatic.

Ten-year-olds can use numbers beyond 100 with understanding; they can use simple fractions; repeat 6 digits forward; know how many minutes are in a fraction of an hour and repeat a 20-syllable sentence.

Eleven Years Old

By this age the girls are falling behind boys somewhat in physical strength and endurance. Girls are apt to be taller than boys at this age and for the next two to three years, owing to the earlier adolescent growth spurt in the female. Membership in groups and clubs is increasing in importance. Children of this age group enjoy taking part in school and community "drives," e.g., paper collection, Red Cross collection, etc. Team games are very popular. If present, shyness may increase and be a difficult problem for some parents to understand. The child is more critical of the products of his labors than ever before. There is an increasing urge for some financial independence from the parents, with the result that he or she will readily take on small jobs after school and during vacations.

He can define some abstract terms, e.g., "justice," "honesty" and "revenge"; he can point out the meaning or moral in fables and can explain the necessity of hygienic measures such as covering the mouth when coughing. It must be realized that by this age the variability of individual interests and the diversity of intellectual pursuits render standardization by simple tests very difficult and of questionable value for the average child.

The Adolescent Child

Since nearly every person who writes about adolescence has his own definition of the word, the reader is requested to refer to Chapter 9, section on adolescence and puberty, for this author's definition and the description of the physical and physiologic changes that occur at this time.

In the last two decades there has been a decided change in the psychologic and social pattern of adolescents in the United States, and to some extent, similar developments have taken place in other developed countries of the western hemisphere. There are many reasons for these changes. Some of the major issues can be briefly outlined.[87, 88]

The multigenerational and stable family unit is quickly disappearing, and an increasing number of children are living in single-parent homes.

There have been monumental changes in the school systems. The great increase in teenagers beginning in the 1950s placed considerable pressure on the secondary schools. This combined with the relatively long compulsory education period forced more and more children into a narrower and narrower age group with increasing isolation.

World and regional armed conflicts, social and racial inequalities, and dishonesty in government have led to disillusionment and then rejection of ideas and opinions from parents and other adults.

Improved means of communication, and especially television, have permitted a greater dissemination of information, both good and bad, giving a false sense of knowledge and sophistication.

Other factors which have played a lesser part are the failure of religion to assume any kind of leadership for youth, the atmosphere of permissiveness in rearing children that prevailed from 1940 to 1970 and the rapid technologic progress following World War II that seemed to promise solutions to many social, economic and educational problems.

The isolation and the disillusionment have led to an adolescent peer society as a semiautonomous social world, with its own set of values and activities. Peers are looked to as the model for dress, music, entertainment and life style. Peer group relationship is prized over all other associations. Increasing numbers of youngsters, as of 1975–77, continue to leave the mainstream of life, at least temporarily.

It is impossible to say how many teenagers represent the extreme of the mood described above. Both the numbers and the degree of withdrawal depend upon attitudes in the family and in the community. Most individuals manage to pass through adolescence without overt problems, but it is a time of stress.

All adolescents at some time, and in various ways, resolve their own identity crises in order to enter and adjust to the adult world.[15, 30] It is important to understand that "adjust" does not imply acquiescence. Even the most conforming of children seek a measure of independence from parents, which they feel is a necessary step toward the attainment of adulthood.

The process of sexual maturation not only involves structural and physiologic changes but brings with it a series of perplexing and sometimes highly disturbing emotional and social problems. Personal appearance of the individual becomes in many children a source of great conflict. There is apt to be a greater emphasis on "good looks" and on a "normal" physique and anatomy than at any other period in life. Perhaps unfortunately, society in general has so impressed the child with normality that he becomes overanxious about his own body and its functions and yet is most reticent to converse about it.

The end of childhood is recognized by many different rituals or physiologic changes as well as by legal and chronologic indices. In primitive societies it is prescribed on the basis of age by an elaborate ceremonial event. In some religious organizations, it is determined by dogma of the church e.g., bar mitzvah. Menarche is often used as a point determining pre- and postpuberty even though conception may not be possible for another one or two years. Social indications of the end of childhood may be the act of sexual intercourse. Relative to this is the fact that in the United States one fifth of all pregnancies occur in women under 19 years of age, approximately one half of these in adolescents 17 years or younger. More than 66% of these pregnancies are conceived out of wedlock. An opinion held by many adolescents is that improved methods of contraception and treatment for venereal diseases have removed many of the hazards of acting out sexual impulses.

The adolescent is easily hurt when criticized. He feels that he is "grown up," but lacks the experience and knowledge of the adult. He will fluctuate between resentment of parental advice and his desire to fall back on his family when he has some problem. He may develop rather romantic ideas about people or become somewhat obsessed with certain ideals. The adolescent girl is apt to have "crushes" on her teachers. There may be certain social difficulties in the schoolroom owing to the fact that at this time the girls usually are two or three years ahead of the boys in stature and emotional development.

Many of the individual difficulties which appear at this age are the result of conflict between the child and other members of society. Pressure is put on him to assume various adult responsibilities, and his own desires about his future form still another, and perhaps more important, "inner" pressure. The outer pressure may come from parents, friends or society in general. Limitations to the accomplishments of the individual are the results of these two pressures plus his socioeconomic status, his level of intelligence and what he is able to achieve throughout this period. It is this relationship between his own aims in life, the aims that others force upon him, his current or past performances and his sense of satisfaction or frustration pertaining to these performances that will greatly influence his emotional development. The tendency of the adolescent, continually faced with failure owing to the conventions of society or parental misunderstanding, is to react with aggressive rebellion. This leads to further difficulties, and a vicious circle results. Maladjustments are much greater among boys and girls who do not have close, harmonious relationships with their parents and among those whose parents are in discord with each other.

For the normally developing adolescent, acceptance by the social group in which he lives is a very dominant and personal drive. When he is deprived of this acceptance and has not found some measure of success in his group, he often withdraws into himself. Such a child needs help in improving social techniques, or perhaps it would be best to transfer him to a more congenial or otherwise more suitable group. The method of "buying" him into the social group by furnishing him with the biggest and best bicycles, automobiles, etc., a method sometimes used by parents, usually ends in failure for the child. If the boy or girl, with the aid of understanding parents, can objectively see his own successes and failures throughout childhood, he or she can nearly always take minor failures in stride in the more sensitive period of adolescence. Children should be taught to make a sensible evaluation of their liabilities and assets progressively throughout childhood. They should also be acquainted with the fact that there are both "good" and "bad" in the world, that there are privilege and underprivilege, honesty and dishonesty, charity and wicked selfishness. A realistic philosophy of life is needed, but also one that furnishes them with a motivation to accomplish the best of which they are capable.

Erikson[15] points out that the prime problem and potential danger of adolescence is identity confusion which can express itself in an excessively long moratorium or in an impulsive attempt to end that moratorium. Erikson sees the identity crisis as a normative stage in the human life cycle. The end of childhood is characterized by marked physical growth, genital maturation and increased social awareness. Youth is faced with the decision of choices to follow in his or her sexual, social and occupational roles as an adult. Some adolescents will not make a decision for themselves and become members of activist groups in religion, enter radical politics or become anarchists or drifters and "drop outs." The appeal of totalitarianisms is another solution in which decisions are made for one.

Early acting out of sexual activities may be an attempt to prove identity in a search for self, but often becomes "genital combat" void of any intimacy. Erikson contends that honest intimacy is possible only when identity is well established in terms of both friendship and love in sexual relationship. The adolescent is perplexed with the physiologic and genital maturation that indicate adulthood and the uncertainty of the part he will play in the adult roles ahead. "It is the inability to settle on an occupational identity which most disturbs young people."[15]

Sex is not a problem limited to the adolescent period, yet it is often felt to be of prime importance at this time. The sexual education of the child has proceeded some considerable degree before adolescence is reached, whether or not this is accomplished by the parents. The first questions, particularly when a new baby arrives, are most likely to come at about 3 or 4 years. Until the preadolescent years it is probably wisest to give information only when it is sought. The answer should be straightforward and in terms simple enough for the child to understand. Detailed explanations are not needed, for the child requires only a simple statement and is not yet interested about details. If the parents feel incompetent to answer such questions because of emotional or idealistic conflict or because of inability to give a concise forthright answer, the physician should be consulted. Ideally, before adolescence is reached the child should be well oriented as to the anatomic and functional differences of the sexes. Such information may best be given as a part of the general instruction in anatomy and physiology, which naturally must be kept on an easily understood level. A clear conception should be given of ovulation, fertilization, pregnancy and birth. Menstruation should be explained before, not after, it occurs in the girl.

Nocturnal emission may better be explained to the boy as he approaches puberty. However, one must not overstimulate latent interests unduly, and good judgment concerning each individual must be used. For instance, in dealing with masturbation, no good is served unless anxiety is alleviated, but too permissive an attitude tends to break down the normal defense against such activity.

The traditional idea that marriage must be delayed until economic independence is obtained is one of the difficulties which modern society has placed in the path of the adolescent. Further, any sexual activity before marriage is socially and religiously forbidden in many groups. Early in the adolescent period each boy or girl often experiences a homosexual period of development. During this time romantic and emotional attachments are formed with a person of the same sex and usually of the same age. Hero worship of an older person may also occur. Overt sexual experiences among boys are not uncommon, and a smaller number of girls may have similar participation. When there is an adequate association with the opposite sex, the homosexual phase is rapidly passed through and the heterosexual phase is entered. It is unfortunate that at this time many questions arise regarding the sex role but adequate and good information is not readily available. Too often misinformation is supplied by peers and is accepted. Even though the phenomena of sexuality is more openly discussed by today's youth, sources of information, including many parents and physicians, are often inadequate or judgmental. Caution is necessary in order not to disgust or frighten these future parents by unwarranted lectures on the sins of sex and the horrors of venereal disease. Parents are frequently in need of education to an equal degree with their children. It has been repeatedly stressed that the background experienced by the child, as reflected in parents' attitudes and behavior, is an extremely important element in his or her sexual adjustment.

The most important obligation of the physician during this period of life is to realize the conflict that is going on in the child. As Thom[18] has so well stated, it is the physician who must attempt to help the child over this difficult hurdle. He must help the child grasp the idea that freedom carries with it obligations and responsibilities; he must in turn help parents to understand that the ultimate goal is to train their child to live happily and efficiently in a world that will grant no special concessions.

Parents must recognize and accept changing relationships between themselves and their children. This amounts to a steadily growing equality. In addition parents and educators must realize that social, economic, and moral values change with each new generation and that these are dynamic, not static. One psychologist points out that many of the rules for adolescents are set up by adults who have never satisfactorily established a set of rules for themselves. The adult must serve as an experienced guide who has the advantage of mature ability and greater information in most spheres, and there must at the same time be an equality of human dignity and personal integrity between the adult and the child.

In conclusion, a word of caution should be offered to the reader. It might appear from what has been said that the adolescent period is one of great storm and stress. Although this may be true in isolated cases, it should be emphasized that the majority of children go through this time of life with comparative ease and with few serious scars carried over into adult life. Overemphasis to parents or children as to the possible difficulties that may be encountered has frequently done more harm than good. A common-sense attitude must be taken and individual problems appropriately dealt with as they arise.[12, 18]

Sleep

Periods of sleep and wakefulness in the newborn infant are disorganized and alternate at brief intervals. By the fourth week a definite pattern emerges with sleep predominating at certain times in a 24-hour period. At this same time the intervals of both sleep and wakefulness lengthen. During the third month a constant periodicity begins to develop with the greatest amount of sleep occurring at night. A term baby will sleep from 15 to 18 hours a day with individual intervals lasting 3–5 hours and awake periods a maximum of 2 hours.[36]

Recent polygraphic studies have increased our knowledge of sleep and its related physiologic phenomena.[23, 37, 55-57, 59] Sleep can be divided into several stages but these fall into two generally recognized categories. *Active* sleep is characterized by rapid eye movements (REM), irregular heart rate and breathing, facial and body movements and inhibition of tendon and some other reflexes. Rapid awakening after a period of active sleep is associated with good dream recall in adults. Cerebral blood flow and brain temperature increase during active sleep. In both the premature as well as the term neonate, apnea is more commonly associated with active sleep. *Quiet* sleep has no rapid eye movements, no facial or body movements except an occasional startle; regular respiration and heart rate and normal muscular tonus is present.

With active sleep there is a low-voltage, fast-frequency pattern in the EEG, while during quiet sleep there is high voltage and a slow frequency. In Chapter 9 the relationship between sleep patterns and rate of secretion of the pituitary hormones is described, e.g., during quiet sleep there is an increased secretion of growth hormone. Drugs that alter the sleep pattern will also alter hormone production.

It has been hypothesized that active sleep is accompanied by increased protein synthesis in the brain. This is supported by the increased cerebral circulation and temperature. It may also help to explain why active sleep is relatively increased in early infancy.

From 50 to 60% of sleep in the newborn is of the active type. With increasing age the amount of quiet sleep increases and averages 80% in the young adult. This is accomplished by a reduction of the number of intervals of active sleep from 7 in children to 4 in adults per night, and some shortening of each interval.[8]

In preterm infants of less than 30 weeks gestation there are long periods in which it is not possible to identify which type of sleep is present from polygraph tracings. Active sleep is the first pattern to clearly emerge. Not until near the end of normal gestation does the fetus manifest quiet sleep. In certain pathologic states there is a retention of the immature pattern well into the neonatal period. Such patterns may be found in babies of diabetic mothers, small-for-date infants and following birth trauma.

At approximately 3 months after birth the infant EEG for the first time shows the presence of "sleep spindles" (low amplitude and increased frequency). In older children and adults these spindles are a constant finding during quiet sleep. Along with the decrease in the amount of active sleep there is a decrease in muscular activity during sleep, from 60% at birth to 25% by 6 months.

At age 1 and 2 years most of the required sleep can be obtained at night, but one or two daytime naps lasting from 1 to 3 hours are still necessary. The requirement of a nap may be waived for a few children as early as $3^1/2$ years, but more often it is not omitted until the child approaches 5 years. By the time nursery school age has been reached (4–5 years), the child may be napping only three to five times a week. The amount of sleep necessary then gradually declines so that the average is 9–10 hours at 12 years and 8–9 hours at 17 years. Any given child may vary in his requirements from day to day.

It is impossible to answer the question, "How long should my child sleep?" Perhaps the best plan, and certainly the one which reduces the number of so-called behavior problems related to it, is that of self-regulation. This takes into account the individual requirements and allows for normal maturation. To promote sound sleep it is always wise to avoid overstimulation before the child goes to bed. Nor should being put to bed be used as a form of punishment, as this immediately sets up a highly undesirable association which may last a long time. Dreams and nightmares or night terrors are not uncommon in mild form, beginning about the second or third year and often subsiding to a great extent by the fifth or sixth year. The child may be restless or even awaken crying due to such episodes. Unless they occur frequently and are persistent, such behavior need not be considered alarming. Awakening due to wetting of the bed is not uncommon during late infancy and early childhood. By 3 or 4 years the child usually sleeps through the night without having to get up to urinate. By 5 years and thereafter sleep through the night is usually deep, quiet and peaceful.

Polygraph studies have revealed that some of these sleep disturbances have a definite relation to various stages of sleep. Both nocturnal enuresis (except in the extremely rare instances of organic etiology) and night terrors, *pavor nocturnus*, are associated with emergent or arousal sleep stage transmissions from deep to light. This pattern often precedes entrance into a REM cycle. Often there is a family history of similar disturbances. Total amnesia of the episode is characteristic of both, and they tend to occur in the first few hours after falling asleep.

In contrast to the above, nightmares occur during REM sleep and there is usually total or partial recall of the events of the dream. They often follow some stressful situation during the day. Because the young child cannot easily distinguish between dreams and reality, he may be so frightened that he resists returning to sleep. Normally increasing ego development and distinction between fantasy and reality, as the child grows older, reduces the problem.[89]

At 18 months sleep may be resisted for some time after the child is put to bed. He often delays sleep by crying for his mother or, a little later, by demanding a drink of water and the like. Taking a favorite toy or some other object to bed with him is common from about 1½ through 3 or 4 years. Certainly no harm can arise from such a practice, and it often serves to quiet the child and better prepare him for sleep. Various methods are resorted to by the young child to resist sleep in addition to those enumerated. These may include head rolling, head banging, singing, talking and thumbsucking. They are so common and occur in so many well-adjusted children that they hardly deserve more attention than mere mention of the fact that they do occur and eventually are given up. The use of restraints or punishment to abolish such behavior always leads to further management difficulties. If let alone the child will "outgrow" these mannerisms by 3 or 4 years of age, although an occasional brief lapse into such action may again appear at times of emotional tension, such as the arrival of another sibling.

Basic Needs of Every Child

Nearly every child psychologist and pediatrician has at one time or another attempted to formulate what he considers to be the basic needs or emotional requirements of the child. The author does not pretend that the following list is complete or the final answer to the problem but feels that recognition of these factors is an important step in the attainment of a happy and well-adjusted child.

1. Security and a feeling of belonging to the family and social group. Each child needs not only love but also firm, kindly guidance. Letting the child do whatever he wants to do whenever he wants to do it must eventually lead to a feeling that his adults are unconcerned, and he develops a sense of insecurity.

2. Adaptability or learning to live with the world as it is. In part this means conforming with the group. In part it means facing reality. It does not mean complete and unquestioned acquiescence to the forces of environment.

3. Self-expression and freedom to show one's individuality. Each child should be allowed to "daydream" and use his imagination. Perhaps one of the greatest faults of modern educational methods is the rigidity of planned activity which allows little time for the child's own self-directed activity. Guidance does not mean planning or constant direction and advice. Experience is still a good teacher, though sometimes a hard one.

4. Achievement of success in both large and small matters. Allowing the child some self-expression often leads to his finding his own best capabilities. Praise on the part of the parents and teachers should be real and always commensurate with the task achieved. False praise seldom fools a child.

REFERENCES

1. Prechtl, H. F. R.: Patterns of Reflex Behavior Related to Sleep in the Human Infant, in Clemente, C. D., Purpura, D. P., and Mayer, F. E. (eds.): *Sleep and the Maturing Nervous System* (New York: Academic Press, 1972).
2. Thomas, A., Chesni, Y., and St. Anne Dargassies, A.: *Examen Neurologique du Nourrison* (Paris: La Vie Medicale, 1955).
3. Aldrich, C. A., and Hewitt, E. S.: Outlines for well baby clinics: Development for the first twelve months, Am. J. Dis. Child. 71:131, 1946.
4. Aldrich, C. A., and Norval, M. A.: Developmental graphs in the first year of life, J. Pediatr. 29:304, 1946.
5. Bloom, L.: Language development, Rev. Child Devel. Res. 4:245, 1975.
6. Gesell, A., and Amatruda, C. S.: *Developmental Diagnosis*, Knobloch, H., and Pasamanick, B. (eds.) (3d ed.; New York: Harper & Row Publishers, Inc., 1975).
7. Touwin, B. C. L.: The Neurological Development of the Infant, in Davis, J. A., and Dobbing, J. (eds.): *Scientific Foundations of Paediatrics* (Philadelphia: W. B. Saunders Company, 1974).
8. Karacan, I., Anch, M., Thornby, J. I., Okawa, M., and Williams, R. L.: Longitudinal sleep patterns during pubertal growth: Four year follow-up, Pediatr. Res. 9:842, 1975.
9. Ainsworth, M. D. S.: The development of infant-mother attachment, Rev. Child Devel. Res. 3:1, 1973.
10. Hogan, G. R., and Milligan, J. E.: The plantar reflex of the newborn, N. Engl. J. Med. 285:502, 1971.

11. Kanner, L.: *Child Psychiatry* (Springfield, Ill.: Charles C Thomas, Publisher, 1935).
12. Daniel, W. A.: *The Adolescent Patient* (St. Louis: C. V. Mosby Company, 1970).
13. Brazelton, T. B.: *Neonatal Behavioral Assessment Scale* (London: William Heinemann Medical Books Ltd., 1973).
14. Olson, W. C.: *Child Development* (Boston: D. C. Heath & Company, 1949).
15. Erikson, E. H.: *Identity, Youth and Crisis* (New York: W. W. Norton and Company, Inc., 1968).
16. Klaus, M. H., and Kennell, J. H.: *Maternal-Infant Bonding* (St. Louis: C. V. Mosby Company, 1976).
17. Lillywhite, H. S., Young, N. B., and Olmstead, R. W.: *Pediatrician's Handbook of Communication Disorders* (Philadelphia: Lea and Febiger, 1970).
18. Thom, D. A.: Psychologic aspects of adolescence, J. Pediatr. 19:392, 1941.
19. Martin, B.: Parent-child relations, Rev. Child Devel. Res. 4:463, 1975.
20. Ringler, N. M., Kennell, J. H., Jarvella, R., Navojosky, B. J., and Klaus, M. H.: Mother-to-child speech at 2 years, effects of early postnatal contact, J. Pediatr. 86:141, 1975.
21. Lenneberg, E. H.: *Biological Foundations of Language* (New York: John Wiley & Sons, Inc., 1967).
22. McCarthy, D.: Language Development in Children, in Carmichael, L. (ed.): *Manual of Child Psychology* (2d ed.; New York: John Wiley & Sons, Inc., 1954).
23. Schulte, F. J.: The Neurological Development of the Neonate, in Davis, J. A., and Dobbing, J. (eds.): *Scientific Foundations of Paediatrics* (Philadelphia: W. B. Saunders Company, 1974).
24. Schulte, F. J.: Neonatal Brain Mechanisms and the Development of Motor Behavior, in Stave, V. (ed.): *Physiology of the Neonatal Period*, Vol. II (New York: Appleton-Century-Crofts, Inc., 1970).
25. Bloomer, H. H.: The Child with Speech and Language Disorders, in Michal-Smith, H. (ed.): *Management of the Handicapped Child* (New York: Grune & Stratton, Inc., 1957).
26. Metraux, R. W.: Speech profiles of the pre-school child 18 to 54 months, J. Speech Hear. Disord. 15:37, 1950.
27. Sameroff, A. J., and Chandler, M. J.: Reproductive risk and the continuum of caretaking casualty, Rev. Child Devel. Res. 4:187, 1975.
28. Kagan, J.: Emergent themes in human development, Am. Sci. 64:187, 1976.
29. Senn, M. J. E., et al.: *Psychologic Aspects in the Care of Infants and Children*, a report of the 21st Ross Pediatric Research Conference (Columbus, O.: Ross Laboratories, 1956).
30. Erikson, E. H.: *Childhood and Society* (New York: W. W. Norton & Company, Inc., 1950).
31. Finch, S. M.: *Fundamentals of Child Psychiatry* (New York: W. W. Norton & Company, Inc., 1960).
32. Freud, A.: *The Ego and the Mechanisms of Defense* (New York: International Universities Press, Inc., 1946).
33. Freud, A.: Adolescence, in *The Psychoanalytic Study of the Child*, Vol. XIII, (New York: International Universities Press, Inc., 1958), p. 255.
34. Freud, S.: in Brill, A. A. (ed.): *The Basic Writings of Sigmund Freud* (New York: Random House, Inc., 1938).
35. Spiegel, L. A.: Comments on the Psychoanalytic Psychology of Adolescence, in

The Psychoanalytic Study of the Child, Vol. XIII, (New York: International Universities Press, Inc., 1958).

36. Parmelee, A. H.; Schulz, H. R., and Disbrow, M. A.: Sleep patterns of the newborn, J. Pediatr. 58:241, 1961.
37. Debré, R., and Doumic, A.: *Le sommeil de l'enfant* (Paris: Presse Universitaire de France, 1959).
38. Knobloch, H., and Pasamanick, B.: The Distribution of Intellectual Potential in an Infant Population, in *The Epidemiology of Mental Disorder: A Symposium in Celebration of the Centennial of Emil Kraepelin* (Washington: American Association for the Advancement of Science, 1959), pp. 249–272.
39. Pasamanick, B., Knobloch, H., and Lilienfeld, A. M.: Socioeconomic status and some precursors of neuropsychiatric disorder, Am. J. Orthopsychiatry 26:594–601, July, 1956.
40. Knobloch, H., and Pasamanick, B.: Predicting intellectual potential in infancy: Some variables affecting the validity of developmental diagnosis, Am. J. Dis. Child. 106:43, 1963.
41. Goodenough, F., and Harris, D.: *Goodenough-Harris Drawing Test* (New York: Psychological Corporation, 1964).
42. Thorndike, R. L. (ed.): *Research Problems and Techniques*. AAF Aviation Psychological Program, Res. Rep. No. 3 (Washington, D.C.: U.S. Government Printing Office, 1947).
43. Wechsler, D.: *Wechsler Intelligence Scale for Children—Revised* (New York: Psychological Corporation, 1974).
44. White, B. L.: *The First Three Years of Life* (Englewood Cliffs, N.J.: Prentice-Hall, Inc., 1975).
45. Bender, L.: A visual motor Gestalt test and its clinical use, Res. Monogr. Am. Orthopsychiatry A., no. 3, 1938.
46. Graham, F. K., and Kendall, B. S.: Memory-for-designs test: Revised general manual, Percept. Mot. Skills, Monogr. supp. 2, 7:147, 1960.
47. Gibson, R., Sullivan, D., and Dickinson, D.: Intelligence in hydrocephalus with and without meningocele (unpublished).
48. Gibson, R.: A comparison of the Leiter and the Binet Intelligence Scales in children with central nervous system dysfunctioning (unpublished).
49. Terman, L., and Merrill, M.: *Stanford-Binet Intelligence Scale: Manual for the Third Revision, Form L-M* (Boston: Houghton Mifflin Company, 1960).
50. Knobloch, H., and Pasamanick, B.: Prediction from Assessment of Neuromotor and Intellectual Status in Infancy, in Zubin, J. (ed.): *Psychology of Mental Development* (New York: Grune & Stratton, Inc., 1967).
51. Knobloch, H., Pasamanick, B., and Sharard, E. S.: A developmental screening inventory for infants, Pediatrics 38:1095, 1966.
52. Piaget, J.: *Six Psychological Studies* (New York: Random House, Inc., 1967).
53. Piaget, J.: *The Psychology of the Child* (New York: Basic Books, Inc., 1969).
54. Cameron, J., Livson, N., and Bayley, N.: Infant vocalization and their relationship to mature intelligence, Science 153:331, 1967.
55. Kohler, W. C., Coddington, R. D., and Agnew, H. W.: Sleep patterns in 2-year-old children, J. Pediatr. 72:228, 1968.
56. Stern, E., Parmelee, A. H., Akiyama, Y., Schultz, M. A., and Wenner, W. H.: Sleep cycle characteristics in infants, Pediatrics 43:65, 1969.
57. Ross, J. L., Agnew, H. W., Williams, R. L., and Webb., W. B.: Sleep patterns

in preadolescent children: An EEG-EOG study, Pediatrics 42:324, 1968.

58. Birch, H. G., and Gussow, J. D.: *Disadvantaged Children: Health, Nutrition and School Failure* (New York: Harcourt, Brace & World, Inc., 1970).

59. Gould, J. B., Lee, A. F. S., James, O., Sander, L., Teager, H., and Fineberg, N.: The sleep characteristics of apnea during infancy, Pediatrics 59:182, 1977.

60. Wolf, P. H.: Critical periods in human cognitive development, Hosp. Pract. 5:77, 1970.

61. Rabin, A. I.: Infants and children under conditions of "intermittent" mothering in the Kibbutz, Am. J. Orthopsychiatry 28:577, 1958.

62. Geschwind, N.: The organization of language and the brain, Science 170:940, 1970.

63. Bloomer, H. H., and Prins, T. D.: Speech and Language Disorders in Children, in Brennemann-Kelly (ed.): *Practice of Pediatrics* (New York: Harper & Row Publishers, Inc., 1967).

64. Neligan, G. A., and Prudham, D.: Family factors affecting child development, Arch. Dis. Child. 51:853, 1976.

65. Howell, M. C.: Effects of maternal employment on the child, Pediatrics 52:327, 1973.

66. Johnston, C. M., and Deisher, R. W.: Contemporary communal child rearing, Pediatrics 52:319, 1973.

67. Doyle, A. B.: Infant development in day care, Dev. Psychol. 11:655, 1975.

68. Deutsch, C. P.: Social class and child development, Rev. Child Devel. Res. 3:233, 1973.

69. Weinberg, W. A., Dietz, S. F., Penick, E. C., and McAlister, W. H.: Intelligence, reading achievement, physical size and social class, J. Pediatr. 85:482, 1974.

70. Werner, E. E., Bierman, J. M., and French, F. E.: *The Children of Kauai* (Honolulu: University of Hawaii, 1971).

71. *Intellectual Development of Children by Demographic and Socioeconomic Factors* (Washington, D.C.: U.S. Dept. of Health, Education and Welfare, Public Health Service, 1971).

72. Belmont, L., and Marolla, F. A.: Birth order, family size and intelligence, Science 182:1096, 1973.

73. Werner, E. E.: Infants around the world: Cross-cultural studies of psychomotor development from birth to two years, J. Cross-Cultural Psych. 3:111, 1972.

74. Money, J., and Ehrhardt, A.: *Man and Woman, Boy and Girl: The Differentiation and Dimorphism of Gender Identity from Conception to Maturity* (Baltimore: Johns Hopkins University Press, 1972).

75. Herzog, E., and Sudia, C. E.: Children in fatherless families, Rev. Child Devel. Res. 3:141, 1973.

76. Bruner, J. S.: The course of cognitive growth, Amer. Psychol. 19:1, 1964.

77. Bruner, J. S.: On perceptual readiness, Psychol. Rev., 64:123, 1957.

78. Piaget, J.: Development and learning, J. Res. Sci. Teaching, 3:176, 1964.

79. Thorpe, H. S.: *Developmental Appraisal of the Preschool Child: Ages Three to Six* (Davis, Calif.: University of California, Davis, 1973).

80. Frankenburg, W. K., and Dobbs, J. B.: The Denver developmental screening test, J. Pediatr. 71:181, 1967.

81. Bayley, N.: *Bayley Scales of Infant Development: Birth to Two Years* (New York: Psychological Corporation, 1969).

82. Illingworth, R. S.: *The Development of the Infant and Young Child, Normal and Abnormal* (5th ed.; Baltimore: Williams & Wilkins Company, 1972).

83. Boothman, R., White, E. M., and Sweenie, S.: Predictive value of early developmental examination, Arch. Dis. Child. 51:430, 1975.

84. Lewis, M., and McGurk, H.: Evaluation of infant intelligence, Science 178:1174, 1972.

85. *Intellectual Maturity of Children as Measured by the Goodenough-Harris Drawing Test* (Washington, D.C.: U.S. Dept. of Health, Education and Welfare, Public Health Service, 1970).

86. Appleton, T., Clifton, R., and Goldberg, S.: The development of behavioral competence in infancy, Rev. Child Devel. Res. 4:101, 1975.

87. Clausen, J. A.: The young as outsiders, Science 187:637, 1975.

88. Millar, H. E. C.: *Approaches to Adolescent Health Care in the 1970s* (Washington, D.C.; Public Health Service, 1975).

89. Anders, T. F., and Weinstein, P.: Sleep and its disorders in infants and children: A review, Pediatrics 50:312, 1972.

90. Schwartz, E. M., and Elonen, A. S.: I.Q. and the myth of stability: A 16-year longitudinal study of variations in intelligence test performance, J. Clin. Psychol. 31:687, 1975.

91. O'Connor, S. M., Vietze, P. M., Hopkins, J. B., and Altemeir, W. A.: Postpartum extended maternal-infant contact: Subsequent mothering and child health, Pediatr. Res. 11:380, 1977.

7 / Organ Development

DEVELOPMENT implies an increase in complexity, in differentiation, and in function. The term is used in opposition to growth, which means an increase in size. It is possible to have considerable development with very little growth in size, as, for example, during the first days following fertilization of the ovum before implantation has occurred and in instances when the growth of a child is checked by a pathologic condition such as rickets. Each individual is endowed by heredity with certain potentialities for growth and development, which may be more or less than average.

The Embryo

During the fourth week of development, when the ovum is about as large as a grape, the main organ systems become established.[45] The neural folds come together and, by fusing, form the neural tube from which the central nervous system is derived. The remaining parts of the germ disk become the skin (ectoderm) that covers the body of the embryo, portions of it contributing to the special sense organs and to the buccal cavity. The dorsal portion of the yolk sac provides the gut (entoderm), later forming pharyngeal structures, lungs, and hepatic tissue. The mesoblast cells between entoderm and ectoderm, by proliferation and differentiation, form the somites, body cavities, circulatory system, and supporting tissues.

The processes of differentiation are wavelike, in a craniocaudal direction. When the embryo is 9 mm long (6 weeks), its primary anatomy is established and the arm buds are just appearing. During the second month occur those changes in form and differentiation that convert the 3–4 mm embryo to the 30-mm fetus.

Development of Enzyme Systems

All of the body's metabolic processes, including those responsible for growth and development, are mediated through *enzyme* systems. At present we do not know all of the enzymes that can exist, and the development of these systems is still under study. The importance of these is so great in an understanding of living organisms that some discussion of them is necessary. A few examples will be given, with no attempt at completeness.

Enzymes are organic (protein) catalysts produced by living cells. They act by varying the rate of chemical reactions without themselves being changed or finally altered by the reaction. A normal living organism is an orderly integrated succession of enzyme reactions. Although the rate of a reaction may be influenced by the amount of an enzyme present, the concentration of the substrate and the substance resulting from its action have a more direct relationship. One therefore usually speaks in terms of activity rather than in measured amounts of enzymes. Some enzymes require for their function the presence of certain organic, usually not protein, compounds, small in molecular size and thermostable. These are called *coenzymes;* the group of B complex vitamins, necessary in many oxidation reactions, are examples.

There is evidence that enzymes appear in response to the presence of their normal substrates, provided the appropriate gene is present, the raw materials are present for enzyme synthesis and a suitable source of energy is available. It is presumed that this induction of one enzyme may lead to the induction of another, leading to sequential induction. The metabolism of embryonic tissue is characterized mainly by the activity of enzymes concerned in synthesizing proteins and lipoproteins.[124] These systems are much more active in the embryo than in the adult, where growth has ceased and only repair is present. It is sometimes difficult to distinguish between proteins with enzymic activity and those with a structural role, and it is possible that such a line of division is not always there. Some enzyme precursors may be activated by hormones, and the intensity or rate of activity is influenced by them under certain circumstances. Induction or change in activity can occur at any stage in development or with age. The lack of sufficient concentration of a substrate may result in decrease in amount or even disappearance. Conversely, as with the removal of the placenta at birth and a resulting accumulation of a substance, a new enzyme may be formed.

Glucose-6-phosphatase is necessary for the conversion of glucose to glycogen. Glycogen first appears in the fetal liver at about 12 weeks. No glycogen is stored in that organ until after that time, the placenta producing the enzymes and regulating the concentration of glucose in fetal blood until the liver is able to do so.[125]

In the prematurely born infant tyrosine is present in the urine in fairly large amounts but is absent in the term infant. The liver of the immature infant does not contain a number of the enzymes necessary for complete metabolism of tyrosine, especially the oxidizing system and transaminase. If large amounts of vitamin C are given, the deficient enzymes are activated and the tyrosinuria disappears.[126] Some enzymes, such as intestinal glycosidase, are activated at the time of birth regardless of the degree of maturity. Erythrocyte and plasma lactate dehydrogenase and plasma glutamic oxalacetic transaminase are examples of enzymes that have a higher rate of activity in the newborn infant than later in life.[127, 128] When bone growth is essentially complete, by late adolescence, there is a corresponding fall in circulating alkaline phosphatase.

Cystathionase activity is not present in the liver of prematurely born infants, and may not appear for several weeks, depending upon the degree of immaturity. This enzyme is important in the synthesis of the essential amino acid cystine. This information raises the question of whether it is the amount of cystine rather than the total amount of protein in a diet that is the limiting factor for protein synthesis and growth.

The cerebral cortex has been studied in a number of animals, including man. Enzyme activities of oxidative metabolism were shown to follow a very interesting pattern. The activity appeared earlier in those animals with earlier maturity. In the guinea pig, who is independent a few days after birth, activity increased by the 41st day of gestation, while in the rat, who is very dependent for the 1st few weeks after birth, enzyme activity increased during the 2d week of extrauterine life. Furthermore, the caudal and phylogenetically older areas of the cortex showed the increased activity first. Concomitant with the change in enzyme development there was a decrease in the resistance to injury from anoxia.[127]

Of considerable importance from a practical standpoint is the rate of development of enzymes used by the body to metabolize and detoxify various drugs. The interference of synthetic vitamin K with the conjugation of bilirubin in the newborn is such an example. The greater toxicity of salicylates and morphine in young infants as compared with older infants is a further example showing the significantly reduced enzymatic activity in the immature subject. The slower rate of inactivation and possibly of renal excretion of a long list of drugs is well established.[129]

Musculature

The development of muscle fibers takes place in premuscular mesodermic tissue. The early growth of voluntary muscle is both hyperplastic and hypertrophic, for the fibers increase both in number and in size. From the middle of prenatal life to early maturity the growth of skeletal muscle forms the largest part of the increment of the body. In the middle of prenatal life skeletal musculature forms about one sixth of the body weight; at birth, one fifth to one fourth; in early adolescence, one third; and in early maturity, two fifths. The gain in musculature in childhood and adolescence is about equal to the growth of all other organs, systems, and tissues combined.[57]

It can be seen that the maximal growth in muscle mass occurs relatively late and follows chronologically the maximal growth in height. It has been found that strength virtually doubles between 12 and 16 years, but the peak increase tends to follow the major increments of height and weight. Tests of motor ability and coordination do not confirm the widely held view that a loss of motor control and awkwardness are associated with the adolescent growth spurt. On the contrary, there is a constant and steady improvement during this period.

Cutaneous Structures

The epidermis (skin) of the one-month-old fetus consists of a single layer of ectodermal cells. Within another 2 weeks a second layer, termed the stratum germinativum, is added. By 4 months the fetal skin has 3 distinct regions: a periderm, an intermediate layer, and the stratum germinativum. At this time there is considerable accumulation of glycogen which persists until late fetal life, but is never present in postnatal skin unless injury occurs. The anaerobic glycolytic pathway is apparently the major energy source for rapid epidermal growth. By 9 months gestation, the characteristic 5 layers typical of the adult are present. These consist of the stratum germinativum (or basal layer), stratum spinosum (or prickle layer), stratum granulosum and the stratum corneum. Palmar and plantar surfaces are considerably thicker by virtue of an extra layer, stratum lucidum, beneath the corneum. The red transparent appearance of the prematurely born infant is largely attributable to the thin and poorly developed stratum granulosum. At this time it contains very little keratohyalin granules characteristic of the older child and adult. In the neonate the stratum corneum is thin and virtually fused with the vernix caseosa, which is an excellent reason to avoid too vigorous an attempt to wash away the vernix. Later the corneum will become the effective barrier of the cornified epidermis. With increasing age there is increasing content of fibers rich in collagen in the dermis which lies beneath the epidermis. It is the increasing thickness and collagen content that characterize the skin changes associated with advancing age.[10, 15, 176]

The secretory or coiled portion of the sweat glands are in the dermis. The eccrine glands are present over most of the body surface and are not associated with hair follicles. These glands are fully developed by the 7th month of gestation, but do not function effectively for many weeks after birth. Adult level of function is not reached until about 2 years. Since the glands are anatomically mature and since they respond mainly to neurogenic stimulus, it may be a functional immaturity of the central nervous system that is responsible for this inefficiency. Because no new sweat glands are added after birth, with the increase in surface area caused by growth there is a corresponding decrease in their density per unit of surface area. The glands on the palms and soles respond to psychogenic stimuli, those on the forehead and axilla to psychic and thermal stimuli, while all other parts of the body respond only to thermal influence.

Apocrine sweat glands are larger, are associated with hair follicles, and are limited to special areas. The largest concentration is in the axilla. Other sites are the anogenital area, the auditory canal (ceruminal glands) and the areolae of the breasts. Both structural and functional maturity occur during adolescence. Like the sebaceous glands, they respond to hormonal stimulus and epinephrine. The ceruminal glands are an exception to this.

Eccrine sweat is largely water, about 99%, and urea. The amount of sodium chloride present increases with age, being 2–3 times more concentrated in the adult as compared to a year-old child. The concentration also increases in proportion to the salt content of the diet. Eccrine sweat is clear and has little odor. Apocrine sweat is cloudy, contains both lipids and proteins and is odoriferous.

Sebaceous glands are appendices of hair follicles and are distributed over all of the body except the palmar and plantar surfaces. They are acinous glands embedded in the dermis, and their secretion is holocrine in type, consisting of lipids and cellular debris. The lipids are unique in comparison to any other synthesized in the body. This uniqueness and complexity may serve in some protective manner to limit the types of microorganisms that can survive in the skin. This uniqueness may also have served some function in sexual attractiveness and may serve to identify an individual to a pet by a distinctive odor. The glands over the head and upper chest are larger than elsewhere. As previously noted, following birth the amount of secretion remains minimal until androgen production increases just prior to puberty. The problem of acne will be discussed in Chapter 9.

The pH of the skin surface drops from a neutral 7.4 at birth to arround 5.5 in a period of 3–5 days. Little further change occurs until puberty when the pH, most notably in the axilla, rises again to a near neutral value. The significance of these changes is not clear.[15]

The finger- and toenails of the premature infant are very soft and thin. In contrast, the full-term baby has well-formed nails which are firm. In a number of chromosomal abnormalities there are conspicuous changes in the nails, e.g., narrow and hyperconvex in Turner's syndrome and marked hypoplasia in the 18 trisomy syndrome.

Hair follicles are apparent by the 3d to 4th fetal month. Maturation progresses on a parallel with the sebaceous glands, and just prior to birth there is an abundant amount of very fine silky hair over most of the body called *lanugo hair*. During the 9th month of gestation this is lost and most of the follicles over the body regress into a resting phase. On the scalp, in contrast, at birth about 80% of the hair follicles are in an actively growing phase. With increasing age, and especially during adolescence, hair growth is accelerated and it becomes coarser. The first appearance of significant quantities of hair in the pubic area and axilla in both sexes, and over the face and chest in males, is influenced by sexual development. (See also Chapter 9.) Increase in the amount and coarseness of hair over the shoulders, back and thighs continues well into adult life. Since normal growth and development of hair is dependent upon adequate nutrition, attempts have been made to use morphologic changes in hair as a means to measure dietary adequacy. Newborn babies who are small for their gestational age, presumably due to fetal undernutrition, have scalp hair shafts of narrower diameter than their normal controls and the hair follicle is more often in a resting phase.[21]

The cheeselike material vernix caseosa covers the normal-term infant in varying amounts. It represents a product resulting from sebaceous gland secretion by the skin and amniotic fluid. The sebaceous glands are not only well developed but are functioning at this time. A short time following birth these glands become relatively dormant until stimulated by the increased amount of circulating sex hormones associated with adolescence. Greenish staining of the vernix, the nails and the umbilical cord are strongly indicative of severe fetal distress. The premature infant may be covered with fine lanugo hair which has been lost by term infants. Small areas of capillary hemangiomas are present in more than half of newborn infants. Typically they appear as small red areas with rather indistinct margins most commonly on the upper eyelids, bridge of the nose and nape of the neck. "Angel's kiss" was an old-fashioned term applied to them and indicates their importance, for they either completely involute or disappear by reason of thickening of the skin during the first two years of life. They can be easily distinguished from the more severe port wine nevus which is more intense in color, has sharp margins and does not blanch with pressure.

Toxic erythema is a skin condition limited to the neonatal period which appears in 30–50% of full-term infants between 24 to 48 hours after birth. It is rarely seen in babies with a gestational age under 32 weeks. The lesions are firm, slightly raised, irregular, erythematous patches occurring singly or in groups and varying in size, but averaging about 1.5 cm in diameter. The lesion has an appearance resembling urticaria and may or may not have a central white papule. They last from several hours to a few days. The etiology is unknown but the tissue is heavily infiltrated with eosinophils. Any body surface may be involved. It is completely benign.

Since the neonate has been subjected to hormonal influences prior to birth there is often some sebaceous gland hyperplasia and secretion of sebum. This is manifested by multiple white-to-yellow 1 mm papules over the nose, cheeks and forehead. It is observed in about half of newborns and is self-limited. The term *milia* is sometimes applied to it. *Miliaria* is a lesion associated with an excessively warm environment and results from obstruction of the sweat glands, which become inflamed, forming small erythematous papules over the trunk and face.

In the normal full-term infant, desquamation is not present at birth and does not begin until a few days later. Desquamation in the premature infant is often delayed for some weeks after birth. Desquamation in the postmature syndrome is often obvious at birth.

Mongolian spots are dark areas, often with a bluish cast, having poorly defined borders and found over the lumbar and sacral areas. They may be single or multiple and are macular in character. They are present in 90% of black, oriental and American Indian infants at birth. They are less common in other ethnic groups. The pigmentation results from an increased number of melanocytes in the dermis. The pigment in these areas usually becomes inconspicuous within one to two years. Pigmentary changes of the skin associated with sexual development are discussed in Chapter 9.

Spider nevi, small red areas with thin capillary "legs" spreading distally, begin to appear at the end of the first year in about 10–20% of the population. The number in any individual may increase until puberty. They have no clinical significance and no genetic factors are apparent.[131]

The prepuce is usually adherent to the glans and remains so for some time after birth. The skin of the external genitalia, axillae and areolae becomes pigmented with the development of secondary sexual characteristics associated with the beginning of adolescence. Adhesions between the labia minora are seldom seen at birth but are not uncommon between 2 and 6 years.[2] They may represent the result of irritation and mild infection, also the lack of estrogenic influence, since the condition is not seen in adolescence.

We have seen that one of the prominent changes in the last trimester of gestation is the addition of subcutaneous fat. Along with a poorly developed sweating mechanism, the failure to accumulate a full quota of subcutaneous fat is a real liability to the premature in maintaining an even body temperature. Such tissue is an important means of insulation against environment. The thickness of the subcutaneous fat increases throughout the first year. It is this accumulation plus the prominent abdomen that gives the infant his rotund appearance. During the second year there is a definite decrease in this tissue. It is important for both the physician and the parents to realize that this change takes place and that it often coincides with the period when the infant begins to display lack of interest in his food. There is a more gradual loss of adipose tissue during the next few years. At the beginning of adolescence and throughout this period there is a reaccumulation of subcutaneous fat, which is more pronounced in girls than in boys. In estimating total body fat in adolescent boys, it was found that between 12 and 18 years a 50% loss of body fat's contribution to body weight occurs.[130] From this one can presume a change in the total content of fat in the body as well as its distribution in comparison to an earlier age. Skin calipers and roentgenograms have been used to evaluate the amount of subcutaneous tissue present, and an effort has been made to equate these findings with levels of nutrition, including obesity.

Dermatoglyphics, the study of the pattern and number of dermal ridges on the palms and fingers or soles and toes, has been used as a diagnostic device in detecting or supporting the diagnosis of a number of dysmorphic syndromes.[24, 25] At least 30 entities have been described, but many of these are not sufficiently unique to be very useful. Some examples may be helpful to acquaint the reader with the technique. Multiple low arches formed by the ridges on the fingertips are seen in trisomy 18. A decreased number of ridges on the fingers is a finding in some patients with Turner's syndrome. Trisomy 21 (mongolism or Down's syndrome) has a number of characteristics including: the convergence of three sets of ridges near the middle of the palm to form a triradius of unusual position, finger loops opening to the radial side of the 4th and 5th finger and the absence of either a loop or a whorl in the hallucal area of the sole. Seldom have these patterns proven to be pathognomonic for a particular condition. In addition to the dermal ridges, the palmar creases may be helpful, such as the so-called simian line or crease in trisomy 21.

Central Nervous System

The structure and function of the nervous system are more readily understood if we review some of its phylogenetic and embryonic development. In more primitive forms of life, such as the jellyfish, only a diffuse network of neurons exists. Stimulation of such an animal produces a diffuse and often inefficient response. In the earthworm a chain of ganglions has developed, and in the early chordate forms a simple neural tube associated with segmental nerves is present. Response to irritation in both of these forms increases in complexity and in the latter is segmental and more purposeful than the diffuse response displayed by lower forms of organisms. All vertebrates have an enlargement of the cephalic end of the neural tube, i.e., a brain, and in progress upward in the evolutionary scale the brain becomes relatively larger. In higher vertebrates the forebrain, especially the cerebral cortex, assumes a dominant role, reaching its greatest degree of complexity in man. With development of the brain there is superimposed on the segmental system a controlling influence. A repetition of this phylogenetic development can be seen in man.[26, 37]

The initial steps in the formation of the nervous system take place very early. An infolding of the thickened dorsal plate of the embryo forms the neural groove and then the neural tube with coincident separation from the parent ectoderm. Certain cells lying near the margin remain independent and assume a position on either side of the tube and just dorsal to it. They are the primordia of the sensory ganglions of the spinal and cranial nerves and indirectly of the sympathetic ganglions. The neural tube rapidly dilates anteriorly as the primordia of the brain; posteriorly it remains relatively uniform in size as the forerunner of the spinal cord.

Initially there are three regional divisions of the brain: forebrain, or prosencephalon; midbrain, or mesencephalon; and hindbrain, or rhombencephalon (Fig 7–1). By 6 weeks further division of the forebrain and hindbrain results in a five-vesicle stage, the components being the telencephalon, dien-

Fig 7–1.—Development of the fetal brain. **I,** at 3 weeks, three regions of the cephalic prominence can be made out. **II,** at 7 weeks, further division has taken place and the five major areas of the human brain are present. **III,** by 11 weeks of gestation, the brain has taken on more definitive form. (Modified from Patten.[45])

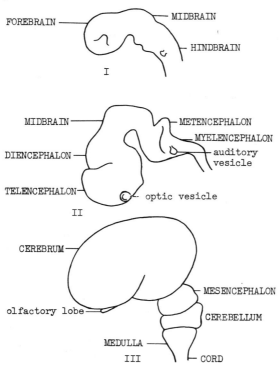

cephalon, mesencephalon, metencephalon, and myelencephalon, which remain as the major regions of the adult brain.[45]

The myelencephalon becomes the medulla oblongata of the adult, and its central dilatation, with that of the metencephalon, forms the fourth ventricle. Within the substance of the myelencephalon are the nuclei of the sixth to twelfth cranial nerves.

In the metencephalon are found the nuclei of the fifth cranial nerves. It is interesting that the first of the suprasegmental structures to assume recognizable form is the vestibular apparatus of the hindbrain, the flocculonodular lobe of the cerebellum. The pons, which is composed largely of fibers leading to the cerebellar hemispheres, appears late in phylogeny and reaches its height of development only in primates. Such fiber paths appear relatively late in the embryo.

Phylogenetically the mesencephalon is farther advanced than the metencephalon. Three major regions develop in this portion of the brain. In the roof are found the corpora quadrigemina, which are the correlation centers for visual and somatic impulses and visual and auditory impulses. Connections with the cerebral cortex are also present. The middle portion of the mesencephalon gives rise to the third and fourth cranial nerves and the red nucleus. This last structure serves as a relay station for impulses from the cerebellum to both upper (cortical) and lower neuron centers. Late in development in phylogeny is the substantia nigra, which is related to descending tracts from the cerebral cortex. Neither medullation of the tracts nor pigmentation is completed until after birth, the melanin deposits not being complete until about puberty.[45]

In the walls of the diencephalon are found important aggregations of cell bodies known collectively as the thalamus. Proprioceptive impulses—deep pressure, temperature and pain—are projected to the thalamus. Auditory and visual pathways enter the thalamus also, and all are in turn relayed to the cerebral cortex. In addition important centers of visceral control (body temperature, heart rate, etc.) are found in this area and are mediated through the autonomic nervous system.

The vesicles of the telencephalon become the lateral ventricles with the connecting foramina of Monro and the small third ventricle. Phylogenetically and ontogenetically the cerebral cortex is the last to appear and the last to mature. In the ventrolateral walls of the telencephalon the corpus striatum forms, which contains the basal ganglions. Its connections are most complex, and it is primarily concerned in the coordination of fine and intricate muscular activities. Superimposed on neuron chains in the more stereotyped reactions are mechanisms affording a wide choice of behavior in response to stimuli entering over the various afferent pathways. The centers for these most plastic and highest responses are found in the cortex. It is not until the seventh fetal month that the six cell layers of the cerebral cortex are completely differentiated. At birth the cortex is approximately one-half as thick as it is in the adult brain.[17, 45]

Externally certain typical landmarks begin to make their appearance by the third or fourth fetal month. At this time the sylvian fissure is recognizable. During the fifth and sixth months the central, parieto-occipital and calcarine fissures become apparent. All of the primary fissures, or sulci, are present by the eighth intrauterine month, but secondary folds continue to appear for several months after birth.[26, 45]

Postnatal growth of the brain is characterized by its rapidity during infancy and early childhood, a much more gradual increment during the middle and late years of the first decade, and a very small terminal increase throughout adolescence. It is not unusual to find the average brain weight in children of 10 years of age as great as that of adults. Nearly half the postnatal growth of the brain has been accomplished by the end of the first year, three-fourths by 3 years and nine-tenths by the seventh year[57] (see Fig 7–7 and Table 7–11). The postnatal growth of the cerebral hemispheres is due mainly to an increase in white matter.

The cerebrum shows a gain in weight until the later part of intrauterine existence and a slight decline in rate of growth thereafter through the first decade. The human cerebellum begins its growth spurt relatively late, at about 30 gestational weeks, and ends it much earlier, around the first birthday, than that of the rest of the brain. This high growth velocity may increase its vulnerability to nutritional or other insults at the time. The brain stem is relatively large in the young fetus, declines in proportionate size until the end of the first year, then shows a small relative gain. There are no marked changes in the relative proportions of these parts after the tenth year. The relative weight of the entire central nervous system is high in early life, being one-fourth the total body weight in the second fetal month and one-tenth at birth. At about age 5 it comprises one-twentieth the total weight and at full maturity averages one-fiftieth.[50, 174]

Histologically the development of the brain occurs in three successive stages: neuroblastic cell proliferation and growth (especially in the first 3 months following conception), rapid growth of neurons with ending of proliferation (in the third trimester), proliferation of glial tissue, myelinization and the vast elaboration of the dendritic processes (during the last portion of fetal life and extending throughout the next 4 years). The fetus of 6–7 months has all or most of the neurons that will ever be present throughout life.[174, 175] In contrast to nearly all other organ systems in the body, there is no adolescent spurt of growth in the central nervous system. After all of the myelin has been deposited, it remains one of the most inactive tissues in the body from a metabolic standpoint.[132] The misinterpretation of this may well have led to the often quoted observation that in marasmic diseases the brain is "spared." The myelin's function appears to be to increase conduction velocity of the axon.[133]

Myelinization begins by the fourth fetal month and appears first in the tracts that are oldest phylogenetically (ventral and dorsal spinal roots). Corticospinal and tectospinal tracts do not acquire myelin, on the average, until shortly after birth. Last to receive this investment are the correlation fibers of higher centers, e.g., cerebral cortex and thalamus. Some tracts are not completely myelinated until several years after birth, and even after being completely covered, the sheath continues to grow in thickness for many years. Myelinization in the cord follows a cephalocaudal direction.*

As the vertebral column is formed, the neural arches grow and enclose the spinal cord in the neural canal. Up to about the third fetal month the neural canal and the spinal cord are coextensive, and the segmentally arranged nerves pass outward through the intervertebral spaces directly opposite their point of origin. After this period differential growth is such that neither the vertebral column nor the neural tube keeps pace with the expansion of the posterior part of the body, and the spinal cord lags farther behind than does the vertebral column. Since the cephalic portion of the nervous system is fixed in the developing cranial vault, the effect of this differential growth is to pull the cord cephalad within the canal. The spinal nerves appear to be dragged caudally from the cord and pass backward through the neural canal until they enter the intervertebral space, which was originally opposite their point of origin. The extent of this displacement is progressively greater in the more caudal regions. In the newborn infant the spinal cord, except for the vestigial filum terminale, ends at the upper border of the third lumbar vertebra, or about one or two vertebral levels below that found in the adult. It is therefore apparent that the differential growth continues until maturity. The cord doubles its weight in the first six months after birth, quadruples in weight in five years and has increased eightfold by the time adult life is reached.[45, 57]

The choroid plexuses are well formed early in embryonic life, and cerebrospinal fluid is present. From chemical studies of the blood and cerebrospinal fluid in animals and man it has been postulated that during the first half of intrauterine life the fluid is an ultrafiltrate of the blood and thereafter assumes gradually the character of a secretion. It is probable that the blood-brain barrier is more permeable during the first few months of life than later.[62] The amount of cerebrospinal fluid in the newborn infant has been

---

*The sequence in which the function of the various structures develops undoubtedly corresponds to the sequence in which they become myelinated; however, some function is possible in the absence of myelin.

estimated to range from 30 to 60 ml; in the child of 10 years the upper limit has been estimated at 200 ml. The cerebrospinal fluid protein and the number of cells present are considerably increased in the neonatal period as compared to later life. Findings in the newborn period for normal spontaneous delivery and the absence of abnormal physical findings in one study were as follows[167]:

	DAY 1		DAY 7	
	RANGE	MEAN	RANGE	MEAN
Red blood cells	0–620	23/mm^3	0–48	3/mm^3
Polymorphs	0–26	7/mm^3	0–5	2/mm^3
Lymphs	0–16	5/mm^3	0–4	1/mm^3
Protein	40–148	73 mg	27–65	47 mg
Sugar	38–64	48 mg	48–62	55 mg
Chloride	680–760	720 mg	720–760	720 mg

Values for protein content in the premature and small-for-date infant are higher on the first day (60–180 mg) and elevated levels persist for a longer time than in the term newborn.[44] Normal adult values are recorded by age 3 months. Some xanthochromia is present in the fluid after birth and parallels in intensity the serum bilirubin level.

In about 10% of children beyond the 10th year the pineal body contains enough calcium to be visualized by roentgenologic examination. Since this structure occupies the midline, it is valuable as a point of reference. In adults of advanced age the pineal body is calcified in 80% of the examinations.

Shurtleff and his co-workers[134] have described a valuable technic for estimating the thickness of the cerebral mantle (outer surface of cortex to inner surface of the lateral ventricle) by x-ray with air contrast studies. Although careful standardization is necessary, this estimation is not difficult to accomplish. Between the age of 3 months to adulthood there was an increase of 1.3 cm. The mean at 3 months was 3.5 cm; at 12 months, 3.9 cm; and 5 years, 4.8 cm, with 2 standard deviations averaging 0.6 cm for each age. There was no further increase in thickness after 5 years.

The brain depends upon glucose as its only source of energy and requires a relatively large supply of oxygen for normal metabolism. In the adult the requirement is about 3.5 ml of oxygen for each 100 gm of tissue per minute, making it the adult organ with the highest metabolic rate. In the newborn infant these requirements are increased by the rapid growth that is taking place at that time. Estimates of oxygen requirements range from 5.0 to 8.0 ml/100 gm. Pyridoxine, a coenzyme, is a necessary nutrient aiding in the formation of aminobutyric acid from glutamic acid. Following birth there is a marked increase in the amount of aminobutyric acid in the brain. It has an inhibitory effect on neuronal excitability. Convulsions will result in infants kept on a pyridoxine-free diet.[132]

Both animal and human studies indicate that there may be critical periods of brain growth when an insult or injury may result in irreversible damage. It is important to emphasize that the times of rapid growth in total mass are not necessarily related to the period of rapid proliferation of neural tissue. It is also important to understand that periods of rapid growth and differentiation relative to the time of birth differ greatly in different species. The effect of undernutrition upon the neonatal rat's brain growth will be much more profound than upon a newborn pig or human because this is a period of major proliferation of neurons in the rat but not for the other two animals. Maternal malnutrition would have its major effect in the human in the final trimester when fetal growth begins to approach the limits of function of the placenta. Malnutrition during infancy may reduce brain weight and this may be reflected in a less-than-normal rate of increase in head circumference. Reduced head circumference may be due to a decreased number of cells in the brain (as measured by DNA content).[168] As pointed out in Chapter 4, a small head is often associated with reduced intelligence. All of these facts taken together would appear to make a very open and shut case that late fetal and infant malnutrition can be held responsible for mental retardation. However, brain growth that is taking place in late fetal and early infancy periods occurs after all of the neurons are present and, therefore, the brain should be less vulnerable. Irradiation and rubella, for instance, have little influence on fetal development after the 1st trimester. The reduction in DNA means primarily a reduction in glial cells which are not considered to be very vital to intellectual functions. Nor can one ignore the impact of a poor socioeconomic environment that so often accompanies poor nutrition.

Dobbing[174] has proposed that there may indeed be two critical periods in human brain development. One is in the embryonic or early fetal period when neural cell proliferation is most rapid and when such accidents as intrauterine infections are most devastating. The second, and a much longer period, is during late fetal life and infancy. Brain growth in total mass during this time is great, though decelerating within a few weeks after birth. The loss of cell numbers at this time may result in a lag in myelinization, and, due to a decreased width of the cortical mantle, an increased density of neurons. Some interference with important aspects of cell migration might occur. Perhaps most important of all is evidence that there is risk to dendritic arborization and the establishment of synaptic conductivity.[175] (See also Chapter 11.)

The electroencephalogram has provided some additional information on the maturation of the brain.[135-137] Prior to 26 weeks following conception the EEG tracing is very irregular and shows no obvious periodicity. Slow waves alternate with periods of no electrical activity. Following this there appear regular bursts of 4–7 seconds' activity with amplitudes of 50–150 microvolts. By 6–7 months the bursts assume some regularity, and this is associated with an increase in enzymatic activity in the brain. By 8 months 16–18 cycles-per-second impulses predominate with a low amplitude. These changes are very typical of the premature infant regardless of birth weight, and there is little or no difference between the periods of being awake and asleep. One of the major differences between the immature and mature baby is the definite change in the EEG between periods of wakefulness and sleep. The changes that occur in the early years of life are the gradual disappearance of a predominantly slow rhythm of 2–4 cycles per second and its replacement by one of 4–7 cycles. At age 5 years the faster activity of the occipital regions begins to dominate, with impulses of 8–12 cycles, and the alpha rhythm of the mature brain emerges.

Sensory Development

Motor function precedes sensibility, as shown by the response of the embryo to direct muscle stimulation. Conel[17] states that there is evidence that the motor cortex matures earlier than the special sensory areas.

TACTILE SENSATION. — With growth more receptors are found in the skin over a wider area and in closer proximity. In early prenatal life the first response to touch is elicited in the region of the face, more particularly the lips. Later responses may follow tactile stimulation of the limbs and finally of the trunk in a cephalocaudal progression. However, even at full term touch and pain are not well differentiated.[12, 16]

The response to painful stimuli (pinprick) follows a fairly definite pattern of development. During the newborn period the stimulus must be strong to cause any response. This hypesthesia lasts about a week. The most characteristic response is immediate, diffuse, with general body movements and crying, and possibly reflex withdrawal of the stimulated member. At age 1 or 2 months the response is more delayed, there is a diminution of the diffuse body movements and reflex withdrawal is less common. When the child reaches 7–9 months there results a generalized localization of the point of irritation. Deliberate withdrawal movements occur which are directed away from the stimulus. Gradually the infant's ability to localize the point of irritation becomes more specific. By 12–16 months the response is one of carrying the hand directly to the point, rubbing the area or pushing the stimulus away, and the eyes will fix on the area if this is possible. This last development shows the beginning of cortical participation in behavior of this type.[37]

Proprioceptive receptors are fairly well developed by midfetal life. Stretching, tapping and causing a change in amniotic fluid pressure will elicit a response in the fetus.[62] These responses carry through into postnatal life and gradually come under the influence of higher centers.

VISUAL SENSATION.—The three primary functions of vision are: light perception, color discrimination and the determination of the size and shape of images. The latter, form vision, is especially concerned with the retinal fovea which has a more complex relationship with the visual cortex than does the peripheral retina. The visual cortex of the occipital lobe has begun differentiation before birth and is complete by 3 months. The EEG reveals some photic response at birth in the visual cortex but by 6 months these responses are very frequent and the pattern fairly regular to flashing stimuli. By 16 weeks the macula and fovea have completed their structural differentiation and myelinization of the visual fibers is well advanced. Final maturation of the macula is not reached until 6 years.[40] During the first weeks of life there is preferential fixation upon some specific patterned stimuli and similarly preference for specific shapes. These findings strongly imply that the visual perception system functions in a fairly complex manner at the time of birth and is capable of processing information. By 2 months there is preferential looking at novel visual stimuli and size and shape discrimination are clearly evident.[183]

The light sense is one of the most primitive of all visual functions and is a mechanism of the rods and visual purple. The portion of the retina with the greatest number of rods is fully developed by the seventh fetal month. The pupillary response is present in late fetal life. Even the smallest prematures apparently have some ability to differentiate light and dark.

Color perception is a function of the cones, which are in greatest number in the macula lutea. By means of grasp-and-reward methods of testing, it is believed that color perception for red, yellow, green and blue are present at 3–5 months. It is difficult to rule out the factor of brightness in all such tests.

The eye is small and therefore hyperopic (farsighted) in the newborn and throughout early childhood. The globe doubles in volume from birth to adult life. Visually, the small size of the globe is partly compensated by the greater convexity of the lens in early life. Although the lens is very soft and pliable, the accommodation-convergence reflex is not consistently present until approximately 6 months of age. With advancing age the lens flattens, reaching a steady state after puberty. The anterior and posterior cortical layers of the lens increase at a rate of 0.007 mm per year throughout life making it possible to "date" the occurrence of insults resulting in permanent lesions.

The continued anterior-posterior growth of the eyeball and the flattening of the lens eventually result in the decrease of the physiologic hyperopia of early life and the establishment of emmetropia in most children by the age of 10–12. Visual acuity at different ages is not universally agreed upon by all investigators but average figures are: 20/200 at 4 months, 20/100 at one year, 20/40 at 2 years and 20/20 between 4 and 5 years.[172]

At birth there is a moderate photophobia and the eyes are usually kept closed. The pupils are miotic but within weeks begin to enlarge and continue to do so for a few years. Psychosensory pupillary reflexes, absent at birth, become apparent at a few weeks. The lacrimal glands are not fully developed at birth but some tearing does occur though the crying reflex is absent for one or two months. Psychic weeping does not develop until the middle of the first year. Temporary obstruction of the lacrimal duct may cause overflow of tears associated with mild inflammation of surrounding skin and conjunctivitis. Spontaneous canalization nearly always occurs by 6–8 months.

Depth sense (visual stereognosis) requires the coordinated use of the two eyes and the fusion faculty of the brain. Fusion is not present at birth and does not appear until central vision is established. Depth sense is developed as the visual acuity grows sharper, as the ocular muscles become coordinated, and as the brain learns to fuse images. Binocularity is clearly established by 6 months of age with generally synchronous movements of the eyes. At about the same time early evidence of depth perception becomes manifest but is still poorly developed. Not until 6 or 7 years is depth perception very accurate and improvement continues until the early teens. Commonly at about 2 years esotropia (convergence) makes its first appearance. If this is monocular, medical attention may be indicated to prevent amblyopia.[171]

Most normal newborn infants will respond to an adequate visual stimulus, such as a bright object (5 cm diameter ball at less than 100 cm distance), by brief fixation of eyes, decreased motor activity, and changes in respiration. Some pursuit of moving objects with appropriate eye and head movements is found in a large number of newborn infants.[138] Very deliberate coordinated following of a moving object is always present by 16 weeks. By 4–5 months a visual-motor stage is reached, and the infant makes approaching movements with the upper extremities. Such development proves the establishment of connections between the visual and the neuromuscular mechanism. Not until the sixth to seventh month is a deliberate reaching, prehensile stage reached. It is not until 3 years that the child can look away from the object before completion of the neuromuscular activity and that the digits begin to extend just before they reach the object to be grasped. The child now is able to appraise the location and size of the object without undue effort. Such behavior displays the advancing maturation of cortical areas and their influence on the visual mechanism.

Further evidence of associations between sight and higher centers is shown by the baby at about 3 months when he recognizes familiar objects such as his bottle. By this time also the movements of the eyes are fairly well coordinated. At 5 or 6 months visual impulses are retained (memory) so that there is an increasing recognition of familiar objects and faces and the response of fear to an unfamiliar face appears.[37]

AUDITORY SENSATION.—The development of the membranous labyrinth occurs early. Its essential gross parts are well defined by the second month of fetal life. Ossification of the periotic capsule begins in the fifth month. At birth the bony investment is complete and there is little if any change in the internal ear thereafter; but later additions increase the size of the petrous bone, tending to bury the labyrinth more deeply. In general defects of bone or sense organs are more common in the cochlea than in the labyrinth.

The internal ear takes up sensations and passes them to the brain for elaboration and appreciation. The middle ear, concerned with the collecting and transmitting of sound waves to the internal ear, is practically of adult size at birth, although the drum membrane may be smaller and more oblique. The external canal is wholly cartilaginous at birth and much shorter than in the adult. The eustachian tube is shorter and more horizontal at birth. Its shortness, like that of the external auditory canal, is due to the slight development of its bony portion as compared with the cartilaginous.[50]

Hearing, as manifested by an overt response to loud (80–90 decibels) noise, is present in the term and premature infant as soon as amniotic fluid and debris drain from the middle ear. Until 3–4 months the response is primarily reflex in nature, such as a startle response. Grimacing, crying, eye blinking or change in respiratory pattern are other types of activity elicited. Localization attempts by eye movements or head turning are first evident at about 3 months. Less intense sounds, e.g., soothing voice, toy bell or rattle, are not consistent in eliciting a response but may cause changes in physical activity or stop crying. After 4 months most new sounds (as opposed to ambient sounds) will call forth searching activities. These will include looking, head turning, reaching and ambulation toward the sound. Speech stimulation from parents, siblings and self become obvious. Pleasurable sound-making and the auditory-tactile feedback of these experiences occupy an increasing amount of the infant's time. Sounds become more complex and between 4 and 6 months babbling is a prominent part of vocal play. This is followed by imitative vocalization and finally, toward the end of the first year, by words with a specific meaning.

The period that follows the end of the first year is characterized by the refinement of listening skills. This includes language development through imitating sounds and perfecting control over speech musculature and increasing ability to discriminate the subtleties of sounds in language. Very important is the gradual increase in attention span and the selective listening abilities. (The last is often an aspect causing consternation and dismay to parents of the 3- and 4-year-old.) The basic auditory skills are completely mastered by the 3-year-old and further development, as it applies to communication competence, involves integration, association and manipulation of those skills.

TASTE SENSATION. —Taste is present at birth, but it is doubtful that there is differentiation of sour, salt and bitter. By 2 or 3 months taste is acute, and the infant will notice a change in the amount of carbohydrate in his formula or a change in milk mixtures and demonstrate by evident displeasure certain substances which are disagreeable to his sense of taste. It is natural for the infant to explore his environment by this method until his other senses, particularly tactile, are better developed. Mouthing of toys is the usual pattern until late in the first year, when, except for thumbsucking, handling and visual inspection become the more common pattern of approach.[37, 48]

OLFACTORY SENSATION. —In the premature and term infant observers have obtained evidence of olfactory function. However, it is poorly developed in early infancy and becomes more acute with advancing age.[48]

DISTURBANCES OF THE SPECIAL SENSES. —These are usually reflected in the total behavior pattern (see Chapter 6). The two senses most commonly affected are sight and hearing. Absence of protective blinking to a strong light, absence of the pupillary reflex and failure to follow moving objects with appropriate eye and head movements constitute sufficient evidence of partial or complete blindness. Strabismus of the nonparalytic type may develop from a deficiency in the ability to fuse the image or may arise from reduced visual acuity in the deviating eye.

The deaf infant may show few signs of his defect for several months. A decrease in vocalization is one of the first changes noted, and accompanying this may be diminished laughter and smiling. What vocalization is present is often monotonal and unmodulated. Extreme visual attentiveness may be a suggestive symptom. Loss of contact with his environment affects the entire behavioral development of the deaf child and threatens his personality more than his intellect. As a result, behavior problems arise which may have been present for some time before the true cause is realized.

Circulatory System

Growth of the heart in weight is characterized by a very slow increment in the first 4 months of gestation and a steady, more rapid increment thereafter. Then for 4–6 weeks after birth there is little change in heart size. After this period the heart grows steadily. During the first year its weight is doubled; by 5 years it is increased fourfold and by 9 years, sixfold. From 9 to 16 years there is a second period of rapid growth concomitant with the increased general growth of this period.

In the full-term infant the heart lies midway between the crown of the head and the buttocks, and the axis is more nearly transverse than in later life. As in the adult, the greater part of the anterior surface of the heart is formed by the right auricle and ventricle. Except for the transverse axis and the absence of the shadow of the aortic knob, the roentgenologic picture of the heart does not differ greatly from the outline of the adult's.[54] By the end of the second or third year practically no differences exist between adult and childhood cardiac shadows (Fig 7–2).

All of the components found in the adult electrocardiogram (ECG) are also present from the fetal age of about 5 weeks.[62] By 11–12 weeks of gestation the fetal ECG can be accurately recorded through the abdominal wall of the mother, which is about 6 weeks earlier than auscultatory perception is possible.[139] Fetal viability can be diagnosed by this technic in the face of marked obesity, and it decreases the danger of radiation exposure by avoiding the use of x-ray. For several months after birth there is a right ventricular preponderance (right axis deviation). In the premature infant the general configuration of the ECG resembles that observed in full-term infants of comparable age.[140, 141] A lower voltage is present in all of the major complexes. The smaller the heart and the more rapid the rate, the shorter will be the P-R interval. In infants this may be as brief as 0.08 second. At 6 years the range is from 0.12 to 0.17 second, and at 14 years, from 0.13 to 0.19 second. The amplitude of the various segments or waves increases only slightly beyond that found in early infancy. In the precordial leads, V_1 and V_2, the T wave is usually inverted and often diphasic throughout childhood.[20, 31, 51]

Fig 7–2.—The cardiac shadow at different ages as seen by roentgenography in the anteroposterior position. **I,** early infancy; **II,** 4-year-old child; **III,** adult. *RA,* right auricle; *RV,* right ventricle; *A,* aorta; *P,* pulmonary conus; *LV,* left ventricle.

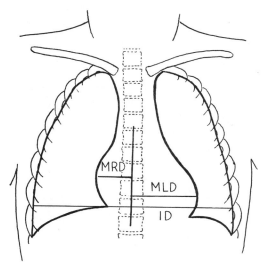

Fig 7–3.—Cardiac roentgenology: method for obtaining measurements of the cardiothoracic index from a teleroentgenogram. See text for details. (From Caffey.[14])

The *size of the heart* is best determined by use of the cardiothoracic index[14] (Fig 7–3). This is obtained from a teleroentgenogram made by placing the patient upright in a full frontal plane with the anterior chest wall against the x-ray film cassette. The exposure is made midway between inspiration and expiration. Tube-film distance is 72 in. The cardiothoracic index equals the total diameter of the heart ($MRD + MLD$) divided by the internal diameter of the chest at the level of the dome of the diaphragm (ID). During the first 3 years of life the index may be above 0.5 (0.62–0.40), but after this the index of a normal child will be less than 0.5.[5] When cardiac size is measured by this method, care must be taken in interpreting the result, for different phases of respiration from the peak of inspiration to the peak of expiration may change the index by a value exceeding 0.2. Position of the patient may also influence the result. Therefore a standard technique must be rigidly adhered to.[14]

In the evaluation of cardiac function and measurements of chamber size, valve positions, etc. there are presently available several very sophisticated techniques. These include cardiac catheterization, vectorcardiography and phonocardiography. Although the results of studies using such methods are recorded here as part of normal values, indications for their use and interpretation of results is beyond the scope of this book.

The growth in caliber of *arteries* seems related to the volumes or weights of the regions they supply. In the fetus the vessels springing from the main trunk grow in direct proportion to the parts of the body they supply, and those to the placenta grow in proportion to the vascular bed. After birth the trunks to the placenta become fibrotic and close completely in 2–5 days. These changes in fetal circulation also affect the arch of the aorta. Before birth blood passes to the arch of the aorta from the heart and through the ascending aorta and the ductus arteriosus. Secondary to the closure of the ductus, the ascending aorta grows rapidly, and this growth during early infancy is one of the most striking changes in chest structure in this period (Fig 7–4).

At term 15–25% of the circulating fetal blood volume is in the placenta. Under usual circumstances the ductus venosus, which carries blood from the placenta to the vena cava, closes immediately after birth. Functional closure of the foramen ovale occurs very shortly after birth.[99] With the onset of respiration the pressure in the left atrium (auricle) rises because of the great

Fig 7–4.—The circulation before and after birth. **Left,** fetal circulation; **right,** normal postpartum circulation. *A,* aorta; *AL,* atelectatic fetal lung; *DA,* ductus arteriosus; *DV,* ductus venosus; *EL,* expanded lung; *HA,* hypogastric artery; *HUE,* head and upper extremities; *IV,* inferior vena cava; *L,* liver; *LA,* left auricle; *LV,* left ventricle; *P,* placenta; *PA,* pulmonary artery; *RA,* right auricle; *RV,* right ventricle; *SV,* superior vena cava; *TLE,* trunk and lower extremities; *UA,* umbilical arteries; *UV,* umbilical vein. The foramen ovale between the auricles in the fetal circulation is not labeled. *Arrows* indicate direction of blood flow. The degree of oxygen saturation of the blood is indicated according to the key: *AB,* arterial; *MB,* mixed; *VB,* venous blood.

increase in pulmonary flow. A fall in pressure in the right atrium results from diminished venous return with the interruption of the placental circulation. Anatomic closure does not take place for several weeks, and increased pressure in the right atrium, as from crying, may cause a temporary shunt from right to left. Most infants show a left-to-right shunt during the first 24 hours, which gradually decreases to a small percentage by 8 days.[142] The time of closure of the ductus arteriosus is still the subject of controversy. Its patency is almost certainly responsible for a large portion of the shunting of blood during the first day of life, and many studies indicate that it remains open for weeks after birth.[52, 99] There is good evidence that constriction of the ductus takes place in response to the degree of oxygen saturation of blood passing through it. With an increase in blood oxygenation there is an increase in constriction.[52] There is an average reduction of 25% in heart volume from birth to the second day as a result of the fluid shift from the vascular compartment,[100] a reduction in volume upon cessation of placental circulation and, possibly, the decreasing size of the shunt across the ductus arteriosus. The gradual change of decreasing right ventricular preponderance in the electrocardiogram is due to left-sided growth and considerable involution of the muscle mass on the right. The right ventricular muscle outweighs the left by 13% at birth; they become equal by the fourth or fifth month; and by age 7 the adult relationship has become established, with the left wall two to three times thicker than the right.

Because of the frequency with which it is encountered and the resultant morbidity and mortality, the hemodynamics of the respiratory distress syndrome will be given brief consideration. Early in the condition, pulmonary vascular obstruction predominates and a right-to-left shunt occurs at the foramen ovale. In most, if not all, of these infants there is a persistent left-to-right shunt in the ductus with the volume of flow increasing with increasing respiratory difficulty. Thus, until the respiratory problem abates and the pulmonary vascular obstruction subsides, there is virtually a persistence of the circulatory pattern found in the fetus.[55]

Early or late clamping of the cord will cause a number of differences in the circulatory dynamics of the newborn. With so-called placental transfusion from late clamping, there is an expansion of blood volume, increase in heart size, higher systolic blood pressure and an increased respiratory rate, as compared to the controls with no transfusion. These changes persist for about 48 hours. Pulmonary rales and transient cyanosis are encountered more frequently in the group with late clamping.[143, 144] The increase in blood volume by using this technic may average 166 ml, or an increase of close to 60%. The value to the infant, if any, of one method over the other has yet to be determined.

The volume of fetal pulmonary circulation is greater than was formerly thought. About 12% of the total cardiac output is in the pulmonary flow. Until the third week of life pressure in the pulmonary artery is higher than the average value for older children. Growth of the small fetal pulmonary arterioles is accomplished after birth by an increase in the lumen and a relative decrease in media.

The thickness of the walls of the great veins is doubled between birth and puberty, and their lumens increase two and a half times by early maturity. The growth of the venous trunks, like that of the arterial trunks, tends to follow the increment of the parts they supply.[50]

The etiology of *congenital defects of the heart* has not been thoroughly investigated. It is, however, generally believed that congenital defects are developmental arrests in which growth processes have started along normal lines but failed to progress to completion. The reverse of this may occur, with a structure growing beyond its proper proportions. Structures molded by secondary changes may become defective by reason of resorption progressing too far or insufficiently. Other structures may form out of their proper relations.[54]

The fetal *heart rate* is usually between 130 and 160 in health. The heart rate is quite variable throughout life, with a wider variation between the extremes in younger persons. Rates differ only slightly between the sexes, with a slightly higher one predominating in girls at all ages (the increase averages about five beats a minute). It should be obvious that valid figures can be obtained only when the child is fully cooperative, quiet and not emotionally stimulated. Table 7–1 lists average heart rates obtained from several sources for children at rest but not sleeping.[20, 101, 102]

Heart rates during infancy are more variable, the younger the more so, than in later life. Part of this is due to the uncertainty of determining differences between the waking and sleeping status of babies. Both rates and variability are least in deep sleep. Mean rates at 1 week are 128 asleep, 163

TABLE 7–1.—AVERAGE HEART RATE
FOR INFANTS AND CHILDREN AT REST

AGE	AVERAGE RATE	2 SD
Birth	140	50
1st mo	130	45
1–6 mo	130	45
6–12 mo	115	40
1–2 yr	110	40
2–4 yr	105	35
6–10 yr	95	30
10–14 yr	85	30
14–18 yr	82	25

awake; at 1 month, 138 asleep, 167 awake; at 6 months, 114 asleep, 149 awake.

Sinus arrhythmia is to be considered a physiologic phenomenon in infancy and childhood.[23] The degree of arrhythmia is somewhat less in the infant, however, than in the older child. This finding is so constant that its absence should be looked upon as suggestive of abnormality. Investigations have shown that the presence and degree of arrhythmia are considerably less in children with rheumatic or congenital heart disease than in healthy ones. Extrasystoles appear frequently in clinically healthy subjects below age 14, but they are relatively more frequent in those with myocardial damage or heart disease. "Escaped heart beats" and mild degrees of sinoauricular block are not common but may be observed in otherwise healthy children. It may be concluded that sinus arrhythmia indicates good heart function, whereas in heart disease the responsible reflex mechanism is for some reason impeded, a condition expressed by regular pulse.[23, 101]

Blood pressure in infants may vary from day to day, and the standard deviation from the mean is relatively greater than in children and adults. There is a general trend to increase both systolic and diastolic pressures with age (Table 7–2). The pressures in premature infants are less than for term infants, an average of 10 mm Hg lower for both systolic and diastolic values for a weight of 2,000 gm as compared to a normal-weight baby.[145] A drop in blood pressure the first hour after delivery is usual and averages about 15 mm Hg. This may be a reflection of the readjustment of blood volume with the increase in pulmonary circulation.[146] Males continue to have a rising

TABLE 7–2.—NORMAL BLOOD PRESSURE FOR VARIOUS AGES
(mm Hg)

INFANTS		AGE	SYSTOLIC	2 SD	DIASTOLIC	2 SD
1st day	50	1 day	78	14	42	14
4th day	65	1 mo	86	20	54	18
10th day	65	6 mo	90	26	60	20
2d mo	65	1 yr	96	30	65	25
8th mo	76	2 yr	99	25	65	25
The figures for		4 yr	99	20	65	20
infants represent		6 yr	100	15	60	10
averages by the		8 yr	105	15	60	10
flush method		10 yr	110	17	60	10
described in the		12 yr	115	19	60	10
text.		14 yr	118	20	60	10
		16 yr	120	16	65	10

The figures under 1 year were obtained by the Doppler method. From 1 year on, the figures were obtained by auscultation, using the first change in sound to indicate diastolic pressure.

blood pressure with increasing age until about 20 years. Girls reach a plateau between 15 and 17 years.[28] To obtain accurate blood pressures, the cuff width should cover at least two thirds of the upper arm. A small cuff will give an erroneously elevated reading, while a wide cuff's main disadvantage is one of inconvenience. Within fairly wide limits, height and weight do not affect blood pressure.[22] Values found by the auscultatory method in children agree very well with intravascular arterial measurements.[169]

Because of poor cooperation, the obtaining of an accurate blood pressure by the usual technique of auscultation is often difficult during infancy. At least two alternate methods have been devised to remedy this situation. One is called the "flush method" and is carried out as follows: the hand or foot is compressed by the examiner's hand, or a pressure dressing is used to compress most of the blood from the part. The cuff is inflated to a pressure just beyond the expected reading. Compression of the hand or foot is removed, and the pressure in the cuff is slowly reduced. The abrupt return of normal color, flush, to the anatomic part indicates the blood pressure reading. The method gives a single value that lies midway between systolic and diastolic values and is quite accurate.[67, 68] A second technique is known as the "Doppler method" and utilizes a transducer in the cuff to transmit ultrasound waves to a recording device. It detects movements of the arterial wall, thus providing very accurate systolic and diastolic pressures.[58] Values in the neonatal period, but several hours postdelivery, are systolic 78, diastolic 42, and 2 standard deviations being 14 mm Hg. Throughout infancy and childhood there are no differences in mean blood pressures between blacks and whites.[51]

Such factors as emotional problems, crying and moving will modify the blood pressure, especially the systolic. Patience on the part of the examiner is important and, when indicated, sedation may be used to obtain a more reliable reading. Short of anesthesia, blood pressure is relatively little changed by sedatives.

Heart sounds during infancy and childhood are of a higher pitch, shorter duration and greater intensity than during later life. The first sound is typically the louder over the entire precordium and has a muscular quality or dull characteristic in distinction to the second sound, which is sharp in quality. Until adolescence the pulmonary second sound is regularly louder than the aortic. Innocent or functional murmurs are quite common during childhood. However, there is little agreement as to the actual frequency and considerably more agreement concerning their significance. In the neonatal period the shorter the period of gestation the more often murmurs are present. A single examination during the newborn period revealed an incidence of 1.7%.[70] Examinations repeated as often as hourly, indicated a frequency of greater than 50% during the first 48 hours of life.[66] Many of these probably represent a transient condition such as an incompletely closed ductus arteriosus or a patent ventricular septal defect.[101] Repeated examinations at 6–12 months indicate a frequency of murmurs at around 10%. After this time there is a rapid rise and at some time approximately 50% of children will have murmurs with the peak incidence between 6 and 9 years.[23, 69] Some children will retain their murmurs well into adolescence. Richards et al.[70] followed a large group of children for several years and found that a murmur present at birth had a probability of being a congenital lesion in a ratio of 1:12. However, if the murmur persisted to 6 months, the chance for association became 1:3. When a murmur was first heard at 12 months, the probability was 1:50. More than half of the murmurs heard at birth were gone by 6 months, and the same was true at 1 year for those noted initially at 6 months.

Innocent systolic murmurs are commonly designated as vibratory, pulmonic ejection and venous hum. The first two are most important because they may more easily be confused with murmurs indicating cardiac disease. The exact means by which the vibratory murmur is produced is not known. It occurs early in systole and is maximal in the third and fourth intercostal spaces from the sternum to the apex of the heart. It is low-pitched and is usually loudest in a reclining position. It does not obscure the other heart sounds. The pulmonic ejection murmur is due to turbulence in the outflow tract of the right ventricle. It is loudest in the left second and third intercostal spaces parasternally and early systolic in time. Both murmurs do not exceed grade III in intensity and are not transmitted to other areas. It is not always possible from auscultation alone to distinguish innocent from pathologic murmurs, especially if the murmur is of an intensity of grade III.

A "venous hum" is a common phenomenon found in children and is continuous in character. It is present parasternally, may be either sub- or supraclavicular in location and is usually accentuated in the upright position.

In the clinical examination of children there is perhaps nothing more subject to variable interpretation than heart sounds, including murmurs. Failure to recognize organic heart disease is indeed a serious error. However, just as serious is the error of alarming parents solely on the basis of a "heart murmur." Proper evaluation must be made in all cases in which disease is suspected, and this should include the past and present history, other aspects of the physical examination and laboratory data, including electrocardiography and roentgenologic studies.

Circulation at Different Ages

The ventricles in early life fill more slowly and are assisted more materially by a relatively more powerful auricular contraction than in later life. As long as the heart rate remains above 100 there is no interval of diastasis, the ventricles being in the act of either filling or discharging during the entire cardiac cycle. The figures for cardiac output of the neonate are 2–3 times greater than for the adult over a given period of time. With growth there is relatively greater development of the left compared to the right ventricle and continued descent of the diaphragm. These changes result in a more vertical position of the heart. Slowing of the heart with age follows increasing vagal control.

Several important physiologic and anatomic features characterize the transitional circulatory pattern in the change from fetal to adult pathways. Some of these have already been mentioned. There is continued patency of the foramen ovale with possible right-to-left shunting. Continued patency of the ductus arteriosus makes possible shunts in either direction. There is the unusual characteristic of the pulmonary vessels which constrict in response to hypoxia or metabolic acidosis. A lowered systemic arterial blood pressure persists for several hours after birth. Finally, the right ventricular muscle is as thick as the left. The essential elements of the change are the reduction in tone of the pulmonary vascular bed during the first several hours following delivery and an increase in tone of the ductus arteriosus. Within 24 hours the healthy term infant has a functionally closed ductus arteriosus and a mean pulmonary arterial pressure considerably below the systemic arterial value.[99, 101]

Except in the neonatal period the blood volume, relative to weight, does not fluctuate greatly throughout life. Recent studies on newborn infants are not in complete agreement with regard to average blood volumes and the direction in which the volume shifts during very early life.[100, 103, 104] At least a part of this disagreement may relate to the time at which the cord was clamped. If large amounts of blood come from the placenta (often more than 160 ml), redistribution may follow a course much different than would be true if the placental transfusion had not taken place.[147] The size of the infant may also influence the dynamics to some extent.[148] Most investigations support the theory that very soon after birth there is a shift of a large quantity of plasma, as much as 25% of the total, from the vascular compartment. This results in an increased concentration of red cells, with a rise in hematocrit. These changes are believed to occur within a matter of hours, and the mechanism of the shift is not known. Obviously the degree and rapidity of these changes will affect any studies carried out on the blood. The change in plasma volume may be one explanation for the variable results obtained in studies on hemoglobin concentrations or extracellular volumes done in the past. With these facts in mind, it can be said that in the newborn infant the total blood volume ranges from 80 to 110 ml/kg during the first several days. In the premature infant an average figure would be 100 ml/kg, and this falls steadily during the first several weeks.[52] In the older infant and child there is a further decrease to between 75 and 90 ml/kg,[71] and in the adult the average value lies within the range of 70–85 ml/kg (approximately 20–40 ml/lb). Using a dye method for their determinations, Brines and coworkers[11] found that total blood volume averaged 200 ml at birth and doubled by the end of the first year. There was little difference between the sexes until puberty, when the volume in the male increased rapidly. Average value for an adult male was 5,500 ml and for an adult female 4,200 ml. There was no direct relationship between volume and body length or surface area.

Lymphatic System

The number of lymph nodes and the amount of lymphoid tissue are considerable at birth and increase steadily during childhood but undergo a relative reduction after puberty.[50] Comparable figures hold for most of the lymphatic tissues throughout the body. An interesting German study cited by Scammon[50] revealed that by age 12 cervical and inguinal nodes were palpable in 100% of a series of children. The number of nodes varied but averaged from seven to nine in each area mentioned. Scammon's curves of organ growth (see Fig 7–7) portray the marked hypertrophy that occurs during childhood and the involution or atrophy that takes place during adult life. Tonsils and adenoids, being a part of the lymphogenous ring of Waldeyer, undergo similar changes, and one should realize that hypertrophy of these structures is a normal physiologic process.[33] The maximal development of these tissues during the time when acute infections of the respiratory and alimentary tracts are most common, and during the period of greatest increase in weight and height, has led to the conclusion that they are a part of a natural defense mechanism. They may have an important part in the total pattern of immune body formation (see "Development of Immunity"). Statistical studies have been equivocal regarding the defensive value of the tonsils and adenoids, and it is admitted that little is known of their function in infancy, when they may be most active as a protective mechanism.

The spleen and thymus are phylogenetically the earliest elements of the lymphoreticular system. By the fourth fetal month the spleen has assumed the general structural characteristics it will maintain. At birth it is larger in relationship to body size than at any other time, but it continues to grow, increasing its weight 12-fold by adult life. At the time of birth very few primitive lymphoid follicles are present, and no germinal centers. By 1 year many follicles are apparent and the germinal centers are well developed. Unlike other organs of the lymphatic system, the spleen does not undergo atrophy during adult life.[50, 149] The function of the spleen is the production of immunoglobulins, and it has a special phagocytic role in that it is the primary

Fig 7–5.—Roentgenography of the infant mediastinum. **A,** pronounced widening of mediastinal and cardiac shadows on nearly complete expiration with the diaphragms high. **B,** same infant a few seconds later, showing change in mediastinal and cardiac shadows produced by inspiration with the diaphragms low. **C,** an apparently abnormal right upper mediastinal shadow caused by improper rotation of the patient. **D,** same infant in normal antero-posterior position.

organ of bacterial sequestration. These protective abilities appear to play an especially important role in the first few years after birth.

The average weight of the thymus at birth is between 12 and 15 gm, but there are wide limits of normal.[8, 50] The birth weight is doubled at 6 months, tripled at 7 years, then remains constant until puberty. The observations of Boyd[8] and others[50] have proved that the lower weights mentioned in the early literature were probably based mainly on specimens which had undergone involution secondary to infection or malnutrition. Such involution may take place rapidly, and a large part of the thymus weight may be lost before the body weight is seriously affected. The thymic tissue, like the lymphatic structures in general, is most abundant when the general nutrition of the individual is at its best. As a general rule, underweight and malnourished children have small thymic shadows on roentgenologic study, and overweight subjects have relatively large thymic shadows.[14] It should be emphasized that there are pronounced variations in the size of the thymic shadow in normal children. Widening of the superior mediastinum on expiration is a normal finding during infancy, and such evidence should not be misinterpreted as an "enlarged thymus." Even in later childhood the organ may have assumed a flat and wide pattern, rather than the more usual narrowing and thickening, giving the impression of a large thymus on roentgenologic examination. Figure 7–5 shows examples of normal thoraxes in which apparent supracardiac widening had no clinical significance.

The function of the lymphoid tissue is primarily to protect against noxious agents, especially the microorganisms. The formation of antibodies is largely accomplished by various parts of the lymphoid system. In addition, structures such as the spleen and peripheral nodes have a filtering action to remove foreign substances from the circulation. During infancy and childhood this tissue characteristically responds to infection by hyperplasia which may outlast the infection for relatively long periods. With advancing age these changes become less pronounced.

Hemopoietic System

The first blood cells to appear in the embryonic circulation arise from the blood islands of the yolk sac. All of the first-formed corpuscles are nucleated, but with continued maturation they assume more and more the character of cells found after birth, and by the tenth fetal week about 90% of the cells in the circulating blood are non-nucleated. In succession, the blood-forming organs are: the yolk sac for the first 2 fetal months, the liver throughout the remainder of the fetal period and the bone marrow, which starts hematopoiesis about halfway through gestation and continues throughout the rest of life. At birth only the lymphocytes are found outside the marrow.

However, the liver and spleen, and possibly other organs, retain the ability to make blood cells for some time after birth and in hemopoietic crises may again manufacture cells until early childhood is reached.[45] During the first few days of life the number of normoblasts found in the bone marrow is reduced considerably. At birth they make up about 36% of the cells, but by the end of the first week the number approaches 17% as an average and then remains at this level throughout childhood. There is a relatively slight change in the number or maturity of the granulocytic series; however, there is a general trend for an increase in the number of lymphocytes found in the marrow, from 6–8% in the newborn to 35–45% at one year and then dropping back to 10–15% at 11 years.[72] In the marrow of the long bones there is an increasing replacement of blood tissue with adipose tissue as age advances. Microscopically this fat appears by age 3 or 4 and grossly by age 7. In the adult very small amounts of red marrow remain in the long bones. Red

TABLE 7–3.—AVERAGE NORMAL BLOOD VALUES AT VARIOUS AGES*

AGE	RBC, MILLION/ CU MM	HGB GM	WBC/ CU MM	POLY., %	LYMP., %	MONO., %	RETIC., %	PLATE/ CU MM
1 day	5.5	21	20,000	70	20	10	3.0	350,000
6 days	5.3	20	15,000	62	31	7	0.7	325,000
2 wk	5.0	18	12,000	31	63	6	1.0	300,000
1 mo	4.7	16					0.5	
2 mo	4.0	12					1.0	
3 mo	4.0	11					2.0	
6 mo	4.5	11.5	10,000	32	60	6	0.8	300,000
1 yr	4.6	12.5	10,000	38	55	6	1.0	300,000
2 yr	4.7	13.0	10,000	45	49	6	1.0	300,000
5 yr	4.7	13.0	8,000	54	40	6	1.0	300,000
10 yr	4.7	13.0	8,000	60	34	6	1.0	300,000

	MCV, μ†	MCH, $\mu\mu_G$	MCHC, %	MCD, μ	HCT
1 day	106	38	36	8.6	53
6 days	103	36	35		49
2 wk	96	33	34		46
1 mo	90	30	33	8.1	43
6 mo	77	26	33	7.4	37
1 yr	78	25	32	7.3	37
2 yr	77	25	32		38
5 yr	80	27	34	7.4	40
10 yr	80	27	34	7.4	42
Adult	87	29	34	7.5	45

*From Wintrobe.[63] Note that there may be a wide range within normal limits.
† MCV = mean corpuscular volume
MCH = mean corpuscular hemoglobin
MCHC = mean corpuscular hemoglobin concentration
MCD = mean corpuscular diameter
HCT = hematocrit

marrow is present in the ribs, vertebrae, sternum, skull and innominate bones throughout life.

In order to maintain the normal cellular equilibrium in the circulating blood, the blood-forming organs are furnished with effective reserves sufficient for all demands. At birth there is a very small reserve of cells at or near the stage of definitive maturation, all bone marrow showing hyperplasia of maturing cells at every stage of development. In early fetal life the concentration of red cells and hemoglobin is low, with the red cells larger than normal and often nucleated. As the fetus grows, there is a gradual rise in hemoglobin content and number of red cells, with reduction in red cell diameter and the number of nucleated forms. At birth the values for red cells and hemoglobin exceed those characteristic of adult life. Shortly after birth the number of red cells and the hemoglobin content fall and reach the lowest point at the eighth to tenth week of life. In the next two years there is a gradual rise in hemoglobin level, which then normally remains stationary[5, 46, 63] (Tables 7–3 and 7–4).

The cellularity of the marrow normally decreases during the first week after birth and attains normal adult levels by the third to fourth month. The greatest change is in the reduction of the erythroid elements, as already noted. Simultaneous with this change is the disappearance of erythropoietin from the plasma. A rise in erythropoietin during the third week coincides with the resumption of marrow activity noted at that time. This glycoprotein, produced in the kidney, is an important hormonal factor influencing red cell production. It is synthesized in increased amounts in response to hypoxia, whether this is due to ischemia, anemia or decreased oxygenation.[5]

TABLE 7–4.—AVERAGE VALUES FOR RED CELLS, HEMOGLOBIN AND VOLUME OF PACKED RED CELLS IN MALES AND FEMALES*

AGE	RED CELLS, MILLION/CU MM	HGB, GM	VOL. PACKED CELLS, %
10 yr			
Male	4.7	13	38
Female	4.7	13	38
14 yr			
Male	5.0	14	41
Female	4.7	13	39
17 yr			
Male	5.3	15.5	45
Female	4.7	13.5	40
Adult			
Male	5.3	16	47
Female	4.7	14	42

*From Wintrobe.[63] Note differences between male and female values after menarche.

The type of hemoglobin present in the late fetus and newborn differs considerably from that found later in life. This early type is called "fetal" hemoglobin in contrast to "adult" hemoglobin. Several chemical differences are known and make possible fairly precise quantitative analysis of the two types. Physiologically the main difference is that fetal hemoglobin has a greater affinity for oxygen than does adult hemoglobin. In the hemoglobin dissociation curve the fetal type is considerably to the left of the adult, i.e., the degree of saturation with oxygen is greater in fetal hemoglobin for the same partial pressure of oxygen as compared with adult hemoglobin. Cord blood contains an average of about 80% of fetal hemoglobin. Adult hemoglobin is first detected in the fetus at about the 13th week of gestation and gradually increases until birth. If anoxia in the fetus exists, a compensatory increase in hemoglobin occurs, and this is mainly of the fetal type.[76] There is evidence that this type is found mainly in the larger red blood cells.[73] Two weeks following birth the average amount of fetal hemoglobin is about 75% of the total, at 5 weeks 55% and by 20 weeks 5%. These are average figures, as there is considerable variation.[74, 75] The life span of the red cells formed during the late fetal and the early neonatal period and containing large amounts of fetal hemoglobin is between 65 and 100 days, compared to 120 days for adult cells.[150] (Using different methods, investigators in the field of cell survival have arrived at different figures, but the shorter life of the cell containing fetal hemoglobin seems well established.)

The blood values found during the first few days to weeks of life may be influenced by several factors.[19, 30] In babies whose cords have been clamped early after delivery the values for hemoglobin, red cells and hematocrit are significantly lower on the first and third days of life than those of babies whose cords were clamped after placental separation. For hemoglobin the average difference between the groups is 3 gm; for red cell count the difference amounts to 1,000,000 cells/mm^3 and for hematocrit 7%. The reticulocyte count is higher after early cord ligation than after delayed clamping, the average being 5.9 in the former and 2.7 in the latter. In infants allowed full benefit of the placental blood the icteric index is higher on the third day than in those whose cord was clamped early. It has also been demonstrated that blood values differ in the newborn with the source of the sample.[19] In general capillary blood will give higher values for hemoglobin, red cells and hematocrit than will venous blood. A third factor to be considered is the time after birth when the blood specimen is obtained. There may be a slight rise in the red blood cell count for a day or two, but this is followed by a rather substantial drop (see Table 7–3). All or some of these factors may account for the differences in values reported for the neonatal period. Nucleated red blood cells, not in excess of 5% of the total number of nucleated cells, may be present normally for several days after birth. Macrocytosis and hyperchromia are characteristic of this period.

Values for hemoglobin in the cord vary from 12 to 22 gm in apparently normal babies. In one series studied there was no relationship between the maturity of the infant and the level found. When these subjects were re-examined at age 2 months, the average hemoglobin level was 11 gm, and this level existed regardless of the value found in the cord at birth.[77] It may be important to point out that the possible benefit from increased stores of iron with the higher initial values would not be evident by 2 months. The reticulocyte count at birth ranges from 3 to 7% in full-term infants but is higher in the premature, sometimes reaching values of 16%.[78] These high counts drop rapidly during the first week but rise slightly again about the end of the second month in response to the physiologic anemia of infancy.

At about 6 years the peripheral blood picture resembles that of the adult. From Table 7–3 it can be seen that the early high leukocyte count of the newborn declines rapidly and that a similar phenomenon occurs with the granulocytes. From age 2 weeks to about 4 years there is a preponderance of mononuclear cells in the peripheral circulation, and for another 3–4 years the number of these cells remains higher than in the adult.

Cells in the circulating blood reflect accurately the marrow activity with regard to both leukocytes and erythrocytes (see Table 7–3). A relative leukopenia has been found in black children and adults. This difference between the white and black is apparent by one year of age and is unrelated to geographic or other environmental influences. The mean total is 1,000 per cu mm less in blacks at all ages after the first year. The lower count is primarily due to a decreased number of neutrophils.[177]

Platelets are derived from megakaryocytes which are present in the yolk sac during early embryonic development, in the liver during the hepatic phase of hematopoiesis and lastly in the marrow. Platelets are present in the circulation as early as the 11th week of gestation and at birth the megakaryocytic activity in the bone marrow and the platelet count in peripheral blood is similar to that of older children and adults. Although one study[151] indicated that the platelet count was considerably decreased in the smallest of premature babies, most other studies have failed to confirm this.[5, 114] A decreased or impaired platelet aggregation has been found in some term and an even higher percentage of premature newborns. Initially platelets adhere to the collagen exposed by injury to a blood vessel. Adenosine diphosphate (ADP) is released by these platelets which leads to further aggregation. It now appears that poor platelet aggregation is present only in infants born to mothers who received acetylsalicylic acid (aspirin) or chlorpromazine, both of which interfere with release of ADP.[5]

In spite of relatively low levels of factors II (prothrombin, a globulin converted to thrombin by calcium that produces the clot by modifying fibrinogen to fibrin), VII (a plasma factor necessary to convert prothrombin to thrombin), IX (a globulin that participates in formation of thromboplastin) and X (a factor essential to thromboplastin formation) bleeding tendencies in the neonate are very rare. All of the above factors necessary for clot formation require vitamin K for their formation. Full-term infants have plasma levels from one-half to one-third those found in older children, and the shorter the gestation period the lower the value. Unless there has been a marked vitamin K deficiency, clotting is adequate to prevent any hemorrhagic disease. The complications of vitamin K deficiency almost never occur in breast-fed infants. Although fibrinogen (factor I) may be at comparatively reduced concentrations in the premature, it is very adequate in amount.

The isoagglutinogens determining blood grouping are present in the red blood cells in early fetal life, although they increase in strength during both intra- and extrauterine existence.[52] The isoagglutinins also follow a rising curve, but are of relatively less importance from a clinical standpoint. The serums of some infants also have agglutinins passively acquired from the mother, and these may be of such type that they would render transfusion of blood from the mother very unwise. Finally, there is evidence that the red cells of the fetus may pass across the placenta and induce specific responses in the maternal serum. In erythroblastosis fetalis (hemolytic disease of the newborn), hemolysins induced in the mother's serum by this means may cross the placental barrier and produce severe blood destruction in the fetus. The RH factor is the best known of the specific agglutinogens of the fetus responsible for such a train of events.

Development of Immunity

Resistance to infection includes a large number of protective devices that are common to all infants and children and are nonspecific. These include the skin, which acts as a physical barrier, plus its secretions, which have antibacterial properties. The lining mucosa of the intestinal, respiratory and genitourinary tracts also act as barriers by the nature of their physical structure, enzymes and other materials secreted and, in some areas, by ciliary action. Intestinal motility is one of the most important factors in controlling the excessive multiplication of bacteria within the small intestine. Normal indigenous intestinal flora are valuable deterrents to the overgrowth of pathogens.[154] Various cells in the body can function as phagocytes to bacteria, viruses and their products. For the cells circulating in the blood stream, this action is greatly aided or perhaps completely dependent upon the presence of either *complement* or *opsonins* or both. As the infant's passive immunity conferred by his mother wanes and before he has manufactured his own catalog of immune globulins, all of these mechanisms assume major proportions.

Interferon is another of the relatively nonspecific products of the organism useful against viral infections.[155] This is a protein substance made in living cells following their exposure to a virus, not necessarily a living virus. It can be produced by all types of living tissue beginning in fetal life, and the proficiency of its synthesis does not appear to be influenced by age. It is of interest to note that the environmental changes that enhance in vitro production of interferon are found in inflamed tissue—a decreased pH, lowered oxygen tension and elevated temperature. The mechanism of action in inhibiting virus reproduction is through its effect upon the host cell, preventing the formation of ribonucleic acid (RNA), necessary for virus replication. Although interferon is species-specific, only one type is produced by each of the species of animals so far examined which inhibits growth of all homologous and heterologous viruses.

The immunologic system has two functions which are under the control of two different but interacting lymphoid systems. One protects the body against invading microorganisms by the synthesis of specific antibodies released into the serum or occasionally other cellular secretions. The other functions through a cell-mediated mechanism of immunity which is responsible for resistance to some specific bacterial, mycotic and viral infections, and for the surveillance of aberrant cell differentiation in the individual.[82]

The origin of these two systems arises from the stem cell of the yolk sac which differentiates into a thymic-influenced group, or T cells, and another group that subsequently is derived from the bone marrow and is designated as B cells. The thymus develops from the third branchial cleft and is actively producing cells as early as the second month of gestation. It is the lymphoid cells under the influence of the thymus that will be responsible for the cell-mediated immunities. Animals, including man, without a thymus or a T cell lymphoid system cannot survive in the usual pathogen-laden environment. Cells of the two systems can now be identified and in healthy persons the B lymphocytes account for 20–25% of the circulating lymphocytes and T cells for 75–80%. During the first year of life the percentage of B cells is slightly higher.[34] There is some evidence that T cells produce a product that assists the B cells in responding effectively in antibody synthesis.

The thymus-derived lymphocytes tend to be distributed selectively in certain regions of the lymphoid tissue. In nodes they occupy the deep cortical areas and the white matter of the spleen. In the circulation they are the small lymphocytes. Of the B cells, those that produce IgA and IgE will be located in subepithelial regions. The circulating B lymphocytes are larger than the T cells. In the lymph nodes they are in the cortical areas and along the medullary cords. Upon antigenic stimulation, they transform to plasma cells with marked cytoplasmic development including endoplasmic granular production and an accentuated Golgi apparatus. These changes appear to be the morphologic changes necessary for the production of antibody synthesis.

In a germ-free environment neither plasma cells nor germinal centers in the spleen or nodes appear. The thymus is vital for the maturation and function of the lymphoid system during a considerable period after birth. In animals, if thymectomy is done at birth, there is marked impairment of antibody production, in the development of delayed hypersensitivity and in the rejection of homografted tissue.

The T lymphocyte is primarily responsible for the cell-bound site of immune mechanisms and the phenomenon of delayed hypersensitivity. These are clinically manifested in contact hypersensitivity, homograft rejection, the tuberculin reaction and some forms of drug allergy.

Specific immunity depends upon the integrity of the lymphoid tissues and their ability to respond to a specific stimulus (antigen) with the complementary antibody. A distinguishing feature of this response is memory. Once an individual has interacted with an antigen, what was learned concerning the synthesis of an antibody is recalled upon another exposure to the same antigen. Normally these mechanisms react only to exogenous substances; but injury, drugs, infection and possibly other factors may induce, on rare occasions, specific antibodies against the host's own tissues. The result is referred to as an *autoimmune disease.*

The first stage in the specific response to an infecting organism is ingestion by a phagocyte, either fixed (macrophage) or motile (leukocytes and histiocytes), with subsequent digestion and release of an antigen which passes to the lymphoid cells. These undergo hyperplasia and hypertrophy with the formation of follicles in lymph nodes, spleen and tonsils. With the initial exposure there is also the first appearance of plasma cells. These cells synthesize five recognizable immunoglobulins. The nature of three of the best understood are indicated in Table 7–5.

Gamma G contains most of the antibacterial immunoglobulins, and since these are genetically specific, they can stimulate the formation of isoantibodies. Passage across the placenta is by active transport, with an increased rate toward the end of gestation. It is for this reason that the premature infant may have a lower level of gamma G than that present in the term infant, which equals that of his mother. The passive immunity acquired by the newborn subject will reflect the mother's past experiences with clinical or subclinical infections and active immunizations. This acquired immunity will protect for 6–9 months following birth.

The low frequency of plasma cells in normal human fetuses during the last trimester and the fall in the level of gamma G globulin, reaching a nadir at

TABLE 7–5.—THE IMMUNOGLOBULINS

Standard nomenclature	Gamma G	Gamma A	Gamma M
Other nomenclature	IgG	IgA	IgM
Molecular weight	165,000	150,000–400,000	900,000
Sedimentation rate	7S	7–11S	19S
Half-life, days	28	5	5
Adult percentage of immunoglobulins	70–80	15–25	3–10
Placental passage	Yes	No	No

3–4 months is the result of absence of stimulation, rather than an inefficient antibody response. In fact, in appropriate conditions the fetus and neonate can respond to antigenic stimulation by the proliferation of plasma cells and antibody production. (It is significant that patients with agammaglobulinemia have no plasma cells.) Exposure to an increasing array of antigens, as time progresses, results in an increase in the number and quantity of specific antibodies found in the serum. Normal adult levels are usually reached by the second year (Fig 7–6). This immunoglobulin is the major one produced in combating infections.

Gamma A is present in the serum in lower concentrations in the child than in the adult and may be absent in the newborn. This immunoglobulin may

Fig 7–6.—The average level of circulating gamma globulin during the first 2 years of life. Note the rapid fall in the first months of life and the slow rise back to adult levels by the second birthday. (From Orlandini et al.[79])

represent a first line of defense against many infections. It has antibody properties similar to those of gamma G but is present in the serum only incidentally. It is synthesized by plasma cells adjacent to epithelial surfaces. There is some evidence that antigens applied locally, e.g., oral poliovirus and influenza virus, may invoke an increased production of specific antibody. This immunoglobulin is found in the intestinal mucosa, in nasal secretions, in colostrum and milk, in bronchial secretions and in tears.[154, 165]

Gamma D has not been identified with a specific action. *Gamma E* is found in the serum in very small amounts. Much higher levels, possibly of diagnostic value, are found in association with severe allergic diseases and parasitic infestation.[18]

Gamma M is found in low concentrations in uninfected fetuses as early as the 20th week of gestation. The source of antigens responsible for its production at this time is not known. In normal newborns, synthesis of this immunoglobulin continues at a rapid rate for the next month and then at a slower rate to reach adult levels by the end of the first year. This information plus other observations indicates that both the fetus and neonate have an increased ability to make IgM, in comparison to IgG and IgA. In fact, the response of IgM to antigenic stimulation remains more rapid than IgG throughout most of the first year. Since IgM is the only antibody found in large amounts in the neonate, regardless of gestational age, who has suffered from an intrauterine infection, it has become an important indicator of that fact. The mean level at birth in the absence of infection is 10–11 mg/100 ml of serum. A level above 20 mg/100 ml is strongly indicative of present or past infection. In congenital rubella, toxoplasmosis, and cytomegalic infections, levels in excess of 100 mg/100 ml are not uncommon.[80, 82] Antibodies in gamma M also include those responsible for the Wasserman and heterophile tests, the rheumatoid factor and the somatic antigens of some gram-negative organisms. A very high level of IgM following congenital rubella, as an example, may reduce the ability to synthesize IgG and thus increase the infant's susceptibility to other infections. The high concentration of passively acquired IgG from the maternal organism also serves to depress fetal and neonatal production of that immunoglobulin. Delay of active immunization of infants until after the first year is advisable for rubeola due to interference of maternal antibodies prior to that time.

Cellular immunity arising from the T lymphocytes appears to be well developed in the newborn. In contrast, maternal lymphocytes at delivery are poor responders against allogenic stimuli. This reduced cellular immunity may be an important factor during pregnancy in protecting the fetus against an immunologic attack by the mother.[82]

The detailed analysis of antibody structure has provided a basis for studying the molecular genetics of the immune response, and an understanding of both the diversity and the commitment of each cell to the synthesis of only one kind of antibody. Immunoglobulins consist of a basic unit comprising two pairs of polypeptide chains, named, according to their molecular weight, "light" and "heavy" chains. The unit of the globulin is formed by two identical heavy and two identical light chains. The heavy chains give the molecule its class distinction, i.e., gamma A, gamma G, gamma M, etc. At the terminal portion of each chain is a variable region in which the sequential arrangement of amino acids changes, a different pattern for each specific antibody. The possible combinations are as infinite as the number of antibodies that will be triggered by each antigen[115] (Table 7–6).

Opsonins, factors in serum that facilitate phagocytosis, appear to be functional during fetal life and are adequately present at birth in full-term infants. In low birth weight infants the activity is decreased, proportionate to the gestational age, toward the following bacteria *Serratia marcescens, Escherichia coli, Pseudomonas aeruginosa* and *Staphyloccocus aureus*.[149]

The *complement system* is a complex of at least 9 different serum proteins closely associated with the humoral antibody system. They usually function in a kind of chain reaction or cascade to facilitate phagocytosis, in a manner that would classify some as opsonins. Most importantly, the reaction sequence is set off by the binding of a specific IgG or IgM antibody to its antigen (cell) which results in the complement C1 binding to the antibody. The end result is cell lysis which cannot be accomplished by the antibody alone nor by the complement system alone.[149] Prematurely born babies have lower levels of measurable complement than term infants who have levels about half that of adults. Adult levels are usually reached at around 6 months.[38]

Macrophages arise primarily from bone marrow, circulate briefly as monocytes, migrate to tissue and there mature functionally to become typical histiocytes. They function as a major part in host defenses by destruction of viruses, intracellular bacteria and parasites. They also play an important role in removing the tissue debris of wound healing, senile cells and tumor cells. Their phagocytic activity may be enhanced by the specific action of an-

TABLE 7–6.—IMMUNOGLOBULINS:
RANGE OF SERUM LEVELS AT
DIFFERENT AGES (in mg/100 ml)

AGE	IgG	IgM	IgA
Newborn	650–1200	5–20	0–10
1 mo	300–500	20–45	10–35
6 mo	400–800	20–60	15–50
1 yr	500–1000	30–80	30–90
10 yr	500–1300	40–120	75–150
Adult	500–1300	70–120	150–250

tibodies and complement as well as by other opsonins and nonspecific stimuli such as BCG. The severity of infections in the newborn period with the *Herpes simplex* virus and *Listeria monocytogenes,* as well as some other evidence, has been attributed to a lack of maturity of macrophage function. How long this ineffectiveness lasts is not presently known, but probably not more than several weeks in the normal infant.[152]

Immunologic competence in the normal infant improves with age. This is likewise true for the low birth weight infant who has no other complications. Splenectomy and thymic irradiation early in life may interfere with the usual maturation of this competence resulting in a possibly lethal susceptibility to infections or malignancy.[38, 82] The reduction in the manufacture of IgG due to fetal rubella can be cited as another example of interference with normal development of immunologic competence. Fetal malnutrition, when severe and prolonged, causes delayed rise in IgG levels, a poor response in antibody titers to some antigens and a reduction in number as well as function of T cells.[163]

Maternal milk contains immunoglobulins of the secretory IgA category, complements C3 and C4, interferon and living leukocytes. In addition to these immunologic components there are additional host-protective factors including lactoferrin, an iron-binding protein, other proteins that bind B_{12} and folic acid, a fatty acid that inhibits growth of staphylococci and complex sugars that promote growth of *Lactobacillus bifidus.* The levels of these substances are particularly high in colostrum. Infections with enteropathic *Escherichia coli* are reported to be much reduced in breast-fed infants compared to those ingesting cow's milk. In vitro studies have shown that lactoferrin removes the iron necessary for growth of a number of organisms including staphylococci. Infants breast-fed by mothers with high serum antibody titers for Coxsackie and poliomyelitis viruses are relatively resistant to oral infections by these organisms. For these reasons many European investigators have advocated the use of breast milk for the vulnerable premature infant.[181, 182]

Maturation of tissue may influence immunity and reaction to antigenic stimuli. In spite of heavy exposure, infection with Brucella abortus in young children is as uncommon as that infection is in calves. Apparently immature tissue will not harbor the infectious agent. Allergic reactions in infants usually are manifested by changes in the skin (eczema), which seldom last longer than two years. The more common response in the older child is in a different tissue, the respiratory tract.

During the newborn period septicemia is far more common than at any other age. There is little tendency to localization of the infection or striking elevation of the temperature. Such symptoms as anorexia, vomiting, diarrhea and subnormal or erratic temperatures are much more reliable signs of infection in this age group. Some viral infections are noted at this time almost to the exclusion of all other ages—e.g., cytomegalic inclusion disease and the generalized forms of Coxsackie and herpes simplex viruses. All are serious, with a high mortality rate. Infections later in life by the latter two viruses are, by contrast, mild and localized. Only in early infancy does one encounter an enteritis from certain strains of *Escherichia coli*. Other pathogens encountered almost exclusively in the neonate or in early infancy include group B streptococci, Proteus, Klebsiella and *Listeria monocytogenes*. Staphylococcal infections may be responsible for severe disease at all ages. Later in infancy and early childhood infections of the upper respiratory tract, including otitis media, are most common. The number of such infections increases each year for the average child until the age of 5–6 years. The total incidence for any one child will vary depending upon such factors as home conditions and opportunity of sibling exposure. These infections are often characterized by high fever, and not infrequently lead to convulsions. Evidence of growing immunity is exemplified by the rarity of serious infections with *Hemophilus influenzae* in children past 3 or 4 years of age. During the school years the various exanthems make their appearance. The hyperpyrexia with convulsions seen earlier is now uncommon. Possibly because of previous sensitization of tissue by past infections, acute hemorrhagic nephritis and rheumatic fever come into prominence at this time. Rarely do these complications of infection by the hemolytic streptococcus occur before 4 years or after 20 years.

Normal Constituents of Blood

Besides the formed elements, the blood contains many substances in solution or in the form of colloids. The blood content of many of them reflects in a large measure the workings of organs or organ systems, especially the kidneys, lungs and liver. Table 7–7 shows the trends of the various constituents with change in age or maturation. It must be emphasized that each laboratory has its own procedures and consequently its own normal values, which may differ slightly from those given. Furthermore, for some age groups and for some substances the number of determinations has been quite small. Most of the estimations were made on capillary blood. This has been done because such methods are becoming increasingly popular in hospitals and laboratories where large numbers of children are examined; because much smaller quantities of blood are necessary, making such procedures more practical, and, finally, because we are more familiar with these micromethods.

We are becoming increasingly aware of the individual differences in normal or average blood chemistry values and of a surprisingly wide range of

TABLE 7–7.—NORMAL VALUES FOR CONSTITUENTS OF BLOOD*

SUBSTANCE	PREMATURE	NEONATE	INFANT	5–15 YR
Aldolase, IU	(6.0–18.0)	(7.2–20.0)	(3.6–10.0)	(1.8–4.9)
Ammonia, μg/100 ml	(100–250)	(90–150)	(45–80)	(45–80)
Urea N, mg/100 ml	(20–47)	19 (10–30)	(6–20)	(6–15)
NPN, mg/100 ml	(24–63)	45 (25–62)	35 (25–45)	(25–35)
Uric acid, mg/100 ml	3.25	3.5 (2.7–5.1)	3.0	3.0
Amino acid				
nitrogen, mg/100 ml		(3.0–4.0)	(3.0–4.5)	(3.0–4.5)
Creatinine, mg/100 ml	(0.5–3.0)	(1.0–2.0)	(1.0–2.0)	(1.0–2.0)
Serum protein,				
gm/100 ml	5.6 (4.5–6.0)	6.1 (5.0–6.9)	5.9 (5.0–6.6)	(6.5–8.0)
Albumin	(2.5–3.5)	(3.0–4.5)	(3.8–5.0)	(4.5–6.0)
Globulin	(1.0–2.2)	(1.3–2.4)	(1.4–2.4)	(2.0–3.0)
Gamma globulin	(0.5–0.9)	(0.8–1.0)	(0.3–0.6)	(0.9–1.3)
Fibrinogen	0.4	(0.2–0.4)	(0.2–0.4)	(0.2–0.4)
Glucose				
(fasting), mg/100 ml	(27–90)	(47–102)	(70–120)	(70–120)
Total lipids, mg/100 ml		(100–600)	470	(500–700)
Cholesterol, mg/100 ml	(45–100)	(45–170)	(70–180)	(130–240)
Electrolytes, mEq/L				
Total base	159 (152–171)	153 (148–160)	152	152
Sodium	(138–159)	144	144	144
Potassium	(4.0–7.0)	(4.0–7.0)	(4.0–5.5)	(4.0–5.5)
Chloride	(104–120)	(102–110)	(100–107)	(100–107)
Bicarbonate	(12.7–25.3)	(18–27)	(23–28)	(23–28)
Serum calcium,				
mg/100 ml	(7.8–9.0)	(8.0–10.0)	(10–12)	(10–12)
Serum phosphorus,				
mg/100 ml	(6.0–8.5)	(6.5–8.5)	6.0	5.0
Alkaline phosphatase,				
IU	···	(70–225)	(50–150)	(50–250)
Serum bilirubin, mg/100 ml	(1.5–7.5)	(1.4–6.0)	(0.2–0.8)	(0.2–0.8)
Lactic acid, mg/100 ml	(15–30)	17	10	10
Thyroxine,				
T_4, μg/100 ml	(5–13)	(7–15)	(5–10)	(5–10)
17-ketosteroids,				
μg/100 ml	···	(60–300)	(0–50)	(0–120)†
17-OH steroids,				
μg/100 ml	···	(5–10)	(5–15)	(5–15)
Iron, serum, μg/100 ml	···	(60–140)	(30–90)	(50–100)
Lactate dehydrogenase, IU	···	(308–1500)	(200–800)	(100–180)
Phospholipids, μg/ml	···	(1.0–1.8)	(2.0–3.5)	(2.4–4.4)
Transaminase				
SGOT, units	···	(10–120)	(5–50)	(5–45)
SGPT, units	···	(10–90)	(5–50)	(5–50)

*Average figures are given as a single value; the range is enclosed in parentheses. Data from various sources.

†The higher levels are found during and after adolescence.

values for many constituents. Particularly during the neonatal periods of both the full-term infant and the prematurely born infant, the ranges are wide and the fluctuations within the individual are great. When it is realized that this is a period of great instability for all of the physiologic mechanisms of the organism, such findings need not confuse. The time of day, number of days after birth and ingestion of food may also affect the values obtained. As examples, we know that during the first few days after birth blood calcium levels, glucose levels and the quantitative prothrombin time are all reduced but reach higher levels in a short time. The phosphorus value, on the other hand, remains relatively elevated in many cases for weeks or months after delivery. The reasons for such changes are not always clear, but the interpretation of seemingly abnormal values from a clinical standpoint must be made with caution in the light of these observations.

During infancy there is an increasing tendency toward stabilization in the healthy subject. After the first year of life the child has become relatively homeostatic so far as most organ functions are concerned. Throughout this chapter we have discussed the relations of organ functions to age and to a limited extent have drawn attention to the blood levels of various substances. Reference should be made to these sections, as well as to Chapter 11, for further examples of blood chemistry and interpretation.

Digestive System

Some aspects of the embryologic development of the gastrointestinal tract are important to an understanding of various congenital anomalies.[45] During the fifth and subsequent fetal weeks there is a conspicuous elongation of the gut which results in a long loop extending ventrally into the belly stalk (the future umbilicus). At the end of this loop is found the yolk sac, which forms a valuable reference point for orientation in following the rotations of the lower intestinal tract. When the gut tract is viewed in ventral aspect, a counterclockwise twisting of the loop is seen. This initial rotation is the primary factor in establishing the positional relations of the large and small intestine. Referring to the yolk sac, that portion of the gut caudal to its attachment becomes the large intestine and a small portion of the distal ileum, while that portion cephalically located becomes the duodenum, jejunum and the remainder of the ileum. By the 10th fetal week the abdominal cavity becomes large enough to accommodate the intestines, and at this time the cecum is found in the left upper quadrant. Rotation continues so that the cecum normally passes over the duodenum first to the right upper quadrant and finally descends to its usual position in the right lower quadrant. Descent is not completed until some time after birth. With this rotation is carried the mesentery and the distal portion of the ileum.

If growth of the abdominal cavity is disturbed to the point that it cannot hold all of the mass of the intestines, they may remain protruding into the belly stalk as an umbilical hernia or, if protruded to a severe degree, as an omphalocele. With persistence of the yolk stalk the anomaly of Meckel's diverticulum occurs. This may take several forms. It may remain attached to the abdominal wall as a fibrous cord or may remain patent so that the contents of the ileum have a fistulous opening at the umbilicus. Finally, it may be a simple sacculation of the ileum. Not infrequently the lining of these diverticula contains mucosa typical of gastric mucosa, leading to ulcer formation.

Incomplete rotation of the gut is not uncommon, and the cecum and adjacent structures may be found in adult life at any position along the path normally followed. Malrotation results from a reversed twisting of the primary gut loop; the small intestine lies ventral to the transverse colon instead of dorsal to it. Such a developmental anomaly causes volvulus in a high percentage of cases; it may be present at birth or not occur until a later age.

Toward the end of the second fetal month the epithelial lining of the gut tends to grow so exuberantly that complete occlusion results. Such changes are particularly apt to take place in the esophagus, upper part of the small intestine and in the rectum.[45] If for some reason the lumen is not reestablished, congenital atresia results. If recanalization is partial, stenosis occurs. Bremer[9] has hypothesized that if two epithelial lumens are formed rather than one, and if this condition persists, duplicate tubes are formed, resulting in the curious anomaly of reduplication of the gut—for example, ileum duplex.

Small pearl-white round areas are rather commonly found in the oral cavity of the newborn infant over the posterior portion of the hard palate. From one to more than half a dozen may be present. They probably represent retention cysts and usually disappear by the 10th day of life. They are sometimes called Epstein's pearls after the Prague physician who first described them. Occasionally petechiae are found over the soft and hard palate; these are rapidly resorbed. They are more commonly found in babies who have had their mouths and pharynges wiped by the gauze-covered finger of the obstetrician following birth.

Although sufficient salivation takes place in the newborn to maintain adequate moisture, many of the cells of the salivary glands do not mature until the third month or later. Drooling, resulting from lack of frequent swallowing, becomes prominent in some infants at about the third month and may increase with the eruption of the first teeth. A protruding tongue, normal in a small percentage of infants during the first several months of life, may accentuate this condition. A short lingual frenum restricting the protrusion of the tongue seldom causes symptoms at any age and rarely, if ever, interferes with nursing or speech development. To the best of our knowledge, we have not seen a true "tongue-tie."

The position of the esophagus in the newborn is the same as in the adult except for its relation to the vertebral column, being one vertebral level higher, with the superior limit at the fourth or fifth cervical vertebra and inferior limit at the ninth thoracic vertebra. At birth it is lined with stratified squamous epithelium five to six cell layers thick. Ciliated cells appear between 12 and 16 weeks of fetal life as a transient condition. Esophageal glands are present at birth but become more complex during later life.[50]

Embryologically, the stomach has the subdivisions and form found in the adult. In the infant the stomach lies with its long axis in the transverse plane of the body. In the second to third year the "cow's horn" form is most frequent. By the seventh to ninth year the "fish hook" type is seen, and from 10 to 12 years onward the stomach is similar to that of an adult.[57] Growth of the stomach is most rapid between birth and the third month of life. At other times the increase in mucosal area is slow and even. Most of the figures in the literature on the capacity of the stomach at various ages are based on postmortem studies and are therefore fallacious. The capacity is fixed only by the maximal limits of distention and varies widely with the size of the infant, the amount of ingested material, and the amount of swallowed air. Very rough approximations are 30–90 ml at birth, 90–150 ml at 1 month and 210–360 ml at 1 year. By age 2 capacity is 500 ml, and in later childhood the average capacity is between 750 and 900 ml.

The length of the small intestine in the newborn varies from 300 to 350 cm, increases about 50% in the first postnatal year and is doubled by puberty. The annular type of duodenum is the form most commonly found in the newborn and young infant.[57] The cecum of the infant is much smaller than that of the adult. The appendix is relatively the same length at birth as later, but it grows rapidly during the first year. The ascending colon is relatively shorter in the newborn than in the adult; the transverse colon is relatively long and may be thrown into folds. The sigmoid colon is usually filled with meconium and is thrown far upward in the abdominal cavity, but it regains its usual position a year after birth.

The salivary glands are said to increase threefold in weight during the first 6 months of life and fivefold in the first 2 years, and by this time to have acquired all the histologic characteristics of the adult.[57]

At birth the pancreas is at the level of the second or third lumbar vertebra. It assumes adult histologic appearance by the end of the first year though it is functionally capable of secretion from midpregnancy on. By this time granules appear in pancreatic cells and enzyme activity is present in the form of insulin, alpha-amylase, lipase, trypsin, chymotrypsin, carboxypeptidase, ribonuclease, desoxyribonuclease, phospholipase, elastase, collagenase and leucine aminopeptidase. Trypsin and lipase activity are lower in premature than in full-term infants and lower at birth than in later life. The levels of most of these enzymes gradually increase to reach adult levels at 3 to 4 years.[32, 65]

In the newborn infant the liver occupies nearly two fifths of the abdominal cavity. The lobulated structure is poorly developed at birth, and lobulation does not become complete until after early childhood. The liver at birth forms 4% of the body weight, and by puberty weighs 10 times as much. A palpable liver edge is very common throughout infancy and early childhood. The gallbladder of the infant increases in size rapidly during the first two years of life.

Sucking in the neonate occurs first in small bursts of only three or four at a time in response to the stimulus of touching the lips. Very quickly, longer and more efficient attempts result. In the mature newborn this maturation may take only a few hours, but in the premature it may require a few days. With sucking there are contractions of the esophagus and peristaltic waves; but unless there is actual passage of material into the upper esophagus, these shortly disappear. It is assumed that this early motility is secondary to neuronal immaturity.[157] The tone of the inferior esophageal sphincter is poor throughout infancy, resulting in repeated regurgitation of gastric contents into the esophagus. This gradually diminishes in frequency and quantity so that it rarely persists past the first birthday.

Roentgenologic studies of the intestinal tract of the normal newborn infant reveal that a gas bubble is visualized in the stomach with the first cry. This gas passes rapidly down the tract, entering the ileum within 2 hours and reaching the rectum by 3 or 4 hours on the average.[84] If none is present in the sigmoid by 24 hours, it is reasonable to assume that some obstructive lesion is present.[14] The esophagus of the infant may be sinuously curved, and after a few swallows of barium there may be a rather pronounced retention of the material in the lower end for several minutes. Gas bubbles passing upward from the stomach frequently push the barium back, causing regurgitation.[1] In the stomach of an infant less than 3 months old there is seldom evidence of a true peristaltic wave, the stomach appearing to contract as a whole. The gastric emptying time during infancy may vary greatly, normally occurring in from 2 to 6 hours with barium mixtures. Longer periods are found following milk feedings in comparison to water or glucose-water feedings. In premature infants the emptying time is slightly, but significantly, faster than in term babies fed in a similar fashion. In the premature, on a milk formula, the median time is 5 to 6 hours.[105] Examination of the small and large intestines reveals little difference from those of the adult except for the relatively high position of the cecum throughout early infancy and the redundant sigmoid, previously mentioned. However, until age 4 or 5 the colon appears disproportionately large, and megacolon has been mistakenly diagnosed in many normal children as a result of failure to recognize this characteristic. Muscular spasm in the colon is rather frequently observed and has no significance in the absence of other findings.[109]

In the normal full-term infant, saliva has been found in the mouth before food has been taken. Gastric juice is secreted by the mucous membrane of the stomach, and hydrochloric acid is present before birth. There is great variation in the amount of free acid in the infant's gastric secretions, but achlorhydria is rare, except possibly in premature infants, of whom as many as one-third have no measurable gastric acidity for at least several days after birth.[112] Secretion of acid by the stomach is under hormonal control of gastrin which is produced by cells of the antrum glands. Stimulation for gastrin involves that by the vagus nerve, triggered by food intake, and the physical stretching of the stomach. Immediately after birth, gastrin in the blood of neonates is significantly higher than in the maternal circulation. This level is further increased with the first feeding. As a result there is a high output of hydrochloric acid right after birth with pH values of gastric juice averaging around 5. Possibly lower values might be found in the absence of swallowed amniotic fluid. After the first feeding, pH values drop as low as 2.2. There follows a gradual fall in output of acid during the next 2 weeks, followed by a rise to adult levels by the end of the fourth month.[27, 85] Because sick infants often develop a relative achlorhydria, vomiting does not result in a decrease in the plasma chloride. With pyloric stenosis, where the obstruction is a purely mechanical one, vomiting can result in a marked reduction in chloride and an electrolyte shift characteristic of metabolic alkalosis.

Both pepsin and renin are present in the fetal stomach and reach adult levels a few months after birth.

Concentrations of duodenal bile acids increase with advancing age throughout infancy. Taurine conjugated bile acids predominate at birth but in the older infant they are mainly conjugated with glycine.[64] Bile acids are essential for the optimal absorption of dietary fat by the small intestine. The low concentration of bile acids and the decreased duodenal concentration of lipase may account for the relatively poor tolerance of fat by some infants.

Our knowledge of hepatic function in early infancy indicates there is some physiologic immaturity.[49, 52]

1. The physiologic hyperbilirubinemia of the newborn is due to several factors, including the normal hemolysis of the excess of red blood cells, but most importantly to liver immaturity. Adequate excretion of bilirubin is possible only after conjugation of the free form (indirect) with glucuronide to form the soluble direct form. The ability to perform this conjugation depends on an enzyme, transferase, which is quantitatively at a very low level

in the newborn and remains so for several days or weeks. This finding is even more marked in the premature infant, who is usually more intensely jaundiced than the full-term infant. Approximately 50% of normal term infants will have visible jaundice in the first week of life, and 80% of the prematurely born. Chemicals or drugs that compete with the transferase as a conjugating agent will often augment the hyperbilirubinemia. Pregnanediol, a steroid found in the breast milk of a small number of women, is one of the naturally occurring substances that may interfere with conjugation of bilirubin and increase the icterus or prolong it.[110] The relationship of severe forms of hyperbilirubinemia to kernicterus and resulting brain damage is well established.

2. During infancy the bile excreted is of low concentration compared to that excreted in later life.

3. The prothrombin level at birth is 20–40% of the normal adult level. It slowly rises to the adult level at the end of the first year. The prothrombin time by Quick's method, which measures the time necessary for the formation of thrombin from prothrombin, is about normal at birth and falls by the second or third day, to return to normal by the sixth day. Prothrombin is formed in the liver.* Recent studies indicate that such a simple explanation for the coagulation defect seen in some newborn infants is no longer adequate. A complex series of factors is involved in the conversion of prothrombin into thrombin. In many newborns several of the so-called vitamin K factors may be low, especially factor VII, in addition to a low concentration of prothrombin.[123] (See "Hemopoietic System," this chapter.)

4. The blood protein values, especially albumin and globulin, are low throughout early infancy. The amino acid levels are essentially the same throughout infancy as in the adult; so one can assume that there is some lag in synthesis.

5. The low blood sugar levels found during the first few days of life may in part be due to lowered gluconeogenesis from protein. It has also been demonstrated that conversion of other sugars (i.e., galactose and fructose) to glucose is slower in the newborn infant.[106]

6. Cholesterol esters are formed chiefly in the liver. The low serum content of these substances during the first year or more may reflect hepatic immaturity.

7. Excretion of Bromsulphalein depends upon two factors of liver metabolism: (1) direct excretion of the free substance and (2) conjugation followed by excretion into bile. Throughout the first week of life from 20 to 30% retention in the 45-minute test is experienced. In the premature infant even

---

*Another factor to be considered is the reduced synthesis of vitamin K in the gut owing to decreased bacterial flora in the neonatal period.

higher values are found.[111] By the end of six weeks normal values of less than 10% retention are present.

8. A number of liver function tests that depend upon changes in circulating blood protein, usually associated with disease in older subjects, will give positive reactions for varying periods of time in the newborn. The response to the cephalin cholesterol flocculation test is often positive in the neonate for several days. It is interesting to note that during the first few months of life the response to this test will remain negative, even though liver damage is present to such an extent that it would cause a positive reaction in an older subject. The thymol turbidity test may show a positive reaction for a brief period. The significance of these findings is presently obscure and they do not necessarily imply functional immaturity.

At birth the lower intestine is filled with meconium, a viscid material greenish-brown to black in color and giving a positive result to tests for occult blood. The normal infant passes some fecal material by 24 hours. In one recent study[87] 69% of the infants had a stool by 12 hours and 94% before 24 hours. The number of stools varies considerably during the first week; they are most numerous between the third and sixth days, when a mean average of 5 in 24 hours is reached. At this time little difference is noted between breast-fed and bottle-fed infants.[88] From the fourth to the seventh day the infant passes transitional stools which are thin, sour, slimy, brown-to-green and may contain remnants of meconium. The stools of the breast-fed infant are homogeneous, sour, pasty, and yellow. The number of stools during early infancy varies considerably, usually numbering two to four a day for the breast-fed infant and one to three for the bottle-fed baby. As the diet becomes more varied and the relative amount of milk is diminished, the fecal material becomes more formed and darker and by 2 years does not differ greatly from the adult stool.

The first meconium passed is sterile, but within a few hours all material passed through the intestinal tract contains bacteria. Within a few days a profuse flora is established in the mouth and the large intestine. The small bowel remains relatively sterile throughout life. The intestinal flora of the breast-fed infant is fairly simple with a high preponderance of *Lactobacillus bifidus* and small numbers of enterococci and coliform bacilli. Breast-milk feedings produce this type of intestinal flora, in contrast to modified cow's-milk feedings, because of its high lactose content, low protein and therefore low buffering action on intestinal contents, and possibly because colostrum and human milk contain some immunoglobulins that influence bacterial growth. Bottle-fed and postweaning stools predominate in anaerobic *Bacteroides* species and aerobic organisms such as *Escherichia coli*, *Klebsiella* and *Streptococcus faecalis*. In the older child and adult, staphylococcus, streptococci and yeasts are found in the lower intestinal tract.[178]

Shortly after birth the microorganisms in the infant mouth correspond in type to those in the maternal vagina. By 2–5 days the oral and nasal flora consist of *Streptococcus viridans,* coliform bacteria, diphtheroids and non-pathogenic diplococci, e.g., *Neisseria catarrhalis.*[178]

Respiratory System

By the sixth week of fetal life the trachea, bronchi and lung buds can be clearly differentiated and their migration toward the thoracic area has begun. This migration is almost completed by the third fetal month, and thereafter the lungs descend very slowly. From its first appearance the right primary bronchus is somewhat larger than the left and is situated at a more acute angle. Although these differences become less marked with growth, they remain sufficient postnatally to account for the fact that foreign bodies more often enter the right bronchus than the left.[45]

The absolute dimensions of the larynx at birth are approximately one-third those of the adult, but relative to the rest of the body it is as large as or larger than at maturity. The cavity of the larynx is short and funnel-shaped throughout infancy. Until age 2 or 3 years the growth of these structures is rapid; then there is a slower increment until puberty. At that time, particularly in males, there is again a rapid increase in all dimensions. From about the third year on, the larynx is longer and wider in boys than in girls. In the newborn the upper end of the epiglottis lies at the level of the first cervical vertebra and is easily seen during physical examination. It gradually descends so that at puberty it is opposite the lower half of the third cervical vertebra.[50]

The trachea in the newborn infant is about 4 cm long, roughly one third the adult length. Both diameters, anteroposterior and lateral, increase nearly 300% from birth to puberty. The small lumen explains the respiratory difficulty associated with the inflammations of this organ in the young child. At birth the bifurcation of the trachea lies at the level of the third or fourth thoracic vertebra, at 4 years at the level of the fifth thoracic vertebra and at 12 years between the fifth and sixth thoracic vertebrae.[50]

The weight of the lungs of a newborn infant in whom respiration has been established is not significantly greater than that in a stillborn infant.[50, 52] This would seem to show that there is no great or sudden influx of blood into the pulmonary bed with the beginning of respiration. However, with the opening of the alveoli there is a vast increase in the pulmonary capillary bed, and the lungs soon accept the entire output of the right heart which was previously shunted through the ductus arteriosus into the aorta. Besides preparing the way for a greater blood volume, the expansion of the lungs and associated unfolding of the coiled capillaries has the effect of lowering the pulmonary vascular resistance. The pulmonary arterial pressure immediately after birth rises abruptly and exceeds the systemic arterial pressure by a considerable degree. During the first several hours, this favors the shunting of blood from left to right across the ductus arteriosus. By the end of the first day the pulmonary pressure has fallen to approximately half of the mean systemic pressure, and it continues to fall but reaches stable levels before the end of the first week.[13, 99] The weight of the lungs is doubled in the first 6 months, tripled by age 1 year and increased 20 times by adult life. There is little change in topography of the lungs, fissures or pleura from infancy to maturity. Anteriorly there is slow descent of the lung margin from the fifth to the sixth rib during growth.

In the premature infant several important anatomic features of the respiratory system differ from those of the mature newborn.[35, 61] There may be a conspicuously impoverished pulmonary vascular bed in the immature infant, and this may explain the impediment to gaseous diffusion and the tendency to cyanosis. There may also be a sparsity of pulmonary elastic tissue, contributing to the persistent atelectasis in the premature infant. And finally, the feeble musculature and the soft bony thoracic cage augment the respiratory difficulties.*

Many of the aspects of respiratory physiology in the fetus and newborn are still under study, and many of the facts now known are interpreted in different ways. Recent monographs with excellent reviews should be consulted by the interested reader. These include works by Smith,[52] Lind and associates[99] and Avery.[158]

The long controversy concerning whether or not regular respiratory movements normally take place in utero seems to have been answered through the development of sophisticated methods to study the problem. By the use of ultrasound techniques it can be demonstrated that movement of the fetal chest, at a frequency of 40–70 per minute, is present about 70% of the time during the last half of gestation. Such movements can be detected sporadically as early as 13 weeks' gestation. There may be diminution of these movements with hypoxia or hypoglycemia. Tactile stimulation will cause reflex gasping as early as 11–12 weeks.[6, 62]

Both the fetus and the newborn have an excessive amount of hemoglobin that differs qualitatively from that found after a few weeks of extrauterine life. Both the quantitative and the qualitative characteristics allow more oxygen to be carried per unit of blood and a greater uptake of oxygen from the lungs. (See also p. 238 for the characteristics of fetal hemoglobin.) However, there may be a resultant lessened efficiency in the release of oxygen to

---

*A relatively decreased (immature) vascularity in the respiratory center of the brain may also be responsible for a reduced sensitivity to stimuli in the smaller premature infants.[35]

the tissues. A third characteristic of neonatal blood is the relatively small amount of carbonic anhydrase. This tends to retard liberation of carbon dioxide and acquisition of oxygen in the lungs.[52, 59] The clinical importance of a low anhydrase level has yet to be completely evaluated.

The transfer of the respiratory function from the placenta to the lungs is related to umbilical cord occlusion. The stimulus for breathing is mediated through blood gas changes and possibly an added factor of tactile stimulation. In actual measurements these are: arterial P_{O_2} falls from 80 to 15 mm Hg; arterial P_{CO_2} rises from 40 to 70 mm Hg; arterial pH falls below 7.35; the tactile stimulation of pressure in the vaginal passage and cooling by exposure are also factors. The rapidity of these changes may be equally as important as the absolute levels. Failure to respond is nearly always secondary to central nervous system depression (as by drugs) or injury.

The most important stimulus to the onset of breathing is probably anoxia resulting from the interruption of the oxygen supply carried by the umbilical vessels. Such changes result in the accumulation of acid metabolites in the respiratory centers of the medulla, and the resulting fall in the pH furnishes the true stimulus.* The metabolic acid-base status of infants of all birth weights are similar.[159] Asphyxia in both premature (low birth weight) and term infants leads to a reversible metabolic acidosis; and if this is associated with hypoventilation, respiratory acidosis is added. The former appears to be a direct consequence of the hypoxia with accumulation of normally combustible organic acids (chiefly lactic). Other factors, such as the transfer of H^+ ions from cell to plasma, are not well documented. With hypoventilation the retention of carbon dioxide in the lung and then in blood leads to the respiratory acidosis. At the time of birth most of the alveoli are collapsed, and those that are open are filled with fluid. In addition there is a definite cohesive force of the moist surfaces of the smaller bronchi and alveoli. Wilson and his associates[59, 60] concluded that the first breath may be the most difficult and that for a variable period after birth vigorous inspirations should be maintained. Some degree of persistent primary atelectasis may be present roentgenologically for more than a week in a normal infant, and in the premature may last several weeks.[14, 60] It is believed that such atelectasis, when present, is normally slight.

Anatomic growth of the lung is characterized by an individual pattern for the airways, alveoli and blood vessels. The airways (bronchi, bronchioli and alveolar ducts) grow predominantly antenatally. The bronchial tree is developed by the 16th week of intrauterine life. The alveoli develop after

---

*It is quite possible that the aortic and carotid chemoreceptors play a more important role in initiation of the stimulus to respiration than does the center in the medulla. A sufficiently prolonged period of anoxia following birth may so disturb the mechanisms involved that they cannot function properly.[99]

birth, increasing in number until approximately eight years and in size until the chest wall ceases growing as an adult. The diameter in fixed specimens increases by 3–4 times from early infancy to puberty. During the first 3 years of life the increase in lung size is mainly due to alveolar multiplication. During the last 3 months of gestation, in addition to the development of distal (respiratory) bronchioli, terminal saccules with flattened epithelium are formed. Respiratory exchange or function is possible at this time. Just prior to birth, primitive alveoli can be detected in the walls of the saccules which will become the alveolar ducts. Until 11–12 years of age there is very sparse elastic tissue present, then a fairly rapid increase to adult proportions occurs.[185]

Vessels associated with the airways and with the alveoli have their independent growth patterns and follow the development of the related structures. Cell types and cell numbers of the respiratory epithelium are established by 6 months gestation and little change ensues with advancing age.[158, 185]

The volume of air taken in the first breath varies considerably but averages about one half of the estimated vital capacity of the 2- or 3-day-old infant, which ranges from 130 to 160 ml. The pressure exerted by the initial inspiration ranges from 10 to 70 cm H_2O, which may serve as practical limits to guide us in the use of artificial respiration.[116] The alveolar CO_2 tension in the normal newborn is below that found after 2–3 weeks of life and may reflect the effect of a patent ductus recirculating blood through the lungs without picking up additional tissue CO_2.[117] During this period there is also increasing alveolar ventilation and oxygen uptake.

Before birth the bronchi and alveoli contain liquid, which is predominantly produced by the lungs themselves. The liquid is different from amniotic fluid in several respects, including a lower urea nitrogen content and the presence of a lipoprotein surfactant, which lowers surface tension and thus maintains the small air spaces and increases the space for available gas exchange once expansion has occurred. After the initial large inspiration, successive breaths have intermediate-sized pressure swings and volume changes. The ratio of the volume expired to that inspired rises, and the rhythm is irregular. Within 10 minutes after the first inspiration the normal infant has acquired some 50–70% of his normal residual capacity. After 30 minutes the lungs are essentially free of excess fluid and the lungs are well expanded. After the first day a continuing regular pattern ensues with some episodic variations related to crying, sleeping, feeding, etc. Prolonged (15 seconds) apneic periods are seldom encountered in the normal newborn infant.[158, 164]

Respiration in infants is largely diaphragmatic in character and continues so until the fifth to seventh years of life, when the costal element becomes more prominent.[31] The rate and depth of breathing are extremely variable in infancy, and the younger the subject the greater the variations. Table 7–8 shows variations in respiration with changes in age. One of the most common respiratory patterns in the premature infant is periodic breathing. This is characterized by periods of apnea in a sequence of ventilatory movements. The pattern of duration and frequency of apnea from infant to infant or in the same infant at different times undergoes great variation.[158] With increasing maturity more regular respiration occurs.

Recent work involving the study of apnea in the preterm infant has lead to a number of discoveries concerning respiratory regulation. The specific neurons in the brain stem that act to fire rhythmically and generate the efferent impulses to the musculature controlling involuntary respiration are highly dependent upon afferent impulses incident to those neurons. The type of breathing—regular, periodic or apneic—depends upon both the inherent activity of the medullary centers and the nature of messages received by those centers. Producing hypoventilation through influence on the centers are hyperthermia, hyperinflation of lungs, vigorous nipple-feeding and catheter suction of the pharynx. Decreasing input to the centers may also decrease their efferent outflow resulting in periodic breathing, hypoventilation and apnea. This may result from hypoxia over an extended period, anemia, hypoglycemia, central nervous system depressants, sepsis and other factors. Immaturity of the centers has already been mentioned as an important element in this respect. In summary, apnea and periodic breathing are characteristically present in early infancy, decrease in frequency and duration with age, occur predominantly in periods of active (REM) sleep, and in the neonatal period are observed more often in premature than in term infants. Apnea in excess of 15 seconds at any level of development may be a

TABLE 7–8.—VARIATIONS IN RESPIRATION
WITH AGE

AGE	RATE/MIN	TIDAL AIR, CC	VITAL CAPACITY, L*
Premature	40–90	12	—
Newborn	30–80	19	—
1 yr	20–40	48	—
2 yr	20–30	90	—
3 yr	20–30	125	—
5 yr	20–25	175	1.0
10 yr	17–22	320	2.0
15 yr	15–20	400	3.7
20 yr	15–20	500	3.8

*These represent mean figures from several sources for both sexes. Vital capacity for boys averages about 6% greater than for girls.

harbinger of cardiopulmonary or central nervous system pathology.[41, 184]

Both term and preterm infants are obligatory nose breathers. The normal response to nasal obstruction, whatever its cause, is to open the mouth to retain the airway. This reflex is absent for a period of several weeks following birth, even to the point of producing cyanosis and eventual asphyxia.

The change in the relative measurements of the chest with age has been discussed (p. 80). The conical shape of the adult chest is not attained until near puberty. Functional tests of lung growth during childhood have been compiled.[160]

Auscultation over the chest of the infant reveals that the breath sounds are loud, harsh and seem near to the ear. These characteristics are due to the fact that the tracheal and bronchial sounds are more distinct and are transmitted through less tissue than in the adult. For the same reasons, the percussion note over the lung fields of the infant and young child is more resonant, even tympanitic, than in the older child or adult.

Bronchovascular shadows in roentgenograms of infants and children are often difficult to read properly. They are relatively more prominent than in the adult, and studies have shown that there is no very exact correlation between the size and density of the hilar shadows and the incidence of upper respiratory infections. There is considerable variation among children, so that simple comparison has little value. Evaluation of these markings by the inexperienced has no doubt frequently led to the erroneous diagnosis of bronchitis and even bronchiectasis. It should be remembered also that shadows extending from the hilus are normally more dense in the inferior segments than above. Owing to the heart shadow, they are relatively more prominent on the right side. As in roentgenographic study of the mediastinum, the phase of respiration influences lung markings, and both phases should be observed when examination is made to find pathologic conditions, especially atelectasis, emphysema and nonopaque foreign bodies.[14]

Malformations of the respiratory tract are relatively rare.[45] Agenesis of one lung or congenital cysts of the lungs may occur. Congenital laryngeal stridor may be the result of small size or abnormal proportions and of a peculiar weakness of the musculature. The most common tracheal anomaly of serious clinical significance is a tracheoesophageal fistula, frequently associated with the cephalic portion of the esophagus ending in a blind pouch.

Urinary System and Water Balance

It is the function of the kidneys to help in regulation of the internal environment of the body. They accomplish this in the following manner:

1. Excretion of nitrogenous waste products, mainly in the form of urea.

2. Stabilization of osmotic pressure by selective excretion and reabsorption of electrolytes, sugar, etc.

3. Stabilization of chemical composition by the mechanism of "renal threshold" and selective excretion and reabsorption.

4. Regulation of extracellular fluid volume, which is partly dependent on (2), also through the action of the posterior lobe of the pituitary body in regulating total fluid output.

5. Maintenance of acid-base balance by electrolyte and osmotic regulation, excretion of excessive accumulation of either acid or alkali and the formation of ammonia in the kidneys to neutralize acid and conserve base.

These actions of the kidneys are supplemented and influenced by other organs or systems, especially the following: lungs, through loss of fluid and excretion of bicarbonate; posterior lobe of the pituitary body, by regulation of water and electrolyte excretion from the kidney; and, finally, the adrenal cortex, through control of sodium, potassium and chloride metabolism.

In the discussion on fetal growth we have seen that after birth there is no pronounced change in the proportion of total body water to body weight. However, there is considerable change in the location of that fluid from birth until maturity. The extracellular fluid volume of the newborn infant is nearly double that of the adult, about 40% of the body weight being extracellular fluid in the newborn and 20% in the adult. (These figures are based on methods measuring the sodium space of the body, which is not strictly extracellular.) Evidence so far obtained reveals that the decrease in extracellular volume of fluid occurs mainly at two different periods of rapid growth. There is a great decrease during early infancy and a less pronounced decrease during adolescence. The intervening period is relatively constant (Table 7–9).

Not only does the infant have a greater content of extracellular fluid than the adult, but the rate at which fluids are exchanged is much greater. The average adult takes in and excretes about 2,000 ml of water daily, representing about 5% of his total body fluid, or 14% of his extracellular fluid. The infant's daily exchange of 600–700 ml of water, in contrast, represents about

TABLE 7–9.—DISTRIBUTION OF WATER IN THE
BODY AT DIFFERENT AGES

AGE	TOTAL BODY WATER	EXTRACELLULAR WATER	INTRACELLULAR WATER
Birth	72	40	32
1 mo	68	32	36
1 yr	64	24	40
Adult	60	20	40

Each figure is the percentage of body weight.

TABLE 7–10.—DAILY WATER REQUIREMENTS

AGE	BODY WEIGHT, KG	WATER REQUIREMENT, ML/KG
3 days	3.0	80–100
10 days	3.2	100–150
3 mo	5.5	140–160
1 yr	9.5	120–140
6 yr	20.0	90–100
12 yr	38.0	60– 80
Adult	70.0	20– 40

20% of the total, or nearly 50% of his extracellular volume. Of the water lost, some is by surface evaporation and some through the lungs. In preterm low birth weight infants, insensible water loss is inversely proportional to gestational age. The higher loss in small infants is due to increased heat expenditure. Term infants in the first 3 days will have an insensible water loss approximating 1 ml/kg/hr, while an infant of 28 weeks' gestation may lose twice as much. (An average adult at rest will have a loss of about 0.4 ml/kg/hr.) The daily excretion of water by the gastrointestinal tract will average 200–500 ml for an infant and 100–300 ml for an adult. It should come as no surprise to learn that control of this rapid water exchange by the infant is less precise than that achieved by the older child or adult, and consequently one sees more severe dehydration or overhydration, in the face of illness, in the less mature organism. An additional risk, in sick infants and young children, is the occasional inappropriate secretion of the antidiuretic hormone (ADH) leading to excessive water retention and hyponatremia. It is not always easy to differentiate this entity from mismanagement of fluid and electrolyte balance by the medical crew. Table 7–10 gives daily water requirements for different ages. It is offered not as a therapeutic index but as a means of illustrating the progressive changes that occur in normal subjects.

The composition of the body fluids also has some tendency to differ with age.[36, 42] The total electrolyte concentration in extracellular fluid tends to be slightly greater in the newborn subject than in the adult (as judged from blood analyses). There is a greater concentration of sodium, chloride, phosphates and organic acids. These differences are even more striking in the premature baby. On the other hand, the concentration of bicarbonate ions is lower in the newborn infant than in the older child, and there is mild acidosis, manifested by a slightly lowered pH. These variations, plus a lowered plasma protein level, cause a reduced colloidal osmotic pressure of the vascular compartment and favor an accumulation of fluid in the tissue spaces and an increased filtration rate of the kidneys. In health these differences between the infant and the adult do not maintain themselves beyond a few weeks or months. The premature and normal newborn infant are usually in a state of well-compensated acidosis and in a state of potential or, in prematures especially, manifest edema. A study of the growth of the urinary system will aid in a better understanding of these facts.

The growth of the kidneys is slow in the early part of prenatal life and rapid in the later part. Kidney weight is doubled in the first 6 months after birth, trebled by age 1 year and increased five times by 5 years. By puberty the increase is 10 times that of the birth weight of these organs. Formation of the last renal tubules has been estimated to take place from the eighth month of gestation to the end of the first month of life. It is probable that no new glomeruli are formed after the ninth month of gestation, but throughout fetal and neonatal life the glomerular tuft is covered by a much thicker layer of cells than at any later time. This anatomic feature may explain the lowered glomerular filtration rate found during the first nine months of life, in spite of the lowered osmotic pressure of the plasma. The lower blood pressure of the infant may also play a part. All of the glomeruli increase in size after birth, but the peripheral ones grow more rapidly.[94]

At birth the kidneys occupy a large portion of the posterior abdominal wall owing to their relatively large size. Fetal lobulation persists throughout the first year. The ureters in the infant are relatively and absolutely shorter than in the adult. In the newborn the bladder lies close to the abdominal wall, and the lower level is behind the middle of the symphysis pubis. During childhood the bladder descends into the pelvis.[50]

In the fetus glomerular filtration apparently precedes tubular function, and large volumes of urine are passed into the amniotic sac from an early state of development. As tubular activity begins, an initially hypotonic and later a hypertonic urine is produced. The maximal osmolarity of the urine is low by adult standards, due to low solute excretion. Ability to form acid urine is limited, in part due to an inability to utilize phosphate buffers. This limitation continues into early postnatal life.[120] The water exchange between mother and fetus and between amniotic fluid and mother are approximately the same in early pregnancy. As pregnancy progresses, more of the fluid transfer from the amniotic sac is accomplished through the fetus.

In comparison to adult levels of renal function, neonate physiologic immaturity is evident as indicated by the following observations.[36, 53, 56, 98, 180]

1. Glomerular filtration rate is only about 30 to 50% of that of the adult and does not reach normal adult levels until late in the first year. This function is important in removing nitrogenous and other waste products from the blood. The decreased filtration is due to some or all of the following reasons: a low arterial blood pressure in the glomerulus, the smaller volume and surface area of the glomerulus available for filtration for months after birth and the fact that many of the glomeruli are not yet morphologically well

developed and are not available for physiologic function. Fortunately, much of the infant's ingested protein is totally metabolized for growth and the amount of urea presented to the kidney for removal is small.[122] Urea and inulin clearance are conventional tests in the laboratory used to measure this function.

2. A decreased ability to excrete an excessive sodium load resulting in a hypotonic urine compared to plasma. This persists throughout the neonatal and early infancy period. This may lead to an abnormal increase in weight, generalized edema and a rise in serum sodium levels. In the mature child such a load stimulates the kidney to increase glomerular filtration and decrease tubular reabsorption of sodium with consequent increase in excretion of sodium in the urine. The high concentration of aldosterone in the plasma in early infancy may play a part in this apparent lack of response of the immature kidney.

3. A decreased ability to excrete a water load which is reflected in the urine as an inability to increase urinary volume. This ability improves rapidly over the first few weeks and reaches adult capabilities by one month. A poor response to the antidiuretic hormone (ADH) is present in early infancy, and there is some evidence that the ability to produce ADH in response to its usual stimuli is decreased for a few months after birth.[170]

4. An inability to concentrate urine even when the infant is given little or no fluids. This is thought to be due to the anatomic immaturity of the loop of Henle resulting in a decreased degree of solute gradient between it and the medullary portion of the kidney. The great variability between the degree of maturity of glomeruli and tubules in the immature kidney may account for this as well as other physiologic findings.

5. The plasma threshold for glucose is lower in newborn infants than in adults and is probably accounted for by the greater nephron heterogenity.

6. Sodium-potassium activated adenosinetriphosphatase activity is lower in the immature kidney than in the mature kidney. This enzyme is an important link in the energy required for sodium reabsorption by the tubules.[92] At the moment, less is known about the maturation of other enzyme systems necessary for tubular transport.

7. The distribution of blood within the kidney varies with age and this may have functional implications. In infants up to a few months of age, a greater proportion of blood flow goes to the medullary nephrons. In adults subjected to a saline load there is a shift of blood to the cortex which apparently facilitates sodium excretion. This temporary unique distribution of blood to the medullary area may improve the infant's ability to conserve sodium, but also interferes with the excretion of it.[36]

The finding of a relatively high hydrogen ion concentration, the limitations of the kidneys' capacity to regulate internal environment and the lowered plasma osmotic pressure suggest that young infants have a very slight chemical margin of safety. Consequently, any disturbance such as diarrhea, infection or improper feeding can lead rapidly to severe acidosis and abnormal fluid balance manifested by dehydration at one extreme or edema at the other. Proper recognition of these factors is vitally important from a therapeutic point of view.[121]

Although small amounts of urine are usually found in the bladder at birth, the newborn may not void for 12–24 hours or longer (Tabel 7–11). Excretion after this period is frequent. The specific gravity of the urine during the first few days is higher than during the remainder of infancy, when the average values for healthy subjects range from 1.002 to 1.008. By age 5 or 6 this value differs little from that for adults. Fluid intake and other factors obviously influence the results. The reaction of the initial urine of the newborn is acid but later approaches neutrality. Throughout the first year of life the urea content is relatively low. However, on the basis of body weight, the amount of urea excreted in 24 hours is greater in childhood than in adult life. As might be anticipated from the foregoing discussion, the concentration of phosphates, chlorides and sulfates is low early in life but gradually increases with age, especially as more solid food is added to the diet. The percentage of uric acid found in the urine in the neonatal period is much higher than it is subsequently.[3, 52] The cause of this is not known. The excretory rate of uric acid remains relatively high throughout early childhood. The relation of urinary uric acid to urea is 1:14 in the newborn and 1:70 in the adult. Creatine is excreted in variable but large amounts by the infant and to a lesser degree by children to the time of puberty, when it ceases in males and is markedly decreased in females. Creatinine output, conversely, increases throughout the growing period, the quantity being directly related to the amount of body musculature.[52] The quantity excreted by the newborn is about 1–3 mg/kg of body weight daily, 10–20 mg at age 2 years and 20–40 mg at maturity.

TABLE 7–11.—AVERAGE
DAILY SECRETION OF
URINE

AGE	ML/24 HR
1 and 2 days	15–50
3–10 days	50–300
10 days to 2 mo	250–400
2 mo to 1 yr	400–500
1–3 yr	500–600
3–5 yr	600–750
5–8 yr	700–1,000
8–14 yr	700–1,500

The Genital Organs*

The relative weight of the testes is the same in the newborn and the adult. The periods of greatest growth are in infancy and again during adolescence, with relatively slow increase in weight between these periods. There is a fourfold increase in all three dimensions from birth to adult life. The seminiferous tubules at birth are solid but during childhood acquire lumens and increase in size. With puberty they enlarge more rapidly. The spermatogonia increase in size and number during childhood and at puberty begin to show the process of maturation.

The testes lie at the site of the future abdominal (internal inguinal) ring from the fourth to the seventh fetal month. During the latter month they become enclosed in the tunica vaginalis, pass through the inguinal canal, and by the middle of the eighth month are usually attached to the fundus of the scrotum. In over 90% of newborns the testes are found in their final position in the scrotum. The canal is obliterated in part or in toto in more than 80% of infants over 2 months of age.[50] In a recent study by Scorer,[162] it was found that while 96% of testes were in the scrotum at birth in fully mature male infants, only 70% were descended in the prematurely born. However, in both groups, 50% of the undescended gonads did come down into the scrotum by the end of the 1st month of life. At the end of 1 year the incidence of undescended testicles was less than 1%, and subsequent examinations revealed no further changes.[162]

The ovaries grow rapidly during early postnatal life and have doubled their weight by age 6 months. Between the ages of 12 and 15 years their weight is again doubled (see Table 9–7). The cortex of the ovary, consisting mainly of primordial follicles, forms a thicker portion in the newborn than in later life. It has been estimated that there is a decrease of 90% in the number of ova from birth to maturity. Undeveloped and atretic graafian follicles are common in childhood.

During the first weeks of life the uterus undergoes involution, and its weight is decreased by one-half from that at birth. The hypertrophy originally present is due to hormone stimulus from the mother. The birth weight of the organ is not regained for about 10 or 11 years. Until adolescence the length of the cervix is twice that of the body of the uterus. Normal relationship is brought about by growth of the corpus uteri while the cervix remains relatively stationary.[50] In adults the lengths of the lumens of the cervix and uterus are about equal. The uterine and cervical glands are simple and tubular until adolescence, when they become longer and branched and undergo the changes characteristic of menstruation.

---

*Further discussion of these organs, particularly endocrine relationships, will be found in Chapter 9.

Increments of Growth

The measurement of the body at regular intervals during its period of growth reveals certain trends in the rate of change common to all normal children. Fetal curves show a phase of slow growth in the early period, a rather marked change in rate about the middle of fetal life and a rapid growth thereafter to birth (see Fig 3–1). Growth curves of children from birth to adult life have been presented in Chapter 4.

Certain organ systems also undergo fairly definite patterns of growth. The organs of respiration, circulation, digestion and excretion follow the pattern set by the body as a whole, as exemplified by height or weight curves of a child. Rapid postnatal growth, which slows in later infancy and ceases before puberty, is characteristic of the central nervous system, the eye and much of the auditory apparatus; this is known as the *neural type* of growth. The *genital type* of growth, typical of the sex organs, shows little increase during early life but a rapid development just before and coincident with puberty. The *lymphoid type* of growth is characterized by rapid growth throughout infancy and childhood, ceasing at about the time of puberty and followed by

Fig 7–7.—Organ growth curves, drawn to a common scale by computing their values at successive ages in terms of their total (average) postnatal increments. (From Harris, J. A., et al.: *The Measurement of Man* [Minneapolis: University of Minnesota Press, 1930].)

TABLE 7–12.—AVERAGE WEIGHTS OF ORGANS AT
DIFFERENT AGES (gm)

	NEWBORN	1 YR	6 YR	PUBERTY	ADULT
Brain	350	910	1,200	1,300	1,350
Heart	24	45	95	220	300
Thymus	12	20	24	30	0–15
Kidneys (both)	25	70	120	170	300
Liver	150	300	550	1,500	1,600
Lungs (both)	60	130	260	410	1,200
Pancreas	3	9	20	40	90
Spleen	10	30	55	95	155
Stomach	8	30	50	80	135

involution. This last type is typical of the tonsils and adenoids, thymus, splenic follicles, lymph nodes and the lymphatic tissue of the intestines. The four types of growth curves are illustrated in Figure 7–7.

Table 7–12 shows the weights of various organs at different ages. (Similar figures for the endocrine organs are given in Table 9–2.)

Summary of Organ Development

Musculature Throughout the span of growth there is an increase in muscle mass, with greatest increase during adolescence. Increase in skill, which involves musculature, is more intimately related to maturation of the nervous system.

Skin At birth the appearance of the skin is an accurate indicator of the length of gestation. Although sweat and sebaceous glands are present at birth, the former do not function efficiently for several months and sebaceous gland function reaches maturity only with the advent of puberty.

Nervous system Growth and maturation of the central nervous system are most rapid during infancy and early childhood, reflected in part by rapid growth of the head during this time. Increased permeability of the blood-brain barrier shortly after birth is reflected in the physical and chemical differences of the cerebrospinal fluid during early infancy and later life.

Special senses Most of the special senses are well developed at birth, although their association with higher centers comes about gradually during early life. Vision, owing to continued growth and development of the eyes, does not assume adult level until after the middle of childhood.

Circulatory system With birth there is considerable change in the paths and relative volumes of blood flow, reflected in the loss of certain fetal structures and changes in the heart and major vessels. Variations in pulse rate, blood pressure, heart sounds (including functional murmurs) and rhythm characterize development of the circulatory system. There is a steady increase in blood volume throughout the growing period, but this is not directly related to size.

Lymphatic system

The entire lymphatic system is characterized by considerable growth throughout childhood, followed by involution as maturity is approached. Hyperplasia and hypertrophy may be pronounced during early life in response to infection.

Blood

Not until midchildhood does the peripheral blood picture become the the same as that of the adult. The differences are apparent in the numbers and types of cells as well as response to infection and noxious agents. Chemical components of the blood fluctuate during the neonatal period, but stabilization and homeostasis are slowly achieved during the first year of life and are relatively well maintained thereafter in health.

Immunity

At birth the infant has received the most important immune globulins across the placenta at levels that are qualitatively and quantitatively equal to those of its mother. For a period of several months after delivery, although there is some ability to synthesize antibodies, the infant is immunologically less competent than in later life. For this and other reasons, there is a changing pattern of infectious disease with increasing age.

Digestive system

Although there is considerable evidence that the digestive system is immature at birth, in usual circumstances there is no impairment of absorption or utilization of the main foods except fat. Liver function, based on adult standards, is definitely immature. Roentgenographic studies of the intestinal tract reveal some changes in position of parts with growth, and some mechanical differences appear with advancing age.

Respiratory system

Initiation of respiration and the associated changes are among the most important events occurring at birth. The newborn infant possesses some immunity to anoxia; nevertheless, beyond a certain point, function of the central nervous system is jeopardized by anoxia. Breathing at first is irregular, in both rate and depth; this persists beyond the neonatal period. Until about the sixth year respiration is largely maintained by the diaphragm; subsequently the thorax plays an equally important role. Anatomic differences between child and adult are of considerable clinical importance relative to symptomatology and physical examination.

Urinary system

The kidneys are physiologically immature at birth and for nearly a year thereafter. This accounts for the ease with which fluid and electrolyte imbalances may occur during infancy with illness. Both the premature and the full-term newborn infant are in a state of well-compensated acidosis due to borderline renal function.

REFERENCES

1. Bakwin, H., Galenson, E., and Levine, B. E.: Roentgenographic appearance of the esophagus in normal infants, Am. J. Dis. Child. 68:243, 1944.

2. Huffman, J. W.: Disorders of the external genitalia and vagina, Pediatr. Clin. North Am. 5:35, 1958.
3. O'Brien, D., Ibbott, F. A., and Rodgerson, D. O.: *Laboratory Manual of Pediatric Micro-biochemical Techniques* (4th ed.; New York: Harper & Row, 1968).
4. Sturman, J., Gaull, G., and Räshä, N. C. R.: Absence of cystathionase in human fetal liver, Science 169:74, 1970.
5. Oski, F. A., and Naiman, J. L.: *Hematologic Problems in the Newborn* (2d ed.; Philadelphia: W. B. Saunders Company, 1972).
6. Bonar, B. E., Blumenfeld, C. M., and Fenning, C.: Studies of fetal respiratory movements: I. Historical and present day observations, Am. J. Dis. Child. 55:1, 1938.
7. Nicolaides, N.: Skin lipids: Their biochemical uniqueness, Science 186:19, 1974.
8. Boyd, E.: Weight of the thymus gland in health and in disease, Am. J. Dis. Child. 43:1162, 1932.
9. Bremer, J. L.: Diverticula and duplications of the intestinal tract, Arch. Pathol. 38:132, 1944.
10. Solomon, L. M., and Esterly, N. B.: *Neonatal Dermatology* (Philadelphia: W. B. Saunders Company, 1973).
11. Brines, J. K., Gibson, J. G., Jr., and Kunkel, P.: The blood volume in normal infants and children, J. Pediatr. 18:447, 1941.
12. Haynes, H., White, B. L., and Held, R.: Visual accommodation in human infants, Science (London) 148:528, 1965.
13. Emmanouilides, G., Moss, A. J., Duffie, E. R., and Adams, F. H.: Pulmonary arterial pressure in human newborn infants from birth to 3 days of age, J. Pediatr. 65:327, 1964.
14. Caffey, J.: *Pediatric X-Ray Diagnosis* (6th ed.; Chicago: Year Book Medical Publishers, Inc., 1972).
15. Behrendt, H., and Green, M.: *Patterns of Skin pH from Birth through Adolescence* (Springfield, Ill.: Charles C Thomas, Publisher, 1971).
16. Coghill, G. E.: *Anatomy and the Problems of Behavior* (New York: The Macmillan Company, 1929).
17. Conel, J. L.: *The Postnatal Development of the Cerebral Cortex: Vol. I. The Cortex of the Newborn* (Cambridge, Mass.: Harvard University Press, 1939).
18. Hamberger, R. N.: Allergy and the immune system, Am. Sci. 64:157, 1976.
19. McCue, C. M., Garner, F. B., Hurt, W. G., Schelin, E. C., and Sharpe, A. R.: Placental transfusion, J. Pediatr. 72:15, 1968.
20. Ziegler, R. F.: *Electrocardiographic Studies in Normal Infants and Children* (Springfield, Ill.: Charles C Thomas, Publisher, 1951).
21. Bradfield, R. B.: Hair tissue as a medium for the differential diagnosis of protein-calorie malnutrition, J. Pediatr. 84:294, 1974.
22. Downing, M. E.: Blood pressure of normal girls from three to sixteen years of age, Am. J. Dis. Child. 73:293, 1947.
23. Epstein, N.: The heart in normal infants and children: Incidence of precordial systolic murmurs and fluoroscopic and electrocardiographic studies, J. Pediatr. 32:39, 1948.
24. Mulvhill, J. J., and Smith, D. W.: The genesis of dermatoglyphics, J. Pediatr. 75:579, 1969.
25. Stough, T. R., and Seely, J. R.: Dermatoglyphics in medicine, Clin. Pediatr. 8:32, 1969.
26. Ford, F. R.: *Diseases of the Nervous System in Infancy, Childhood and Adoles-*

cence (5th ed.; Springfield, Ill.: Charles C Thomas, Publisher, 1966).

27. Berger, L., Henrichs, I., Raptis, S., Heinze, E., Jonatha, W., Teller, W. M., and Pfeiffer, E. F.: Gastrin concentration in plasma of the neonate at birth and after the first feeding, Pediatrics 58:264, 1976.

28. Moss, A. J., and Adams, F. H.: *Problems of Blood Pressure in Childhood* (Springfield, Ill.: Charles C Thomas, Publisher, 1962).

29. Harper, R. M., Hoppenbrouwers, T., Sterman, M. B., McGinty, D. J., and Hodgman, J.: Polygraphic studies of normal infants during the first six months of life. I. Heart rate and variability as a function of state, Pediatr. Res. 10:945, 1976.

30. Moss, A. J., and Monset-Couchard, M.: Placental transfusion: Early versus late clamping of the umbilical cord, Pediatrics 40:109, 1967.

31. Vaughan, V. C., and McKay, R. J.: *Nelson Textbook of Pediatrics* (10th ed.; Philadelphia: W. B. Saunders Company, 1975).

32. Gryboski, J.: *Gastrointestinal Problems in the Infant* (Philadelphia: W. B. Saunders Company, 1975).

33. Kaiser, A. D.: The Tonsil and Adenoid Problem, in Brennemann, J. (ed.): *Practice of Pediatrics*, Vol. II (Hagerstown, Md.: W. F. Prior Company, Inc., 1947), Chapter 4.

34. Fleisher, T. A., Luckasen, J. R., Sabad, A., Gehrtz, R. C., and Kersey, J. H.: T and B lymphocyte subpopulations in children, Pediatrics 55:162, 1975.

35. Levine, S. Z., and Gordon, H. H.: Physiologic handicaps of the premature infant, Am. J. Dis. Child. 62:274, 1942.

36. Loggie, J. M. H., Kleinman, L. I., and Van Maanen, E. F.: Renal function and diuretic therapy in infants and children, J. Pediatr. 86:485, 1975.

37. McGraw, M. B.: *The Neuromuscular Maturation of the Human Infant* (New York: Columbia University Press, 1943).

38. Janeway, C. A.: Progress in immunology: Syndromes of diminished resistance to infection, J. Pediatr. 72:885, 1968.

39. McMurray, L., Roe, J. H., and Sweet, L. K.: Plasma protein studies on normal newborn and premature infants, Am. J. Dis. Child. 75:265, 1948.

40. Mann, I. C.: *Development of the Human Eye* (New York: The Macmillan Company, 1928).

41. Schulte, F. J., Busse, C., and Eichhorn, W.: Rapid eye movement sleep, motoneurone inhibition, and apneic spells in preterm infants, Pediatr. Res. 11:709, 1977.

42. Edelmann, C. M., and Spitzer, A.: The maturing kidney, J. Pediatr. 75:509, 1969.

43. Wilson, G. S., and Miles, A. A. (eds.): *Topley and Wilson's Principles of Bacteriology and Immunity* (4th ed.; Baltimore: Williams & Wilkins Company, 1955).

44. Otila, E.: Studies on cerebrospinal fluid in premature infants, Acta Paediatr. (suppl. 8) 35:3, 1948.

45. Patten, B. M.: *Human Embryology* (3d ed.; New York: McGraw-Hill Book Company, Inc., 1968).

46. Smith, C. H.: *Blood Diseases of Infancy and Childhood* (St. Louis: C. V. Mosby Company, 1960).

47. Pratt, E. L., Bienvenu, B., and Whyte, M. M.: Concentration of urine by young infants, Pediatrics 1:181, 1948.

48. Pratt, K. C., Nelson, A. K., and Sun, K. H.: *The Behavior of the Newborn*

Infant, Ohio State Univ. Studies, no. 10 (1930).

49. Dawkins, M. J.: Biochemical aspects of developing liver function, B. Med. Bull. 22:27, 1966.

50. Scammon, R. E.: A Summary of the Anatomy of the Infant and Child, in Abt, I. A. (ed.): *Pediatrics,* Vol. I (Philadelphia: W. B. Saunders Company, 1923), Chapter 3.

51. Schachter, J., Lachin, J. M., Kerr, J. L., Wimberly, F. C., and Ratey, J. J.: Heart rate and blood pressure in black newborns and in white newborns, Pediatrics 58:283, 1976.

52. Smith, C. A., and Nelson, N. M.: *The Physiology of the Newborn Infant* (4th ed.; Springfield, Ill.: Charles C Thomas Publisher, 1976).

53. Smith, H. W.: *The Physiology of the Kidney* (2d ed.; New York: Oxford University Press, 1951).

54. Walsh, S. Z., Meyer, W. W., and Lind, J.: *The Human Fetal and Neonatal Circulation* (Springfield, Ill.: Charles C Thomas, Publisher, 1974).

55. Brown, R., and Pickering, K.: Persistent transitional circulation, Arch. Dis. Child. 49:883, 1974.

56. West, J. R., Smith, H. W., and Chasis, H.: Glomerular filtration rate, effective renal blood flow and maximal tubular excretory capacity in infancy, J. Pediatr. 32:10, 1948.

57. White House Conference on Child Health and Protection: *Growth and Development of the Child:* Pt. II. Anatomy and Physiology (New York: Century Company, 1933).

58. Hernandez, A., Goldring, D., and Hartman, A. F.: Measurement of blood pressure in infants and children by the Doppler ultrasonic technique, Pediatrics 48:788, 1971.

59. Wilson, J. L.: Initiation of respiration in the newborn infant, J. Pediatr. 23:485, 1943.

60. Wilson, J. L., and Farber, S.: Pathogenesis of atelectasis of newborn, Am. J. Dis. Child. 46:590, 1933.

61. Wilson, J. L., Long, S. B., and Howard, P. J.: Respiration of premature infants: Response to variations of oxygen and to increased carbon dioxide in inspired air, Am. J. Dis. Child. 63:1080, 1942.

62. Windle, W. F.: *Physiology of the Fetus* (Philadelphia: W. B. Saunders Company, 1940).

63. Wintrobe, M. M.: *Clinical Hematology* (6th ed.; Philadelphia: Lea & Febiger, 1967).

64. Challacombe, D. N., Edkins, S., and Brown, G. A.: Duodenal bile acids in infancy, Arch. Dis. Child. 50:837, 1975.

65. Gschwind, R.: Behavior of pancreatic enzymes in premature infants, Ann. Paediatr. 175:169, 1950.

66. Burnard, E. D.: The cardiac murmur in relation to symptoms in the newborn, Br. Med. J., 1:134, 1959.

67. Forfar, J. O., and Kibel, M. A.: Blood pressure in the newborn estimated by the flush method, Arch. Dis. Child. 31:126, 1956.

68. Moss, A. J., Liebling, W., Austin, W. O., and Adams, F. H.: An evaluation of the flush method for determining blood pressure in infants, Pediatrics 20:53, 1957.

69. Fogel, D. H.: The innocent (functional) cardiac murmur in children, Pediatrics 19:793, 1957.

70. Richards, M. R., Merritt, K. K., Samuels, M. H., and Langmann, A. G.: Frequency and significance of cardiac murmurs in the first year of life, Pediatrics 16:169, 1955.

71. Russell, S. J. M.: Blood volume studies in healthy children, Arch. Dis. Child. 24:88, 1949.

72. Sturgeon, P.: Volumetric and microscopic patterns of bone marrow in normal infants and children: I. Volumetric pattern. II. Cytologic pattern, Pediatrics 7:577 and 642, 1951.

73. Walker, J., and Turnbull, E. P. N.: Hemoglobin and red cells in the human fetus. III. Foetal and adult hemoglobin, Arch. Dis. Child. 30:111, 1955.

74. Cook, C. D., Brodie, H. R., and Allen, D. W.: Measurement of fetal hemoglobin in newborn infants: Correlation with gestation age and intrauterine hypoxia, Pediatrics 20:272, 1957.

75. Janix, J. H. P., and Visser, H. K. A.: Determination of low percentages of fetal hemoglobin in blood of normal children, A.M.A. Am. J. Dis. Child. 92:588, 1956.

76. Karlberg, P., and Lind, J.: Studies of the total amount of hemoglobin and the blood volume in children, Acta Paediatr. 44:17, 1955.

77. Marks, J., Gairdner, D., and Roscoe, J. D.: Blood formation in infancy: III. Cord blood, Arch. Dis. Child. 30:117, 1955.

78. Seip, M.: The reticulocyte level and the erythrocyte production judged from reticulocyte studies in newborn infants during the first week of life, Acta Paediatr. 44:355, 1955.

79. Orlandini, O., Sass-Kortsak, T. A., and Ebbs, J. H.: Serum gamma globulin levels in normal infants, Pediatrics 16:575, 1955.

80. Henley, W.: The immunoglobulins, Pediatr. Ann. 5:372, 1976.

81. Saito, M., Gittleman, I. F., Pincus, J. B., and Sobel, A. E.: Plasma protein patterns in premature infants of varying weights on the first day of life, Pediatrics 17:657, 1956.

82. Bach, F. H., and Good, R. A.: *Clinical Immunobiology*, Vol. I (New York: Academic Press, 1972).

83. Gell, P. G. H., and Coombs, R. R. A.: *Clinical Aspects of Immunology* (Philadelphia: F. A. Davis Company, 1968).

84. Frimann-Dahl, J., Lind, J., and Wigelius, C.: Roentgen investigations of neonatal gaseous content of the intestinal tract, Acta Radiol. 41:256, 1954.

85. Thompson, J.: The volume and acidity of the gastric contents in the unfed newborn infant, Arch. Dis. Child. 26:558, 1951.

86. Halbrecht, I., and Brzoza, H.: Evaluation of hepatic function in newborn infants by means of chemical study of cord blood, A.M.A. Am. J. Dis. Child. 79:988, 1950.

87. Sherry, S. N., and Kramer, I.: The time of passage of the first stool and first urine by the newborn infant, J. Pediatr. 46:158, 1955.

88. Nyhan, W. L.: Stool frequency of normal infants in the first week of life, Pediatrics 10:414, 1952.

89. Graham, B. D., and Wilson, J. L.: Chemical control of respiration in newborn infants, A.M.A. Am. J. Dis. Child. 87:287, 1954.

90. Jones, H. E.: The vital capacity of children, Arch. Dis. Child. 30:445, 1955.

91. Ferris, B. G., Jr., and Smith, C. W.: Maximum breathing capacity and vital capacity in female children and adolescents. Pediatrics 12:341, 1953.

92. Yoshida, T.: Substrate metabolism and renal function, Pediatr. Clin. North Am. 23:627, 1976.

93. McCance, R. A., and Widdowson, E. M.: Protein catabolism and renal function in the first two days of life in premature infants and multiple births, Arch. Dis. Child. 30:405, 1955.

94. McCrory, W. W.: *Developmental Nephrology* (Cambridge: Harvard University Press, 1972).

95. Prindull, G.: Maturation of cellular and humoral immunity during human embryonic development, Acta Paediatr. Scand. 63:607, 1974.

96. Fellers, F. X., Barnett, H. T., Hare, K., and McNamara, H.: Change in thiocyanate and sodium²⁴ spaces during growth, Pediatrics 3:622, 1949.

97. Slater, R. J., and Sass-Kortsak, A.: The turnover and circulation of the plasma proteins in the body, Am. J. Med. Sci. 231:669, 1956.

98. Howell, R. R.: Diagnostic enzymology, in Cook, R. E. (ed.): *The Biological Basis of Pediatric Practice* (New York: McGraw-Hill Book Company, Inc., 1968).

99. Lind, J., Stern, L., and Wegelius, C.: *Human Foetal and Neonatal Circulation* (Springfield, Ill.: Charles C Thomas, Publisher, 1964).

100. Gairdner, D., Marks, J., Roscoe, J. D., and Berttell, R. O.: The fluid shift from the vascular compartment immediately after birth, Arch. Dis. Child. 33:489, 1958.

101. Nadas, A. S., and Fyler, D. C.: *Pediatric Cardiology* (3d ed.; Philadelphia: W. B. Saunders Company, 1972).

102. Reeve, R., and DeBoer, K.: Sinus arrhythmia: Data and patterns from groups of individuals followed from 1 month to 23 years of age, Pediatrics 26:402, 1960.

103. Sisson, T. R. C., and Whalen, L. E.: The blood volume of infants, alterations in the first hours after birth, J. Pediatr. 56:43, 1960.

104. Clark, A. C. L., and Gairdner, D.: Postnatal plasma shift in premature infants, Arch. Dis. Child. 35:352, 1960.

105. Schell, N. B., Karelitz, S., and Epstein, B. S.: Radiographic study of gastric emptying in premature infants, J. Pediatr. 62:342, 1963.

106. Cornblath, M., and Schwartz, R.: *Disorders of Carbohydrate Metabolism in Infancy* (Philadelphia: W. B. Saunders Company, 1966).

107. Hemmings, W. A.: Protein transfer across the fetal membranes, Br. Med. Bull. 17:96, 1961.

108. Valadian, I., Stuart, H. C., and Reed, R. B.: Patterns of illness experiences, Pediatrics 24:941, 1959.

109. Singleton, E. B.: *X-Ray Diagnosis of the Alimentary Tract in Infants and Children* (Chicago: Year Book Publishers, Inc., 1959).

110. Hsia, D. Y-Y.: Bilirubin metabolism, Pediatr. Clin. North Am. 12:713, 1965.

111. Oppe, T. E., and Gibbs, I. E.: Sulphobromophthalein excretion in premature infants, Arch. Dis. Child. 34:125, 1959.

112. Ames, M. D.: Gastric acidity in the first ten days of life of the prematurely born baby, Am. J. Dis. Child. 100:252, 1960.

113. Borgstrom, B., Lindquist, B., and Lundh, G.: Enzyme concentration and absorption of protein and glucose in duodenum of premature infants, Am. J. Dis. Child. 99:338, 1960.

114. Sell, E. J., and Corrigan, J. J.: Platelet counts, fibrinogen concentrations, and factor V and factor VII levels in healthy infants according to gestational age, J. Pediatr. 82:1028, 1973.

115. Edelman, G. M.: Antibody structure and molecular immunology, Science 180:830, 1973.

116. Karlberg, P.: The adaptive changes in the immediate postnatal period, with

particular reference to respiration, J. Pediatr. 56:585, 1960.

117. Stahlman, M., and Sexton, C.: Ventilation control in the newborn, Am. J. Dis. Child. 101:216, 1961.

118. Lyons, H. A., Tanner, R. W., and Picco, T.: Pulmonary function studies in children, Am. J. Dis. Child. 100:196, 1960.

119. Bernstein, I. L., Fragge, R. G., Gueron, M., Kreindler, L., and Ghory, J. E.: Pulmonary function in children: I. Determination of norms, J. Allergy Clin. Immunol. 30:514, 1959.

120. Alexander, D. P., and Nixon, D. A.: The foetal kidney, Br. Med. Bull. 17:112, 1961.

121. Edelmann, C. M., and Barnett, H. L.: Role of the kidney in water metabolism in young infants, J. Pediatr. 56:154, 1960.

122. McCance, R. A.: The maintenance of stability in the newly born, Arch. Dis. Child. 34:361, 1959.

123. Van Creveld, S.: Coagulation disorders in the newborn period, J. Pediatr. 97:633, 1959.

124. Richter, D.: Enzymic activity during early development, Br. Med. Bull. 17:118, 1961.

125. Driscoll, S. G., and Hsia, D. Y-Y.: The development of enzyme systems during early infancy, Pediatrics 22:785, 1958.

126. Kretchmer, N.: Enzymatic patterns during development, Pediatrics 25:606, 1959.

127. Sereni, F., and Principi, N.: The development of enzyme systems, Pediatr. Clin. North Am. 12:515, 1965.

128. Pojerova, A., and Tovarek, J.: On enzymatic activity in the neonatal period, Acta Paediatr. 48:213, 1959.

129. Done, A. K.: Developmental pharmacology, Clin. Pharmacol. Ther. 5:432, 1964.

130. Heald, F. P., Hunt, E. E., Schwartz, R., Cook, C. D., Elliot, O., and Vajda, B.: Measures of body fat and hydration in adolescent boys, Pediatrics 31:226, 1963.

131. Wenzel, J. E., and Burgert, E. O.: The spider nevus in infancy and childhood, Pediatrics 33:227, 1964.

132. Kennedy, C.: Physiologic characteristics of growth of the human brain, J. Pediatr. 59:928, 1961.

133. Davison, A. N., and Dobbing, J.: Myelination as a vulnerable period in brain development, Br. Med. Bull. 22:40, 1966.

134. Shurtleff, D. B., Foltz, E. L., and Chapman, J. T.: Ventriculo-skull distance, Am. J. Dis. Child. 111:262, 1966.

135. Fois, A.: *The Electroencephalogram of the Normal Child* (Springfield, Ill.: Charles C Thomas, Publisher, 1961).

136. Engel, R.: Maturational changes and abnormalities in the newborn electroencephalogram, Dev. Med. Child Neurol. 7:498, 1965.

137. Rosen, M. G., and Satran, R.: The neonatal electroencephalogram, Am. J. Dis. Child. 111:133, 1966.

138. Brazelton, T. B., Scholl, M. L., and Robey, J. S.: Visual response in the newborn, Pediatrics 37:284, 1966.

139. Mattingly, R. F., and Larks, S. D.: The fetal electrocardiogram, J.A.M.A. 183:245, 1963.

140. Vanoni, R. P.: Rilievi electrocardiografici del neonato immaturo, Minerva Pediatr. 10:1041, 1958.

141. Levine, O. R., Griffiths, S. P., and Levine, A.: Electrocardiographic findings in healthy premature infants, Pediatrics 30:361, 1962.
142. Jegier, W., Blankenship, W., Lind, J., and Kitchin, A.: The changing circulatory pattern of the newborn infant studied by the indicator dilution technique, Acta Paediatr. 53:541, 1964.
143. Buckels, L. J., and Usher, R.: Cardiopulmonary effects of placental transfusion, J. Pediatr. 67:239, 1965.
144. Oh, W., Lind, J., and Gessuer, I. H.: The circulatory and respiratory adaptation to early and late cord clamping in newborn infants, Acta Paediatr. Scand. 55:17, 1966.
145. Moss, A. J., Duffie, E. R., and Emmanouilides, G.: Blood pressure and vasomotor reflexes in the newborn infant, Pediatrics 32:175, 1963.
146. Young, M.: Blood pressure in the newborn baby, Br. Med. Bull. 17:154, 1961.
147. Steele, M. W.: Plasma volume changes in the neonate, Am. J. Dis. Child. 103:42, 1962.
148. Usher, R., and Lind, J.: Blood volume of the newborn premature infant, Acta Paediatr. Scand. 54:419, 1965.
149. Winkelstein, J. A.: Opsonins: Their function, identity and clinical significance, J. Pediatr. 82:747, 1973.
150. Garby, L., Sjolin, S., and Vuille, J.-E.: Studies on erythro-kinetics in infancy: V. Estimation of the life span of red blood cells in the newborn, Acta Paediatr. 53:165, 1964.
151. Medoff, H. S.: Platelet counts in premature infants, J. Pediatr. 64:287, 1964.
152. Albrecht, R. M., and Hong, R.: Basic and clinical considerations of the monocyte-macrophage system in man, J. Pediatr. 88:751, 1976.
153. Haworth, J. C., Norris, M., and Dilling, L.: A study of the immunoglobulin in premature infants, Arch. Dis. Child. 40:243, 1965.
154. Walker, W. A.: Host defense mechanisms in the gastrointestinal tract, Pediatrics 57:901, 1976.
155. Glasgow, L. A.: Interferon: A review, J. Pediatr. 67:104, 1965.
156. Miller, J. F. A. P.: The thymus and the development of immunologic responsiveness, Science 144:1544, 1964.
157. Gryboski, J. D.: The swallowing mechanism in the neonate: Esophageal and gastric motility, Pediatrics 35:445, 1965.
158. Avery, M. E., and Fletcher, B. D.: *The Lung and Its Disorders in the Newborn Infant* (3d ed.; Philadelphia: W. B. Saunders Company, 1974).
159. Kildeberg, P.: Disturbances of hydrogen ion balance occurring in premature infants, Acta Paediatr. 53:505, 1964.
160. De Muth, G. R., Howatt, W. F., and Hill, B. M.: The growth of lung function, Pediatrics 35:161, 1965.
161. Lawson, J. S., and Hewstone, A. S.: Microscopic appearance of urine in the neonatal period, Arch. Dis. Child. 39:287, 1964.
162. Scorer, C. G.: The descent of the testes, Arch. Dis. Child. 39:609, 1964.
163. Chandra, R. K.: Fetal malnutrition and postnatal immunocompetence, Am. J. Dis. Child. 129:450, 1975.
164. Phelan, P. D., and Williams, H. E.: Ventilatory studies in healthy infants, Pediatr. Res. 3:425, 1969.
165. Smith, R. T.: Gamma A immunoglobulins and the concept of local immunity, Pediatrics 43:317, 1969.
166. Editorial comment: Measurement of skinfold thickness in childhood, Pediatrics 42:538, 1968.

167. Naidoo, B. T.: Cerebrospinal fluid in healthy newborn infants, S. Afr. Med. J. 42:933, 1968.
168. Winick, M.: Malnutrition and brain development, J. Pediatr. 74:667, 1969.
169. Park, M. K., and Guntheroth, W. G.: Direct blood pressure measurements in brachial and femoral arteries in children, Circulation 41:231, 1970.
170. Janovsky, M., Martinek, J., and Stanincova, V.: Antidiuretic activity in the plasma of human infants after a load of sodium chloride, Acta Paediatr. Scand. 54:543, 1965.
171. Dayton, G. O., Jones, M. H., Rawson, R. A., and Rose, M.: Developmental study of coordinated eye movements in the human infant, Arch. Ophthalmol. 71:865, 1964.
172. Keeney, A. H.: Development of Vision, in Falkner, F. (ed.): *Human Development* (Philadelphia: W. B. Saunders Company, 1966).
173. Ross, E. D., Velez-Borras, J., and Rosman, N. P.: The significance of the Babinski sign in the newborn—a reappraisal, Pediatrics, 57:13, 1976.
174. Dobbing, J.: The Later Development of the Brain and Its Vulnerability, in Davis, J. A., and Dobbing, J. (eds.): *Scientific Foundations of Paediatrics* (Philadelphia: W. B. Saunders Company, 1974).
175. Purpura, D. P., and Shofer, R. J.: Principles of Synaptogenesis and Their Application to Ontogenetic Studies of Mammalian Cerebral Cortex, in Clemente, C. D., Purpura, D. P., and Mayer, F. E. (eds.): *Sleep and the Maturing Nervous System* (New York: Academic Press, 1972).
176. Moynahan, E. J.: The Developmental Biology of the Skin, in Davis, J. A., and Dobbing, J. (eds.): *Scientific Foundations of Paediatrics* (Philadelphia: W. B. Saunders Company, 1974).
177. Caramihai, E., Karayalcin, G., Aballi, A. J., and Lanzkowsky, P.: Leukocyte count differences in healthy white and black children 1 to 5 years of age, J. Pediatr. 86:252, 1975.
178. Williams, R. F.: Colonization of the Developing Body by Bacteria, in Davis, J. A., and Dobbing, J. (eds.): *Scientific Foundation of Paediatrics* (Philadelphia: W. B. Saunders Company, 1974).
179. Dawes, G. S.: Breathing before birth in animals and man, N. Engl. J. Med. 290:557, 1974.
180. Kenney, R. A.: Renal function, Pediatr. Clin. North Am. 24:651, 1976.
181. Ford, J. E., Law, B. A., Marshall, V. M. E., and Reiter, B.: Influence of the heat treatment of human milk on some of its protective constituents, J. Pediatr. 90:29, 1977.
182. Goldman, A. S., and Smith, C. W.: Host resistance factors in human milk, J. Pediatr. 82:1082, 1973.
183. Fantz, R. L., and Miranda, S. B.: Newborn infant attention to form and contour, Child. Dev. 46:224, 1975.
184. Kattwinkel, J.: Neonatal apnea: Pathogenesis and therapy, J. Pediatr. 90:342, 1977.
185. Reid, L.: Influence of the pattern of structural growth of lung on susceptibility to specific infections in infants and children, Pediatr. Res. 11:210, 1977.

8 / Osseous Development

BONE ALWAYS DEVELOPS by the transformation of preexisting connective tissue. One of these tissues is mesenchyme and the other is cartilage. Bone formation in mesenchyme is referred to as intramembranous ossification and forms the skull, face, ribs and vertebral bodies. Bone formation in cartilage is known as endochondral ossification and is best exemplified in the bones of the extremities. The models, primordial mesenchyme or cartilage, of the pectoral girdle and upper limb bones appear slightly before those of the pelvic girdle and lower limbs, thus following the cephalocaudal pattern of development. Calcification begins at 8–9 weeks and this event is used in establishing the end of the embryonic period and the beginning of the fetus.[13]

The human skeleton passes through the successive stages of connective tissue, cartilage and bone, and only articular cartilage in the joints persists into adult life as a remnant of the original primordial tissue. Initial ossification appears near the center of the shaft of long bones. In the middle of the bone endochondral tissue produces the matrix which subsequently undergoes ossification. Simultaneously, on the surface, the periosteum is producing its matrix for eventual bone formation. Both processes are important in remodeling which continues throughout the life span. As growth proceeds, cartilaginous concentrations appear at the ends of each bone to become the epiphyses. At birth, ossification has taken place along the shafts, diaphyses, of all of the long bones and thus they are radiologically visible. With only a few exceptions, most epiphyses become calcified after birth and in a largely predictable order. Linear growth continues as long as there is proliferation of cartilage cells in the epiphyseal plate. These cells, as with other endochondral tissues, lay down the matrix for future osseous formation. Growth ceases when the epiphyseal plate becomes calcified and the diaphysis and epiphysis become fused. These changes are very useful as indicators of maturation of the growing organism.[5-7, 15]

From birth to 4 years the cut surface of a long bone shows a pink texture of trabeculae interspersed with rich red marrow. From 4 to 7 years fat gradually accumulates in droplets, and by 7 years the bony trabeculae have given place to a real marrow cavity. Between 12 and 14 years there is a patch of fat in the midlength of the bone, extending toward both extremities. Changes in the epiphyses of the long bones are comparable to those in the shaft, but the bone trabeculae do not become absorbed and fatty changes are completed by 19 or 20 years. These changes closely parallel the dates of fusion of the epiphyses except in the upper part of the femur. Tibia, sternum, pelvic bones and vertebrae contain red marrow throughout life, and adult distribution is attained at about 25 years, which roughly corresponds to the date of fusion of their epiphyses.

Measuring Skeletal Maturation

Roentgenologic study of the bones may be of great aid to the pediatrician in evaluating physical development from birth through adulthood. Essentially the record of osseous development depends on two features: growth of the area undergoing ossification, and deposition of calcium in that area. The two do not necessarily keep pace with each other, nor are they always present together. In this chapter will be discussed various methods which have been successfully used in the study of osseous development and their application to measurements of normal growth and development of the child.

The appearance and union of the various centers of ossification follow a fairly definite pattern and time schedule from birth to maturity. This process provides, through x-ray studies, a valuable criterion for estimating normal and abnormal growth. The skeletal maturity of any individual is known as the *bone age*. It must be realized that in this field, as in others in which measurements of growth are made, there is no simple formula for deriving or evaluating growth trends.

Normal osseous development may be disturbed by a number of abnormalities that are specific as to cause and effect, and by others that are less specific in relation to bone but affect the entire organism. The specific factors may be outlined as follows:

1. Inability to respond to the growth hormone. The most striking example of this is achondroplasia, in which proliferation of cartilage is disturbed and linear growth and maturation are retarded.
2. The formation of normal bone matrix is compromised. Since the matrix is made up of protein, a very low protein intake, as experienced in the underdeveloped countries, may cause deficiencies in formation. Scurvy is a classic example of a condition with poorly formed bone matrix. Excesses of corticosteroids in Cushing's disease or with therapy interfere with normal matrix formation.
3. Abnormal mineralization of bony matrix. Several possibilities must be considered here.
   a) Deficiency of the enzymes which free calcium and phosphorus from their

organic combinations and allow them to be deposited. Hypophosphatasia is an inborn error of metabolism resulting in poor mineralization due to nearly complete absence of alkaline phosphatase in all tissues. In both hypothyroidism and scurvy, phosphatase content is markedly decreased, which undoubtedly contributes to the delayed mineralization so characteristic of these diseases.

b) Acidosis (lowered pH of the blood), as seen in chronic renal failure, interferes with mineralization by increasing the ionization of calcium and its solubility product so that its deposition does not occur in the protein matrix.

c) Concentrations of various substances in the serum bathing the bony matrix will influence the deposition of calcium and phosphorus. The relation of the parathyroid glands in this respect will be discussed in the following chapter. Renal abnormalities associated with low serum phosphorus, e.g., resistant rickets ("phosphate diabetes"), or renal failure associated with low serum calcium will decrease mineralization. Howland's rule that the product of serum calcium and phosphorus must exceed 35 for the healing of rickets, though subject to some question, still applies in general to these conditions. Relative excesses of serum protein, by binding the calcium, will also interfere.

d) Lack of absorption of the necessary constituents of bone from the intestinal tract is another factor. Vitamin D deficiency and the various malabsorption syndromes are examples of such conditions.

Bone maturation is particularly influenced by the androgenic and estrogenic hormones. Precocious development associated with adrenal hyperplasia, gonadal or brain tumors and iatrogenic causes invariably will advance skeletal development. Obesity is another condition in which there is slight but definite acceleration of the bone age. Chronic malnutrition, chronic or repeated severe infections and hypogonadism produce some degree of retardation. The most marked delay in skeletal maturation is seen in hypothyroidism (see Figs 8–20 and 8–21). Intrauterine infections, especially rubella, and many of the chromosomal abnormalities are associated with a retarded bone age as well as with other bony anomalies. Most other genetic causes of variations in skeletal development have more subtle effects.[12, 16]

Equally as important as dealing with the more severe forms of pathology, is the study of normal variations if we hope to establish standards that will be useful in the clinical care of children, the anthropologic studies of populations or epidemiologic evaluations of environmental influences. There is little question that certain aspects of the order and rate of maturation are under genetic control. The black, for example, shows a more rapid maturation than the white.[14] Interestingly enough, if one studies individual bones in each race, one finds that all bones are not uniformly ahead or behind, e.g., the phalanges in blacks are slightly behind those of white children.[36] From early childhood girls are ahead of boys by a few months and the difference increases with advancing age[5, 14, 24] (Tables 8–1 and 8–2).

TABLE 8–1.—PRESENCE OF SIX OSSIFICATION CENTERS IN ROENTGENOGRAMS OF NEWBORNS*

OSSIFICATION CENTER	BIRTH WEIGHT, GM					
	UNDER 2,000	2,000–2,499	2,500–2,999	3,000–3,499	3,500–3,999	4,000 OR MORE
Calcaneus						
White boys	100%					
girls	100					
Black boys	100					
girls	100					
Astragalus						
White boys	72.7	100%				
girls	83.3	100				
Black boys	90.9	100				
girls	100	100				
Dist. femoral epiphysis						
White boys	9.1	75.0	85.3%	100%	100%	
girls	50.0	91.7	98.0	100	100	
Black boys	18.2	88.5	90.7	94.0	100	
girls	50.2	93.8	99.0	100	100	
Prox. femoral epiphysis						
White boys	0.0	18.8	52.9	78.8	84.1	97.1%
girls	0.0	54.2	75.5	85.7	90.7	90.5
Black boys	0.0	38.5	62.7	76.0	80.0	92.9
girls	14.3	40.6	76.7	88.1	86.4	100
Cuboid						
White boys	0.0	6.2	14.7	39.8	44.3	60.0
girls	0.0	37.5	57.1	65.2	70.4	76.2
Black boys	0.0	23.1	43.8	58.0	68.2	100
girls	21.4	37.5	68.0	78.2	81.8	75.0
Head of humerus						
White boys	0.0	7.7	13.8	41.9	49.0	59.1
girls	0.0	5.6	25.8	41.9	69.4	86.7
Black boys	0.0	0.0	15.2	27.6	48.4	63.6
girls	0.0	10.7	22.7	52.6	38.9	100

*Modified from Christie.[3] Figures in each column are percentage of infants in whom the center was present. With some variations, incidence is higher in black than in white infants and in girls than in boys for a particular weight group.

TABLE 8–2.—PERCENTAGE OF CHILDREN IN WHOM SPECIFIED CARPAL BONES HAVE APPEARED*

BONE	SEX	AGE, YR																
		B	1	2	3	4	5	6	7	8	9	10	11	12	13	14	15	16
Capitate	F	8	96	100														
	M	2	98	100														
Hamate	F	8	96	100														
	M	2	98	100														
Triangularis	F	0	20	52	79	100												
	M	0	22	50	57	92	84	93	100									
Lunate	F		8	32	50	80	91	99	100									
	M		8	18	36	64	64	87	98	99	100							
Navicular	F				12	30	61	95	99	100								
	M				4	17	34	51	75	92	99	100						
Multangulum maj.	F			4	18	53	74	94	99	100								
	M				4	14	33	51	72	88	96	97	100					
Multangulum min.	F				15	40	65	95	100									
	M				4	22	29	48	81	95	100							
Pisiform	F								1	19	50	79	96	100				
	M									2	6	22	28	66	95	99	99	100

*From Nelson,[10] after Flory.

283

The methods for assessment of skeletal maturation or bone age can be divided into three categories with some additional variations.

1. Roentgen films of the subject being studied are compared to a standard atlas of the same anatomical part.[18, 27, 28] The atlases have been compiled from a large number of children selected at 3-to-6-month age intervals and accounting for sex differences. The advantages of this method are: it is well established; it is simple in technique; since only one anatomical area is used, the exposure to radiation is minimal. The disadvantages include: the wide chronologic age variation included in the individual atlas standard; the necessity of sometimes using relatively insignificant and unreliable changes in moving from one age standard to the next; a fairly wide variation in each individual's interpretation of the differences between standards and between the standard compared to the film in question (see Figs 8–5 to 8–21).

2. A method which totals the time of appearance of a number of secondary (epiphyseal) centers and attributes a maturity rating or age level to the number present.[11] It was initially thought that using a large number of centers would eliminate some of the problems posed by the use of atlases. This is doubtful. Since all areas must be considered, undue attention can be attributed to the appearance or lack of appearance of calcification, or its size, of centers that have been found to have such normal variations as to be very unreliable as predictors. An additional disadvantage is that multiple areas are exposed to radiation.

3. In this method, a scoring system is based upon such factors as appearance of calcification, degree of radiopacity, size, shape and fusion of epiphyses and diaphyses.[5, 8, 32] In some instances specified areas were designated as being the most reliable for different age ranges. Most authorities using these techniques found that often the carpals and tarsals, featured prominently in some of the atlases, were quite unsuitable indicators of maturity. Consequently, specific bones and detailed descriptions of stages of development that can be seen on the films are used in the scoring. Although these methods seem highly reliable in the hands of the investigators, in the usual clinical setting they have as many errors of prediction as do the others described above. The means of interpretation are more complex and, therefore, the method is more difficult to teach to others. It takes a considerably greater amount of time to reach a conclusion.[1, 4]

As a result of the attempts to develop the ideal approach to determining skeletal maturity and interpreting its significance, a number of very important findings have resulted.[2, 3, 5] The variations in sex and race have been pointed out and are apparent in some of the tables in this chapter. The standards established by Greulich and Pyle,[18] undoubtedly the most frequently used method in the United States, have been shown to be slightly in advance of the average child in the present generation. This is a finding of the recent USPHS survey.[35, 36] When assessed against the atlas standards, the skeletal ages of the boys were less than their chronologic ages by 2.5

months at 6 years and 13.8 months at 11 years. The differences in girls were similar but not as great: 1.0 month at 6 years and 9.8 months at 11 years.

The correlation of chronologic age with skeletal age is slightly better for girls than for boys, in part, because there is a narrower range of normal variability in the pattern of bone development. It has also been found that this range of variability is more affected by adverse circumstances, e.g., malnutrition, in boys than in girls. Using Sheldon's terminology of body type (Chapter 4), there is a tendency for the endomorphic girl and the mesomorphic boy to have more advanced bone age than other body types of the same sex.[5] The association of advanced skeletal maturity in long-existing obesity is well recognized.[5, 30]

Less easily defined are some of the genetic influences on growth and skeletal maturation unrelated to sex or race. Some children are normally slower in realizing their growth potential than most of their peers. They remain small, but usually above the lowest percentiles on the standard growth charts. Their bone age is compatible with their height age and this finding can usually be interpreted as a reassuring indication of normal adult stature. See also the discussion of delayed adolescence (constitutional slow growth) in Chapter 13. Bayley[15] and her co-workers have supplied us with a useful means of predicting adult height based on present height and present bone age (see Figs 4–8 and 4–9). How much variation can be found in the degree of skeletal maturation in normal children? This will vary depending upon the technique used. The Greulich and Pyle[18] atlas gives a standard deviation of 6 months at 3 years and 16 months by 11 years. Added to this is the variation in interpretation by individual radiologists which may be considerable when evaluating identical films.[20] Figure 8–18 is an excellent example to illustrate two principles. The apparent asymmetry between the right and left side of the body may seem very great and has been used as an argument against using a roentgenograph of a single area, such as the wrist. If, however, one recognizes that the variability of the carpal bones is too great to make them useful in such evaluations, the apparent discrepancy is resolved.[8, 32]

Although the USPHS survey did not reveal any geographic differences in the United States,[36] international studies have indicated the need for separate standards for children of different racial and geographic backgrounds.[25, 26, 34] Especially in anthropomorphic studies and serial evaluations used to study cultural and other environmental influences, one must establish one's own base lines. An interesting observation supporting this concept pertains to a group of black African children. In the early months of life their bone development (hand) was accelerated over that of European children of the same age, but by 18 months this relationship was reversed. The older the African child became in chronologic age, the further he or she

Fig 8–1.—Fetal ossification centers, showing average time of appearance in fetal weeks or months. (From Caffey.[2])

Fig 8–2.—Secondary ossification centers, showing average time of appearance. (From several sources.)

fell behind in bone age. Similarly, the statural growth rate was initially faster, but before the end of the first year it had dropped below that of European counterparts.[25]

All of the primary ossification centers for the tubular bones appear during fetal life (Fig 8–1). The secondary centers usually appear after birth, except the distal epiphysis of the femur, where ossification takes place during the last two fetal months. Therefore, absence of this center is good presumptive evidence of prematurity. The center in the proximal epiphysis of the tibia is present in approximately two thirds of full-term infants at birth. In infants with fetal malnutrition (see Chapter 3), the distal femoral epiphysis is frequently absent even though the gestational age is full term.[29] The time

Fig 8–3.—Ossification centers of the hands and feet, showing time of appearance. Note the wide range of "normal" and compare with Table 8–2. (From Caffey,[2] modified from Scammon in *Morris' Human Anatomy*.)

PRIMARY CENTERS

HAND

Phal. III 2-4 f.m.
Phal. II 2-6 f.m.
Phal. I 2-4 f.m.
Metac. 2-4 f.m.
Hama. b.-6 m
Capit. b.-6 m
M.min. 2.5-9 y
M.maj. 1.5-10 y
Navicu. 2.5-9 y
Trique. 6 m. - 4 y
Luna 6 m. - 9.5 y
Pisif. 6.5- 16.5 y

SECONDARY CENTERS

HAND

Appear   Fuse

5 m. - 2 y.
5 m. - 2 y.
}14-21 y
5 m. - 2 y.
10 m. - 2 y.
3 - 18 m.
}15-25 y
4 - 9 y.

FOOT   PRIMARY CENTERS

Phal. III 2 - 3.5 f.m.
Phal. II 10 f.w. - 7 y.
Phal. I 2-4 f.m.
Metat. 2-4 f.m.
Cun. III 9 f.m. - 3.5 y.
Cun. II 9 m. - 5 y.
Cun. I 9 m. - 4 y.
Cuboid 6 f.m.- 1 y.
Navi. 3 m. - 5 y.
Talus. 3.5 f.m. -2 m.
Calca. 3 f.m. - 1 m.

FOOT   SECONDARY CENTERS

Appear   Fuse

1-2 y.   11-22 y.
9-24 m.}
6-24 m.} 12-22 y.
6-24 m.   13-22 y.
5-12 y.   12-22 y.

f.m. = fetal months; m. = post natal months; y. = year

BOYS   GIRLS

Fig 8–4.—Normal maturation of the bones of the feet from birth to age 1 year expressed as percentiles. (From Caffey,[2] according to Stuart.)

schedule of appearance of some important secondary centers is shown in Figure 8–2.

Figures 8–3 and 8–4 show the normal maturation of the bones of the hands and feet in both sexes. Rarely, one or more carpals are present at birth. Table 8–2 shows the time of appearance of carpal bones in both sexes, and Figures 8–5 to 8–19 show graphically the sequence of appearance of the carpal centers. The author would again like to point out that the calcification of carpal bones may be easily recognized, but they are rather poor indicators of age-related skeletal maturation. The average time of complete calcific union of epiphyses and diaphyses is given in Table 8–3.

The stage of osseous development correlates better with sexual maturation, including menarche, than chronologic age, height or weight.[23, 24] Most girls have their first menstrual period when their roentgenographic record of skeletal age is between 13 and 13.5 years.

Any list of conditions with which disturbances of osseous development occur should be qualified (Table 8–5). There are individual variations in the reaction to disease so far as skeletal structures are concerned. In general, endocrine abnormalities cause more profound changes than infection or malnutrition. Almost any form of disease which influences height and weight will result in some interference in bone maturation. This interference may be manifest in narrow bands of dense bone in the metaphysis called *lines of arrested growth*. They probably indicate that osteoblastic activity in the region continues, but chondroplasia and linear growth are markedly slowed.[10]

Probably the most extreme example of poor nutrition is seen in kwashiorkor and this is associated with pronounced slowing in skeletal maturation. In this condition, as well as in other causes of deviation in bone development, correction of the underlying etiology will result in catch-up bone maturation just as it does in statural growth.

Roentgen films will often reveal other abnormalities associated with specific causes of retarded skeletal maturation. Examples are the short 4th metacarpal in Turner's syndrome, the irregular mineralization known as epiphyseal dysgenesis in hypothyroidism or longitudinal streaks of poor ossification in the long bones in congenital rubella. Serial films may be useful in evaluating the effectiveness of therapy or as part of a survey to study the results of a disease upon growth.

The rate of linear growth of tubular bones may be of some value when a rapid method of appraisal of bone development is needed, as in the evaluation of response to treatment. Examples are measurement of recovery from malnutrition or progress of therapy in cretinism.[17] Linear growth of the radius is normally 0.25 cm/month for the first year, 0.20 cm/month from 12 to 18 months and 0.12 cm/month from 18 to 24 months. Table 8–4 gives

Fig 8–5 (top left).—Newborn; no carpal bones are present, and epiphyses are not calcified.

Fig 8–6 (top right).—One year; the capitate and hamate are well developed and first appear by age 6 months.

Fig 8–7 (bottom left).—Two years; the distal epiphysis of radius is present in 85% by this age, and one or more epiphyses of the phalanges appear.

Fig 8–8 (bottom right).—Three years; the third carpal, triangularis, is present, and epiphyses of most of the metacarpals and phalanges are added.

Fig 8–9 (top left).—Four years; a fourth carpal appears, and complete appearance of all epiphyses of the phalanges is present.

Fig 8–10 (top right).—Five years; from five to seven carpals are present (females slightly in advance of males), and the proximal ends of the metacarpals begin to acquire definitive molding.

Fig 8–11 (bottom left).—Six years; all carpals except the pisiform are present, and the distal ulnar epiphysis may appear in 60% of girls and 30% of boys.

Fig 8–12 (bottom right).—Seven years; the distal epiphysis of the ulna is present in all but 10% of boys. The carpals are undergoing considerable molding with assumption of articulatory surfaces.

Fig 8–13 (top left).—Eight years; no further ossification centers appear, but growth and molding continue. The width of the epiphyses of most phalanges now equals the width of the shafts.

Fig 8–14 (top right).—Nine years; the styloid of the ulna becomes prominent. In girls the pisiform may be present.

Fig 8–15 (bottom left).—Ten years; the pisiform is present in 50% of girls and rarely in boys. The styloid process of the ulnar epiphysis is well developed, and the epiphyses of the phalanges are wider than their shafts.

Fig 8–16 (bottom right).—Thirteen years; the pisiform is present (beneath the triquetral), and the carpals have assumed their definitive shapes.

Fig 8–17 (top).—By 17 years the epiphyses of the metacarpals and pha-langes have united, and within a year the epiphyses of the radius and ulna unite with their respective diaphyses.

Fig 8–18 (bottom).—Right and left wrists of a normal boy of 5 years show-ing a possible variation. There are four carpal centers in the right extremity and six in the left.

Fig 8-19 (top).—Wrist of a 5½-year-old normal boy (average height, weight, mental development and normal physical examination). A sibling at the same age showed similar apparent retardation of bone development. Both children subsequently developed normally.

Fig 8-20 (bottom left).—Wrist of a cretin, age 5, who had been treated for several months. Note failure of appearance of carpal centers, the disturbed pattern (distal epiphysis of radius and metacarpal centers appearing before carpal centers) and uneven calcification.

Fig 8-21 (bottom right).—Same patient. Note absence of head of the fibula (normally present by age 5), uneven calcification of the epiphyses (epiphyseal dysgenesis) and so-called lines of arrested growth in shafts of the long bones.

TABLE 8–3.—AVERAGE AGE OF UNION OF THE
MORE IMPORTANT EPIPHYSES

| AGE, YR | | UNION OF EPIPHYSES |
BOYS	GIRLS	
6	6	Head and greater tuberosity of humerus
7	7	Ischium and pubis
12	12	Trochlea and capitellum of humerus
14	13–14	Olecranon and ulna
14	13–14	Epiphysis of calcaneus
15–17	14–16	Proximal epiphysis of radius
15–17	14–16	Trochanter and head of femur
16–18	15–17	Epiphyses of metacarpals and metatarsals
17	16	Coracoid
18–20	17–19	Distal epiphysis of radius
18–20	17–19	Distal epiphysis of ulna
18–20	17–19	Distal epiphyses of tibia and fibula
18–20	17–19	Acromion
18–20	17–19	Head and greater tuberosity of humerus
18–20	17–19	Distal epiphysis of femur
18–20	17–19	Proximal epiphyses of tibia and fibula

the average length of several long bones at different ages. The author has not been impressed with the value of using measurements of bone growth as a means of assessing treatment.

Practical Applications

A number of carefully compiled standards are available for determining the existing degree of skeletal maturation in children through radiologic examination. Unfortunately all have their faults or limitations when applied to the evaluation of growth of a specific individual. A large share of the difficulty, one might say disappointment, rests with the clinician who fails to recognize the limits of the information that can be obtained from such an examination, due largely to the inherent variability present in the developing human. Nevertheless, the discriminating use of these standards has been of great value in studying the growth and development of children, both normal and abnormal. Often they can be of considerable aid in the diagnostic appraisal of a particular individual. In this respect they may have some advantage over more complicated procedures because the results are relatively easily and promptly obtained. One must be aware that conclusions drawn from statistically significant differences of large groups are often insignificant when applied to an individual. As in the use of other measurements of growth, the normal genetic variability of bone maturation is considerable and must always be considered when making the final judgment.

TABLE 8-4.—MEAN LENGTH (cm) OF LONG BONES (SHAFT)*

	0-2		0-6		1-0		2-0		AGE, YR = MO 4-0		6-0		8-0		10-0		12-0	
	B	G	B	G	B	G	B	G	B	G	B	G	B	G	B	G	B	G
Humerus	7.3	7.1	8.8	8.7	10.5	10.4	13.0	12.8	16.2	16.2	19.0	19.0	21.6	21.5	23.9	24.0	26.3	26.8
Radius	5.9	5.7	7.0	6.7	8.2	7.9	9.8	9.5	12.3	12.0	14.3	14.0	16.2	15.9	17.9	17.7	19.6	19.8
Ulna	6.7	6.5	7.7	7.6	9.1	8.8	10.9	10.7	13.5	13.3	15.8	15.5	17.7	17.5	19.5	19.4	21.3	21.8
Femur	8.6	8.7	11.2	11.2	13.6	13.4	17.2	16.9	22.4	22.2	26.9	26.9	31.1	31.2	34.9	35.0	38.4	39.3
Tibia	6.9	7.0	8.9	8.9	10.9	10.8	13.9	13.8	18.3	18.2	21.9	21.8	25.2	25.3	28.4	28.6	31.4	32.2
Fibula	6.6	6.6	8.5	8.5	10.6	10.5	13.7	13.5	18.2	18.0	21.7	21.6	24.9	25.0	27.9	28.3	30.7	31.3

*Modified from Maresh.[9] B = boys, G = girls.

TABLE 8–5.—PATHOLOGIC CONDITIONS ASSOCIATED WITH ABNORMALITIES OF OSSEOUS DEVELOPMENT

Conditions associated with *advanced* osseous development:
  Hyperthyroidism (acceleration is not a constant finding)
  Adrenogenital syndrome (tumor or hyperplasia of the adrenal cortex)
  Pubertas praecox (Fluhmann)
  Tumors of the ovary (granulosa cell, thecoma, teratoma)
  Interstitial cell tumor of the testes
  Pineal gland tumor (male only)
  Tumors of the third ventricle involving the hypothalamus
  Simple obesity associated with statural overgrowth
  McCune-Albright syndrome (polyostotic fibrous dysplasia)

Conditions associated with *delayed* osseous development:
  Hypothyroidism
  Addison's disease
  Hypopituitarism (dwarfism)
  Pituitary cachexia (Simmonds' disease)
  Prolonged malnutrition
  Chronic illness
  Fröhlich's syndrome (adiposogenital dystrophy)
  Chondrodystrophy (achondroplasia)
  Hurler's syndrome (lipochondrodystrophy)
  Some cases of mental deficiency and mongolism
  Gonadal agenesis (Turner's syndrome)
  Hypogonadism

REFERENCES

1. Graham, C. B.: Assessment of bone maturation—methods and pitfalls, Radiol. Clin. North Am. 10:185, 1972.
2. Caffey, J.: *Pediatric X-Ray Diagnosis* (6th ed.; Chicago: Year Book Medical Publishers, Inc., 1972).
3. Christie, A.: Prevalence and distribution of ossification centers in the newborn infant, Am. J. Dis. Child. 77:355, 1949.
4. Roche, A. F., Eyman, S. L., and Davila, G. H.: Skeletal age prediction, J. Pediatr. 78:997, 1971.
5. Acheson, R. M.: Maturation of the Skeleton, in Falkner, F. (ed.): *Human Development* (Philadelphia: W. B. Saunders Company, 1966).
6. Rubin, P.: *Dynamic Classification of Bone Dysplasias* (Chicago: Year Book Medical Publishers, Inc., 1964).
7. Vaughan, V. E., and McKay, R. J.: *Nelson Textbook of Pediatrics* (10th ed.; Philadelphia: W. B. Saunders Company, 1975).
8. Garn, S. M., Rohmann, C. G., and Silverman, F. N.: Radiographic standards for postnatal ossification and tooth calcification. Med. Radiogr. Photogr. 43:45, 1967.
9. Maresh, M. M.: Linear growth of long bones of extremities from infancy through adolescence, A.M.A. Am. J. Dis. Child. 89:725, 1955.
10. Park, E. A.: Bone growth in health and disease, Arch. Dis. Child. 29:269, 1954.
11. Wilkins, L.: *The Diagnosis and Treatment of Endocrine Disorders in Childhood and Adolescence* (3d ed.; Springfield, Ill.: Charles C Thomas, Publisher, 1965).

12. Sontag, L. W., and Lipford, J.: The effect of illness and other factors on the appearance pattern of skeletal epiphyses, J. Pediatr. 23:391, 1943.
13. Patten, B. M.: *Human Embryology* (3d ed.; New York: McGraw-Hill Book Company, Inc., 1968).
14. Garn, S. M., Sandusky, S. T., Nagy, J. M., and McCann, M. B.: Advanced skeletal development in low income Negro children, J. Pediatr. 80:965, 1972.
15. Bayer, L. M., and Bayley, N.: *Growth Diagnosis* (Chicago: University of Chicago Press, 1959).
16. White House Conference on Child Health and Protection: *Growth and Development*, Pt. IV. Appraisement of the Child (New York: Century Company, 1933).
17. Woolley, P. V., Jr., and McCammon, R. W.: Bone growth in congenital myxedema, J. Pediatr. 27:229, 1945.
18. Greulich, W. W., and Pyle, S. I.: *Radiographic Atlas of Skeletal Development of the Hand and Wrist* (2d ed.; Palo Alto: Stanford University Press, 1959).
19. Krogman, W. M.: *The Physical Growth of Children: An Appraisal of Studies 1950–1955*, Child Development Publications (Lafayette, Ind.: Purdue University, 1956).
20. House, R.: A summary of 49 radiologists' opinions on the skeletal age limits of apparently normal six year old children, Am. J. Roentgenol. 64:442, 1950.
21. Dreizen, S., Snodgrasse, R. M., Webb-Peploe, H., Parker, G. S., and Spies, T. D.: Bilateral symmetry of skeletal maturation in the human hand and wrist, A.M.A. Am. J. Dis. Child. 93:122, 1957.
22. Mainland, D.: Evaluation of the skeletal age method of estimating children's development. I. Systemic errors in the assessment of roentgenograms, Pediatrics 12:114, 1953.
23. Hansman, C. F., and Maresh, M. M.: A longitudinal study of skeletal maturation, Am. J. Dis. Child. 101:305, 1961.
24. Pyle, S. I., Reed, R. B., and Stuart, H. C.: Patterns of skeletal development in the hand, Pediatrics 24:886, 1959.
25. Mackay, D. H.: Skeletal maturation in the hand: A study of development in East African children, Trans. R. Soc. Trop. Med. Hyg. 46:135, 1952.
26. Falkner, F.: Physical Growth, in Gairdner, D. (ed.): *Recent Advances in Pediatrics* (Boston: Little, Brown & Company, 1958), Chapter 5.
27. Pyle, S. I., and Hoerr, N. L.: *Radiographic Atlas of Skeletal Development of the Knee* (Springfield, Ill.: Charles C Thomas, Publisher, 1955).
28. Hoerr, N. L., Pyle, S. I., and Francis, C. C.: *Radiographic Atlas of Skeletal Development of the Foot and Ankle* (Springfield, Ill.: Charles C Thomas, Publisher, 1962).
29. Scott, K. E., and Usher, R.: Epiphyseal development in fetal malnutrition syndrome, N. Eng. J. Med. 27:822, 1964.
30. Maresh, M. M.: Bone, muscle and fat measurements, Pediatrics 24:971, 1961.
31. Kopczynska, J.: Determination radiologique de la maturation osseuse, Ann. Radiol. 7:308, 1964.
32. Tanner, J. M., Whitehouse, R. H., and Healy, M. J. R.: *A New System for Estimating Skeletal Maturity from the Hand and Wrist*. Part II. *The Scoring System* (Paris: Centre International de l'Enfance, 1962).
33. van der Werff Ten Bosch, J. J.: *Somatic Growth of the Child* (Springfield, Ill.: Charles C Thomas, Publisher, 1966).
34. Andersen, E.: Skeletal maturation of Danish school children in relation to

height, sexual development and social conditions, Acta Paediatr. Scand. (suppl.) 185:1, 1968.

35. *Skeletal Maturity of Children 6–11 Years, United States* (Washington, D.C.: U.S. Dept. of Health, Education and Welfare, Public Health Service, 1974).

36. *Skeletal Maturity of Children 6–11 Years: Racial, Geographic Area and Socioeconomic Differentials, United States* (Washington, D.C.: U.S. Dept. of Health, Education and Welfare, Public Health Service, 1975).

9 / Role of the Endocrine Glands in Normal Growth and Development

IT IS NOT the function of this text to give a detailed biochemical review of the mechanism of action of the various hormones involved in growth and development. It does seem necessary to at least acquaint the reader with some of the intricacies involved for a clearer understanding of this very complex field. Perhaps more than any other factor in growth and development, the hormones can effect the most profound changes.

Hormones interact with specific receptors in cellular plasma membranes. In a number of instances, including the trophic hormones of the pituitary, parathyroid hormones and calcitonin, the hormone-receptor complex influences the membrane enzyme adenylate cyclase which in turn influences the rate of synthesis of cyclic adenosine 3, 5-monophosphate (cyclic AMP) from intracellular adenosine triphosphate. Cyclic AMP regulates a number of intracellular processes; in many situations this involves the activation of protein kinases that phosphorylate cellular constituents. For instance, an increased synthesis of cyclic AMP has been shown to increase ribosomal phosphate content which may be a factor in protein production, both qualitative and quantitative. The effect of the hormones may be either stimulatory or inhibitory.

The steroid and thyroid hormones use a different method of information transfer. They gain access to the intracellular space where they are bound by specific cytoplasmic protein receptors and are then transported to the nucleus. Once in the nucleus the hormone exerts its effect, which has been shown to include alterations in chromatin structure and the template activity of DNA.[33]

Growth hormone, somatomedin, prolactin and insulin have mechanisms of action that presently remain obscure. It might be significant to note that this group, in common with thyroid hormones, influences a very broad spectrum of tissues in contrast to the trophic hormones which affect only specific target organs.

Hormones may be released in a free active form, e.g., insulin, or bound to a specific protein moiety such as globulin, e.g., cortisol, growth hormone, estrogens and thyroid. In some cases the binding is very loose (cortisol) and in others firm (thyroid). During pregnancy maternal thyroid-binding globulin increases, resulting in a considerably elevated total thyroxine level compared to normal. This type of binding may also be partially responsible for the minimal passage of maternal thyroid hormones across the placenta.

With the exception of insulin and somatomedin, which compete for the same receptor sites, each hormone is identified with a highly specific protein receptor in the cell membrane or in the cytoplasm. This accounts for the very high concentrations of some of the hormones in target organs, e.g., estrogen in the uterus and other portions of the genital tract.

The active half-life in the circulation of the different hormones varies

Fig 9–1.—A diagram showing the relationships of the pituitary gland to the hypothalamus and various target organs. Stimulus to production of the pituitary hormones arises from neurosecretions or releasing factors in the hypothalamus; there is a specific one for each hormone. With the possible exception of the growth hormone, all have reciprocal regulatory influences, represented by *broken lines,* back to the pituitary (or hypothalamus) through the hormones secreted by the target organs. In the case of the antidiuretic hormone (vasopressin, ADH), the feedback mechanism is indirect by virtue of changes in plasma osmolality. Since aldosterone production by the adrenal cortex functions largely independently of ACTH, it is omitted. (From Lowrey, G. H.: Consideration of Pituitary Endocrine Dysfunction, in Kahn, E. (ed.): *Correlative Neurosurgery* [Springfield, Ill.: Charles C Thomas, Publisher, 1969]).

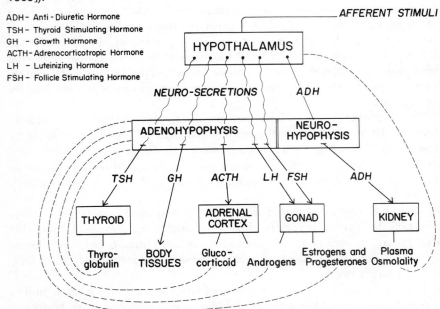

ADH – Anti - Diuretic Hormone
TSH – Thyroid Stimulating Hormone
GH – Growth Hormone
ACTH – Adrenocorticotropic Hormone
LH – Luteinizing Hormone
FSH – Follicle Stimulating Hormone

AFFERENT STIMULI

HYPOTHALAMUS

NEURO-SECRETIONS   ADH

ADENOHYPOPHYSIS   NEURO-HYPOPHYSIS

TSH   GH   ACTH   LH FSH   ADH

THYROID   ADRENAL CORTEX   GONAD   KIDNEY

Thyro-globulin   BODY TISSUES   Gluco-corticoid   Androgens   Estrogens and Progesterones   Plasma Osmolality considerably and is somewhat related to the duration of its effect upon a particular tissue. Growth hormone has a half-life of only 20 minutes, while thyroid hormones have 6–7 days and cortisol has about 48 hours. Therapeutically, giving a single dose of 5–10 mg of growth hormone once a week is equally effective as divided doses given daily to hormone-deficient patients. One must conclude, therefore, that the effectiveness in a cell is considerably longer than the measurement of half-life would seem to indicate.

All of the hormones are subject to a negative feedback mechanism which is responsible for the control of the amount of secretion into the circulation. In a normal individual, the level of circulating hormone is the usual stimulus or inhibitor for further secretion. If the amount present temporarily exceeds the physiologic requirements, the feedback is able to decrease the amount released and/or synthesized. If the circulating amount is insufficient, the reverse message is conveyed through this system and increased hormone secretion occurs. The degree of sensitivity of feedback varies with age (maturation) with some hormones. As we shall see later in discussing the gonadotropic hormones, the fetal hypothalamus is very insensitive to gonadotropic levels, during early childhood it is exquisitely sensitive, and then as puberty approaches, the hypothalamus becomes more permissive which allows for the events of sexual maturation. The feedback mechanism for some of the hormones is related entirely or partially to blood levels of chemical substances. Examples are ionizable calcium for the parathyroids and glucose for insulin (Fig 9–1).

Effects of Maternal and Placental Hormones on the Fetus

There is some doubt at present as to just what hormones can pass across the placenta to the fetus and in what quantities. Most of the protein molecules from the anterior pituitary probably do not pass with any degree of ease from the maternal circulation to the fetal circulation. This is also believed to be true of thyroglobulin, which has a molecular weight of approximately 700,000. Some experimental work has indicated that thyroid hormone may pass, but that it is not in free equilibrium between mother and fetus.[39] Clinical evidence to support this is present in the fact that cretins seldom appear to be hypothyroid until several weeks after birth. However, retardation of osseous development is present at the time of birth, and some of these infants will suffer irreparable neurologic damage even though adequate therapy is begun within the first month or two. It is therefore postulated that the developing fetus must supply his own thyroid hormone in order to have completely normal development. About 75–80% of cretins have no demonstrable thyroid gland, thus making them excellent subjects for observation.

As outlined in Chapter 3, the placenta is capable of producing estrogen, progesterone and a gonadotropin, all of which pass to the fetus.[82] In addition, as early as the end of the first trimester the fetal pituitary is synthesizing the gonadotropins FSH (follicle-stimulating hormone) and LH (luteinizing hormone). These trophic hormones do have a definite stimulatory effect upon the developing ovaries and testes with some sex hormone production.[40] As one author [83] has expressed it, "The human fetoplacental unit at midpregnancy may be characterized as a balanced system of physiologic enzyme deficiencies."

The phenomenon of breast hypertrophy and "witch's milk" in the newborn infant is an example of the estrogenic effect. The number of infants actually secreting milk in any group varies, depending upon the observer, from 15 to 80%. There is often considerable increase in size of the labia and a "milky" discharge from the vagina. Definite estrogenic changes also are present in the vaginal mucosa, which at birth resembles that of the adult in morphology, glycogen content and surface pH. During the few weeks following delivery desquamation of the epithelium takes place and the squamous cells are replaced by a single layer of cuboidal cells, the glycogen disappears and the pH becomes alkaline. In about 2–3% of female newborns some vaginal bleeding results from the effect of abrupt withdrawal of estrogen on the endometrium. The elevated blood levels of estrogens, progesterones and prolactin found in the newborn rapidly fall.[20, 22] In the male some hypertrophy of the prostatic utricle and urethra may be present at birth, though this seldom has clinical significance.

Urine pregnanediol excretion is high in the immediate newborn period but rapidly disappears. This compound is derived largely from the placentally synthesized progesterone and, in contrast to estriol content in maternal urine, has little significance relative to viability of the fetus.[41] Studies of endometrial changes in the female newborn show considerable variation in the presence or degree of the proliferative phases and these changes are unrelated to fetal ovarian morphology.[42] Definite follicular formation in the newborn ovary is not uncommon and probably reflects placental and/or fetal gonadotropic stimulation.

The fetal pituitary has the capacity to synthesize growth hormone (GH) by the end of the first trimester.[30] The GH content of the gland steadily increases, as does its size and the number of acidophil cells, until the last 10 weeks of gestation. At this time inhibitory influences become operative as the neurophysiologic mechanisms of the hypothalamus mature. At midgestation the amount of GH in the pituitary is nearly equal to that of a one-year-old child. Serum levels of GH are considerably elevated above childhood normals in the neonate and remain so for several weeks.[58] The functional importance of GH to the fetus or during infancy remains obscure. Evidence from the study of anencephalic fetuses and children with a confirmed diagnosis of growth hormone deficiency indicates it is not essential for physical growth during fetal life or for the first 12–18 months following birth. It is possible that the hormone may play a role in neonatal homeostasis in preventing hypoglycemia.[44, 99]

The relatively high levels of prolactin found in the fetal pituitary and in the serum have no clearly understood function at the present time.

Thyroid-stimulating hormone (TSH) in the fetal pituitary follows a pattern similar to the production of GH. The rising levels through midgestation are accompanied by elevated free and globulin-bound thyroxine in the serum. The levels establish a plateau during the last half of pregnancy but they remain elevated for a few days after birth.[58]

Grumbach[40] has hypothesized that early in gestation there is hyperactivity and relatively unrestrained secretion of releasing factors by the hypothalamus. Later, with increasing maturation, inhibitory influences from the central nervous system play a greater role. In part, the fetal secretions of the thyroid and testicle may have some influence in bringing about the change in sensitivity of the releasing centers as a part of the maturational process.

The administration of large doses of testosterone to the mother has caused virilization of the female fetus. Some types of synthetic progesterones have relatively strong androgenic properties and when given to mothers have produced some degree of masculinization.[63] Rarely the administration of synthetic estrogens to pregnant women has resulted in a virilizing effect on the external genitalia of female babies.[64] It is postulated that maternal, placental or fetal metabolism can alter these steroids to produce a hormone with a greater androgenic effect than the original steroid.

In summary, the infant at birth has already been exposed for some time to potent hormonal substances produced by the mother, the placenta and the fetus. The last two are the more important in influencing development. All of the endocrine glands of the normal neonate have received physiologic stimuli and have synthesized their respective hormones in considerable amounts. Further maturation consists primarily in the further refinement of feedback controls and alterations in sensitivity to stimuli and inhibitors.

The Central Nervous System and Pituitary Gland

Considerable progress has been made in defining the role of the central nervous system in the regulation of pituitary function.[9, 51, 59, 65, 69] Influence upon the anterior pituitary is mediated by neurohumoral substances transported to the gland by the hypophyseal-portal system originating in a capillary network in the median eminence of the hypothalamus. At least four specific releasing factors have been identified as arising in the hypothalamus. All are small polypeptides containing from 8 to possibly 20 amino acids. Not all have been chemically identified as yet. Known stimulators are related to adrenocorticotropic hormone (ACTH), TSH, GH and a single one for both gonadotropins (FSH and LH). Two inhibitors have been identified: one for prolactin and *somatostatin* for the growth hormone. Somatostatin not only inhibits growth hormone production but also glucogen by the alpha cells of the pancreas. This latter finding shows considerable promise in treating juvenile onset diabetes mellitus, since suppression of glucagon decreases insulin requirements and prevents development of ketosis. Figure 9–1 indicates the interrelationship of the releasing factors to the other trophic hormones of the pituitary.

All of the pituitary hormones are secreted in an episodic but rhythmical manner throughout a normal 24-hour day.[25] In the absence of stress, either emotional or physical, the secretion of ACTH, cortisol, GH and the gonadotropins is largely dominated by the daily sleep-wake pattern. Good correlation exists between the stages of sleep (see Chapter 6), electroencephalographic tracings and the blood levels of these hormones. Throughout childhood the maximum production and secretion of GH occurs in association with deep sleep, stages 3–4. In fact, stimulant medications that prevent deep sleep, when used chronically, will interfere with a child's growth.[32] ACTH and cortisol release are greatest just prior to awakening several hours after the maximal GH level is reached. Prior to puberty, gonadotropic levels are at a low and steady state. Just coincident with early sexual changes the level rises and the greatest increase occurs throughout sleep. With sexual maturation completed, secretion occurs equally without a circadian rhythmicity. In women, there are some modifications associated with the menstrual cycle.

Less clearly understood is the relationship of higher centers to the function of the pituitary. It is a fact that both emotional and physical stress result in an increased production of ACTH with a corresponding increase in blood cortisol. This has been termed an energy-mobilizing action converting proteins into carbohydrates. The release of gonadotropins may be influenced by sexual behavior. In most primates, and probably in man, the effect upon the developing brain and subsequent behavior is very definitely related to the kind and amount of sex hormone present in the fetus.

The anterior and posterior lobes of the pituitary are formed from separate ectodermal primordia. The anterior portion comes from the stomodeal depression known as Rathke's pouch, which appears about the fourth fetal week. The time at which this tissue becomes physiologically active is not known, but by the twelfth fetal week its glandular character is apparent on histologic examination.[19]

During growth the histologic appearance of the anterior pituitary changes, reflecting the changes in the products synthesized by the gland. It is probable that all secretory cells are derived from a small chromophobe stem cell. Newer techniques can now differentiate the specific function of cells and make obsolete the old acidophil-basophil-chromophobe nomenclature. At birth, delta cells, which are the producers of gonadotropins, are easily identified. This is followed by their virtual disappearance until about 10 years of age when they increase in number until adulthood. These changes undoubtedly reflect the fetal and then the pubescent exposure to hypothalamic stimulation and its documentation of the high levels of gonadotropins found in the blood. One cell type probably produces both FSH and LH. It is known that a single cell type is responsible for the synthesis of both prolactin and GH and another one for ACTH and the melanocyte-stimulating hormone (MSH). Only TSH is produced individually by one cell type. With the exception of the delta cells, there are no major shifts in the number of cell types with age.[4, 61]

Six hormones are recognized as arising from the anterior pituitary. These are: GH, TSH, ACTH, prolactin and two gonadotropins—FSH and LH (also termed "interstitial cell stimulating hormone"). All have been identified as being polypeptides of relatively high molecular weight (20,000–30,000). ACTH and GH are the only hormones that have been synthesized in the laboratory. Growth hormone is unique in that it is very species-specific. Hormone obtained from any species lower than a primate is ineffectual in man. This fact has obvious clinical significance because it means the supply is very limited.

The normal physical growth of an individual depends upon an adequate secretion of the growth hormone and the genetic ability to respond. Growth hormone is present in the blood throughout all of the growing period and well into adult life. Normal levels vary considerably in response to the circadian rhythm and fluctuations in normal stimuli or inhibitors. Levels in very early infancy may be 10 or more times higher than later in life. Average fasting early A.M. levels will be 2–5 ng/ml. It is estimated that requirements for normal growth will approximate 1 mg per day. Some workers have found slightly higher daytime levels in adolescents, while most have found no fluctuation with age other than that referred to above.[7, 8, 65, 71] The content of GH in the pituitary also remains constant regardless of age. In terms of growth, only the central nervous system, and possibly the adrenals and gonads, are unaffected by the hormone. Normal growth of the fetus occurs in the absence of GH, either from its own pituitary gland, from the mother's or from both. It is highly unlikely that the placental "growth" hormone plays any part (see Chapter 3). Although the half-life of pituitary GH is only 20 minutes, its activity after becoming fixed in tissue almost certainly continues.

From clinical and laboratory studies the principal action of this hormone appears to be one of stimulating DNA synthesis and cell multiplication. It is difficult clearly to separate all of the important factors influencing human growth, and perhaps there is considerable overlap in functions.[86] At the risk of oversimplification, the following plan seems to fit our interpretation of the available facts. Embryonic and fetal growth seem largely independent of hormonal influence, though the sex hormones have great impact at this time on ultimate sexual differentiation (see "Gonadal Influences on Growth and Development", p. 316). Adequate nutrition, maternal care and placental development with its intricate vascularity are included; these are most important for both cell multiplication and cell growth in the fetal and early infancy periods. After this critical period nutritional deprivation has its greatest effect on cell size. Growth hormone has its major influence on increasing the number of cells of the body (except in those systems already noted) from late infancy until adulthood. Its metabolic functions continue until death. Adequate thyroid hormone is necessary for normal increase in cell size and also for cell multiplication. As with nutrition, it appears that in late fetal and early infant development thyroid hormone plays an important role in cell multiplication and later in life in cell size. At the time of adolescence the sex hormones exert their influence. Androgens—male hormones—primarily cause an increase in cell size, while estrogens may stimulate cell size but also may restrict cell multiplication.

Some of the more important metabolic effects of growth hormone will be outlined.[7, 8] It stimulates the transport of amino acids across cell membranes and the synthesis of protein. Secondary to this action is the decreased excretion of urinary nitrogen. Growth hormone promotes the growth of cartilage. Total fatty acid catabolism is increased and free fatty acids are mobilized, causing a delayed increase in their level in serum. Immediately after administration blood glucose levels fall and there is a decreased insulin sensitivity with a prolongation of the disappearance rate of glucose given intravenously. Newborn infants have higher levels of growth hormone than older children or adults. In contrast to the latter, the newborn infant reacts to an increase in blood sugar with an increase in plasma GH. It is postulated that this ability may ensure the mobilization of fat needed to supply energy.[96] Furthermore, the hormone has been used with some measure of success to treat neonatal hypoglycemia. A slight drop in the respiratory quotient probably is a reflection of the effects upon carbohydrate and lipid metabolism. Sodium, potassium and inorganic phosphate are retained, but there is an increased rate of urinary calcium excretion.

Other factors than sleep are responsible for fluctuations in the secretion of GH. Exercise and physical or emotional stress act as stimulants. Hypoglycemia and prolonged fasting cause an increased production. Very high serum levels are found in most patients with kwashiorkor. Arginine and some other amino acids, by infusion, are strong stimuli as are pyrogens.

L-Dopa and norepinephrine through their catecholaminergic effect stimulate production and may represent the fundamental mechanism resulting from pyrogens and hypoglycemia.[65]

A powerful inhibitor of growth hormone production is *somatostatin*, a 14 amino acid polypeptide produced in the hypothalamus. Although it may serve as a regulator of GH secretion, its role in normal growth and development has not been clear from available work. Moderate to large amounts of corticosteroids given steadily will eventually interfere with growth. This is probably through interference with the action of somatomedin.[29] Interrupted dosage is much less harmful to growth (see Fig 13–3).

Human GH given to dwarfs with pituitary insufficiency will result in accelerated growth and a positive nitrogen balance during the period in which it is administered. Assays of GH in the serum of patients with acromegaly are markedly elevated. For further discussion of abnormal growth and deviations from normal in GH secretion, see Chapter 13.

Linear growth is due to growth of the long bones of the extremities. This occurs as a result of proliferation of cartilage in the epiphyseal plates which is dependent upon GH. The rate of this process may be estimated by measuring the uptake of isotope labeled sulfur into the chondromucoprotein of cartilage. Growth hormone in vitro will not produce the proliferation in the absence of normal serum. The ingredient in the serum was originally designated *sulfation factor* but is now termed *somatomedin*. Somatomedin is a stable peptide with a molecular weight of about 8,000 that enhances not only incorporation of sulfate into chondromucoprotein but thymidine into DNA and uridine into RNA. Its origin appears to be from the liver and is essential to the effectiveness of GH upon bone growth.[60]

The posterior lobe of the adenohypophysis (pars nervosa) is a part of the neurosecretory system that includes the supraoptic and paraventricular nuclei of the hypothalamus.[45] The hormones vasopressin or antidiuretic hormone (ADH) and oxytocin are produced in these areas and then reach the posterior lobe by the hypothalamo-hypophysial nerve tracts, where they are stored until released into the systemic circulation. Oxytocin is primarily concerned with uterine muscle contracture and has little relevance to growth and development. Vasopressin is discussed in Chapter 7 under the subject of water balance.

Insulin

Insulin is a powerful anabolic hormone which in many respects resembles growth hormone. The pancreas is well developed and secreting insulin by the end of the third trimester. Insulin's most important function is to increase the transport of glucose and amino acids across the cellular plasma membrane. In contrast to GH, which is lipolytic, insulin enhances the uptake of free fatty acids by the cell. It appears to increase the synthesis of DNA and RNA in target tissues such as muscle and bone. In its absence, cell ribosomes become less efficient in protein synthesis.

Although there is some evidence that the fetal pancreas and beta cells do not respond to hyperglycemia, the newborn infant of a diabetic mother manifests a number of features that indicate maternal hyperglycemia has influenced fetal insulin production. Often there is pancreatic hyperplasia of the beta cells. The infants are large with a surplus of adipose tissue and visceromegaly. They are at considerable risk to develop neonatal hypoglycemia.

The Thyroid Gland

The thyroid gland is probably second only to the pituitary in relative importance in its influence on growth and development.

The thyroid makes its appearance toward the end of the fourth fetal week as a bilobed diverticulum from the floor of the pharynx. Toward the end of the fourth month colloid can be found in the center of the cell mass, and there is evidence that shortly after this time the gland becomes physiologically active. Accessory thyroid tissue may be found along the course of the thyroglossal duct from the base of the tongue to the root of the neck. Occasionally thyroid glands are found substernally.[19]

The thyroid hormones consist of thyroxine (T_4) and triiodothyronine (T_3). It is believed that the latter is the active hormone and that T_4 is converted to T_3 in peripheral tissue. T_3 is about four times more potent than T_4 but it usually constitutes only about 5–10% of circulating hormones. Both are transported in blood in strong association with globulin, and small amounts with albumin. Secretion of the hormones is stimulated by pituitary TSH which functions in the thyroid cell through a cyclic AMP mechanism. Although TSH is under control of a hypothalamic releasing factor, the major negative feedback of thyroid hormones is dependent upon specific receptors in the pituitary. Normal levels of serum T_4 at birth are 7–15 μg/100 ml and from midinfancy on are 5–10 μg/100 ml. Except for a brief period after birth (see below), T_3 levels range from 90 to 170 ng/100 ml throughout all of childhood.

Early in the second trimester there is an increase of TSH in the fetal serum and a progressive increase in T_4 to a level that exceeds that found in maternal serum at the same time.[84] This differential is maintained until delivery. Immediately following birth there is a marked surge in TSH production by the newborn's pituitary and a response by the capable thyroid. Some workers relate the surge of TSH to neonatal cooling while others feel clamping of the cord in some way is responsible. Mean cord levels of TSH are 10 μU/ml which rises to a mean of 35 μU/ml by 2 hours and is followed by a drop to the same values found at birth by 72 hours. Mean cord levels of T_4 are 12 $\mu g/100$ ml which rise to a maximum of 25 $\mu g/100$ ml by 2–5 hours and then slowly fall over the next 6–10 days to the same values found at birth. Blood levels of T_3 parallel TSH values: 35 ng/100 ml at birth, 220 ng/100 ml at 2 hours and 146 ng/100 ml at 72 hours. The neonate is relatively hyperthyroid by virtue of elevations of both T_3 and T_4, though the T_3 elevation is a very brief one. Premature infants follow a similar pattern but the initial surge and response is reduced proportionate to the degree of immaturity.[43, 48, 101] Throughout most of infancy, T_4 levels remain slightly higher than those found later in life. During middle to late adolescence T_4 levels are lower than at any other time throughout childhood.[36]

Thyroid hormones are necessary for the production of all forms of RNA and their presence in the cell stimulates ribosome production and protein synthesis. They also promote oxidative phosphorylation in mitochondria of most cells. The hormones are important for normal maturation of the brain, their absence causing a delay in cell differentiation and at least a transient decrease in cell numbers. They are required for physical growth and development, and, along with the sex hormones, they occupy an essential role in bone development and linear growth. In relationship to pituitary GH they play a permissive role. In their absence GH is relatively ineffective. In the absence of GH, the thyroid hormones may promote some degree of maturation, but no growth.

In contrast to GH, which has little influence on fetal and neonatal growth, thyroid function has very great influence.[85] As already mentioned, in its absence there is lack of brain development and this is manifested in delayed behavioral development. Retardation in bone maturation in thyroid deficiency is often profound and is such a constant finding that the presence of a normal "bone age" almost excludes the diagnosis.[47] The lack of growth of osseous tissue is also reflected in a reduced serum content of alkaline phosphatase. If hypothyroidism occurs before or during adolescence, sexual maturation is delayed or absent.

Absence or deficiency of thyroid secretion at birth results in the clinical entity of cretinism. This is characterized by stunted growth with shortened extremities, pale and mottled skin, thickened facial features, umbilical hernia, large tongue, constipation, noisy respiration and generally lethargic behavior. Adequate therapy will correct the physical abnormalities but may not be able to amend the effects of lack of fetal thyroid function on the brain.[10, 47]

The Adrenal Glands

The adrenal medulla originates from cells of the neural crest which also form the sympathetic ganglions. Very early in embryonic life these cells may be differentiated from the ganglion cells by staining with chromic acid, which they retain; this has led to the term "chromaffin cells." Similar clusters of chromaffin cells found along the aorta persist for many years following birth. The cells of the adrenal cortex arise from the splanchnic mesoderm. Early in fetal life two distinct layers of the cortex can be made out. The inner portion of the cortex, called the reticular zone, becomes mature and well differentiated by the third fetal month, and vacuoles are formed in these cells. The outer portion remains a thin layer and is undifferentiated until after birth. In the neonatal period the adrenal gland has approximately 20 times the relative size found in the adult; this is due to persistence of the fetal reticular layer. By the end of the first month of life the number of these cells has decreased greatly; the final adult character of the adrenal cortex is not attained until about the third year. The adult reticular cells are derived by a process of differentiation from the fetal cells.[15] [19] By the end of the third week after birth the adrenals have lost half of their initial weight. Following this period there is slow increase in weight, and by the third or fourth year the adrenals have regained their original size. The cause of these striking changes, especially the retention of the fetal layer throughout the late fetal development, is not at present known. It has been theorized that some trophic substance from the pituitary or placenta may maintain it until birth.[49] It has also been postulated that this fetal reticular zone is responsible for the relatively large quantities of 17-ketosteroids excreted by the infant in the first few days after birth (Table 9–1).

The adrenal cortex produces three groups of steroid hormones. According to their physiologic functions they are designated as: mineralocorticoids (aldosterone), glucocorticoids (cortisol or hydrocortisone) and androgens (testosterone). During the neonatal period corticosterone is the major glucocorticoid secreted, but this is quickly replaced by cortisol. Small and physiologically unimportant amounts of estrogen and progesterone may be produced by the adrenal cortex.

The first group, mineralocorticoids, mainly influence water, sodium and potassium balance. They control sodium and potassium excretion by the kidneys through the mechanism of reabsorption. With a deficiency of these hormones there is an excessive loss of sodium from the body and an increase in serum potassium content. Secondarily the serum chloride level is lowered due to excessive chloride excretion. The extracellular fluid volume is depleted as a consequence of the electrolyte loss when water is carried off. Dehydration, weakness, microcardia and circulatory collapse are the end results. Conversely, an excess of aldosterone increases the reabsorption of sodium in the kidney, leading to elevation of the serum sodium level. Serum potassium content falls owing to excessive excretion, and intracellular potassium also is depleted. With the sodium retention there is an increase in the

TABLE 9–1.—NORMAL URINE OR PLASMA
CONTENT OF VARIOUS HORMONES OR
THEIR METABOLITES

ASSAY	NEONATE	CHILD	ADULT
17-hydroxysteroids urine, mg/24 hr	0.2–3.5	0.5–5.0	1.5–9.0
17-ketosteroids urine, mg/24 hr	1.5–2.5	0.1–1.0	5–12 female 6–22 male
Aldosterone urine, ng/24 hr	1–2	2–10	5–20
Testosterone* plasma, ng/100 ml	230–300	3–10	300–500
Estradiol† plasma, ng/100 ml	100–300	2–4	10–200‡
LH plasma, ng/ml	4–10	0–4	6–20
FSH plasma, ng/ml	0–2	0–4	6–20
Thyroxine (T_4) plasma, μg/100 ml	7–15	5–10	5–10
GH plasma, ng/ml	20–40	2–5	2–5

*Male only.
†Female only.
‡The wide range of values is a reflection of changing levels throughout the menstrual cycle.

extracellular fluid volume, with resulting edema. Sodium tends to replace the intracellular potassium in order to maintain osmotic balance. If this exchange reaches any degree of magnitude, degenerative changes appear and weakness, paralysis and cardiac failure occur. To bring about further extracellular-intracellular ionic balance, the extracellular chloride concentration is decreased. This in turn is compensated for by a rise in serum bicarbonate content. The final result is slight hypernatremia, hypokalemia, hypochloremia and increased serum bicarbonate content. Eventually hypertension may be present. In a normal individual the hormone output is such that these factors are kept in balance and are related to the sodium and potassium intake and to blood volume. If the volume falls, this causes an increased secretion of aldosterone; conversely, an increased blood volume inhibits hormonal production. It is believed that the juxtaglomerular apparatus of the kidney plays a key role in the rate of secretion of aldosterone. Reduced blood flow in the kidney is followed by an increased release of renin and angiotensin-stimulated aldosterone secretion.

The group of glucocorticoids control carbohydrate-protein balances in the body. They differ chemically from the first group in having an oxygen atom attached to the eleventh carbon atom in the steroid nucleus. These hormones promote catabolism and gluconeogenesis from protein. When in excess they inhibit carbohydrate utilization by the body tissues and tend to cause increased fat deposition. This inhibiting action also produces a relative hyperglycemia which is resistant to insulin. These hormones also are important in times of severe stress, such as infection, burns, mental strain, and so on. At such times relatively large amounts of these are found in the circulation and in the urine as the 17-hydroxycorticosteroids (17-OHCS). They also constitute the group of anti-inflammatory agents. It is possible that the excessive secretion of these hormones during illness in children accounts for the temporary arrest in growth which is often noted by increased nitrogen catabolism and inhibition of normal carbohydrate metabolism. In addition to causing these changes, the glucocorticoids depress the number of circulating eosinophiles, cause involution of lymphatic tissues and depress normal immune responses.[10, 22]

Androgens constitute the third and final group. Experimental and clinical evidence indicates that these substances originate in the reticular layer of the cortex. In their physiologic action they resemble androgens from the testes since they promote both masculinization and nitrogen retention. In the female all androgens are derived from the adrenal cortex, whereas in the male a small but relatively potent portion comes from the testes as adolescence progresses.[31] Plasma levels of testosterone remain somewhat elevated for a few months after birth and then decrease to prepubertal values. There appears to be a persistence of fetal levels of LH stimulating the testes. There is no evidence that the adrenals contribute to this.

The adrenocorticotropic (ACTH) hormone from the pituitary determines the amounts of secretion of the corticoids and the androgens. The water and electrolyte controlling hormone aldosterone is secreted largely independently of ACTH and responds to blood volume. ACTH can respond quickly by increase in stressful situations, which may well be lifesaving under some circumstances. Under usual conditions there is a sensitive "feedback" or inhibiting action of cortisol and corticosterone upon the release of ACTH from the pituitary. This permits a very excellent balance and regulation of adrenal cortical function. There is very little inhibitory effect of the androgens on the production of ACTH. The circadian variations in the plasma levels of cortisol have already been described.[15, 25] Depending somewhat on the methods for determination,[46] the adult plasma levels of 17-OHCS normally range between 4 and 10 μg, for the 17-KS between 60 and 100 μg. At birth and for a few days after, the levels of 17-KS in the infant are from 2 to 5 times higher than in the adult. This is especially significant when it is realized that the mother's level is usually considerably reduced at parturition compared with her nonpregnant state. Urinary excretion for a few days is correspondingly elevated in the newborn. The exact source of this increase in the infant is not certain, but it does parallel the involution of the fetal reticular layer previously described. It is important to understand that testosterone is not one of the androgens recoverable in the 17-KS fraction of either plasma or urine.

Some confusion exists in the literature relative to the functional ability of the adrenal cortex of the young child or infant to perform under normal circumstances and under stress. Part of this confusion undoubtedly was due to ignorance of the existence of the many different steroids formerly lumped under headings such as 17-ketosteroids and 17-hydroxycorticosteroids. Conclusions were sometimes formed upon total urinary excretion of a group of steroids rather than on the basis of units per time per weight. Plasma levels probably have greater physiologic significance than urine levels, but this was not appreciated. Good reviews of our present knowledge are available and will be briefly outlined.[38, 70, 72, 73]

Continuing throughout all of childhood, there are enzymatic changes in the adrenal cortex which are characteristic and similar to such changes in other tissues. Although the fetus can synthesize and metabolize steroids, his ability to make the ones considered biologically potent is limited. For normal development of the fetal cortex, fetal ACTH is needed. (Most anencephalic monsters have poorly developed adrenals.) In the premature and term infant, large amounts of 17-ketosteroids are present in the blood and urine. These fall rapidly to the low levels expected in infants, with one exception. The blood levels in the premature remain higher for longer periods, presumably due to slower metabolism and excretion. Separation of the 17-ketosteroids indicates that those present at birth are considerably different from those present a few weeks later; e.g., dehydroepiandrosterone is present at birth and does not reappear in the urine until age 8 or 9. Although some studies indicate transient inability in the neonate, especially the premature, to produce adequate quantities of potent corticosteroids,[56] most authors conclude that, on the basis of size, there is neither an inability to synthesize these hormones nor any decreased response to stimuli. If vaginal delivery occurs, the mother's plasma levels of cortisol are some 3–10 times higher than the infant's at birth. The blood levels quickly readjust and remain constant throughout life.

The important role of glucocorticoids in lung maturation and production of surfactant has been discussed in Chapter 5.

Aldosterone production in premature and newborn infants may lag behind levels found later in life if no stimulation is supplied. If, however, salt restriction is introduced, the response is very adequate at all ages.[91] Rarely in the newborn infant the response of the kidney to administered aldosterone may be briefly paradoxical in relation to sodium and potassium retention. This probably reflects renal immaturity.[37]

The functional status of the adrenal medulla in infancy and childhood appears to have little influence on growth and development except in pathologic states. This statement may indicate more ignorance than knowledge, since adequate levels of catecholamines in the blood are important to maintain vegetative functions such as heart rate, blood glucose levels and vascular tone. On the basis of weight versus urinary excretion, the levels of epinephrine and norepinephrine are similar at all ages, except for infancy and early childhood, when slightly greater amounts are produced.[90] (See also Chapter 10 for role of norepinephrine in temperature control.)

Gonadal Influences on Growth and Development

Sex differentiation from the primordial gonad into testis or ovary is determined by genetics (Chapter 2). The adrenal and gonadal tissues arise from cells of similar origin, the former from the cephalic end of the mesonephric ridge and the latter from the adjacent gonadal ridge located on the ventral border of the mesonephros. Thus the two steroid-producing glands have an intimate genesis. In the future female the earliest and most significant changes occur in the cortex, with greater growth and prominence of these cells, whereas in the future male the medullary areas undergo similar early development at the expense of the cortex.

In the presence of a Y chromosome the predominant phenotype will be male. Even in the rare occurrence of more than one X chromosome, as in XXY Klinefelter's syndrome, the external genitalia are typically male and testes are present. The absence of a Y chromosome results in phenotypic female genital development. The fetal testes produce two important hormones relative to sexual development. One, testosterone, is responsible for the differentiation of the primordial wolffian ducts into the epididymis, vas deferens, seminal vesicles and prostatic gland. The other hormone is protein in nature and causes regression of the müllerian ducts. In the absence of the fetal testes, the wolffian ducts regress and the müllerian duct system progresses to form the fallopian tubes, uterus and proximal portion of the vagina. In a sense, female development is a negative procedure since the fetal ovary remains poorly differentiated at the same time that male organogenesis is well underway.[36]

In contrast to the unipotential of the primordia of the gonaducts, the primordia of the external genitalia are bipotential and may differentiate into either male or female type. The direction taken depends upon the predominance of estrogens or androgens. Comparable parts form the following structures: male glans penis/female glans clitoridis, male corpora cavernosa penis/female corpora cavernosa clitoridis, male corpus spongiosum/female bulb of the vestibule, male ventral portion of penis/female labia minora, male scrotum/female labia majorum. Identification of sex from appearance of the external genitalia is usually not possible until about the 10th or 11th week of gestation.[19]

Future reproductive physiology and certain behavioral aspects of maleness and femaleness depend upon the early (fetal and neonatal) exposure of the brain to the sex hormones. One of the major actions of androgens during development is to organize (imprint?) the immature central nervous system into a male direction.[34] The development following duct differentiation includes the appearance of interstitial (Leydig) cells in the testis which are capable of producing androgenic hormones. It is interesting to note that these cells become dormant and atrophic from 4 to 6 weeks following birth and they are not morphologically recognizable again until puberty is approached.

Early in gestation the fetal gonads are capable of stimulation by the abundent chorionic gonadotropin produced by the placenta. The fetal pituitary begins synthesis of gonadotropins late in the first trimester reaching a peak of production at midgestation and then decreasing until birth. As a result, serum testosterone levels in the male fetus are very high for some time around midgestation and then drop off, but not to the usual prepubescent values, until 4–6 months after birth. At term, the LH value is still elevated while FSH is often not detectable. There are significant sex differences with the serum levels of FSH and LH, both being higher in the female. The high level of testosterone in the male fetus, and approximately equal estrogens in both sexes, may result in a difference in the sensitivity of the negative feedback mechanism (maturation ?) which accounts for the differences in the gonadotropins[40, 68] (see Table 9–1).

In many animals, including primates, if a male animal is castrated in the neonatal period, the pituitary release of gonadotropins (FSH and LH) becomes cyclic in the adult and is indistinguishable from that of the normal female. If an ovary is transplanted into such an adult male, cyclic ovulation occurs. If, however, a single injection of androgen is given following the castration, the ovulation does not take place. Furthermore, if the normal newborn female animal is given a single injection of androgen, she will be acyclic. Passivity and sexual receptivity characterize the male newborn castrate treated with estrogens as he enters adult life. Conversely, the androgen-treated female newborn becomes more aggressive in behavior, resembling the normal male.[67] Such evidence supports the concept that early exposure to these hormones, even if transient, profoundly influences subsequent development of the brain and its influence upon sex-related behavior and gonadal function.

Even in the young child the ovaries vary considerably in size, and this variation is due primarily to the number and size of small follicular "cysts." Gradual changes in the germinal epithelium at the cortex convert it from a tall columnar type to the thin endothelium-like layer more characteristic of the mature organ. Just before and during adolescence ovarian growth occurs at a fairly rapid rate, and follicular formation increases. The follicles go through the cycle of increasing in size, forming the corpus luteum and the eventual atresia which is characteristic of the mature female. It is probable that ovulation does not take place for several months or years after morphologic maturity is attained.

The male gonads undergo little differentiation or growth after the neonatal changes are completed. For the first 6–7 years the tubular epithelium is poorly developed. The connective tissue is abundant and resembles mesenchyme. At approximately 10 years of age the Leydig cells reappear, the tubular cells undergo early differentiation and the tubules increase in size. Sertoli cells are well developed and spermatids are present. Beyond age 12 the Leydig cells become larger, and the cytoplasm becomes vacuolated and more intensely stained than previously. Basal membranes of the tubules are well formed, and Sertoli cells become mature. These maturational steps have considerable practical importance, since they are lacking in the undescended testicle. Varying degrees of fibrotic replacement also take place in the undescended testicle. The time chosen for operative procedures for cryptorchism cannot be arbitrary when based on these facts.[66]

The normally functioning gonad is necessary for proper development of the child. The effects of prepubertal castration demonstrate this: the muscles are less well developed, there is a greater deposition of fat in them and the bones are longer owing to failure of the epiphyses to close.[4] The time of closure of the epiphyses is closely correlated with the advent of puberty, and the average child grows about 7.5 cm after its onset. With this fact in mind, it is interesting to note that the castrate stops growing at the time puberty normally would have occurred. The same picture results whether the ovaries or the testes are removed. Overactivity of the testicular tissue in prepubertal boys, as in interstitial cell tumors, results in early development of secondary sexual characteristics, a shortened growth span and a final stature less than his genetic potential. In girls similar symptoms result from granulosa cell tumors in the ovary.[20]

The androgens secreted by the interstitial cells of the testes are activated by the gonadotropins from the pituitary. Their physiologic properties are not essentially different from those previously described for the adrenal cortex. In boys the testes certainly are the most important source of androgens.

Like testosterone, the ovarian estrogens normally are not secreted in physiologic amounts until shortly before puberty. Estrogens do not have any anabolic properties. Their major effect is in accomplishing the development of sexual maturity in girls and accelerating maturation which can be measured as bone age. Further discussion of the role of the gonads in growth and development will be found in the section on adolescence and puberty in this chapter.

The Parathyroid Glands

The importance of the parathyroid glands to normal growth and development can be appreciated when it is realized that these glands are responsible for normal bone development, which, in turn, is the limiting factor for statural growth. The parathyroid glands to a great degree regulate calcium and phosphorus metabolism in the body. Other important factors are the production of the parathormone antagonist calcitonin by special cells in the thyroid, the dietary intake of calcium and phosphorus, the availability of vitamin D, the status of physical exercise and the ability of the kidneys to respond to existing metabolic requirements.[1, 3, 4, 75] (See also Chapter 8.)

Bone consists of an organic matrix in which is deposited a calcium-phosphate-carbonate complex called dahllite. All bone has both resorbing surfaces, under the influence of osteoclast cells, and bone-forming surfaces, under the influence of osteoblast cells. The osteoblasts are believed to elaborate the enzyme phosphatase. The fluid in contact with bone is normally maintained, in relation to the concentration of its constituents, by the kidneys. Under usual conditions these body fluids are in a state of incomplete saturation so far as calcium and phosphorus are concerned. Consequently, there is a constant dissolution of calcium and phosphorus from the resorbing surfaces even in growing bone. Bone deposition occurs in response to stresses and strains wherever bone is needed and also in the growing ends of long bones. This deposition consists in the laying down of an organic matrix or cartilage rich in phosphate due to the presence of osteoblasts. Phosphorylase, an enzyme present in growing cartilage and in bone tissue, is also important. This enzyme catalyzes the reaction in which inorganic phosphate is freed from organic esters. Thus, phosphatase and phosphorylase are responsible for increasing the concentration of phosphate ions on the surface where bone is forming. When the product of phosphate ions and calcium ions is sufficiently great, dahllite is deposited. This whole mechanism makes for efficient skeletal formation which is strong but not bulky. The factor, or factors, involved in the final limits of bone growth, which therefore limits stature, is not known, but some proposed theories will be discussed.

The calcium and phosphorus content of body fluids is of vital importance in bone growth. The calcium in serum is composed of three fractions: (1) calcium ions, (2) calcium bound to protein and (3) a very small un-ionized portion in solution. Under normal conditions of protein content and hydrogen ion concentration, about 50% of the calcium is in an ionized form in the serum. Recent work indicates that the primary action of the parathyroid hormone is to liberate calcium from bone, making it available to the circulation. This may be accomplished through the use of the citric acid, which keeps the calcium in soluble form both through its effect on the pH as an acid and as a chelating agent.[1, 3] In addition to the direct effect on bone, the hormone enhances calcium absorption from the gut in the presence of vitamin D. Finally, it increases the renal tubular reabsorption of calcium and the excretion of phosphate. The net result of the action of parathormone (PTH) is to increase the serum level of calcium and decrease phosphorus. In normal circumstances the adjustment of the serum calcium to the serum phosphorus level is such that the product of the two, expressed as mg/100 ml, is between 40 and 55 in growing children (30–40 in adults). This fact, plus clinical experience, is the basis for the law of Howland and Kramer, which states that rickets will be present in children if the product is below 35 and that rickets will heal if the product rises above 40.

Calcitonin is a polypeptide containing 32 amino acids and is formed by parafollicular C cells found in the thyroid, thymus and parathyroids. It is secreted in response to hypercalcemia resulting in a lowered serum calcium and phosphate. This is accomplished by inhibition of bone resorption. Its onset of action is more rapid than PTH.[14, 17] Its physiologic importance appears to be one of balancing the homeostatic mechanisms for serum calcium.

Bone growth, then, depends on the local condition of the tissues and the serum or body fluids which act as a substrate for the tissues. If some disturbance occurs to diminish the elaboration of the enzymes (phosphatase, phosphorylase), the concentration of phosphate ions will not be sufficient to exceed the solubility product of the complex calcium-phosphate-carbonate salt, and deposition will not take place. However, even though the enzymes may be present in sufficient quantity, if the concentration of calcium or phosphate in the serum is low, the solubility product of the salt cannot be exceeded. Therefore, bone growth may be disturbed in two ways in the process of mineralization. Other factors, too, may interfere, such as poor matrix formation due to abnormality of protein metabolism. Finally, it is known that a lowered pH of the serum, as in chronic acidosis, favors decalcification by its effect on the ionization of the calcium (See pp. 280–281).

The clinical picture of hyperparathyroidism is characterized by decalcification of bone with resultant softening and malformation. Cysts may form in the bone and fractures occur. All of these may contribute to statural abnormality and relative dwarfism.

At birth the parathyroid glands appear to be morphologically similar to those of the adult. Some authors state that hypertrophy is occasionally present late in the first week of life and believe this is caused by the high phosphate content of cow's milk and its effect on serum levels. The relatively low calcium and elevated phosphate levels in the serum of the newborn infant have been attributed, in part, to cow's-milk feedings.

The classic description of the functionally depressed or immature parathyroids being responsible for the low calcium–high phosphorus ratios found in the neonatal period is open to question. Although some work indicates that small-for-gestational-age and premature neonates have depressed parathyroid function leading to hypocalcemia,[54, 55] others have found that serum calcitonin levels were markedly elevated in infants with low calcium levels.[100] The high values of calcitonin in the newborn are consistent with the increased number of C cells found in the thyroid at that time. There is no evidence of impaired renal function being at fault for the associated hyperphosphatemia. Serum concentrations of PTH indicate a slightly reduced level for the first few days of life when compared to older infants, but essentially no change with age thereafter.[3]

Adolescence and Puberty

Adolescence is that period of life associated with accelerated growth in height and weight, the appearance of sexual characteristics and ability to reproduce and then a rapid deceleration of growth which is terminated by the final maturation of bone with fusion of epiphyses and metaphyses. It is the period of transition from childhood to adulthood. Shakespeare wrote of it in *Twelfth Night:*

> Not yet old enough for a man
> nor young enough for a boy;
> as a squash is before 'tis a
> peascod, or a codling when
> 'tis almost an apple: 'tis
> with him in standing water,
> between boy and man.

Adolescence has no sharp end points at the beginning or end, and it lasts almost a decade. There is considerable variability in the chronologic ages at which these events occur.

Puberty (from the Latin *pubertas,* meaning adulthood) refers to that time when sexual reproduction is possible. Common law and most legal statutes refer to the word in a similar manner. Developmentally, this is usually considered to coincide with the appearance of dark curly pubic hair. Menarche is often used as the dividing line between pre- and postpuberty in the female, though ovulation and the ability to reproduce is often not present for another year or two. Nocturnal emissions in the male are no better indicators of the presence of mature sperm. On the average, puberty is assumed to take place about two years later in boys than in girls. The "adolescent spurt" of growth is steroid- (sex hormone) mediated and is greater in quantity and longer in duration in boys.

This period is accompanied by important psychologic changes that are deeply influenced by the physical alterations. These aspects of adolescence and puberty are discussed in Chapter 6.

Generally speaking, the sooner puberty occurs the sooner will the rate of growth decline and finally stop.[27] This can be nicely shown in girls by charting two subjects on the same graph. If the onset of menarche occurs earlier in one, her growth curve levels off sooner than that of the other subject under study. This growth curve may be representative of height, weight or of body dimensions in general (Fig 9–2). At the same age, the mean height and weight of boys or girls who are more mature sexually are significantly greater than of those who are less mature (Fig 9–3), and the onset of puberty is better correlated with these measurements than with chronologic age.[6] It should be pointed out that growth curves based on cumulative data of large numbers of subjects are misleading or misrepresent the shape of the curve for the individual at the time of adolescence. The curve for the large numbers appears relatively smooth because it covers a number of years for the growth spurt. The curve for the individual is usually relatively abrupt in change at the beginning and end of the growth spurt and covers a time

Fig 9–2.—Relation of growth and onset of menarche. The *blocks* in the curves represent the time of menarche in two groups of girls. Girls with early menarche, and presumably reaching maturity early, have a more accelerated growth curve than girls with late menarche, but duration of their growth is shorter. As a result of this growth pattern girls with late maturation are taller, on the average, when final stature is attained. (From Holt, L. E., Jr., and McIntosh, R. (eds.): *Diseases of Infancy and Children* [11th ed.; New York: Appleton-Century-Crofts, Inc., 1941].)

Fig 9–3.—Average height and weight curves for boys and girls. The earlier increase at the time of adolescence for the girls is clearly shown. The fact that most girls are larger than most boys between ages 11 and 13 is probably due to the earlier influence of the sex hormones on physical growth.

measured in months rather than in years. The maximal yearly increase in height occurs the year before menarche in most girls.

That growth may proceed to some considerable extent after menarche is graphically indicated in Figure 9–4. The average increase after this time was about 3 in. (7.5 cm) in a group of American girls, with a range from under 1 in. to nearly 7 in. Obviously, one must be cautious in giving advice as to how much further increase in stature will occur after the onset of menstruation. A further interesting observation based on this material is that final height was not predictable from the amount of growth taking place following menarche. There is some trend in the direction of the tallest girls' having the greatest amount of post-menarche growth, but many variables are apparent.

Fig 9-4.—Growth following menarche in 68 normal American girls. The *dark line* indicates the final height and the *shaded areas* the inches grown after menarche. The point at which the dark line crosses a shaded column represents that specific girl's postmenarchial growth and final height. It can be seen that the shortest girls (far left of chart) did not show the least amount of growth after menarche, and the same absence of correlation is generally true of the tallest girls (right), who did not necessarily have the greatest postmenarchial growth.

Until very recently in the United States, and possibly other developed nations, each succeeding generation of girls experienced an earlier age of the menarche. As with the past history of increasing height in succeeding generations, we may have reached an ultimate limit. For at least two decades, menarche is not occurring earlier and adult height is not increasing. (See also Chapter 2.) There do appear to be some genetic factors involved in the normally wide variation found among healthy girls (Table 9–2).[50, 80, 81]

Previous indications that hot climates brought about earlier menarche and other evidences of sexual maturation have been put aside as purely anecdotal.

The pubertal acceleration in height occurs earlier, is of shorter duration and of lesser magnitude in girls than in boys.[87] Although the peak of statural growth in boys or girls cannot be associated with any particular stage of sexual development, all girls will have begun the decelerating phase of growth before menarche.[88] The age at which each stage of adolescence is

TABLE 9–2.—AGE AT MENARCHE

AGE, YR	ALL RACES*	WHITE	BLACK
6–9	0.2	0.2	0.2
10	1.2	0.8	4.0
11	12.8	11.6	21.3
12	43.3	41.7	51.2
13	73.2	72.9	74.1
14	91.7	91.4	93.5
15	98.3	98.2	98.7
16–17	99.7	99.6	100.0

*Percentage of girls whose menstrual periods had started, in a survey in the United States by race and age.[12]

reached follows the usual sequence (Tables 9–3 and 9–4) in more than 60% of children; this still permits nearly 40% to deviate from the expected. As an example, breast development in girls reaches stage II or III before any appearance of pubic hair in 75% of subjects, but pubic hair reaches stage II or III in approximately 10% of girls before the breasts reach stage II.

Not only is there much variation in the ages at which the various sequences of puberty begin, there are also considerable differences among children in the rapidity with which each progresses from one stage to the next. One may remain at one stage for less than 6 months while another occupies the same stage for 2 years. The average adolescent will pass through all stages in approximately 4 years, but normal variations range from 18 months to 8 years. The rate of passage is unrelated to the age of onset of the earliest changes.

The causes of the onset of puberty are not at all clear. An interesting postulation is that of Frisch and her co-workers.[6] They believe that there are meaningful correlations between total body mass (lean body weight) and the predictability of the age of menarche. When a critical weight is reached the mechanisms responsible for menarche begin. In support of this hypothesis is the observed secular trend in height and weight over the past 150 years with the decreasing age at menarche.

Hormonal assays have shown the relationship of increased release of pituitary gonadotropins LH and FSH with the advancing stages of adolescent development, gonadal growth and function, and osseous maturation.[26, 31, 93-95] The postulated steps in this complicated interrelationship are suggested in the following outline:

1. Following midgestation of the fetal period, maturation of the hypothalamic-pituitary-gonadal axis begins.

2. Throughout late infancy and most of prepubescent childhood the

TABLE 9-3.—STAGES OF SEXUAL DEVELOPMENT: FEMALE

AGE	STAGES
0–12	I. Preadolescent. Female pelvic contour evident, breast flat, labia majora smooth and minora are poorly developed, hymenal opening small or absent, mucous membranes dry and red, vaginal cells lack glycogen.
8–13	II. *Breasts:* Elevation of nipple, small mound beneath areola which is enlarging and begins pigmentation. *Labia majora* become thickened, more prominent and wrinkled, *labia minora* easily identified due to increased size along with clitoris, urethral opening more prominent, mucous membranes moist and pink, some glycogen present in vaginal cells. *Hair:* First appears on mons and then on labia majora about time of menarche, still scanty, soft and straight. *Skin:* Increased activity of sebaceous and merocrine sweat glands and initial function of apocrine glands in axilla and vulva begin.
9–14	III. Rapid growth peak is passed, menarche most often at this stage and invariably follows the peak of growth acceleration. *Breasts:* Areola and nipple further enlarge and pigmentation more evident, continued increase in glandular size. *Labia minora* well developed and vaginal cells have increased glycogen content, mucous membranes increasingly more pale. *Hair* in pubic region thicker, coarser, often curly (considerable normal variation including a few girls with early stage II at menarche). *Skin:* Further increased activity of sebaceous and sweat glands with beginning of *acne* in some girls, adult body odor.
12–15	IV. *Breasts:* Projection of areola above breast plane and areolar (Montgomery) glands apparent (this development is absent in about 20% of normal girls). Glands easily palpable. *Labia:* Both majora and minora assume adult structure, glycogen content of vaginal cells begins cyclic characteristics. *Hair* in pubic area more abundant, axillary hair present (rarely present at stage II, not uncommonly present at stage III).
12–17	V. *Breasts:* Mature histologic morphology, nipple enlarged and erect, areolar (Montgomery) glands well developed, globular shape. *Hair* in pubic area more abundant and may spread to thighs (in about 10% of women it assumes "male" distribution with extension toward umbilicus). Facial hair increased often in form of slight mustache. *Skin:* Increased sebaceous gland activity and increased severity of *acne* if present before.

hypothalamus and pituitary are highly sensitive participants in the negative feedback system with resulting suppression of any gonadal activity.

3. As the time of early adolescence is approached the sensitivity of the hypothalamus and pituitary decline. This permits increasing synthesis by the gonads of the sex hormones and an increasing release of LH and FSH by the pituitary. As the sex hormones reach higher levels in the circulation their biologic effect is manifested in the physical changes of sexual development (Table 9–5).

4. In females, increasing amounts of estrogen appear now to exert a posi-

TABLE 9–4. — STAGES OF SEXUAL DEVELOPMENT: MALE

AGE	STAGES
0–14	I. Preadolescent
10–14	II. Increasing size of *testes* and *penis* is evident (testicle length reaches 2.0 cm or more). Scrotum integument is thinner and assumes an increased pendulous appearance. *Hair:* First appearance of pubic hair in area at base of penis. *Skin:* Increased activity of sebaceous and apocrine sweat glands and initial function of apocrine glands on axilla and scrotal area begins.
11–15	III. *Testes* and *penis:* Further increase in size and pigmentation apparent. Leydig cells (interstitial) first appear at stage II, are now prominent in testes. *Hair:* In pubic area more abundant and present on scrotum, still scanty and fine textured, axillary hair begins. *Breasts:* Button-type hypertrophy in 70% of boys at stages II and III. *Larynx:* Changes in voice due to laryngeal growth begin. *Skin:* Increasing activity of sebaceous and sweat glands with beginning of *acne,* adult body odor.
12–16	IV. *Testes:* Further increase in size, length 4.0 cm or greater, increase in size of *penis* greatest at stages III and IV. *Hair:* Pubic hair thicker and coarser and in most ascends toward umbilicus in typical male pattern, axillary hair increases, facial hair increases over lip and upper cheeks. *Larynx:* Voice deepens. *Skin:* Increasing pigmentation of scrotum and penis, *acne* often more severe. *Breasts:* Previous hypertrophy decreased or absent.
13–17	V. Rapid growth peak has occurred. *Testes:* Length greater than 4.5 cm. *Hair:* Pubic hair thick, curly, heavily pigmented, extends to thighs and toward umbilicus. Adult distribution and increase in body hair (chest, shoulders, thighs, etc.) continues for more than another 10 years. Baldness, if present, may begin. *Skin:* Acne may persist and increase. *Larynx:* Adult character of voice.

tive feedback (stimulating) on the hypothalamic gonadotropic-releasing center, triggering an LH surge at midcycle. As this mechanism matures, the surge becomes sufficient to induce ovulation (see Tables 9–3 and 9–4).

Socioeconomic factors are important in the determination of the time of onset of puberty. In nearly every society the more well-to-do girls experience earlier menarche than their peers. The secular changes referred to in Chapters 2 and 4 almost certainly have resulted from improvement in nutrition, decreases in severity and frequency of diseases, and the beneficial influence of other amenities that have occurred through the years. Still another factor may be the increased hybridization resulting from greater genetic mixes than was possible previously. Race, age of maternal menarche and other genetic factors appear to have some, but relatively minor, influences. Malnutrition, chronic disease and blindness all tend to delay the appearance

TABLE 9–5. — HORMONES INVOLVED IN ADOLESCENT DEVELOPMENT

LUTEINIZING HORMONE RELEASE FACTOR

Activity: stimulates pituitary to release gonadotropins (LH and FSH)
Source: hypothalamus
Nature: decapeptide

LUTEINIZING HORMONE

Activity: preparation and ripening of ovarian follicle, may stimulate release of progesterone, role not clear in prepubertal girl; in male stimulates interstitial (Leydig) cells of testes to secrete testosterone
Source: pituitary
Name: LH, a glycoprotein

FOLLICLE-STIMULATING HORMONE

Activity: in female, develops ovarian follicle to antrum stage, increases estrogen secretion from follicle; in male, matures sperm and may influence growth of seminiferous tubules
Source: pituitary
Name: FSH, a glycoprotein

ESTROGENS

Activity: feminizing, cause breast development, uterine growth, vaginal maturation, bone maturation, no effect on somatic growth
Source: mainly ovarian but small and possibly significant amounts from adrenal cortex and testes
Names: estrone, estradial, estriol

ANDROGENS

Activity: virilizing, cause penile and prostatic development; promote hair growth of pubic, axillary, facial and general body areas; bone maturation; laryngeal development; sebaceous and sweat gland development; stimulus to somatic growth
Source: testicles, adrenal cortex, small amounts from ovary
Names: dehydroepiandrosterone, testosterone, epitestosterone, androstenedione

PROGESTERONES

Activity: block estrogen effect on endometrium, stimulate endometrial gland secretion, stimulate lobule-alveolar breast formation and growth
Source: mainly from ovarian corpus luteum, small amounts from testes and adrenal cortex (large amounts from placenta)
Names: progesterone, pregnenolone

of puberty.[5, 89] Some of the pathologic conditions associated with abnormalities of sexual development are indicated in Table 9–6.

The occurrence of diffuse nontoxic goiter is sufficiently common among adolescents to warrant some discussion. These goiters do have an increased frequency during the adolescent growth spurt, but the relationship, if any, of one to the other remains obscure. The inclusion of iodine in table salt plus the interregional transportation of foods has not eliminated iodine-deficient

TABLE 9–6. — PATHOLOGIC CONDITIONS
ASSOCIATED WITH ABNORMALITIES OF SEXUAL
DEVELOPMENT*

Conditions associated with *delayed onset* of puberty
    Pituitary dwarfism
    Hypothyroidism
    Hypogonadism (agenesis, atrophy, surgical or traumatic castration)
    Acromegaly (rare)
    Any severe chronic illness
    Hypothalamic lesions (Frölich's syndrome)
Conditions associated with *precocious* sexual development
    Adrenal cortex tumors or hyperplasia
    Interstitial cell tumors of the testes
    Ovarian tumors (granulosa cell and thecoma)
    Pineal gland tumors (in males only)
    Third ventricle tumors of the brain
    Hydrocephalus (rare)
    Postencephalitis (rare)
    McCune-Albright syndrome (polyostotic fibrous dysplasia)

*Besides the endocrine glands, it will be noted that the central nervous system (hypothalamus) may also be involved.

goiter though its frequency in this country has been dramatically reduced in comparison to the early 1900s. Recent surveys indicate that about half or more of all adolescent goiters are due to chronic lymphocytic thyroiditis.[46, 79] This is a form of autoimmune disease secondary to an initial low-grade infection in the gland which is responsible for the liberation of the antigenic stimuli. Of the various methods used to identify the significant antibodies, an immunofluorescent technique seems to be the most reliable.[98]

The influence of the endocrine glands on the ultimate stature of human beings depends on several factors. Maturational influences of estrogens and androgens in limiting growth have been mentioned. Very soon after the union of the shafts and the epiphyses of the long bones has taken place, linear growth ceases. The sex hormones have great influence in this category. The fact that eunuchs usually stop growing at the time when puberty would normally occur would suggest that secretion of the pituitary growth hormone diminishes at this time. That this is not true is well established. The quantities of this hormone that are present in the pituitary and in the blood are approximately equal in children and adults. Only in the acromegalic and the pituitary dwarf are there variations from this, higher levels being found in the former and the lower levels in the latter. The thyroid hormone and insulin also act synergistically with the growth hormone; both are necessary for normal stature, but neither alone promotes growth. We must conclude that some change occurs in the end organs, making them resistant to normal quantities of the growth hormone when full maturity is achieved.

The development of secondary sexual characteristics usually follows a fairly set pattern, although there may be considerable individual variation (see Tables 9–3 and 9–4).[5, 13, 26, 94, 95] Many have observed that the development of sexual characteristics is much more closely correlated with bone maturation than with chronologic age. There is likewise a better correlation between maturation and measurements of height and weight than with age. Enlargement of the breasts and rounding of the contours of the hips are the first discernible changes in girls. Accumulation of subcutaneous fat in girls may be noted in the regions of the thighs, buttocks, chest, lower abdomen and the mons veneris. By the time of menarche the small budding breasts have progressively enlarged to assume a conical shape. The mature or rounded form gradually develops during the next two to four years. The first appearance of pubic hair precedes menarche by a year or more; it becomes more deeply pigmented and coarser throughout adolescence and into adult life. In approximately 10% of normal girls, pubic hair is present before significant hypertrophy of the breasts occurs. The initial growth of axillary hair may follow menarche or occur shortly before it.[76]

Growth of the breasts is evoked by the increase in amount of circulating estrogens. The initial response is elongation and thickening of the ducts. When progesterone is added, the distal ends of the ducts enlarge to form the lobule-alveoli. The source of the progesterone is the corpus luteum formed following ovulation. In the absence of pituitary growth hormone, however, the effectiveness of these steroids is minimal. With pregnancy there is a marked increase in the steroid hormone which augments the lobule-alveolar development and prepares the breast for lactation. Milk production results from the addition of prolactin by the placenta and the anterior pituitary.

In about 70% of boys, some hypertrophy of the breasts occurs. The peak incidence is between the fourteenth and fifteenth years, after the appearance of pubic hair and the growth of the genitalia has started. As adolescence advances, this *gynecomastia* gradually disappears, but it may persist for as long as two years.[78] Some degree of tenderness, particularly following even minor trauma, is not uncommon. Asymmetric enlargement may be present. Pubic hair first appears with the beginning increase in size of the penis. Axillary and facial hair come shortly thereafter. Puberty is said to be reached in the male when the pubic hair becomes darker, coarser and begins to curl. Other body hair in the male undergoes similar changes, but these are much later and continue well into adult life. The characteristic hairline on the forehead in men is one of the last developments of sex maturation. Deepening of the voice, due to growth of the larynx in the ventrodorsal diameter, occurs at midadolescence (average 14–16 years) in boys.[13, 21, 24]

Acne vulgaris is so common during adolescence that it has come to be regarded as physiologic rather than pathologic.[11, 97] It is present to some degree in 75–90% of children before 18 years of age. It is the result of androgenic stimulation of the sebaceous glands. Circulating testosterone is taken up by the sebaceous gland and converted by enzyme action to dihydrotestosterone, which causes hypertrophy of the gland and increases production of sebum. At the same time there is altered keratinization within the follicular canal resulting in varying degrees of obstruction. The obstructed pilosebaceous unit is called a *comedo*. Two types of comedones are formed: incompletely obstructed ones are termed blackheads and completely obstructed ones are whiteheads. It is the latter that are responsible for the major lesions. These are small elevated papules just beneath the skin surface in early stages. As more sebum is produced the follicle expands and eventually ruptures dispersing its contents into the adjacent dermis. This initiates the inflammatory lesion which may be severe because of the highly irritating nature of the fatty acids found in sebum. As the disorder increases in intensity, papules, pustules, nodules or cysts develop. Primary sites for acne are the face, chest, back and shoulders. As fibrous tissue forms to encapsulate the inflamed area, some degree of scarring and cicatrix result in both pitting and keloid scars in the more unfortunate individuals. There does seem to be an indication that the more severe forms follow a dominant inheritance. Acne appears equally in both sexes and all races. It tends to start after menarche and increases in intensity with the degree of development of secondary sex characteristics in both boys and girls.

Increased pigmentation of the skin progressively increases with advancing sexual maturation in the axillary, areolar, circumanal, scrotal, penile and labial areas. Another fairly common change found in the skin of adolescents is "colored" striae. These are most frequently seen over the gluteal areas, thighs and lower abdomen. They are red-purple when first present but fade later to become almost invisible. They are not necessarily associated with obesity, occur in about one third of these children and are more evident in those with the most severe acne.[18]

Muscular development, including strength, progresses rapidly in both sexes, but is more pronounced in the male. Involution of the lymphatic system, reduction in tonsil and lymph node sizes, as well as decreased reaction to most infections, begins at this time and continues for several years. The differences between the sexes at this time in red blood cell counts and hemoglobin values have been noted in Chapter 7.

Some descriptions have already been given of the development of the primary sex organs. A few additional statements are necessary. The vaginal mucosa changes from columnar to squamous shortly before menarche. Concurrent with this change there is an increased glycogen content of the mucosa and the pH becomes lowered. As a result, the bacterial flora of the vagina changes. It is probable that during the first one or two years following

TABLE 9–7.—AVERAGE WEIGHT (gm) OF ENDOCRINE
GLANDS AND SOME SEX ORGANS AT VARIOUS AGES*

	NEWBORN	1 YR	6 YR	14 YR	ADULT
Pituitary	0.1	0.2	0.3	0.4	0.5–0.8
Thyroid	2.0	3.0	7	14	18
Adrenals (2)	6–8	4.5	7	10	10–20
Parathyroids	—	—	—	—	0.65
Testes (2)	1.5	1.5	1.6	7	35
Ovaries (2)	0.3	0.6	1.9	6	11
Uterus	3.9	1.4	2.8	30	50
Prostate	0.8	0.8	1.3	3.3	17

*From several sources.

menarche the menstrual periods of most girls are anovulatory. The first
several menses are often irregular and the interval is longer or shorter than is
characteristic of later life.[20, 22]

REFERENCES

1. Deftos, L. J., Roos, B. A., and Parthemore, J. G.: Calcium and skeletal
   metabolism, West. J. Med. 123:447, 1975.
2. Albright, F., and Reifenstein, E. C.: *The Parathyroid Glands and Metabolic
   Bone Disease* (Baltimore: Williams & Wilkins Company, 1948).
3. Root, A., Gruskin, A., Reber, R. M., Stopa, A., and Duckett, G.: Serum concentrations of parathyroid hormone in infants, children and adolescents, J.
   Pediatr. 85:329, 1974.
4. Ezrin, C., Godden, J. O., Volpe, R., and Wilson, R.: *Systematic Endocrinology*
   (Hagerstown, Md.: Harper & Row Publishers, Inc., 1973).
5. Tanner, J. M.: *Growth at Adolescence* (2d ed.; Oxford: Blackwell Scientific
   Publications, 1962).
6. Frisch, R. E.: A method of prediction of age of menarche from height and
   weight at ages 9 through 13 years, Pediatrics 53:384, 1974.
7. Raben, M. S.: Growth hormone, N. Engl. J. Med. 266:31, 82, 1962.
8. Root, A.: Growth hormone, Pediatrics 36:940, 1965.
9. Nalbondov, A. V. (ed.): *Advances in Neuroendocrinology* (Urbana: University
   of Illinois Press, 1963).
10. Bacon, G. E., Spencer, M. L., and Kelch, R. P.: *A Practical Approach to
    Pediatric Endocrinology* (Chicago: Year Book Medical Publishers, Inc., 1975).
11. Hurwitz, S.: Acne vulgaris, Pediatr. Ann. 5:55, 1976.
12. *Age at Menarche, United States* (Washington, D.C.: U.S. Dept. of Health,
    Education and Welfare, Public Health Service, 1973).
13. Stolz, H. R., and Stolz, L. M.: *Somatic Development of Adolescent Boys* (New
    York: The Macmillan Company, 1951).
14. Williams, R. H. (ed.): *Textbook of Endocrinology* (4th ed.; Philadelphia: W. B.
    Saunders Company, 1968).
15. Ganong, W. F., Alpert, L. C., and Lee, T. C.: ACTH and the regulation of
    adrenocortical secretion, N. Engl. J. Med. 290:1006, 1974.
16. Federman, D. D.: *Abnormal Sexual Development* (Philadelphia: W. B. Saun-
    ders Company, 1967).

17. Winter, J., and Faiman, C.: Pituitary-gonadal relations in female children and adolescents, Pediatr. Res. 7:948, 1973.
18. Sisson, W. R.: Colored striae in adolescent children, J. Pediatr. 45:520, 1954.
19. Patten, B. M.: *Human Embryology* (3d ed.; New York: McGraw-Hill Book Company, Inc., 1968).
20. Huffman, J. W.: *The Gynecology of Childhood and Adolescence* (Philadelphia: W. B. Saunders Company, 1968).
21. Schonfeld, W. A.: Primary and secondary sexual characteristics: Study of their development in males from birth through maturity, with biometric study of penis and testis, Am. J. Dis. Child. 65:535, 1943.
22. Villee, D. B.: *Human Endocrinology, A Developmental Approach* (Philadelphia: W. B. Saunders Company, 1975).
23. Heald, F. P., Masland, R. P., Sturgis, S. H., and Gallagher, J. R.: Dysmenorrhea in adolescence, Pediatrics 20:121, 1957.
24. Shuttleworth, F. K.: *The Adolescent Period: A Graphic and Pictorial Atlas,* Monogr., Soc. Res. Child Dev., Vol. III, no. 3 (Washington, D.C.: National Research Council, 1938).
25. Weitzman, E. D.: Biologic rhythms and hormone secretion patterns, Hosp. Pract. 8:79, 1976.
26. Root, A. W.: Endocrinology of puberty, J. Pediatr., 83:1, 1973.
27. Stuart, H. C.: Physical growth during adolescence, Am. J. Dis. Child. 74:495, 1947.
28. Stuart, H. C.: Normal growth and development during adolescence, N. Engl. J. Med. 234:666, 693 and 732, 1946.
29. Loeb, J. N.: Corticosteroids and growth, N. Engl. J. Med., 295:547, 1976.
30. Matsuzaki, F., Irie, M., and Shizume, K.: Growth hormone in human fetal pituitary glands and cord blood, J. Clin. Endocrinol. 33:908, 1971.
31. August, G. P., Grumbach, M. M., and Kaplan, S. L.: Hormonal changes in puberty: correlation of plasma testosterone, LH, FSH, testicular size, and bone age with male pubertal development, J. Clin. Endocrinol. 34:319, 1972.
32. Safer, D. J., Allen, R. P., and Barr, E.: Growth rebound after termination of stimulant drugs, J. Pediatr. 86:113, 1975.
33. Chan, L., and O'Malley, B. W.: Mechanism of action of the sex steroid hormones, N. Engl. J. Med. 294:1322, 1976.
36. Gardner, L. I.: *Endocrine and Genetic Diseases of Childhood and Adolescence* (2d ed.; Philadelphia: W. B. Saunders Company, 1975).
37. Klein, R.: Adrenocortical control of sodium and potassium excretion in newborn period, J. Clin. Invest. 30:318–324, March, 1951.
38. Aarskog, D.: Cortisol in the newborn infant, Acta Paediatr. Scand., vol. 54, supp., 158, 1965.
39. Grumbach, M. M., and Werner, S. C.: Transfer of thyroid hormone across the human placenta, J. Clin. Endocrinol. 16:1392, 1956.
40. Grumbach, M. M., and Kaplan, S.: Fetal Pituitary Hormones and the Maturation of Central Nervous System Regulation of Anterior Pituitary Function, in Gluck, L. (ed.): *Modern Perinatal Medicine* (Chicago: Year Book Medical Publishers, Inc., 1974).
41. Roby, C. C., Ober, W. B., and Drorbaugh, J. E.: Pregnanediol excretion in the urine of newborn male infants, Pediatrics 17:877, 1956.
42. Ober, W. B., and Bernstein, J.: Observations on the endometrium and ovary in the newborn, Pediatrics 16:445, 1955.
43. Brien, T. G., Fay, J. A., and Griffin, E. A.: Thyroid status in the newborn

infant, Arch. Dis. Child. 49:225, 1974.

44. Humbert, J. R., and Gotlin, R. W.: Growth hormone levels in normoglycemic and hypoglycemic infants born small for gestational age, Pediatrics 48:190, 1971.
45. Hays, R. M.: Antidiuretic hormone, N. Engl. J. Med. 295:659, 1976.
46. Wilkins, L.: *The Diagnosis and Treatment of Endocrine Disorders in Childhood and Adolescence* (3d ed.; Springfield, Ill.: Charles C Thomas, Publisher, 1965).
47. Lowrey, G. H., Aster, R. H., Carr, E. A., Ramon, G., Beierwaltes, W. H., and Spafford, N. R.: Early diagnostic criteria of congenital hypothyroidism: A comprehensive study of forty-nine cretins, A.M.A. Am. J. Dis. Child. 96:131, 1958.
48. Lieblich, J. M., and Utiger, R. D.: Truodothyronine in cord serum, J. Pediatr. 82:290, 1973.
49. Gardner, L. I.: Adrenocortical metabolism of the fetus, infant and child, Pediatrics 17:897, 1956.
50. Provis, H. S., and Ellis, R. W. B.: An anthropometric study of Edinburgh schoolchildren, Arch. Dis. Child. 30:328 and 432, 1955.
51. Frohman, L. A.: Neurotransmitters as regulators in endocrine function, Hosp. Pract. 4:55, 1975.
52. Blodgett, F. M., Burgin, L., Iezzoni, D., Gribetz, D., and Talbot, N. B.: Effects of prolonged cortisone therapy on statural growth, skeletal maturation and metabolic status of children, N. Engl. J. Med. 254:636, 1956.
53. Fluhman, C. F.: Menstrual problems of adolescence, Pediatr. Clin. North Am. 5:51, 1958.
54. Tsang, R. C., Chen, I. W., Friedman, M. A., and Chen, I.: Neonatal parathyroid function: Role of gestational age and postnatal age, J. Pediatr. 83:728, 1973.
55. Tsang, R. C., Light, I. J., Sutherland, J. M., and Kleinman, L. I.: Possible pathogenetic factors in neonatal hypocalcemia of prematurity, J. Pediatr. 82:423, 1973.
56. Cranny, R. L., and Cranny, C. L.: The urinary excretion of 17-hydroxysteroids by premature infants, Am. J. Dis. Child. 99:344, 1960.
57. Ulstrom, R. A., Colle, E., Burley, J., and Gunville, R.: Adrenocortical steroid metabolism in newborn infants: I. Urinary excretion of free and conjugated 17-hydroxycorticosteroids in normal full-term infants. II. Urinary excretion of 6-beta-hydroxycortical and other polar metabolites, J. Clin. Endocrinol. 20:1066, 1080, 1960.
58. Sack, J., Fisher, D. A., and Wang, C. C.: Serum thyrotropin, prolactin, and growth hormone levels during the early neonatal period in the human infant, J. Pediatr. 89:298, 1976.
59. McEwen, B. S.: The brain as a target organ of endocrine hormones, Hosp. Pract. 5:95, 1975.
60. Daughaday, W. H.: Regulation of skeletal growth by sulfation factor, Adv. Intern. Med. 17:237, 1971.
61. Swanson, H. E., and Ezrin, C.: The natural history of the delta cell of the human adenohypophysis, in childhood, adulthood, and pregnancy, J. Clin. Endocrinol. 20:952, 1960.
62. Deanesly, R.: Fetal endocrinology, Br. Med. Bull. 17:91, 1961.
63. Wilkins, L.: Masculinization of female fetus due to use of progestins, J.A.M.A. 172:1028, 1960.

64. Bongiovanni, A. M., DiGeorge, A. M., and Grumbach, M. M.: Masculinization of the female infant associated with estrogenic therapy alone during gestation, J. Clin. Endocrinol. 19:1004, 1959.
65. Martin, J. B.: Neural regulation of growth hormone secretion, N. Engl. J. Med., 288:1384, 1973.
66. De la Balze, F. A., Mancini, R. A., Arrillaga, F., and Andrada, J. A.: Puberal maturation of the normal human testis: A histologic study, J. Clin. Endocrinol. 20:266, 1960.
67. Jones, H. W., and Scott, W. W.: *Hermaphroditism, Genital Anomalies and Related Endocrine Disorders* (Baltimore; Williams & Wilkins Company, 1958).
68. Penny, R., Olambiwonnu, O., and Frasier, S. D.: Follicle stimulating hormone (FSH) and luteinizing hormone-human chorionic gonadotropin (LH–HCG) concentrations in paired maternal and cord sera, Pediatrics 58:41, 1974.
69. Kahana, L., Lebovitz, H., Lusk, W., McPherson, H. T., Davidson, E. T., Oppenheimer, J. H., Engel, F. L., Woodhall, B., and Odom, G.: Endocrine manifestations of intracranial extrasellar lesions. J. Clin. Endocrinol. 22:304, 1962.
70. Green, O. C.: Steroid metabolism in the fetus and the newborn infant, Pediatr. Clin. North Am. 12:615, 1965.
71. Lazarus, L., and Young, J. D.: Radioimmunoassay of human growth hormone using ion exchange resin, J. Clin. Endocrinol. 26:213, 1966.
72. Hillman, D. A., and Giroud, C. J. P.: Plasma cortisone and cortisol levels at birth and during the neonatal period, J. Clin. Endocrinol. 25:243, 1965.
73. Paulsen, E. P., Sobel, E. H., and Shafran, M. D.: Urinary steroid metabolites in children: I. Individual 17-ketosteroids in children with normal sexual development, J. Clin. Endocrinol. 26:329, 1966.
74. Copp, D. H.: Parathyroids, calcitonin and control of plasma calcium, Recent Prog. Horm. Res. 20:59, 1964.
75. Avioli, L. V., and Haddad, J. G.: Vitamin D: Current concepts, Metabolism 22:507, 1973.
76. Heald, F., Daugela, M., Brunschuyler, P.: Physiology of adolescence, N. Engl. J. Med. 268:299, 1963.
77. McNeill, D., and Livson, N.: Maturation rate and body build in women, Child Dev. 34:25, 1963.
78. Nydick, M., Bustos, J., Dale, J. H., and Rawson, R. W.: Gynecomastia in adolescent boys, J.A.M.A. 178:449, 1961.
79. Nilsson, L. R.: Adolescent colloid goitre, Acta Paediatr. Scand. 55:49, 1966.
80. Young, H. B., Zoli, A., and Gallagher, J. R.: Events of puberty in 111 Florentine girls, Am. J. Dis. Child, 106:568, 1963.
81. Lee, M. M. C., Chong, K. S. F., and Chan, M. M. C.: Sexual maturation of Chinese girls in Hong Kong, Pediatrics 32:389, 1963.
82. Conly, P. W., Morrison, T., Sandberg, D. H., and Cleveland, W. W.: Concentrations of progesterone in the plasma of mothers and infants at time of birth, Pediatr. Res. 4:76, 1970.
83. Diczfalusy, E.: Steroid Synthesis and Catabolism in the Human Fetoplacental Unit, in Waisman, H. A., and Kerr, G. (ed.): *Fetal Growth and Development* (New York: McGraw-Hill Book Company, Inc., 1970).
84. Gitlin, D., and Biasucci, A.: Ontogenesis of immunoreactive thyroglobulin in the human conceptus, J. Clin. Endocrinol. 29:849, 1969.

85. Fisher, D. A., Hobel, C. J., Garza, R., and Pierce, C. A.: Thyroid function in the preterm fetus, Pediatrics 46:208, 1970.
86. Cheek, D. B.: *Human Growth: Body Composition, Cell Growth, Energy and Intelligence* (Philadelphia: Lea & Febiger, 1968).
87. van der Werff Ten Bosch, J. J.: *Somatic Growth of the Child* (Springfield, Ill.: Charles C Thomas, Publisher, 1966).
88. Marshall, W. A., and Tanner, J. M.: Variations in pattern of pubertal changes in girls, Arch. Dis. Child. 44:291, 1969.
89. Zacharias, L., and Wurtman, R. J.: Age at menarche, N. Engl. J. Med. 280:868, 1969.
90. Voorhess, M. L.: Urinary catecholamine excretion by healthy children, Pediatrics 39:252, 1967.
91. Weldon, V. V., Kowarski, A., and Migeon, C. J.: Aldosterone secretion rates in normal subjects from infancy to adulthood, Pediatrics 39:713, 1967.
92. Rosenfield, R. L., and Eberlein, W. R.: Plasma 17-ketosteroid levels during adolescence, J. Pediatr. 74:932, 1969.
93. Yen, S. S. C., Vicic, W. J., and Kearchner, D. V.: Gonadotropin levels in puberty, J. Clin. Endocrinol. 29:382, 1969.
94. Sizonenko, P. C., Burr, I. M., Kaplan, S. L., and Grumbach, M. M.: Hormonal changes in puberty. II. Correlation of serum luteinizing hormone and follicle stimulating hormone with stages of puberty and bone age in normal girls, Pediatr. Res. 4:36, 1970.
95. Burr, I. M., Sizonenko, P. C., Kaplan, S. L., and Grumbach, M. M.: Hormonal changes in puberty. I. Correlation of serum luteinizing hormone and follicle stimulating hormone with stages of puberty, testicular size, and bone age in normal boys, Pediatr. Res. 4:25, 1970.
96. Wolf, H., Stubbe, P., and Sabata, V.: The influence of glucose infusion on fetal growth hormone levels, Pediatrics 45:36, 1970.
97. *Skin Conditions of Youths 12–17 Years, United States* (Washington, D.C.: U.S. Dept. of Health, Education and Welfare, Public Health Service, 1976).
98. Monteleone, J. A., Danis, R. K., Tung, K. S. K., Ramos, C. V., and Peden, V. H.: Differentiation of chronic lymphocytic thyroiditis and simple goiter in pediatrics, J. Pediatr. 83:381, 1973.
99. Lovinger, R. D., Kaplan, S. L., and Grumbach, M. M.: Congenital hypopituitarism associated with neonatal hypoglycemia and microphallus, J. Pediatr. 87:1171, 1975.
100. Dirksen, H. C., and Anast, C. S.: Hypercalcitonemia and neonatal hypocalcemia, Pediatr. Res. 11:424, 1977.
101. Fisher, D. A., and Burrow, G. N. (eds.): *Perinatal Thyroid Physiology and Disease* (New York: Raven Press, 1975).

10 / Energy Metabolism

THE KNOWLEDGE of metabolism in infants and children has been used as a practical tool in studies of nutrition such as determining caloric requirements, establishing or ruling out such diagnoses as hypothyroidism, hyperthyroidism and simple obesity, defining optimal conditions of environment for newborns and prematures, establishing better norms for growth and development and, finally, improving understanding of the processes of living matter.

Heat is produced in all tissues of the body by oxidative and nonoxidative reactions. In the adult, skeletal muscle produces the greatest portion, even during rest. When external temperature is markedly reduced, the muscle is called upon to produce more heat by shivering. For several months after birth, the infant is unable to shiver or is very inefficient in producing heat by that method. The liver produces more heat than any other internal organ, about 25% of the total body heat at basal levels. The infant is unique in that the brain contributes some 50–60% of the total at birth. At approximately 5 years the brain's contribution is 35% and reaches about 24% in the adult.[22] The decline is due principally to an ever-slower growth of the high energy-producing cell mass relative to total body weight. The recognition of the metabolic needs of the brain in early life is an important aspect in planning the optimal nutrition of the neonate.

Temperature Regulation

Temperature regulation is obviously essential to man because wide variations, no matter what the etiology, may cause death. This subject is of vital importance in the study of metabolism.

Heat is lost from the body of an adult[3, 12] by:

Radiation, conduction and convection	70%
Evaporation (skin and lungs)	27
Warming inspired air	2
Urine and feces	1
	100%

337

The same values for heat loss by evaporation have been found in the new-born and premature.[7] These factors are influenced by environment, such as air temperature, humidity, clothing and metabolism. Body control of these factors is through:

1. Redistribution of blood: vasodilatation and constriction influencing skin temperature.

2. Variations in blood volume: rise in temperature causing an increase from tissue fluid dilution of the blood.

3. Secretion of sweat and exhalation of water vapor.

4. Metabolism: the metabolic rate rising when environmental tempera-ture falls much below body temperature. Shivering, already mentioned, is a factor which may cause an increase of 180% in the rate over basal levels.

The regulatory centers for temperature control are located in the hypothalamus and are apparently influenced by skin temperature and by temperature of the blood flowing through them. The thyroid gland and adrenals also play a role in regulating heat production. Removal of either or both causes a lowering of body temperature, whereas administration of thyroid extract or epinephrine increases metabolism and raises body temper-ature. In cretins and in patients with Addison's disease the body tempera-ture is low.

In the newborn the mechanisms of sweating and shivering are imperfectly developed. Physiologically the sweat glands are immature (see Chapter 7). The relatively large surface area compared to body mass, and the meager amount of insulating subcutaneous fat, all contribute to considerable instabil-ity of body temperature which is typical of the neonatal period. At the time of birth the infant has a very slightly higher temperature than the mother. Immediately the baby's temperature falls, regardless of the means taken to protect against it. Cold-induced peripheral vasoconstriction is well de-veloped before the time of birth. However, an increased oxygen uptake in response to cold is considerably less pronounced in the first postnatal hour in comparison to what it will be later.[29] Heat loss due to evaporation of amniotic fluid probably contributes to the quick cooling off of the skin. In a nursery with a room temperature between 25 and 28 C, there was a drop of 1.8 C by the third hour as an average for 20 infants.[13] Cooling an infant in a similar fashion in the second postnatal hour results in a smaller decline of rectal temperature and the rate of fall is much slower.[14] Recovery to a "normal" body temperature is relatively prompt, seldom taking more than 2–4 hours in term neonates. Ambient temperature, humidity and clothing will obvi-ously have some influence. The rapid recovery would indicate that there is no physiologic immaturity of the hypothalamic center. Crying is a fairly efficient means of increasing the infant's body temperature by increasing the metabolic rate; in some infants this may result in as much as a 180%

increase over basal levels. In general, the more mature the baby or the greater the birth weight, the more stable will be the body temperature.

The skin thermoreceptors of the newborn infant are highly sensitive, and a slight decrease in the average skin temperature provokes a prompt peripheral vasoconstriction.[29, 30] Similarly, a change in temperature in the opposite direction causes vasodilatation and some sweating. There does not appear to be a very marked difference between the vascular response in the premature infant, the term infant or the adult. However, the ability to sweat is considerably reduced in the smallest infants and is still quite inefficient in the normal newborn.[31] Sweating, as a response to intradermal nicotine or epinephrine, is considerably less in the low birth weight infant as compared to the full-term infant.[41] These observations suggest that small and premature infants have failed to develop axon reflex sweating. Shivering is an efficient mechanism for increasing metabolism and raising body temperature in the adult and child. Either this mechanism is not well developed in the neonate or other means are more reliable. Many observers have commented upon the rarity of shivering in premature infants. If the environmental temperature is lowered below the *neutral temperature* range,* restlessness and increased movements do occur. The neutral temperature for infants is higher and has a narrower range than for adults.[32] Studies of heat production in adults subjected to continuous moderate cooling show only a very slight increase in basal metabolic rate. In the full-sized and underweight newborn infant similar studies show a decided increase in oxygen consumption, which returns to the normal rate only when the environment is readjusted to the neutral temperature.[34, 35, 36] This is true even though there may be some lag in the body temperature returning to normal. The oxygen consumed may be treble the basal levels. This response to chilling has been referred to as chemical or nonshivering thermogenesis and is a phenomenon unique to early infancy. (The adult human or animal responds similarly only when exposed to much greater degrees of change.) If the baby's body temperature is further depressed, a point may be reached where the response of increasing metabolism is no longer possible. Factors that have been noted to interfere with thermogenesis are: the respiratory distress syndrome,[34] extreme prematurity, intracranial hemorrhage, hypoglycemia and some drugs.[36]

The nature of the mediator of nonshivering (chemical) thermogenesis appears to be unique to the time of early infancy. Recent studies indicate that norepinephrine secretion is a major mechanism for this adaptation. On exposure to cold there is a consistent increase in urinary norepinephrine and

---

*Neutral temperature range is defined as that set of thermal conditions in the environment in which the oxygen consumption (metabolism) is at a minimum and body temperature is in the normal range of 37 C ±0.5.

plasma nonesterified fatty acids. The response in premature infants is quantitatively less than in full-term babies. The infusion of norepinephrine in newborn infants does cause an increased oxygen consumption and rise in rectal temperature.[39, 42]

The site of chemical thermogenesis in the infant is brown adipose tissue.[14, 32, 37] Although present in very small amounts in the adult, it makes up a considerable quantity of the total fat present in the full term as well as in the premature baby. The largest depots are found in the intrascapular area, but some is present in the thorax and in the perirenal areas. In contrast to white adipose tissue, it has a rich nerve and blood supply and a higher content of mitochondrial cytochromes; it contains multilocular lipid cytoplasmic inclusions instead of the single lipid inclusions. Morphologically it can be differentiated by 26 weeks. Although intrauterine malnutrition is usually associated with a marked depletion of white fat, brown fat is spared. Studies in animals and man indicate that it is metabolically very active under cold stress. Under such environmental conditions, for the first 4 to 6 months of life in human infants, the intrascapular area has the highest skin temperature.[14] It has been suggested that brown adipose tissue serves as a thermogenic source under cold stress, and in response to norepinephrine, by warming the blood as it comes from peripheral structures. The norepinephrine increase is the initial chemical step to the activation of a lipase which hydrolyzes the brown fat. The resulting fatty acids are then oxidized in a highly exothermic reaction. Plasma levels of glycerol, resulting from lipase activity, are elevated as a result of cold exposure in the neonatal period.[5]

In the low birth weight infant the skin and rectal temperature parallel each other rather closely, and fluctuate with extremes of environmental temperature. The survival rate of such infants was significantly higher if they were kept in a thermoneutral (30–32.5 C) environment for the first few days as compared to slightly cooler conditions.[27, 28, 31] In a comparative study of two groups of low birth weight infants treated equally except for a difference of 1.5 C ambient temperature, the babies exposed to the cooler environment for their first two weeks had a much better ability to maintain a deep body temperature upon subsequent exposure to cold than did the controls. However, the rate of increase in body weight and length was significantly faster in the warmer condition, presumably due to decreased energy expenditure.[40] There is evidence that supplementing the diet of the group raised in the cooler environment would overcome the growth differences.[24] Brief periods of exposing the term or premature neonate to a slightly cooler than neutral temperature during the first few days also appears to accelerate the ability to adapt to future thermal changes.[2, 5]

The possibility that a higher ambient temperature than neutral might have some advantages has received some attention.[20, 43] Using an environmental temperature of 37 C it has been demonstrated to reduce the metabolic rate and therefore to decrease the nutritional caloric requirements. Term, premature and small-for-date infants could adapt to the higher temperature by increasing their evaporative heat loss, with the degree of sweating being related to gestational age. The premature was the least able to reach and maintain a new thermal equilibrium with any further increase in temperature.

Within fairly wide limits, the humidity of the environment exerts little influence on survival, although low values may contribute to heat loss by increasing evaporation or insensible loss.

Even in the older child temperature regulation is less exact than in the adult. Bayley and Stolz[25] found that relatively high rectal temperatures predominated in young children, with a gradual decrease beginning at age 2 years. This trend continued through puberty, tending to stabilize at 13 to 14 years in girls and some 4 years later in boys.[26] At 18 months the average temperature was 99.8 F (37.7 C), and 50% of the subjects had temperatures of 100 F (37.8 C) or higher. Daily variations were considerable—as much as 3 F (1.8 C) at 6 years. Such variations were not influenced greatly by the time of day. Active play, however, tended to produce a slight rise. When recordings were properly carried out (mainly referring to adequate time), very little difference was noted between oral and rectal temperatures. Except for the changes at puberty, no differences were noted between the sexes. The following table indicates average body temperatures in well children under basal conditions.

Such fluctuations and apparent deviations from "normal" temperature should be recognized by physicians in order to avoid unnecessary diagnostic procedures and therapy. A few children appear to have consistently high normal body temperatures, and a smaller number have consistently low normal body temperatures. It has been mentioned that the younger child reacts more violently to infection than the older one, exhibiting higher fever and sometimes convulsions—so-called febrile convulsions. Dehydration and

AGE	TEMPERATURE		STANDARD DEVIATION	
	F	C	F	C
3 mo	99.4	37.5	0.8	0.4
6 mo	99.5	37.5	0.6	0.3
1 yr	99.7	37.7	0.5	0.2
3 yr	99.0	37.2	0.5	0.2
5 yr	98.6	37.0	0.5	0.2
7 yr	98.3	36.8	0.5	0.2
9 yr	98.1	36.7	0.5	0.2
11 yr	98.0	36.7	0.5	0.2
13 yr	97.8	36.6	0.5	0.2

disturbed electrolyte balance may result, especially in the infant and young child. Associated findings with fever are tachycardia and hyperpnea; in the very young the latter may be quite pronounced. A mild glycosuria is occasionally seen in infants with fever in whom the carbohydrate metabolism is otherwise normal.

Respiratory Metabolism

"Metabolism is the term employed to embrace the various chemical processes occurring within the tissues upon which heat production and growth of the body depend and from which the energy for muscular activity and for the maintenance of vital function is derived."[3] Heat produced by an animal is largely the result of oxidation of food, and by measuring the oxygen consumed one can compute the metabolism of the body.

The respiratory quotient (RQ) has an important bearing on many phases of metabolism. It is the ratio of the volume of carbon dioxide produced to the volume of oxygen used: $RQ = CO_2/O_2$. For the complete combustion of carbohydrates the respiratory quotient is 1.0. For fat the value is 0.71, and for protein, 0.80. Thus the respiratory quotient can be taken as an indication of the type of food being metabolized by the organism. In man, on a mixed diet, the quotient is around 0.85. A diet high in carbohydrates will raise it, and a diet high in fat will lower it.*

Careful studies of the respiratory quotient in the newborn have, in general, revealed high values for the first day. For three or four days after birth there is a drop to rather low levels, followed by a rise to near the adult quotient. These figures give good evidence that during the first day of life carbohydrate is used almost exclusively as the source of energy. The stores of glycogen are soon exhausted, and until breast milk or a formula is taken well, by the fifth or sixth day, fat is utilized for energy needs. This reasoning is substantiated by the observation that the blood sugar content of the newborn is quite low and for a brief period remains low. Table 10–1 shows this rather dramatic change in the respiratory quotient for the first few days of life.[13]

In general, the respiratory quotient for premature infants remains low for a longer period and then rises to a slightly higher level than does that of a more mature infant.[4, 13]

To maintain basal needs of about 1.7 calories/kg (0.8 calories/lb)/hour and, in addition, to provide an allowance for activity, growth, fecal loss and specific dynamic action, the total food requirement is estimated as 80

---

*The RQ for a premature or newborn may not truly reflect the source of energy being used, for in both anaerobic metabolism may form some considerable part of the heat production mechanism.

TABLE 10–1.—CHANGES IN RESPIRATORY QUOTIENT IN THE NEWBORN

DAY OF LIFE	RQ	% OF TOTAL ENERGY FROM CHO	FAT
1st few hours	0.90	66	34
1	80	30	70
2	74	8	92
3	73	5	95
4	75	12	88
5	79	26	74
6	82	38	62
7	81	34	66
8	81	34	66

calories/kg/day (36 calories/lb/day). However, the spontaneous intake of newborns to the point of satiety by the first day averages 90 calories and by the eleventh day over 100 calories/kg.[13] When a proper caloric intake is being estimated, the baby's activity must be considered. It has already been pointed out that strenuous crying may increase the basal level of metabolism by 180%, so a very active infant will require a higher caloric intake than one who is more lethargic.

The premature infant has a greater requirement, estimated as high as 150 calories/kg. However, Levine and Gordon[7] have shown that 120 calories/kg (55 calories/lb) in a low-fat formula produced excellent results and adequate weight gain when given after the fifth to eighth day of life.

Basal Metabolism in Children

It will be readily realized that in infants and small children many of the criteria cannot be met for obtaining a true basal metabolic rate, e.g., fasting conditions, no muscular activity, and other factors inherent in a true basal condition. However, we can obtain nearly basal levels, and the lacking factors can be considered in the final evaluation. As in an adult, a single reading has little value, but repeated recordings may be a considerable aid. In infants and children under 4–5 years the chamber method or direct calorimetry must be used.

Norms of metabolism can be presented only in terms of averages, for the metabolism of the great majority of individuals does not agree exactly with any accepted standard. The following factors, responsible for variations from the normal, must be carefully evaluated.

1. PULSE RATE.—Muscular exercise is usually accompanied by an increase in the pulse rate and heat production.

2. CLIMATE. — Hot weather usually reduces body heat production; the converse is true of cold weather.

3. GROWTH. — The two stages of rapid growth in childhood, during the first year of life and at puberty, are associated with a greater relative heat production than at any other time. This "growth factor" is most important in comparisons of metabolism of children and adults. The complexities of the relationship of growth and metabolism are not well understood, but we do know that the rate of growth does not necessarily correlate well with the various changes in metabolism. (See also under "Age.")

4. FOOD INTAKE. — An insufficient diet causes not only a loss of weight but a lowered metabolic rate. In a normal individual the ordinary mixed diet raises the metabolic rate about 6% above the basal level; overfeeding may raise it as much as 40%. This factor, called specific dynamic action, must be considered in the nonfasting child. However, Murlin[11] stated that in children under age 1 year an average feeding increased metabolism very little or not at all over basal levels. In infants fed milk with a very high protein content (40% of the total caloric intake) the metabolic rate may increase as much as 25%. This condition is, of course, rarely to be considered.

5. AGE. — This is a most important factor for the pediatrician. The younger the individual, the greater will be the tendency to variation from the average. Heat production increases with age so long as growth continues; there follows a period of relative stability corresponding to active maturity, and finally a definite decline which begins about the fifth decade.[1, 3]

Premature infants. — During the first few weeks of life the heat production of the premature may be very low (between 46 and 92 calories for 24 hours). On the basis of body surface the averages are generally lower than those for a mature newborn. Further, the premature infant may produce less heat on his expected birth date than does the full-term infant during any day of his first week of life. Activity, when manifested by a premature, increases the heat production above the basal level by an average of 40%, compared with 65% for the normal newborn. Until height and weight are normal for age, the metabolic rate of the premature remains below that of the normal infant.[7, 13]

Small-for-date infants. — The growth-retarded and/or malnourished neonate has a significantly higher metabolic rate than that of preterm infants of similar weight. This finding is in agreement with the concept of the relatively greater susceptibility of such infants to hypoglycemia. The larger and metabolically very active brain is undoubtedly an important factor.

Full-term infants. — Depending on the weight of the baby, his vitality, and the amount of fat tissue present, the average figures range from 125 to 165 calories produced per 24 hours. It is interesting to note that the smallest baby does not necessarily produce the least amount of heat. For a fairly large series of infants the average figure was 42 calories/kg/24 hours, or about 28 calories/sq m/hour. Judged by weight, the infant at birth is more active metabolically than is the adult but less so than the child of 1–3 years.

Older infants and children. — Most data indicate that physical development rather than age determines the metabolic rate. Most observers agree that there is an increase in the metabolic rate associated with puberty and that it is related directly to the growth spurt rather than to any identifiable item in sexual maturation.[6, 8, 14] Tables 10–2 and 10–3 give some representative figures of metabolic rates for different ages based upon the more commonly used standards.

6. SEX. — Until age 8 there is only a slight difference between the sexes. At approximately this time boys have a slightly higher rate than girls. The rise at puberty, when present, occurs about two years sooner in girls than in

TABLE 10–2. — AVERAGE BASAL METABOLIC RATES FOR PREMATURE AND TERM NEWBORNS AND ADULTS ACCORDING TO DIFFERENT STANDARDS*

	TOTAL BASAL, PER HR	AV. CALORIES	
		PER SQ M/HR	PER KG/HR
Premature infants	6.48	26.25	2.04
Term infants	6.67	29.16	2.00
Adults	. . .	35–40	1.00

*From Smith.[13]

TABLE 10–3. — RESULTS PICKED AT RANDOM SHOWING GENERAL TRENDS OF BMR FOR NORMAL SUBJECTS*

AGE	WEIGHT, KG	HEAT/24 HR	HEAT/SQ M/HR	HEAT/KG/HR
2 days	3.45	162	32.1	1.91
5 days	3.34	150	30.5	1.88
6 mo	5.40	353	40.0	2.75
10 mo	9.37	479	37.7	2.12
2½ yr	11.5	585	51.9	2.20
5 yr	15.5	720	52.4	2.01
9 yr	22.0	898	44.9	1.70
10 yr	30.6	1,065	41.3	1.43
14 yr	40.2	1,300	39.2	1.35
18 yr	65.6	1,700	32.8	1.08
Adult	70.0	1,400†	35–40.0†	1.00†

*Mainly from data of Lewis, Murlin and Talbot.
†Average figures.

boys. At the end of the second decade of life there is usually more than 10% difference in favor of the males.

The selection of the most nearly ideal standards for children has been an important part of the studies of metabolism in the pediatric age group. Height, weight, age, surface area and level of creatinine excretion, either alone or in combination, are the references commonly used in the past. Surface area, based on the Du Bois formula, has become the accepted standard for adults and probably is still the one most used in children. This method, however, has proved to be unsatisfactory. There are several reasons for this. The number of infants and children in whom accurate measurements of surface area have been carried out is less than half a dozen, if normal subjects alone are considered. Widely divergent results have been obtained for children of atypical body build when the basal metabolic rate has been calculated on the basis for surface area.[9, 20, 23] The variability of estimated area must take into consideration the fact that small human beings

TABLE 10–4.—STANDARD TOTAL CALORIES FOR WEIGHT*—
GIRLS AND BOYS†

WEIGHT, KG	TOTAL CALORIES PER 24 HR		WEIGHT, KG	TOTAL CALORIES PER 24 HR	
	GIRLS	BOYS		GIRLS	BOYS
3.0	136	150	36.0	1,173	1,270
4.0	205	210	38.0	1,207	1,305
5.0	274	270	40.0	1,241	1,340
6.0	336	330	42.0	1,274	1,370
7.0	395	390	44.0	1,306	1,400
8.0	448	445	46.0	1,338	1,430
9.0	496	495	48.0	1,369	1,460
10.0	541	545	50.0	1,399	1,485
11.0	582	590	52.0	1,429	1,505
12.0	620	625	54.0	1,458	1,555
13.0	655	665	56.0	1,487	1,580
14.0	687	700	58.0	1,516	1,600
15.0	718	725	60.0	1,544	1,630
16.0	747	750	62.0	1,572	1,660
17.0	775	780	64.0	1,599	1,690
	802	810	66.0	1,626	1,725
	827	840	68.0	1,653	1,765
20.0	852	870	70.0	1,679	1,785
22.0	898	910	72.0	1,705	1,815
24.0	942	980	74.0	1,731	1,845
26.0	984	1,070	76.0	1,756	1,870
28.0	1,025	1,100	78.0	1,781	1,900
30.0	1,063	1,140	80.0	1,805	. . . . .
32.0	1,101	1,190	82.0	1,830	. . . . .
34.0	1,137	1,230	84.0	1,855	2,000

*Calories produced under basal conditions compared to weight.
†From Talbot.[16]

have greater surface area in comparison with their weight than do larger subjects. For instance, the newborn infant has 16% as much surface area as an adult, but weight is only 5% that of an adult.

Talbot[16] carefully worked out standards based on height and weight and largely ignored age and surface as standards. He stated that evidence better supported the concept that the heat production "regulator" was the active mass of tissue in the infant's and child's body, that is, muscle.[14] This was substantiated by the findings that there was a good correlation between creatinine excretion and total basal caloric output[18] (Tables 10–4 and 10–5). Creatinine as a reference standard is impractical owing to the difficulty of collecting 24-hour urine specimens in the smaller children.

Wetzel[19] has advocated using "developmental level" as the most satisfactory standard for basal heat production. By use of the Wetzel grid the developmental level can be plotted, and the normal heat production is then read from one of the ordinates of the auxodrome. Wetzel and others who

TABLE 10–5.—STANDARD TOTAL CALORIES FOR HEIGHT* (OR TOTAL CALORIES FOR EXPECTED WEIGHT)—GIRLS AND BOYS†

HEIGHT, CM	TOTAL CALORIES PER 24 HR		HEIGHT, CM	TOTAL CALORIES PER 24 HR	
	GIRLS	BOYS		GIRLS	BOYS
48	134	. . .	92	681	725
50	159	. . .	94	695	740
51	. . .	160	96	709	755
52	186	175	98	722	765
54	214	200	100	735	785
56	246	225	105	770	805
58	278	260	110	807	830
60	309	300	115	846	875
62	341	315	120	894	935
64	373	360	125	942	990
66	404	390	130	987	1,045
68	433	420	135	1,057	1,105
70	462	450	140	1,130	1,165
72	489	480	145	1,208	1,220
74	515	510	150	1,294	1,290
76	539	535	155	1,386	1,380
78	560	565	160	1,477	1,480
80	581	590	165	1,544	1,570
82	601	612	170	1,584	1,655
84	619	635	175	1,596	1,720
86	636	660	180	1,600	1,800
88	652	685	190	. . . .	1,900
90	666	705			

*Calories produced under basal conditions compared to height. Since the height standard is based on a normal weight, this can also be called expected weight.
†From Talbot.[16]

Fig 10–1.—Curves comparing growth and heat production. All curves are plotted against a common abscissa, age. Ordinates for each curve are different, and are properly indicated. For Z the ordinate is weight in kg; for Z', kg/yr. All curves are based on averages. Note that the curves for theoretical weight and daily rate of basal heat production follow similar patterns, lending support to the selection of weight as the most suitable criterion for the basis of energy (metabolism) studies during growth. The curves also show that

have used this method claim considerable accuracy for it. Our own studies have not shown as good a correlation with the Wetzel grid as with height or weight for age based on Talbot's tables, and Eichorn,[21] using the grid, discovered many discrepancies in a group of adolescents.

Figures 10–1 through 10–4 and Tables 10–2 through 10–5 illustrate the various standards used and the results obtained from some of the more complete studies.

If physical development is average, the number of calories produced per kilogram will equal that of normal children of the same age, sex and physique. If the proportion of inactive body substance (fat, bone and body fluids) is small, the caloric output per unit of weight will be greater. Conversely, if there is a greater amount of inactive tissue, as in obese children, the number of calories produced per unit of weight will be less than the average. When data obtained from obese but otherwise normal children were compared with body surface as one standard and height-weight as the other standard, the difference between the sets of figures amounted to over 25% in many instances. The author made three satisfactory determinations of oxygen consumption on a moderately obese, but otherwise normal, boy. Averaging the three determinations, the basal metabolic rate according to several different standards, was as follows:

STANDARD OF COMPARISON	BMR
Body surface (Mayo Clinic)	−19%
Height (Talbot)	+10%
Expected weight for age (Talbot)	− 5%
Wetzel grid	−10%

Formerly basal metabolism determinations were extensively used in evaluating thyroid function. Precise measurements of thyroid and pituitary

---

heat production and growth are so closely related as to be part of the same biologic processes. Birth occurs at the peak of the curve for "rate of gain" under normal conditions; the premature must attain this peak in the less favorable conditions of extrauterine existence. Some difficulties of rearing premature infants can thus be attributed to stresses of growth in a relatively adverse environment. Note also that between ages 3 and 4 the average child has reached a low point in rate of gain, a leveling off of theoretical weight and a relative decrease in heat production (whether measured as total calories or based on unit of weight). In this period physiologic anorexia is common. Curve U is said to represent true metabolism. The high metabolism of infants is ascribed to "cellular synthesis" and "heat of dissipation" by Wetzel, or to the rapid growth and differentiation that take place during these years. Even during the prepubertal spurt of growth this curve undergoes a steady decline, reaching its lowest level when growth ceases. (From Wetzel.[19])

Fig 10-2.—Metabolism curve for boys, based on total calories produced at basal levels referred to surface area (sq m). (From Benedict and Talbot.[1])

hormones are more accurate as an indication of thyroid status. Although a low basal metabolic rate may be characteristic of intrauterine dwarfism and indicates a guarded prognosis for complete growth recovery,[9] there are other techniques for making the diagnosis which are both simpler and more reliable. Although still of value in research projects such as determining nutritional needs, metabolic rate per se has little to offer as a diagnostic aid.

Practical Applications

To maintain normal and stable body temperatures in the neonate, the environmental temperature must be higher and in a narrower range than for older subjects. The reasons for this are the greater surface area in relation to mass and the increased thermal conductance of the infant, which results in a greater heat loss. The infant's primary response to a chilling environment is

Fig 10–3.—Metabolism curve for boys, based on total calories produced at basal levels referred to weight. (From Benedict and Talbot.[1])

Fig 10–4.—Metabolism curves for boys and girls, based on calories produced per hour per square meter referred to age. Note particularly the tendency to a leveling off in the prepubertal years. (From Lewis et al.[8])

by nonshivering thermogenesis, manifested in an increased oxygen consumption, and later by increased movement. Brown adipose tissue may be an important source of this increase in metabolism. For optimal care of the low birth weight baby continuous monitoring is essential. Skin temperatures are equally valid to rectal temperatures for this purpose. Humidity plays a very secondary role, as compared to temperature, in the survival of the premature infant.

In the older child there is a normal range of fluctuation of the body temperature. This range becomes progressively narrower with increasing age, and the mean value drops approximately one degree from shortly after birth until adolescence.

Determinations of basal metabolism have been of great value in the study of growth and development, but no completely satisfactory standard for children of different ages, shapes and sizes has been devised. The use of basal metabolism as a diagnostic tool throughout childhood has little merit.

REFERENCES

1. Benedict, F. G., and Talbot, F. B.: Carnegie Inst. of Washington Pub. no. 233, 1915.
2. Evans, H. E., and Glass, L.: *Perinatal Medicine* (Hagerstown, Md.: Harper & Row Publishers, Inc., 1976).
3. Kleiber, M.: *The Fire of Life: An Introduction to Animal Energetics* (New York: John Wiley & Sons, Inc., 1961).
4. Gordon, H. H., and Levine, S. Z.: Respiratory metabolism in infancy and in childhood: Respiratory exchange in premature infants; basal metabolism, Am. J. Dis. Child. 52:810, 1936.
5. Perlstein, P. H., Hersh, C., Glueck, C. J., and Sutherland, J. M.: Adaptation to cold in the first three days of life, Pediatrics 54:411, 1974.
6. Johnston, J. A.: Factors influencing retention of nitrogen and calcium in period of growth, Am. J. Dis. Child. 59:287, 1940.
7. Levine, S. Z., and Gordon, H. H.: Physiologic handicaps of the premature infant: I. Their pathogenesis, Am. J. Dis. Child. 64:274, 1942.
8. Lewis, R. C., Duval, A. M., and Iliff, A.: Effect of adolescence on basal metabolism of normal children, Am. J. Dis. Child. 66:296, 1943.
9. Krieger, I., and Woolley, P. V.: The basal metabolic rate in growth failure of prenatal onset, Am. J. Dis. Child. 127:340, 1974.
10. Lewis, R. C., Kinsman, G. M., and Iliff, A.: The basal metabolism of normal boys and girls from 2 to 12 years old, Am. J. Dis. Child. 53:348, 1937.
11. Murlin, J. R.: Energy Metabolism, in Abt, I. A. (ed.): *Pediatrics* (Philadelphia: W. B. Saunders Company, 1923).
12. Newburgh, L. H., Johnston, M. W., and Newburgh, J. D.: *Some Fundamental Principles of Metabolism* (Ann Arbor, Mich.: Edwards Bros., Inc., 1945).
13. Smith, C. A., and Nelson, N. M.: *The Physiology of the Newborn Infant* (4th ed.; Springfield, Ill.; Charles C Thomas, Publisher, 1976).
14. Rylander, E.: Age-dependent reactions of rectal and skin temperatures of infants during exposure to cold, Acta Paediatr. Scand. 61:597, 1972.
15. Talbot, F. B.: Basal metabolism of girls, Am. J. Dis. Child. 52:1, 1936.

16. Talbot, F. B.: Basal metabolism standards for children, Am. J. Dis. Child. 55:455, 1938.
17. Talbot, F. B., Wilson, E. B., and Worcester, J.: Basal metabolism in girls: Physiologic background and application of the standards, Am. J. Dis. Child. 53:275, 1937.
18. Talbot, F. B., Worcester, J., and Stewart, A.: New creatinine standards for basal metabolism and its clinical application, Am. J. Dis. Child, 58:506, 1939.
19. Wetzel, N. C.: Growth, in Glasser, O. (ed.): *Medical Physics*. Vol. I (Chicago: The Year Book Publishers, Inc., 1944).
20. Sulyok, E., Jequier, E., and Prod'hom, L. S.: Respiratory contribution to the thermal balance of the newborn infant under various ambient conditions, Pediatrics 51:641, 1973.
21. Eichorn, D. H.: A comparison of laboratory determinations and Wetzel grid estimates of basal metabolism among adolescents, J. Pediatr. 46:146, 1955.
22. Holliday, M. A.: Metabolic rate and organ size during growth from infancy to maturity and during late gestation and early infancy, Pediatrics 47:169, 1971.
23. Lamb, M. W., and Michie, J. M.: Basal metabolism of 19 children from two to ten years old, J. Nutr. 53:93, 1954.
24. Glass, L., Lola, R. V., Jaiswal, V., and Nigam, S. K.: Effect of thermal environment and caloric intake on head growth of low birth weight infants during the late neonatal period, Arch. Dis. Child. 50:571, 1975.
25. Bayley, N., and Stolz, H. R.: Maturational changes in rectal temperatures of 61 infants from 1 to 36 months, Child Dev. 8:195, 1937.
26. Iliff, A., and Lee, V. A.: Pulse rate, respiratory rate and body temperature of children between two months and 18 years of age, Child Dev. 23:238, 1952.
27. Silverman, W. A., and Blanc, W. A.: The effect of humidity on survival of newly born premature infants, Pediatrics 20:477, 1957.
28. Miller, H. C., Behrle, F. C., Hagar, D. L., and Denison, T. R.: The effect of high humidity on body temperature and oxygen consumption of newborn premature infants, Pediatrics 27:740, 1961.
29. Brück, K.: Temperature regulation in the newborn infant, Biol. Neonate 3:65, 1961.
30. Moss, A. J., Duffie, E. R., and Emmanouilides, G.: Blood pressure and vasomotor reflexes in the newborn infant, Pediatrics 32:175, 1963.
31. Day, R. L., Caliguiri, L., Kamenski, C., and Ehrlich, F.: Body temperature and survival of premature infants, Pediatrics 34:171, 1964.
32. Oliver, T. K.: Temperature regulation and heat production in the newborn, Pediatr. Clin. North Am. 12:765, 1965.
33. Oliver, T. K., and Karlberg, P.: Gaseous metabolism in newly born human infants, Am. J. Dis. Child. 105:427, 1963.
34. Miller, H. C., Behrle, F. C., Nieman, J. L., Driver, R., and Dudding, B. A.: Oxygen consumption in newborn premature infants, Am. J. Dis. Child. 103:71, 1962.
35. Adamsons, K., Gandy, G. M., and James, L. S.: The influence of thermal factors upon oxygen consumption of the newborn human infant, J. Pediatr. 66:495, 1965.
36. Scopes, J. W.: Metabolic rate and temperature control in the human body, Br. Med. Bull. 22:88, 1966.
37. Hull, D.: The structure and function of brown adipose tissue, Br. Med. Bull. 22:92, 1966.

38. Silverman, W. A., Agate, F. J., and Fertig, J. W.: A sequential trial of the nonthermal effect of atmospheric humidity on survival of newborn infants of low birth weight, Pediatrics 31:719, 1963.
39. Stern, L., Ramos, A., and Leduc, J.: Maturation of chemical thermogenesis in premature infants, Pediatr. Res. 2:317, 1968.
40. Glass, L., Silverman, W. A., and Sinclair, J. C.: Effect of thermal environment on cold resistance and growth of small infants after the first week of life, Pediatrics 41:1033, 1968.
41. Green, M., and Behrendt, H.: Sweating capacity of neonates, Am. J. Dis. Child. 118:725, 1969.
42. Schiff, D., Stern, L., and Leduc, J.: Chemical thermogenesis in newborn infants: Catecholamine excretion and plasma non-esterified fatty acid response to cold exposure, Pediatrics 37:557, 1966.
43. Sulyok, E., Jequier, E., and Prod'hom, L. S.: Thermal balances of the newborn infant in a heat-gaining environment, Pediatr. Res. 7:888, 1973.

11 / Nutrition in Normal Growth

THE INFANT, child and adolescent must have food for growth and for maintenance and repair of body tissues. To supply the caloric requirement alone is not sufficient to promote optimal growth. It is essential to consider quantitatively the basic foodstuffs: proteins, fats, carbohydrates, minerals and vitamins. In this chapter we will outline our present knowledge of the influence of nutrition on growth and development. Fetal growth and nutrition are considered in Chapter 3 and the development of the central nervous system as related to nutrition is discussed in Chapter 7. Obesity is presented in Chapter 13.

Since there is no adequate definition for "optimal growth" there can be no "optimal diet" for growth. In attempting to designate a near ideal, or even just a satisfactory dietary intake, a number of important variables and unknowns are encountered. These include the individual variations in total energy output from day to day or from year to year. The individual differences in the utilization of food, composition of feces, urine and blood, and changes in body weight. Indeed, day-to-day changes for a single person of any of these items can be considerable. Finally, much of our knowledge in this field has been derived from animal experiments which may not be directly applicable to man.

In the following pages the definition of *requirement* is that proposed by Foman, "The least amount of that nutrient that will promote an optimal state of health."[10] It is not always possible to arrive at a specific quantity which all experts would agree fulfills the above definition; nevertheless, the variation would not be very great.

Total Caloric Requirements

In this chapter 1 calorie = 1 large calorie = 1 Cal = 1 kcal.

The caloric requirements of children are traditionally divided into (1) basal metabolism, (2) growth, (3) muscular activity, (4) caloric loss in excreta and (5) specific dynamic action of foods (S.D.A.).

During the first year to 18 months the daily requirement for basal metabolism averages about 55 calories/kg (25 calories/lb). After this period the basal requirements tend to become gradually less (when based on weight), approaching the adult level of 25–30 calories/kg.[14, 20] The premature infant's basal requirements are slightly lower than those of the normal newborn. The small-for-date neonate's requirements will be greater than those of the prematurely born and should be met promptly to prevent hypoglycemia.

The specific dynamic action of food requires from 5 to 7 calories/kg on the average diet. When the diet contains a large proportion of protein, the requirement may be more than doubled.

Approximately 10% of the daily intake is lost in the excreta of the bottle-fed baby and older child and about 8% for the breast-fed child. Most of it is lost in the feces.

The requirements for activity may vary tremendously per individual, at different age levels, and for the two sexes. An average allowance during the first year is 20 calories/kg (9 calories/lb)/day. For the premature or phlegmatic infant this amount may be about halved, whereas for an extremely active infant the requirements may be more than doubled. During adolescence the requirement may also be proportionately high, especially for active boys.

Daily growth requirements are variable since growth is a dynamic process and, for practical purposes, represents calories stored. During the early months of life 20–40 calories/kg (10–18 calories/lb) may be stored. By the end of the first year this allowance has fallen to 5–15 calories/kg. There follows a gradual decline in relation to body weight, with a temporary increase occurring during the spurt of growth which takes place before puberty.[10, 12]

In the low birth weight infant the requirements for growth may be considerably greater than are those for the normal newborn. Especially in the premature infant, where the growth rate can be expected to follow the intrauterine pattern until the time of expected delivery, the caloric demand may be high. Due to marginal renal function in the premature baby, careful monitoring will be required so that fluid and electrolyte balance are normally maintained. Decreased absorption of fat by the premature infant must be taken into account in estimating adequacy of the total caloric intake.

Requirements of the adolescent will vary widely and better correlations exist with physiologic stages of development (Chapter 9) than with chronologic age. The added requirements to meet the demands of the acceleration of physical growth may be relatively short in duration for any one individual but the quantity may be surprisingly large, nearly double those preceding the growth spurt (Table 11–1). An inadequate diet may put such a child into a negative nitrogen (protein) balance. For the average American girl the peak increase would be between 11 and 14 years and for boys between 13 and 16 years.[12, 28] It must be recognized that there is as much or more variability in the physiologic demands of the body at this time than at any other, and our knowledge concerning nutrition for the adolescent is extremely meager. The youngster's appetite remains our best index of need.

Table 11–1 shows the distribution of total caloric requirements based on age. In obese and undernourished children one should calculate the total caloric allowance on the expected rather than on the actual weight of the subject, taking care to avoid "nutritional breaks" by any sudden or drastic changes in the diet.

Although the immediate or acute effect of malnutrition in retardation of growth has long been recognized, the fact that permanent impairment may result has been only recently accepted. Particularly disturbing have been the studies showing the effect upon the growth and development of the central nervous system and the potential damage to intellectual and personality development.[39, 40, 42] Work in animals demonstrated that permanent growth retardation could be accomplished as a result of underfeeding early in life. No matter how adequate the nutrition following this critical period, complete recovery was not possible. Additional observations indicated an apparent greater susceptibility to infections and a reduced mental awareness in the deprived animals. If undernutrition was delayed until after the neonatal period, although the growth rate showed a very similar interruption, subsequent adequate nutritional intake permitted complete recovery. Similar findings in man were suspected but more difficult to prove.[36, 38, 43, 52, 53]

Early restriction of calories, in the late fetal and neonatal periods, slows the rate of cell multiplication. The findings are similar in a gross way for animals and human infants.[43, 45, 47, 50] Unfortunately, the type of cell most influenced at these chronologically similar times may be quite different in different species because of the marked maturational variations that are present. For example, at birth the degree of rat brain maturation is much less advanced than that of man. Probably more significant is the effect that malnutrition may have upon human cell migrations and synapse formation

TABLE 11–1. — TOTAL CALORIC REQUIREMENT PER DAY
(CAL/KG)

AGE	8 WK	10 MO	4 YR	14 YR	ADULT
Basal	55	55	40	35	25
S.D.A.	7	7	6	6	6
Excreta	11	10	8	6	6
Activity	17	20	25±	20±	10±
Growth	20	12	8–10	14	0
	110	104	87–89±	81±	47±

and function at these crucial times.[43, 46, 50] Additional findings have included deficient and delayed myelination, changes in the EEG and poor performance on some types of intelligence tests.[47, 52] As pointed out in Chapter 3 and Chapter 7, malnutrition is often associated with a reduction in brain weight and in head circumference. If severe, both of these physical findings may be an initial indication of mental retardation.

Compounding the problem is the recognition that persons of small size and mental incompetence are productive of offspring with similar findings. In most circumstances, the nutritional deprivation is combined with varying degrees of socioeconomic deprivation and often with infections, especially chronic ones. Where one finds constant hunger, one does not have to look far to discover other undesirable social conditions. A vicious pattern of events can easily be appreciated for the underprivileged child and his family: hunger leads to learning apathy, and a constant anxiety about food will certainly dilute and impair any intellectual pursuits.[24, 44]

Suffice it to say that the long-range effects of one isolated episode or of chronic malnutrition can be understood only in the context of the human ecologic conditions including biologic, social and economic factors which the child and his family have experienced. A number of studies suggest that an episode of severe malnutrition in infancy may cause little, or only temporary, intellectual impairment in the context of a lifetime of generally favorable experiences for child development.[11, 13, 53] If, however, severe malnutrition occurs in an ecologic situation that is generally unfavorable for intellectual development, then that early nutritional deprivation will likely have a clear relation to impaired intellectual performance. The prevention will undoubtedly involve considerable political, economic and social evolution.

The association of an inadequate intake of calories and protein with an increased incidence of acute or chronic infection has long been recognized, but the precise relationship of cause and effect has been difficult to establish. With the increased knowledge of the mechanisms of host defense, it is now possible to quantitate some of the immunologic deficiencies seen in chronic malnutrition.[63, 64] Normal response in antibody production to antigen stimulus is usual for gamma globulin (IgG) but is frequently reduced for the surface secretory IgA on mucous membranes. All lymphoid organs are grossly reduced in malnutrition, the thymus being most severely affected. The thymus-dependent areas of lymph nodes are depleted. The T lymphocytes are considerably reduced in the peripheral blood and the expected delayed hypersensitivity reactions, an indication of cellular immunity, are absent or markedly reduced. This condition can be rapidly corrected by adequate nutrition. Impaired function of serum complement and opsonic activity has been reported in children with severe deficiencies of calories and protein in their diet. As with most studies of malnutrition, it is difficult to delineate the effect of specific nutrients or the influence of the infections themselves upon the host defense. There does seem to be little doubt, however, that chronic nutritional deficiency reduces a child's resistance to infection and some specific immunologic inadequacies can now be identified.

Protein

Proteins are normal constituents of all animal cells and body fluids except bile and urine. They are important in the regulation of osmotic relations of the intracellular and extracellular fluids and play an important role in the fluid balance of the body. Many of the body's enzymes have the properties of proteins, and a considerable number of the hormones are proteins or protein derivatives. Many of the substances associated with immunologic and antigenic phenomena are proteins. In addition to these many functions found in the adult, this foodstuff serves the special function in the child of providing basic building materials for the manufacture of tissues during growth.[17]

Protein needs for growth are both qualitative and quantitative. Our knowledge concerning these needs comes from dietary surveys, measurements of nitrogen balance and creatinine excretion and estimations of the rate and composition of growth at different ages. An adequate protein intake may be defined as one which contains all of the essential amino acids in sufficient amounts to satisfy maintenance needs and to provide the surplus compatible with normal growth. The absolute amounts and percentages of the amino acids conducive to optimal human growth are not known. From the practical standpoint of feeding infants and children, the protein foodstuffs of animal origin in common use (milk, meat, fish and eggs) supply all of the essential amino acids, and some foods of vegetable origin supply most of them in fairly high concentrations.

The amino acid level in the serum during the first few weeks of life is higher than in the older child or adult. The total quantity of amino acids found in the urine is also elevated for a short time after birth, being higher in the low birth weight infant than in the normal newborn. In terms of milligrams excreted per day per kilogram of body weight, the average figures are: premature, 8.8; term infant, 7.6, and older child, 2.5. These findings suggest a transient enzyme deficiency.[41]

Studies of all age groups from prematures to adults show that in "normal" amounts proteins are readily digested and assimilated.

For the normal newborn infant a positive nitrogen balance and maintenance of adequate albumin in serum is obtained with a protein intake of 2.2 gm/kg/day. The requirement of the breast-fed baby may be slightly less owing to the high "biologic value" of lactalbumin.[10, 32] Unmodified cow's milk as obtained in most stores or reconstituted evaporated cow's milk contains 3.3% protein and 4.8% lactose. Human milk has considerable variability, especially if feeding continues beyond 2–3 months, but an average set of values at 2–3 weeks after birth would indicate 1.2% protein and 7.0% lactose. Both milks contain approximately 67 calories/100 ml. Some of the immunologic properties of human milk are discussed in Chapter 7 under "Development of Immunity."

Levine and Gordon[15, 16] were among the first to suggest that a higher protein intake than supplied by human milk could be of real benefit to the premature infant. Their studies indicated a more rapid weight gain and a higher magnitude of nitrogen balance if these babies were supplied with a formula containing 3–4 gm/kg/day of protein. They pointed out that to maintain a similar nitrogen balance from human milk, there would be an excessive fluid intake and possibly an amount of dietary fat in excess of the infants' tolerance. An adequate intake of carbohydrate results in a better weight gain and increased nitrogen retention as well as a lowering of the blood urea nitrogen.[29] The addition of carbohydrate offers more expendable body water and spares protein breakdown, with corresponding decrease in nitrogenous waste products that must be handled by already marginally functioning kidneys.

It has been emphasized that the optimal quantity and quality of protein for low birth weight infants remains undefined and work in the field continues. Unusually high levels of protein in the diet of these babies (6.0–7.0 gm/kg/day) may provoke anorexia and fever as an immediate effect and may have some deleterious influence upon the central nervous system.[22] Large amounts of cow's milk protein also increase the renal solute load and increase the chances for metabolic acidosis. Finally, some recent studies indicate that with an adequate caloric intake more modest levels of protein intake can produce equally satisfactory weight gains.[54]

A possible further reason for limiting the protein intake of cow's milk in the preterm baby is his inability to completely metabolize several of the amino acids, especially the sulfur-containing ones. Absence of the enzyme cystathionase is found in both liver and brain. This enzyme is necessary for the conversion of methionine to cystine. As a result there are higher levels of several amino acids, including methionine, in plasma and urine of preterm babies fed relatively high-protein cow's-milk formulas as compared to those fed breast milk. Some investigators postulate such levels indicate the formula exceeds the capacity of these infants to utilize the protein. It is also theorized that elevated levels of some amino acids may have a detrimental influence upon brain development.[59]

As the body matures, it becomes richer in protein. At birth the average nitrogen content is about 2% (Fig 11–1). By 4 years the adult proportions are reached, wherein the body contains 3% of nitrogen. Retention of nitrogen

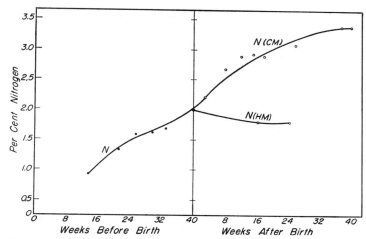

Fig 11-1.—Nitrogen content of the body before and after birth. *N(CM)*, nitrogen content of infants fed cow's milk; *N(HM)*, nitrogen content of infants fed human milk. (Fom Stearns.[23])

decreases rapidly during this period. It is approximately 204 mg/kg/day at age 1 month but only 11.0 mg/kg/day at age 4 years. The marked retention in the early months and years of life that is reflected in these figures is attributed not only to the construction of new tissue but to the maturation of existing tissue.[33] These figures are for average diets, for it has been demonstrated that in young infants simply increasing the protein content of the diet will result in increased nitrogen retention for prolonged periods. In older children such an increased retention is observed for only a brief period. In neither infants nor older children is growth in terms of height or weight greatly influenced by these differences in nitrogen retention.

From the end of the first year until the adolescent growth spurt, protein requirements are fulfilled by an allowance of 1.5–2.0 gm/kg/day. It can be demonstrated that children on relatively high caloric diets require less protein to maintain a positive nitrogen balance and growth.

Ingestion of very large portions of protein over a long period may have detrimental results, with diminished growth and diminished nitrogen retention. A very low content of protein in the diet eventually leads to a poor appetite. In children with kwashiorkor, the lack of desire to eat complicates the management. Children who are undernourished but receive adequate protein will continue to have a good appetite.[47]

Table 11–2 shows the average caloric, protein and water requirements at different ages.

TABLE 11–2.—AVERAGE CALORIC, PROTEIN AND
WATER REQUIREMENTS PER DAY

AGE, YR	CAL/KG	PROTEIN, GM/KG	WATER, ML/KG
Premature	120	3.0–4.0	150
Infancy	110	2.0	150
1–3	100	2.0	125
4–6	90	3.0	100
7–9	80	2.5	75
10–12	70	2.0	75
13–15	80	1.5	50
15+	50	1.0	50
Adult	45	0.8	50

Carbohydrate

Carbohydrates supply the greatest percentage of calories and bulk of the average diet but constitute less than 1% of the total body weight. The relatively small amount stored in the liver and muscles as glycogen is rapidly depleted in periods of starvation. Carbohydrate combined with protein in nucleotides and nucleoproteins may be found in every living cell. It is found combined with fat as cerebrosides and also is present in all connective tissue.

The main function of carbohydrate is to supply readily available energy for heat and muscular work. It spares protein and also exerts an antiketogenic effect by sparing rapid utilization of fat. Carbohydrate not oxidized or stored as glycogen is converted into fat and stored in the various fat depots.

Judging from the respiratory quotients and the blood levels of both term newborn and premature infants, carbohydrate stores are rapidly exhausted in the first few hours of life. However, the infant gastrointestinal tract easily digests and assimilates the disaccharides (milk and cane sugar) and monosaccharides (dextrose) from the time of birth, and once normal feedings have started, the relative hypoglycemia (40–80 mg/100 ml) of the first few days of life disappears and the respiratory quotient also rises.[37]

Congenital lactase deficiency is a very rare inborn error of metabolism. The commonest type of lactase deficiency is that which develops in older children, adolescents or young adults, among some blacks and orientals. Though free of gastrointestinal symptoms in early life they develop diarrhea and cramping after ingesting milk when they are older. Characteristically the stools have a pH less than 6 and sugar is present. Transient lactase deficiency is not uncommonly associated with any gastroenteritis that can damage intestinal epithelium during infancy.[10, 30]

Carbohydrate metabolism in the neonate is unique in a number of ways and has been the object of considerable study. Especially important is the recognition and prevention of hypoglycemia which may cause permanent as well as temporary impairment of central nervous system function. Term infants with blood glucose levels below 30 mg/100 ml within the first 6–8 hours following delivery have been reported at an incidence of about 10%. The frequency is twice as great in preterm or small-for-date babies. The longer the period of fasting after parturition the higher the incidence. Although many of these infants will exhibit no obvious manifestations of the low blood sugar at the time, this is not a reliable indication that no damage has taken place. The pathogenesis of this potentially dangerous situation is often multiple and may vary in different infants. Glucose is essential for normal brain metabolism. Carbohydrate stores, mostly in the liver, are rapidly depleted by the brain and other glucose-dependent tissues. Glucose-sparing substrates, such as fatty acids and glycerol, are inadequate or poorly utilized. Relative or absolute hyperinsulinism may be present, as in the diabetic mother. An added factor may be poor aerobic oxidation secondary to asphyxia or cold stress. Oral or parenteral administration of glucose is necessary until this usually transient condition is corrected.[37]

The relative requirements of children for carbohydrates do not differ from those of adults and are aimed at supplying a readily available source of energy. In general, it may be stated that not more than about 40% of the total calories in an infant's formula should be in the form of carbohydrates. Later in life the optimal range is believed to be between 40 and 60% of the total caloric intake.[10]

Lipids

The amount of fat present in the body varies with each individual. It is derived from ingested fat and from conversion of carbohydrate and protein in the body. In addition to its most commonly emphasized role as a source of concentrated energy, fat provides structural components for the repair and building of many body tissues, serves as a vehicle for the absorption of the fat-soluble vitamins (A, D, E and K), spares protein and is essential in the synthesis of the steroid hormones. There is some evidence that the highly unsaturated fatty acids are essential to life, and these cannot be synthesized by the body.

As a dietary component the lipids impart palatability to food. In addition to the metabolic roles listed above they play a very essential part in maintaining body temperature. Passively they act as an efficient insulator against the environmental temperature. The unique nature and metabolism of brown fat in preserving body temperature has been described in Chapter 10.

Few experiments have been carried out on children using low-fat diets, but those few have indicated that fat is essential to normal growth and development. In the rat and dog, diets deficient in linoleic and arachidonic acids caused retarded growth and eczematoid skin lesions. Hansen et al.[8] believe that some infantile eczema is benefited by the addition of the fatty acids to the diet.

Retention of ingested fat is lower in the newborn than in the older infant or child. With mother's milk the retention is very close to 100%. With cow's milk it is 75–85%. The premature infant may lose from 30 to 50% of the ingested fat in the stool, the larger amounts for the most immature. The premature may absorb unsaturated fats or medium-chained triglycerides as well as the more mature infant, but he absorbs saturated fats poorly. By about 2 months of age there is no difference between the infant and adult in fat absorption. A possible reason for this improvement is the increased concentration and the change in composition of the bile salts which are necessary for fat digestion. Formulas for the premature infant are usually recommended to contain minimal amounts of saturated fats.[7, 15, 55, 56]

Once the newborn infant has depleted his available glycogen stores (usually within the first day) he begins to depend on reserves of fat for energy, as demonstrated by a reduction in the respiratory quotient. During this process there is an increased transport of fat substances in the blood and nearly a twofold increase in the blood lipids between birth and the second week of life, although the total is still lower than in the child or adult.

Although the breast-fed infant obtains nearly 50% of his caloric intake from fat, it is the general consensus that after breast feeding is stopped, not over 35% of the total caloric intake should be in the form of fat either for the infant or for the older child. Diets having very low fat contents lead to excessive carbohydrate intake, hunger and early fatigue.[10, 19] When low-fat diets are prescribed, as in celiac disease or cystic fibrosis of the pancreas, it is customary to supplement them with addition of vitamins, especially A and D.

The value of a diet low in saturated fats in an attempt to reduce the development of atherosclerosis in later life has not been determined. At this time, it seems safe to recommend that the ingestion of saturated fats should be limited but not curtailed to the extent of the "low cholesterol diet" now advised by some nutritionists for all adults. This advice may be especially applicable to children in a family with a known history of myocardial infarction. The tendency to elevated serum cholesterol can be modified to an appreciable extent by a restricted saturated fat diet.[19]

Summarizing our knowledge of the role of proteins, carbohydrates, and lipids in nutrition, we may state that all three are essential to optimal growth. The allowance for protein should be higher for the artificially fed infant than for the breast-fed infant. The infant fed cow's milk has a relatively greater retention of nitrogen and greater muscle mass than the infant fed human milk, but there is no evidence that this is of any great benefit. There is some evidence that properly prepared cow's milk is better suited to the premature infant than is human milk. Carbohydrate is well utilized as food at all ages and is the main source of energy. Lipids are the least well tolerated of any of the three basic foods; the younger the child the less the tolerance.

Minerals

The minerals are essential to normal body structure and function. The child requires at least 12 minerals in proper amounts for formation of new tissues and body fluids. At birth the mineral content of the body is 3% of the total weight. Throughout childhood there is a steady increase, both absolute and relative, so that in the adult 4.35% of the body weight is mineral ash.

The minerals may be divided into three main groups. The important electropositive ions are sodium, potassium, calcium, and magnesium. The electronegative ions are chlorine, phosphorus, and sulfur. Iron and iodine and the trace elements represent a separate group physiologically.

Sodium is found chiefly in the extracellular fluids of the body, with a small amount in muscle, cartilage and bone cells. With chloride, bicarbonate, protein and phosphate it regulates the osmotic pressure and ionic equilibrium of body fluids. With calcium, potassium and magnesium it aids in control of the irritability of the neuromuscular system. The sodium content of the body is regulated by amounts ingested balanced against excretion under control of aldosterone. Except under extreme degrees of dehydration, hydration or loss from the intestinal tract, the body's control of water and electrolyte balance is very precise. The average daily requirement is met by 1–2 gm. This amount is normally found in the content of the food eaten.

Potassium is the most important electropositive intracellular ion. Its functions are almost identical with those of sodium except that the latter is largely extracellular. In addition, it influences the irritability and conductivity of the heart muscle. Potassium metabolism is influenced by the adrenal cortical hormone, possibly by the parathyroid hormone, and by ionic equilibrium of calcium, sodium and protein.

Since most foods contain an abundant supply of this mineral, a diet low in potassium is difficult to prepare. Between 1 and 2 gm is required daily.

Calcium occurs in the body to a far greater extent than any other positive mineral element. Ninety-nine per cent of it is found in combination with phosphates and carbonates as bone. Most of the remainder is found in the plasma, half of this being bound with protein and the other half in ionizable form.

Calcium furnishes important material for structure and growth of bones and teeth, and it supplies ions which function in muscle contraction, in the control of irritability of nerve cells and in the coagulation of blood and milk. It plays a minor role in electrolyte balance.

Calcium is easily absorbed as a soluble salt from the upper alimentary tract. The degree of absorption is influenced by the amount in the diet, the calcium : phosphorus ratio, the acidity or alkalinity of the intestinal tract and the presence of vitamin D. The calcium plasma level, which is quite constant at all ages, except in the premature infant at birth when levels are low, is influenced by the parathyroid glands and the acid-base balance. Metabolism, mainly concerned with deposition in bone, is under the control of hormones from the parathyroids, pituitary, adrenal cortex and the sex glands as well as vitamin D.[2, 10, 21] The role of calcitonin in calcium metabolism is discussed in Chap. 9.

The amount of calcium retained by the growing child is about 25% of that ingested, under ordinary conditions. During the first year, with an adequate vitamin D intake there is a greater storage in the body, both relative and absolute, when cow's milk is the source of food than when the source is human milk; however, there is no indication that this "supermineralization" is beneficial to the growing child. Levine believes this fact may be of some value in preventing rickets in the premature infant. It should be remembered that when the vitamin D supplement is inadequate, calcium and phosphorus absorption and retention are greater from human milk than from

Fig 11–2.—Calcium content of the body before and after birth. *CM*, calcium content of infants fed cow's milk; *HM*, calcium content of infants fed human milk; *Prem*, calcium content of prematures fed human milk. (From Stearns.[23])

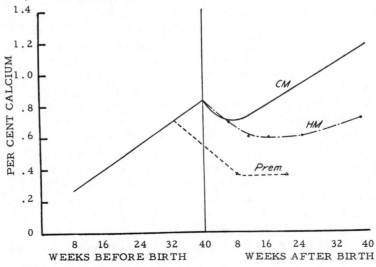

cow's milk. Therefore, in such instances rickets will be less common in the breast-fed infants (Fig 11–2).[10, 23]

The quantity of calcium required by the growing child is estimated at between 50 and 70 mg/kg/day. In general, 1 gm/day with a calcium:phosphorus ratio of 1:1.5 appears satisfactory.

Magnesium is found in all body cells, but about 75% is in the skeleton, and a fairly large quantity is in muscle. Knowledge regarding the function of magnesium is meager. It serves as a catalyst in phosphorus and pyruvic acid metabolism and has a role in maintaining the electrolyte balance. It also is concerned with the regulation of nerve impulses and muscle irritability. Magnesium deficiency may occur in severe diarrhea and in malabsorption syndromes. During infancy it may be associated with hypocalcemic tetany. The fact that correcting the low calcium level in the serum does not result in cessation of the tetany is a possible clue to hypomagnesemia. According to Macy,[18] about 15–20% of the intake is retained. Requirements are given in Table 11–3. Serum magnesium is maintained normally at 1.5–1.8 mEq/L. Parathormone (PTH) increases renal tubular reabsorption of magnesium. Low serum concentrations increase the release of PTH.

Phosphorus is distributed in the body as organic compounds and inorganic phosphate. About 70% of the phosphate is found in the skeleton combined with calcium. With potassium, phosphorus forms the most important intracellular mineral constituent of the body. In the organic form it is found in combination with fat, protein, and carbohydrate.

Phosphorus is an important component of bone, muscle, and nerve tissue. It plays a role in the absorption of carbohydrates and their transformation in muscular activity, in the transportation of fatty acids and as a buffer in the acid-base equilibrium. As cephalin it is essential to the formation of thrombin.

After birth the storage of phosphorus depends on the amount avilable in the diet, the stimulus to absorption and deposition offered by added vitamin D and the depression of absorption by large amounts of calcium or fats in the diet.[21]

With adequate vitamin D intake, an infant should have a phosphorus intake of about 0.2–0.5 gm daily, children 2–10 years 1.0 gm daily and adolescents up to 1.5 gm daily. There is no known ill effect from an excess intake of phosphorus.

Chlorine, as the chloride, is a component of all body secretions and excretions. With sodium it constitutes the most important electrolyte in the extracellular fluid, maintaining acid-base and water balances. Chloride excretion is influenced by the antidiuretic factor of the posterior pituitary gland and by the adrenal cortical hormone; however, these influences are probably secondary to water metabolism.

TABLE 11–3. — RECOMMENDED DAIL*

	AGE, YR	WEIGHT, KG	HEIGHT, CM	ENERGY, KCAL	PROTEIN, GM	VITAMIN A ACTIVITY, IU	VITA-MIN D ACTIVITY, IU	VITA-MIN E ACTIVIT* IU
						FAT-SOLUBLE VITAMINS		
Infants	0.0–0.5	6	60	kg × 117	kg × 2.2	1400	400	4
	0.5–1.0	9	71	kg × 108	kg × 2.0	2000	400	5
Children	1–3	13	86	1300	23	2000	400	7
	4–6	20	110	1800	30	2500	400	9
	7–10	30	135	2400	36	3300	400	10
Males	11–14	44	158	2800	44	5000	400	12
	15–18	61	172	3000	54	5000	400	15
	19–22	67	172	3000	54	5000	400	15
	23–50	70	172	2700	56	5000		15
	51+	70	172	2400	56	5000		15
Females	11–14	44	155	2400	44	4000	400	12
	15–18	54	162	2100	48	4000	400	12
	19–22	58	162	2100	46	4000	400	12
	23–50	58	162	2000	46	4000		12
	51+	58	162	1800	46	4000		12

*See reference 14.

In normal conditions the intake of chloride does not require special consideration because it is abundantly supplied in many foods.

Sulfur is a constituent of all body protein in the form of amino acids. It is also found in combination with lipids and as inorganic sulfur. It occurs in melanin, vitreous humor, heparin, cartilage, nerve tissue, insulin, thiamine and enzymes of cellular respiration.

In general, the metabolism of sulfur is linked with protein metabolism since the greater part of the sulfur ingested is in the form of amino acids. Sulfur, as amino acid sulfur, is essential to growth. An adequate protein intake assures a sufficient allowance of sulfur; the ideal intake has not been established.

Iron is found in the body in relatively small amounts—approximately 3 gm in the normal adult. Fifty-eight per cent is in hemoglobin, 7% in muscle hemoglobin, 15% as chromatin in the cells and in cytochrome, and the remaining 20% stored in the liver, spleen, bone marrow, and to less extent in other tissues. Almost 75% of the total body iron of the newborn is found in the hemoglobin.[34] It is evident that the chief function of iron is to carry oxygen to the tissues and to aid in oxidation processes carried on by the cells. All cells contain iron as heme proteins. Mitochondrial heme proteins function in utilization of oxygen in production of cellular energy in the form of ATP (adenosine triphosphate). Other cytochromes are found in the endoplas-

DIETARY ALLOWANCES, REVISED 1974*

	WATER-SOLUBLE VITAMINS							MINERALS					
ASCOR-BIC ACID, MG	FOLA-CIN, μG	NIA-CIN, MG	RIBO-FLAVIN, MG	THIA-MIN, MG	VITA-MIN B_6, MG	VITA-MIN B_{12}, μG	CAL-CIUM, MG	PHOS-PHORUS, MG	IODINE, μG	IRON, MG	MAG-NESIUM, MG	ZINC, MG
35	50	5	0.4	0.3	0.3	0.3	360	240	35	10	60	3
35	50	8	0.6	0.5	0.4	0.3	540	400	45	15	70	5
40	100	9	0.8	0.7	0.6	1.0	800	800	60	15	150	10
40	200	12	1.1	0.9	0.9	1.5	800	800	80	10	200	10
40	300	16	1.2	1.2	1.2	2.0	800	800	110	10	250	10
45	400	18	1.5	1.4	1.6	3.0	1200	1200	130	18	350	15
45	400	20	1.8	1.5	2.0	3.0	1200	1200	150	18	400	15
45	400	20	1.8	1.5	2.0	3.0	800	800	140	10	350	15
45	400	18	1.6	1.4	2.0	3.0	800	800	130	10	350	15
45	400	16	1.5	1.2	2.0	3.0	800	800	110	10	350	15
45	400	16	1.3	1.2	1.6	3.0	1200	1200	115	18	300	15
45	400	14	1.4	1.1	2.0	3.0	1200	1200	115	18	300	15
45	400	14	1.4	1.1	2.0	3.0	800	800	100	18	300	15
45	400	13	1.2	1.0	2.0	3.0	800	800	100	18	300	15
45	400	12	1.1	1.0	2.0	3.0	800	800	80	10	300	15

mic reticulum of the liver. Some of these are important in oxidative breakdown of drugs and in catabolism of endogenous compounds.[5]

Between the seventh and ninth gestational months, liver iron increases from 5 to 30 mg. Immediately after birth this may rise to 80–100 mg, reaching a peak at 2–3 months. At this time there is an increase in erythropoiesis and a steady decrease in liver iron ensues for the next couple of years. In addition there is a paucity of hemosiderin in bone marrow during most of childhood. These observations indicate that iron depots, except for the first 2–3 months, are marginal. It is not surprising, then, to find that a deficiency of iron in the diet rapidly leads to anemia, and that the two categories of children most susceptible are preschoolers in a low socioeconomic situation and the adolescent girl.[6, 12]

Small amounts of iron are present in the serum bound to a beta globulin *transferrin*. There is an excess of this protein and normally about 66% of serum transferrin is in a free state. When the degree of saturation falls below 15% very little iron will be available for hemoglobin synthesis or for the important cytochrome enzymes. Iron deficiency does not cause a purely hematologic problem but may involve cellular functions resulting in lowered host defense and interfering with optimal neurologic function.[1, 3, 57] The mean values representative of iron and iron-binding capacity during life are shown in the table on page 370.

AGE		SERUM IRON, μG/100 ML	IRON-BINDING CAPACITY, μG/100 ML
Newborn		190	225
1 day		50	50
2 wk		125	230
3 mo		50	250
1 yr		70	250
2 yr		100	250
10 yr		110	280
Adult:	female	110	330
	male	125	300

During periods of rapid growth the need for iron is greater than at other periods of life in order to avoid hypochromic microcytic anemia. The anemia of prematurity, occurring about two to four months after birth, cannot be prevented by giving iron prophylactically, but the severity and duration may be influenced to some extent by early administration of iron. The cause of this anemia is believed to be twofold: (1) the greater portion of storage of iron by the fetus occurs during the last trimester (Fig 11–3), and (2), more important, the premature infant grows relatively rapidly during a short span of time.[5] It has recently been demonstrated that an important percentage of normal infants fed untreated (heat) homogenized whole cow's milk will develop a milk-induced enteric blood loss, often resulting in a reduced iron storage and a mild but definite iron-deficiency anemia. Heating the milk, or substituting a prepared formula, reversed the changes.[49] The American Academy of Pediatrics recommends the use of iron-fortified formulas throughout the first year as a prophylaxis against iron-deficiency anemia.

The iron accumulated by the fetus is sufficient only for the first few months of life, and the supply may be even less adequate in the case of a maternal iron deficiency, multiple birth or prematurity. Neither human nor cow's milk contains enough iron to meet the requirements of the infant after the fourth month, so foods supplying this need, such as meat, are a necessary part of the diet by this time. It is of interest to note that 70% of the hemoglobin iron at age 1 year is still derived from fetal stores and 40% at 2 years.[31] These figures emphasize the ability to reuse the available supply. There is evidence that some of the transplacental iron acquired from maternal sources is stored and not utilized until late in the first year.[31] The iron requirements for the growing child vary between 0.5 and 1.0 mg/kg/day during early life and between 0.2 and 0.4 mg for the older child.[18]

The amount of iron in food that can be absorbed depends upon the nature of that food or its combination with other components in the diet. Much of the phosphorus in cereals and legumes is present as phytic acid which forms an insoluble salt with iron and greatly decreases absorption. Similarly, the iron and phosphoproteins in egg yolk form a complex that impedes its availability. Since the iron in meat is primarily present in protein, hemoglobin or myoglobin, it is less influenced by other ingredients in the diet and is more readily assimilated. These factors are important in explaining the high incidence of iron-deficiency anemia among the poor, especially in the underdeveloped countries.

Iodine is necessary for the formation of the thyroid hormone and thus plays a vital part in body metabolism. It is readily absorbed from the alimentary tract in either organic or inorganic form. After absorption it is rapidly taken up by the thyroid gland. The amount retained by the body depends on the intake and the amount already stored.[21]

The work of Marine has well established the routine use of iodine

Fig 11–3.—Nitrogen, iron, calcium, and phosphorus content of the human fetus. It is apparent that the fetus retains the greatest proportion of all four of these substances during the final trimester. (From Swanson, W. W. and Iob, V.: Am. J. Obst. Gynecol. 38:383, 1939.)

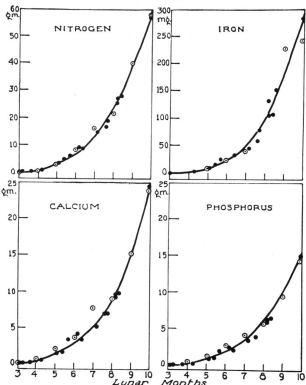

prophylactically in a "goiter belt" area to prevent simple goiter. Iodized table salt usually supplies adequate iodine in the so-called goiter areas. For infants and children the daily requirements are stated to be 40–100 μg and for adolescents 100–200 μg.

The following minerals, found in very small amounts in the human body, are essential to normal growth and development.[20, 21, 23] *Fluorine* is apparently necessary for good tooth enamel formation. It is also found in bone, but its function here is poorly understood. Nutritional surveys continue to find dental caries to be the most prevalent disease throughout all of childhood, and that the administration of fluoride is a safe and effective means of reducing its incidence.[58] *Copper* is found in larger quantities in the liver of the fetus than in the child after birth, and it is found in larger quantities in the bone marrow after birth than in the liver or bone marrow of the fetus. Since the liver of the fetus and the bone marrow of the infant are the chief sources of red blood cells, these variations lend support to the theory that copper is necessary for hemoglobin synthesis. It is also found in the enzymes tyrosinase and ascorbic oxidase. Since the normal diet contains traces of copper, its deficiency is not to be anticipated in the normal child. *Zinc* is necessary for normal growth and sexual maturation. Although deficiency states are rare, a syndrome found in African and Asian children is associated with marked reduction in the zinc content of plasma, urine, sweat and tissues. These children are retarded in statural growth, have delayed bone age and retarded genital development with minimal or absent sexual maturation and a poor response of growth hormone to hypoglycemia. A major factor in the etiology is the diet which contains large amounts of phytate which binds zinc and makes it unavailable. Phytate is a common ingredient in most grains. Supplementing the diet with zinc for these subjects corrected the growth failure. Since a number of enzymes contain the element, it is probably essential for nucleic acid and protein synthesis.[51]

Vitamins

The vitamins are so well known that they will be considered very briefly and in outline form (see Table 11–3). It is certain that they are essential to normal growth and development. A well-rounded diet usually supplies adequate amounts of them, but during infancy and nutritional disturbances some of them should be given to supplement the diet. Neither human nor cow's milk supplies sufficient amounts of vitamins C and D, so they should be added to the infant's intake.

Present knowledge of the vitamins indicates that their major role is to act as coenzymes that activate enzymes in basic metabolic processes. Not all enzymes require coenzymes for their activation. Most coenzymes containing vitamins are not synthesized in the body and must be supplied in the diet. Some of the B complex vitamins can be derived from specific amino acids, and vitamin K and biotin are obtained from the action of intestinal flora under normal conditions. Both folic acid and B_{12} are important in protein metabolism, being involved in the transfer of single carbon units, and folic acid plays a major role in the formation of nucleoproteins. Megaloblastic anemia may be caused by a deficiency of either vitamin. Pyridoxine is an essential coenzyme to a number of enzymes essential for amino acid metabolism, including decarboxylase and transaminase as well as others. Deficiency of this vitamin has led to convulsive seizures in infants and neuropathies in older persons. Pantothenic acid is a constituent of coenzyme A which is involved in acetylation reactions of the three main food elements. The specific actions of biotin, inositol, choline and possibly other vitamins are not yet clearly delineated, nor is it certain at present that these should be so classified. The daily requirements of all of the water-soluble vitamins considered in this paragraph but not outlined in Table 11–3 have not been defined.

Vitamins A, D and K are fat-soluble; therefore the ability to absorb fat must be present before they can be adequately absorbed. Vitamins A and D may be stored in the liver, so that large quantities given at one time are effective for relatively long periods. Vitamin D is also available in water-soluble form (activated ergosterols).[3, 4, 10]

The body has very poor ability to store any of the water-soluble vitamins; consequently, these vitamins must be ingested frequently in adequate amounts. In general, the factors of the B complex occur together in nature, so that a deficiency of any one is usually associated with a deficiency of the others.

The figures usually given for the requirements of the vitamins have been more or less arbitrarily chosen. Factors such as illness, malnutrition and increased activity are not considered. Finally, it has recently been demonstrated that some foods have a sparing action on vitamins of the B complex whereas others have an opposite effect. The amounts suggested in Table 11–3 are generally considered to give a wide margin of safety.

In the foregoing paragraphs we have indicated in a general way what substances are thought necessary and the quantities required, when known, for optimal growth and development. Alone, however, the figures are insufficient, for we must have some means of determining whether a child is or is not receiving the best nutrition possible. Actually, no such method is available. Average stature and weight are not necessarily proof that the state of nutrition is satisfactory. Investigations on vitamins, for instance, have shown that somatic growth alone is not an adequate index of certain important deficiencies in nutrition.[3, 26]

Food Habits

As the child grows, he develops food habits. These change with increasing maturation of body and mind and are related to his nutritional requirements, to his personal satisfactions and dissatisfactions and to the impact of the society around him. The psychologic reaction of the child to the offering of food is receiving much attention at present, and properly so.

The foundations of eating behavior rest on the physiologic mechanisms of hunger and appetite and their gratification. Hunger contractions almost certainly occur in the stomach of the newborn. This is an unpleasant sensation and is relieved by the ingestion of food. The infant, at this time and later on, does not tell when he is hungry by looking at the clock, as do most adults. It seems advisable, therefore, to have a feeding schedule flexible enough to coincide with hunger time. This establishes good feeding behavior at the outset and may avoid trouble later on. It might be well to add at this point that the amount offered should be sufficient to satisfy. Many cases of "colic" in infants are related to underfeeding and poor feeding technique.[25]

The time to add solid food to the infant's diet comes when he is prepared for it and may vary over a wide range from one to perhaps four months. There is no valid indication that immaturity of the gastrointestinal tract precludes the introduction of solid food in the diet even before this, but little is to be gained and the chances of aspiration are certainly increased. The time at which chopped or more coarse food should be added depends on the child's rate of progress and, from a purely nutritional standpoint, makes little difference. An adequate diet may be secured in a variety of ways, and either forcing or overly delaying new food experiences is hardly to be desired. Most "chopped" or "junior" foods need little mastication, so that dentition is not a particularly important consideration until even coarser foods are introduced.

As motor skills increase, the child needs less and less help in eating. Some children are fairly proficient in feeding themselves by 18 months, but in many this skill comes later. The child should be allowed some choice in his diet by this time, and his likes and dislikes should be respected. By age 5 he can handle a knife and fork quite well, although he still needs occasional help. It is important throughout childhood that mealtime be a happy time in order to ensure good habits.

It is common during the second or third year, sometimes sooner, for the parents to be overly concerned with the child's appetite. This is often a period of psychologic anorexia. It must be realized that by this time the rapid growth which characterized infancy is over. The rate of weight gain reaches its lowest point during this time, and the metabolic rate is at a relatively low level. In addition, this is a period in the child's life when he is becoming aware of himself as an individual and as a part of the family group. His interests are not as concerned with eating as they formerly were. He may like to exert his authority by seeing the effect of his not eating on his parents, especially if they appear worried about it. If these facts are explained to parents and they are assured that no healthy child (physically and mentally) will starve himself if food is available, many disagreeable behavior problems will be avoided. Often asking the child to participate in preparing the food or the table will renew interest. Smaller helpings may also be desirable and make the goal of "cleaning the plate" more easily attained.

During adolescence the appetite is usually increased. Growth in both height and weight is accelerated. Increased fat deposition occurs as a part of sexual maturation in both sexes, though it is more pronounced in females. Unfortunately, adolescence is also a period when food fads are often begun and promoted by false conceptions of nutrition and its relationship to maturational changes. Youth are particularly susceptible to food fads as a means of correcting problems which may include acne, real or imagined ailments, delay in sexual development or as solace for unfulfilled needs. As we have seen in the psychological development of teenagers, they are strongly influenced in their behavior by their peers, many of whom may follow food cults. They are easy targets for quackery which can result in either excesses of certain nutrients or deficiencies in minerals, calories or vitamins. Avoidance of animal products may be practiced due to fear of additives, such as hormones and antibiotics, or contamination by radioactive fallout. Although a well-planned vegetarian diet can easily supply all necessary nutrients, many adolescent vegetarians have been found to have inadequate caloric, protein and iron intakes. Fluid restriction, as found in the Zen macrobiotic diets, has led to serious renal problems. Especially worrisome is the pregnant teenager and the following care of the infant if parents are pursuing a food fad or cult.[60]

Often the adolescent is "too busy" to eat a well-balanced meal and resorts to between-meal snacks, which may constitute more than one fourth of the recommended caloric intake. Often such foods lack both iron and protein content and contribute an important share to dental caries. Parents and other counselors may find it difficult to reform such practices, and mild degrees of dietary deficiencies are not uncommon.[35, 48]

Recent surveys in the United States indicate the overall nutritional status of infants and children is reasonably good.[61, 62] Not surprising was the finding of a direct correlation between the nutritional status and income or socioeconomic level. Both stature and weight were lowest in the poorer population groups. Iron deficiency and iron-deficiency anemia were the most commonly encountered specifically identified problems. In children under 5 years the incidence was as high as 30% in some areas for iron deficiency (transferrin saturation below 20%) and 26% for anemia (hemoglobin below 10 gm). Ethnic and geographic variations in regard to other nutrients were noted but did not constitute major problems.

The effect of illness on appetite is well recognized. The fact that some anorexia may persist beyond the time of obvious signs and symptoms of illness must also be realized to avoid the introduction of poor food habits. Fatigue, excitement and temporary emotional disturbances occur in every normal child at one time or another, and their interference with appetite should be respected. The small child has a short attention span and often has great difficulty in sitting still during a meal. All of these factors play a part in development related to food intake, and a reasonable attitude toward them is essential.

The environment in which the child eats may also influence him. Some of the more important factors pertain to the economics of the family, the cultural food pattern of the family, the availability of food and the attitude of the family toward food in general or toward particular preferences or prejudices.

It is apparent that nutrition in children is more than a simple matter of chemistry and physiology based on laboratory studies. The other factors, though only briefly considered, should constantly be kept in mind by the person who must guide parents and children in establishing good habits.

Dietary Requirements

The complexity of the newer knowledge of the nutrition of children has only been touched on in this chapter. We have made no attempt to outline the actual preparation of formulas or diets, since this is done in most textbooks of pediatrics or in dietary manuals. Owing to common demand by those who reviewed this chapter during its preparation, we present some basic data in Table 11–4.

TABLE 11–4.—REQUIREMENTS OF SOME ESSENTIAL NUTRIENTS

Estimation of total caloric requirements, daily
     Infancy: 100–120 calories/kg expected weight for age.
     Childhood: 1,000 calories basic plus 100 calories for each year; e.g., a boy aged 9 should have
         1,000 plus 900, or 1,900 calories daily.
Estimation of protein requirements, daily
     Infancy: 2 gm/kg; an adequate amount is assured if the infant consumes 100 ml whole milk/kg.
     Childhood: 1.5 gm/kg until puberty, when slightly more is desirable.
     If about 20% of the required caloric intake is protein, the requirement will be met.
Minerals, daily
     Calcium, 1–1.5 gm
     Phosphorus, 0.5–1.0 gm
     Iron, 16 mg
     Iodine, 100–200 mg (trace)

TABLE 11–4—*Continued*

Vitamins: see Table 11–3
Composition of daily diet to satisfy basic growth needs

Milk	600–800 ml
Meat, poultry, fish	1 serving (5–6 weekly)
Liver	1 serving weekly
Eggs	1 (5–6 weekly)
Vegetables, 1 raw, 1 pigmented	2 servings
Fruit, fresh, 1 citrus	2 or more servings
Butter	2 tsp
Bread (enriched or whole grain) and cereals	enough to meet caloric needs
Salt (iodized)	seasoning
Vitamin D	approximately 500 units

REFERENCES

1. Buckley, R. H.: Iron deficiency anemia: Its relationship to infection susceptibility and host defense, J. Pediatr. 86:993, 1975.
2. Root, A. W., and Harrison, H. E.: Recent advances in calcium metabolism, J. Pediatr. 88:1, 1976.
3. Beaton, G. H., and McHenry, E. W. (ed.): *Nutrition* (New York: Academic Press, Inc., 1965).
4. Wasserman, R. H., and Taylor, A. N.: Metabolic roles of fat-soluble vitamins D, E and K, Am. Rev. Biochem. 41:179, 1972.
5. Oski, F. A., and Naiman, J. L.: *Hematologic Problems in the Newborn* (2d ed.; Philadelphia: W. B. Saunders Company, 1972).
6. Owen, G. M., Kram, K. M., Gary, P. J., Lowe, J. E., and Lubin, A. H.: A study of nutritional status of preschool children in the U.S., 1968-70, Pediatrics 53:597, 1974.
7. Räihä, N. C. R.: Biochemical basis for nutritional management of preterm infants, Pediatrics 53:147, 1974.
8. Hansen, A. E., Knott, E. M., Wiese, H. F., Shaperman, E., and McQuarrie, I.: Eczema and essential fatty acids, Am. J. Dis. Child. 73:1, 1947.
9. Jackson, R. L., Hanna, F. M., and Flynn, M. A.: Nutritional requirements of infants and children, Pediatr. Clin. North Am. 9:879, 1962.
10. Foman, S. J.: *Infant Nutrition* (2d ed.; Philadelphia: W. B. Saunders Company, 1974).
11. Wharton, B. A.: Child Health and Nutrition, in Apley, J. (ed.): *Modern Trends in Paediatrics* (London: Butterworth, 1970).
12. Young, C. M.: Adolescents and Their Nutrition, in Gallagher, J. R., Heald, F. P., and Garell, D. C. (eds.): *Medical Care of the Adolescent* (New York: Appleton-Century-Crofts, 1976).
13. Lloyd-Still, J. D., Hurwitz, I., Wolff, P. H., and Shwachman, H.: Intellectual development after severe malnutrition in infancy, Pediatrics 54:306, 1974.
14. National Research Council Food and Nutrition Board: *Recommended Dietary Allowance* (8th ed.; Washington, D.C.: National Academy of Sciences, 1974).
15. Levine, S. Z.: Protein nutrition in pediatrics, J.A.M.A. 128:283, 1945.
16. Levine, S. Z., and Gordon, H. H.: Physiologic handicaps of the premature infant, Am. J. Dis. Child. 64:297, 1942.

17. Holt, L. E., and Snyderman, S. E.: Protein and amino acid requirements of infants and children, Nutr. Abstr. Rev. 35:1, 1965.
18. Macy, I. G.: *Nutrition and Chemical Growth in Childhood*, Vol. I, Evaluation (Springfield, Ill.: Charles C Thomas, Publisher, 1942).
19. Hennekens, C. H., Jesse, M. J., Klein, B. E., Gourley, J. E., and Blumenthal, S.: Cholesterol among children of men with myocardial infarction, Pediatrics 58:211, 1976.
20. Goodhart, R. S., and Shils, M. E. (eds.): *Modern Nutrition in Health and Disease* (Philadelphia: Lea and Febiger, 1973).
21. Shohl, A. T.: *Mineral Metabolism*, Am. Chem. Soc. Monogr. Ser. (New York: Reinhold Publishing Corporation, 1939).
22. Goldman, H. I., Goldman, J. S., Kaufman, I., and Liebman, O. B.: Late effects of early dietary protein intake on low-birthweight infants, J. Pediatr. 85:764, 1976.
23. Stearns, G.: Mineral metabolism of normal infants, Physiol. Rev. 19:415, 1939.
24. Graham, G. G.: Environmental factors affecting the growth of children, Am. J. Clin. Nutr. 25:1184, 1972.
25. Stevenson, S. S.: The adequacy of artificial feeding in infancy, J. Pediatr. 31:616, 1947.
26. Stuart, H. C.: Need for observations of growth in appraising adequacy of nutrition in childhood, J. Pediatr. 7:320, 1935.
27. Windle, W. F.: *Physiology of the Fetus* (Philadelphia: W. B. Saunders Company, 1940).
28. Heald, F. P.: *Adolescent Nutrition and Growth* (New York: Appleton-Century-Crofts, 1969).
29. Calcagno, P. L., and Rubin, M. I.: Effect of added carbohydrate on growth, nitrogen retention and renal excretion in premature infants, Pediatrics 13:193, 1954.
30. Christopher, M. L., and Bayless, T. M.: Role of the small bowel and colon in lactose induced diarrhea, Gastroenterology 60:845, 1971.
31. Smith, C. A., Cherry, R. B., Maletskas, C. J., Gibson, J. G., Raby, C. C., Caton, W. L., and Reid, D. E.: Persistence and utilization of maternal iron for blood formation during infancy, J. Clin. Invest. 34:1391, 1955.
32. Holt, L. E.: Nutritional requirements in early life, Pediatrics 17:578, 1956.
33. Holt, L. E., György, P., Pratt, E. L., Snyderman, S. E., and Wallace, W. M.: *Protein and Amino Acid Requirements in Early Life* (New York: New York University, 1960).
34. Schulman, I.: Iron requirements in infancy, J.A.M.A. 175:118, 1961.
35. Everson, G. J.: Bases for concern about teenagers' diets, J. Am. Dietet. A. 36:17, 1960.
36. Tanner, J. M.: Relationships of different bodily tissues during growth and in the adult, in *Diet and Bodily Constitution* (Ciba Foundation Study Group) (Boston: Little, Brown & Company, 1964).
37. Cornblath, M., and Schwartz, R.: *Disorders of Carbohydrate Metabolism in Infancy* (2d ed.; Philadelphia: W. B. Saunders Company, 1976).
38. Smith, C. A.: Prenatal and neonatal nutrition, Pediatrics 30:145, 1962.
39. McCance, R. A.: Some effects of undernutrition, J. Pediatr. 65:1008, 1964.
40. McCance, R. A.: Food, growth and time, Lancet 2:621, 671, 1962.
41. Waisman, H. A., and Kerr, G. R.: Amino acid and protein metabolism in the developing fetus and the newborn infant, Pediatr. Clin. North Am. 12:551, 1965.

42. Widdowson, E. M.: Early Nutrition and Later Development, in *Diet and Bodily Constitution* (Ciba Foundation Study Group (Boston: Little, Brown & Company, 1964).
43. Dobbing, J., and Sands, J.: Vulnerability of developing brain; IX: The effect of nutritional growth retardation on the timing of the brain growth spurt, Biol. Neonate 19:363, 1971.
44. Scrimshaw, N. S.: Synergism of malnutrition and infection: Evidence from field studies in Guatemala, J.A.M.A. 212:1685, 1970.
45. Winick, M.: Malnutrition and brain development, J. Pediatr. 74:667, 1969.
46. Chase, H. P., Dorsey, J., and McKhann, G. M.: The effect of malnutrition on the synthesis of a myelin lipid, Pediatrics 40:551, 1967.
47. Chase, H. P., and Martin, H. P.: Undernutrition and child development, N. Engl. J. Med. 282:933, 1970.
48. Hodges, R. E., and Krehl, W. A.: Nutritional status of teenagers in Iowa, Am. J. Clin. Nutr. 17:200, 1965.
49. Woodruff, C. W., and Clark, J. L.: The role of fresh cow's milk in iron deficiency, Am. J. Dis. Child. 124:18, 1972.
50. Cheek, D. B., Graystone, J. E., and Read, M. S.: Cellular growth, nutrition and development, Pediatrics 45:315, 1970.
51. Halstead, J. A., Ronaghy, H. A., Abadi, R., Haghshenass, M., Amirhakemi, G. H., Barakat, R. M., and Reinhold, J. G.: Zinc deficiency in man, Am. J. Med. 53:277, 1972.
52. Stock, M. B., and Smythe, P. M.: 15-year developmental study on effects of severe undernutrition during infancy on subsequent physical growth and intellectual functioning, Arch. Dis. Child. 51:327, 1976.
53. Richardson, S. A.: The relation of severe malnutrition in infancy to the intelligence of school children with differing life histories, Pediatr. Res. 10:57, 1976.
54. Räihä, N. C. R., Heinonen, K., Rassin, D. K., and Gaull, G. E.: Milk protein quantity and quality in low-birth-weight infants: Metabolic responses and effects on growth, Pediatrics 57:659, 1976.
55. Katz, L., and Hamilton, J. R.: Fat absorption in infants of birth weight less than 1,300 gm, J. Pediatr. 85:608, 1974.
56. Holt, P. R.: The roles of bile acids during the process of normal fat and cholesterol absorption, Arch. Intern. Med. 130:574, 1972.
57. Dallman, P. R.: Iron, vitamin E and folate in the preterm infant, J. Pediatr. 85:742, 1974.
58. Report of American Academy of Pediatrics Committee on Nutrition: Fluoride as a nutrient, Pediatrics 49:456, 1972.
59. Gaull, G. E., Rassin, D. K., Räihä, N. C. R., and Heinonen, K.: Milk protein quantity and quality in low-birth-weight infants, J. Pediatr. 90:348, 1977.
60. Robson, J. R. K.: Food faddism, Pediatr. Clin. North Am. 24:189, 1977.
61. Garn, S. M., and Clark, D. C.: Nutrition, growth, development and maturation: Findings from the Ten-State Nutrition Survey of 1968–1970, Pediatrics 56:306, 1975.
62. Owen, G., and Lippman, G.: Nutritional status of infants and young children: U.S.A., Pediatr. Clin. North Am. 24:211, 1977.
63. Chandra, R. K.: Immuno-competence in undernutrition, J. Pediatr. 81:1194, 1972.
64. Katz, M., and Stiehm, E. R.: Host defense in malnutrition, Pediatrics 59:490, 1977.

12 / Facial Growth and Dentition

The Craniofacial Skeleton

THE EMBRYONIC ORIGIN of the bones making up the cranium and face are a mixture of intramembranous ossification and endochondral ossification (see Chapter 8). This mixture permits the marked variations in the rate and pattern of growth in this area as well as explaining some of the peculiarities of the malformations, congenital or acquired, that are encountered. The teeth, in part derived from ectodermal tissue, also have considerable influence on facial growth. For purposes of discussion, we shall divide the skull into the neurocranium, a protective enclosure for the brain, and the viscerocranium, the main skeleton of the jaws.

The neurocranium consists of an endochondral portion that forms the base of the cranium as the occipital bone, the sphenoid, the ethmoid, and the petrous and mastoid portions of the temporal bone. The intramembranous ossification forms the cranial vault. During fetal life and well into childhood, the bones of the vault are separated by dense connective tissue membranes, the sutures and fontanels (see Figs 4–3 and 4–4). The softness of the bones and their relatively pliable sutures enable the skull to undergo considerable molding during birth (Fig 12–1). The same construction also permits rapid brain growth.[3]

The endochondral portions of the viscerocranium originate in the first two branchial arches to form the malleus, incus and stapes of the middle ear and the styloid process of the temporal bone. Some endochondral ossification also occurs in the condyle of the mandible. Intramembranous bone formation occurs within the boundaries of the first branchial arch to form the maxilla and premaxilla, the zygoma, the squamous portion of the temporal bone and the mandible.

The primitive buccal cavity is bounded by the frontonasal process and the maxillary and mandibular processes of the first branchial arch. The frontonasal process elaborates into paired median and lateral nasal folds which form the nares. The palate develops from two parts, a median process extending from the premaxilla and two lateral processes from the maxilla. Normally development begins at the 5th week of gestation and is completed

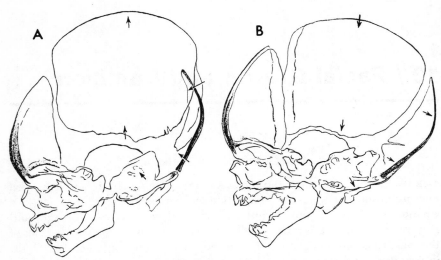

Fig 12–1.—A, tracing of roentgenogram of neonatal skull on first day of life, demonstrating molding of bones of the calvarium with overlapping of their edges and narrowing of sutures caused by compression during passage of head through the birth canal. Parietals are displaced upward, and temporals and occipital are rotated counterclockwise. **B,** tracing of roentgenogram on third day of life, showing re-expansion of cranium and widening of sutures and fontanels, as compared with **A,** after parietal, occipital, and temporal bones have returned to normal positions. (Courtesy of Dr. H. C. Moloy; from Caffey.[4])

by fusion of all three processes at 12 weeks. Fusion occurs in an anterior-to-posterior direction. At the same time they also fuse with the nasal septum. The posterior portions of the lateral processes do not become ossified and form the soft palate and uvula.[30]

Failure of fusion results in the condition of cleft palate and the degree of failure can vary considerably. The resulting intercommunication of both nasal and oral cavities leads to serious phonation problems and frequent infections which include the middle ear. Since normal swallowing depends upon juxtaposition of tongue and palate, feeding is a real problem during infancy.

The anlagen of the sinuses are first found during the third fetal month when the face is assuming some definitive characteristics. Although present at birth, major growth and development is postnatal (Fig 12–2). Their presence is very influential in facial growth. In the neonate the maxillary sinuses and ethmoid cells are so small that radiologic identification is virtually impossible. The frontal sinuses originate, as do the maxillary sinuses, by the

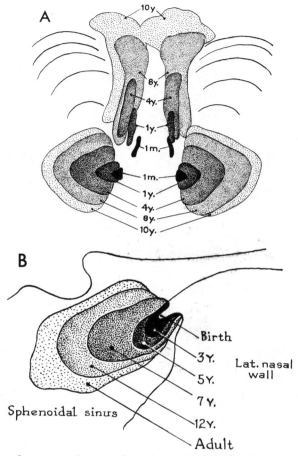

Fig 12–2.—A, composite drawing showing changes in size and shape of maxillary and frontal sinuses during infancy and childhood; *m,* month; *y,* year. **B,** diagram illustrating postnatal growth of sphenoid sinus from birth to maturity. (Redrawn from Scammon in Abt's *Pediatrics;* from Caffey.[4]) *(Continued.)*

direct extension of nasal mucosa and growth takes place by further evagination and concurrent resorption of bone. On the average, the frontal sinuses are apparent on radiologic examination by age 3 years and extend upward to the orbital roof by 6 or 7 years. Maxillary sinuses can often be visualized by the end of the first year.[20]

At birth, pneumatization of the temporal bone has barely begun, and there is but a single cell, the mastoid antrum, in communication with the

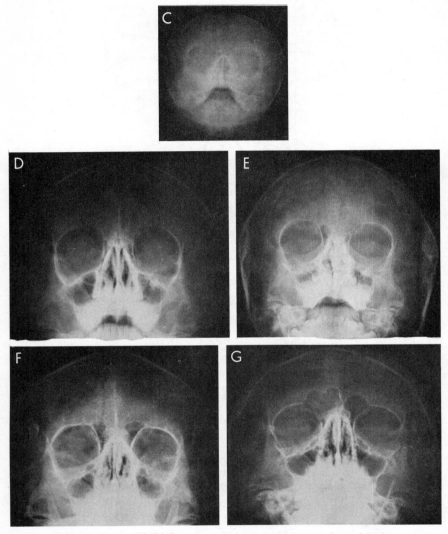

Fig 12–2 (cont.).—**C–G,** dorsoventral projections; sphenoid sinuses not visualized. **C,** newborn. **D,** 2 years. **E,** 4 years; definite budding upward from the ethmoids, the beginning of the frontal sinuses. **F,** 9 years; frontal sinuses have penetrated to a point above the supraorbital ridges. **G,** 12 years; sinuses are fully defined and pneumatization of zygoma appears as air-containing slits above maxillary antrums.

superior part of the middle ear. Further pneumatization occurs through outgrowth of air cells from the mastoid antrum into the solid bone which reach the tip by about 5 years.[4]

At birth the skull is large in proportion to the rest of the skeleton and the face is small compared to the cranium (see Fig 4–3). The small jaws and lack of development of paranasal sinuses account for the apparent disproportion.

Growth of the cranial vault is rapid during infancy and early childhood, though at a constantly decelerating rate. The mechanism that produces normal suture closure and cessation of neurocranial growth is poorly understood. Spreading of the sutures, due to increased intracranial pressure, can occur until late adolescence when final ossification takes place. Premature closure (synostosis) of the sutures may be congenital and leads to some bizarre head shapes. The more common ones include: scaphocephaly associated with the sagittal suture, oxycephaly with the coronal suture and microcephaly with multiple sutures. Often these are found in combination with other anomalies.[34]

Skull bones are soft at birth and remain so through early infancy. The asymmetry of the head from molding at delivery will be self-limiting. Congenital torticollis and persistent positioning of an infant may result in some flattening of the cranial vault which usually disappears, or is greatly modified, if normal growth follows.

The inclination of the sutures determines the direction of growth of the maxilla, which is forward and downward (Fig 12–3). Remodeling and appositional bone growth result from enlargement of the maxillary and frontal sinuses and the alveolar ridges and cause the eventual mature facial contour.

Fig 12–3.—Paired parallel sutures of nasomaxillary complex. The resultant vector of growth at these sutures is downward and forward in a direction similar to the growth vector of the mandible.

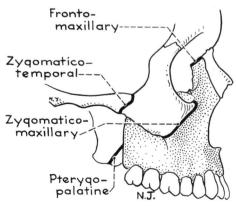

TABLE 12–1.—PERCENTAGE OF ADULT FACIAL AND CRANIAL
DIMENSIONS ACHIEVED AT DIFFERENT AGE LEVELS

AGE, YR	CRANIUM OF ADULT DIMENSIONS				FACE OF ADULT DIMENSIONS			VOLUME RATIO CRANIUM: FACE
	WIDTH	HEIGHT	LENGTH	BIZYGO-MATIC WIDTH	BIGONIAL WIDTH	HEIGHT	LENGTH	
0				56		38	40	8:1
2	86	92	86	80		68	70	5:1
6	92	96	90	83	83	80	80	3:1
12	98	99	96	90	93	89	87	2.5:1
			max. attained by 15 yr					
18	100	100	100	100	100	100	98	2:1

In the newborn infant the mandible is poorly developed with small alveolar processes, short rami and short condyles. The main growth center of the mandible is in the condyles. It is interesting to note that, unique to the human, the deep portion of the condyle has endochondral bone formation while its outer layers are membranous. Growth results in an increase in overall mandibular length as well as increase in height and width of the rami. As with the maxilla, the vector of growth is forward and downward. In both the upper and lower alveolar processes, the teeth develop at a rapid rate and their size has considerable influence on the pattern of growth. With increasing age the mental region of the mandible becomes more prominent resulting in a well-developed chin in the adult.

The varying speeds with which each dimension of the face and cranial vault is accomplished are given in Table 12–1. It can be seen that cranial size is completed much earlier than any portion of the face.[24]

Growth of the Teeth

The entire process by which a human being gets his teeth constitutes a highly interesting interaction of the ectodermal and mesodermal tissues throughout the early years of life.

Precisely, the basal layer of cells of the stratified squamous epithelium lining the oral cavity begins to proliferate rapidly about the 34th day of embryonic life and develops a ridge along the free margins of the jaws, the dental lamina. About the sixth week of intrauterine life 10 ovoid swellings appear at intervals about this ridge of ectodermal tissue, the tooth buds of the 10 primary teeth (Fig 12–4, left). Continuing rapid proliferation of the epithelial cells leads to the development of a budlike "invasion" of the underlying mesodermal connective tissue. A concomitant stimulation of this embryonic connective tissue leads to a rapid proliferation of its cells, which produces the dental papilla, the organ responsible later for the formation of

Fig 12–4.—Left, section through mouth of human embryo about 6 weeks old. Opposing collections of cells in upper and lower jaws are the beginnings of primary tooth buds. Invagination has already started. *T,* tongue; *A,* arch of mandible; *UJ,* upper jaw; *LJ,* lower jaw. **Right,** section through developing tooth—advanced "bell stage"—in fetal mandible at about 4 months. By the time of birth the crowns of all 20 primary (deciduous) teeth are in the process of calcification and enough inorganic calcium has been deposited to permit their detection on x-ray films (see Fig 12–8). *CT,* connective tissue of mandible; *OEE,* outer enamel epithelium; *SR,* stellate reticulum; *SI,* stratum intermedium; *IEE,* inner enamel epithelium; *DP,* dental pulp. It should be remembered that both primary (deciduous) and secondary (permanent) teeth are fully formed and their crowns calcified months to years before they erupt.

the dentin and pulp. The continued proliferation of the epithelium produces a caplike enamel organ surrounding the outer end of the dental papilla.

Further proliferation of the epithelial cells at the deep margins of the cap leads to the development of a bell-shaped enamel organ (Fig 12–4, right). The innermost layer of cells (the interior of the bell) later will produce the specialized tall, hexagonal, columnar cells, the ameloblasts, which will lay down the enamel matrix. A large portion of the dental papilla becomes enclosed in this invaginated bell, and the outermost layer of its peripheral cells then undergoes differentiation to the tall, columnar odontoblasts. The basement membrane separating the layer of ameloblasts of the enamel organ from the odontoblasts of the dental papilla later becomes the dentoenamel junction of the calcified crown. The remaining embryonic connective tissue of the interior of the dental papilla becomes the dental pulp. The outer layer of enamel epithelium of the bell-like ectodermal invasion and the stellate cells which separate it from the inner specialized layer of ameloblasts begin to serve as a nutritive mechanism as soon as calcification begins. This occurs between the fourth and the sixth month of uterine life at the dentoenamel junctions of the 20 primary teeth. It then reduces to a thin layer of cells on the completion of the enamel, the reduced enamel epithelium. The remnants of the remaining ameloblasts degenerate to a thin, acellular, chitinous membrane on completion of the enamel, but the layer of odontoblasts remains around the periphery of the pulp as a permanent mechanism for the formation of secondary dentin.

Following the laying down of dentin and enamel, activity of the deepest margins of the invaginated bell (the epithelial root sheath) initiates the formation of the root or roots and molds their shape. Continued extension of the original ridgelike dental lamina lingually and distally leads similarly to a cycle of developmental events which produces the permanent teeth. The tooth germs of the succedaneous permanent teeth appear lingually to those of the primary teeth from the 5th month in utero (central incisors) to 10 months after birth (second bicuspids), and the tooth germs of the three permanent molars appear progressively distal to those of the second primary molar from 4 months of fetal life (first molar) to the 4th or 5th year of life (third molar).[17, 21, 26, 29]

With the development of the roots of the primary teeth the crowns move occlusally until the reduced enamel epithelium fuses with the oral epithelium, the epithelium over the tips of the cusps of the crowns degenerates and the crown gradually erupts into occlusion with its opponent from the opposite arch. The remnant of the inner layer of cells of the bell, now a thin degenerated membrane, the enamel cuticle, gradually wears away, and the sole remaining evidence of the original fetal invasion of ectodermal tissue, now returned to the oral cavity, is the enamel, without cells, without nerve supply, without blood supply, hence without any direct systemic connection. As a child grows the crowns of the permanent teeth develop, the roots of the primary teeth resorb, the permanent teeth, both succedaneous and molars, erupt, occlusion of the permanent teeth in the two arches establishes and the attrition of the enamel of the crowns begins.

This life cycle of dental histophysiologic events now may be summarized briefly into six periods for diagnostic purposes: (1) growth; (2) calcification and maturation; (3) eruption of primary teeth; (4) resorption of roots of primary teeth; (5) eruption of permanent teeth, and (6) attrition. The period of growth may be divided further into five distinct but overlapping periods of rapid change prior to the second period of the cycle, the period of calcification and maturation. These five periods are (1) initiation, the development of the dental lamina and tooth buds; (2) proliferation, the rapid growth of cells by which the initiated tooth develops through the stages of the bud, cap and bell, along with the concomitant changes of the dental papilla; (3) histodifferentiation, the development of the specialized cells, the ameloblasts and odontoblasts; (4) morphodifferentiation, the stage of development of final characteristic contour and size of the crowns of the various teeth, and (5) apposition, the deposition of the matrix of the enamel progressively outward along the length of the ameloblast from the dentoenamel junction. This activity terminates in the external contour of the crown and the deposition of the matrix of the dentin inward, an activity which reduces the size of the pulp by reducing the size of the pulpal chamber.[27, 28]

Factors Influencing Normal Tooth Growth and Development

Although the preceding description of normal dental histophysiologic events follows a known sequence, it tells nothing of the biologic factors which may influence the rate of development, the dimensions, the morphology, the number and the eruption sequence of the teeth.

Recent investigations have revised the chronology of the various events which make up the pattern of the development of the individual teeth. It should be of interest to one who would regularly observe the development in the oral cavity to be familiar with these factors and to understand the causes of seeming irregularities which may occur in the dynamic individual known as the "growing child."

There is considerable range of time in tooth development and eruption, as indicated in Tables 12–2 and 12–3. Although there is some correlation of advancement and retardation in both osseous and dental development, it is not a very close one. Calcification and eruption of teeth do occur at a slightly earlier age in girls than in boys but not to the same degree as in bony maturation.[11, 12] There are genetic influences in dental growth as exemplified by a closer correlation of time of calcification and eruption in siblings than in unrelated individuals. Also, within the boundaries of the United States, black children have slightly more advanced permanent tooth eruption than do whites. Although tooth development and eruption may be delayed, as in hypothyroidism, or advanced, as in the adrenogenital syndrome, endocrine influences are less marked and less reliable diagnostically in dental tissue than in osseous tissue.[10, 15]

Genetic factors are the major determinants of tooth size and morphology which vary distinctly in different population groups. Tooth morphology and size play an important role in the etiology of malocclusions. It has been suggested that in population areas where there is considerable mixture of

TABLE 12–2. — CHRONOLOGY OF DEVELOPMENT OF THE HUMAN DENTITION*

PRIMARY DENTITION

TOOTH	CALCIFICATION BEGINS MAXILLA	MANDIBLE	CROWN COMPLETED MANDIBLE (MO)	MAXILLA (MO)	ERUPTION MAXILLA (MO)	MANDIBLE (MO)	EXFOLIATION MAXILLA (YR)	MANDIBLE (YR)
Central incisor	14 wk in utero	$14\frac{1}{2}$ wk in utero	$1\frac{1}{2}$	$2\frac{1}{2}$	$9\frac{1}{3}$	$7\frac{1}{2}$	6–7	6–7
Lateral incisor	16 wk in utero	$16\frac{1}{2}$ wk in utero	$2\frac{1}{2}$	3	11	$13\frac{1}{4}$	7–8	7–8
Cuspid	17 wk in utero	17 wk in utero	9	9	$19\frac{1}{2}$	$19\frac{2}{3}$	10–12	9–12
1st molar	5 wk in utero	$15\frac{1}{2}$ wk in utero	6	$5\frac{1}{2}$	$15\frac{2}{3}$	16	9–11	9–11
2d molar	19 wk in utero	18 wk in utero	11	10	28	$26\frac{1}{2}$	10–12	10–12

PERMANENT DENTITION

TOOTH	CALCIFICATION BEGINS MAXILLA	MANDIBLE	CROWN COMPLETED MAXILLA (YR)	MANDIBLE (YR)	ERUPTION MAXILLA (YR)	MANDIBLE (YR)	ROOT COMPLETED MAXILLA (YR)	MANDIBLE (YR)
Central incisor	3–4 mo	3–4 mo	$4\frac{1}{2}$	$3\frac{1}{2}$	7–$7\frac{1}{2}$	6–$6\frac{1}{2}$	10–11	$8\frac{1}{2}$–10
Lateral incisor	10–12 mo	3–4 mo	$5\frac{1}{2}$	4–$4\frac{1}{2}$	8–$8\frac{1}{2}$	$7\frac{1}{4}$–$7\frac{3}{4}$	10–12	$9\frac{1}{2}$–$10\frac{1}{2}$
Cuspid	4–5 mo	4–5 mo	$5\frac{1}{2}$–$6\frac{1}{2}$	$5\frac{1}{2}$–6	11–$11\frac{2}{3}$	$9\frac{3}{4}$–$10\frac{1}{4}$	$12\frac{1}{2}$–15	12–$13\frac{1}{2}$
1st premolar	$1\frac{1}{2}$–$1\frac{3}{4}$ yr	$1\frac{3}{4}$–2 yr	$6\frac{1}{2}$–$7\frac{1}{2}$	$6\frac{1}{2}$–7	10–$10\frac{1}{3}$	10–$10\frac{3}{4}$	$12\frac{1}{2}$–$14\frac{1}{2}$	$12\frac{1}{2}$–14
2d premolar	2–$2\frac{1}{4}$ yr	$2\frac{1}{4}$–$2\frac{1}{2}$ yr	7–$8\frac{1}{2}$	7–8	$10\frac{3}{4}$–$11\frac{1}{4}$	$10\frac{3}{4}$–$11\frac{1}{2}$	14–$15\frac{1}{2}$	$14\frac{1}{2}$–15
1st molar[17]	32 wk in utero	32 wk in utero	4–$4\frac{1}{2}$	$3\frac{1}{2}$–4	6–$6\frac{1}{3}$	6–$6\frac{1}{4}$	$9\frac{1}{2}$–$11\frac{1}{2}$	10–$11\frac{1}{2}$
2d molar	$2\frac{1}{2}$–3 yr	$2\frac{1}{2}$–3 yr	$7\frac{1}{2}$–8	7–8	$12\frac{1}{4}$–$12\frac{3}{4}$	$11\frac{3}{4}$–12	15–$16\frac{1}{2}$	$15\frac{1}{2}$–$16\frac{1}{2}$
3d molar	7–9 yr	8–10 yr	12–16	12–16	$20\frac{1}{2}$	20–$20\frac{1}{2}$	18–25	18–25

*From several sources, see text.

TABLE 12–3. — ERUPTION AGES (MONTHS) FOR PRIMARY TEETH*

PERCENTILES	EARLY MIN.	10	30	AVERAGE 50	70	LATE 90	100
Mandibular central incisor	4	5	6	7.8	9	11	17
Maxillary central incisor	5	6	8	9.6	11	12	15
Maxillary lateral incisor	6	7	10	11.5	13	15	21
Mandibular lateral incisor	6	7	11	12.4	14	18	27
Maxillary 1st molar	8	10	13	15.1	16	20	28
Mandibular 1st molar	8	10	14	15.7	17	20	27
Mandibular cuspid	8	11	16	18.2	19	24	29
Maxillary cuspid	8	11	17	18.3	20	24	29
Mandibular 2d molar	8	13	24	26.0	28	31	34
Maxillary 2d molar	8	13	24	26.2	28	31	34

*From Horowitz and Hixon.[14]

ethnic and racial groups, the incidence of malocclusions rises.[17, 23] There is also a definite difference in the average size of teeth between the sexes.[9]

Tooth agenesis, except in such conditions as ectodermal dysplasia, is relatively rare. The teeth most frequently missing in the permanent dentition are: third molars, mandibular bicuspids and maxillary incisors.[14]

The biologic event of permanent tooth eruption in the normal individual is probably more related to root age than to any environmental influence. Under unusual circumstances, exceptions to the above statement have been noted. Prolonged undernutrition may delay eruption of the permanent teeth. Premature loss of primary teeth due to caries may accelerate eruption (Fig 12–5).[13, 18, 25, 32]

Probably more relevant to future prevention of malocclusion problems is a normal sequence of appearance of the permanent dentition. Ordinarily the mandibular teeth erupt ahead of the maxillary except in the cuspid-bicuspid region (Table 12–4).

TABLE 12–4. — NORMAL SEQUENCE OF ERUPTION OF PERMANENT TEETH[19]

MANDIBLE	MAXILLA
1. First molar	2. First molar
3. Central incisor	5. Central incisor
4. Lateral incisor	6. Lateral incisor
7. Cuspid	8. First bicuspid
9. First bicuspid	10. Second bicuspid
11. Second bicuspid	12. Cuspid
13. Second molar	14. Second molar

The numbers indicate the usual sequence of eruption.

The Development of Occlusion

Development of Primary Occlusion

Interdentation of the primary teeth occurs before age 3 in most instances. There is less variability in occlusal relations in the primary than in the permanent dentition; however, some of the variations seen are of great clinical significance.

The mandibular denture occludes within the maxillary denture throughout its circumference. Most primary arches are ovoid, and there seems to be less variation in conformation than in permanent arches. Usually there is generalized spacing of all the anterior teeth, although there are somewhat wider spaces mesial to the maxillary cuspids and distal to the mandibular cuspids—termed primate spaces, since they are particularly prominent in the dentitions of certain lower primates.

Fig 12–5 (top).—Boy, age 7; periapical radiograph showing early eruption of permanent (bicuspid) teeth following premature loss of the primary molars due to carious abscesses. Note the very incomplete root formation.
Fig 12–6 (bottom).—Age 5 years; normal primary occlusion.

Contrary to popular opinion, the spacing between the primary teeth is not due to growth in width, for little increase in this dimension is seen. Spacing is either present or absent in primary dentitions; it does not increase with age.

It will be observed (Fig 12–6) that each mandibular tooth occludes one cusp anteriorly to the corresponding tooth in the maxilla. This is normal, and any deviations from this pattern are symptomatic of malocclusion. The most posterior surfaces of the second primary molars usually form a straight terminal plane. Interproximal cavities, sucking habits, or a deformity of the facial skeleton may cause development of a terminal plane with a step. This plane largely determines the occlusal relationship of the first permanent molars which erupt just behind the second primary molars.

The primary occlusion is usually very stable, showing fewer anomalies than either the mixed or the permanent dentition. The most typical malocclusion is that caused by a severe sucking habit. Many children engage in sucking habits during the first three years of life with little damage; still, such habits can give rise to severe problems in the development of occlusion. An anterior open bite is typical. An open bite may also lead to a perverted tongue thrust during the swallowing act, which may further compound the malocclusion as well as producing defects of speech. If the anteroposterior relationship remains normal and the habit ceases by age 4, the condition is self-correcting most of the time. If the mandibular teeth are occluding one cusp posteriorly, the problem seldom resolves itself and severe malocclusion may result in the permanent dentition.

Development of the Permanent Occlusion

1. MIXED DENTITION STAGE. — That period when both primary and permanent teeth are in the mouth is known as the *mixed dentition*. Those permanent teeth which follow into a place in the arch once held by a primary tooth are called *successional* or *succedaneous teeth*, e.g., incisors, cuspids, bicuspids. Those permanent teeth which erupt posteriorly to the primary teeth are termed *accessional teeth*.

With the arrival of the first permanent tooth begins the hazardous process of transition from the primary to the permanent dentition. During this period, which normally lasts from age 6 to 12 years, the dentition is highly susceptible to environmental changes.

2. FIRST MOLAR ERUPTION. — In most children the first molars are the first permanent teeth to erupt. Before their eruption the primary arches should display a straight terminal plane (vertical tangent touching the distal surfaces of both second primary molars) or, more favorably, a mesial step

(distal surface of the lower second primary molar mesial to the distal surface of the upper second primary molar).

3. INCISOR ERUPTION.—*a*) Mandibular incisors. The eruption of the first permanent molars is followed almost immediately by the eruption of the mandibular central incisors. They, in turn, are followed by the mandibular lateral incisors. Some have claimed that the incisors frequently erupt before the molars in the permanent dentition and that this predisposes to malocclusion. Lo and Moyers[19] found this sequence to occur so rarely that it has little significance. The mandibular incisors develop lingually to the resorbing roots of the primary incisors, the latter being moved labially as they are exfoliated. If the roots of the primary teeth are not properly resorbed, the permanent incisors may erupt into the oral cavity behind the primary incisors. Removal of the primary incisors allows the tongue to push the permanent incisors labially to their correct position. When the normal primary spacing is present, the permanent incisors erupt without showing crowding and attain good alignment. Lack of spacing in the primary anterior segment may be the result of a narrow alveolar arch. The permanent incisors, then, are more apt to be crowded on eruption.

b) Maxillary incisor eruption. The maxillary central incisors erupt just after the mandibular central incisors. They may also follow the lower lateral incisors. There is a marked change in incisal angulation with the eruption of the permanent central incisors, the almost vertical primary tooth being replaced by a permanent one with a decided labial inclination. The central incisors erupt with a slightly distal inclination and some space between them. This is diminished with the eruption of the lateral incisors and completely closed as the cuspids wedge their way into place.

The maxillary lateral incisors may experience more difficulty in assuming their normal position. As they erupt, they are often seen slightly labial to the central incisors. As the cuspid erupts, it releases its pressure against the root of the lateral incisor, permitting the latter to fall into line.

4. CUSPID AND BICUSPID ERUPTION.—The favorable development of occlusion in this region is largely dependent on two factors: proper tooth size–arch length ratio and maintenance of a desirable sequence of eruption.

a) Mandible. The most favorable eruption sequence in the mandible is cuspid, first bicuspid, second bicuspid. All three should precede the second molar.

If the teeth are too large for the alveolar space, the second bicuspid may have insufficient room and be forced to erupt lingually. A similar malocclusion is seen when the primary molars have been destroyed by caries or when they are exfoliated prematurely. The early loss or destruction of the primary molars permits the permanent molars to tip forward, decreasing the amount of space available for the cuspids and bicuspids.

b) Maxilla. The eruption sequence, it will be remembered, is different in the maxilla, i.e., first bicuspid, second bicuspid and cuspid. The maxillary anterior segment is not prone to collapse lingually, since it is supported by the mandibular arch. It is, however, very easily displaced labially, e.g., by thumbsucking or a tongue thrust.

When the maxillary primary molars are lost prematurely, the cuspid is blocked out of position labially. Extreme labial malpositioning of maxillary cuspids and lingual malpositioning of mandibular second bicuspids are often signs of the same problem—insufficient space. The malocclusion varies with the jaw because of the difference in eruption sequence. In each instance the last tooth to erupt in front of the first molar is the tooth forced out of position.

5. SECOND MOLAR ERUPTION.—The second molars should erupt after all teeth anterior to them are in position, the mandibular tooth preceding the maxillary.

6. THIRD MOLAR ERUPTION.—The third molars erupt so late that they are almost solely a problem of the adult. It has been contended that the eruption of the third molars forces the dentition forward, causing crowding of the teeth, but the evidence to support this theory is unconvincing.

The Origin of Malocclusion

Malocclusions are of three general types: skeletal or osseous (genetic), dental and functional, or muscular.

1. The mixing of races seen on this continent has resulted in many genetic combinations not favorable to the production of harmonious facial development. Many malocclusions are due to unfavorable or disharmonious bone growth. The commonest problems are mandibular retrognathism, mandibular hypertrophy, and asymmetry of the face. In addition there may be insufficient bony support for the dentition, i.e., the bones are not big enough for the teeth, or the teeth are too large for their bony base.

2. Improper care of the primary dentition may result in premature loss of deciduous teeth, permitting drifting of the permanent teeth or tooth buds (Fig. 12–7). Pernicious pressure habits can also cause malpositioning of teeth.

3. A malrelationship of the mandible causes malocclusion. Most functional malrelationships of the mandible are due to reflexes learned to avoid malpositioned teeth. For example, functional mandibular retraction is frequently seen when the maxillary dental arch is narrowed. The muscles sim-

Fig 12–7.—Periapical radiographs, showing premature loss of the primary second molars, which has allowed the permanent molars to shift in a forward direction, causing the permanent second biscuspid to be impacted in their line of eruption.

ply retrude the lower jaw to permit occlusion with a wider portion of the maxilla.

It is thus seen that not all malocclusions have a similar etiologic history. Because of the variance in origin, the prognoses are not the same. It is much easier to correct tooth malpositions and functional malrelationships due to muscle reflexes than it is to overcome inherent genetic patterns of bone growth. Early diagnosis is the first step in minimizing the effects of malocclusion.

The Teeth in Clinical Appraisal of a Child's Development

For clinical estimation of dental ages Table 12–2 can be used in connection with an examination of the child's mouth to ascertain the number of erupted and exfoliated teeth along with a careful examination of the development of the posterior mandibular teeth as exhibited in a size no. 2 posterior bitewing or in a lateral jaw radiograph.

Average dental development of children, beginning with the full-term infant at birth, is shown in Figures 12–8 through 12–13 and summarized in Table 12–5.

Nolla[25] recently completed a serial radiographic study (by yearly increments of growth) of 25 boys and 25 girls at the University of Michigan's

---

Figs 12–8 to 12–13.—Stages in development and eruption of teeth. To a certain extent a physician, like a veterinarian, can tell the age of his patient by looking at the teeth. X-rays help in this estimation.

Fig 12–8 (top left).—Newborn; lateral radiograph of jaws. Enough inorganic calcium has matured in crowns of all 20 primary teeth so that incisal and occlusal surfaces are outlined.

Fig 12–9 (top right).—Age 16 months; lateral radiograph of jaws. Primary first molars have erupted (12–14 months); primary cuspids are erupting, and crowns of their permanent successors are about one-fifth calcified. Primary second molars will erupt to complete preschool dentition at 20–24 months. Crowns of first and second bicuspids (position indicated by radiolucent follicles between roots of lower primary molars) have not begun to calcify, and crowns of first permanent molars are about one-third calcified.

Fig 12–10 (bottom left).—Girl, age 4 years; lateral jaw radiograph. Primary second molars have erupted to complete preschool dentition (2–2¹/₂ years). Crown of permanent first molar has completed calcification; root beginning. Crown of first bicuspid beneath roots of primary first molar is about one-third calcified, and calcification of the crown of the second bicuspid and permanent second molar has begun.

Fig 12–11 (bottom, left center).—Boy, age 6; lateral jaw radiograph. Permanent first molar is erupting into occlusion. Crowns of both bicuspids are nearing completion of calcification. Crown of permanent second molar is two-thirds complete in calcification.

Fig 12–12 (bottom, right center).—Boy, age 10; lateral jaw radiograph. The lower primary cuspid and primary first molar have exfoliated, and the permanent cuspid and permanent first bicuspid are erupting. Normally the permanent cuspid erupts ahead of the first bicuspid in the mandible. Note that the apical ends of the erupting permanent teeth have not completed their full development.

Fig 12–13 (bottom right).—Age 11¹/₂ years; lateral jaw radiograph. Both lower bicuspids have erupted, and the permanent second molar has begun to erupt. The apical ends of the permanent first molar have completed their development. Note the congenitally missing maxillary permanent second bicuspid.

TABLE 12–5.—RADIOGRAPHIC DETERMINATION OF SERIAL DEVELOPMENT OF MANDIBULAR POSTERIOR TEETH

AGE LEVEL	CORONAL CALCIFICATION	ERUPTED	COMPLETION OF ROOTS
Birth	*Primary* 3/5, incisors 1/3, cuspids Tips of cusps calcified in united ring, 1st molar Tips of cusps calcified, still isolated in separate centers of calcification, 2d molar *Permanent* Sometimes traces in tips of mesial cusps, 1st molars	None	None
9-10 mo	*Primary* Enamel completed all teeth *Permanent* Tips of cusps calcified still isolated, 1st molars Trace of incisal edges, centrals, laterals Tips of cuspids	*Primary* Centrals Laterals	None
1 yr	*Permanent* (balance of table) Cusps united in ring, 1st molars 1/5-1/4, centrals, laterals 1/7-1/6, cuspids	Add *primary* 1st molars	None
16-18 mo	1/3, 1st molars 1/4-1/3, centrals, laterals 1/6-1/5, cuspids Tip of cusp, some 1st bicuspids	Add *primary* cuspids	*Primary* Centrals and laterals completed
2 yr	1/2-2/3, 1st molars 2/5-1/2, centrals, laterals 1/4, cuspids Tips of cusps, all 1st bicuspids Tips of cusps, some 2d bicuspids	Add *primary* 2d molars	None added

Age			
2½-3 yr	Completed, 1st molars 2/3, centrals, laterals 3/8, cuspids 1/2, 1st bicuspids 1/6, 2d bicuspids Trace, tips mesial cusps, 2d molars	Add none	*Primary* 1st and 2d molars completed Some cuspids completed
4½ yr	3/4-5/6, 1st bicuspids 5/8-3/4, 2d bicuspids 5/8-3/4, cuspids 1/3, 2d molars	Add none	*Primary* All cuspids completed *Permanent* (balance) 1/3, 1st molars 3/8-1/2, 1st molars
6-7 yr	Completed, centrals and laterals Completed, 1st, 2d bicuspids, cuspids 2/3, 2d molars	*Permanent* (balance) 1st molars Centrals Add laterals	1/2-2/3, 1st molars 6/7, centrals 3/4, laterals Variable amt., 1st, 2d bicuspids, cuspids
7-8 yr	Completed, 2d molars Trace tips of cusps, some 3d molars		Completed centrals, laterals, 1st molars
9-10 yr	Beginning calcification, most 3d molars	Add most cuspids, many 1st bicuspids	1/2, 1st bicuspid 1/3, 2d bicuspid 1/4, 2d molar
12 yr	1/4-5/6, 3d molars	Add 2d bicuspids, most 2d molars	Completed, many cuspids, 1st bicuspids 2/3, 2d bicuspids 1/3, 2d molars

TABLE 12-6, A.—AGE NORMS FOR MANDIBULAR TEETH FOR BOYS*

AGE	CENTRAL INCISOR 1/1	LATERAL INCISOR 2/2	CUSPID 3/3	1ST BICUSPID 4/4	2D BICUSPID 5/5	1ST MOLAR 6/6	2D MOLAR 7/7	3D MOLAR 8/8	ALL TEETH EXCL. 3D MOLAR	ALL TEETH INCL. 3D MOLAR
4	71.5	68.6	42.7	34.8	20.4	64.4	20.8	0	323.2	323.2
5	75.5	71.9	51.5	43.0	33.1	71.5	30.8	0	377.3	377.3
6	79.5	76.1	57.4	51.6	42.7	76.9	40.7	0	424.9	424.9
7	88.8	83.2	65.9	60.8	53.6	83.3	51.5	8.8	487.1	495.9
8	95.0	90.4	73.5	68.8	62.4	89.5	59.4	14.2	539.0	553.2
9	95.9	95.4	79.7	75.4	70.3	94.5	66.8	18.1	578.0	596.1
10	98.5	98.5	85.5	81.1	76.5	97.9	73.2	20.9	611.2	632.1
11	100.0	100.0	90.9	87.8	83.4	99.0	78.9	27.6	640.0	667.6
12	100.0	100.0	95.8	94.1	89.5	99.5	84.6	35.2	663.5	698.7
13	100.0	100.0	98.5	96.9	93.7	100.0	89.3	44.9	678.4	723.3
14	100.0	100.0	99.5	98.8	96.5	100.0	93.9	53.9	688.7	742.6
15	100.0	100.0	100.0	100.0	99.0	100.0	96.6	62.8	695.6	758.4
16	100.0	100.0	100.0	100.0	100.0	100.0	99.9	71.1	699.9	771.0
17	100.0	100.0	100.0	100.0	100.0	100.0	100.0	76.1	700.0	776.1
18	100.0	100.0	100.0	100.0	100.0	100.0	100.0	79.3	700.0	779.3

*Note: 0-100 = percentages of tooth development; at 60% crown is complete.

TABLE 12–6, B.—AGE NORMS FOR MANDIBULAR TEETH FOR GIRLS*

AGE	CENTRAL INCISOR 1/1	LATERAL INCISOR 2/2	1ST CUSPID 3/3	1ST BICUSPID 4/4	2D BICUSPID 5/5	1ST MOLAR 6/6	2D MOLAR 7/7	3D MOLAR 8/8	ALL TEETH EXCL. 3D MOLAR	ALL TEETH INCL. 3D MOLAR
4	69.3	66.9	56.5	39.1	28.6	70.2	26.7	0	357.3	357.3
5	75.5	71.7	61.8	50.5	38.3	74.4	39.4	0	411.6	411.6
6	84.5	79.2	67.1	60.2	47.1	80.3	50.3	23.5	468.7	492.2
7	93.4	86.0	72.4	67.2	57.6	86.1	60.4	18.8	523.1	541.9
8	98.8	94.7	77.9	72.9	65.6	92.7	67.2	21.1	569.8	590.9
9	100.0	99.5	83.4	79.6	73.2	98.2	73.5	23.2	607.4	630.6
10	100.0	100.0	90.4	84.8	79.2	99.7	78.6	32.9	632.7	665.6
11	100.0	100.0	96.4	91.7	85.0	100.0	82.6	37.7	655.7	693.4
12	100.0	100.0	99.7	97.1	91.9	100.0	88.6	47.7	677.3	725.0
13	100.0	100.0	100.0	100.0	93.7	100.0	95.0	58.5	688.7	747.2
14	100.0	100.0	100.0	100.0	93.8	100.0	97.4	65.6	691.2	756.8
15	100.0	100.0	100.0	100.0	96.5	100.0	97.8	69.9	694.3	764.2
16	100.0	100.0	100.0	100.0	99.7	100.0	98.7	75.6	698.4	774.0
17	100.0	100.0	100.0	100.0	100.0	100.0	99.0	80.3	699.0	779.3
18	100.0	100.0	100.0	100.0	100.0	100.0	100.0	80.5	700.0	780.5

*Note: 0–100 = percentages of tooth development; at 60% crown is complete.

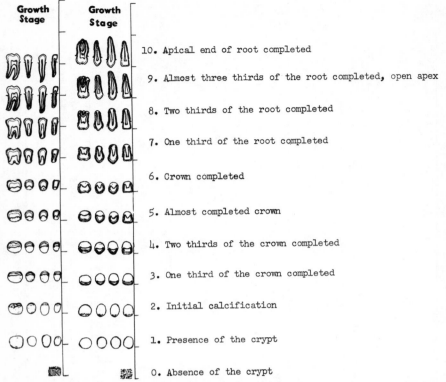

Growth Stage		Growth Stage		
			10.	Apical end of root completed
			9.	Almost three thirds of the root completed, open apex
			8.	Two thirds of the root completed
			7.	One third of the root completed
			6.	Crown completed
			5.	Almost completed crown
			4.	Two thirds of the crown completed
			3.	One third of the crown completed
			2.	Initial calcification
			1.	Presence of the crypt
			0.	Absence of the crypt

Drawings made from roentgenograms of developing permanent teeth, to be studied in conjunction with Tables 12–6, A and B. Beginning with stage 1 (of Nolla's 10 stages assigned to developing teeth), in which the tooth bud is hardly more than a ring of cells, the tooth develops to stage 10, where it is complete. Note that the crown develops much sooner than the root, as seen in Figure 12–9, where the 6-year molar has a well-developed crown but no roots as yet. A value of 60 (6 in the drawings) indicates that the crown of the particular tooth is complete.

Elementary School (Tables 12–6, A and B). Beginning her study of the 50 children at 4 years (48 months) of age, Nolla computed the percentage of completion for the teeth through 18 years (216 months). A value of 60.0 indicates that development of the crown is complete (see values in boldface). Girls, it will be noted, are about one year ahead of boys in dental development but advance at the same annual rate.

Returning to the chronology of dentition (see Table 12–2), a few examples may be cited to illustrate the use of such a table. Individual children may be expected to vary considerably from any average established for a population, and for this reason considerable advance or retardation should be permitted as a range of normality. The premature infant may be expected to be considerably retarded if development is measured from date of birth, whereas the full-term infant with a family history of early dental development may be born with the two mandibular incisors erupted or erupting. Unless these two prematurely erupted incisors are obviously malformed supernumerary teeth and the diagnosis is confirmed radiographically, they should *not* be extracted.

If one who is studying a radiograph of a child's mandible notes that the crown of the first permanent molar is completed, and the crowns of the second bicuspid and the second permanent molar have just begun to exhibit calcification, he concludes that this child has a dental age of $2^1/_2$–3 years. If a mother asks whether a severe illness at age 6 years caused the irregular, hypoplastic incisal edges of her daughter's newly erupted centrals, the answer obviously is "No"; the incisal edges of the mandibular incisors are calcified by 16–18 months and the entire crowns by 4–5 years.

The Dental Anomalies

Interference during any stage of the growth of teeth, as well as interferences during the periods of calcification, the eruption or the exchange of the two dentitions, will lead to anomalous development which may involve one or more teeth but not necessarily the child's occlusion. For example, a disturbance during initiation may produce too many or too few teeth; during proliferation, extra cusps or roots, twinning, fusion and dental tumors; during histodifferentiation, odontomas and dentinogenesis imperfecta (opalescent dentin); during morphodifferentiation, peg-shaped teeth, Hutchinson's incisors and unusually small or unusually large teeth; during apposition, hypoplasia of tetany, rickets and heredity; during calcification, mottled enamel, vital staining and amelogenesis imperfecta, and during eruption, impaction, ectopy and ankylosis. Most of these anomalies gradually are being shown to exhibit a familial pattern of development.

Probably a more useful classification of the dental anomalies can be made on the basis of their characteristic appearance rather than on the basis of the period of initiation. These deviations in development, then, may be grouped as anomalies of number, of shape, of texture and of position. It would be beneficial to the children concerned if most of these anomalies could be detected early and the children referred promptly to a children's dentist or an orthodontist.

1. ANOMALIES OF NUMBER. —Of the missing teeth, the absence of maxil-

lary lateral incisors (Fig 12–14) and the mandibular second bicuspids most frequently is detected in children. The absence of either creates a problem of occlusion. Supernumerary teeth occur most often in the midline of the maxillary arch, where they interfere with eruption and alignment of the normal incisors (Fig 12–15). Extra teeth may accompany cleidocranial dysostosis.

A few children exhibit the bizarre condition known as ectodermal dysplasia, in which many surface structures may be involved as a syndrome of ectodermal deviations. Along with variations or complete absence of sweat and sebaceous glands, adult hair, eyebrows, eyelashes and fingernails, the teeth may be totally or partially missing. Those anterior teeth which do erupt are characteristically conoid.

2. ANOMALIES OF SHAPE. — Not infrequently the maxillary laterals fail to

Fig 12–14 (top).—Periapical radiograph showing a maxillary midline supernumerary tooth which remained unerupted.

Fig 12–15 (bottom).—Occlusal radiograph illustrating how congenitally missing maxillary lateral incisors permit a wide diastema to remain between the maxillary central incisors.

develop as typical incisors but erupt as small, cone-shaped, "peg" teeth. The crowns of the late-maturing bicuspids may not even resemble teeth; hutchinsonian permanent incisors and molars have been described in many textbooks; a number of anterior permanent teeth may erupt malformed from a traumatic episode which has involved the primary predecessor; attention already has been called to the conoid teeth that accompany ectodermal dysplasia, and it should be kept in mind that extensive irradiation of the jaws during the period of growth of the teeth halts dental development at the particular level reached.

3. ANOMALIES OF TEXTURE. —Two hereditary anomalies of development alter the structure of teeth in a unique pattern. One anomaly, involving odontoblasts, produces dentinogenesis imperfecta, or hereditary opalescent dentin. Most of the affected teeth exhibit a peculiar amber color, abrade early and extensively and, radiographically, exhibit roots which appear rather small for their crowns but with highly calcified or completely missing pulpal chambers and root canals. Amelogenesis imperfecta, on the other hand, involves maldevelopment by the ameloblasts. Such teeth develop and erupt (infrequently they fail to erupt) with very little, imperfectly formed enamel. The frail enamel stains and abrades or wears until the teeth become quite disfiguring. The only solution usually is extraction of the teeth and preparation of complete dentures early in life, or a full mouth reconstruction. Rarely are either of these conditions accompanied by caries; in fact, most of the involved members of the families studied at the School of Dentistry of the University of Michigan have submitted samples of saliva which provide negative counts of lactobacilli.

Staining and hypoplasia of tooth enamel has long been recognized as a hazard of tetracycline therapy in infancy and early childhood. The staining occurs only if the drugs are used during the period of crown calcification and the degree is related to the amount used (frequency and dosage). To spare the more visible anterior teeth, tetracyclines should be avoided, whenever possible, during the first 6–7 years.[31]

4. ANOMALIES OF POSITION. —Radiographic examination frequently detects a first permanent molar erupting ectopically into the distal roots of the second primary molar. Unless the dentist interferes at an early period, pressure of its crown results in resorption of the roots of the primary molar, premature exfoliation of that tooth and serious loss of space in the arch. In another type of anomalous development a number of children are found with the roots of the primary molars apparently ankylosed while the bony arches increase in their occlusal dimension, due to an elaboration of the alveolar bone which provides support for the developing permanent teeth. Such ankylosed primary molars actually have been found completely submerged

Fig 12–16.—Periapical radiograph showing an ankylosed primary second molar which is no longer at the occlusal level. Note also the congenitally missing permanent second bicuspid.

(Fig 12–16). A dental anomaly of position also accompanies the syndrome of craniocleidodysostosis; the primary teeth are retained into adulthood and the permanent teeth remain unerupted.

Since most of the dental anomalies which have been described have deleterious implications for a child's appearance or the alignment of his teeth, it appears pertinent to re-emphasize their early detection and the referral of the patient for treatment. It is of interest to note, too, that the anomalies of dental development may accompany anomalous development in other areas of a child's body. Amelogenesis imperfecta, for example, has been associated with failure of the permanent teeth to erupt, tremendous overgrowths of the fibrous tissue of the gingivae, degenerative macules of the retina and the annoying dermal condition, epidermolysis bullosa.

Certain other systemic pathologies may produce uncommon deviations in the growth and development of the dentition, such as overretention of the primary teeth, producing a very delayed eruption of the permanent teeth. This deviation may be seen in the mongoloid child (trisomy 21).

REFERENCES

1. Avery, J. K.: Compiled mimeographed material, Department of Oral Histology, School of Dentistry, University of Michigan.
2. Broadbent, B. H.: The face of the normal child, Angle Orthod. 7:209, 1937. (Report of the classic studies done in the growth of the face by the Bolton Foundation at Western Reserve University; a special cephalometric study.)
3. Brodie, A. G.: On the growth pattern of the human head from the third month to the eighth year, Am. J. Anat. 68:209, 1941.
4. Caffey, J.: *Pediatric X-Ray Diagnosis* (6th ed.; Chicago: Year Book Medical Publishers, Inc., 1972).
5. Friel, S.: The development of ideal occlusion of the gum pads and the teeth, Am. J. Orthod. 39:196, 1954.

6. Garn, S. M., and Lewis, A. B.: Relationship between sequence of calcification and the sequence of eruption of the mandibular molar and premolar teeth, J. Dent. Res. 36:992, 1957.

7. Garn, S. M., Lewis, A. B., and Polacheck, D. L.: Variability of tooth formation, J. Dent. Res. 38:135, 1959.

8. Finn, S. B.: *Clinical Pedodontics* (4th ed.; Philadelphia: W. B. Saunders Company, 1973).

9. Garn, S. M., Lewis, A. B., and Kerewsky, R. S.: Sex differences in tooth size, J. Dent. Res. 43:306, 1964.

10. Garn, S. M., Lewis, A. B., and Blizzard, R. M.: Endocrine factors in dental development, J. Dent. Res. (suppl.) 44:243, 1965.

11. Garn, S. M., Lewis, A. B., and Kerewsky, R. S.: Genetic, nutritional and maturational correlates of dental development, J. Dent. Res. (suppl.) 44:228, 1965.

12. Garn, S. M., Lewis, A. B., Kerewski, R. S., and Jegart, K.: Sex differences in intra-individual tooth size communalities, J. Dent. Res. 44:476, 1965.

13. Grøn, A.-M.: Prediction of tooth emergence, J. Dent. Res. 41:573, 1962.

14. Horowitz, S. L., and Hixon, E. H.: *The Nature of Orthodontic Diagnosis* (St. Louis: C. V. Mosby Company, 1966), Chapters 5 and 9.

15. Hurme, V. O.: Ranges of normalcy in the eruption of permanent teeth, J. Dent Child. 16:11, 1949.

16. Korf, S.: Eruption of permanent incisors following premature loss of their antecedents, J. Dent. Child. 32:39, 1965.

17. Kraus, B. S., and Jordan, R. E.: *The Human Dentition before Birth* (Philadelphia: Lea & Febiger, 1965), p. 109.

18. Lauterstein, A. M.: A cross sectional study in dental development and skeletal age, J. Am. Dent. Assoc. 62:161, 1961.

19. Lo, R. T., and Moyers, R. E.: Studies in the etiology and prevention of malocclusion: I. The sequence of eruption of the permanent dentition, Am. J. Orthod. 39:460, 1953.

20. Maresh, M. M.: Paranasal sinuses from birth to adolescence, Am. J. Dis. Child. 60:58, 1940.

21. Meredith, H. V.: Order and eruption for the deciduous dentition, J. Dent. Res. 25:43, 1946.

22. Meredith, H. V.: Relation between the eruption of selected mandibular permanent teeth and the circumpuberal acceleration in stature, J. Dent. Child. 26:75, 1959.

23. Moorrees, C. F. A.: *The Aleut Dentition* (Cambridge, Mass.: Harvard University Press, 1957).

24. Enlow, D. H.: *The Human Face, An Account of the Postnatal Development of the Craniofacial Skeleton* (New York: Harper & Row Publishers, Inc., 1968).

25. Nolla, C. M.: *The Development of the Permanent Teeth* (M. S. thesis [University of Michigan, Ann Arbor, 1952]).

26. Robinow, M., Richards, T. W., and Anderson, M.: The eruption of the deciduous teeth, Growth 6:127, 1942.

27. Turner, E. P.: The Growth and Development of the Teeth, in Davis, J. A., and Dobbing, J. (eds.): *Scientific Foundation of Paediatrics* (Philadelphia: W. B. Saunders Company, 1974).

28. Schour, I., and Massler, M.: Development and growth of teeth, in Orban, B. (ed.): *Oral Histology and Embryology* (St. Louis: C. V. Mosby Company, 1944).

29. Weinmann, J. P.: Eruption of the teeth, in Orban, B. (ed.): *Oral Histology and Embryology* (St. Louis: C. V. Mosby Company, 1944).

30. Moore, K. L.: *The Developing Human* (Philadelphia: W. B. Saunders Company, 1973).

31. Grossman, E. R., Walchek, A., and Freedman, H.: Tetracyclines and permanent teeth: Relation between dose and tooth color, Pediatrics 47:567, 1971.

32. Garn, S. M., Sandusky, S. T., Nagy, J. M., and Trowbridge, F. L.: Negrocaucasoid differences in permanent tooth emergence at a constant income level, Arch. Oral Biol. 18:609, 1973.

33. *An Assessment of the Occlusion of the Teeth of Children, 6–11 Years* (Washington, D.C.: U.S. Dept. Health, Education and Welfare, Public Health Service, 1973).

34. Smith, D. W.: *Recognizable Patterns of Human Malformation* (2d ed.; Philadelphia: W. B. Saunders Company, 1976).

13 / An Outline of Abnormal Growth

STRICTLY SPEAKING, any outline of abnormal growth must include almost all of the many congenital anomalies and dystrophies, for they represent abnormalities of growth. Our outline, however, is limited primarily to the aberrations of statural growth in infancy and childhood. Obesity also is discussed.

In the preceding chapters the major factors that influence normal growth have been considered. Much of our knowledge has resulted from studies of abnormal subjects. This chapter is included mainly to help the reader to a better understanding of the potentialities of growth and how growth may deviate from the usual pattern; it is not meant to be an exhaustive treatise.

Dwarfism

The schema in Figure 13–1 will suggest many possible causes of small stature, most of which are discussed in this chapter. Very often it is difficult if not impossible to designate the primary cause, and combinations of factors often exist, e.g., malnutrition and anemia. Some are difficult to evaluate in terms of degree of effectiveness, e.g., psychologic implications of lack of tender loving care (T.L.C. in the figure). The purpose of this diagram is to point out the multiplicity and diversity of etiologic conditions leading to retarded growth.

Some authors and most laypeople will make a distinction between the terms *dwarf* and *midget,* referring to the former as small but disproportioned and the latter as small and well proportioned in all physical aspects. No distinction will be made in this discussion.

Talbot[12] has used the term "dwarf" to designate any child moderately or conspicuously shorter than 90% of children in the community of the same chronologic age. Retarded growth may be due either to a slow rate or to an unusually short period of growth.[10, 11] The diagnosis of dwarfism will depend on a number of factors, one of the most important being the age of the child. The achondroplastic child would be placed in this category at an early age. An individual with Turner's syndrome would probably not be recognized as

Fig 13–1.—Conditions frequently leading to small stature.

being unusually short until late childhood or adolescence. In the person with the adrenogenital syndrome the first impression is of overgrowth; but as adolescence is approached short stature becomes prominent, unless proper therapy has been instituted earlier. The boy or girl who has a delayed onset of the adolescent growth spurt, often associated with some delay in osseous maturation, may be considered a "dwarf" by family or self until the mechanisms that set off the long-awaited adolescence finally begin to work.

The most common causes of short stature as seen in our clinic are listed below in the order of their frequency.

1. Delayed onset of adolescence (constitutional delay in growth)
2. Dwarfism secondary to severe chronic disease
3. Primordial (genetic)
4. Turner's syndrome (gonadal dysplasia)

5. No diagnosis established
6. Hypothyroidism
7. Hypopituitarism

In attempting to determine the etiology of retarded stature, a number of approaches may be necessary. Even after exhaustive studies, a definite conclusion may be impossible unless the child can be followed through his entire growth period.

HISTORY. — History and examination of the growth pattern followed in the past can be very helpful. Many syndromes are associated with small size at birth, including multiple births, many of the chromosomal abnormalities and intrauterine undernutrition. In congenital hypothyroidism (cretinism) a slow rate of growth may go unnoticed for several months, and is associated with a very placid personality, constipation and the delayed appearance of developmental milestones. Retardation of statural growth in Turner's syndrome may be so gradual that parents become aware of it only after several years. A past history of medications is important since some medications can have a deleterious influence on growth. The use of large amounts of glucocorticoids in conditions such as asthma or rheumatoid arthritis (Fig 13–2) can cause growth failure. Prolonged and continuous use of central nervous system stimulants, as in the hyperkinetic syndrome, can disturb the important sleep-growth hormone release pattern with resulting slowing of statural growth (Chapter 9). Hurler's syndrome, refractory rickets and a host of other metabolic diseases associated with short stature are among those with hereditary backgrounds. Investigation of relatives with unusual heights may be rewarding in establishing the origin of these genetic conditions. In the families of most children with delayed onset of puberty, a history of similar growth pattern is found in a sibling, parent or grandparent. Malnutrition, chronic and recurrent disease and physical abuse or neglect are diagnoses established more readily through the history than by other parts of the examination.

PHYSICAL EXAMINATION. — This must be carefully done, with special reference to measurements of dimensions or proportions and attention to details. The determination of body proportions (trunk-extremity length) will aid in the differential diagnosis of hypothyroidism with a high ratio, as compared to primordial dwarfism with a normal ratio. Small head circumference is an outstanding feature of the "bird-headed" dwarf, while a large head is characteristic of many patients with achondroplasia. Children with congenital heart disease or with metabolic abnormalities often appear chronically ill, in contrast to many cases of statural retardation with other causes where the child appears healthy and happy. Some diseases are associated with quite specific findings that help to identify them — e.g., webbing of the neck and

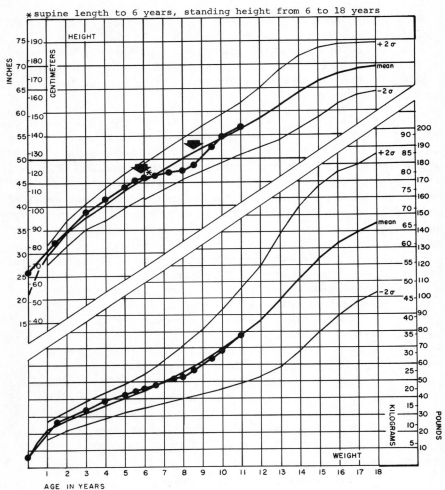

Fig 13–2.—Iatrogenic dwarfism of a temporary nature from corticosteroid treatment for rheumatoid arthritis. Normal development until shortly before his sixth birthday, when he developed low-grade fever and swelling and pain in both knees. Laboratory tests were negative. For approximately 3½ years large doses of corticosteroids (prednisone) were used, which were successful in relieving his symptoms but retarded statural growth and caused a cushingoid appearance. Note the recovery after withdrawal of the drug, with a short period of actual acceleration in growth rate until his former level was obtained. Recently an arthritic patient was seen who had been on corticosteroids from age 2 to 14 and whose height was only 45 in. at the latter age.

lymphedema of hands and feet in Turner's syndrome, short extremities and redundant skin in classic achondroplasia, ectodermal abnormalities (skin, hair, nails and teeth) in Hutchinson-Gilford syndrome, bowing and other deformities of the long bones in rickets of all types and the typical facies in cretinism, Hurler's syndrome, Cockayne's syndrome or the severe form of metaphysial dysostosis. Multiple anomalies are associated with the majority of the chromosomal abnormalities, frequently involving all three germinal layers.

ROENTGENOLOGIC EXAMINATION.—This may be limited or extensive enough to cover the entire skeleton and certain soft-tissue areas. Minimal examination should include hand and wrist films for "bone age." The most severe retardation is found in hypothyroidism, while less marked delay is present in hypopituitary dwarfing and Turner's syndrome. Often films of this area will add other information. Short metacarpals are characteristic of pseudohypoparathyroidism and of Turner's syndrome, while in Hurler's syndrome other changes occur which are pathognomonic. Skull films are useful in eliminating craniopharyngiomas which may cause growth retardation through hypothalamic dysfunction. In about 80% of cases there is abnormal intracranial calcification. In many bone diseases (Table 13–1) a complete skeletal examination may be necessary. Especially early in life, the findings may be subtle and difficult to interpret. When indicated, of course, studies of the heart, lungs, kidneys or other systems should be obtained.

LABORATORY EXAMINATION.—These will vary and depend upon the findings available from the history and physical examination. Anemia and severe renal disease can be rather promptly investigated without elegant equipment. Other systemic diseases may be more difficult to verify and require elaborate testing. Some of the endocrinopathies can be attacked directly; others, only by indirect means. A buccal smear or chromosome count is indicated in all girls of short stature. It must be remembered that not all patients with Turner's syndrome will have all the typical findings of the "textbook case." Tests for thyroid function are mandatory if bone maturation is relatively more delayed than statural growth. An increasing number of centers are now able to determine growth hormone levels. A single determination has little value. Presently used screening tests to determine whether further investigation of growth hormone synthesis is indicated include stimulation with estrogen, glucagon and L-dopa.[9] Gonadotropic hormone analysis has value after adolescence has begun. If growth hormone deficiency does exist, there is often an associated deficiency of one or more of the other pituitary hormones.

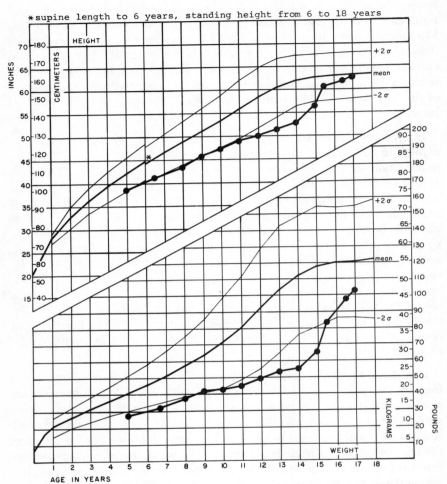

Fig 13-3.—Delayed adolescence in a girl. Normal delivery and birth weight of 7 lb 4 oz was followed by a slow but steady growth rate. General health was good. At age 12 a careful evaluation of her growth failure gave no clue to a possible cause. Significantly, at that time her "bone age" was estimated at 9 years, which equaled her "height age." Menses began at 15 years, which also had been true of her mother. (Growth charts used in Figures 13-2 to 13-11 based on Stuart and Meredith's data as described in Chapter 4.)

Constitutionally Delayed Growth

The most common type of small stature has been designated either as "delayed onset of adolescence" or "constitutionally delayed growth." It occurs in either sex, although boys are seen in clinics more often than girls. From infancy, most of these children will be smaller than their peers and make up the lower percentiles of the growth curves. Puberty and its associated growth spurt is delayed by 2–4 years. Bone age studies will indicate that the degree of maturation is compatible with the height but behind the chronologic age (Fig 13–3). In the majority of families a sibling or parent has followed a similar pattern of growth. The patient eventually attains a height which is commensurate with his or her genetic potential.

Bone Diseases

1. ACHONDROPLASIA (CLASSIC CHONDRODYSTROPHY). — This disorder follows a dominant type of inheritance or may occur sporadically. The primary pathologic changes are limited to parts of the skeleton which develop from cartilage. The cartilage cells appear to mature less rapidly than normal, and the patterns of growth are very irregular. The disturbance of proportion and the retardation of growth begin during intrauterine existence. The major clinical feature is the pronounced shortness of all the long bones of the extremities and consequent dwarfism. The skull is frequently large and indicates a mild degree of hydrocephalus, although seldom resulting in mental retardation. The nose is somewhat flattened. The development of the trunk is essentially normal, but lordosis is often prominent. The skin of the extremities is loose and forms folds. In the hyperplastic type the ends of the long bones widen in mushroom fashion.

There are probably mild or forme fruste variants; but in older individuals, not previously examined by roentgen techniques, these may be indistinguisable from other syndromes, such as multiple epiphysial dysplasia (see Table 13–1).

2. MORQUIO'S DISEASE (OSTEOCHONDRODYSTROPHY). — Inherited as a recessive trait, this syndrome is characterized by joint deformities with contractures becoming more severe with increasing age. With the exception of the skull, all bones are involved. There is decreased growth of articular cartilage, and secondary to this, there is retardation of metaphysial development with shortening of the long bones and "degenerative" joint changes. Shortening and gradual fixation of all vertebrae contribute to the dwarfing. Kyphosis and scoliosis are common. The mental development is normal. This is now included in the mucopolysaccharidoses.

TABLE 13-1.—DISEASES OF BONE CAUSING DWARFISM

DISEASE	GROWTH RETARDATION	PHYSICAL CHARACTERISTICS	ROENTGEN FINDINGS	CHEMICAL FINDINGS
Achondroplasia	+++	Short extremities, large head. Genetic dominant.	Tubular bones short and thick, often metaphysial flaring. All bones involved, including skull and pelvis.	Normal.
Morquio's disease, osteochondrodystrophy	++	Often obvious only after second or third year. All joints have increasing loss of mobility with age. Short neck, kyphosis, scoliosis. Genetic recessive.	All the epiphyses show irregularity, fragmentation, but shafts are normal.	Normal (mucopolysaccharides in urine in rare instances; see Gargoylism below).
Ollier's disease, dyschondroplasia, enchondromatosis	+ to +++	Dwarfing varies with the bones involved. First evident after infancy. Firm tumor of bone with growth failure in length of involved bone. Rarely genetic.	Radiolucent tumors, especially of hands, feet, long bones of arms and legs. Often asymmetrical.	Normal.
Albers-Schönberg disease, osteopetrosis congenita	+ to +++	Great variety. In most severe cases, death occurs in early childhood. Small, gracile habitus, delayed puberty. Hepato- and splenomegaly. Intracranial pressure and cranial nerve palsy occasionally. Genetic dominant and recessive types.	Dense and sclerotic bone, narrow marrow space, metaphysial widening. All bones involved.	Normal.
Osteogenesis imperfecta, fragilitas ossium	+ to +++	Considerable variety. Most severe form may have intrauterine fractures. Growth failure dependent upon frequency and severity of fractures. May resemble achondroplasia. Blue scleras. Genetically dominant.	Thin, delicate cortex of all bones. General decreased mineralization. Number of, and deformity from, fractures depends upon severity.	Normal.
Rickets (see text for various types)	0 to ++	The earlier present and longer the duration, the more severe growth retardation. In some of the renal forms, complete correction of growth may not occur. Some deformity, usually bowing, accompanies dwarfing. All bones involved. Sporadic and sex-linked dominant in refractory type.	Bone demineralized, trabeculae prominent, metaphysial end flattened or cupped and frayed appearance, increased distance between epiphyses and metaphysis.	Vitamin D deficient—low P, elevated alkaline phosphatase (serum). Refractory—low P, elevated alkaline phosphatase. Renal failure—high P, low Ca, acidosis, high BUN, etc.

Disorder		Clinical	Radiographic	Chemical
(...hypophosphatasia)	0 to +++	Several types or variations. The earlier manifested, the more severe. Earliest forms have marked deformities of extremities and skull, hypertension, renal failure, mental retardation. Mild forms resemble vitamin D deficient rickets. Genetic recessive.	Nearly complete to slight lack of ossification and calcification, premature closure of sutures in skull, widening of metaphyses.	Alkaline phosphatase very low or absent, high Ca (serum), phosphorylethanolamine (urine).
Gargoylism, Hurler's and Hunter's syndrome, dysostosis multiplex	+ to +++	Facial features coarse, progressive flexion deformities of joints (especially in hands), hepatomegaly, splenomegaly, corneal opacity, mental retardation, short life span. Genetic recessive, both autosomal and sex-linked.	Tubular bones shortened, thickened and epiphysial plates irregular. More marked in upper extremities. Phalanges and metacarpals become tapered. Skull is scaphoid and sella "boot"-shaped.	Mucopolysaccharides (urine).
Multiple epiphysial dysplasia, chondrodystrophia calcificans	+ to +++	The earlier manifested, the more severe the dwarfing and joint contractures. Mildest forms resemble mild achondroplasia. Genetic recessive.	Long bones, vertebrae and hands and feet involved. Stippled or punctate epiphyses in severe form, irregular and small epiphyses in mild form. Long bones short and slight thickening.	Normal.
Metaphysial dysostosis	+ to +++	Mild to severe forms. Dwarfing secondary to decreased bone growth plus deformities from bowing and contractures. Micrognathia and hypertelorism often present. Genetics unknown.	Metaphysial portion irregular, cystic, widened and showing varying degrees of deformity. Resembles severe rickets, but epiphyses are normal.	Normal (some reports of abnormalities have appeared but are not consistent).
Hyperparathyroidism	0 to +++	Short stature only in severe forms with long bone deformity, convulsions, mental retardation.	Bone demineralization, cysts, variable deformity of long bones.	Elevated Ca, low P, progressive renal failure.
Diastrophic dwarfism[40]	++ to ++++	Short extremities, hip dysplasia, equinovarus deformity of feet, short fingers, abducted thumbs, malformed ears.	Flattened epiphyses, short long bones, underdeveloped metacarpals and phalanges.	Normal.

3. OLLIER'S DISEASE (DYSCHONDROPLASIA).—There is an excess of hypertrophic cartilage at the growing ends of the long bones involved in this disease. Normal resorption does not take place, and linear growth is decreased. Single or multiple lesions may exist in an asymmetrical or symmetrical pattern. The degree of statural retardation depends entirely upon the severity of the condition, and some degree of asymmetry is usually present. Inspection and palpation, as well as roentgenology, disclose the nature of the tumors.[22]

4. ALBERS-SCHÖNBERG DISEASE (OSTEOPETROSIS).—In the more severe forms of this disease, death occurs in infancy. Statural growth is not markedly affected in most circumstances and probably is secondary to anemia, lowered resistance to disease and the influences of central nervous system damage due to some encroachment of the thickened skull. The primary defect is failure of the transformation of spongiosa to cancellous bone, and all bones assume a dense and thickened appearance. Growth failure probably resembles that found in any chronic illness. Splenomegaly and hepatomegaly are commonly found.

5. OSTEOGENESIS IMPERFECTA (FRAGILITAS OSSIUM).—This condition goes through a wide spectrum of bone changes from very severe, even causing fetal death, to mild, with the first appreciation of its existence only in adolescence. Dwarfism, if present, is the result of numerous fractures of the extremities with impactions, angulations and overlapping of fragments. Associated findings are: large cranial vault of extreme thinness (crane à rebord), poor dentition and blue scleras. Occasionally the appearance resembles achondroplasia, but x-ray examination corrects this impression. The pathologic change is failure of periosteal intramembranous bone formation due to lack of osteoblasts. The condition is inherited as a dominant trait in the less severe forms.

6. RICKETS.—The changes in the bone that are recognized by x-ray examination as rickets can be caused by a number of different conditions; but in all instances the essential feature is lack of calcification of the organic matrix of bone. In "ordinary" rickets there is a deficiency of vitamin D intake and a poor absorption of calcium from the gut, with a level of extracellular calcium too low to permit deposition in bone. Vitamin D may also promote reabsorption of phosphorus from the kidney, tending to balance the extracellular rise of calcium. In rickets the blood calcium levels are normal or low, the phosphorus levels are always low until healing is complete and the alkaline phosphatase levels are elevated in active disease. As we have seen (Chapter 8), the products of calcium and phosphorus must be above a certain

level, at a normal pH, before they are deposited in the bone. Even though osteoblastic activity is increased in rickets, as shown by the high alkaline phosphatase, it will not free enough phosphorus on the bone surface to exceed the solubility product of the calcium-phosphorus salts. The resulting softness of the bone leads to the characteristic deformities and consequent reduction in stature.

In "refractory rickets," tubular function of the kidney is altered so that normal reabsorption of phosphorus is not obtained. For this reason the descriptive term *phosphate diabetes* has been used. The blood level of phosphorus is often very low, often below 2.0 mg/100 ml while the calcium level is normal and the alkaline phosphatase is elevated. In some patients there is an associated aminoaciduria. Doses of vitamin D that cure ordinary rickets are not effective; but when large doses—often exceeding 500,000 units daily—are given, healing takes place.[6, 19] However, one seldom is able to obtain normal levels of phosphorus, and the patient usually has some growth retardation.

Rickets associated with renal acidosis will be described under organic disorders (p. 423).

7. HYPOPHOSPHATASIA. — This is an inborn error of metabolism in which the tissues cannot synthesize alkaline phosphatase. Structural changes in the bone occur which roentgenologically resemble severe rickets with resulting dwarfism. Variants of the disease exist which are related to age and severity. If symptoms appear in early infancy, hypercalcemia, hypertension, renal failure and mental retardation accompany the retarded growth, and life expectancy is low. In the milder forms that are first manifest at an older age, structural as well as biochemical findings are less severe. The presence of phosphorylethanolamine in the urine is unique to this disease. The pattern of inheritance is recessive.

8. METAPHYSIAL DYSOSTOSIS. — This bone dysplasia is known in 2 forms, which actually may represent different entities, since the cause is unknown. The more severe form results in extreme deformities of the bones, owing to softness. The other form often seems to appear later in childhood, and the deformities are less marked. X-ray examination gives typical findings, with involvement of the metaphysial areas and sparing of the epiphyses. The findings may resemble mild rickets or progress to severe widening and demineralization with severe bending.

9. DISEASES OF THE SPINE. — Infection, hemivertebrae and lytic lesions, such as tumors or Cushing's disease, may result in growth failure or actual collapse of vertebrae with reduction in stature.

Generalized Diseases

Many diseases of infants and children may cause either temporary or permanent retardation of growth. Only a few will be outlined here.

1. Galactosuria. — This is one of the so-called inborn errors of metabolism. The fault lies in the inability of the body to change galactose and lactose, the milk sugars, into glucose and glycogen. The enzymes necessary for this change are absent, and when these milk sugars reach high levels, they act as toxic agents. This is a relatively rare congenital disease accompanied by retarded growth, mental retardation and cataracts in the more severe cases. Hepatomegaly is often pronounced, owing to cirrhosis. As a result, glycogen storage is reduced, causing hypoglycemia of such degree that it may represent the most prominent physiologic abnormality and cause the major symptomatology. It is probably this disturbed carbohydrate physiology which accounts for the retarded growth. Galactosuria and galactosemia are universal findings in these cases.

2. Glycogen storage disease (von Gierke's disease). — There are several types of glycogen storage disease, all of which have certain clinical similarities. All are caused by the deficiency of specific enzymes which are necessary for either the storage of glycogen or for the mobilization of the glycogen stored in the liver, muscle, kidney and other organs. In one of the more common forms of the disease the error of metabolism is the relative absence of glucose-6-phosphatase, which permits glycogen conversion into glucose. Excessive glycogen storage results. In another type of the disease the debrancher enzyme necessary to break the complex chains of glycogen to simpler forms is absent. In yet another form an abnormal type of glycogen is produced which is resistant to normal glycogenolysis. Retarded growth characterizes all forms of glycogen storage disease, and hepatomegaly, cirrhosis and hypoglycemic symptoms may occur.

3. Diabetes mellitus. — Children with severe and poorly controlled diabetes may show a reduction in both height and weight.[3] In refractory diabetes dwarfism may be pronounced. With improved methods of control, including close attention to adequacy of diets, one rarely sees pronounced statural abnormalities in diabetic children today. Some authors have stated that the height of the average diabetic child is greater than normal at the time of onset of the disease, but other workers in the field have published contradictory figures.

4. Gargoylism (Hurler's syndrome, dysostosis multiplex). — This is another inborn error of metabolism resulting in storage of abnormal quantities of mucopolysaccharide in many organs. Pathologic changes in-

clude slow and irregular cartilage growth, hepatomegaly, splenomegaly, changes in the central nervous system with progressively lowered mentation, and often clouding of the cornea. Kyphosis is present in some patients. The name of the disease best describes the appearance of these unfortunate dwarfed children. Mucopolysaccharide can be found in the urine of many, but not all, of these patients, which suggests the possibility of different metabolic errors. Recently a number of patients have been described who show most of the characteristics of Morquio's disease (see section on this disease) but who excrete a mucopolysaccharide which differs from that found in gargoylism.[23, 24] In addition, some of the former patients demonstrate minimal corneal opacities. It is obvious that several different diseases can now be defined that formerly were included under a single category.

5. THE LIPOIDOSES.—There are a number of specific diseases in this group all of which are characterized by systematic disorders of fat metabolism with storage of abnormal lipid products in various organ systems. The more commonly encountered include Niemann-Pick's, Gaucher's and Fabry's diseases. Retarded physical growth is usually present and mental retardation is common, except in Fabry's disease. The prognosis for life is poor although patients with Gaucher's disease and Fabry's disease may become adults. Hypothalamic as well as pituitary involvement may be the cause of dwarfism.[14]

6. NUTRITIONAL PRIVATION.—Nutritional deficiency probably contributes to a large number of entities, as well as being a primary cause of stunted growth. As pointed out in previous chapters, the deprivation may occur in utero due to maternal malnutrition or placental malfunction, or it may occur after birth. The earlier it takes place, especially if severe in degree, the more likely it is to cause permanent growth retardation, probably by actual reduction in total cell number. If growth is impaired by an unsatisfactory diet, other poor socioeconomic factors are apt to be present. The result is an adult who is often less healthy than average, and in women there is an inferior obstetric record and the production of small babies who tend to grow to be small adults and perpetuate the trend.[42] Poor nutrition may further complicate other conditions. Fatigue and respiratory distress may interfere with adequate oral intake in congenital heart disease.[38] A number of children have been studied who suffered from psychologic deprivation associated with unusual eating patterns and extremely short stature. Growth hormone levels were abnormally low, even following usual methods of stimulation. Improving the environment resulted in a more normal food intake, resumption of statural growth and a return to normal of growth hormone levels.[39]

It is quite possible that the small size often observed in the child and adult with mental retardation is associated with mild but chronic undernutrition.

There is no evidence that decreased stimulation of the pituitary by the higher central nervous system plays a part.[37]

7. CHRONIC INFECTIONS. — A large number of diseases could be listed under this classification. A few examples are hookworm infestation, malaria, dysentery, pulmonary disease, syphilis and osteomyelitis. Gardiner-Hill[7] stated that such diseases may cause a premature "senescence of growing cartilage" with calcification. Growth failure may be either temporary or permanent.

Organic Disorders

1. CONGENITAL HEART DISEASE. — The greatest extent of retardation of growth occurs in diseases of the cyanotic group, including tetralogy of Fallot, complete transposition of the great vessels and a condition in which both great vessels arise from the same ventricle. The acyanotic group shows growth retardation most severely in ventricular septal defects with pulmonary hypertension and in complicated atrial septal defects. Even in the less involved abnormalities some degree of growth failure usually is present.[25] In nearly all of these the failure of growth, when present, is believed to be due to anoxia hampering cellular metabolism. In a recent study of growth of children with congenital heart disease corrected by surgery, Adams et al.[15] found that many did not regain normal stature or weight even after relatively long periods of observation. An associated growth defect of a genetic basis was postulated as a possible explanation. It seems more likely that early impairment of growth results in metabolic changes that become irreversible at the cell level.[38]

2. HEPATIC INSUFFICIENCY. — Prolonged hepatic insufficiency, as in cirrhosis and congenital atresia of the biliary passages, notoriously slows growth and may be associated with rickets due to poor absorption of fat-soluble vitamins.

3. MALABSORPTION SYNDROMES. — Children who have the celiac syndrome and pancreatic cystic fibrosis may simply remain small without showing rickets, or rickets may be superimposed on the primary disease. In both diseases there is poor absorption of ingested foodstuffs, particularly fats, and to less extent proteins. Consequently, vitamins A and D are poorly absorbed. In pancreatic cystic fibrosis there is the additional factor of the chronic pulmonary infection that retards development. Recently added to the list of causes for malabsorption are the deficiencies of sugar-splitting enzymes, which result in diarrhea with strongly acid stools due to bacterial fermentation of the sugars as they pass into the lower gut. One interesting

observation that has been made in many of these severely malnourished children is the small head circumference. This measurement was considerably below 2 standard deviations for either their age or in comparison to their height. Psychometric evaluation following successful treatment did not indicate an appreciable lowering of mentation while still in early childhood. Delay in bone maturation is commonly associated with severe nutritional privation from whatever cause.

4. RENAL DWARFISM. — Several different syndromes may be included under this classification. It is recognized that any chronic renal insufficiency of a severe grade may impair growth. Such impairment may be seen with chronic nephritis and chronic urinary tract infection and as a result of congenital abnormalities. The retention of abnormal metabolites and the usual accompanying acidosis so change the internal environment that optimal cellular function is impossible. The resulting dwarfism usually is accompanied by retarded ossification but may or may not result in the syndrome known as renal rickets.

In a few patients with renal insufficiency of long duration the condition may be associated with generalized bone disease. Roentgenologically these changes are not easily distinguished from vitamin D deficient rickets; hence the term "renal rickets" has been applied. In these individuals there is always a marked retention of phosphorus, and this is said to be responsible for the hyperplasia of the parathyroid glands that is nearly always present. Because of this finding at autopsy, it has been postulated that renal rickets is secondary to hyperparathyroidism.

The Fanconi syndrome, a type of renal acidosis, may lead to a clinical picture resembling rickets and causing dwarfism. The syndrome as usually described is characterized by a family history (often consanguinity), impaired growth at an early age, "rickets," albuminuria, an increase in urinary glucose, organic acids, ammonia, phosphorus and calcium, a persistently alkaline urine reaction, hypophosphatemia but normal calcium levels in the blood and lowered blood bicarbonate content without uremia. Degenerative changes in the renal tubules represent the main morphologic change. The condition has been ascribed to abnormal tubular function with failure of resorption of certain important solutes. It would appear that the bone changes in this condition are due to the acidosis caused by increased urinary excretion of base secondary to increased excretion of organic acids. An added feature is the low serum phosphorus content.

Brief mention should be made of another type of renal acidosis sometimes associated with rickets-like bone changes. In this condition there is no glomerular pathology as in renal rickets. The fundamental change is due to damage or anomaly of the tubules. In the presence of damaged kidney tubules ammonia is not formed to be excreted in combination with acid and, furthermore, an acid urine is not easily formed. In this eventuality calcium, being a base, is in demand and appears in increased amounts in the urine. The serum calcium level tends to fall, and consequently parathyroid hyperplasia results. This tends to counteract the low serum calcium level but causes hypophosphatemia. In the presence of a low or normal serum calcium content and a low serum phosphorus level, calcium is not deposited in osteoid tissue. It should be explained that this condition and renal rickets differ not only in their pathologic physiology in relation to the kidneys but also in the mechanism by which the bone changes are produced. In the simplest terms, renal rickets is caused by bone destruction, whereas osteomalacia due to renal acidosis is caused by lack of bone formation (or lack of calcification, exactly as in vitamin D deficient rickets).[21]

5. ENDOCRINE DISORDERS. — The significance of the role played by the endocrine glands in normal growth has been discussed in Chapter 9. Dwarfism may result from a deficiency of either the anterior pituitary's growth hormone or the thyroid hormone. The hypothyroid dwarf usually displays relative and absolute shortness of the extremities. The skin lacks normal turgor and appears thick and dry. Anemia is fairly common. If the condition is not quickly recognized and adequately treated, mental retardation is pronounced. Roentgenologic studies of the bones show severe delay in maturation (Fig 13–4). Laboratory evidence of decreased thyroid function is present.[17]

There are a number of different kinds of pituitary dwarfism depending upon which pituitary hormones are absent. It may be that a large percentage of so-called pituitary deficiencies are really hypothalamic releasing hormone deficiencies (see Chapter 9). For the purpose of discussion, it is useful to divide the types into two categories: isolated growth hormone deficiency and multiply pituitary hormone deficiencies. Clinically the most commonly encountered is that of multiple deficiencies which is most evident by lack of sexual maturation as well as short stature. Most cases are either idiopathic or secondary to a specific lesion such as an intracranial tumor. The bone age is retarded, severely so after puberty, and growth may continue at a very slow rate until the age of 30 years or more because the epiphyseal plates never ossify.

Pituitary dwarfism with normal sexual maturation is usually due to isolated growth hormone insufficiency. It may have a genetic basis, since it can appear more than once in a family; it is probably autosomal recessive.[43] Bone age is only slightly retarded, and in addition to small stature, there is slow maturation of facial development and the skin tends to wrinkle prematurely. Linear growth is often fairly normal for 18–24 months after birth and then

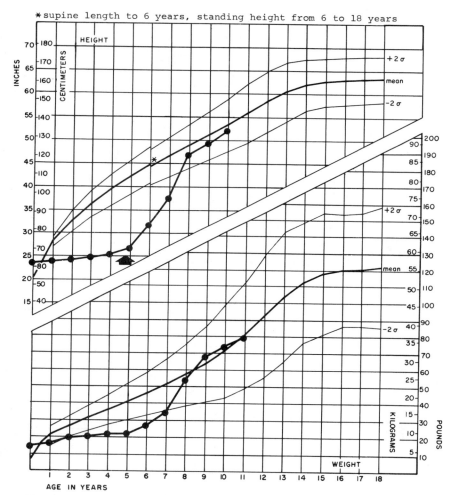

Fig 13–4.—Hypothyroidism causing severe growth retardation; corrected by adequate therapy. Growth and mental retardation were apparent when child was examined at 4³/₄ years for a chief complaint of "not walking." Bone maturation was found to be under 1 year by x-ray examination, and PBI was 1.2 μg per cent. Desiccated thyroid was started, as indicated by arrow, and was gradually increased to a daily dose of 180 mg. There was improvement in growth and bone maturation, but mentation remained at a low level. It is of interest to note that accelerated growth gradually leveled off as normal height for age was approached.

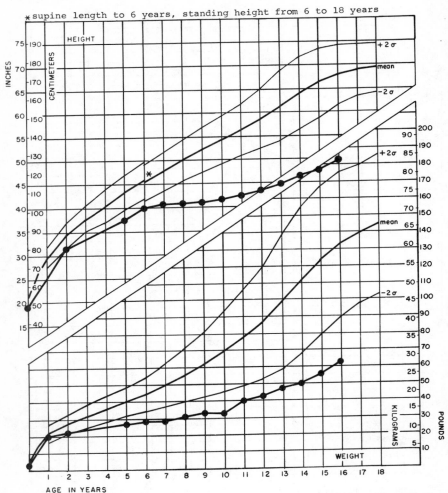

Fig 13–5.—Probable pituitary dwarf. Although growth never ceased, the pattern of a near normal rate during infancy followed by a decided slowing down is typical of many pituitary deficiencies. On several occasions, tests for thyroid and adrenal cortex function and the integrity of the pituitary-adrenal axis were normal. Bone maturation persisted at about 2–3 years behind chronologic age. When this boy was last seen, at age 16, he still appeared very immature and there was no evidence of sexual maturation.

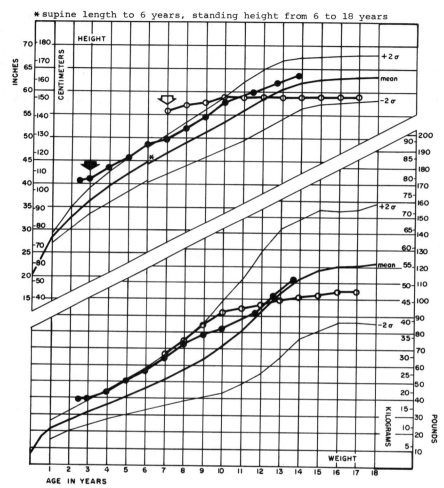

* supine length to 6 years, standing height from 6 to 18 years

Fig 13–6.—Adrenogenital syndrome in sisters, showing the effectiveness of early therapy as compared to late therapy. Virilization was apparent in both at birth; but until pubic hair, acne, and accelerated growth were noted, the diagnosis was not entertained. At the time suppressive treatment with hydrocortisone was begun *(arrows)*, the older girl's bone maturation was estimated at 15 years and the younger sibling's at 7 years. Before therapy both had elevated urine contents of 17-ketosteroids.

becomes markedly retarded (Fig 13–5). The incidence of isolated growth hormone deficiency is presently unknown but in one survey was estimated at one in 30,000 births.[26]

Another rare type of dwarfism is characterized by a high plasma level of growth hormone and low or absent somatomedin factor. As discussed in Chapter 9, somatomedin is an intermediate substance needed to promote the incorporation of sulfate into chondroitin sulfate and thymidine into DNA of cartilage under stimulation of the growth hormone. Children with this disorder have short stature, increased subcutaneous fat, a high-pitched voice, acromicria, sparse hair and dental dysplasia. It is more common in consanguineous marriages.[36]

Studies of the African pygmies indicate they have an end-organ resistance to growth hormone and they do not lack the somatomedin factor. They have normal circulating amounts of growth hormone.

Hyperfunction of the adrenal cortex, as in the adrenogenital syndrome, will result in a temporarily accelerated rate of growth with virilization, due to increased secretion of androgens. However, premature union of the epiphyses and diaphyses eventually precludes further increase in length, so that the final stature falls short of the expected norm. Adrenal tumors, with onset later in life, may produce a similar disturbance* (Fig 13–6).

Gonadal tumors with hormonal function are extremely rare in boys and are uncommon in girls. Precocious sexual development in such instances is associated with accelerated bone maturation; so the pattern of growth that is followed will be similar to that just described for adrenal cortical hyperfunction except that the precocity is isosexual—i.e., masculinizing in boys and feminizing in girls. Tumors of the hypothalamus and other lesions in this area may cause precocious sexual development. Except for the early onset and rapid development of secondary sex characteristics plus the usual signs of an intracranial lesion, the pattern of development is the same as that normally followed by each sex as puberty is approached (Fig 13–7). Pineal tumors in boys produce a similar syndrome.

Polyostotic fibrous dysplasia (McCune-Albright syndrome) is characterized by cystic bone changes which tend to be asymmetrical, brown pigmented areas of the skin and precocious growth and sexual development. Most of the cases so far described with the endocrine changes have been in females. In all instances noted the premature epiphysial union, which is invariably a part of the precocity, results in stature below normal by the time growth ceases.

Hypogonadism of a congenital nature is seen in Turner's syndrome, which is caused by an XO-chromosome distribution. The external genitalia are

---

*A few cases have been reported of feminizing adrenal tumors in boys.

Fig 13-7.—Precocious sexual development and overgrowth secondary to a hypothalamic tumor surgically removed at 10 years of age. From the growth pattern it seems certain that the tumor had been present since age 6 years. Enlargement of genitalia (both phallus and scrotum), pubic hair, acne and deepening of the voice preceded progressive loss of vision and headaches, which finally brought the boy to the clinic. At age 10 bone maturation was 5 years advanced, the urine content of 17-ketosteroids and gonadotropins were at late adolescent levels.

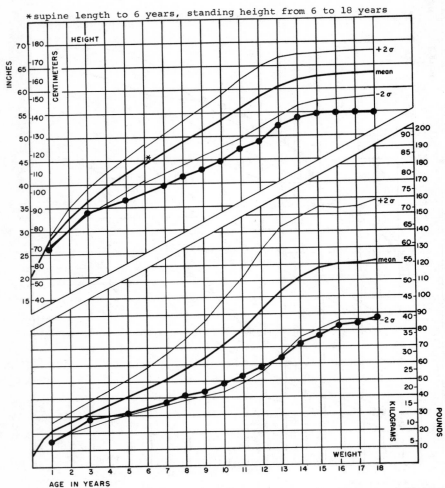

AGE IN YEARS

Fig 13-8.—Turner's syndrome (gonadal agenesis). Note especially the gradual deviation below the normal with increasing age. At birth it was observed that this girl had lymphedema of the hands and feet, which slowly disappeared over the period of infancy. Webbing of the neck and micrognathia were also present. Sexual maturation occured at 15 years, after estrogen therapy was begun. The "bone age" was 3 years behind chronologic age at 15 years. Buccal smears did not contain any chromatin body, and the urinary gonadotropins were considerably elevated.

typically female, but the cells lack the chromatin body associated with a normal genetic female. The internal genital organs are quite rudimentary, often being fibrous bands. Such children are dwarfed, lack sexual development and frequently have other anomalies, such as webbing of the neck, increased carrying angle of the arms, micrognathia, mild mental retardation, pigmented nevi and congenital heart defects. As the chronologic time of puberty approaches, the levels of urinary gonadotropins are elevated above normal, but estrogen levels remain very low or absent (Fig 13–8). A very similar syndrome in which no chromosomal abnormalities have been identified has been described in boys.[8] The genitalia are underdeveloped with absent (to palpation) or small and often undescended testes.

Hyperparathyroidism may cause dwarfism as a result of the changes in bone—softening with decalcification, cyst formation and fractures leading to severe malformations. In this condition, lowered serum phosphate and increased calcium and phosphatase contents are typical.

Although it cannot be stated at this time that the condition termed pseudohypoparathyroidism fits into the classification of endocrine dwarfism, it can be stated that an endocrine dysfunction exists in this syndrome, first described by Albright. The blood and physical changes are those of hypoparathyroidism, and in addition there are short stature and other anomalies. The interesting feature which sets these children apart from others with hypoparathyroidism is that they do not respond to parathyroid hormone therapy. It is this inability of the body to respond that has led to the present nomenclature of the disease. Short stature, tendency to obesity, characteristic round face, striking shortening of the metacarpals and the occasional finding of exostoses are typical of this syndrome.

Hereditary and Primordial Dwarfism

The best examples of hereditary dwarfism are to be found in isolated areas of Africa, India, Melanesia and the Philippine Islands. It is not certain whether more than one race is involved. All individuals have dark skin and curly hair; but the facial features, such as thickness of the lips, flatness of the nose and breadth of the face, differ among the African pygmies, the Asian pygmies and the Negritos.[28] The average adult height of the male is under 5 feet (128 cm). Birth weight is less than normal compared to other races, but seldom would be classified as "premature." It must be admitted that statistics are meager. The pattern of growth is apparently normal, although slow, and with very little prepuberal spurt; however, the appearance of secondary sex characteristics follows the usual course.

Most authorities refer to the primordial dwarf as the small individual with normal proportions who undergoes sexual maturity at the expected age and shows no evidence of any endocrine disorder. Essentially the diagnosis is made by exclusion. Although the true incidence of this type of retarded stature is unknown, it would appear to be very small, with the exception of the hereditary dwarfs. Most of the sporadic, as well as familial, types of dwarfism have other abnormalities—some of a serious nature, similar to those described below. However, many cases cannot be classified in our present state of ignorance.

Other Types of Dwarfism

Many different syndromes associated with remarkably short stature have been described—some sporadic, some familial—but often having certain findings that are repeated sufficiently often in different patients to make one think that there could be a common pathogenesis. Many eponyms have resulted, which may be confusing; but it is often difficult to find an adequate scientific label that is both brief and descriptive. A few representative types are indicated below, with only the major features being outlined.[7, 10, 18, 20, 29, 30]

1. ASSOCIATED RENAL ABNORMALITIES.—Syndromes described by Lowe, Lightwood and Fanconi now bear their names. Fanconi's syndrome has already been referred to previously (Fig 13–9). Lowe's syndrome is evident shortly after birth, with mental retardation, cataracts, glaucoma and rickets. It appears only in males, and metabolic abnormalities include acidosis and aminoaciduria. Lightwood's syndrome also manifests itself in early infancy, with failure to thrive, metabolic acidosis, hyperchloremia, hypokalemia and inability to form acid urine or urinary ammonia.[21]

2. ASSOCIATED SKIN MANIFESTATIONS.—The Hutchinson-Gilford syndrome is typical of a class of dwarfism associated with progeria. Ectodermally derived structures are severely affected. The skin is thin and smooth, and alopecia and poorly enameled teeth are present. Arthritic changes occur early in life. The face is small with a prominent nose. Bone maturation is normal. No obvious familial tendency exists. Syndromes associated with pigmentation of the skin and hypersensitivity to light, similar to xeroderma pigmentosum but milder, have been described by Cockayne, Rothmund-Thomson and Werner. In Cockayne's syndrome, progeria and cataracts are present, and often neurologic findings, such as deafness and low mentality, are noted. Arthritic changes and early graying of the hair are common. Dwarfing becomes apparent in early childhood. The condition described by

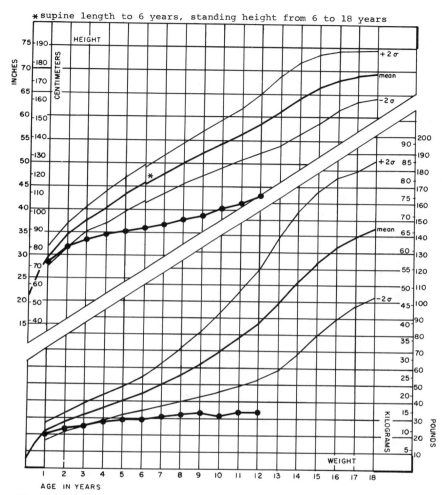

Fig 13-9.—Dwarfism secondary to severe renal disease (Fanconi's syndrome with cystinosis). Metabolic abnormalities present in this boy were proteinuria, glucosuria, aminoaciduria, metabolic acidosis, and cystine crystals in the cornea and bone marrow. Clinically the child appeared chronically ill and had a very poor appetite. Just before death occurred after his 12th birthday, his BUN reached 110 mg/100 ml.

Fig 13–10.—Primordial dwarfism of the intrauterine type. Birth weight was 5 lb, but pregnancy was estimated to be full term. The only abnormalities noted were microcephaly (below 2 standard deviations for both age and height) and mild mental retardation, evidenced by her being placed in a special education class. Sexual maturation was slightly delayed, but menarche occurred at 16 years. Bone maturation at 8, 10 and 16 years matched chronologic age.

Rothmund-Thomson resembles that of Werner except for earlier age of onset. Because of this difference, the dwarfism is more pronounced in the former syndrome. Skin becomes pigmented and is light-sensitive. Nails and hair are dysplastic, and teeth have poor enamel formation. Lack of subcutaneous fat and atrophic skin lends to the appearance of senility. Cataracts develop in more than half of the patients.

3. ASSOCIATED BONE CHANGES. — Cornelia de Lange first described the syndrome that now bears her name.[29] Severe growth and mental retardation with microbrachycephaly, some degree of micromelia or phocomelia, espe-, cially of the upper extremities, and hirsutism are typical findings. Genitalia in males are small, but no patient has yet been followed into adolescence to determine development at that time. Facial features include heavy eyebrows growing over the midline, an anteverted nose due to nasal cartilage hypoplasia and thin lips with the angles of the mouth turning down. Evidence now present supports a recessive type of inheritance. The Ellis-van Creveld syndrome is also called "chondroectodermal dysplasia." There is a symmetrical and progressive distalward shortening of the extremities, and the tubular bones appear short and thick by x-ray examination. Both the nails and the teeth are poorly formed. Polydactylism of the hands is a constant finding. Inconstant features are congenital heart disease and mental retardation. Genetic influences are not known.

4. INTRAUTERINE DWARFISM. — A large number of dwarfs would probably fit into this category, including some already described in which low birth weight is a common finding (Fig 13–10). At least three types have been differentiated by some authors. All are characterized by very small size at birth but normal duration of pregnancy and continued slow growth thereafter, with normal maturation of osseous tissue and sexual development. Virchow-Seckel[20] syndrome is best described by the synonym "bird-headed dwarf." Microcephaly and some degree of mental defectiveness is usual. Russell described a dwarfism associated with a large cranium and a relatively small and undeveloped face. Silver first brought our attention to a group of dwarfs with asymmetry of the body (similar to hemiatrophy) and precocious sexual development with early elevation of the urinary gonadotropins.[47]

5. CHROMOSOMAL ABNORMALITIES. — In the past few years many different malformations associated with chromosomal abnormalities have been reported. In most two findings were common: growth retardation and mental retardation. Many other associated anomalies have been described, with some tendency to repeat if the autosomal defect was the same in the different patients. It would serve little purpose to go through the long list.[11, 47]

Giantism

The pathogenesis of giantism is less complicated than that of dwarfism, owing to the fact that there are fewer causes. The following classification covers the majority of cases seen in any clinic.

Hereditary Giantism

In hereditary giantism there is usually abnormal height in one or both parents or in close relatives. Such individuals are well proportioned, although they may have somewhat longer extremities than the average person. Bone maturation follows a normal course of growth. As with hereditary dwarfs, Africa furnishes the best examples of this type of giantism in the Dinka tribe of the Sudan and the Watutsi of Ruanda-Urundi. In both of these the male often reaches a height of over 7 ft (196 cm).

Pituitary and Hypothalamic Giantism

Hyperfunction of the eosinophilic cells of the anterior pituitary before fusion of the epiphyses will cause excessive growth. In many of the cases recorded abnormal growth started just before or at the time of puberty, and the abnormal height was attained in the next few years. Such giants may grow to a height of 8 ft or more. Usually some degree of acromegaly is superimposed on the giantism. Frequently there are signs of intracranial tumor with expansion of the sella turcica. Pituitary giantism has been described in infancy but is extremely rare.[9]

A number of patients with giantism and signs of neurologic abnormalities but without evidence of direct involvement of the pituitary have been described by Sotos et al.[31] The author has followed four such patients, two into puberty. These children have mild to moderate degrees of mental retardation, and some, but not all, have abnormal pneumoencephalograms with hydrocephalus. Very early in life it was noted that growth was excesssive, and then by about 4–6 years of age a normal rate was maintained so that the relative excess in size was not lost. In two of the patients bone maturation proceeded at a normal pace and adolescence occurred at the expected time. Adult height in each· was above the 97th percentile. Mild acromegalic changes were present—large hands and feet and prognathia—which exaggerated the awkwardness associated with the neurologic deficit (Fig 13–11). The etiology of this type of giantism is not presently known but may well reflect an abnormality of the central nervous system, especially the hypothalamus, and its control over the secretion of growth hormone from the pituitary. Fasting blood assays on three patients in our laboratory have been in the normal range.

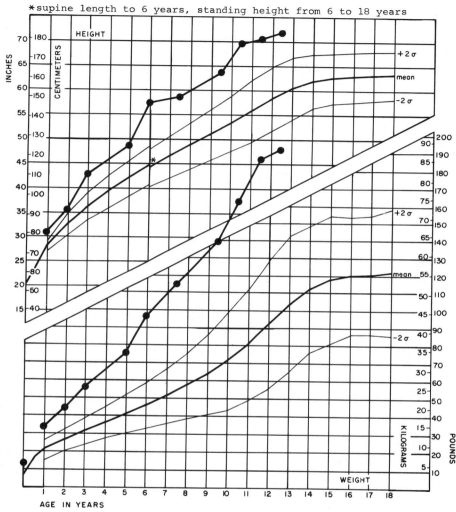

*supine length to 6 years, standing height from 6 to 18 years

Fig 13–11.—Giantism of the cerebral type. In addition to the large size of this girl, she had some acromegalic features, with large hands and feet and moderate prognathism. Mental retardation was severe, but repeated x-ray examinations of the skull failed to show evidence of abnormality. Bone maturation was compatible with age, and breast development was well advanced and pubic hair present at 12$^{1}/_{2}$ years.

Marfan's Syndrome

Most patients with Marfan's syndrome are enough taller than the average for their age so that it is very noticeable. Although sporadic cases exist, the usual mode of inheritance is autosomal dominant. In addition to excessive linear growth, these children are thin and have disproportionately long arms, legs, fingers and toes (arachnodactyly). The skull may be long and narrow. Associated findings that are less constant than those just described include subluxation of the lens; a number of deformities of the heart and great vessels; scoliosis and kyphosis; and arthrogryposis.

Eunuchoid Giantism

In the experience of the author this is a rare type of giantism, and the medical literature gives little support to its existence. The cases described have invariably been males in which the hypogonadism was primary or secondary. Such boys are tall, with long extremities and delayed or absent sexual maturation. Presumably because of late fusion of the epiphyses growth is prolonged, leading to increased height. The urinary excretion of androgens is low, while gonadotropins are elevated.

Obesity

A universally accepted definition of obesity is probably an impossibility. It would differ in every cultural group and among the different races. The genetic background determining body type would be an important factor. Age would be considered an essential variant by many people. If one uses most of the modern growth tables or curves, obesity may be considered to exist in any child who weighs 20% or more above the mean for his height.

Obesity may be encountered at any age but is most often brought to the attention of the clinician during adolescence. Most of these children are found to have been overweight since infancy or early childhood but have become more sensitive about it as they grow older. Among high school children in the United States its frequency has been estimated at 15–20%.

The changing pattern of subcutaneous fat deposition in the first two decades of life is very interesting. Until age 4–5 years the amount present remains relatively steady. In males there is loss beginning at this age and lasting for 3–5 years. No such loss usually takes place in the female. Both sexes experience a preadolescent gain which continues to adult life in girls, but is followed by a brief loss of fat in the late adolescent boy. At all ages boys are more lean than girls with the greatest contrast following puberty.[2]

Animal experiments and clinical observations in man suggest that the lateral and ventromedial hypothalamus together determine, to a great degree, the regulation for body fat. Isolated destruction of the ventromedial centers results in hyperphagia and obesity. Isolated destruction of the lateral centers causes loss of appetite and loss of weight. It has been postulated that the ventromedial centers act as satiety controls to inhibit the lateral centers. In both man and animals obesity produces insulin resistance and higher than normal levels of circulating insulin. Cell receptors for insulin may be modified or their number diminished in liver and muscle but not in the fat tissue of obese subjects. Only the fat cells can react in a normal fashion resulting in shunting glucose from muscle and liver glycogen synthesis to lipid production. Since vagotomy or pancreatic destruction can block ventromedial obesity, it has been suggested that the function of the centers is mediated through control of insulin release.[44]

Aside from the abnormal metabolic changes associated with insulin resistance, there are none other consistently present in obese persons. Elevated blood lipids are common, but not universal.

Furthermore, all of the enumerated changes found by some workers, and the insulin resistance, are reversible with adequate weight reduction. Obesity is a threat to health since it is a prime factor in causing hypertension, coronary heart disease, cerebrovascular disease and diabetes mellitus. It also greatly increases the risks of major surgical procedures. Perhaps equally important is the psychologic trauma that it causes to the child and his family.[45]

Children as well as adults follow the law of conservation of energy, and the only possible way to increase weight is to take in more calories than are expended.[16]

There are still many misconceptions about obesity. The fact that most of these children are referred to an endocrinologist for diagnosis and treatment indicates this. Only a small fraction of the total are actual endocrine problems. Hypothyroidism as a factor in obesity is extremely rare. We have seen only one in which the two conditions coexisted. Wilkins[18] stated that he had seen only two in more than 200 hypothyroid children. As a matter of fact, most children with thyroid deficiency are below normal in weight for their age, and virtually all are below normal for stature. This is certainly true for the congenital group in every instance. This is in direct contrast to the usual obese child, who is taller than the average for his age.

Cushing's syndrome, due to tumor or hyperplasia of the adrenal cortex, is seldom seen in the pediatric age group. These subjects are obese but nearly always shorter than normal, owing to the excessive output of corticoids, osteoporosis and collapse of vertebral bodies. In addition there are hirsutism, hypertension, glycosuria and a diabetic type of glucose tolerance curve. None of these findings is present in simple obesity. The skin striae found in Cushing's syndrome are similarly found in many adolescents with no abnormalities. Steroid determinations in the urine will confirm the diagnosis if doubt exists.

Another rare type of obesity is Fröhlich's syndrome. Unfortunately, this term has been much abused and often incorrectly used. The condition is a specific entity associated with a lesion of the hypothalamus causing, in addition to obesity, short stature, retarded or absent sexual development, visual failure, headaches and other signs of intracranial pressure. In the same category, i.e., obesity due to intracranial lesions, we can include the Laurence-Moon-Biedl syndrome. Other findings in this condition are mental retardation, syndactylism and retinitis pigmentosa. It is extremely rare. Also, one might mention the obesity occasionally seen with other forms of mental retardation, although the psychologic factor may play a part, in that such children may find excessive eating one of the few forms of pleasure.

When all of these rare types are pooled, they make up less than 1% of the total of overweight children.

Often the child, parents or physician believes that prepubescent boys have genitalia that are too small, and when this is associated with obesity, it is often concluded that some glandular abnormality is present. If the pubic fat pad is pushed back and the chronologic age rather than the overall body size is taken into consideration, it will be seen that the genital organs are quite normal. It must be remembered that these organs undergo very little growth until adolescence is well along. Furthermore, size of body is not a good index of maturity. Most of these boys will have normal development and often a drop in weight as they approach puberty without any therapy.

It has been stated that obesity occurring early in life is associated with fat cell hyperplasia, while that occurring later in childhood causes fat cell hypertrophy.[46] Some authorities assume obesity that begins in early life is more intractable to treatment due to the differences in the number of lipid cells present. The author would point out that fat is equally mobilizable from big as well as small cells. Weight reduction can be accomplished on the same diet at the same rate in both subjects, all other factors being the same, e.g., age, exercise, etc. The emotional problems associated with the greater degree of habituation in the child with the early onset are not to be denied.

A number of important physical findings are frequently present in obese children when this is due to increased caloric intake alone. They tend to be slightly taller than their peers. Bone maturation and sexual development are more advanced. In girls, menarche occurs earlier than in those of average weight.

Interesting social and psychologic findings have been reported from a number of clinics.[2, 16, 46] Obesity is more prevalent in the lower socioeconomic classes. This is especially true for girls. It is more common in the United States in the children of first and second generation immigrants. It is found more often in the firstborn and among bottle-fed than breast-fed children. It is more apt to occur in infants and children whose mothers had excessive weight gain during the pregnancy. In 70–80% of the families at least one other member is obese.

Unfortunately many people still associate some degree of obesity with good health during infancy and early childhood. Mothers become upset when their 2- or 3-year-old is more interested in exploring the world than in eating. It should be recalled that in contrast to early infancy, growth is relatively slow and energy requirements are low. The normal child at this age also assumes a more mature body build and proportions which are much different in appearance than that of the infant.

One of the most disturbing findings of the majority of these studies is the fact that fat infants often become fat children who become fat adolescents who become fat adults.[4, 16, 33, 35, 41]

The psychologic factors in obesity have been well analyzed by a number of workers who have emphasized their importance.[16, 33, 46] Many of the children have feelings of insecurity and are overprotected by their parents. Very frequently other personality problems are evident; these include nocturnal enuresis, severe school difficulties and social problems with few or no intimate friendships of their own age. The onset of obesity following some surgical procedure is not uncommon, according to parental histories. Most of these children have had the onset of this overweight problem early in childhood, often by 4 or 5 years of age. Perhaps because parents are prone to accept a little "pudginess" at this age as a reflection of good health, they are not concerned until many more years have passed. In fact, many parents deny that their children were overweight at the early ages until proof is obtained by plotting past weights upon a standard growth curve. Such children often eat to excess because it gives them a feeling of pleasure and satisfaction that is difficult to obtain in other ways. It is not unusual to find that the mothers have rejected them but feel that their duty has been well done if the children are fed adequately. This pattern of substituting food for love may go back to infancy, or it may begin at age 3 or 4 in response to the frequent "feeding problems" present at this time.

Many of these boys and girls lead sedentary lives, especially the adolescent girl, and lack of exercise may be a contributing factor.[2] Sometimes it is difficult to distinguish which came first. Is the decreased exercise due to the awkwardness and embarrassment caused by the obesity, or does the decreased exercise itself lead to accumulation of adipose tissue?

In conclusion, a number of important facts need emphasis. Most obesity has its onset early in life, often in the first few years.[32, 33, 34] The association of this with psychologic problems is very significant in these children, and the combination often leads to a vicious circle in which each problem augments the other. To many parents obesity in the preschool child represents an indication of healthfulness. To attain this deceptive goal, poor eating habits are well established by the time the overweight child desires to correct the situation. Finally, it is agreed that those who are obese as juveniles will make up a very large percentage of the grossly obese adults.[34, 35]

REFERENCES

1. Arnaud, C. D.: Parathyroid hormone: Coming of age in clinical medicine, Am. J. Med. 55:577, 1973.
2. Garn, S. M., and Clark, D. C.: Trends in fatness and the origins of obesity, Pediatrics 57:443, 1976.
3. Boyd, J. D., and Kantrow, A. H.: Retardation of growth in diabetic children, Am. J. Dis. Child. 55:460, 1938.
4. Fisch, R. O., Bilek, M. K., and Ulstrom, R.: Obesity and leanness at birth and their relationship to body habitus in later childhood, Pediatrics 56:521, 1975.
5. Caffey, J.: *Pediatric X-ray Diagnosis* (6th ed.; Chicago: Year Book Medical Publishers, Inc., 1972).
6. DeLuca, H. F.: Vitamin D: A new look at an old vitamin, Nutr. Rev. 29:179, 1971.
7. Gardiner-Hill, H.: The abnormalities of growth and development: The clinical and pathological aspects, Br. Med. J. 1:1241 and 1302, 1934.
8. Gardner, L. I.: *Endocrine and Genetic Diseases of Childhood and Adolescence* (2d ed.; Philadelphia: W. B. Saunders Company, 1975).
9. Bacon, G. E., Spencer, M. L., and Kelch, R. P.: *A Practical Approach to Pediatric Endocrinology* (Chicago: Year Book Medical Publishers, Inc., 1975).
10. Warkany, J.: Dwarfs and other little people: An overview, Semin. Roentgenol. 8:135, 1973.
11. Felson, B. (ed.): Dwarfs and other little people, Semin. Roentgenol. 8:133, 1973.
12. Talbot, N. B.: Dwarfism in children, Bull. New England M. Center 7:117, 1945.
13. Dorst, J. P., Scott, C. I., and Hall, J. G.: The radiologic assessment of short stature-dwarfism Radiol. Clin. North Am. 10:393, 1972.
14. Bernsohn, J., and Grossman, H. J. (eds.): *Lipid Storage Diseases: Enzymatic Defects and Clinical Implications* (New York: Academic Press, Inc. 1971).
15. Adams, F. H., Lund, G. W., and Disenhouse, R. B.: Observations on the physique and growth of children with congenital heart disease, J. Pediatr. 44:674, 1954.
16. Lowrey, G. H.: Obesity in adolescence, Am. J. Public Health 48:1354, 1958.
17. Lowrey, G. H., Aster, R. H., Carr, E. A., Ramon, G., and Beierwaltes, W. H.: Early diagnostic criteria of congenital hypothyroidism, Am. J. Dis. Child. 96:131, 1958.
18. Wilkins, L.: *Diagnosis and Treatment of Endocrine Disorders in Childhood and Adolescence* (3d ed.; Springfield, Ill.: Charles C Thomas, Publisher, 1965).
19. Fraser, D., and Salter, R. B.: The diagnosis and management of the various types of rickets, Pediatr. Clin. North Am. 4:417, 1958.
20. Seckel, H. P. G.: *Bird-Headed Dwarfs* (Springfield, Ill.: Charles C Thomas, Publisher, 1960).

21. McCrory, W. W.: Symposium on disorders in growth arising from renal tubular dysfunction, J. Pediatr. 57:1, 1960.
22. Rubin, P.: *Dynamic Classification of Bone Dysplasias* (Chicago: Year Book Medical Publishers, Inc., 1964).
23. Schenk, E. A., and Haggerty, J.: Morquio's disease: A radiologic and morphologic study, Pediatrics 34:839, 1964.
24. McKusick, V. A.: *Heritable Disorders of Connective Tissue* (2d ed.; St. Louis: C. V. Mosby Company, 1960).
25. Mehrizi, A., and Drash, A.: Growth disturbance in congenital heart disease, J. Pediatr. 61:418, 1962.
26. Parkin, J. M.: Incidence of growth hormone deficiency, Arch. Dis. Child. 50:904, 1975.
27. Kaplan, S. A.: *Growth Disorders in Children and Adolescents* (Springfield, Ill.: Charles C Thomas, Publisher, 1964).
28. Coon, C. S.: *The Origin of Races* (New York: Alfred A. Knopf, Inc., 1963).
29. Ptacek, L. J., Opitz, J., Smith, D. W., Gerritsen, T., and Waisman, H. A.: The Cornelia de Lange syndrome, J. Pediatr. 63:100, 1963.
30. Husson, G. S., and Parkman, P.: Chondroectodermal dysplasia (Ellis-Van Creveld syndrome) with complex cardiac malformation, Pediatrics 28:285, 1961.
31. Sotos, J. F., Dodge, P. R., Muirhead, D., Crawford, J. D., and Talbot, N. B.: Cerebral gigantism in childhood: A syndrome of excessively rapid growth with acromegalic features and a nonprogressive neurologic disorder, N. Engl. J. Med. 271:109, 1964.
32. Robertson, A. F., and Lowrey, G. H.: Overweight children, Mich. Med. 63:629, 1964.
33. Börjeson, M.: Overweight children, Acta Paediatr. (suppl. 132) 51:1, 1962.
34. Heald, F. P., and Hollander, R. J.: The relationship between obesity in adolescence and early growth, J. Pediatr. 67:35, 1965.
35. Charney, E., Goodman, H. C., McBride, M., Lyon, B., and Pratt, R.: Childhood antecedents of adult obesity, N. Engl. J. Med., 295:6, 1976.
36. Najjar, S. S., Khachadurian, A. K., Ilbawi, M. N., and Blizzard, R. M.: Dwarfism with elevated levels of growth hormone, N. Engl. J. Med., 284:809, 1971.
37. Lowrey, G. H., Bacon, G. E., Fisher, S., and Knoller, H.: Fasting growth hormone levels in mentally retarded children of short stature, Am. J. Ment. Defic. 73:474, 1968.
38. Naeye, R. L.: Anatomic features of growth failure in congenital heart disease, Pediatrics 39:433, 1967.
39. Silver, H. K., and Finkelstein, M.: Deprivation dwarfism, J. Pediatr. 70:317, 1967.
40. Stover, C. N., Hayes, J. T., and Holt, J. F.: Diastrophic dwarfism, Am. J. Roentgenol. 89:914, 1963.
41. Eid, E.: Follow-up study of physical growth of children who had excessive weight gain in first six months of life, Br. Med. J. 2:74, 1970.
42. Thomson, A. M.: Adult Stature, in van der Werff Ten Bosch (ed.): *Somatic Growth of the Child* (Springfield, Ill.: Charles C Thomas, Publisher, 1966).
43. Sheikholislam, B. M., and Stempfel, R. S.: Hereditary isolated somatotrophin deficiency: Effects of growth hormone administration, Pediatrics 49:362, 1972.
44. Keesey, R. E., and Powley, T. L.: Hypothalamic regulation of body weight, Am. Sci. 63:558, 1975.

45. Mann, G. V.: The influence of obesity on health, N. Engl. J. Med., 291:178, 1974.
46. Winick, M. (ed.): *Childhood Obesity* (New York: John Wiley and Sons, 1975).
47. Smith, D. W.: *Recognizable Patterns of Human Malformation* (2d ed.; Philadelphia: W. B. Saunders Company, 1976).

Appendix

The following tables give values which are frequently used in the appraisal of infants and children. References for these tables will be found under the appropriate chapter and section in the main text.

AVERAGE HEAD CIRCUMFERENCE
OF AMERICAN CHILDREN

AGE	MEAN IN.	MEAN CM	STANDARD DEVIATION IN.	STANDARD DEVIATION CM
Birth	13.8	35	0.5	1.2
1 mo	14.9	37.6	0.5	1.2
2 mo	15.5	39.7	0.5	1.2
3 mo	15.9	40.4	0.5	1.2
6 mo	17.0	43.4	0.4	1.1
9 mo	17.8	45.0	0.5	1.2
12 mo	18.3	46.5	0.5	1.2
18 mo	19.0	48.4	0.5	1.2
2 yr	19.2	49.0	0.5	1.2
3 yr	19.6	50.0	0.5	1.2
4 yr	19.8	50.5	0.5	1.2
5 yr	20.0	50.8	0.6	1.4
6 yr	20.2	51.2	0.6	1.4
7 yr	20.5	51.6	0.6	1.4
8 yr	20.6	52.0	0.8	1.8
10 yr	20.9	53.0	0.6	1.4
12 yr	21.0	53.2	0.8	1.8
14 yr	21.5	54.0	0.8	1.8
16 yr	21.9	55.0	0.8	1.8
18 yr	22.1	55.4	0.8	1.8
20 yr	22.2	55.6	0.8	1.8

AVERAGE CHEST CIRCUMFERENCE AND
INTERCRISTAL WIDTH OF AMERICAN CHILDREN

AGE	CHEST CIRCUMFERENCE IN.	CM	PELVIC BICRISTAL DIAMETER IN.	CM
Birth	13.7	35	3.2	8
3 mo	16.2	40	4.3	11
6 mo	17.3	44	4.8	12
1 yr	18.3	47	5.1	13
18 mo	18.9	48	5.5	14
2 yr	19.5	50	6.0	15
3 yr	20.4	52	6.2	16
4 yr	21.1	53		
5 yr	22.0	55	7.2	18
6 yr	22.5	56		
7 yr	23.0	57	8.2	20
8 yr	24.0	59		
9 yr	24.5	60	8.5	21
10 yr	25.1	61		
12 yr	27.0	66	9.0	22
14 yr	29.0	72	11.0	28
16 yr*	31.0	77		
18 yr*	33.0	82	12.2	31
20 yr*	34.5	86	12.6	32

*Males only.

WEIGHT AND HEIGHT PERCENTILE TABLE: BOYS (BIRTH TO AGE 18)

WEIGHT IN LB			WEIGHT IN K			AGE	HEIGHT IN IN.			HEIGHT IN CM		
10%	50%	90%	10%	50%	90%		10%	50%	90%	10%	50%	90%
6.3	7.5	9.1	2.86	3.4	4.13	Birth	18.9	19.9	21.0	48.1	50.6	53.3
8.5	10.0	11.5	3.8	4.6	5.2	1 mo	20.2	21.2	22.2	50.4	53.0	55.5
10.0	11.5	13.2	4.6	5.2	6.0	2 mo	21.5	22.5	23.5	53.7	56.0	60.0
11.1	12.6	14.5	5.03	5.72	6.58	3 mo	22.8	23.8	24.7	57.8	60.4	62.8
12.5	14.0	16.2	5.6	6.3	7.3	4 mo	23.7	24.7	25.7	60.5	62.0	65.2
13.7	15.0	17.7	6.2	7.0	8.0	5 mo	24.5	25.5	26.5	61.8	65.0	67.3
14.8	16.7	19.2	6.71	7.58	8.71	6 mo	25.2	26.1	27.3	63.9	66.4	69.3
17.8	20.0	22.9	8.07	9.07	10.39	9 mo	27.0	28.0	29.2	68.6	71.2	74.2
19.6	22.2	25.4	8.89	10.7	11.52	12 mo	28.5	29.6	30.7	72.4	75.2	78.1
22.3	25.2	29.0	10.12	11.43	13.15	18 mo	31.0	32.2	33.5	78.8	81.8	85.0
24.7	27.7	31.9	11.2	12.56	14.47	2 yr	33.1	34.4	35.9	84.2	87.5	91.1
26.6	30.0	34.5	12.07	13.61	15.65	2½ yr	34.8	36.3	37.9	88.5	92.1	96.2
28.7	32.2	36.8	13.02	14.61	16.69	3 yr	36.3	37.9	39.6	92.3	96.2	100.5
30.4	34.3	39.1	13.79	15.56	17.74	3½ yr	37.8	39.3	41.1	96.0	99.8	104.5
32.1	36.4	41.4	14.56	16.51	18.78	4 yr	39.1	40.7	42.7	99.3	103.4	108.5
33.8	38.4	43.9	15.33	17.42	19.91	4½	40.3	42.0	44.2	102.4	106.7	112.3
35.5	40.5	46.7	16.1	18.37	21.18	5 yr	40.8	42.8	45.2	103.7	108.7	114.7
38.8	45.6	53.1	17.6	20.68	24.09	5½ yr	42.6	45.0	47.3	108.3	114.4	120.1
40.9	48.3	56.4	18.55	21.91	25.58	6 yr	43.8	46.3	48.6	111.2	117.5	123.5
43.4	51.2	60.4	19.69	23.22	27.4	6½ yr	44.9	47.6	50.0	114.1	120.8	127.0
45.8	54.1	64.4	20.77	24.54	29.21	7 yr	46.0	48.9	51.4	116.9	124.1	130.5
48.5	57.1	68.7	22.0	25.9	31.16	7½ yr	47.2	50.0	52.7	120.0	127.1	133.9
51.2	60.1	73.0	23.22	27.26	33.11	8 yr	48.5	51.2	54.0	123.1	130.0	137.3
53.8	63.1	77.0	24.4	28.62	34.93	8½ yr	49.5	52.3	55.1	125.7	132.8	140.0
56.3	66.0	81.0	25.54	29.94	36.74	9 yr	50.5	53.3	56.1	128.3	135.5	142.6
58.7	69.0	85.5	26.63	31.3	38.78	9½ yr	51.4	54.3	57.1	130.6	137.9	145.1
61.1	71.9	89.9	27.71	32.61	40.78	10 yr	52.3	55.2	58.1	132.8	140.3	147.5
63.7	74.8	94.6	28.89	33.93	42.91	10½ yr	53.2	56.0	58.9	135.1	142.3	149.7
66.3	77.6	99.3	30.07	35.2	45.04	11 yr	54.0	56.8	59.8	137.3	144.2	151.8
69.2	81.0	104.5	31.39	36.74	47.4	11½ yr	55.0	57.8	60.9	139.8	146.9	154.8
72.0	84.4	109.6	32.66	38.28	49.71	12 yr	56.1	58.9	62.2	142.4	149.6	157.9
74.6	88.7	116.4	33.84	40.23	52.8	12½ yr	56.9	60.0	63.6	144.5	152.3	161.6
77.1	93.0	123.2	34.97	42.18	55.88	13 yr	57.7	61.0	65.1	146.6	155.0	165.3
82.2	100.3	130.1	37.29	45.5	59.01	13½ yr	58.8	62.6	66.5	149.4	158.9	168.9
87.2	107.6	136.9	39.55	48.81	62.1	14 yr	59.9	64.0	67.9	152.1	162.7	172.4
93.3	113.9	142.4	42.32	51.66	64.59	14½ yr	61.0	65.1	68.7	155.0	165.3	174.6
99.4	120.1	147.8	45.09	54.48	67.04	15 yr	62.1	66.1	69.6	157.8	167.8	176.7
105.2	124.9	152.6	47.72	56.65	69.22	15½ yr	63.1	66.8	70.2	160.3	169.7	178.2
111.0	129.7	157.3	50.35	58.83	71.35	16 yr	64.1	67.8	70.7	162.8	171.6	179.7
114.3	133.0	161.0	51.85	60.33	73.03	16½ yr	64.6	68.0	71.1	164.2	172.7	180.7
117.5	136.2	164.6	53.3	61.78	74.66	17 yr	65.2	68.4	71.5	165.5	173.7	181.6
118.8	137.6	166.8	53.89	62.41	75.66	17½ yr	65.3	68.5	71.6	165.9	174.1	182.0
120.0	139.0	169.0	54.43	63.05	76.66	18 yr	65.5	68.7	71.8	166.3	174.5	182.4

GROWTH AND DEVELOPMENT

WEIGHT AND HEIGHT PERCENTILE TABLE:
GIRLS (BIRTH TO AGE 18)

WEIGHT IN LBS			WEIGHT IN KG			AGE	HEIGHT IN IN			HEIGHT IN CM		
10%	50%	90%	10%	50%	90%		10%	50%	90%	10%	50%	90%
6.2	7.4	8.6	2.81	3.36	3.9	Birth	18.8	19.8	20.4	47.8	50.2	51.0
8.0	9.7	11.0	3.3	4.2	5.0	1 mo	20.2	21.0	22.0	50.4	52.8	55.0
9.5	11.0	12.5	4.1	5.0	5.8	2 mo	21.5	22.2	23.2	53.7	55.5	59.6
10.7	12.4	14.0	4.85	5.62	6.35	3 mo	22.4	23.4	24.3	56.9	59.5	61.7
12.0	13.7	15.5	5.3	6.2	7.2	4 mo	23.2	24.2	25.2	59.6	61.0	64.8
13.0	14.7	17.0	5.9	6.8	7.7	5 mo	24.0	25.0	26.0	60.7	64.2	67.0
14.1	16.0	18.6	6.4	7.26	8.44	6 mo	24.6	25.7	26.7	62.5	65.2	67.8
16.6	19.2	22.4	7.53	8.71	10.16	9 mo	26.4	27.6	28.7	67.0	70.1	72.9
18.4	21.5	24.8	8.35	9.75	11.25	12 mo	27.8	29.2	30.3	70.6	74.2	77.1
21.2	24.5	28.3	9.62	11.11	12.84	18 mo	30.2	31.8	33.3	76.8	80.9	84.5
23.5	27.1	31.7	10.66	12.29	14.38	2 yr	32.3	34.1	35.8	82.0	86.6	91.0
25.5	29.6	34.6	11.57	13.43	15.69	2½ yr	34.0	36.0	37.9	86.3	91.4	96.4
27.6	31.8	37.4	12.52	14.42	16.96	3 yr	35.6	37.7	39.8	90.5	95.7	101.1
29.5	33.9	40.4	13.38	15.38	18.33	3½ yr	37.1	39.2	41.5	94.2	99.5	105.4
31.2	36.2	43.5	14.15	16.42	19.73	4 yr	38.4	40.6	43.1	97.6	103.2	109.6
32.9	38.5	46.7	14.92	17.46	21.18	4½ yr	39.7	42.0	44.7	100.9	106.8	113.5
34.8	40.5	49.2	15.79	18.37	22.32	5 yr	40.5	42.9	45.4	103.0	109.1	115.4
38.0	44.0	51.2	17.24	19.96	23.22	5½ yr	42.4	44.4	46.8	107.8	112.8	118.9
39.6	46.5	54.2	17.96	21.09	24.58	6 yr	43.5	45.6	48.1	110.6	115.9	122.3
42.2	49.4	57.7	19.14	22.41	26.17	6½ yr	44.8	46.9	49.4	113.7	119.1	125.6
44.5	52.2	61.2	20.19	23.68	27.76	7 yr	46.0	48.1	50.7	116.8	122.3	128.9
46.6	55.2	65.6	21.14	25.04	29.76	7½ yr	47.0	49.3	51.9	119.5	125.2	131.8
48.6	58.1	69.9	22.04	26.35	31.71	8 yr	48.1	50.4	53.0	122.1	128.0	134.6
50.6	61.0	74.5	22.95	27.67	33.79	8½ yr	49.0	51.4	54.1	124.6	130.5	137.5
52.6	63.8	79.1	23.86	28.94	35.88	9 yr	50.0	52.3	55.3	127.0	132.9	140.4
54.9	67.1	84.4	24.9	30.44	38.28	9½ yr	50.9	53.5	56.4	129.4	135.8	143.2
57.1	70.3	89.7	25.9	31.89	40.69	10 yr	51.8	54.6	57.5	131.7	138.6	146.0
59.9	74.6	95.1	27.17	33.79	43.14	10½ yr	52.9	55.8	58.9	134.4	141.7	149.7
62.6	78.8	100.4	28.4	35.74	45.54	11 yr	53.9	57.0	60.4	137.0	144.7	153.4
66.1	83.2	106.0	29.98	37.74	48.08	11½ yr	55.0	58.3	61.8	139.8	148.1	157.0
69.5	87.6	111.5	31.52	39.74	50.58	12 yr	56.1	59.8	63.2	142.6	151.9	160.6
74.7	93.4	118.0	33.88	42.37	53.52	12½ yr	57.4	60.7	64.0	145.9	154.3	162.7
79.9	99.1	124.5	36.24	44.95	56.47	13 yr	58.7	61.8	64.9	149.1	157.1	164.8
85.5	103.7	128.9	38.78	47.04	58.47	13½ yr	59.5	62.4	65.3	151.1	158.4	165.9
91.0	108.4	133.3	41.28	49.17	60.46	14 yr	60.2	62.8	65.7	153.0	159.6	167.0
94.2	111.0	135.7	42.73	50.35	61.55	14½ yr	60.7	63.1	66.0	154.1	160.4	167.6
97.4	113.5	138.1	44.18	51.48	62.64	15 yr	61.1	63.4	66.2	155.2	161.1	168.1
99.2	115.3	139.6	45.0	52.3	63.32	15½ yr	61.3	63.7	66.4	155.7	161.7	168.6
100.9	117.0	141.1	45.77	53.07	64.0	16 yr	61.5	63.9	66.5	156.1	162.2	169.0
101.9	118.1	142.2	46.22	53.57	64.5	16½ yr	61.5	63.9	66.6	156.2	162.4	169.2
102.8	119.1	143.3	46.63	54.02	65.0	17 yr	61.5	64.0	66.7	156.3	162.5	169.4
103.2	119.5	143.9	46.81	54.2	65.27	17½ yr	61.5	64.0	66.7	156.3	162.5	169.4
103.5	119.9	144.5	46.95	54.39	65.54	18 yr	61.5	64.0	66.7	156.3	162.5	169.4

EXPECTED INCREMENTS IN WEIGHT AND HEIGHT*

AGE	WEIGHT, KG		HEIGHT, CM	
0–1 mo	0.64		3.8	
1–3 mo	1.54		6.1	
3–6 mo	1.77		6.4	
6–9 mo	1.36		4.6	
9–12 mo	1.00		4.1	
12–18 mo	1.40		6.6	
18–24 mo	1.22		5.6	
24–30 mo	1.04		4.8	
30–36 mo	0.95		4.3	
36–42 mo	1.04		3.8	
42–48 mo	0.95		3.6	
48–54 mo	1.09		3.6	
54–60 mo	1.00		3.3	
60–66 mo	1.14		3.6	
66–72 mo	1.18		3.3	
	BOYS	GIRLS	BOYS	GIRLS
6–7 yr	2.2	2.1	6.1	5.8
7–8 yr	2.4	2.4	5.6	5.6
8–9 yr	2.5	2.5	5.6	5.6
9–10 yr	2.7	2.8	5.1	5.3
10–11 yr	2.5	3.5	5.1	5.8
11–12 yr	3.0	4.5	5.1	6.4
12–13 yr	4.1	5.1	5.6	6.6
13–14 yr	5.5	4.3	7.2	5.1
14–15 yr	5.1	2.3	5.8	2.5
15–16 yr	4.5	1.8	5.1	2.0
16–17 yr	3.2	1.2	3.8	0.8

*Data represent averages from several sources.

AVERAGE HEART RATE FOR INFANTS AND CHILDREN AT REST

AGE	AVERAGE RATE	2 SD
Birth	140	50
1st mo	130	45
1–6 mo	130	45
6–12 mo	115	40
1–2 yr	110	40
2–4 yr	105	35
6–10 yr	95	30
10–14 yr	85	30
14–18 yr	82	25

NORMAL BLOOD PRESSURE FOR VARIOUS AGES (mm Hg)

INFANTS		AGE	SYSTOLIC	2 SD	DIASTOLIC	2 SD
1st day	52	1 day	78	14	42	14
4th day	70	1 mo	86	20	54	18
10th day	80	6 mo	90	26	60	20
2d mo	95	1 yr	96	30	65	25
8th mo	95	2 yr	99	25	65	25
The figures for		4 yr	99	20	65	20
infants represent		6 yr	100	15	60	10
averages by the		8 yr	105	15	60	10
flush method		10 yr	110	17	60	10
described in the		12 yr	115	19	60	10
text.		14 yr	118	20	60	10
		16 yr	120	16	65	10

The figures under 1 year were obtained by the
Doppler method. From 1 year on, the figures were
obtained by auscultation, using the first change
in sound to indicate diastolic pressure.

VARIATIONS IN RESPIRATION WITH AGE

AGE	RATE/MIN	TIDAL AIR, CC	VITAL CAPACITY, L*
Premature	40–90	12	—
Newborn	30–80	19	—
1 yr	20–40	48	—
2 yr	20–30	90	—
3 yr	20–30	125	—
5 yr	20–25	175	1.0
10 yr	17–22	320	2.0
15 yr	15–20	400	3.7
20 yr	15–20	500	3.8

*These represent mean figures from several sources for both sexes.
Vital capacity for boys averages about 6% greater than for girls.

ERUPTION AGES (MONTHS) FOR PRIMARY TEETH

PERCENTILES	EARLY MIN.	10	30	AVERAGE 50	70	90	LATE 100
Mandibular central incisor	4	5	6	7.8	9	11	17
Maxillary central incisor	5	6	8	9.6	11	12	15
Maxillary lateral incisor	6	7	10	11.5	13	15	21
Mandibular lateral incisor	6	7	11	12.4	14	18	27
Maxillary 1st molar	8	10	13	15.1	16	20	28
Mandibular 1st molar	8	10	14	15.7	17	20	27
Mandibular cuspid	8	11	16	18.2	19	24	29
Maxillary cuspid	8	11	17	18.3	20	24	29
Mandibular 2d molar	8	13	24	26.0	28	31	34
Maxillary 2d molar	8	13	24	26.2	28	31	34

NORMAL SEQUENCE OF ERUPTION OF PERMANENT TEETH

MANDIBLE	MAXILLA
1. First molar	2. First molar
3. Central incisor	5. Central incisor
4. Lateral incisor	6. Lateral incisor
7. Cuspid	8. First bicuspid
9. First bicuspid	10. Second bicuspid
11. Second bicuspid	12. Cuspid
13. Second molar	14. Second molar

The numbers indicate the usual sequence of eruption.

IMPORTANT LABORATORY VALUES FOUND IN INFANTS AND CHILDREN

AVERAGE NORMAL BLOOD VALUES AT VARIOUS AGES

AGE	RBC, MILLION/ CU MM	HGB, GM	WBC/ CU MM	POLY., %	LYMPH., %	MONO., %	RETIC., %	PLATE/ CU MM
1 day	5.5	21	20,000	70	20	10	3.0	350,000
6 days	5.3	20	15,000	62	31	7	0.7	325,000
2 wk	5.0	18	12,000	31	63	6	1.0	300,000
1 mo	4.7	16					0.5	
2 mo	4.0	12					1.0	
3 mo	4.0	11					2.0	
6 mo	4.5	11.5	10,000	32	60	6	0.8	300,000
1 yr	4.6	12.5	10,000	38	55	6	1.0	300,000
2 yr	4.7	13.0	10,000	45	49	6	1.0	300,000
5 yr	4.7	13.0	8,000	54	40	6	1.0	300,000
10 yr	4.7	13.0	8,000	60	34	6	1.0	300,000

	MCV, μ*	MCH, $\mu\mu_G$	MCHC, %	MCD, μ	HCT
1 day	106	38	36	8.6	53
6 days	103	36	35		49
2 wk	96	33	34		46
1 mo	90	30	33	8.1	43
6 mo	77	26	33	7.4	37
1 yr	78	25	32	7.3	37
2 yr	77	25	32		38
5 yr	80	27	34	7.4	40
10 yr	80	27	34	7.4	42
Adult	87	29	34	7.5	45

*MCV = mean corpuscular volume
MCH = mean corpuscular hemoglobin
MCHC = mean corpuscular hemoglobin concentration
MCD = mean corpuscular diameter
HCT = hematocrit

AVERAGE VALUES FOR RED CELLS, HEMOGLOBIN AND VOLUME OF PACKED RED CELLS IN MALES AND FEMALES

AGE	RED CELLS, MILLION/CU MM	HGB, GM	VOL. PACKED CELLS, %
10 yr			
Male	4.7	13	38
Female	4.7	13	38
14 yr			
Male	5.0	14	41
Female	4.7	13	39
17 yr			
Male	5.3	15.5	45
Female	4.7	13.5	40
Adult			
Male	5.3	16	47
Female	4.7	14	42

NORMAL URINE OR PLASMA CONTENT OF VARIOUS HORMONES OR THEIR METABOLITES

ASSAY	NEONATE	CHILD	ADULT
17-hydroxysteroids urine, mg/24 hr	0.2–3.5	0.5–5.0	1.5–9.0
17-ketosteroids urine, mg/24 hr	1.5–2.5	0.1–1.0	5–12 female 6–22 male
Aldosterone urine, ng/24 hr	1–2	2–10	5–20
Testosterone* plasma, ng/100 ml	230–300	3–10	300–500
Estradiol† plasma, ng/100 ml	100–300	2–4	10–200‡
LH plasma, ng/ml	4–10	0–4	6–20
FSH plasma, ng/ml	0–2	0–4	6–20
Thyroxine (T_4) plasma, μg/100 ml	7–15	5–10	5–10
GH plasma, ng/ml	20–40	2–5	2–5

*Male only.
†Female only.
‡The wide range of values is a reflection of changing levels throughout the menstrual cycle.

NORMAL VALUES FOR CONSTITUENTS OF BLOOD*

SUBSTANCE	PREMATURE	NEONATE	INFANT	5–15 YR
Aldolase, IU	(6.0–18.0)	(7.2–20.0)	(3.6–10.0)	(1.8–4.9)
Ammonia, μg/100 ml	(100–250)	(90–150)	(45–80)	(45–80)
Urea N, mg/100 ml	(20–47)	19 (10–30)	(6–20)	(6–15)
NPN, mg/100 ml	(24–63)	45 (25–62)	35 (25–45)	(25–35)
Uric acid, mg/100 ml	3.25	3.5 (2.7–5.1)	3.0	3.0
Amino acid				
Nitrogen, mg/100 ml		(3.0–4.0)	(3.0–4.5)	(3.0–4.5)
Creatinine, mg/100 ml	(0.5–3.0)	(1.0–2.0)	(1.0–2.0)	(1.0–2.0)
Serum protein,				
gm/100 ml	5.6 (4.5–6.0)	6.1 (5.0–6.9)	5.9 (5.0–6.6)	(6.5–8.0)
Albumin	(2.5–3.5)	(3.0–4.5)	(3.8–5.0)	(4.5–6.0)
Globulin	(1.0–2.2)	(1.3–2.4)	(1.4–2.4)	(2.0–3.0)
Gamma globulin	(0.5–0.9)	(0.8–1.0)	(0.3–0.6)	(0.9–1.3)
Fibrinogen	0.4	(0.2–0.4)	(0.2–0.4)	(0.2–0.4)
Glucose				
(fasting), mg/100 ml	(27–90)	(47–102)	(70–120)	(70–120)
Total lipids, mg/100 ml		(100–600)	470	(500–700)
Cholesterol, mg/100 ml	(45–100)	(45–170)	(70–180)	(130–240)
Electrolytes, mEq/L				
Total base	159 (152–171)	153 (148–160)	152	152
Sodium	(138–159)	144	144	144
Potassium	(4.0–7.0)	(4.0–7.0)	(4.0–5.5)	(4.0–5.5)
Chloride	(104–120)	(102–110)	(100–107)	(100–107)
Bicarbonate	(12.7–25.3)	(18–27)	(23–28)	(23–28)
Serum calcium,				
mg/100 ml	(7.8–9.0)	(8.0–10.0)	(10–12)	(10–12)
Serum phosphorus,				
mg/100 ml	(6.0–8.5)	(6.5–8.5)	6.0	5.0
Alkaline phosphatase,				
IU	…	(70–225)	(50–150)	(50–250)
Serum bilirubin, mg/100 ml	(1.5–7.5)	(1.4–6.0)	(0.2–0.8)	(0.2–0.8)
Lactic acid, mg/100 ml	(15–30)	17	10	10
Thyroxine,				
T_4, μg/100 ml	(5–13)	(7–15)	(5–10)	(5–10)
17-ketosteroids,				
μg/100 ml	…	(60–300)	(0–50)	(0–120)†
17-OH steroids,				
μg/100 ml	…	(5–10)	(5–15)	(5–15)
Iron, serum, μg/100 ml	…	(60–140)	(30–90)	(50–100)
Lactate dehydrogenase, IU	…	(308–1500)	(200–800)	(100–180)
Phospholipids, μg/ml	…	(1.0–1.8)	(2.0–3.5)	(2.4–4.4)
Transaminase				
SGOT, units	…	(10–120)	(5–50)	(5–45)
SGPT, units	…	(10–90)	(5–50)	(5–50)

*Average figures are given as a single value; the range is enclosed in parentheses. Data from various sources.
†The higher levels are found during and after adolescence.

CEREBROSPINAL FLUID VALUES AT DIFFERENT AGES

| | DAY 1 | | DAY 7 | | AFTER FIRST YEAR |
	RANGE	MEAN	RANGE	MEAN	RANGE
Red blood cells	0–620	23/mm^3	0–48	3/mm^3	0/mm^3
Polymorphs	0–26	7/mm^3	0–5	2/mm^3	0–1/mm^3
Lymphs	0–16	5/mm^3	0–4	1/mm^3	0–4/mm^3
Protein	40–148	73 mg	27–65	47– mg	15–40 mg
Sugar	38–64	48 mg	48–62	55 mg	50–90 mg
Chloride	680–760	720 mg	720–760	720 mg	650–750 mg

ORGAN WEIGHTS

AVERAGE WEIGHTS OF ORGANS AT DIFFERENT AGES (gm)

	NEWBORN	1 YR	6 YR	14 YR	ADULT
Brain	350	910	1,200	1,300	1,350
Heart	24	45	95	220	300
Thymus	12	20	24	30	0–15
Kidneys (2)	25	70	120	170	300
Liver	150	300	550	1,500	1,600
Lungs (2)	60	130	260	410	1,200
Pancreas	3	9	20	40	90
Spleen	10	30	55	95	155
Stomach	8	30	50	80	135
Pituitary	0.1	0.2	0.3	0.4	0.5–0.8
Thyroid	2.0	3.0	7	14	18
Adrenals (2)	6–8	4.5	7	10	10–20
Parathyroids	—	—	—	—	0.65
Testes (2)	1.5	1.5	1.6	7	35
Ovaries (2)	0.3	0.6	1.9	6	7
Uterus	3.9	1.4	2.8	30	50
Prostate	0.8	0.8	1.3	3.3	17

Index